CONSTRUCTING THE SEXUAL CRUCIBLE

CONSTRUCTING THE SEXUAL CRUCIBLE

An Integration of Sexual and Marital Therapy

David M. Schnarch, Ph.D.

DEPARTMENTS OF PSYCHIATRY AND UROLOGY
LOUISIANA STATE UNIVERSITY SCHOOL OF MEDICINE
NEW ORLEANS, LOUISIANA

W · W · *Norton & Company* · *New York* · *London*

Permission to reprint quotations:
Figure from The Annual Review of Sex Research, a publication of The Society for the Scientific Study of Sex. From *The Art of Intimacy* by Thomas Patrick Malone, M.D., and Patrick Thomas Malone, M.D. Copyright © 1987. Reprinted by permission of the publisher Prentice Hall, a division of Simon & Schuster, New York. From *Loneliness* by Clark E. Moustakas. Copyright © 1989, 1966. Reprinted by permission of the publisher Prentice Hall, a division of Simon & Schuster, Englewood Cliffs, NJ. From *Taking Sides: Clashing Views on Controversial Issues on Human Sexuality, First Edition*, edited by Robert T. Francoeur. Copyright © 1987 by the Dushkin Publishing Group, Inc., Guilford, CT. Reprinted by permission. Taking Sides® is a registered trademark of the Dushkin Publishing Group, Inc. Chart from p. 37 of *Object Relations and the Developing Ego in Therapy* by Althea J. Horner, 1979. Reprinted by permission of Jason Aronson Inc., Publishers. From *Grammatical Man* by Jeremy Campbell. Copyright © 1982 by Jeremy Campbell. Reprinted by permission of Simon & Schuster, Inc. From *The Tree of Knowledge* by Humberto R. Maturana and Francisco J. Varela. Copyright © 1987 by Humberto R. Maturana and Francisco J. Varela. Reprinted by arrangement with Shambhala Publications, Inc., Boston, MA.

Printed in the United States of America.

Library of Congress Cataloging-in-Publication Data

Schnarch, David M., 1946–
    Constructing the sexual crucible : an integration of sexual and
marital therapy / David M. Schnarch.
        p.   cm.
    "A Norton professional book."
    Includes bibliographical references and index.
    ISBN 0-393-70102-6
    1. Sex therapy.   2. Marital psychotherapy.   3. Sex Behavior.
4. Sex Counseling—methods.   5. Sex Disorders—therapy.   I. Title.
    [DNLM: 1. Marital Therapy.   WM 55 S357c]
    RC557.S3   1991   616.85'830651—dc20   91-31835

W.W. Norton & Company, Inc., 500 Fifth Avenue, New York, NY 10110

W.W. Norton & Company, Ltd., 10 Coptic Street, London WC1A 1PU

            8 9 0

To my wife, Ruth,
my daughter, Sarah,
and
my parents, Stan and Rose Schnarch

In Memory of
Bill Kell
David Schnarch
Sigmund Schnarch

I must conquer my loneliness
alone.

I must be happy with myself
or I have
nothing
to offer you.

Two halves have
little choice
but to
join;
and yes,
they do
make a
whole.

But two
wholes
when they coincide . . .
that is
beauty.

That is
love.

Peter McWilliams (1970)

Acknowledgments

I should warn you of the inherent paradox of reading books on intense intimacy and profound eroticism. Anyone who has taken the time to author such a book has no recent firsthand knowledge of what he or she writes. Without my beloved wife's gentle patience, I would certainly not have had the time to create this. Without her tremendous personal strength and integrity to bang my head against, I would never have learned about the importance of begrudging respect in marriage.

Writing this book has been the third best thing I have done in my life; marrying Ruth and having my daughter, Sarah Elizabeth, are the first two. Sarah has taught me more about how people develop than she will ever know. My parents have done the same; their love for each other and their continuing personal development have been more of a blessing for me than *they* will ever know. It's easy to see where they got it from: My 92-year-old grandmother, Estelle Schnarch, is a good teacher about the courage to love.

I have been blessed by teachers who nurtured me as I was becoming a man, and I am respectful and grateful. Bill Kell, William Mueller, and Ben Hoffman are master therapists and my admiration of them has driven my own development forward. There is one special man whose impeccable integrity will not permit mention of his name; I have become who *I* am because of who *he* is and his love.

There are other men whose friendship I cherish; these are my friends-for-life, and I don't use that term loosely. They are Ted Urban, Barry Lester, John Ducat, Dave Levert, and André Stern. André straddles both these groups of men, a professional in his own right who shared his mind and heart unselfishly on long walks during the formative stages of my thinking.

To all those who tolerated my long hermitage writing this book, my constant preoccupation, my slowness in corresponding, my memory and considerateness lost in an avalanche of ideas and references: I thank you. I am truly blessed by you all, and I give thanks for having known you in my lifetime. I hope that you find this book particularly gratifying, since it bears your collective thumbprint.

Writing a book of this magnitude certainly teaches who one's professional friends are; I, fortunately, have also been blessed with these too. André Stern, M.S.W., struggled through my earliest versions. More people were enlisted for the semi-final version: Elizabeth David, M.D. (LSU School of Medicine, New Orleans), offered expertise on object relations theory, challenging collegiality and encouragement. William Masters, M.D. (Masters and Johnson Institute), Bernard Apfelbaum, Ph.D. (Berkeley Sex Therapy Group), and Bernie Zilbergeld, Ph.D., had already given much to me (and the field of sex therapy) through their own writing. Bernie Apfelbaum was generous with his support and succinct suggestions throughout; Bernie Zilbergeld's review of the quantum model smoothed its presentation. The summaries preceding each chapter developed from William Masters' suggestions.

Don-David Lusterman, Ph.D., and Judy Lusterman were kind enough to tell me that my writing lacked coherence. This final version is much improved; I regret not writing it even better. Bernard Goldstein, Ph.D. (UCLA), critiqued the biological dimensions of this material; like the others, his comments pushed me to further refine my thinking. Robert Francoeur, Ph.D. (Fairleigh Dickinson University), and Rev. Raymond J. Lawrence, Jr., reviewed the material on sexuality and spirituality; their own work provided the stimulus for much of the discussion that appears. Joshua Golden, M.D., and Peggy Golden, B.A. (UCLA), offered comments that substantially shaped the book. I followed their suggestions the same way that I enjoy their friendship: closely. I alone, however, am responsible for the final version.

I talked about this book for several years with Susan Barrows of Norton Professional Books before undertaking to publish it with Susan as editor. It was a very deliberate act on both our parts, although in retrospect neither of us anticipated that it would involve what it has. Susan says I "win the award," although when she says it I know it is a dubious honor. Her experience editing sexuality books, her elegant personal style, wisdom, patience, and ability to handle authors have all been drawn upon. Her encouragement to speak out, and our mutual respect for the erotic, have allowed this book to evolve into what it is.

The other people who helped prepare the manuscript also deserve awards for endurance and composure in the face of frustration. Margaret Farley at Norton no longer has to receive my phone calls "last one at night and first in the morning." The typesetters at Bytheway Typesetting Services no longer pull their hair out with final changes. And Barbara McDowell, my administrative assistant and good friend, no longer needs to track down references in arcane places or go blind making galley corrections; my office can now go back to "normal" (although I doubt it ever will).

Thanks to Tricia Nolan, Assistant Professor of Medical Bibliography, LSU Medical Center, for proofreading.

Finally, I thank my patients. I thank them for allowing me to witness their triumphs and agonies, honoring me through the intimacy of our shared experiences. What you read here are their chronicles, what I have learned by what I have seen them do. They have taught me about the resilience of the human spirit and the quest for growth and goodness; most of all they have taught me about the wondrousness of sexual potential. I give special thanks to Sarah and Paul (whom you will meet later in this book) for allowing their story to be told and for directing me to resource material on spirituality; they epitomize the indwelling spirit of life in which they believe so strongly.

Contents

Introduction

Edgar Levenson (1972) pithily noted that writing a book is much like losing a mountaineering companion down a glacier crevasse. The friend eventually emerges from the foot of the glacier, frozen in time, far younger than the partner who returns to look at his trailmate. Levenson hoped that he had matured since the conclusion of his own book, which reflected his development at a moment in process.

It has taken over five years to write this book. It began with installing a computer in my office, into which I entered observations after particularly interesting sessions. After collecting ideas and clinical material for several years, it was time to figure out what I was thinking. This book, as well as its companion soon to follow, *The Intimacy Paradigm*, is the outgrowth of that process.

But it's not just my tendency to procrastinate in the face of anything wonderful that has taken this labor of love five years to come to maturity. It has taken that long for my own professional and personal maturity to reach the point that writing this book was possible. While Paul Masson winemakers tout that they "sell no wine before its time," it is another thing for an author to delay publication, knowing that his work has not ripened sufficiently. Perhaps this material would have been more striking if published some three years ago, when many of the concepts were already well developed. In the intervening period, sex therapy has matured somewhat and this book may be seen as an articulation of scattered thoughts many sexual and marital therapists have had; it will still be startlingly different to others.

Now I am glad that I have not rushed to publication (although my wife, friends, and editor would hardly consider it rushing). There is an elegance to life and the human experience—an elegance that is hard to recognize and almost impossible to articulate. As I become more mature, I find something spiritual in the way my patients play out their unwitting but deliberately and painstakingly created dramas of personal development. I am grateful for the opportunity I've had to write this book and, in the process, to learn what I have about life, relationships, intimacy, and sexuality.

When first starting to deal with patients' sexual concerns, I thought the problem was that I couldn't treat sexual dysfunctions; then I realized the real problem was that this was *all* I could do. Modern sex therapy conceptually divides people into two groups (without realizing it): people who have sexual dysfunctions, and those who don't (i.e., people who are *functional*). It's all too easy to assume that sexually *dysfunctional* people have lousy sex, never recognizing what common sense and experience say about *functional* people: Everyone whose body successfully completes the sexual response cycle (including orgasm) isn't having *wall-socket sex*. It turns out there are *three* categories: the sexually *dysfunctional*, the sexually *functional*, and the *blessed few* who have profoundly erotic intimate experiences. When one realizes this, one becomes more observant of "knowledge" about sex, marriage, and sexual-marital therapy.

When men and women pledge marriage "for better and for worse, in sickness and in health," they do so in the hope of pursuing the *best* that marriage has to offer. Modern sex and marital therapy, on the other hand, is predicated on the amelioration of *dysfunction*—we treat "sickness" and make the "worse" more tolerable. We offer little to facilitate the "better" and the "health."

This shows up in the most subtle ways, which also happen to demonstrate that we have a lot to learn about sexual "problems" as well. Treating "inhibited sexual desire," for example, presupposes a knowledge of "uninhibited sexual desire"; non-problematic desire, however, is not addressed by modern sexology. Folks commonly complain of boredom "while doing 'it,'" but desire *during* sex (e.g., passion and eroticism) is what therapists know the *least* about. We don't really know much more about *intimacy*. The procedures that contemporary sex and marital therapy developed to achieve *functional* sex and emotional "communication" are almost *antithetical* to profound interpersonal contact. One doesn't often hear of people romping around in bed during cadaver-like "non-demand non-genital touch."

Constructing the Sexual Crucible is an attempt to help the *functional*, the *dysfunctional*, and increase the ranks of the *blessed few*. It offers a new three-dimensional model of sexual desire, thorough consideration of eroticism, and a two-stage model of intimacy. These are presented with a constant eye towards clinical relevance and utility. My goal is to create a *paradigm shift*: not simply increasing the ideas in a burgeoning clinical literature, but creating an alternative way of seeing (and *doing*) sexual-marital therapy in which existing information takes on new meaning.

The emphasis of this book is on health and growth rather than pathology; absence of pathology does not create the type of marriage folks think they want. Eroticism and intimacy in marriage (and marriage itself) are adult *developmental* tasks. Thus, this book shifts from the deficit focus pervading many treatment approaches to an asset model; this shift also reflects my faith in human potential, including sexual potential. My patients would tell you, however, there is nothing about this approach that reflects *naivete*. We sometimes talk about *goodness*, but we also talk about *hatred* and *normal marital sadism*; it is very much a "hardball" approach.

Intensely intimate and erotic experiences are hard to get, and hard to tolerate when one has them. It's difficult for couples to have sex at the level of personal involvement that biblical prohibitions against *carnal knowledge* take for granted. Couples who *know* each other at this level during sex have reached one of the pinnacles of human development. The bible *is* correct, however, that this is the realm in which folks integrate sexuality and spirituality; unfortunately, most folks don't make it.

My patients never believe this until they experience it for themselves, and I have given up trying to explain it at the outset. I will do the same here: Having offered this provocative thought, I encourage you to read on to consider this for yourself in depth.

When this book addresses treatment of dysfunction, it does so in a way that doesn't interfere with additional development beyond "non-pathological" levels. More accurately, the crucible approach focuses on sexual potential from the outset, because doing so facilitates spontaneous resolution of sexual dysfunction along the way. This paradigm shift is one of the most profound performance-anxiety-reducing interventions possible.

People can develop the capacity for *self-validated* intimacy (required for intense eroticism) in the crucible of seeing eye to eye (i.e., literally having sex with prolonged eye contact); this, however, is not enough. The really important step involves having sex "*I*" to "*I*": letting oneself see and be seen *behind* the eyeballs (i.e., looking *inside* one another). However, folks spontaneously avoid "*I*" contact: Their eyelids are up, but their emotional "shades" are drawn; you can't see past their retinas. You can tell when you are really seeing *inside* someone, and they know they are letting you *see*. Couples can (re)learn to look *into* each other during sex; we train ourselves not to because the implications are often overwhelming.

These few observations give an inkling about the concept of the sexual crucible. A crucible is a resilient vessel in which metamorphic processes occur;

a secondary meaning refers to Christ's crucifixion. Both apply to the therapeutic crucible, recognizing that marital conflict is often the crossroad of personal development.

As the concept of the therapeutic crucible developed, the means of "therapeutic solution" shifted: No longer was the goal to unravel the Gordian knot of interlocking claims and counterclaims through negotiation and "communication." The goal became to help each spouse go *through* his or her elaborate construction rather than derail or avoid it. As therapy became the crucible containing the couple's drama, it also became the cradle of adult functioning.

The dynamics of marriage itself fuel the crucible. Couples stay together by concurrence, but separation or divorce is a unilateral option; marriage is a nonenforceable commitment. *One spouse, however, can always force the other to choose between holding onto the marriage and holding onto his/her integrity.* This is an adults-only realization, worlds away from "happily ever after." There is nothing wrong with this common mettle-melting development; it is part of marriage's *utility.* Marriage (and the marital bed) is the crucible of adult human development.

The *sexual* aspect of the crucible addresses the way couples play out their individual, dyadic, and family dynamics in the sexual dimension of their relationship. The style and emotional ambiance of the actual behavioral exchanges *always* reflect drama taking place on other levels, even when neither party has difficulty reaching orgasm. This permits the use of sexuality as an *elicitation window*: Looking at oneself *through one's* spontaneous sexual behavior is often a stunning experience.

Changing one's sexual style can both highlight and resolve nonsexual issues of personal development and relational deadlock. Couples are shocked that this doesn't involve negotiation or communication (and often loses this broader impact if it does); it involves *differentiation* (a growth process of primary importance in the sexual crucible). This approach produces leaps in sexual pleasure and intensity that still amaze me from time to time, and always amaze patients. This amazement forced me to reconceptualize the possibilities of human sexual development; the result is the concept of *sexual potential.*

The sexual crucible is an intimacy- and eroticism-based treatment approach; it departs from the sensate-prescription focus of modern sex therapy, and the a-erotic ambiance of contemporary marital therapy. It embraces a non-reciprocity model of intimacy which (a) *uses* sexuality as a vehicle for growth, (b) is readily operationalized through sexual behavior, and (c) helps people mature enough to explore the limits of their sexual potential. This approach integrates sex therapy and marital therapy, which have developed as more-or-less separate disciplines. Prior attempts to integrate the two fields have subordinated one discipline's framework and contribution to the predominant focus of the other. They are treated here with equality and integrated to such a degree that the outcome is metamorphic.

Modern society and modern therapists tend to agree about sexual technology: "Making love" is a behavior; if one does particular behaviors, then one should feel a particular way as a result. In this case, it involves the belief that intercourse is inherently intimate, arousing, and physically and emotionally satisfying. This book takes an alternate approach: Sex is only a way of conveying things that one must be capable of feeling and expressing, independent of specific behaviors. Given this ability, one can express them in an *anatomy-independent* fashion.

This book doesn't focus much on "techniques" by contemporary standards. Modern sex therapy has tended to be seen as a simplistic behavior-modification system of "canned" prescriptions and cookie-cutter outcomes; in part, this perceived shallowness is well deserved. Those looking for another "how to" book of sex therapy (or sex) techniques will be disappointed with *Constructing the Sexual Crucible*. At some points you may think, "OK, now that I *see* the problem, what do I do about it?" I have addressed that question at some points, noting at others that detailed coverage of relevant treatment techniques appears in the companion book to follow. *The Intimacy Paradigm: An Elicitation Approach to Sexual-Marital Therapy* focuses much more on actual interventions. Actually, *Constructing the Sexual Crucible* grew out of the process of writing *The Intimacy Paradigm*. It became increasingly clear that the conceptual underpinnings of the clinical approach needed to be explicated in advance, to convey the richness of the interventions and save clinicians and the public from yet another wave of technocracy.

The metaphor of the sinew-testing sexual crucible goes beyond describing the alchemy that integrated sexual-marital therapy offers people. Somewhat ambivalently, I must report that it also describes (a) the trials of professional/personal development awaiting therapists who seek to help patients fulfill their sexual potential, and (b) a therapist's in-session experience while doing so. Therapists generally undergo a gut-wrenching differentiation from their most dearly cherished personal beliefs and professional practices; it requires journeying forth from the promised land of modern sex therapy.

Clinicians' "comfort level" with sexuality varies greatly; one's own isn't obvious until it is exceeded. Consider, for example, the level at which one accepts one's *parents'* eroticism: Even those who can imagine their parents' "making love" don't generally see a lusty bed-squeaking encounter with panting and groaning; at best it is a silent movie with fuzzy focus, bad lighting, stilted acting, and of mercifully short duration. The point at which the image has technicolor, noise, action, and *style—this* is the comfort level and degree of involvement that therapists must achieve.

I acknowledge having not finished this growth process either. I had considerable difficulty writing the descriptions of sexuality at the limits of sexual potential you will encounter later on. Sexuality texts of serious merit are generally so devoid of eroticism that one would never expect to blush. One reads such books at night to put one to sleep, not before practicing what one preaches to patients. At some points, this book may have the opposite effect; the goal is not to titillate, but rather, to provide an honest look at what marital sexuality can really be.

There isn't much in modern sex therapy that addresses the therapist's use of *self*. Likewise, nothing in professional training provides sex or marital therapists greater knowledge or capacity for intimacy or sexual intensity (or a better marriage) than the average individual. From time to time, you may feel the same "crucible effect" as did people described in this book: suddenly seeing the limitations of one's own relationships revealed in one's personal (and clinical) practices. I have increasing respect for therapists who push themselves to the level of development necessary to fulfill their professional responsibilities.

I have the same response towards my patients. I admire folks who have very solid control over a *very* powerful eroticism. I respect self-mastery (rather than self-abnegation). I respect, most of all, people who have the strength and integrity to use their sexuality as a vehicle for their own development. I have learned more about eroticism and intimacy from my patients (particularly those over age 50) than anything I have ever read.

I think these pages reflect the cutting edge of sexual and marital therapy today. It is certainly the cutting edge of my own development. Putting this out for you to read is an incredibly intimate act: You will know how I understand intimacy per se, and how and what I see as a clinician and as a human.

I strongly suggest you read through the brief summaries preceding each chapter before beginning Chapter One; it will provide a more detailed conceptual overview in which to locate yourself when you start to read in earnest.

Like any good intimate, I neither expect your concurrence nor fear your disagreement. Writing this is a declaration of my own existence and my wish to make a small difference for having walked on this earth. I find myself forever curious, however, about what will be going on in *your* head as you read on.

D. M. S.
July 19, 1991

CONSTRUCTING THE SEXUAL CRUCIBLE

CHAPTER ONE

Leaving the Promised Land

We begin by looking at the contradiction between evolving expectations for intimacy and sexual satisfaction, and the paradigms of modern sex and marital therapy. Mutual completion of the sexual response cycle is not the same thing as intimacy. We must relinquish the modern sex therapy paradigm, which emphasizes genital (dys)function and overlooks eroticism and emotional meaning, if we are to develop as a discipline.

What does it take to change irrevocably the fundamental paradigms in which sexual-marital therapy is conducted?

Perhaps we should start from where Maturana and Varela (1987) leave off, with the Sufi tale of a society contemplating a move from their familiar island to a new one that promises a healthier and happier life. Some people reject outright the possibility of an alternative way of life, and some are stymied by their fear of crossing the waters. Some more adventurous types train themselves to swim or sail. When one of the former group meets one of the latter, a common dialogue ensues. A fearful type asks an adventurous type how a ton of cabbages can be transported as provisions for life on the new island. Invariably, the other answers that the weight would sink the ship; moreover, the cabbages might be altogether unnecessary upon arrival. "But what you call weight, I call my basic food," says the fearful type. "Suppose this were an allegory," asks the adventurer, "and instead of talking about cabbages we talked about fixed ideas, presuppositions, or certainties?" The response of those fearful of change is always the same: "I think I'll bring my cabbages to someone who better understands my needs!" (Maturana & Varela, 1987).

Modern society promises that intense intimacy and erotic bliss are a natural and inevitable outcome of love. Many couples consult sexual and marital therapists when they do not achieve this outcome. How have therapists evolved the capacity to help people on this journey? How do *they* know the route to this new island of marital bliss? And, are these socially sanctioned

1

"guides" any more willing than their patients to leave behind their own fixed ideas, presuppositions, and certainties?

The concept of marital romantic love is a relatively recent innovation (Bullough, 1976; Murstein, 1974). For most of recorded history, marriages have been arranged on the basis of social, political, and economic alliances, rather than chosen by the individuals themselves. It was not until the troubadours of the Middle Ages that the concept of "heart-breaking" romantic love emerged. Lawrence (1989) suggested that romantic love emerged in response to Christianity's emphasis on chastity and celibacy. Lederer and Jackson (1968) thought just the opposite: that it arose in response to the Crusades, when educated and bored women of the manor embraced "romantic love" as their *escape* from chastity. Contemporary views of intimacy, sexuality, and marriage are more affected by social, economic, and scientific forces than romantics would care to recognize.

Intimacy generally refers to great familiarity and disclosure of important personal information between confidants. A precise definition of intimacy is exceedingly hard to propose; two chapters of this book (Chapters Four and Five) are devoted to accomplishing that goal. And yet we use the word *intimacy* as if all people share an invariant understanding of the concept. We actually know very little about the evolution of intimacy throughout the course of civilization, and even less about its course in the evolution of the human species. As we shall see, this strange phenomenon, which mass marketing now promises as a given (for a price), has existed as a biological *possibility* for only the last 100,000 years. One might say that human intimacy is evolution's most current experimental novelty.

Only sketchy records from antiquity exist regarding how intimacy, sexuality, and marriage were handled in pre-Biblical, pagan-polytheistic, and ancient oriental cultures. We gather from 20,000-year-old sexually explicit cave drawings from Western Europe and tomb paintings from ancient Egypt that sexuality has been a central interest and concern from the earliest eras of civilization. However, the relationship between sexual behavior and intimacy is almost entirely a matter of conjecture.

Keifer (1977) noted that the quest for intimacy is one of the oldest themes in Western civilization. Some authors (e.g., Canter, 1963) have reinforced popular beliefs that the Roman Empire was besieged with sexual excesses and promiscuity; more recent scholars (e.g., Bullough, 1976; Lawrence, 1989), however, have pointed out that this interpretation is highly distorted and biased. The tendency to overlook the contextual meaning of sexuality is apparent in the lens through which every generation views the past. Plato theorized that lovers originally existed as a single entity whose bisection created two incomplete individuals; men and women were doomed to spend their days searching for their "other half" to recreate the original state of fused oneness. This theme of the frustrations and tragedies of romantic desire has been central to Western literature and modern thought. And yet, the context and content of these desires are rarely considered; Plato's view was not a romantic one. His concern was not with finding the perfect mate or "co-dependency" but, rather, with perfection of the soul and liberation of the spirit from its corporeal limits.

Many have criticized Christianity for "the poisoning of Eros" (e.g., Lawrence, 1989). Certainly the evolution of Christian dogma regarding love and intimacy shaped Western civilization's concepts of sexual and intimate gratification. John Money (1985) writes in *The Destroying Angel* of how early Christianity struggled to reconcile the contradiction between the sanctity of virginity, celibacy, and perfect chastity with the sanctity of marriage and childbearing. Love was characterized as good, spiritual, and affiliated with God; passion was evil, carnal, and base. Christian asceticism was a highly successful derivative of sex-negative Greco-Roman stoicism and gnosticism, with its platonic dualism of body as the tomb of the soul.

It is not as though more recent history provides a clearer navigational chart to intimate beatitude. Confusion and debate cloud our understanding of intimacy and sexuality in puritanism and Victorianism. For example, D'Emilio and Freedman (1988) write:

> As Edmund Morgan pointed out over forty years ago, Puritans were more interested in sex and more egalitarian about male and female sexual expression than we previously thought. More recently, scholars have revised the older pictures of the Victorians. One school argues that repression characterized official ideology, but just underneath the surface of society lay a teeming, sexually active underground. Another argument holds that repression did not characterize even the ideology. . . . Finally, one can interpret the work of Michel Foucault to suggest that Victorians were actually obsessed with sexuality, elaborating on its meanings and creating new categories of sexual deviance and identity. (p. xiii)

When one sets out for the new island of intimate bliss, one looks for markers and reference points. We want those reference points stable, so we can reach them or steer clear of them. The notion that these reference points are floating and affected by the same currents that affect us is an unsettling possibility. How does the therapist of today steer others with such certainty when the markers of history that underlie the tools of the trade are constantly being rewritten? If we are unable to maintain a stable picture of even the past two hundred years, how can sexual-marital therapists be freed from the short-sighted splash of pop psychology and contemporary culture, and at the same time remain responsive to it? D'Emilio and Freedman suggest that one major factor creating changing patterns of sexual politics is a window of social instability between the demise of an older social system and the establishment of a new one. Levenson's (1972) articulate discussion of the inherent time-bound nature of psychotherapeutic "understanding" poses thorny questions to the sexual-marital "guide": How does one lead others to new ways of handling intimacy and sex when, on the one hand, such journeys are often embarked upon during times of social transition, and on the other hand, the time-bound paradigms of psychotherapy are tied to that fading social system?

Lederer and Jackson (1968) pointed out that marital and sexual beliefs, attitudes, and ways of behaving are reciprocally determined by and determine the evolution of social conditions. They noted that the family unit is primarily organized around physical survival in all societies in all times when adaptation to a hostile environment is primary. Early hominids required bonding for survival of the species. As recently as the westward settlement of the United States, moreover, clearing the land and battling the weather and Native Americans led people to adopt criteria for a "meaningful relationship" that differ vastly from current conceptualizations. (Those Native Americans had their *own* ideas about intimacy and sexuality, which we are only recently coming to appreciate.) Lederer and Jackson suggest that the main forces confronting and organizing marriage today are primarily emotional:

> The battle for survival in modern societies is usually a battle for emotional survival and the tools of war are correspondingly psychological, aimed at maiming the enemy's self-esteem or causing him shame rather than killing him.
>
> In such psychological warfare (for example, the battle of the sexes between spouses), it is difficult to decide who is the winner and who is the loser. (p. 35)

The current obsessive quest for intimacy did not emerge until the mid 1880s. In the Middle Ages and colonial times, the more common focus was escaping the inexorable intertwining and close physical proximity of other human beings. Formality became a defense against the overbearing intrusiveness of neighbors and the lack of personal space (Gadlin, 1977). Every aspect of daily life was scrutinized and modulated by tightly knit extended family systems and Church dictates.

Fromm (1941) attributed the increasing quest for intimacy to the abolition of serfdom, the rise of metropolitan cities, and the industrial revolution which destroyed the pervasive connective tissue of society within which people defined themselves in relationship to each other. Progressively decreased clarity in role definitions fueled expectations for sexual equality and the need for inner-oriented definitions of self. Faced with the overwhelming awareness of existential loneliness and irrevocable separateness from others, men and women embarked on the search for intimacy as a balm for this anxiety. Like many other authors (e.g., DeLora & DeLora, 1975), Keifer noted:

> Unlike the individual in the earlier community *(Gemeinschaft)* environment who was more or less born into a ready-made set of close acquaintances, an individual living in the modern urban society *(Gesellschaft)* must search selectively and deliberately for those persons who are to become his/her close acquaintances and intimates. (1977, p. 267)

Increased interest in intimacy cannot be attributed to changes in social values per se. Cultural anthropologists point out that changes in customs, values, and behaviors are typically initiated by the introduction of some new material or invention; social policy and attitudes toward the change are a subsequent (rather than preliminary) process. Corresponding drastic shifts in economics and religion have similarly influenced traditional pair bonding. Copernicus' 16th century astronomical revolution challenged the infallibility of Roman Catholic dogma; Luther's Protestant Reformation furthered the process, directly challenging Rome's dictates regarding celibacy and divorce.

In 1769, James Watt's invention of the steam engine laid the groundwork for an industrial revolution that was to shake the very foundations of rural family structure and "traditional" marriage. Part of the shift was the rise of the middle class, made possible by the printing press and widespread distribution of printed material.

> The change in the last four hundred years, then, is not so much a change in the concept of romantic love between men and women, but the wholesaling of this possibility to the masses. History is filled with accounts of great love affairs, frequently between people who married, but they were of the ruling classes and never the peasantry. The industrial revolution and our own egalitarian revolution have raised the expectations of hundreds of millions of people concerning relationships, love, and marriage. Love is expected, and marriage must provide warmth and caring. (Beavers, 1985, p. 135)

Goals and motives concerning sexuality and intimacy in American culture have been quite varied: procreation, power over others, physical pleasure, recreation or sport, personal intimacy, and spiritual transcendence (D'Emilio & Freedman, 1988; Money, 1985).

> In the colonial era, the dominant language of sexuality was reproductive, and the appropriate locus for sexual activity was in courtship or marriage. In the nineteenth century, an emergent middle class emphasized sexuality as a means of personal intimacy, at the same time it reduced sharply its rate of reproduction. Gradually, commercial growth brought sex into the market-place, especially for working-class women and for men of all classes. By the twentieth century, when the individual had replaced the family as the primary economic unit, the tie between sexuality and reproduction weakened further. Influenced by psychology as well as by the growing power of the media, both men and women began to adopt personal happiness as a primary goal for sexual relations. (D'Emilio & Freedman, pp. xv–xvi)

Charles Goodyear's invention of vulcanized rubber in 1839, and the subsequent widespread availability of inexpensive latex condoms in the 1920s triggered increased public acceptance of non-procreative sexuality, and (partial) sexual equality for women. Readily available and effective contraception reduced distracting fears of pregnancy and permitted women to focus on emotional as well as physical gratification during marital and non-marital sex.

However, the industrial revolution and the consequent elevation of applied science have produced yet another revolution—one of heightened expectations. It is not hard to understand how people who have come to believe that "science" can solve all problems may also believe that the science of psychology has a "technology" for helping relationships lacking in intimacy. As patients turn to practitioners to provide this guidance, a paradox emerges. The search for "perfect intimacy" may be seen as a form of narcissism. Campbell (1975) pointed out that our field may add to this paradoxical state: On the one hand modern psychiatry and psychology describe men and women as self-centered, while on the other, they encourage them to be more so.

Perhaps the current divorce rate can be blamed on medical science; declining mortality rates have given new meaning to the notion of a life-long partner. As people live longer, the continuing quest for intimacy places new expectations on long-term relationships. Whereas the later years of life were sometimes thought of as a period of disengagement from intimate relationships (Burr, 1970; Pineo, 1961), research supports the crucial need for intimate relationships during this period (Lowenthal & Haven, 1968). As the impact of stress on the human auto-immune system and the aging process becomes more apparent, the importance of the quality of daily human interaction becomes clearer. Nowhere in the course of human civilization have people expected more gratification and fulfillment out of marriage than today.

The increase in divorce may be seen as a direct result of these heightened and unmet expectations. Some might argue that the current state of divorce and fracture of the family unit reflects the decay of the surrounding social structure. Others argue that it reflects insufficient flexibility and relevance of the institution of marriage to changing social circumstances. If marriage is to change, then certainly the socially designated institutions of marital and sexual expertise and their apostles must change as well.

William Simon (1989) astutely suggests we are experiencing a paradigmatic crisis following the failure of the *naturalized approach* of the 1960s and 1970s "modern" sexual era to produce the discoveries and consolidation it once appeared to herald. The *naturalization* of sex, typified by the Masters and Johnson (1966, 1970) paradigm, produced a focus on orgasm as a hyperreality unto itself with its own physiology, chemistry, and neurology. Once eroticism and sexual desire were viewed as simplistic expressions of biological drive that came as standard equipment with the body, the role of the individual and social context was ignored. Modern sexology approached sexuality, Simon writes, as if the secrets of life could be discovered on the dissecting table.

The result has been the evolution of a sexology which confuses sexual data with phenomenological experience, and overlooks consideration of eroticism, desire, and personal meaning. Simon notes that sexual satisfaction is determined by sociocultural meanings that occasion a sexual encounter; context impacts the way eroticism and desire are experienced and expressed in interpersonal "scripts" and the pleasure derived therein. The failure of naturalized behaviorism to distinguish between eroticism and sexual behavior is nowhere more apparent than in the professional literature; detailed discussion of sensuality and *wet* sex is totally absent.[1]

> At its best, however, the claim that the intensity with which many of us experience the sexual is proof of its "primary" or "primitive" character represents a very selective description of the universe of encounters with sexual desire, very little of which appears in scientific discourse. Between the opaqueness of the

---

[1]Chapter Fourteen offers a depiction of eroticism in sexual behavior that is unusual for a professional text. The role of sexual desire in human sexual response paradigms will be discussed later in this chapter, and in much greater detail in Chapter Nine.

language of drive and the seeming "heroism" of describing observable sexual behavior there is an almost complete silence regarding the specific content of either the desire for sex, the experience of sexual desire or the experience that affords different qualities of emotional production. (Simon, 1989, p. 25)

Shifting to a postmodern denaturalized sexual paradigm, Simon notes, requires resisting the belief that contemporary knowledge has universal applicability or timeless utilty. The need for new conceptualizations stems from the ever-changing contextual basis of sexual realities and not merely from inadequacies of old paradigms. No one likes to give up the precepts that underlie one's clinical practice and professional identity. On the other hand, holding on to old paradigms precludes developing an integrated sexual-marital therapy that considers eroticism, intimacy, and personal meaning in sexual behavior.

Sexual and marital therapists ply their trade with the implicit certainty that contemporary paradigms and practices are tried and true paths for that which people quest. Said differently, therapists imply that contemporary sexual and marital therapy has arrived at the promised land; the application of available technology has discovered the route to marital Mecca and made it easy to follow. So self-assured are clinicians in this belief, that couples are scrutinized for individual pathology and systemic collusion to explain therapeutic failures. Admittedly, it is a little difficult getting hired as a guide to the promised land while acknowledging that one's profession is still trying to find the way. Maintaining self-imposed caveats in the face of an increasingly market-driven profession and a demanding public is even harder:

> The steady popularity of "intimate" themes in the various media, the "pop intimacy" of encounter groups, and, for some, the restless moving in and out of "alternate" life-styles and marriages suggest the need of modern individuals for encounter, for understanding, for self-discovery, and for intimate union. The stresses of modern living—those that bring ulcers, heart attacks, and suicides—are thought to be soluble in the medium of the intimate experience. For many individuals, intimacy has become the new religion.
>
> The age-old attempt of human beings to resolve the separateness of individual existence has for many modern individuals become the frantic *pursuit* of intimacy. (Keifer, 1977, p. 291)

> A stranger to our land might well conclude, after being exposed to a fair sampling of our songs and of our product advertising, that it is the life, liberty and the pursuit of *intimacy* that propel our politico-economic and social system. (Keifer, 1977, p. 268)

THE HELPING PROFESSIONS' QUEST FOR INTIMACY

Wynne and Wynne have noted:

> . . . when we turn to our colleagues and to the literature in family therapy and marital enrichment, we have found that the goal of improved intimacy is currently viewed as a "given" that requires no further explanation. Many marital therapists and marital enrichment programs appear to assume that enhancing experiential intimacy is a direct pathway to improved relationships. Nevertheless, when we consider historical, ethnic and social-class variations in marital relationships, the current public and professional consensus about the importance of intimacy stands in sharp contrast to the rarity with which intimacy has been regarded as important, or has even been identified in other settings and times. As we review the vicissitudes of relatedness in contemporary Western life, we are perplexed by the ephemeral inconsistency of intimacy and impressed by the power and attraction of the phenomenon. All too often, even when intimacy is transiently meaningful, it fails to build into enduring relatedness. (Wynne & Wynne, 1986, p. 384)

These authors suggest that health-care professionals could do more to facilitate intimacy by challenging the quest for it than by promoting it:

> In our view, professionals in the marital and family field should take leadership in challenging the enshrinement of "intimacy" as a primary goal. Somewhat paradoxically, professionals may be more able to enhance the contribution of intimate experience to the quality of life if they do NOT accept what Schaefer and Olsen (1981) have aptly called "the overriding predominance of intimacy as a cultural value" (p. 47). (Wynne & Wynne, 1986, p. 392)

Rimmer (1977) observed that many writers double-talk about intimacy while subtly (and not so subtly) promoting what they know best—physical contact:

> Typical of the confusion in the minds of many of the sexual popularizers who believe, evidently along with Masters and Johnson, that good sex is physical first and mental second, is some of the work by Helen Gurley Brown. Here is a quote from the introduction to *Cosmopolitan* magazine's *Love Guide,* a bedside companion for the confused young female:
>
> > "Here we hope is the ultimate *love* book . . . it is not a sex text—although it *will* revolutionize your sex life if you really do all we tell you. Sexuality is *not* a mechanical thing. If an orgasm were your only goal, an electric vibrator would

help you achieve that, technically. But what any woman really wants is so much more . . . more human, more beautiful, more fulfilling, more magical, more supportive. She craves intimate sharing between two people."

The emphasis is Helen Gurley Brown's. Few females or males would disagree with the last two sentences. But do those sentences jibe with the contents of the book? Here are the chapter titles—and the sheer shuck you get for your money: *Awakening Your Sensuality . . . Sexual Muddles and Fallacies . . . The Erotic Senses . . . Know Your Body Nude . . . How to Excite Yourself . . . How to Make a Man Want You . . . Know His Body Nude . . . Losing Your Virginity without Losing Your Cool . . . That First Night with a New Man . . . Ways to Sustain Passion . . . How to Make Him a Better Lover . . . Sick Sex . . . Continuing to Live Sensuously . . .* topped off with *Your Zodiac Seduction Book.*

Contrast the introduction with the contents and you have the typical guide to what can be the ultimate physical contact any of us can experience in interrelationships. (Rimmer, 1977, pp. 361–2)

Sexual health-care professionals have contributed to this by promulgating the view of sexuality as the same as intimacy, fueling popular assumptions that sexuality is inherently intimate, and reinforcing the pursuit of sexuality as the best or most direct route to intimacy. Malone and Malone (1987) assail sexual health-care professionals who suggest that "sex is sex and has to be seen as such, not as something that has much to do with relationship" (p. 199). Sex therapists earned that stereotype in the early days of the 1960s and '70s when sexual science adopted the mantle of austere, quantifiable scientific "hard science" in an attempted to establish itself as a legitimate scientific discipline. Keifer points out:

Contemporary social scientists, however, have only begun to raise questions regarding intimate processes and have made few attempts to integrate the work of earlier writers. Furthermore, intimacy is an often-used euphemism for sexual behavior, and family specialists have tended to equate intimate with sexual behavior and sexuality. Those who have written about intimate life-styles actually have been referring to a variety of emergent sexual life-styles. Furthermore, there are obvious operational problems in defining and then conducting empirical investigations of intimate processes. (Keifer, 1977, p. 269)

In reinforcing the pursuit of sexuality as both the best or most direct route to intimacy, and an end in itself, the sexual health-care field has fueled preoccupation with sexual functioning.[2] It has reciprocally stimulated and been

---

[2]Of course, that preoccupation exists in many others who are not sexual health-care providers.

stimulated by such "technological advances" as penile implants, papaverine, and "pecker pumps." Not that people have ever needed much encouragement from professionals to be preoccupied with genital functioning. But we often lose sight of the cyclical process by which ordinary people become physicians and therapists who then perpetuate prevailing attitudes in the name of science. *Many health-care providers who promote the latest surgical, chemical, mechanical, and behavioral "advances" believe (explicitly or implicitly) that maintenance of an erection sufficient for intercourse and completion of the sexual response cycle is the most important issue in sexual intimacy.* The underlying assumption that completion of the sexual response cycle or prolonged intercourse is synonymous with sexual bliss is hardly recognized—hardly recognized, that is, until it is pointed out that they themselves may have "adequate" sexual functioning, but frustrating and unfulfilling sexual relationships. The "relational" aspects of sexual relationships are often the most difficult, and the most salient, in terms of "sexual satisfaction."

The subtly expressed attitude that sexual functioning is synonymous with sexual satisfaction is not merely an aberration of the medical model. The entire modern field of sexual therapy is rooted in a focus on *utilitarian* sexual function or, more accurately, on sexual *dysfunction*. In fact, almost all the major textbooks in the field of sexual therapy are organized around discrete genital performance difficulties (or more recently, desire disorders) and their treatment. While often explicitly eschewing a medical model, sex "therapy" has focused on "pathology" and sexual dysfunction and *not* on the promotion of holistic wellness, sexual fulfillment, or intimacy.

Masters and Johnson's Model

The field's obsession with the mechanics of sex results, in part, from Masters and Johnson's concentration on performance problems and the phenomenal impact of their model of human sexual response. Masters and Johnson's (1966) famous four-stage "phase" model of excitement, plateau, orgasm, and resolution focused on genital and peripheral physiological changes and on classification of sexual dysfunctions. Their model's exclusive focus on physiological response has had tremendous impact on the field. It may be that many clinicians have drawn meaning from Masters and Johnson's publications that differ significantly from what these two central figures in modern sex therapy had in mind; the consistency of others' interpretation of their work may shape their legacy more than the actual style of therapy Masters and Johnson evolved. Part of this stems from the absence of a thorough articulation from Masters and Johnson of their actual clinical approach and an integration of it with their model of sexual response.

For example, Masters and Johnson's original diagnostic schema of physiological response disorders overlooked consideration of problems of interest or desire (see Figure 1.1); this absence has led other clinicians to interpret the implications and assumptions of their model. It would appear that Masters and Johnson originally assumed that intensity and salience of sexual experience were correlated with level of physiological arousal, and sexual interest was positively correlated with orgasmic frequency. The idea that sexual feelings follow from sexual function is consistent with their underlying assumption that sexual arousal is most likely to appear when it is ignored.

The absence of subjective arousal and phenomenological experience in their model and the lack of consideration of *desire* reinforced a common view of sexuality held by many clinicians: orgasm was thought to be so intensely pleasurable and self-reinforcing that one would have to be either stupid or significantly disturbed not to go back for a second helping. Masters and Johnson state that their two-week treatment program did not permit time for analysis or appreciation of individual psychosexual development, and that

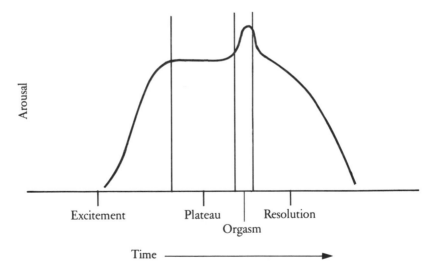

Figure 1.1 Masters & Johnson's Sexual Response Cycle
Derived from Human Sexual Response, 1966, p. 5.

they based their strategy around the assumption that "memory of pleasure in sensate experience probably represents the only *psychological* constant in human sexual response, since all other psychological investment is organized into a highly individualized matrix for every human being" (1970, p. 70). In the case of sexual dysfunctions it was anticipated that, if patients could be helped to have a successful physiological performance, they would continue to want to repeat it in the future. The sum total of such expectations actually increases pressure on patients to want sex and to have orgasms. Yet, Masters and Johnson's clinical emphasis on performance anxiety and the notion of non-demand pleasuring appears to eschew a goal-oriented focus on orgasm.

The field of sexual health-care has given little consideration to the role of treatment *paradigms*, yet this consideration is crucial to whether the eventual goals of interventions are achieved. For instance, the outcome of interventions aimed at reducing performance anxiety (e.g., ban on intercourse) and prescription of non-demand pleasuring is more determined by the paradigm in which it occurs than by something inherent in the behaviors. Is a therapist working within the Masters and Johnson paradigm (or at least the common understanding of their paradigm) giving an underlying paradoxical message when the patient is encouraged *not* to focus on orgasm? Heiman and Grafton-Becker (1989) point out that in spite of seeing the couple as "the patient" and using the couple to treat the sexual problem, Masters and Johnson appear to emphasize etiological factors on the individual level in conceptualizing sexual problems (e.g., religious beliefs, spectatoring). Do such contradictions put the therapist in an unwitting and subtle double-bind, which may never reach consciousness but reduces therapist resiliency and effectiveness?

For another example, consider the implications for professionals engaged in adolescent sex education. It is common for sex education programs to encourage knowledge of human sexuality towards the goal of responsible decision-making and prevention of problem pregnancies. The Masters and Johnson sexual response cycle is often taught as if it were fact, rather than a model. But more importantly, the underlying assumption that completion of the sexual response cycle is the fulfillment of human sexual potential—so pleasurable that it inherently leads to subsequent desire and repetition—is actually antithetical to a sex education approach suggesting that higher cortical processes can control sexual behavior. Moreover, the philosophy that "sex is a natural function" has a different meaning to a teenager than to a middle-aged man with erectile difficulty. To the former, it becomes a rationalization for adolescent sexual experimentation and reinforcement for the common belief that hormones control human sexual behavior; to the latter, it suggests that he *should* have sexual desire and function—if he were competent. The ease with which "sex is a natural function" can be (mis)interpreted as encouragement to "do what comes naturally" fuels support for the mindless "sex is uncontrollable/dangerous" educational approach of "Just Say No!"

The object of this digression is to point out that one's verbally stated attitude (which in the case of Masters and Johnson is clearly toward performance-anxiety reduction and teenage pregnancy prevention) is often antithetical to the subtle implications of one's paradigm. This contradiction, when it occurs, creates a paradoxical message at an unconscious level that, at the least, weakens the intended impact of messages and interventions delivered from within that paradigm.

Williams (1983) noted a similarly striking but apparently unnoticed inconsistency in the Masters and Johnson (1970) approach to sex therapy, resulting from their physiologically based model of sexual response. Masters and Johnson's treatment of retarded ejaculation deviates from their otherwise invariant emphasis on pressure-free, "nondemand" activities. Pressure to perform (ejaculate) is the central thrust of treatment, whereas those very same techniques were specifically proscribed for women with similar orgasmic difficulties. Williams suggested this inconsistency arose from Masters and Johnson's assumption that the retarded ejaculator's ability to maintain an erection was indicative of sexual arousal:

> However, although the penis of the retarded ejaculator is erect, he may not be experiencing the erotic feelings that can be expected to accompany his erection. The absence of erotic feelings is irrelevant to the Masters and Johnson sexual response cycle since their construct rests solely on physiological events. Thus, the retarded ejaculator meets the requirements for the Masters and Johnson excitement and plateau phases even when he lacks the state of heightened sexual arousal which would take him into the orgasm phase. Considering his lack of erotic feelings, his lack of orgasm is not nearly so noteworthy as is his sustained erection. (1983, p. 159)

Williams suggested that Masters and Johnson's report of 82% success with retarded ejaculation patients reflects their ability to force ejaculation while perpetuating the patient's problem of pleasureless physiological arousal. Williams used the term "premature erections" to underscore that physiological response in men cannot be taken as inherently reflective of subjective arousal. Premature ejaculation is a ubiquitous example of physiological response occurring independently of sexual arousal and satisfaction. The corresponding term "premature orgasm" is sometimes used for women who experience multiple orgasms with minimal stimulation and miss the buildup of sexual tension prior to orgasm. These phenomena, once understood, illustrate the need for consideration of sexual satisfaction independent from vasocongestion and orgasm. Likewise, they underscore an implicit and often unrecognized aspect of the paradigm of "modern" sex therapy. Sex therapy focuses on increasing performance by attempting to reduce anxiety about performance; as we shall see when we consider Bernard Apfelbaum's (1983) notion of *response anxiety*, Masters and Johnson's paradigm may actually perpetuate the performance anxiety that it seeks to diminish!

At the time of its original publication, some 25 years ago, Masters and Johnson's physiological model of the human sexual response cycle was a major advance in sexual science. Yet, like all scientific advances, it also reflected conceptual limits. Now that their contribution has become so assimilated into modern society as to be taken for granted as *truth*, it is crucial to explore those limits. What was originally a strength of the model is also its weakness: It is a purely physiological model without space for phenomenological experience. While Masters and Johnson addressed people's feelings in their treatment approach, these are conspicuously absent from their model of human function and dysfunction.

Rosen and Beck (1988) pointed out that both the absence of integration of cognitive-affective states with physiological processes and the practical difficulty of differentiating four discrete stages are significant shortcomings of Masters and Johnson's model. They describe Masters and Johnson's model as an impressive but essentially disjointed description of physiological events.

Others have suggested that Masters and Johnson's exclusive focus on dysfunction has created obstacles to thinking about the relation between performance and subjective arousal:

> The term "sexual dysfunction," introduced in *Human Sexual Inadequacy*, has become so much a part of our language that it can indeed seem strange to be presented with a symptom that is not a dysfunction. Perhaps this makes it easier to notice that the term "sexual dysfunction" carries the assumption that sexual problems are to be defined in terms of behavioral outcomes, erections and orgasms, and that the achievement of these outcomes signifies sexual fulfillment. We have come to associate unimpaired sexual functioning with sexual well-being. Yet consider the way arousal disorders can be masked by non-symptomatic sexual functioning in people whose sexual alienation is less severe than that found in Masters and Johnson's sexual aversives. In fact, in this

Masters and Johnson sample sexual alienation may well have been masked until it reached phobic proportions and then could no longer be ignored. (Apfelbaum, 1977c, p. 95)

On another note, it has taken years for sexual health-care providers to listen to what women have been saying all along. Ann Landers' nonscientific survey of women's preference for coitus or cuddling reflected this: It is not the orgasm they crave, but rather the sense of satisfaction and arousal that is often missing in intercourse. Harold Lief (1988) noted that some people who are orgasmic seemingly don't "remember" their orgasms and have no desire to pursue further sexual experiences. He suggested that the event of orgasm may be so unstimulating that it fails to lead them to desire such pleasure again.

Apfelbaum (1977c) suggested that an artifact of Masters and Johnson's original research for *Human Sexual Response* has made the ability to tune out the partner and perform, the *de facto* reference model of sexual style. He suggested that Masters and Johnson's sexual athletes' ability to ignore the massive intrusions of the laboratory setting, anonymous partners, and artificial phallus should have resulted in the publication's being named *Human Sexual Performance*. We are only emerging from the fog of sexual dysfunction treatment to recognize that people who can function without feeling are not necessarily sexually healthier or more satisfied than those with genital response difficulties.

Kaplan's Triphasic Model

Shortly after Masters and Johnson conceptualized the sexual response cycle as four stages of physiological changes comprising a unitary process, Kaplan (1974) proposed that sexual response was actually a *bi*phasic process composed of two distinct and relatively independent components. Her biphasic model, presented in *The New Sex Therapy*, consisted of (a) genital vasocongestive reaction (excitement) and (b) reflexive clonic muscular contractions (orgasm). Like Masters and Johnson, Kaplan offered a conceptual understanding of the role of human emotion in sexual dysfunction; like her predecessors, she did not integrate it into her physiological model.

Kaplan's next major publication, *Disorders of Sexual Desire*, reflected and fostered growing professional attention to problems of inhibited sexual desire. In it, she attempted to address the issues of erotic arousal and the phenomenological experience of sexual desire that Masters and Johnson had ignored. She noted that frequency of orgasm was uncorrelated with degree of arousal in

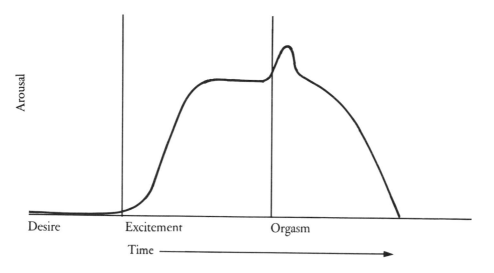

Figure 1.2 A Common Understanding of Kaplan's Triphasic
Concept of Human Sexuality

some women having orgasmic dysfunction or sexual desire problems. Kaplan
was instrumental in the inclusion of such problems in the third edition of the
American Psychiatric Association's *Diagnostic and Statistical Manual of Mental
Disorders (DSM-III)*, (1980).

Whereas there was no role for sexual desire in Masters and Johnson's sexual
response model, Kaplan (1977, 1979) proposed a *triphasic* model (desire,
excitement, and orgasm), placing desire *before* physiological response (see Figure 1.2). Desire was conceived as an appetitive response preceding sexual
arousal and leading to sexual behavior, similar to the popular concept of
"horniness." Her model of desire was quite consistent with notions of *libido*
(sexual drive or energy) in the psychoanalytic framework within which she
primarily operated.

Rosen and Beck (1988) noted that Kaplan's desire stage, although an important contribution to the clinical literature, lacked adequate operational definition and linkage to the stages of excitement and orgasm. Further, Kaplan's
hypothesis of desire as a necessary precondition for excitement and orgasm
was contradicted by research indicating that perhaps one-third of women,
unselected for sexual dysfunction, never experienced spontaneous desire despite adequate arousal and orgasm (Garde & Lunde, 1980).

Yet the most telling feature of Kaplan's model of sexual desire was the aspect that passed unnoticed by most clinicians, perhaps because it was consistent with the prevailing paradigm of modern sex therapy. Kaplan's notion of sexual desire as a *precursor* to sexual arousal or behavior is quite different from desire-as-passion that can occur *throughout* the physiological response cycle. Kaplan's discussion of sexual desire as analogous to *hunger* for food underscores the deprivation/satiation paradigm of modern sex therapy. This has several parts, the first of which is the implicit notion that sexual desire is a function of deprivation. It is consistent with the popular witticism: "Sex is a misdemeanor: the more you miss it, the meaner you get."

The second implication is that, once deprivation is no longer an issue, desire is reduced. That is to say, we expect desire to slack once sexual arousal starts, and certainly once the sexual response cycle has run its course. Widespread adoption of the appetitive model of sexual desire obviated consideration of "burning" and "yearning" sexual passion that can pervade the entire sexual encounter and is not slackened by orgasm. It is the notion of sexual desire as ever-increasing passion that people anticipate, hope for, and demand.[3] The failure of the modern sex therapy paradigm to address issues of passion — instead of performance — paved the way for those who did so by pathologizing it into an "addiction." "Sexual addiction" addresses desire for sexual behavior which is not reduced by orgasm and other forms of attempted satiation. Ironically, many clinicians who vehemently disagree with the conceptualization and marketing of sexual addiction therapy fail to recognize that "hunger" models of sexual desire provided a fertile environment for its emergence.

A further irony exists when sex and marital therapists attempt to address a wife's complaint that her husband rolls over to sleep after he reaches orgasm, leaving her frustrated and deciding whether to kill him or bring herself to climax. This common situation, known as "snorgasms," is consistent with the deprivation/satiation model of desire that prevails in modern sex therapy. By analogy: he was hungry, he ate, and he was satiated . . . so why go on? There is something quite humorous when the husband hoists the therapist on his or her own petard by citing the literature in self-defense.

Although Kaplan's triphasic model was a significant step forward in developing a comprehensive model of human sexual response, the duality between the phenomenology and physiology in sexual response was perpetuated, as in Masters and Johnson's model. Once arousal started, the phenomenological dimension (represented by desire) ceased to be involved in the physiological

---

[3]For a thorough discussion of the concepts of sexual desire, passion, and arousal, see Chapter Nine.

response. As such it was a model of human sexuality that failed to account for that characteristic which most sets human sexuality apart from that of other species and which is itself rooted in biology: the human capacity for intimacy and attaching profound emotional meaning to sexual experience. Although Kaplan discussed many ways in which human emotion could influence physiological response, she failed to integrate it into her model of human sexual function.

Modern sex therapy has lacked a paradigm that fosters high levels of sexual desire and salience. In point of fact, the implicit paradigm of modern sex therapy, with its failure to integrate the biological capacities of humans for both physical response and phenomenological meaning, has had far-reaching and often unrecognized effects—some of them negative, some of them simply contributing to the failure to help people solve the very dilemmas that brought them into treatment. Among these we must underscore difficulties with intimacy, especially intimacy in relation to sexuality. The focus on dysfunction, inherent in modern models of physiological response and the content of the professional sex therapy literature, is not enough.

What is required, and what this book offers, is a paradigm shift in the way that sexual-marital therapy is conceptualized and practiced.

You can tell when a paradigm shift takes place by what happens in the arena of questions. Just prior to a paradigm shift, some questions seem quite bizarre and even heretical. After the paradigm shift, the same questions seem self-evident; in fact, you wonder how you couldn't even see that the question needed to be asked. For example, the paradigm of modern sex therapy encourages clinical consideration to stop at the point of orgasm. But, with a paradigm shift to *sexual potential*, you might look at the sexual response cycle and ask, "What is beyond orgasm?"

This chapter has actually set the stage for the micro and macro levels of exploration that will occur within this book. The paradigm shift will begin on a micro-level in the next chapter with the quantum model, a physiological model of sexual functioning that integrates the role of salience and phenomenological intensity into human sexuality. Then in Chapter Three, we will consider a concept that permits further exploration of phenomenological intensity and salience: the concept of *sexual potential*. In Chapters Four and Five, we will conduct a fundamental reexamination of our understanding of the nature and process of intimacy.

Subsequently, our focus will shift to a more clinical perspective. The *sexual crucible*, grounded in a new *clinical* model of intimacy, represents a complete paradigm shift from "modern" sex therapy to what might be properly considered a "post-modern" paradigm. We will integrate the earlier line of inquiry in this new context, by presenting a multisystemic perspective on factors that contribute to and impede intimacy and the attainment of sexual potential. Along the way we will stop to marvel at the inherent elegance of human functioning on many related levels: the individual, the dyad, and the extended relational system. We will encounter a three-dimensional model of sexual response integrating sexual desire in Chapter Nine, and reconsider the politics of sexual desire and *wanting* in Chapter Ten. Chapter Fourteen will offer an extended case example of sexual desire-as-passion.

Finally, we will return to consideration of the sexual crucible, in terms of both the internal processes of the patients, and the role of the therapist. In our last chapter, we will consider the role of spirituality and sexuality, completing our examination of human sexual potential—from the ridiculous to the sublime. There we will encounter the work of a Benedictine monk who has developed what the minions of sexual health-care professionals have not: a paradigm in which desire, particularly sexual desire, stems from a sense of fullness and completeness rather than deprivation and hunger, and which grows rather than being slackened by fulfillment.

As we prepare to leave the promised land of modern sex therapy, let us be heedful of the Sufi tale: please leave your presuppositions and certainties at the shoreline.

CHAPTER TWO

The Quantum Model of Sexual Function and Dysfunction

We now turn to a model of human sexual response that integrates physiological and psychological dimensions; it offers a foundation for considering intimacy and sexual desire. Psychological processes modulate the impact of tactile stimulation and are, in themselves, a component of total stimulus level. Sexual (genital) response occurs when total stimulation reaches "threshold" levels for tumescence/lubrication or orgasm. Humans are capable of profound sexual experiences, uncorrelated with level of tactile stimulation or vasocongestive response.

The quantum model[1] is a *systemic* framework integrating physiologic and psychological aspects of sexual functioning. It provides an understanding of why bodies function sexually and why sometimes they don't. It offers an alternative to the widespread tendency to conceptualize sexual dysfunctions as separate "diseases," such as one might think of leukemia, high blood pressure, and kidney stones. Many sex therapy textbooks do not escape this compartmentalized approach.

The quantum model also avoids the tendency to dichotomize the causes of sexual dysfunctions into (non-interactive) "orgasmic" and "psychogenic" categories, as commonly occurs in urology, gynecology, and psychiatry texts.

The term *quantum* derives from the Latin word meaning "how much"; in our present context, it concerns the amount of stimulation required to create the physiological changes Masters and Johnson (1966) outlined as the sexual response cycle.

On the level of cellular response, the body conducts electrical impulses from specialized sensors to specialized receptors. Like all electrical processors (and all organisms), the body exhibits "threshold" sensitivity levels below

---

[1]The quantum model is a tentative formulation, offered here for its clinical utility; it is my hope that it will stimulate further development by others. Some of its roots lie in the early writings of Masters and Johnson (1970) and of Mosher (1980).

21

which the receptor does not reliably detect stimulation to trigger its performance. This is analogous to signal detection theory, which was the basis of Bateson's (1951) early work in family therapy.

At its most basic level, the quantum model is an economic model of genital functioning integrating physiological stimulation and intrapsychic processes. In its richest elaboration, it integrates intimacy, emotional meaning, and sexual potential.

Medical students, physicians, and therapists report the model helps organize seemingly diverse data into an integrated system of fluid dynamic processes; it reduces the need to memorize specific questions for diagnostic interviews and increases clinical flexibility. Patients report the model helps them understand sexual difficulties related to medical illness and relationship problems.

THE BASIC CONCEPTS

"Sexual stimulation" is composed of more than just tactile input; emotional and cognitive processes amplify or diminish the effective impact of concurrent tactile stimulation. Moreover, psychological processes comprise a portion of the total amount of an individual's total stimulation; they have stimulus value in their own right. In some cases, psychological stimulation alone is sufficient to create genital response and orgasm.

Total stimulus level differs from physical (tactile) stimulus level; *total* stimulus level is a mind-body interaction, determined by two components:

TOTAL STIMULUS LEVEL = PHYSICAL STIMULI + PSYCHOLOGICAL PROCESSES

TOTAL STIMULUS LEVEL refers to the total amount of sexual stimulation that is less than, equal to, or greater than the threshold level for physiological sexual response.

The term **PHYSICAL STIMULI** refers to the amount of external sexual stimulation received. It is a function of the quality and quantity of tactile input and the capacity of the body to transmit and process it.

PSYCHOLOGICAL PROCESSES refer to the emotional and cognitive processes of the receiver. These include sensate focus abilities, attribution of meaning to sensory experiences, and the impact of anxiety. Psychological processes are modulated by intrapsychic and systemic components.

THRESHOLD refers to the amount of total stimulation required to trigger genital vasocongestive responses associated with arousal and orgasm.

Level of *total* stimulation (rather than tactile stimulation per se) determines whether anticipated changes in sexual physiology occur. Descriptions of human sexual function are often mechanical, devoid of any of the "humanness," complexity, or warmth that most people seek in sex. In fact, most descriptions are apt models of sexual functioning for species lower on the phylogenetic scale.

In humans, sexual functioning involves more than tactile input; the manner in which stimulation is experienced and attended to plays a crucial role in determining the *total* stimulus level and the degree of arousal ultimately achieved. Contrary to contemporary notions of "giving someone an orgasm," or "making someone 'cum'," putting the *human* into human sexuality involves the internal experience of individuals involved.

In actuality, even the partner's psychological processes have an impact on the "receiver's" total stimulus level; metacommunication regarding the partner's pleasure has a marked impact. For centuries, the focus of partners' consciousness has been emphasized by the sexual doctrine of many Eastern religions. This topic will reappear in our subsequent discussion of *sexual potential*, when we consider achieving extreme levels of sexual pleasure (Chapter Three). For now, discussing two sets of psychological processes adds a cumbersome level of complexity; we will consider only the *receiver's* internal focus in our immediate goal of explaining minimal levels of sexual functioning.

The concept of total stimulus level is similar to Weiss' (1972) neurophysiological model of dually innervated erection. Weiss conceptualizes a synergistic interaction of psychogenic and reflexogenic pathways in which the amount of genital stimulation required for erection is reduced when erotic psychic stimulation is present. Conversely, guilt or hostility, even at unconscious levels, could inhibit the erection reflex. Weiss considers psychic stimulation to consist

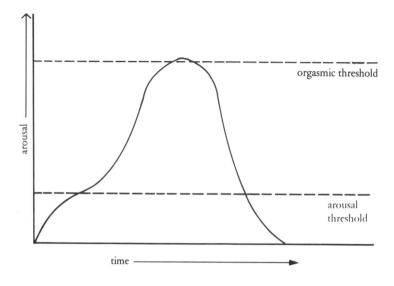

Figure 2.1 Thresholds for Sexual Response

of a variety of components: visual, auditory, tactile, olfactory, gustatory, memory, and imagination. Weiss' model and the quantum model differ in that the former focuses on changes in physiological transmission of stimulation, whereas our emphasis is on "executive functions" which organize and modulate the impact of physical stimulation. Weiss' dual-innervation model and the quantum model represent compatible parallel interactive processes.

SEXUAL RESPONSE THRESHOLDS: AROUSAL AND ORGASM

When total levels of stimulation reach two distinct response "thresholds," physiological changes associated with adequate sexual functioning occur. These two thresholds concern arousal and orgasm (see Figure 2.1). A threshold is nothing more than a stimulus level that must be reached or exceeded to trigger genital and peripheral physiological changes.[2] For example, when sexual stimulation reaches or exceeds the arousal threshold, erection occurs in men

---

[2]In the strict physiological sense, threshold refers to the "all-or-nothing" response of a nerve to a stimulus, which can be experimentally isolated and quantified. In its current usage, threshold refers to an "adequate" level of stimulation, and remains a conceptualization beyond existing psychophysiological measurement techniques.

or vaginal lubrication occurs in women (both caused by increased blood flow to the genital region).

The orgasmic threshold operates in much the same way. Orgasm is basically a reflex, just like the patellar "knee jerk" reflex.[3] Although orgasm is far more complex, feels better, and triggers far more performance anxiety, it is basically the same phenomenon. It is quite possible for a physician to stimulate a patient's kneecap so lightly that the reflex threshold is not achieved. Likewise, if the physician smashes the patient's knee, or if the patient is unable to relax the leg or deliberately overrides the reflexive response, the anticipated response will not occur. Within the sexual domain, the phenomenon known as orgasm occurs when necessary and sufficient *total* stimulation to reach the orgasmic threshold is achieved.[4]

Variations in Thresholds

Stimulus thresholds for sexual response differ; some people are blessed or cursed with relatively low or high thresholds. Genetics and previous experience (conditioning) account for some individual differences. Threshold levels also differ for a given individual over time. Transient fluctuations may result from fatigue, illness, alcohol consumption, prescription or recreational drugs, intermittent borderline diabetes, hormonal fluctuations, and other physiological processes.

Thresholds for sexual response also display long-term patterns of change;

---

[3]The analogy of patellar reflex (a muscle stretch reflex) may be more apt than apparent at first glance. Sherfey (1966, 1974) conceptualizes orgasm as a spinal reflex triggered by pelvic muscle stretch receptors. Orgasm is thought to be triggered by vasocongestive stretching of the pelvic muscles producing powerful reflexive contractions; the result is expulsion of blood trapped in the tissue and venous plexi and the associated sensations of orgasm. Mould (1980) offers an even more sophisticated muscle stretch theory.

Kinsey et al. (1953) suggested that the explosive tension discharge in *sneezing* was the best analogy to orgasm; obviously, this conceptualization emphasizes the individual dimension. The patellar examination metaphor works on both the systemic (dyadic) and individual level; two partners can make each other sneeze, but most people prefer to make each other twitch.

[4]Conceptualization of a stimulus threshold is consistent with prevailing views of sudden discharge of sexual tension through orgasm. It fulfills Rosen and Beck's (1988) suggestion that modern views of orgasm (as a sudden, all-or-nothing change) must account for the striking transition from preorgasmic to orgasmic states. The notion of "threshold" is implicit in the efforts of many clinicians (e.g., Barbach, 1980; Lobitz & LoPiccolo, 1972; LoPiccolo, 1980) to develop orgasmic "triggers," physiological responses (such as voluntary muscle contractions or hyperventilation) that push a highly aroused individual "over the line" into orgasm. Masters and Johnson (1966) postulate that "a trigger-point level of vasocongestive and myotonic increment" (p. 129) is involved in the inception of orgasm. Rosen and Beck (1988) noted that no theory of orgasm to date had considered the possible role of *psychological* events as triggers.

one such change is associated with aging. As an individual ages, more stimulation is required to reach threshold and a corresponding slowing of response is common. Disease, injury, and medications can elevate thresholds. All the above difficulties can have additional psychological effects that reduce total stimulus level, and thus further reduce the likelihood of reaching threshold levels of stimulation.

For the moment, it is sufficient to recognize that little or no (expected) genital response is observed when total stimulus level fails to reach the individual's current threshold. This may occur even when receiving what might have been previously regarded as "sufficient" stimulation.

The distinction between *subjective arousal* vs. *genital response* becomes crucial when people complain of not becoming "aroused." It is quite possible to be desirous of sexual contact and *feel* aroused, even though total stimulation does not reach arousal threshold. This occurrence confuses people about their sexual interest and ability, and generates anxiety in the couple; one partner may feel unattractive or undesirable to the other.

Likewise, an individual experiencing minimal subjective arousal may demonstrate "adequate" genital response. Clinicians' tendency to use genital response as an indication of subjective "arousal" creates further diagnostic confusion; patients use the same guideline when asked if they are "aroused." More properly, genital response is an indication of a particular *level* of arousal.

Like many other physiological processes, sexual response thresholds can be conditioned. The discovery that the autonomic nervous system was conditionable led to rapid advances in treatment of psychophysiological disorders (e.g., migraine headache); biofeedback training has made conscious control of brain waves, peripheral vasodilation, and other physiological processes commonplace.

Masters and Johnson (1970) hypothesize that sex in situations encouraging "getting it over quickly" (e.g., with prostitutes or in backseats of cars) can condition a man to have subsequent premature ejaculation. The notion of threshold conditionability is a relatively unexplored conceptual dimension offering new opportunities for clinical intervention. Threshold conditionability may play a significant role in the sexual difficulties of individuals with posttraumatic stress disorders.

Results with my patients suggest that treatment of rapid ejaculation can be accomplished by raising the man's orgasmic threshold through repeated exposure to *unusually intense* sexual stimulation. This is a more difficult accomplishment than simply reducing anxiety and modulating tactile stimulation below the threshold level; it offers, however, a more resilient resolution and the opportunity to pursue a *far* greater sexual intensity.

ATTAINING THRESHOLD LEVELS OF STIMULATION
Variations in Stimulation

The quantum model highlights the dynamic processes of sexual functioning. Variations in total stimulus level can create intermittent difficulties in sexual performance. For instance, *total* stimulation may be sufficient to exceed the individual's arousal threshold but not the orgasmic threshold. Alternatively, total stimulation may fluctuate above and below the arousal threshold within a given sexual encounter, producing intermittent loss of erection in men or lubricative difficulty in women.

Voluminous research data suggest arousal and orgasm involve different physiological systems (see Rosen & Beck, 1988). The arousal and orgasmic thresholds depicted in Figure 2.1 denote a hierarchical organization; the mechanisms controlling genital performance respond to lower levels of stimulation than do those that control orgasm. Occasionally, however, mechanisms controlling genital response are impaired while orgasmic processes function normally; men, for instance, sometimes ejaculate without an erection.[5]

Total stimulation that quickly exceeds the arousal and orgasmic thresholds produces rapid "premature" orgasm. Women and men who achieve multiple orgasms are able repeatedly to achieve levels of stimulation above their orgasmic threshold. The male "refractory period" can be thought of as temporary increment in threshold, which diminishes in time following orgasm. Acute sensitivity after orgasm can also reduce receptivity to continued stimulation.

Variables Are Additive and Interactive

Within certain limits, a person's psychological processes are greater determinants of total stimulus level than is physical stimulation. From a bioevolutionary perspective it is not surprising that the sexual functioning of a species with highly evolved cortical capacities is greatly influenced by those capacities.

Physical stimulation and the receiver's cognitive/emotional functioning are additive and reciprocally interactive variables. The additive relationship between physical stimulation and the receiver's internal focus, can be stated as follows:

---

[5] The independence of orgasm, ejaculation, and arousal is also evident in some men with "delayed" ejaculation who sometimes report ejaculating without subtractive arousal or pleasure.

> *   A decrease in physical stimulation can be counterbalanced to some degree by increased sensate focus and receptivity, producing an equivalent total stimulus level.

> *   Conversely, a decrease in sensate focus and receptivity can be counterbalanced to some degree by an increase in physical stimulation, maintaining an equivalent total stimulus level.

This relationship is illustrated in Figure 2.2. Patterns A, B, and C depict three different combinations of touch and psychological receptivity leading to threshold levels of total stimulation (either tumescence/lubrication or orgasm).

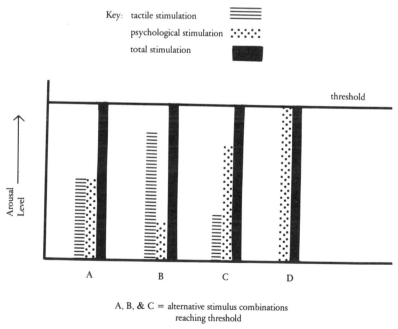

A, B, & C = alternative stimulus combinations
reaching threshold

D = psychological stimulation reaching
threshold (e.g., mental orgasm)

Figure 2.2 Physical Stimulation and Psychological Processes as Components of Total Stimulus Level

In some cases, psychological stimulation is sufficient in itself; the power of psychological processes is evident in anticipatory fantasies that create erection and lubrication, women who fantasize to orgasm, and "wet dreams" (pattern "D," Figure 2.2). Paraplegics who develop new erogenous zones and "mental orgasms" are yet another example.

When the goal is profound sexual experience rather than minimal (threshold) sexual functioning, the complex relationships between particular emotions, psychological functioning, erotic scripts, and sexual behaviors become far more significant than tactile stimulation. We will consider these dimensions in great detail in subsequent chapters; for the moment, let us turn to case examples to illustrate the interaction of physical stimulation and psychological processes in everyday life.

Applications of the Model

Jane and Bob[6]

As a child, Jane, now age 24, was the dual recipient of her father's sexual approaches and her mother's messages about sexual guilt. Her experience of being quickly dropped by her high school sweetheart when she refused to have intercourse with him only reinforced her distrust of men and anxiety about sex. With her current boyfriend, Bob, she has difficulty relaxing. Jane cannot focus on her bodily sensations when Bob touches her, and she tends to think about anything else she can. She often grabs Bob's hand to stop him when he touches her vagina, and then tentatively permits him to start again. She refuses intercourse or any form of oral stimulation. She often finds insertion of a finger into her vagina painful because she has not become aroused enough for spontaneous vaginal lubrication to occur.

Bob comes from a family where his father "runs the show" and his mother and he defer to dad's wishes. Bob expects to replay these dynamics with Jane, including scripting their sexual experiences. Bob is also relatively sexually inexperienced. He tends to rush to touch Jane's vagina. Bob is upset by her dry vagina and complaints of discomfort, which he takes as a negative reflection on his sexual adequacy. He often complains that Jane is "holding out on him." Jane's acute awareness of this only serves to reinforce her anxiety and further distract her from focusing on her own bodily sensations.

---

[6]Names in case material throughout the book have been changed; first names have generally been used for stylistic purposes. In clinical practice, I always refer to patients by their last names at the outset. With many patients, this practice continues throughout the course of treatment. At several points in this book I refer to patients by their last names when they are significantly older than I—to do otherwise simply seems disrespectful and overly familiar.

This case illustrates the reciprocal impact of ineffective physical stimulation and the internal state of the receiver. Because of massive anxiety and distraction in psychological processes, increasing the level of physical stimulation is likely to have negligible benefit on the total levels of stimulation. Fear of inadequacy is the greatest single deterrent to effective sexual functioning because it completely distracts the individual from his or her own kinesthetic sensations of pleasure and arousal (Masters & Johnson, 1970). In this case, both Jane and Bob are probably anxious about their adequacy and feeling insecure. Jane prohibits her partner from providing lots of high quality physical stimulation, and her cognitive and emotional processes further diminish the impact of the stimulation she does permit. For his part, it is doubtful that Bob knows how to provide effective stimulation or could tolerate being taught. It is little wonder that Jane is not able to achieve a total stimulus level sufficient to reach her arousal threshold.

If Jane and Bob are able to construct a relationship system in which either the physical stimulation or a pleasurable focus on sensations (and hopefully both) is allowed to increase, her arousal is likely to improve and vaginal lubrication will occur. Her lubrication and increasing signs of arousal are likely to have a soothing effect on her partner, making him more attentive and invested, thus creating a positive feedback loop in the sexual and emotional relationship.

On the other hand, this is relatively unlikely. Given the low self-esteem and emotional dependency that Jane brings with her as a function of her prior family experiences, she is not likely to gain control of the style and pacing of their sexual interactions. If the negative sexual pattern described above continues, it will exacerbate both partners' concerns and create a downward spiral that will solidify and amplify their respective positions in the relationship. In that case, Jane may develop increased sexual difficulty, including vaginismus (an involuntary contraction of the opening to the vagina).

Carrie and John

Carrie is the same age and has the same unfortunate family background as Jane. Similarly, she is quite nervous and distracted during sex with her boyfriend, John. However, Carrie does not find it necessary to stop John from stimulating her vagina and is willing to receive cunnilingus from him, although she is not totally comfortable with it.

For his part, John is much more sexually experienced than Bob and more sure of himself; he is a technically proficient and relaxed partner. John is capable of providing an emotionally secure environment for Carrie, in part because he eventually had intercourse with his last girlfriend, who presented him with the same situation. He doesn't get upset when Carrie tells him to "slow down," which has a calming effect on her and makes Carrie think John is a "special guy."

Carrie and John had some initial sexual difficulty helping her becoming lubricated. However, she was able to obtain sufficient physical stimulation and establish a facilitative internal focus, creating a total stimulus level that exceeded her arousal threshold. Over the course of time, Carrie readily became aroused and eventually had orgasms through manual stimulation.

It is quite possible that if Carrie had been paired with Bob (Jane's boyfriend), she might have been unable to accomplish this and eventually would have presented the same clinical picture as Jane.

Susan and Bob

Susan is 22. Her major family legacy about sexuality was the common absence of sex education except for menstrual hygiene, injunctions not to get pregnant, and encouragement to postpone intercourse until marriage. After being discovered masturbating as a child, she followed her mother's injunction to never let her mother catch her masturbating again. Susan continued to masturbate privately and became able to bring herself to orgasm with ease.

Susan had intercourse with high-school boyfriends, and was conscientious about using birth control. She was able and willing to focus on her own bodily sensations when receiving stimulation and anticipated that sexual encounters would be enjoyable and positive.

Recently, Susan started dating Bob, Jane's old boyfriend. Bob had broken up with Jane after two years of fighting about premarital intercourse. By the time he started dating Susan, Bob was even more sexually inept and insecure than he was with Jane. He became defensive when Susan instructed him on how she liked to be touched. At first, Susan thought it was exciting and "daring" to talk about how she liked to be touched, but she felt differently when Bob described it as "sleazy." After several encounters, Susan stopped trying to improve Bob's technique. Bob thought everything was wonderful because he got to have intercourse.

Susan was able to partially compensate for the low quality and quantity of physical stimulation by her well-developed ability to sensate focus and fantasize. She was still able to reach her arousal threshold with Bob (or perhaps despite him). In fact, Susan was able to achieve a total stimulus level sufficient for a high level of arousal. Unfortunately, Susan couldn't compensate enough to reach her orgasmic threshold.

Initially, Susan considered this to be a temporary development, hoping they would learn to relax and "communicate" in bed with a little practice. Unfortunately, this did not occur; Susan began having increasing difficulty focusing and relaxing. She became frustrated about being so close to orgasm, knowing that it would happen if she simply touched herself. However, she had yet to do this in front of a partner, and Bob was hardly the candidate for her first attempt.

Thereafter, Susan continued to reach her arousal threshold, but only barely. Her decreased level of arousal and enthusiasm became apparent. Bob began complaining that she did not care for him as much as before and that she used sex to "manipulate" him. Susan subsequently experienced intermittent difficulty reaching her arousal threshold, as well as reduced desire for sex with Bob.

If Susan has the ego strength to maintain herself in the face of Bob's disparaging attitude, she may have the leverage to push for a change in their relationship or the strength to leave him without grabbing onto another partner out of dependency. Either way, Susan is likely to find herself with a more workable partner and provide a self-corrective experience in bed without needing treatment.

On the other hand, consider the additional possibility that Susan's father dies suddenly during this time and that her mother starts dating within a month thereafter. While engulfed in feelings of loss, Susan might become more emotionally dependent on Bob. Should this occur, Susan would be less able to maintain an independently defined position and push for the necessary changes. Therapeutic intervention would more likely be required for Susan to regain her sexual functioning within this relationship.

The above vignettes provide an intuitive illustration of the fluid, dynamic interplay between physical stimulation and the receiver's psychological processes in the determination of total stimulus level, and the role of interpersonal and intrapsychic dynamics. Our focus will now turn to a detailed examination of each of the variables determining total stimulus level: *physical stimulation* and the *receiver's emotional state*.

QUALITY AND QUANTITY OF PHYSICAL STIMULATION
Stimulus Level and Technique

Physical stimulation is a function of location, style, and duration of touch, together with the capability of the body to transmit input from sensors to receptors. To the degree that the person being touched (the receiver) is physiologically intact and emotionally receptive to all forms of stimulation from the partner (the giver), physical stimulus level is determined by the technique of the giver. To the degree that the receiver places restrictions on how and what portions of his or her body may be touched, the receiver also determines "technique" and sets upper limits on the level of physical stimulation received. Moreover, the factors that usually cause the receiver to impose limitations on style or duration also color how that stimulation is experienced by the receiver. Thus, physical stimulation and the receiver's internal processes are not independent.

Physical stimulation is obviously important in reaching high levels of total stimulation. However, the importance of technical proficiency has been disproportionately inflated by the popular media and by clinicians' use of "stock" sex therapy prescriptions. Technical proficiency has generally focused on invariant styles determined by anatomy. To the degree that technique is important, it is specific to the preferences of the current partner. A sex manual and prior experience are of only minor assistance if they are contrary to the preferences of the receiver.

Optimal physical stimulation can be achieved with a receiver willing to make his or her sensations and emotional processes known to the partner during sexual contact. This requires a giver who is willing to be taught and to modify his/her behavior accordingly. The ability to do this during the actual sexual exchange can have the long-term benefit of keeping the psychological processes of the receiver and the giver "in synch." Such styles focus attention on the immediate situation and enhance the experience of intimacy.

While this may seem axiomatic, it requires a measure of intimacy during sexuality that many couples may find disturbing. The receiver may find it difficult to simultaneously communicate and focus on his or her own kinesthetic cues of arousal. For many people, self-disclosure and sexual contact are mutually exclusive events. Likewise, some partners feel criticized, controlled, or demeaned (instead of invited and desired) when the receiver expresses his/her preferences; the resulting defensiveness presents a further barrier to optimizing total stimulus level.[7]

Stimulus Transmission

Problems of stimulus transmission include the physiological impact of congenital defects, traumatic injury, illnesses, and the iatrogenic impact of their treatments (see Table 2.1). Medical problems such as spinal cord injuries may

---

[7]The underpinnings of these common problems are discussed in detail in subsequent chapters and treatment suggestions are offered. A complete treatment approach for resolving such problems is detailed in *The Intimacy Paradigm*.

Table 2.1
Examples of Threats to Transmission
of Sexual Stimulation

Congenital Defects:	Spina bifida
	Cerebral palsy
Trauma:	Stroke
	Amputation
	Spinal injury
Illness:	Lupus erythematosus
	Myasthenia gravis
Iatrogenic Effects:	Medicinal side effects
	Surgical scarring

present relatively permanent barriers to stimulus transmission (but not to sexuality per se), while other conditions such as myasthenia gravis may cause more intermittent disruptions. "Spinal shock" during the first year following spinal cord injury is an example of a temporary impairment in stimulus transmission.

Impairment of stimulus transmission may occur at the site of the sexual stimulation and/or anywhere along the transmission path. Impairment may arise from neurological, hormonal, vascular, or biomechanical processes inherently involved in effective stimulus conduction and response. Impairment may be partial, even in the case of relatively stable difficulty. For example, some men with spinal cord injuries are able to compensate with greatly increased duration and intensity of stimulation and make themselves ejaculate (Ellis, 1980).

Any comprehensive model of sexuality must consider the impact of illness and physical disability in an integrated fashion, rather than as an isolated auxiliary topic. It is common for physical disabilities to impact the receiver's psychological processes during sex, creating secondary barriers to threshold levels of stimulation. These include the distraction of pain, feelings of inadequacy and anger, and the loss of the body as a source of pleasure. However, challenges to physical viability never destroy the capacity or need for sexual contact.

THE RECEIVER'S PSYCHOLOGICAL PROCESSES

The receiver's ability to focus on the quality, quantity, and location of the stimulus, and the phenomenological meanings the receiver applies, minimize or magnify the total stimulus level. This includes the receiver's experience of the emotional climate, congruence with sexual repertoire and gender role, and attributions and unconscious associations based on prior experience and future expected contingencies. The receiver's internal processes are a crucial and often underestimated dimension in the attainment of threshold levels of stimulation.

Sensate Focus

One of Masters and Johnson's enduring legacies was the development of the famous "sensate focus" exercises. Masters and Johnson conceptualized these activities as "authoritative direction structured around use of the common denominator of sensory experience . . . employed in reversal of the presenting sexual distress" (Masters & Johnson, 1970, p. 70). They used the term "sensate focus" to refer to general sensory appreciation of pleasurable sexual stimuli, as well as a set of prescribed therapeutic activities.

Like many innovations that expand clinical thinking, the concept of "sensate focus" has also had a limiting effect. While it may not have been Masters and Johnson's intent, "sensate focusing" has become identified in the minds of many clinicians as a therapeutic invention or assignment. In actuality, sensate focusing is an ongoing internal *process* of kinesthetic feedback that occurs spontaneously in healthy individuals. Sensate focusing is not limited to sexual stimulation; it is, in fact, an integral part of daily mobility, physical dexterity, and body mastery. It is raised to an art form in athletic training, particularly by gymnasts. From the perspective of Maturana and Varela's (1987) model of human development, sensate focus has its roots in the biological evolution of neurocortical functioning. Part of that evolution is the development of the capacity for memory traces of erotic sensory experience to be associated with ontological meaning.

Given the tendency for clinicians to particularize the concept of sensate focusing to Masters and Johnson's techniques, there is some impulse to christen the spontaneous, ongoing, kinesthetic process with another name. However, we will resist the impulse to increase the professional jargon in lieu of arguing for broader conceptualization. The concept of sensate focus, as used in this book, pertains to the natural recursive process that occurs during sexual (and other) activity; when it is used to refer to therapeutic prescriptions, it will be explicitly noted as such.

Sensate focus modifies the effective impact of physical stimulation. This involves subjective attributions the receiver attaches to sensations, as well as heightened awareness of the kinesthetic cues themselves. If the receiver regards the subjective sensations of sexual arousal as pleasant, then sensate focus is self-reinforced and progressive as he or she becomes more aroused.

If (as in the case of sexual aversion) the receiver does not wish to become aroused, he or she will distract him/herself to diminish awareness of pleasurable physical sensations. Anxiety, triggered by arousal, further detracts from effective sensate focus. Paradoxically, individuals who *do* want to become aroused, but who worry about not functioning adequately, also have difficulty maintaining effective sensate focus. As these individuals experience their own cues of arousal, their fears of failure increase concomitantly, destroying effective sensate focus and creating the outcome they seek to avoid. It is important to recognize that sensate focus does not involve merely *tuning out* thoughts and emotions and *tuning in* to one's bodily sensations. Sensate focus also involves attunement of thoughts, emotions, and other attributions about the experience for the enhancement of kinesthetic sensations of sexual pleasure.

The best explanation of sensate focus comes from intuitive experience. The following vignette has been effective with a wide variety of trainees in providing a gut-level appreciation of the psychological processes of the receiver and the role they play in determining total stimulus level:

Your classmates (or colleagues) collect money to provide the ultimate sexual experience for someone in your organization. A lottery is held and you are the lucky winner. The money is used to obtain the services of your current fantasy sex partner (e.g., Julia Roberts, Mel Gibson). According to the provisions of the award, you are brought to a comfortable room where you are blindfolded; you await the entry of your heart throb, who will perform oral sex on you. You figure the blindfold is a little kinky, but you are game for the experience. Even if you are generally uncomfortable with oral sex, this is too good to pass up.

Blindfolded, you recline on the bed. The door opens gently, and you listen as your all-time fantasy partner walks softly towards you and begins to supply the best oral stimulation you have ever imagined or received. You are aroused and can feel the blood pumping in your loins; your breathing is fast. You are starting to sweat, and your genitals are throbbing. You are in seventh heaven, both with the stimulation and with the thought of this lovely creature going down on you. You can hardly believe your good luck.

Just as you are reaching a crescendo of sexual pleasure, a quiet voice comes through a small loudspeaker in a corner of the room. The sexual stimulation continues unabated, and delicious. The voice points out that your classmates are not as altruistic as you might hope. Gently it reveals that the person currently going down on you is not your all-time heart throb, but rather your mother's sister, Aunt Sara. Aunt Sara never stops and doesn't miss a beat.

You are left to your own devices to imagine the impact this shift in understanding has on your total level of arousal. When this story is told in classrooms, the typical response is nervous laughter. Most students become acutely aware of the impact of subjective experience on total stimulation, even when physical intensity is invariant. Most no longer wish to sensate focus; instead, they wish to tune out the physical stimulation that was so enticing only seconds before.

Difficulties with sensate focus can be extreme to the point of aversion, precluding total stimulation from reaching arousal threshold. In other cases partial interference with sensate focus creates a limited handicap in reaching threshold levels of stimulation. This may take the form of invariant or intermittent inability to reach orgasm or simply the requirement of long duration and high intensity of physical stimulation. Commonly, the speed and ease of reaching arousal and orgasm are consistent with partner's expectations, but residual impairment in sensate focus remains. It is often difficult for folks to imagine the possibility of untapped sexual potential as long as their bodies (minimally) complete the sexual response cycle.

Anxiety

Despite all the talk one hears about sexuality and performance anxiety, the role of anxiety in sexual functioning is not well understood. Anxiety plays an important role in determining total stimulation level, through both the physical dimension and the receiver's emotional processes. Overall, the impact of anxiety is level dependent; however, the relationship is *curvilinear* rather than linear.

A *low level of anxiety* appears to augment sexual arousal by increasing attention and focus. Some people find low-level anticipatory anxiety a necessary "internal cue." Hans Selye (1956) considered the role of facilitative stress ("eustress") in his broad conceptualization of the effects of stress on aging and illness. For some, such anxiety may be the result of childhood proscriptions about masturbation or sex play with other children or siblings. For others, low-level anxiety of being discovered becomes an anticipated component through paired-association learning during defiant adolescent sexual exploration. "Being naughty" is often quite arousing.

Some cases of sexual disinterest and "boredom" after marriage are due to reduced anxiety from repetitive contact with a socially sanctioned partner. While anxiety in illicit sexual contact might preclude effective sensate focusing for some individuals, for others it provides the kinesthetic enhancement that makes affairs attractive and sexually "exciting." Low-level anticipatory anxiety enhances sensate focus, when the accompanying autonomic activity is subjectively experienced as pleasure and excitement.

Low-level anxiety is often necessary for personal development. Flexible sexual repertoires emerge from progressive desensitization of anxiety associated with a broad range of sexual scripts and behaviors. Few individuals are anxiety free during their initial experience with intercourse. It is through the progressive mastery of anxiety that people convert what is novel into what is commonplace and *normal*. Without low-level anxiety, desensitization (and sexual development) does not occur.

At *moderate levels*, however, anxiety appears to have a debilitating impact on sexual functioning. In fact, Kaplan (1974) identified three sources of sexual anxiety as immediate causes of sexual dysfunction: fear of failure, performance anxiety, and excessive need to please one's partner. Whether this effect results from physiological changes in stimulus transmission (e.g., the impact of norepinephrine secretion), impairment in sensate focusing, or shifts in phenomenological attributions of sensory experience is not clear. In any case, moderate levels of anxiety appear to diminish the total stimulus value of any physical stimulation being received. The individual's subjective awareness of his/her own anxiety may be further debilitating.

In some experiences of moderate-level anxiety, it remains possible to reach threshold by increasing the level of physical stimulation. In other cases, the negative impact of anxiety is great enough to preclude reaching threshold levels with any amount of stimulation. This is true for arousal difficulties as well as those in reaching orgasm.

For many men, intromission is the time of "put up or shut up," "being on the firing line," and "doing your duty." Given this anxiety and the additional positional demands of the missionary position, it is not surprising that the inception of intercourse is the most common point at which men have difficulty maintaining an erection. Patterns "A" and "B" in Figure 2.3 illustrate the negative impact of anxiety in the etiology of erectile difficulty and "retarded" ejaculation.

For many women, penetration signals the time and technique that she (and her partner) expect to bring her to orgasm. Being rushed into intercourse, fear of not reaching orgasm before her partner ejaculates and loses his erection, decreased clitoral stimulation, and the distraction of vigorous thrusting can easily create problems with lubrication or orgasm (patterns "A" and "B" in Figure 2.3).

However, this conceptualization does not account for the phenomenon of

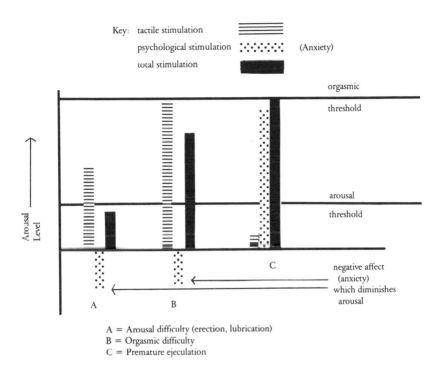

A = Arousal difficulty (erection, lubrication)
B = Orgasmic difficulty
C = Premature ejaculation

Figure 2.3 The Role of Anxiety in Sexual Dysfunctions

rapid ejaculation in men. At least on the surface, "premature" ejaculation seemingly defies the conceptualization of anxiety as antagonistic to high total stimulus levels. How can it be that extremely anxious men are able to reach orgasm, almost against their will?

Pattern "C" (Figure 2.3) presents a different explanation of the role of anxiety in premature ejaculation. The diagram accurately reflects the sexual style many couples use to accommodate this problem. Sexual physical stimulation composes a minor portion of the total stimulation, since men with poor ejaculatory control generally refuse to have their penis touched prior to penetration; they prefer to "save themselves for the main event." Stimulation to the penis is either brief or nonexistent, consisting of several strokes intravaginally; when ejaculation occurs prior to penetration there has often been no tactile stimulation at all.

The body does not appear to distinguish anxiety and sexual arousal. The kinesthetic manifestations of both are quite similar: elevated muscle tension, increased heart rate and hyperventilation, perspiration, increased blood pressure, and increased adrenaline output. Both anxiety and sexual stimulation result in massive autonomic nervous system activation.

In rapid ejaculation the major (or exclusive) "arousal" is the physiological and emotional components of the man's anxiety. When total stimulation exceeds the orgasmic threshold, a pleasureless orgasm occurs. Subsequent experiences of disappointingly rapid ejaculation potentiate the likelihood and speed of future occurrences.

This explains why common self-distraction techniques are ineffective in controlling ejaculation. Sexual stimulation provides such a small proportion of the total stimulation density that distraction affects the physiological process only minimally (although it does diminish enjoyment). Distraction limits total stimulus level based on *sexual* arousal, denying men of a chance to condition their orgasmic threshold.

The reason why anxiety has "additive" rather than antagonistic impact on total stimulation level in some men is not known. Many men who ejaculate rapidly describe their problem as "getting too aroused" rather than "getting too anxious." Such men conceptualize their anxiety as "positive" arousal and only recognize their "negative" fearful experience when it is pointed out to them. Although subjective experience may modulate the impact of anxiety on sexual response, it does not provide a complete explanation; telling men they are anxious rather than "turned on" does not, in itself, cure premature ejaculation.

From this model, several component treatment strategies for rapid ejaculation become obvious. Reduced anxiety permits more sexual stimulation (and more pleasure) prior to ejaculation, even if latency to orgasm is not increased. Further reduction of anxiety often permits greater stimulation and longer latency; this is often the source of short-term progress. Increasing the erotic component of physical stimulation, and the efficacy of the receiver's internal focus often dramatically increases total stimulus levels. In turn, this allows eventual raising (conditioning) of the orgasmic threshold, providing a secondary long-term treatment effect.[8]

The impact of *extreme levels* of anxiety has attracted growing attention in

---

[8]This treatment approach involves another paradigm shift from contemporary sex therapy, and is more involved than a behavioral prescription or technique. In general, the required approach is consistent with the sexual potential paradigm outlined in this book; specific treatment details are elaborated in *The Intimacy Paradigm*.

recent years. Kaplan explored such problems in *Disorders of Sexual Desire* (1979) and in sexual aversion, sexual phobias, and panic disorders (Kaplan, 1987). Schover and LoPiccolo (1982) conceptualized sexual anxiety and avoidance along a continuum, with inhibited sexual desire at the low end of extreme reactions and phobic reactions at the high end; Kaplan (1979) considered sexual aversion and inhibited desire to be qualitatively different phenomena.

Although one might expect that higher levels of anxiety are increasingly debilitating, this does not hold true in all cases. Reports of men who develop and maintain an erection in circumstances of high anxiety, exploitation, and threats of castration (i.e., becoming *scared stiff*) run counter to expectations (Masters & Sarrel, 1986; Sarrel & Masters, 1982). This is not very different from the model of rapid ejaculation presented above, in which anxiety is the major component of threshold levels of stimulation. As another example, consider that anticipatory anxiety of punishment can become a necessary component in the sexual arousal pattern of pedophiles or exhibitionists (Bancroft, 1987). In the next chapter, we will consider the report of a young man with extreme performance anxiety, from which Apfelbaum (1977b) argues that performance anxiety *facilitates* genital functioning.

The role of anxiety in sexual function and dysfunction highlights the relative youth of sexual science. There are few cogent explanations of why anxiety has a decremental impact on arousal in some individuals, while having an additive (although undesired) impact in others. Note that the terms "low," "moderate," and "high" anxiety are meaningful only relative to individuals' threshold levels and emotional makeup; they do not reflect an absolute measure of subjective or physiological activation. However, considering anxiety in the determination of total stimulation is useful in explaining both cause and resolution of common sexual difficulties.

Emotional Agendas and Sexual Styles

The emotional dynamics of the receiver, as soothed or abraded by the current relationship and the extended family system, have a profound effect on sexual functioning.

For some, the context of a "loving committed relationship" is a powerful enhancer of physical stimulation. For others, the same context triggers fears of entrapment that diminish arousal. Sometimes, extremely positive initial sexual encounters are in themselves the trigger for fears of dependency or rejection.

Some people cannot bear the thought of sex after an argument, while others need the anger and hostility to fuel their eroticism. Others need the schism created by the fight to soothe their fears of enmeshment; only then can they permit themselves to be wildly abandoned in bed and relaxed enough to focus.

One of the hallmarks of modern sex therapy has been the ability to improve genital response by enhancing sensate focus on pleasurable physiological cues, despite the presence of broader situational problems or long-term personal issues. Masters and Johnson's treatment approach fixed on diminishing immediate challenges to sensate focus within the couple's pattern of physical interaction and communication.

One might ask, "Isn't it possible that difficulty with sensate focusing might develop or increase from several episodes of performance difficulty, and if so, why is it necessary to look any further in the individuals or the system?" While the proposition is obviously possible, the proposed conclusion is unsatisfying. This line of thinking begs the question of why the sexual difficulty arose in the first place. If sensate focus and sexual dysfunction are invariably related, how does one explain intermittent difficulties of primarily "psychological" etiology? Even if the sexual dysfunction originally had an "organic" basis (e.g., illness or medication that has been terminated) and has since become a self-perpetuating "psychogenic" problem, one might ask why there is insufficient adaptive flexibility to stop the negative spiral.

Why do some individuals experience deficits in effective sensate focus and others do not? While this point once looked moot in the face of short-term treatment efficacy, poor long-term results make this question more pressing. The answer often lies in the recursive aspects of individual personality and relationship development.

Consider, for example, the notion that difficulty with sensate focus results from religious or parental prohibitions about sexual pleasure. Often this is a boondoggle for clinicians, since ubiquitous religious and parental prohibitions are present in the histories of many individuals who do not have difficulty focusing. In such cases where prohibitions appear to be major barriers, one might legitimately wonder: What is it about this individual and/or the relationship that prevents spontaneous detoxification of negative injunctions? More importantly, the presence of stereotypic prohibitions often forecloses clinical consideration of additional (and often more significant) sources of difficulty.

For many individuals, difficulty with sensate focus is a function of *contempo-*

rary systemic variables. Couples who experience marital discord may destroy the "holding environment" they previously established and lose the ability or desire to sensate focus during sexual contact. Often one or both partners are aware of this shift, although they do not appreciate its crucial role in the creation and perpetuation of their sexual difficulty. Once the holding environment is lost, it is often difficult for partners to modify their system of interaction and provide a spontaneous corrective experience.[9]

It is also important to wonder about the makeup of the receiver, which determines his or her response to exigencies of the system. Apfelbaum (1977b) suggests that the individual's response to anxiety and distractions in the sexual situation determines whether sensate focus is efficacious. Some individuals are natural *bypassers*, able to tune out internal and situational "noise" and focus on pleasurable physiological cues and fantasies. Kaplan (1987) actually teaches patients bypassing while Apfelbaum (1983) teaches counter-bypassing (e.g., refocusing on the details of the encounter).

The question of bypass vs. counter bypass becomes particularly important when the goal of treatment extends beyond adequate genital response and includes increased intimacy and eroticism. Bypassing, the more common sexual strategy of the two, is antithetical to intimacy.[10]

Problems of eroticism and sexual dysfunction often surface in relationships where there is disparity in partners' optimal scripts and conditions for sexual functioning. Chapter Seven ("Individual Dimensions of Intimacy and Sexuality") addresses some origins of problems with intimacy and eroticism, while Chapters Eight and Eleven ("The Dyadic Component" and "The Extended Family System") elaborate on the contextual aspects.

The main components of the quantum model have now been articulated. While simple in concept, it provides a backdrop from which to understand the complexities of sexual-marital therapy. Before turning to a final elaboration of the model, let's pause to demonstrate several applications.

---

[9]Winnicott's (1953) concept of a "holding environment" has little to do with physical holding, except perhaps between mothers and infants; the holding environment referred to above concerns the construction of a resilient bond of mutuality that permits minor friction and miscommunication to be self-soothed and forgotten. In sex, it refers to an ambiance in which partners can relax without anticipation of disharmony. Object relations issues, discussed in Chapter Seven, are a major determinant of success.

[10]Common views of intimacy and orgasm suggest that the two are antithetical due to "dimming of consciousness" and "tuning out everything but sensation." This is a critical topic with far-reaching implications; it will be addressed in great detail in Chapter Three when we consider exploration of sexual potential and profound levels of sexual intensity.

ILLUSTRATING THE
DYNAMIC ASPECTS OF THE MODEL
Intermittent Dysfunctions

The quantum model helps explain the occurrence of intermittent dysfunctions in successive sexual encounters or within a single event. Intermittent dysfunctions result from an episodic failure to reach and maintain threshold levels of sexual stimulation. These fluctuations are caused by variations in physical stimulation and stimulus transmission, the receiver's psychological processes, and changes in the thresholds.

Differences Between Partners

Al and Sally (both age 49) have been married for 30 years. Al is increasingly unable to get an erection with Sally, but has no difficulty with his 29-year-old girlfriend, Gwen.

One common explanation might be that his girlfriend is a "better" sexual partner than his wife. "Better" might mean that she is less inhibited in stimulating and touching him. Al's report, "my wife doesn't turn me on," seems to support this assumption. However, sexual contact with Gwen consists exclusively of her passively receiving Al's touch, to which she is readily orgasmic. In fact, she tends to be far more passive in bed than Sally. Gwen offers Al the hero worship and sense of power that he misses in his marriage. Al has more of an erection when he is touching his girlfriend than when his penis is being sucked by Sally.

Al's internal processes may make him a distinctly better receiver with his girlfriend, even when he is the giver. Al has much less difficulty validating his own eroticism and sexual preferences and fewer fears of engulfment with Gwen, due to differences in their age and income and the time-limited nature of the affair. Al is more aroused by "being needed" than by tactile exchange. The need to pay attention to a new partner in order to stay "in synch," the low-level anxiety of illicit sex, and the spice of defying Sally also enhance Al's response. Al has constructed a temporarily more effective psychological state with his girlfriend than with his wife. This viewpoint differs considerably from Al's conceptualization: "Maybe I don't get erections because I don't love my wife."

One year into the affair, Gwen dumps Al for a younger man. Al's erectile difficulty with Sally increases, and he eventually agrees to enter conjoint treatment. While some benefit might be obtained by increasing the level of physical stimulation he receives, addressing intrapsychic and systemic issues in treatment is likely to offer Al the biggest increment in total level of stimulation. Al has sexual beliefs and unresolved issues that limit the intensity of his sexual experience with *any* partner: his need for a women to validate and defer to him, fear of commitment and loss of self, need to "prove" himself through sexual performance, and self-consciousness about his false teeth.

Intermittent Difficulty With One Partner

Joe is a happily married man who initially gets an erection but loses it in the midst of lovemaking. At the outset of foreplay, he is relatively relaxed and a good receiver of his wife's caresses. He rapidly reaches arousal threshold, and erection occurs. However, as his arousal mounts and time spent in foreplay increases, Joe increasingly shifts his attention to anticipating intercourse and fears of not being able to penetrate. Like many men, Joe feels that once he has an erection, he is suppose to "use it" for his wife's pleasure.

His wife senses his anxiety and gets nervous too. Joe has gotten angry and withdrawn on past occasions when he lost his erection. Her touch becomes more tentative, transmitting her anxiety to Joe while also offering less effective physical stimulation. Joe interprets this as her losing confidence in him. Both partners' processes contribute to a significant decrease in total stimulation. At the point that it drops below arousal threshold, Joe loses his erection.

If Joe were able to relax and abandon his focus on intercourse, and if his wife were able to provide higher quality and quantity of stimulation, it is quite likely that Joe would get another erection.

Sometimes when Joe has given up in frustration, his wife has continued stimulating him to show she still cares. When Joe has seen this as a demand to perform, he has been unable to become erect again. On occasion, when Joe has relaxed, he got a second erection. However, as the duration of the second erection increased, Joe again shifted his focus to intromission; the shift in focus decreased the total stimulus level and repeated the pattern of intermittent erectile dysfunction within the single sexual encounter.

Progressive Development of a Dysfunctional Sexual System

Joan learned over the years that her husband, George, didn't like much kissing, fondling, or eye-to-eye contact, especially as an end in itself. He was, however, willing to "do it for her" as preparation for intercourse. George liked the lights out during intercourse. Joan preferred themes of loving affection, while George preferred to "talk dirty." Joan had no difficulty with sex as an erotic event for its own sake, but the repeated absence of bonding and tenderness left her feeling unfulfilled and "used." After coitus was completed, she liked to embrace and talk; George jumped out of bed to "clean up" and attended to other interests.

Over the course of time, Joan perceived foreplay as being "for her," while intercourse was "for him." She felt obliged to have intercourse once George was aroused, although it felt like "paying" for the caresses. After repeatedly feeling alienated and angry, Joan began to think about nonsexual topics during "his turn."

At first Joan began to have difficulty reaching orgasm during coitus, although she could accomplish it if she focused intensely. Progressively, her frequency of orgasm during intercourse diminished. Joan's anger as well as her deliberate self-distraction diminished the total stimulation to a level below her orgasmic threshold, regardless of how long her husband thrusted. Joan knew this deprived George of the gratifications of feeling "wanted" and seeing her aroused. He craved both these things and she secretly enjoyed depriving him.

Up to this point, Joan was always able to reach arousal threshold during foreplay. However, George took her vaginal lubrication as an immediate cue for penetration, communicating the message that he had "paid his dues." Over the course of time Joan was subtly conditioned not to become aroused, since it signaled the end of the activities she desired.

George's response to her attempts to discuss the growing estrangement in their marriage was to complain about her "frigidity" in bed. He became increasingly demanding and verbally abusive, further diminishing his attractiveness to her. In the following year, Joan became increasingly disinterested in foreplay, which was no longer sufficient for her to reach arousal threshold. When she gave into George's badgering, she had pain during intercourse due to reduced lubrication. Some 14 months after Joan flatly refused to have intercourse, George consented to seek treatment "for her problem."

Alternating Multiple Dysfunctions

Figure 2.4 depicts a variety of sexual dysfunctions, illustrating the utility of the quantum model in conceptualizing various sexual difficulties. Item "A" presents the pattern of a man who doesn't get an erection, or a woman who doesn't experience spontaneous vaginal lubrication. Item "B" illustrates the pattern of a man whose erection subsides without achieving orgasm or a woman who initially experiences vaginal lubrication but subsequently experiences a loss of arousal. Item "C" presents a model of rapid orgasm in a man or woman, while item "D" represents difficulty reaching orgasm at all.

Figure 2.4 illustrates that the etiologies of various sexual dysfunctions are not unique and do not represent discrete syndromes. The specific dysfunction a person incurs is determined by the level of total stimulation and the point at which it occurs in the couple's sexual behavior pattern. This holistic perspective is somewhat different from the views of Kaplan and Masters and Johnson. Perhaps owing to their medical backgrounds and interest in diagnostic labeling, these authors tend to discuss sexual difficulties as discrete syndromes.

Moreover, the quantum model's focus on thresholds differs from Masters and Johnson's four-stage model of sexual response, which focuses on the physiological changes that occur between thresholds. Masters and Johnson's

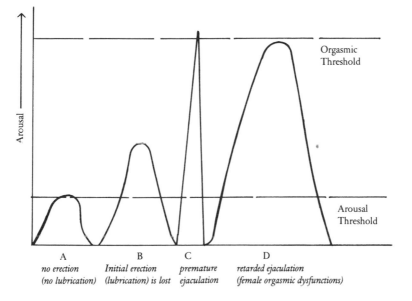

Figure 2.4 A Variety of Sexual Dysfunctions

four-stage model is derived from physiological research on human sexual response, while the quantum model more closely approximates patients' phenomenological experience and functional problems.

A review of Figure 2.4 makes it easy to understand how someone could have two alternating dysfunctions.

From the outset of the sexual encounter, Steve is focused on his fear of not being able to achieve penetration. He is anxious and a poor receiver. Initially, he has difficulty getting an erection. When his patient and considerate partner touches his penis to arouse him, it raises his anxiety even more. He believes "a man should have an erection even before getting into bed" and feels more obligated to have an erection in response to his partner's touch. Generally, Steve is unable to achieve arousal thresholds of total stimulation.

On those occasions when Steve is able to get an erection, his concerns shift to his secondary fear that he will not be able to ejaculate. He is able to maintain his erection once he gets it by rapid thrusting, such that the total stimulation does not drop below arousal threshold. However, he is not able to focus enough to reach his orgasmic threshold. Like many men, Steve thinks that physical stimulation is more important than his emotional processes in achieving orgasm. He mistakenly tries to thrust harder and faster to bring himself to orgasm, which only further diminishes his ability to focus on the sensations in his penis. Steve becomes increasingly fearful of not reaching orgasm as the duration of intercourse increases (just as many women do). After 30 minutes, he gives up in fatigue and frustration.

The result in Steve's case is a pattern of alternating disorders of erectile difficulty and delayed ejaculation. In similar fashion, it is possible for a man to have difficulty with rapid ejaculation in the initial moments of coitus, as well as difficulty with delayed ejaculation if coitus lasts longer.

Given the widespread preoccupation with sexual adequacy, any model of "normative" sexual functioning (such as Figure 2.1, reproduced in Figure 2.5 as pattern "A") can quickly reinforce what Zilbergeld has referred to as "the myth of the hard-driving fuck" (1978, p. 47). It is important to note that sexual patterns often exhibit considerable variation (including brief loss of erection or arousal) without necessarily being problematic (see Figure 2.5). Whether patterns "B," "C," "D," and "E" are regarded as problematic is determined by the frequency of occurrence and the particular expectations of the individuals involved.

INTEGRATING MIND AND BODY IN SEXUALITY

The lay public and health professionals generally maintain a duality between mind and body in sexual functioning. In the absence of an effective integrated model, the importance of psychological and physiological processes in sexual functioning is often recognized but approached in disparate, isolated cogni-

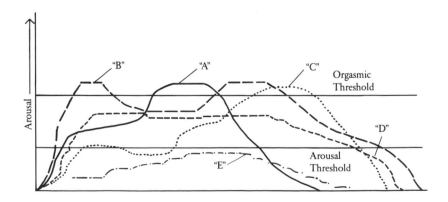

Figure 2.5 Normal Variation in Sexual Patterns

tive "sets." In contrast to Masters and Johnson's four-stage model of sexual functioning (which focused solely on physiological response), the quantum model offers an integration of mind and body in sexual response. This permits the quantum model to be readily integrated with existing detailed models of intrapsychic and dyadic processes in sexual behavior. For example, the domain of the individual's internal psychological processes in the quantum model can be neatly articulated through the model proposed by Byrne (1977) and expanded by Fisher (1986). Their "sexual behavior sequence" addresses a developmental model of learned arousal, affective, and cognitive responses to sexual cues, which in turn determine overt sexual behavior (see Figure 2.6).

The explication of the current quantum model considers the holistic functioning of a single individual. On the dyadic level, one could construct two such models with appropriate interpersonal links. Verhulst and Heiman's (1988) "dyadic interaction system" offers just such a dynamic model of symbolic, affective and sensate exchanges within the couple (see Figure 2.7).

The integration of physiological and psychological dimensions, as additive and interactive processes, has been repeatedly demonstrated in this chapter. One implication of the quantum model is the subtle notion that sexual difficulties are generally an *outcome of a process* rather than a *personal defect*.

Kerr and Bowen's (1988) discussion of the role of additive factors in the emergence of nonsexual symptomatology is useful in understanding the quantitative role of process variables.

> We create the schizophrenia we see around us. We create it by virtue of the way we function everyday. We continually make decisions and do things that tend to impair as well as promote the functioning of others. All of us participate in groups that function in ways that make it more difficult for certain group members to function. This process is most obvious in the family, but it can occur in any group. When the process reaches a certain quantitative level of emotional intensity (sufficient autonomy has been lost), the stage is set for the emergence of clinical schizophrenia or some other serious problem.[11] Thought of in this way, schizophrenia is not the product of a biological "defect" or of something that has "suddenly" gone wrong. It is, rather, an *outcome*. (pp. 12–13)

---

[11]Whether a serious clinical problem emerges depends on more variables than those of the family relationship system. If a person with very little emotional autonomy, for example, has ideal life circumstances, he may never demonstrate any overt symptoms normally associated with clinical schizophrenia. He may, for example, have a support system that is quite available to him, but does not pressure him. While that may result in his being in a childlike position for his whole life, the low stress level would make the more obvious clinical signs and symptoms of schizophrenia less likely to appear. If another person with little autonomy develops a serious alcohol or eating problem, the presence of these problems may "protect" him from developing other types of clinical syndromes.

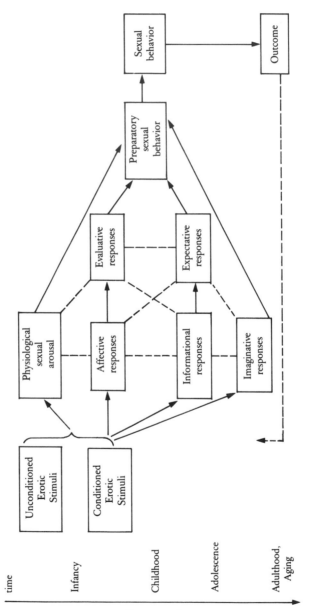

Figure 2.6 The Sexual Behavior Sequence
(Fisher, 1986)

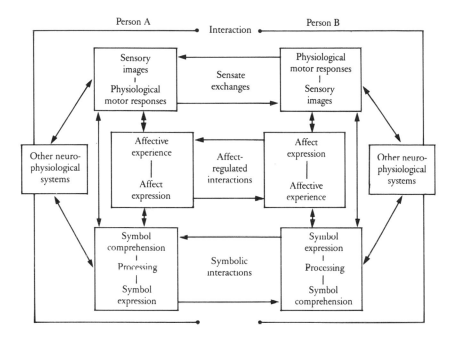

Figure 2.7 The Dyadic Interaction System.
From Verhulst & Heiman, 1988.

The advantages of this viewpoint in establishing a viable treatment paradigm should be obvious. Less apparent, perhaps, are the advantages to the clinician confronted with taking a problem-oriented "sexual history." This viewpoint encourages the clinician to think beyond the immediate stimulus-response situations of sexual encounters to nonsexual situations and to times prior to the emergence of the sexual symptomatology.

Minimal Function Is Not Enough

Enrichment, beyond mere mechanics, must be a standard part of sex therapy. Previous motivators of sexual desire or behavior need to be broadened and replaced, particularly for patients whose eroticism has played a destructive but central role in their lives. Like object relations therapies which aim at integration of "disowned" aspects of the self, sexual-marital therapy must consider the "disowned" aspects of an individual's eroticism, permitting it to be recognized, reorganized, validated, and cherished. Aggressive sexual play, as well as integrating eroticism and intimacy with a loved and valued partner, is an aspect of personal development relevant to symptomatic and asymptomatic partners alike.

Some people devote their lives to the pursuit of "sexual chemistry." Ironically, sexual chemistry is often nothing more than the serendipitous achievement of arousal and orgasmic thresholds by two people with compatible sexual scripts in the early manifestations of interlocking individual issues. When interlocking unresolved object relations and family-of-origin issues eventually become gridlocked, sexual chemistry evaporates. The view that sexual chemistry can be *developed* if both parties are willing to "grow themselves up" constructively tarnishes the fantasy that sexual chemistry is some form of interpersonal "magic."

"Sexual chemistry" often fades away, not because the chemicals are used up, but because they are neutralized in the slowly unfolding interplay of transference projections and homeostatic systems. If partners can maintain their sexual excitement through the disillusionment, anger, and desperate struggle for autonomy that follows "instant intimacy," they may succeed in discovering an alternative formula for sexual chemistry. That formula, derived in the sexual crucible of sexual and marital difficulties, contains the equation for self-sustaining intimacy and sexuality. Self-sustaining individuals are two of the principal factors in that formula.

REACHING RESPONSE THRESHOLDS AND BEYOND
Sexual "Normality" and Sexual Potential

Helping couples exceed the total stimulus level reached in their typical sexual exchanges often requires violating the couple's construction of what is "normal" and proper sexual behavior. This includes styles of interaction and meanings of experience. "Normality" is constructed through repeated sexual contact, in which individual preferences and cultural standards are expressed and validated.

Social prescriptions for "sexual normality" are embedded in sexual humor and the literary and performing arts. "Sexual myths" are examples of prevailing cultural norms that are antithetical to effective long-term sexual functioning. Zilbergeld (1978) has pointed out several popular "myths" :

- All physical contact must lead to sex, and all sex must involve intercourse.
- Sex requires an erection and a real man always wants sex.
- Sex is a linear progression culminating in orgasm.

- Sex should come naturally.
- In sex, as elsewhere, it is performance that counts.
- The man must take charge of and orchestrate sex.
- The preceding myths should no longer have an impact on those who previously believed the myths.

An individual's view of "normality" is more than the internalization of cultural standards as transmitted through the family of origin. It is also the expression of the individual's success and failure in personal development. It reflects the internalization of familial dynamics in terms of object relations and systemic patterns of interaction.

Sexual dysfunctions often evolve gradually and additively. The emergence of symptomatology does not occur until the growing intrapsychic and systemic impairment in total stimulation exceeds the ability to reach threshold. Thus, couples are able to establish a debilitating pattern and label it "normal" because the incapacitating aspects have yet to reach symptomatic levels. Many culturally prescribed sexual values and practices are considered "healthy" because the debilitating aspects do not emerge until later adult life. Some impaired sexual functioning in later life is the insidious result of 30 or more years of practicing "normal" sex, which is then confused with physiological changes of senescence.

There is considerable mythology about "the sexless older years," and many people unfortunately manage to live down to this expectation. While some increased frequency of erectile dysfunction in older men is due to organic problems, such an explanation is simplistic. Consider the fact that many men struggle for years with premature ejaculation and that the most common attempt at delaying ejaculation is self-distraction (a stimulus reduction technique). After years of practice, a man gets quite proficient at reducing the total stimulus value of whatever he is receiving throughout the sexual encounter. Over the course of time, the process becomes an ingrained, habitual response. Now, add to this the fact that both arousal and orgasmic thresholds rise as age increases; Masters and Johnson (1966) described this as "slowing" of the sexual response. You have a "natural" formula for erectile dysfunction in later life.

Figure 2.8 depicts this process. When the level of stimulation necessary for erection (arousal threshold) exceeds the total stimulation derived from the man's customary sexual repertoire, the man will experience erectile dysfunction.

Consider Ed and Connie, who married at age 21; for many years they had a "normal" sexual relationship. Ed usually became erect during initiation, even prior to removing his clothes. He had an ejaculatory latency of about three minutes and preferred that

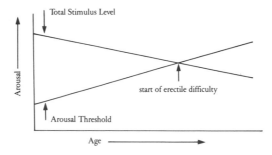

Figure 2.8 Common Etiology of Erectile Dysfunction in Older Men

his wife not touch his penis during foreplay to "save it" for coitus. This was fine for Connie, who was embarrassed and preferred not to touch Ed's penis. For 30 years, foreplay consisted of Ed kissing and "petting" Connie until she was close to orgasm; they then shifted to intercourse so that they could reach orgasm simultaneously. Ed often used distraction to control his ejaculation, a stimulus reduction technique at which he became quite adept.

At age 53, Ed began to have erectile difficulties for which his urologist could find no physical explanation. By the couple's report, the difficulty began intermittently and increased in frequency and severity over an eight-month period. During this period, Ed increasingly focused on his "inability to perform" and feelings of inadequacy. Connie was similarly disappointed, frustrated, and felt unattractive.

Ed was confused because (in his own perception) he had not deviated from his prior "successful" technique. He attributed the difficulty to something he feared: the irreversible physiological decay of aging. Further attempts offered no improvement in genital response and reinforced his erroneous conclusion about the nature of his sexual difficulty. His anxiety decreased the effective impact of physical stimulation even further.

Neither spouse was comfortable with Connie touching Ed's penis during foreplay. This violated their construction of what was normal and "necessary" in a "good sexual relationship." It exacerbated both spouses' anxiety, violated standards for appropriate male and female sexual behavior, and fueled feelings of inadequacy by challenging them to function in a way that left them feeling inept. Ed misinterpreted Connie's anxiety as further demand to produce an erection. Connie and Ed decided that their problem was an indication of being "too old."

"Normal" sexual beliefs and behavior patterns tend to preclude spontaneous remission and surface as resistance to treatment activities in sexual-marital therapy. One role of treatment is to help partners free themselves from the invisible restraints of being "normal," in order to reverse any overt dysfunction and to help them reach higher-than-customary levels of sexual intensity. All cultures facilitate certain aspects of personal development and inhibit others.

The goal of sexual-marital therapy is not to condemn contemporary society, but rather to help people obtain the benefit of what the culture offers, and then to differentiate themselves from it and move beyond.

Ironically, couples who enter treatment for sexual-marital difficulties often don't feel "normal" and cling tenaciously to prevailing cultural standards. Couples who develop sexual dysfunction usually seek treatment to "get back to the way we used to be," without realizing that this is often what caused the problem.

Preoccupation with being "normal" is a powerful point of therapeutic intervention in the initial meeting. Normalizing the difficulty is a rapid way to improve the outlook on their predicament, establish rapport, and improve self-esteem. If this were simply reframing or education, it would be worthwhile. But it is more: Since the construction of "normality" is a powerful determinant of people's behavior and attributional meanings, it can be harnessed into a paradigm shift that is both diagnostic and therapeutic in nature.[12]

Sex Beyond the Orgasmic Threshold

We are a society in which the goal of sexuality is orgasms. For some, quantity of orgasms rather than quality is the key to sexual fulfillment. For others, the goal is extended sexual orgasm. Yet the human body is capable of ecstatic phenomenological experiences beyond orgasm for which there is no known physiological counterpart. While *love* may come to mind, that is not the object of discussion.

Westerners are blind to their assumption that current sexual "enlightenment," reflecting the technical expertise of an industrialized and highly literate world, is the epitome of sexual wisdom. Eastern cultures have advanced sexuality to an art form and a vehicle of religious worship. In Eastern approaches to sexuality, the giver's internal processes rank in equal importance to those of the receiver. This is fundamental to the linking of *chakras*, the essence of male and female sexual energy (Avalon, 1974). In this process, integration of mind and body becomes complete, both between and within sexual partners. These cultures' "primitive" rituals and "lost secrets" are often viewed by contemporary western society as decadent or pathological—and yet alluring. For instance, the practitioner of Tantric Yoga who strives for indefinite delay of ejaculation might be considered masochistic—and still we are intrigued by his ritual.

---

[12]The impact of "sexual normality" is discussed at several points throughout this book (e.g., see Chapters Three, Ten, and Fifteen). *The Intimacy Paradigm* details an intervention strategy (paradigm shift) which exploits common preoccupation with and conception of "normality."

When psychophysiological research is able to explore the biological correlates of profound sexual experience, it will expand awareness of human sexual potential though the cognizance of "something to measure," as well as the data it produces (see Figure 2.9). Biofeedback studies of yogis' meditation and Tibetan monks' chanting triggered a revolution in scientific understanding of mind-body interaction. Studies of profound sexual experience will no doubt do likewise.

Perhaps attainment of profound sexual experience and integration of sexuality with personal development are the two true missions of sexual-marital therapy. To accomplish this goal, the sexual-marital therapist must facilitate personal development beyond the level commonly promoted by existing culture, familial norms, and contemporary professional practice.

Hopefully this traverse of the quantum model has provided a dynamic understanding of sexual function and dysfunction, and redefined the purpose and practice of sexual-marital therapy. Sex therapy can be as plebeian as helping people reach their arousal and orgasmic thresholds; unfortunately for practitioners and consumers, it often is.

Therapists are often accused of debasing sexuality by critics who seek to preserve its sanctity by making it unmentionable. On the other hand, clinicians have conveyed the impression, despite disclaimers, that they are primarily concerned with bodily functions and technique; for many, the image is uncomfortable but true. Sexual-marital therapy can be as rich as the human capacity for eroticism and the conquest of isolation and meaningless. It can be utilized in the absence of any overt dysfunction, as a vehicle for individual development and relational bonding. The sexual crucible represents a treatment approach that embraces these goals.

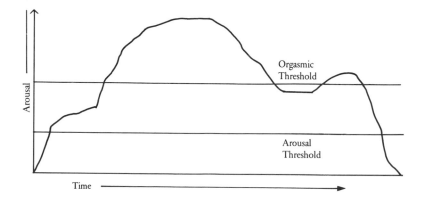

Figure 2.9 Profound sexual experience in conjunction with orgasm.

CHAPTER THREE

Sexual Potential: Actualization of Eroticism and Intimacy

*Unwillingness to recognize the mediocrity of "normal" sexual relationships blocks aware-
ness of human sexual potential. Our examination of sexual styles will illustrate relatively pleasureless "automatic physiological responsiveness"; "nondysfunctional" sex does not
guarantee sexual fulfillment. People actually fit into one of three categories: "sexually
dysfunctional," "sexually functional," and "the blessed few" who experience profoundly
erotic sex. Unfortunately, modern sexual and marital therapy emphasizes the first two
categories, but not the third.*

In discussing the concept of *sexual potential*, three complex questions
arise:

1. Does orgasm represent the limits of human sexual experience? Is
   there some aspect of subjective intensity in sexual experience that
   might be independent of the physiological event of orgasm? If so,
   why are many people seemingly unaware of this?
2. Why don't more people pursue the goal of intensity of experience
   rather than adequate physiological functioning?
3. If untapped potential sexual intensity exists, what does it take to
   actualize it?

Each of these questions will be considered in this chapter.

Profound sexual experience and intimacy are not reducible to mechanical
issues of stimulus level and physical technique. If available psychophysiological
data are any indication, peak sexual experience shows only a limited correla-
tion with physiological arousal. For many people, orgasm is the goal and
measure of sexual fulfillment; this is the *problem* that often goes unnoticed.

The notion that meaningful sex is synonymous with orgasm, or that orgasm defines the limits of human sexual experience, leads to common erroneous assumptions: (a) if one has an orgasm, one has experienced the essence of

sex, or (b) sexual function with orgasm is synonymous with sexual satisfaction. Both assumptions interfere with awareness of sexual potential. While orgasms are undeniably erotic, orgasms and eroticism are quite different things.

On occasion, something cracks the facade of contemporary sexual expectations: People have profound erotic experiences in which they are nowhere near orgasm; sometimes the orgasm occurs like an afterthought, or the intensity of experience interferes with orgasm or erection. Such experiences hold a clue to the actual nature of human sexual processes, much like when men have orgasm and ejaculation independently of each other. However, the invitation to explore the limits of one's sexuality is often declined—people withdraw from the experience rather than learn from it.

The concept of *sexual potential* suggests that subjective intensity of sexual experience is only somewhat correlated with orgasm. It is not reducible to "intensity of orgasm" or "types" of orgasm; such notions provoke outdated debates about vaginal vs. clitoral orgasm in women. Men experience considerable variation in quality of sexual experience as well.

Peak transcendent experience lies at the further reaches of human sexual potential. Because many people's serendipitous initial experience of their sexual potential coincides with orgasm, it is easy to mistakenly assume that these are one and the same; however, phenomenological intensity and salience of arousal are only somewhat correlated with orgasm. Pursuit of intense orgasms per se often interferes with repeated attainment of transcendent eroticism and intimacy. Orgasm can (and often does) occur without profound personal meaning, as many people can unfortunately attest.

Let us start out this discussion by suggesting that it is possible to experience profoundly intense eroticism and intimacy without orgasm and, moreover, to achieve a level of sexual intensity for which there is no (currently) known corresponding physiological counterpart.

WHY IS SEXUAL POTENTIAL AN UNFAMILIAR CONCEPT?

Conceptualization and awareness of sexual potential has been limited through the interaction of three discrete but related components:

- conventional sex roles, normal sexual styles, and typical personal development;
- transgenerational values embodied in social norms;
- limited professional and scientific "knowledge."

The quantum model provides an explanation of how one could reliably reach orgasm and not experience, or even know about, dormant sexual potential. It is possible (and common) to reach threshold levels for genital response and orgasm while significant *noise* remains in the receiver's psychological processes. Unwitting mind-wandering, ineffective cognitions, insecurities, and anxieties either go unnoticed during sexual contact or are so pervasive that they are accepted as normal and "nonproblematic." Moreover, it is possible to reach orgasm while the intensity of physical stimulation or interpersonal contact is less than optimal. To the degree that this is an ongoing state of affairs, the individual has not experienced the limits of his/her sexual potential.

Repetitive sexual experience rapidly becomes baseline "normal" sexual experience. Patients recognize sexual "problems" when they fail to attain threshold levels for genital response and orgasm. Except in cases of marked sexual dysfunction, people generally accept their repeated personal experience as the nature of human sexuality per se. In cases of long-term sexual dysfunction, people accept their experience as reflective of *their* personal nature. Ineffective cognitive-affective processes that limit sexual potential (or give rise to clinical difficulty) become invisible to the couple's scrutiny.

A continuum exists from sexual dysfunction through "nonproblematic" sexual normality to sexual potential; sexual enhancement and development beyond that required for adequate genital functioning often remain untapped. Evolution may have ensured that humans are programmed to perpetuate the species, but there is no evidence that fulfillment of erotic potential and capacity for intimacy are guaranteed. This unique human ability is not inherent in sexual behavior or genital function; it is a potential that must be developed.

Human sexuality *can* be beautiful and wonderful but this is the exception rather than the rule. When therapist's models of human sexual response don't consider biologically determined capacities for *depth* and *meaning* in intimacy, fantasy, and eroticism, is it any wonder that contemporary cultural sexual norms don't either? It requires stepping outside of the prevailing cultural sexual paradigm to recognize that contemporary values *inhibit* the exploration of human sexuality, rather than *support* it.

Eastern approaches to eroticism based on Tantric Yoga emphasize self-discipline in focusing consciousness and sexual energy. Followers of this approach believe that sexual potential, rather than the *fulfillment* of that potential, is natural. It is thought to require practice, discipline, and understanding the interaction among spiritual, emotional, and physical dimensions. Eastern approaches, which appear mystical by Western standards, emphasize spiritual and emotional transcendence rather than orgasm.

The failure to differentiate between sexual potentials and guaranteed outcomes has multiple iatrogenic effects. One is widespread feelings of shame, disappointment, and inadequacy among the many couples who do not experience sex as comfortable, wonderful, or beautiful. Inadvertent encouragement for teenagers to pursue early coital experimentation is another. The notion that intercourse is inherently wonderful fuels teenage curiosity and unrealistic expectations. It leads parents to the almost humorous suggestion that intercourse is *so* wonderful that it should be saved for marriage. More realistically, one has arrived at a pinnacle of human development when sex reaches levels we are taught to take for granted; *tolerating* that level of intensity is another. The suggestion "You are not ready for intercourse if (among other things) you aren't eager to do it with the lights on" is a far more useful deterrent to teenage coital activity. However, by this same standard of preparedness, most adolescents' parents aren't ready for intercourse, either!

The common belief that "intercourse is the most intimate thing that two people can do" reflects a *potential* rather than an experience inherent in genital union. In fact, widespread preoccupation with intercourse reflects the usefulness of that mode of interaction in *limiting* intimacy. People generally do *not* want to do the most intimate things possible.

Csikszentmihalyi (1990) suggests that the enhancement of eroticism is related to sexuality in much the same that athletic sports represent the highest levels of training and performance in physical activity. He notes that romance resembles sports, in that most people are content to hear about it or watch a few experts perform it rather than do it themselves.

Culturally stereotypic sexual behavior reflects normative difficulties in modulating tolerable levels of intimacy and eroticism, while still permitting orgasm. There are too few individuals capable of intense eroticism and intimacy to affect social conventions in a meaningful way; conventional cultural norms support *utilitarian* levels of sexual intensity.

Merely labeling ineffective sexual technique and gender-role sexual behavior as "sexual myths" misses the point. These are *not* myths in the sense that they represent the prevailing norms. Sexual "myths" reflect the way people construct personal reality through personal conduct. The point that "sexual myths" reflect *beliefs* rather than incontrovertible truth is a good one, but one should not overlook *why* such myths are so widespread and tenaciously held. Sexual "ignorance" reflects prevalent unresolved issues which perpetuate and are perpetuated by intergenerationally transmitted norms.

If orgasm insured the achievement of sexual satisfaction, fewer people would self-destruct in the quest for what is believed to come *naturally*. Many people, including clinicians, don't recognize (and don't *want* to recognize) the level of suffering and deprivation that most relationships endure and perpetuate.

The general public and therapists who don't specialize in sex therapy fantasize that this specialty is filled with eroticism, steamy conversations, and struggles for impulse control. What a wonderful denial of the pain and sorrow that fill my office! When therapists have sex with patients, it reflects a commingling of their respective pain and pathology, not unbridled passion. Sexual-marital therapy provides a portal into the lack of closeness or intimacy that pervades many marriages. Curing genital dysfunctions is vastly easier than helping patients *look into each other* while they are having an orgasm; it involves more than doing *it* with the lights on, or seeing each other's body. *The effort required to help couples openly display the depths of their eroticism is vastly underestimated in the professional and popular literature.*

The outset of sex therapy is bathed in feelings of inadequacy, deprivation, and pain. Successful treatment can contain a triumph in self-respect and autonomy, as well as better performance; in the best outcomes, the former is not based on the latter. Self-worth derived from better performance perpetuates the continual need to perform. Improved sexual functioning based on the *refusal* to pander to one's insecurities is what lasting self-esteem and increased capacity for eroticism and intimacy are all about.

The Barrier of Professional and Scientific "Knowledge"

Conventional professional "wisdom" often suggests a path that restricts the awareness and pursuit of sexual potential. Sexual health-care providers and scientists have not offered a developmental model for the far positive end of the continuum of sexual experience. For example, Schover and LoPiccolo (1982) conceptualize a continuum of sexual desire problems from inhibited sexual desire to sexual phobia and panic; difficulty reaching high levels of sexual desire has no place on this continuum.

The contributions of other well-known clinicians offer relatively little insight into the upper limits of human sexual development. Levay and Kagle (1977) characterized sexual maturation as a progression of three levels of sexual development: *pleasure* (the ability to experience satisfaction), *intimacy* (the ability to experience pleasure with another person), and *cooperation* (the ability to work with another for sexual pleasure). The "work" of sexual maturation, as well as how a therapist helps people accomplish it, is never specified. Other clinicians, in contrast, suggest that the ability to *play* is a crucial aspect of sexual maturation (e.g., Scharff, 1982).

Scharff believes that *good enough sex* (1982, p. 132) (analogous to Winnicott's *good enough mothering*) is the necessary ingredient in adult sexual maturation; proper balance of sexual gratification and frustration creates the capacity for whole-object attachment. However, Scharff's concept of "good enough sex" involves a half-truth. On the one hand, accepting the transient quality of sexuality and intimacy *is* important in tolerating intense sex. On the other hand, "good enough sex" is all that most people *can* tolerate.

When sexuality and intimacy improve sufficiently (i.e., above the good enough level), couples back away from it. Struggling with oneself to tolerate ever-increasing levels of physical stimulation and meaningfulness is fundamental to the sexual crucible of human development. "Good enough sex" is insufficient stimulus to trigger the recursive process of personal growth and exploration of human sexual potential. Good enough sex is what sex and marital therapy offers; good enough sex is exactly what traditional gender-role sexual behavior, at its best, provides.

"Sexual Addiction": The Antithesis of Sexual Potential

Since the early 1980s, the sex therapy field has attended to the lower end of the continuum of sexual desire and salient sexual experience. Recently, two divergent currents have emerged to address the upper end of that continuum. One is reflected in such publications as *Enlightened Sexuality* (Feuerstein, 1989), the preface of which states:

> This new orientation makes our conventional approach to sex obsolete. It is broadly sensual, erotic, and even ecstatic. It represents a great alternative to the modern obsession with self-centered genital sexuality and its pursuit of the thrill of orgasm. Truly erotic sexuality is not narrowly focused on a small area of the body—the genitals. Nor is it powered by withdrawal into private fantasies. Instead it requires that in our sexual play we're present as the whole body. . . .
>
> Sex is *not* incompatible with spiritual life. For centuries we have been haunted by the opposite idea, namely that sexuality and spirituality are mutually exclusive. This unenlightened stereotype has traumatized millions of people, and continues to do so. The truth is that if we want to grow spiritually, we cannot merely deny the existence of our genitals, just as we cannot merely succumb to all our self-indulgent whims. Rather we must integrate our sexual urges into our spiritual needs.
>
> Sex can be so much more than a valve for our neurotic need to feel good or

loved. It can be joyous and illuminating. It can be a truly transformative force in our lives. Not only can it reveal to us a depth of pleasure that outdistances the nerve spasms of conventional orgasm, it can also yield a radical intimacy that penetrates the skin of our bodies as it penetrates the boundaries of our ego personalities, until we recognize each other in the Mystery of existence itself. Sensuality and enlightenment do not lie poles apart, as our inherited Victorian morality would have us believe. Sex can be a means to, and an expression of, spiritual enlightenment.

This joyous pursuit of human sexual potential through desire and self-mastery has received increasing attention of late. In *Flow: The Psychology of Optimal Experience*, Csikszentmihalyi (1990) addresses the integration of skill development and personal consciousness that permits transcendent happiness from otherwise pedestrian and banal activities. His notion of *flow* addresses the role of psychological processes in total stimulus density (discussed in Chapter Two, "The Quantum Model").

> The optimal state of inner experience is one in which there is *order in consciousness*. This happens when psychic energy — or attention — is invested in realistic goals, and when skills match the opportunities for action. The pursuit of a goal brings order in awareness because a person must concentrate attention on the task at hand and momentarily forget everything else. These periods of struggling to overcome challenges are what people find to be the most enjoyable times of their lives. A person who has achieved control over psychic energy and has invested it in consciously chosen goals cannot help but grow into a more complex being. By stretching skills, by reaching toward higher challenges, such a person becomes an increasingly extraordinary individual. . . . "Flow" is the way people describe their state of mind when consciousness is harmoniously ordered, and they want to pursue whatever they are doing for its own sake. (p. 6)

A pathology-based counterpart to the concept of sexual potential has emerged in approaches to intense desire: "sexual addiction." Sexual addiction-ology offers very different meaning to peak experiences derived from the pursuit of sex for its own sake. Sexual addiction focuses on *disorder (rather than order)* in consciousness; *dissociation* is sexual addiction's answer to Csikszentmihalyi's observation of focused concentration that obviates awareness of all else. Sexual addictionology represents a subtle return to the disease model of sexuality of prior centuries, pathologizing intense sexual desire. *Sexual addiction and codependency are paradigms antithetical to conceptualization and realization of sexual potential.*

Codependency and sexual addiction are not disease entities. The *symptoma-tology* of codependency reflects low levels of differentiation,[1] while the *ubiquity* of codependency is perfectly consistent with Kerr and Bowen's (1988) assessment that most people remain at this level. The conceptual difference between codependency and differentiation mirrors the difference between "being in denial" and "denying": the creation of a disease from which the person attempts to free him/herself, rather than a less gratifying but sober view of typical human development suggesting widespread emotional immaturity. Conducting "emotional immaturity" groups is less "sexy" and less commercially viable than touting codependency groups.

The difference in these two viewpoints is crucial. The task is not to free oneself from one's partner or a disease, any more than the real struggle of adolescence is to emancipate oneself from one's parents. The struggle is with oneself: to emancipate oneself from one's own immaturity and ambivalence. In this litigious age of "victimization," the notion of being the partner's (or one's own) victim is more palatable than the notion of homeostatic ambivalence. The paradigm of codependency encourages codependence.

Whereas the "sex addict" is perceived as driven by desire for intense gratification, the sexual potential model posits that many people find that difficult to tolerate. Clinical experience treating "sex addicts" suggests they are as intolerant of intense eroticism and intimacy as the average individual. Compulsive sexual behavior, albeit the singularly most gratifying aspect of the "addict's" life, is not the same as transcendent sexuality.

Situational and legal pressures, poor impulse control, and low frustration tolerance drive patients with compulsive sexual behavior into treatment hurriedly and precipitously. They approach treatment and sex the same way: the final outcome is less important than having it when they want it. Treatment often terminates when they fail to receive the gratifying results they anticipated (and were perhaps implicitly promised).

Sexual addiction treatment, itself, presents barriers to sexual potential. People at the lowest levels of differentiation are driven by the avoidance of tension and self-denial, and intolerant of the frustration necessary to achieve the capacity for true relatedness. Scharff's (1982) notion of "good enough sex" is applicable to this point.

Individuals who engage in self-negating compulsive sexual and relationship behaviors are reluctant to give up emotionally destructive sexual patterns or partners, especially those providing the greatest gratification. They might want to be rid of the pain of their lifestyle, but they don't want to go through the

---

[1]The concept of differentiation will be discussed in detail in Chapters Four, Five, and Seven.

pain of giving it up. Sexual addictionology naively reduces motivation to complete treatment by encouraging renouncement of intense sexual gratification as the price of salvation.

Sexual addiction and sexual potential models are antithetical in other ways. Sexual addiction lies at the upper limits of a pathology-based continuum of sexual desire. In the health-based model of sexual potential, the upper limit of sexual desire is where one meets the God-within (Moore, 1985). Since both approaches involve some notion of spirituality, it is instructive to note the differences.

Three basic tenets of "sexual addiction treatment" philosophy involve acceptance (a) of a "higher power" as the road to recovery, (b) that one must look outside oneself for the resources for recovery, and (c) perpetual treatment for a disease that is never "cured." This trilogy is consonant with Friedman's (1990) observation that causes are notorious for the manner in which they permit leaders and followers to abdicate personal responsibility for themselves. It is also consistent with Moore's suggestion that sexual arousal based on feelings of inadequacy and an externalized sense of self "makes us resistant to the spirit of life that would lead us out into a far fuller existence" (p. 80). Moore states:

> From this trauma [of the realization of responsibility for our own lives], we are still trying to recover. We find it difficult to listen to a God who is interested in so much more than recovery. (p. 80)

Moore cites the experience of a "sudden sense of desire for no specific object at all" as the hallmark of heightened spirituality; sex addictionology encourages avoidance of such experiences and acceptance of a higher power that precludes transcendent sexual experience.

Although the visage of God enshrined in sexual addictionology's "higher power" rarely receives critical examination, there is much to be discerned by putting this central feature in context; its pseudo-spiritual flavor is often a significant attraction for people seeking to integrate their spirituality and sexuality (see Chapter Seventeen). Stratton's (1991) analysis of Kierkegaard's views of spiritual development provides a basis for understanding the different spiritual flavor of sexual addictionology vs. the sexual crucible.

In *Fear and Trembling*, Kierkegaard (1946) describes the different paths taken by the Knight of Infinite Resignation and the Knight of Faith on their quests for spirituality. The Knight of Infinite Resignation is epitomized by the biblical story of Job. Job loved and feared God, and strove to impress Him by tolerating trials and burdens. It was a one-way relationship: Job knew his God, but God seemingly did not know him. Job was a plodder, staggering forward on the straight and narrow, one day at a time. Sexual addictionology promotes Knights of Infinite Resignation in the crusade against sexual desire.

On the other hand, the Knight of Faith has a two-way relationship with God. Abraham of the Old Testament was a Knight of Faith; Abraham knew God and God knew Abraham. When God directs Abraham to kill his beloved son Isaac, he transcends the double-bind imposed by his ability to love through a leap of faith: Abraham grasps the inherent paradox of what God is asking, and willingly hurls himself into it. Whereas Job fears that God does not see his toils, Abraham trusts that God is watching when he commits himself. Whereas Job is a plodder, Abraham dances through life with grace. In the end, Job is humbled by God, whereas Abraham receives God's generosity.

If one assumes that both men's sexual relationship with their wives reflected their relationship with God, Job's wife probably had inhibited sexual desire and accused him of being oversexed; Abraham and his wife never took their eyes off each other when they orgasmed. The spirituality of the sexual crucible smiles on sexuality as fundamentally good; sexual addiction's higher power demands resignation and declaration of helplessness in the face of a self-destructive evil.

While the concepts of codependency and sexual addiction might encourage people to examine the nature of their discontent, they also lead to an approach that interferes with a resilient solution. When treatment for various sexual/emotional "addictions" fails, patients often don't abandon the approach; instead, they assume they are more hopelessly codependent and "addicted" than they feared. People who are "codependent" and "emotionally addicted" become dependent on models of codependency and addiction. While this criticism applies to other forms of psychotherapy as well, the very label of "addictions" makes it easy for people to internalize and personalize the limitations of the treatment model itself. Considering the notion that patients reconstruct their unresolved issues in treatment, it seems logical that the final stage of "codependency" and "addiction" treatment would involve rejection of these very concepts.

In contrast, differentiation-based forms of sexual-marital therapy embrace the notion of finite treatment and the assumption of individual responsibility for satisfaction and self-discipline. In fact, self-discipline (in the form of differentiated functioning) is a key to intense levels of eroticism and intimacy.

Unfortunately, "sexual addictionology" has become big business; major hospital corporations have discovered that inpatient "sex addiction" programs are lucrative. The result has fueled society's "addiction to addiction," further diminishing attention to notions of sexual (human) potential.

Mental Health Marketing of Sexuality

Commercialization of sexuality (and sex therapy) creates a misconception that people today are obsessed with increasing sexual intensity and frequency. It would seem no stone has been left unturned, no effort spared, in the pursuit of enhanced sexual attraction, performance, and gratification. Many people feel sexual hype is counterproductive to realization of sexual potential. Sexual health-care professionals are at the vanguard of such a position, for they see the casualties of contemporary "sexual enlightenment." But laymen legitimately note these same clinicians are the unwitting promoters of the performance ethic and genital focus they decry.

Helping people reach their sexual potential is not amenable to franchising and mass marketing. The process of reaching one's sexual potential is not a matter of learning concepts or mastering skills and behavioral techniques. One does not learn it by observing or listening to others. Csikszentmihalyi (1990) noted that optimal experience depends on the ability to control what happens in consciousness moment by moment; each person has to achieve it on the basis of his or her own individual efforts and creativity. The role of the therapist is not to "teach" but rather to assist in the tailoring of a highly idiosyncratic crucible of personal development. Some couples seem able to construct this on their own, but more often it helps to have a therapist who can expedite the process.

The market for helping individuals reach their sexual potential is smaller than one might like to think. Financial opportunities to help people reach *pretty good* sex, as long as it is promoted as *ultimate sex*, are significantly greater. People *want to want* intense eroticism and intimacy, as long as they are safe from having it. *If behavior is a better indication of intent than cognitions, people want good enough sex and tolerable levels of intimacy.* While this viewpoint makes many professionals and laymen uncomfortable, living it without seeing it does not. "Sexual satisfaction" is based on having as-good-as-can-be-tolerated sex rather than as-good-as-it-gets sex. Better-than-can-be-tolerated sex creates its own discomfort.

Does the concept of sexual potential create yet another goal about which one can feel inadequate? If this is the outcome, then its clinical application is self-defeating. Motivation to change out of self-rejection is inherently self-limiting; the drive to grow out of self-acceptance is self-perpetuating.

Contemporary views of sexual "adjustment" subtly reflect the medical model notion of "nonproblematic" sexuality; "healthy" sexual adjustment becomes little more than the absence of "pathology." Nonproblematic sexual adjustment involves "reasonable" levels of sexual desire, the absence of genital dysfunction or orgasmic difficulty, and the presence of some level of sexual pleasure.

Once stated this way, some therapists quickly suggest sexual "health" involves more than lack of problems; they point to the issue of satisfaction. However, if contemporary theory and practice are any reflection, sex therapy pursues nonpathological sexuality (i.e., the elimination of sexual dysfunctions) and assumes positive sexuality will flourish in the vacuum.

"Healthy" (i.e., nonpathological) sexual adjustment differs from satisfying sexual adjustment or achieving one's sexual potential. The fulfillment of sexual potential involves the limits of physiological sensation and the unfettered capacity for intellectual, emotional, artistic, and spiritual appreciation. Sexual experiences at the limits of sexual potential (and what it takes to get there) are often initially disquieting and unsatisfying (in the conventional expectation of the term).

Eroticism and intimacy on the edge of sexual potential vibrate the extended system of personal and systemic unresolved issues. Getting there involves departing from traditional gender-role behaviors during sexual contact, which usually generalizes into broader violation of gender roles previously defined by the dyadic relationship, the extended family, and society in general.[2]

THE RELATIONSHIP BETWEEN EXTREME LEVELS OF SALIENCE AND SEXUAL AROUSAL

What exists in contemporary sexological research of relevance to the concept of sexual potential? The poverty of data substantiating a strong link between psychophysiological response and subjective experience should not be surprising. Most models of sexual response focus on the *normative*, median pattern, whereas the notion of sexual potential focuses on extreme and relatively unusual experiences. Rosen and Beck (1988) note the assumption that sexual arousal follows a predictable sequence is fundamental to sexual response cycle models. They state "however useful and appealing, the concept of a sexual response cycle ought to be viewed as little more than a convenient abstraction, which may mask important variations in response patterns and sequencing from one individual or instance to another" (p. 38).

Byrne (1977, 1983) developed a comprehensive model of sexual arousal,

---

[2]This point will be discussed subsequently in regard to the dyadic system (Chapter Eight), family-of-origin issues (Chapter Eleven), and the politics of sexual desire (Chapter Ten). Clinical application is demonstrated in Chapters Fourteen ("*In Pursuit of Seuxal Potential*") and Fifteen ("*Uses of Inherent Paradox*").

involving reciprocal interaction among external events, transitory emotional mediational responses, and durable personality traits. Based on his laboratory research involving visual sexually explicit stimuli, Byrne focused on the personality trait of willingness to experience erotic stimulation (erotophobia-erotophilia). Barlow (1986) proposed a model involving external stimulation, autonomic arousal, and attentional focus on erotic cues; his central theme was the role of anxiety and cognitive interference.

Both Byrne's and Barlow's models center on cognitive-affective processes that make the difference between *minimal* sexual response or sexual *dysfunction*. Neither model (nor related research) addresses physiological processes at profound levels of erotic experience. Rosen and Beck note most laboratory studies concentrate on physiological correlates of sexual excitement, with a few recent studies on orgasm and even fewer on the nature of sexual desire.

While "mental orgasms" (triggered by imagery in the absence of physical stimulation) have been reported by some women for many years (Hite, 1976; Kinsey et al., 1953), they have only recently been documented in the physiology laboratory. Results indicate that imagery-induced orgasm is accompanied by identical physiological and perceptual events (elevated blood pressure and heart rate, pupil dilation, pain tolerance, and reduced pain detection) as genitally-stimulated orgasms (Whipple, Ogden, & Komisaruk, 1991).

Psychophysiological research has not accounted for what every individual who has had at least two orgasms knows: they differ in intensity. Psychophysiology has not discerned those people who have orgasms but are indifferent to the experience, those who have "crashing orgasms," and those who minimally trigger the reflex. Measurement of psychophysiological response has focused on orgasm per se rather than the quality of that experience—and then only minimally.

We are a long way off from being able to demonstrate things we take for granted, such as how people *feel* sexual "vibes" from each other when they pass on the street. Rosen and Beck point to a number of studies indicating little concordance between treatment outcome, subjective satisfaction, and genital vasocongestion. Response concordance generally becomes highly variable as research subjects' level of sexual arousal increases.

Delineating patterns of response clearly is facilitated when a high degree of concordance exists between these response dimensions [physiological and self-report measures]. In reality, most studies have demonstrated varying degrees of *dissociation* between response components from one individual or situation to another. We should note, however, that this concern is not unique to sexual psychophysiology, but has emerged as a central theme in the laboratory study of emotion generally. . . . (p. 335)

For the clinician interested in helping people achieve the upper limits of sexual potential, research on low-level physiological arousal is of limited help. While psychophysiological measurement is vital and interesting, it can reinforce the misperception of orgasm and repetitive copulatory capacity as the invariant determinant of satisfaction. Subjective arousal is a more useful dimension of sexual satisfaction than physiological response.

But how does one measure such things as the degree of "wonderment"? Beyond the difficulty of establishing a research measure of "profound" erotic experience, there are the problems of being *able* to reliably and ethically create this condition under laboratory circumstances. Were researchers able to do so, one might assume that they would abandon the laboratory and become exceedingly wealthy business people!

Within the limited research on the interaction of physiological and psychological processes, there has been a gradual movement toward cognitive arousal models of sexual response. Rosen and Beck (1988) state:

> More recent research [on physiological indices of peripheral autonomic arousal] has underscored the necessity for placing *subjective experience* in a central position in our definition of the sexual response. Although the physiological substratum is clearly more amenable to empirical definition and measurement than are the subjective components of arousal, it is clear that genital engorgement (or other autonomic changes) should not be viewed as necessary or sufficient in defining the sexual response. Numerous instances have been presented in which sexual arousal may be experienced without genital responding, and vice versa. Despite a growing awareness of the importance of including cognitive and affective components in the definition of sexual arousal, however, there continues to be little consensus in the field regarding the choice of specific cognitive-subjective factors to be studied. (pp. 334–5)

The concept of sexual potential is but another step in grappling with the phenomenological complexity of intensely pleasurable sexual experience. Rosen and Beck anticipate many of the issues psychophysiological research will face:

> Can current laboratory assessment techniques be used to measure psychophysiological changes at increasing levels of arousal during the response cycle? Considering that most laboratory studies to date have been limited to the measurement of changes during the initial stages of sexual excitement, what additional

findings would emerge if such investigations were extended to include higher levels of arousal? For example, in reviewing the studies of anxiety and distraction effects on sexual arousal, it can be questioned whether similar results would have been obtained if the experimental paradigm had included more extended periods of erotic stimulation and subjects had experienced higher levels of arousal prior to the introduction of the anxiety or distraction stimulus. . . . Can the phenomenon of the postorgasmic "refractory period" be adequately explained by means of traditional psychophysiological concepts, such as autonomic balance and parasympathetic rebound? To what extent do ISR [individual specific response] patterns influence the characteristics of the refractory period? (pp. 338–9)

The mere conceptualization of profound erotic and intimate sexual experience offers expanded vision for psychophysiological sex research. Is there a physiological counterpart to the transcendent sexual experience? Maturana and Varela's (1987) view of evolution would suggest so; Eastern religious views of mind-body unity would concur. Is intensity of phenomenological experience directly correlated with degree of synaptic activity in the brain, spinal column, or peripheral organs? Is it related to the length and complexity of component synaptic chains? Is it correlated with the number of discrete synaptic pathways firing concurrently? Is it a function of the degree of harmony or antagonism among concurrent synaptic processes?

Is profoundness of sexual experience correlated with the number of involved portions or processes of the brain? Or a function of the number and degree of human senses involved? Or is it correlated with higher cortical processes, such as the ability to organize these diverse processes into an effective matrix? Will it require a shift from models of linear prediction to *chaos theory* (Gleick, 1987), as occurred recently in explaining the sense of smell (Freeman, 1991)? Answers are more likely to emerge once we see, through the concept of sexual potential, that these questions exist.

Dysfunctionals, Functionals, and the Blessed Few

Another illustration of the independence of sexual arousal and physiological functioning lies buried deep within the catacombs of the sex therapy literature. Not surprisingly, it involves an approach that was antithetical to the focus on dysfunctions that has dominated sexual therapy. Bernard Apfelbaum (1977b, 1977c) presented a perspective fruitful for our discussion. Unlike Masters and Johnson and Kaplan, he did not offer a physiological model of sexual functioning; rather, he developed a conceptual model more focused on conscious phenomenological processes than on physiological response. While other clinicians sought new treatment methodologies, Apfelbaum addressed the independence of sexual arousal and physiological functioning by considering why some people *didn't* have sexual problems:

> Why is it that many patients in general psychotherapy do not have sexual symptoms, despite histories of rape, incest, and other severe early sexual trauma, just like those found in the histories of sex therapy patients? These "remote" factors, to use Kaplan's term, may be severe enough to cause psychosis but not sexual dysfunctions. Is it that early sexual traumas are not as pathogenic as what we can call "late" sexual traumas, the etiological factors stressed by Masters and Johnson? These "late" traumas are initial performance failures resulting from drinking, being rushed (as with prostitutes or as a consequence of lack of privacy), having to fumble in the back seat of a car, fear of pregnancy, or of venereal disease, etc. Although these factors do appear with great regularity in the histories of sex therapy patients, my impression is that like early traumas they can be found with equal frequency in the histories of therapy patients in other than sex therapy. These experiences are common enough to suggest that they may be found with much the same frequency in the nonpatient population as well. (1977b, pp. 50–51)

Apfelbaum noted that many individuals displaying hypothesized causes of sexual dysfunction (e.g., religious orthodoxy, depression, sexual orientation conflicts, communication difficulties, and even extreme relationship discord) often had no sexual symptoms. In fact, why was only one partner sexually symptomatic in couples with severe marital conflict? We shall pursue this line of questioning for the moment because of its intrinsic interest; it will eventually bring us back to the topic of sexual potential.

Kaplan had suggested that the effects of anxiety and stress from these various "remote" and "immediate" factors were general and nonspecific. She considered performance anxiety to be only one of many sources of anxiety and did not accord it a unique role in causing sexual dysfunctions. Kaplan further hypothesized that what distinguished sexually dysfunctional and functional individuals was their *response* to stress.

> The mere thought, "Maybe I won't have an erection tonight," need not necessarily be associated with anxiety of sufficient intensity to drain the penis of blood. In the secure person who has a good relationship, such a thought will not produce impotence, but when there is deeper unrecognized anxiety about sex, then the consciously perceived performance anxiety can tap intense sources of conflict which may be beyond the man's conscious awareness. . . . On a con-

scious level, the patient panics about his ability to perform, while unconsciously he needs to avoid a successful performance. (Kaplan, 1979, pp. 35–36)

Apfelbaum disagreed with Kaplan's assumption that anxiety per se causes sexual dysfunction, pointing out that in some cases general anxiety facilitated sexual functioning. Kaplan's explanation failed to appreciate the essence of performance anxiety in sexual dysfunctions. Noting that the fear of not responding adequately includes having the "right" *feelings* as well as genital response and orgasms, he coined the term *response anxiety* to denote global pressure to perform. Response anxiety is evident in the tendency of some women to fake orgasms; it is also manifest in Zilbergeld's (1978) observation that all people fake feelings at one time or another.

Taking up Kaplan's example of the man with the erectile dysfunction, Apfelbaum disagreed with her basic assumption that the man did not want to perform successfully; the man's response anxiety was tantamount to "the compulsion to perform despite lack of desire" (1977b, p. 53). Another way of looking at response anxiety was to call it *performance-anxiety anxiety*: shame of performance anxiety.

He thinks he shouldn't be anxious. He then tries to hide not only his turned-off state, but his anxiety about it. The result is that he becomes more emotionally isolated from his partner and even more turned off. The less anxious he is about performance anxiety, 1) the less intense it will be, and 2) the more easily he will be able to share the experience with his partner rather than having it isolate him from her. (Apfelbaum, 1983, p. 105)

Apfelbaum's notion of response anxiety positioned him strategically between Kaplan, and Masters and Johnson. On the one hand, Apfelbaum suggested that none of the "immediate" (surface, behavioral) or "remote" (deep, psychoanalytic) factors proposed by Kaplan create performance anxiety in the absence of response anxiety. On the other hand, Apfelbaum disagreed with Masters and Johnson's emphasis on performance anxiety as the cause per se of dysfunctions. Apfelbaum suggested that while performance anxiety may cause sexual dysfunctions in people with sexual dysfunctions, this same performance anxiety creates automatic genital response (without concomitant sexual arousal or desire) in functional populations. And it is at this juncture that Apfelbaum's thesis on the autonomy of physiological response and subjective experience becomes relevant to the notion of sexual potential.

Apfelbaum (1977b) reported one extreme case in which the patient had almost every conceivable thing going wrong and was still able to function. This young man displayed four startling pathogenic factors:

1. a five-year history of intermittent urethral pain with recent prostatitis that created itching and painful orgasm;
2. hospitalization for suicidal depression over the death of his father;
3. an orthodox religious upbringing in an authoritarian Arabic culture, and terror of sexual thoughts throughout his adolescence;
4. intense performance anxiety surrounding his fear of losing his capacity to perform sexually, and several experiences of initial erectile difficulties with women. On each of these experiences the man ultimately pushed himself to perform successfully. He had no erectile difficulty on numerous other encounters and masturbated daily to reassure himself of his abilities, although the experience was unpleasant.

Apfelbaum suggested that it was performance anxiety that allowed this man to function. Some people, he suggested, were capable of *automatic physiological functioning* under the most unpleasant circumstances and the same high levels of anxiety that caused others to become dysfunctional. He cited other cases of genital response occurring autonomously and independently of subjective sexual arousal, living demonstrations of the independence of genital response and satisfaction: men having erection or premature ejaculation with no subjective arousal, as well as sustained erection in men with retarded ejaculation. Kaplan (1974) had also mentioned women who lubricate or reach orgasm without subjective arousal or satisfaction. Commenting that it was such people who confuse our understanding of sexual dysfunction, Apfelbaum wrote, " . . . automatic functioning can mask the effects of all pathogenic influences on sexuality, making these effects appear random, confounding etiological issues, and creating the belief that the causes of both sexual dysfunction and sexual disorder cannot be specified" (1977b, p. 50).

Since (a) performance anxiety seems to be the ubiquitous result of traditional gender roles in sexual behavior, and (b) it is possible to clinically identify *functional* patients, Apfelbaum suggested that performance anxiety cannot be the root cause of sexual dysfunctions. It may, however, be one of two critical and specific factors in the creation of sexual dysfunctions. The second critical factor involves a differential responses to stress.

Kaplan's notion of a differential response to stress considered two possibilities. One was that some individuals and couples have better "defenses" to modulate anxiety than others. This is actually similar to Kerr and Bowen's (1988) symptom production theory in family systems. But unlike Kerr and

Bowen, who proposed that differentiation increases the capacity to modulate anxiety and reduce emergence of symptomatology, Kaplan assumed that "sexually dysfunctional patients are highly vulnerable to stress; this basic vulnerability is not altered by [her approach to] sex therapy" (1974, p. 217). Consequently, the goal of her sex therapy was maximum reduction of anxiety and stress surrounding the sexual situation, since there was no way to reduce the vulnerability itself.[3]

Secondly, Kaplan hypothesized that individuals differ in constitutional vulnerability to somatization under stress. Apfelbaum rejected this alternative as too similar to the "symptom choice" psychosomatic theories of the 1940s, from which modern sex therapy rebelled. Instead, Apfelbaum (1977b) suggested that some individuals have a sexual response *style* that makes it possible to function sexually when anxious or in a stressful relationship.

Kaplan's (1974) treatment approach of *bypassing* utilized a commonly occurring sexual style involving the ability to overlook lack of subjective desire or satisfaction by focusing on physiological sensations in order to function. Basically it involved helping patients ignore disruptive aspects of their relationship and their own psychological processes in order to avoid treatment interruptions for individual psychoanalysis.[4] Bypassing, according to Apfelbaum, was not just a therapeutic technique but rather a general psychological approach during sex involving "the aptitude and the willingness to bypass anything in one's sexual relations that would interfere with sexual performance" (1977b, p. 59). He considers bypassing to be the predominant sexual style; partner-replacement fantasies (i.e., *bypass* fantasies) are the most common fantasy during sex.

> Some people have the motivation and the ability to narrow down their consciousness at will, to hold an exclusive focus on sensation, tuning out any discordant notes in the relationship. Contrary to the slogan that it is not possible to will an erection or an orgasm, these sexual performers are able to accomplish

---

[3]Kaplan's assumption regarding the limited impact of sex therapy, as well as her resultant treatment approach, will be considered in Chapter Six; Kerr and Bowen's theory of differentiation will be discussed in Chapters Four, Five, and Seven.

[4]In her original approach, Kaplan (1974) conceptualized a two-tier approach: Masters and Johnson's (1970) sensate focus techniques were used until "resistance" dictated a brief shift to individual psychoanalytic psychotherapy. In severe cases, sex therapy was terminated altogether in lieu of psychoanalysis. As her approach evolved, Kaplan (1979) made more frequent use of individual psychotherapy, concurrent with sex therapy.

what amounts to that. . . . For the person who works at bypassing it appears possible to function at low levels of arousal or even . . . with no enjoyment at all. Of course, bypassers who must work at their routines are vulnerable to losing interest, to feeling it is not worth the effort. (1977b, p. 60)[5]

Drawing a Conclusion

Apfelbaum's notion of differences in sexual *style* provides an answer to the question why some people with high-risk characteristics *don't* develop sexual dysfunctions: Sexual dysfunction requires (a) the presence of performance anxiety, and (b) the absence of an effective sexual style (i.e., one that "works" for the individual). Moreover, Apfelbaum's insight suggests how men who are sexually assaulted by women (Masters & Sarrel, 1986; Sarrel & Masters, 1982) are "scared stiff." These men, like many others, utilize bypass as their modal sexual style and demonstrate automatic physiological response under conditions of extreme stress.

Since successful performance in the sexually functional individual temporarily relieves, but doesn't eliminate, performance anxiety, such anxiety can be thought of as actually *stimulating*, rather than impairing, performance. That is, subsequent performances are motivated by attempts to reduce performance anxiety. Individuals who learn to effectively bypass internal and external stresses develop "automatic" functioning, usually accompanied by reduced or absent desire and arousal. Apfelbaum (1977c), in fact, distinguished between sexual *dysfunctions* and sexual *disorders*. *This distinction highlights those individuals who are sexually functional in a utilitarian sense, but who lack sexual desire, arousal, or satisfaction.*

The foregoing retrospective yields two significant developments for the concept of sexual potential. First, the identification of sexually *functional* individuals further highlights the independence of sexual response and phenomenological experience. While Apfelbaum's focus lies in the lower levels of sexual profoundness (common to the field of sex therapy in general), it opens up the feasibility of extreme levels of profoundness independent of the limits of sexual arousal and orgasm.

Secondly, this discourse also contains the elements of the paradigm shift we seek. The prevailing conceptual and diagnostic focus, consensually validated in

---

[5]This discussion of sexual styles and bypassing highlights another aspect of "the receiver's psychological processes" and the dynamics of the quantum model (Chapter Two). It foretells our discussion of the etiology of inhibited sexual desire (Chapter Nine).

the DSM-III-R, groups people who have sexual dysfunctions vs. those who don't. With all our focus on dysfunctions, we implicitly (and sometimes explicitly) assume that people who are nondysfunctional are having wonderful, intense sex. However, after reviewing Apfelbaum's work on "sexual functionals," what is usually invisible now becomes obvious.

Rather than divide people into categories of sexually dysfunctional and sexually blissful, we need to think of the sexually dysfunctional, the sexually functional, and the blessed few. The willingness to perceive the mediocre levels of sexual experience that pervade and frustrate the majority of *functional* people opens the door to the concept of sexual potential. (The notion of the "blessed few" will resurface when we undertake an intensive reexamination of the nature of intimacy in the next chapters.)

DIMENSIONS OF DEPTH: PSYCHOLOGICAL DIMENSIONS OF SEXUAL EXPERIENCE

Our discussion of sexual styles provides a natural introduction for Donald Mosher's brilliant "Three Psychological Dimensions of Human Sexual Experience" (1980). Mosher addresses individual and dyadic psychological determinants of profound sexual experience; he approaches them as independent of, but related to, genital response and orgasm.[6]

Mosher proposes that people utilize three main emotional "dimensions" (scripts) in sexual experience: *trance state, role enactment,* and *partner engagement.* Depth of involvement in each dimension can vary from superficial to total absorption.

Trance state is most akin to sensate-focus activities, emphasizing introspective attention to one's kinesthetic cues of arousal. Depth of involvement in sexual trance increases as day-to-day reality fades, replaced by increasing concentration on the sexual reality of the moment. At low levels of depth, the individual is unable to abandon the day-to-day reality, scanning the environment unrelated to the sexual encounter. At moderate levels of involvement, daily reality fades and interest is focused on the sexual interaction; attention is still vulnerable to minor external interruptions as well as distracting cognitions and affects (e.g., performance anxiety and spectatoring). At profound depths of involvement, the individual becomes totally absorbed in the sexual reality and loses awareness of extraneous events (unless there is an emergency).

---

[6]What follows describes yet another aspect of the role of psychological processes in reaching threshold levels of total stimulation (re: Quantum Model, Chapter Two).

Role enactment emphasizes playing out erotic fantasies and "scripts." Depth of involvement in sexual role enactment is a function of sex-role definition, sex-role congruence, and sex-role skill. Sexual self-role refers to sexual behavior and gender identity developed through experience. Sexual role expectations influence depth of involvement by defining what level of involvement is deemed proper or appropriate. Congruence between sexual scripts and sex-role definition facilitates merging self and role; action and affect become automatic and intense when this happens. Sexual role skill refers to aptitude and experience that enable convincing enactment of a particular sexual role.

Minimal depth of involvement in sexual role enactment is marked by avoidance, disinterest, or complete dissociation of self from role. At moderate levels, action is routine and mechanical with some consistency between behavior and script expectations; there is the quality of "faking it" and spectatoring one's performance. At profound levels of involvement, there is an ecstatic sense of preoccupation and transformation in which self and role become one.

Partner engagement emphasizes the unique loving bond between partners. Depth of involvement in partner engagement is a function of the resilience and salience of the bond, the extent of core personal identity involved, and the degree of profound personal meaning embodied in the encounter. Mosher offers a detailed analysis of increasing depths of partner engagement (see Table 3.1).

Mosher also links depth of partner engagement to partner selectivity. He suggests that narrow latitude of partner acceptance is a necessary condition for deeper levels of partner engagement. At *casual* levels of acceptability (low partner engagement) partners may be inappropriate, nonappetitive, or "deviant." *General* acceptability, reflected in "recreational sex," involves selection of socially appropriate, interested, and available partners. *Selective* acceptability narrows partner selection to those with particular physical and emotional qualities; the bond is personalized, pleasurable sex. *Affectionate* acceptability involves fondness for a particular partner. *Unique* acceptance involves a single partner with whom a loving bond is developed. Profound depth of partner engagement requires a partner who has attained highly unique status in one's life.[7]

Mosher suggests that humans have the potential to use all three dimensions

---

[7]Partners sharing repeated intensely intimate experiences often develop unique acceptance of each other; profound intimacy, itself, is another dimension of partner engagement. The nature of intimacy will be considered in the subsequent chapters.

(trance state, role enactment, and partner engagement) simultaneously, each at profound levels of involvement. *Encounters involving profound involvement in all three dimensions have four characteristics*:

1. Role enactments permeate down to nonconscious and nonvolitional levels of responsiveness.
2. The sexual encounter becomes the only possible phenomenological reality for the moment.
3. Intense object relations attachments are formed with the partner.
4. All classic physiological sexual responses occur within a context of profound emotion and meaning.

Mosher's contribution is more than useful in understanding the concept of sexual potential—fulfillment of that potential is at the heart of his model.

Table 3.1
Degrees of Depth in Partner Engagement
(Mosher, 1980)

DEPTH OF PARTNER ENGAGEMENT	CHARACTERISTIC FOCUS
Past-oriented, ego-centered	Hostility overriding; fantasy of revenge and reversal of past events; partner as prop
Present-oriented, ego-centered	Present sensory experience; fantasy-less use of partner as necessary genitalia
Self-oriented, surface-centered	Self-appraisal of appearance and performance; fantasy as secret pornography; partner as necessary alter to own ego
Partner-oriented, surface-centered	Appreciation of partner's appearance and performance; partner's pleasure as important as own; fantasy as shared pornography; willing alter for partner's ego
Partner-oriented, core-centered	Appreciation of partner's core potentialities; self-disclosure and acceptance of partner's self; loving synergy; fantasies are romantic and poetic; partner is loved
Union-oriented, core-centered	Consciousness of self and partner is lost in experience of mystical union; human act of loving is a spiritual sharing that celebrates life itself; partner and self become universal man and woman

Mosher goes beyond suggesting that an individual *can* learn to use all three dimensions of sexual experience; he considers anything short of this to be "unbalanced" involvement. The pattern of unbalanced involvement gives an encounter its particular style and flavor. Chronic unbalanced involvement (i.e., limited actualization of sexual potential) creates routine and circumscribed patterns of sexual interaction, insipid sexual experiences, and conflict between partners regarding sexual ambiance and technique.

Each dimension has its associated preferred sexual style (see Table 3.2). In trance state, continuous methodical non-intrusive stimulation from the partner is preferred. The style is relaxed, passive, sensual, and inwardly oriented. Partner engagement is facilitated through eye contact, kissing, romantic utterances, and peripheral sensuality. The style is affectionate sharing and mutual pleasuring, with romantic fantasies of love and union. Role enactment emphasizes novelty, variety, and skill with oral sex and intercourse in a playful, exhibitionistic atmosphere. The style requires verbal and nonverbal script-congruent expression.

By now, you have probably recognized the ready integration of Apfelbaum's and Mosher's concepts of psychological styles. Apfelbaum's view of *bypass style* is virtually identical to Mosher's *trance state*. Moreover, both authors' assumptions about the effects of restricted sexual style are similar, although at somewhat different ends of the arousal continuum; Apfelbaum addressed the cause of sexual dysfunction whereas Mosher considered roadblocks to profoundly meaningful sexual experience. The negative effects of bypass on arousal and satisfaction, as posited by Apfelbaum, are similar to Mosher's prediction of limited depth of experience due to inability to use partner engagement and role enactment. Whereas Apfelbaum regarded bypass as a coping strategy for problems in the sexual system, Mosher considered restricted range of style an issue of personal development. The dyadic implications are also perfectly clear: partner engagement and role enactment can achieve meaningful depth only in a relationship from which (a) one is not trying to tune out one's partner and (b) the partner is equally adept at playing the corresponding part.

Since Apfelbaum and Mosher began with vastly different interests, their similar conclusions underscore a fundamental aspect of human sexual potential. Taken together, their works articulate some of the intricate psychological processes that create profound sexual experience; contrast this with widespread notions of "good sex" and you have a clearer picture of how the concept of sexual potential is so subtly unappreciated in contemporary sexual norms. Finally, their works contain an important message about the ability to main-

Table 3.2
Characteristics of Three Dimensions of Psychological Involvement in Sex
(Mosher, 1980)

CHARACTERISTICS	SEXUAL TRANCE	PARTNER ENGAGEMENT	ROLE ENACTMENT
Setting	Privacy: freedom from distraction	Psychological: good relationship	Stage: dramatic, exhibitionistic
Mood	Calm, relaxed, serene	Romantic, loving	High self-esteem, playful
Sexual Techniques	Slow pacing and repetitive	Kissing, full body contact, eye contact	Variety and skill in oral sex and intercourse
Style	Passive, sensual, inwardly oriented	Affectionate sharing, mutual pleasuring	Active movement, sound and facial expression
Role Expectations	Non-intrusive, sensitive to ambiance	Loving partner	Complementary and coordinated
Sex Talk	Infrequent, pacing instructions	Romantic endearments	Lusty or directing
Fantasies	Scriptless, visual or sensory images, synesthesia	Romantic, valentines, love songs, face of partner, union, rebirth	Scripted for novelty, drama, exhibition
Conception of Sex	Trip, altered state	Loving merger	Adventure or drama
Criterion of Good Sex	Intense absorption into sensations	Loving union with partner	Ecstatic expression and nonvolition
Orgasms	Intense sensations with faded consciousness	Flowing, loss of self in union	Dramatic, expressive, nonvolitional
Low Meaning	Transported	Love union	Real man or woman
High Meaning	Illumination	Celebration of life	Fulfillment of archetypal role

tain sexual function and arousal in the face of extreme adversity. The broader the range of sexual styles that can be used at profound depth, and the broader the range of sexual behaviors that correspond to this repertoire, the more resilient the couple will be to the inevitable injuries, illness, and traumas that are a fact of life.

FUTURE EXPLORATION OF SEXUAL POTENTIAL

A number of sex therapy outcome studies have shown increases in subjective sexual and relationship satisfaction without corresponding improvements in sexual functioning (DeAmicis et al., 1985; Heiman & LoPiccolo, 1983; Kilmann et al., 1986; Levine & Agle, 1978; LoPiccolo et al., 1985). While this is disappointing to a therapeutic discipline predicated on symptomatic relief of dysfunctions, it bodes well for the goal of *dramatically* enhancing subjective sexual and relationship satisfaction without necessarily creating corollary changes in physiological processes. This doesn't mean that the limits of sexual potential can be achieved without resolution of sexual dysfunctions or that reversal of sexual dysfunctions is not a legitimate goal. Indeed it is, and the approaches outlined in subsequent chapters and *The Intimacy Paradigm* are effective in doing just that.

But, what if the level of total stimulation required to reach the orgasmic threshold is some 30, 20 or even 5% below the potential limits of an individual's experiential capacity? What if the individual is able repeatedly to bypass ineffective intrusive thoughts and affects and continue to function autonomically?

- Is this "pathological"? Certainly not by any conventional definition of normality. In fact, Apfelbaum suggests that this is why the individual is *not* sexually dysfunctional.
- Is this "problematic"? Not by the unaware patient's self-evaluation — that is, not until the chronic impact emerges as lack of arousal, desire or satisfaction. Even then, this development may not be regarded as problematic if it is an acceptable solution to individual or systemic dynamics.
- Is this "wasted potential"? Certainly.
- Is this "important"? That is a matter of opinion.

The quest for unfulfilled sexual potential is akin to the quest for excellence in sound reproduction. The pursuit of experiential realism in high-fidelity sound systems is disproportionately expensive, elusive, and difficult to document by scientific measurement. Yet it is the most meaningful portion of the experience to the true stereophile, who willingly spends every penny in pursuit of his or her subjective experience.

The vast majority of people make do with perfectly adequate, moderately-priced sound systems. Without the opportunity for side-by-side comparison, they are satisfied. Even upon initial exposure, the novice is unlikely to discern the subtle differences that mean everything to the person with a developed ear. The stereophile thinks most people don't know what they are missing. The normal individual thinks the stereophile is a nut. Appreciation of sound reproduction, like sexual potential, is an acquired taste and a matter of perspective. Some people enjoy their orifices more than others.

A Therapy That Encourages People to "Tune In"?

The pursuit of sexual potential is a vital undertaking, but not one supported by traditional sexual and marital therapy. Preoccupation with sensate focus prescriptions has created an inherent paradox: sex therapy's core sexual style does not support profound depths of partner engagement or role enactment. Society has idealized one partner focusing inward while the other touches him/her; the paradigm is prostrate, eyes-closed, "cadaver" sex. Although helpful in learning to sensate focus, tune out one's partner, and achieve utilarian arousal, this pattern is antithetical to collaborative "romping" in bed. In fact, its external appearance (e.g., a "comatose" partner) is commonly a source of relationship conflict.[8]

Eastern approaches to sex encourage partners to develop a mutual focus of psychic energy (Kundalini); sex therapy sensate focus prescriptions, in contrast, advocate that both partners focus on one partner. Said differently, Eastern approaches suggest a centripetal focus of partner's consciousness, whereas traditional sex therapy encourages a centrifugal focus.

The distinction is not merely philosophical. The partner of a man with long-term premature ejaculation learns to be sexually passive (in order not to trigger ejaculation). Likewise, she eventually uses self-distraction to minimize her arousal (in order to minimize further frustration). However, the corollary is often overlooked: *the woman refrains from focusing her erotic energy towards her partner because he can feel it and the additional "charge" will trigger his orgasm.* The result is that neither partner has an experience anywhere near his or her sexual potential.

The notion of "dimming of consciousness during orgasm" promotes another inherent paradox. The "dim" view of orgasm (which reflects many people's experience) is antithetical to intimacy during orgasm; it ignores the *sharpening* of consciousness during orgasm (e.g., Mosher's alternative sexual reality, constructed to varying degrees of profoundness). Heightened awareness of the

---

[8] *The Intimacy Paradigm* presents a paradigm shift in sexual prescriptions that avoids the problems highlighted in this section.

sexual reality is more than disrupted EEG patterns; floods of associations, de-repressions, and paradigm shifts often occur during and after such experiences. Beyond "I'm coming, I'm coming" is the "Eureka!" experience of "I've got it!"

When one stops to examine it, the paradigm of contemporary sexual and marital therapy is shockingly non-erotic; eroticism (and sexual aggression in particular) is perhaps the most avoided aspect of sexual potential. Sexual aggression need not connote brute force or domination and submission; it often involves seduction and the power of "putting one's partner into orbit." It does not require pounding or pile-driving; gentle rhythmic grinding and fluid motion from a highly charged partner is often more effective. Motionless silence and noisy pile-driving can both be devastatingly erotic when conducted in the right ambiance; it is hot, soothing, and hightly intimate. Unfortunately, pile-driving often results from *avoidance* of eroticism, *shallow* levels of partner engagement, and *lack* of comfort with one's body; the impact is not the same.

Sexual aggression, never a particularly comfortable topic, has become even more suspect when viewed through current therapeutic emphasis on sexual victimization. Two vignettes highlight the tremendous need to focus on eroticism, and how rarely it is recognized by health-care professionals.

A recent class of third-year medical students were having a hard time recognizing the difference between genital function and eroticism. The female students were asked to recollect an experience of being in an elevator alone with a stranger, *feeling* him mentally undress her; with some reluctance, they acknowledged this common experience. With much greater enthusiasm, the male students reported doing the corresponding behavior. However, it was the last question that really surprised them all: "Have you ever sent or received that same intensity of erotic jolt while having sex with someone you knew?" Like most people, the students were shocked to realize they showed passing strangers a part of their sexuality that they never used with their partners.

The second example comes from the recent 1991 Annual Meeting of the American Association of Sex Educators, Counselors and Therapists. During my presentation, I asked a room packed with certified sex therapists, "How many of you think treatment is not completed until patients can have eyes-open orgasms?" *Not one single therapist raised a hand.* The question itself took many clinicians by surprise; the surprise arose from suddenly experiencing a paradigm shift in treatment approach.

Many couples show a minor "regression" just prior to termination of treatment; it commonly occurs when couples haven't made sufficient progress in sustaining high levels of eroticism, including sexual aggression. The requisite qualitative leap is important, difficult, and rarely a focus of sexual and marital therapy. Patients who made the transition talk knowingly of "being in the groove" while having sex; it is the antithesis of "being in a rut."

For example, the wife in a couple moving towards termination of a highly successful treatment began to complain she felt "used" by her husband; this was the same complaint she expressed at the outset of treatment.[9] At the outset, however, the husband *couldn't* allow himself to use her; after much work on his part, now he *could* (at least during intercourse). Actually, the wife's half-hearted complaint reflected being somewhat unnerved by the intensity of his erotic energy.

There is an irony to the common complaint "I feel used"; often it reflects bungling ineptitude and restricted eroticism. *All too often a spouse hasn't gotten far enough in his/her sexual development to* really *use a beloved partner*. When one half of a couple has more experience with intense sex than the other, that partner's complaint is actually: "He (she) doesn't know how to really use me *well*; I resent being used *poorly*." There are lots of people who enjoy "being rode hard and put up wet." It involves the ability to say, "Take me, ravish me, do whatever you want"; it has nothing to do with spouse abuse or exploitation.

In the wife's case, the invitation to meet her husband head-on with her own sexual aggression scared her. She described it this way:

> I know that I am holding back, but I really don't want to. But when I can really feel him, I get afraid, even though I really want to meet him at that level. I also know that if I hesitate long enough, he will get frustrated and go back to the way he was, apologizing for his sexuality and not really letting his eroticism loose; I hated it when he did that in the past. The crazy part is that I know that after it happens, I will let myself loose and come on to him; that is, until he really lets himself go with me.[10]

---

[9]It is easy to misinterpret this as "resistance to termination." Sometimes, the couple intuits that some critical task has not occurred; fresh symptomatology keeps the possibility of treatment intervention alive.

[10]When this kind of report is received from individuals having sexual or relationship problems, the possibility of prior abuse or trauma comes to mind. But when it occurs from a high-functioning happy individual with no memory trace of sexual abuse, and whose sexual and marital relationship is vibrant and hitting new highs, the interpretation of "repressed memories of abuse" becomes less parsimonious. Nuances of self-report are often key to accurate diagnosis. In this and *many cases*, the description is indicative of object relations issues triggered by profoundly intense sexuality and intimacy. When patients who *have* been previously abused reach the same point as this woman, it becomes a matter of clinical judgment whether to "go back" to abuse issues or "go forward" to deal with contemporary issues of adult eroticism and intimacy.

It is ironic that this dynamic, expected at *low* levels of arousal from aversive individuals, *invariably surfaces in all couples at high levels of eroticism and intimacy; the problem is helping the couple get far enough in treatment so that it does*. In the above case, the wife successfully made the transition. The result, however, was a shock for the husband: He was equally unnerved when his wife *lustily* performed fellatio on him!

This vignette hints at the level of intensity inside the sexual crucible. Dealing with issues like this is like being *drop forged*—hammering out a sexuality of great strength and integrity. It is a solution for the millions of people whose sexuality is *die cast*: brittle, easily stressed, and shaped like the childhood mold into which it was poured. This is not simply emancipating oneself from childhood prohibitions; once accomplished, one faces *adult* issues of eroticism and intimacy.

Intense sex and intimacy are hard to tolerate. Although our ostensible focus is pleasure, people often find that exploration of sexual potential requires courage and integrity. For example, couples become unnerved when they enjoy sex that straddles the fine line between pleasure and pain. Buddhism teaches that enlightenment involves sitting on the edge of ecstatic pleasure and unbearable pain as one witnesses life. Many people chase after intense sex and intimacy, but few seem truly willing to find it.

What Lies Ahead?

Francoeur (1987b, 1990) noted that Karl Jaspers, Alvin Toffler, Teilhard de Chardin and other commentators on contemporary culture suggest that the world has entered a transitional stage of heightened consciousness:

> The recent conservatism may be seen as marking a time of consolidation during which we can adjust ourselves to the radical and deep cultural changes that began in the 1960's and 1970's. In a few years, a new human may emerge to fly in a world of which the Puritans and Victorians could never conceive. (1987b, p. 313)

In contrast to Leo's (1987) view that the sexual revolution is dead, Kirkendall (1987) suggests that it is just getting started. If Kirkendall is correct, the revolution will occur in the *focus* of sex rather than in fluctuations of conservatism and permissiveness about premarital and extramarital sex. One secondary outcome of the AIDS pandemic may be increased attention to depth and salience in sexual experience; people are more likely to focus on quality than quantity of partners.

Another manifestation of the revolution will surface in the services developed for the handicapped and the elderly; both populations need sexual enhancement services. But this will not result from altruism—it will stem from recent passage of equal access legislation for the handicapped, secondary impact of life-prolonging medical technology, and aging of the baby-boomer generation. These all involve economic and political power, and power has always been a powerful factor in access to sex.

For the handicapped and the aged, maintaining sexuality and self-esteem involves the same tasks facing the rest of society: (1) detaching self-esteem from sex-role behavior, and (2) detaching adequacy and eroticism from physical functioning—that is, developing *anatomy-independent eroticism and intimacy*. Handicapped people who transcend their disability and maintain eroticism and self-esteem intact violate normal social expectations; they trigger anxiety in temporarily able-bodied individuals who cannot do likewise. These latter individuals (including health-care professionals) are confronted with their own physical vulnerability, their anatomy-dependent self-acceptance, and their restricted emotional development.

The joke that, "the most effective form of birth control in later adult life is nudity," reflects the self-rejection implicit in cultural norms. Older adults who refuse to relinquish their sexuality to cultural stereotypes highlight the confusion health-care professionals perpetuate between *sexual prime* and *genital prime*. Most sex books and professional texts state that males reach their sexual prime in late adolescence and that women reach theirs several years later. Unwittingly, such notions imply that sexual prime concerns genital response and firm flesh. This unfortunately validates the piece-of-meat model of sexual intimacy that most people unwittingly practice in daily life.

Most people never come close to their sexual potential and those who do generally do not accomplish this until the fifth and sixth decade of life.

The periods of childhood, adolescence, and adulthood have age-appropriate tasks; advanced age has such tasks as well. But these tasks do not involve the winding down of diminished sexual capacity. The later adult years are the time when the most important exploration of sexual potential occurs.

Whereas younger women struggle to balance displays of sexual interest and eroticism with fears of looking "cheap" or "easy," elderly women can validate their own sexual interest and participate as an equal in displays of eroticism and sexual virtuosity. Adolescent boys, preoccupied with genitally focused issues of masculinity, are often unkind; they are threatened by a partner who is self-motivated and sexually knowledgeable. In contrast, this is where a *mature* older man shines. Sexual intensity is more a function of emotional maturation than of physiological responsiveness. If sexual intimacy is thought to involve the disclosure of core levels of *self*, then *sexual* prime and *genital* prime occur at vastly different ages. *If* older people have learned something about themselves in their days on earth, there is far more *core self* to be brought to sexual intimacy and more differentiation to permit the disclosure of it. Intimacy in later adult life is no longer fraught with anxiety about being dominated or controlled. There is less concern about enduring a less-than-ideal partner or relationship forever. Forever gets shorter and shorter. . . .

Perfect fulfillment of sexual potential, like the achievement of total differentiation, is never achieved. It is a lifelong pursuit of personal development. The sexual crucible is the embodiment of the hero's (and heroine's) quest, of which Joseph Campbell (1949, 1988) has written. It involves the conquest of self in relationship to trials and difficulties, the transcendence of personal limitations, and the dauntless struggle to be fully human with one's partner. When we, as individuals and as a society, recognize and respect these things, we will truly be on our way towards the fulfillment of our sexual potential.

CHAPTER FOUR

The Quest for Intimacy

Our in-depth examination of intimacy begins with the definitions and descriptions that dominate the professional literature. We will find confusion about how intimate relationships actually develop and how to help when they don't. A previously unrecognized contradiction exists between models emphasizing disclosure reciprocity and the existential viewpoint, which emphasizes acceptance of immutable separateness. We will resolve the dilemma by developing a two-stage developmental model of intimacy, in preparation for a rare-as-hen's-teeth clinical model of intimacy (presented in Chapter Five).

The widespread quest for intimacy is like what happens in Russia when there is a rumor that some store has a rare delicacy. People run to get on line, sure that it is worth waiting in the cold for hours if everyone else is; some don't even know what the rumored item is, but don't want to miss out. The fact that the item might not be to one's preference or size is almost inconsequential. One might find some use for it in the future, or trade it for something else, or know someone else who might want it.

While therapists have fueled the public's quest for intimacy, there is precious little of substance on that topic in the professional literature. Intimacy has been promoted as a panacea to mental health consumers, although clinical consideration of the *processes* of intimacy has been relatively superficial and glib. One might ask: What *are* the source and substance of therapists' expertise in the area of intimacy?

The amorphous literature on intimacy can be roughly categorized into three categories: *definitional*, *descriptive*, and *clinical* approaches to the topic. The professional literature abounds with definitions and descriptions (which will be considered first in this chapter). You should be forewarned: there is a distinct poverty of clinical wisdom on the process of intimacy. This fact is both disconcerting and helpful in understanding why sexual and marital therapy has been relatively ineffective in facilitating marital intimacy, sexual and otherwise. *Many therapists conduct treatment unaware they lack any clinical understanding of how intimacy develops or how to help it when it doesn't. Modern sexual and marital therapies have implicitly embraced definitional and descriptive models of intimacy and have thereby been seduced and led astray.*

DEFINITIONAL APPROACH TO INTIMACY

The word *intimacy* itself derives from the Latin *intimus*, meaning "inner" or "inmost," and retains similar meanings in many modern languages (e.g., secret, deep, private) (Hatfield, 1984). Keifer (1977) observed that, although the term has been used intermittently by social scientists for over half a century, an adequate definition is every bit as elusive as the search for intimacy itself. She noted early references to intimacy in Colley's (1909) discussion of intimate aspects of primary groups, Simmel's (1908) thesis of intimate processes, Lewin's (1936) delineation of the self into peripheral and central regions, and Freud's (1914/1949) discourse on narcissism and the transcendence of self.

Discussions of intimacy are hampered by difficulty defining the phenomenon. Reliance on intuitive understanding creates ambiguity when the discussion becomes specific and detailed. When authors do offer definitions, subtle differences are often more significant than commonalities. For example, Lowenthal and Haven (1968) defined intimacy in the simplest terms: confiding in or talking about oneself or one's problems to others. Keifer (1977) defined intimacy as "the experiencing of the essence of one's self in intense intellectual, physical and/or emotional communion with another human being . . . " (p. 267). Hatfield (1984) defined it as a process in which we attempt to get close to another, to explore similarities (and differences) in the ways we think, feel, and behave. As these viewpoints demonstrate, intimacy can be approached from the vantage points of individual phenomenology, interpersonal behavior, and social purpose.

Biddle (1976) conceptualized intimacy as involving variations in *breadth, openness,* and *depth. Breadth* refers to the scope of shared activities and the degree of time spent together. *Openness* refers to degree of self-disclosure. Keifer (1977), one of the few authors to look at the *content* of openness, wrote, "Openness, then, is the *mutual disclosure of the intellectual, physical, and/ or emotional identities of each partner in the process of their interaction*" (p. 274, italics in original). Openness in intimate relationships is often thought to follow a predictable pattern: disclosure proceeds from peripheral to more core aspects of self, and tends to be repetitive (Altman & Taylor, 1973).

Depth refers to the degree to which less readily accessible, core, aspects of an individual are disclosed or shared. Lewin (1936) considered depth as the disclosure of information which "distinguishes him from others, that which is individual in a qualitative sense, as the core value and chief matter of his existence" (p. 126). Such disclosure also distinguishes the person to whom the information is disclosed as having particular status in the life of the discloser. The dimensions of breadth, openness, and depth are highly interdependent, so that a change in one dimension is likely to bring about a change in one or both of the others.

Keifer considered the additional variable of *salience*:

> Some of one's intimate relationships are more important than others. I use the term *salience* to refer to the relative value or importance that any of one's relationships holds for the individual. A relationship that has a great deal of salience assumes relatively high priority in the day-to-day life of the individual. Salience can be seen in the amount of time one spends thinking about the intimate partner and about matters having to do with that relationship. Day-dreams and fantasies are manifestations of salience, as are dreams that take place during sleep and other signs of mental preoccupation with the partner in his or her absence. The time that one spends dwelling on past interaction, whether pleasant or unpleasant, with one's intimate partner or anticipating future inter-action is an indication of salience. . . . The salience of one's various intimate relationships is an overlooked variable in the family literature. (1977, pp. 279–280)

Some authors have addressed the dimensions in which intimacy occurs. Keifer (1977) considered three: *intellectual, emotional*, and *physical*. Hatfield (1984) similarly delineated three dimensions: *cognitive* (revealing and listening to confidences), *emotional* (caring deeply about each other), and *behavioral* (comfort in close physical proximity and touch, eye gazing, leaning towards each other).

Whereas the above authors conceptualize intimacy as having a few dimensions, other authors have taken the opposite route. Waring and Reddon (1983) considered intimacy to be a concoction of identity, sexuality, compatibility, expressiveness, independence, cohesion, affection, and conflict resolution. L'Abate and Talmadge (1987) suggested, "Intimacy in marriage means that each partner brings and participates with ego strength, power, interdependency, vulnerability, touch, trust, mutuality, an understanding of self, and a sharing of the self as known" (p. 29). Clinebell and Clinebell (1970) considered at least 12 "varieties or facets" of intimacy: sexual, emotional, intellectual, aesthetic, creative, recreational, work, crisis, commitment, spiritual, communication, and conflict.

Attempts to define intimacy through exhaustive lists of traits and character-istics are generally overly inclusive. "Buckshot" conceptualizations miss the mark of clearly differentiating the critical and nondivisible salient processes of an intimate relationship from secondary or superficial processes. Often there is more gained by delineating what intimacy is *not*, if the ultimate goal is a *clinical model* of intimacy that facilitates treatment. While there is room in academic inquiry for an "it's in there, somewhere" approach, the clinician must focus time and interventions on the crucial processes involved. "Shotgun" conceptualizations are often indicative of the early efforts of a young science.

Others have similarly recognized the problems of diffuse definitional ap-proaches. Wynne and Wynne (1986) concluded it was not useful to loosely equate intimacy with such terms as closeness, warmth, love, or sexuality. Malone and Malone (1987) similarly commented:

> There are many words used to attempt to describe the functional (useful) human relationship, the healthy, growthful, prototypic dyad. The most com-mon are love, openness, commitment, genuine closeness, supportiveness, af-firming awareness, mature relationship. We speak of being yourself with others, of honestly relating. All of these terms have specific significance and are subtly different from one another. They each describe some particular aspect of relationship. Normally, however, we use them not specifically but interchange-ably: to be open is to be aware; to be aware is to be mature, honest, and committed in relationship; to be all of these is to be genuinely close. This is not true. These different aspects of relationship are each important in their own way, but many of them are not at all what we mean by the term *intimate*. (p. 4)

DESCRIPTIVE MODELS OF INTIMACY

If one wants proof that the clinical study of marriage and adult sexuality is in its adolescence, one need look no further than the topic of intimacy. Scientific consideration of intimacy has been stifled by the view that the uniqueness of individual experience precludes systematic examination (Davis, 1973; Hat-field, 1984). Attempts to study intimacy sometimes trigger a sense of profan-ing or debasing a sacred, transcendent, or quasi-religious experience. Similar views confronted Masters and Johnson at the outset of their explorations of human sexuality. Like many adolescents, we tend to view intimacy in highly abstract and idealized terms.

The abstract quality of descriptions of intimacy is evident, for example, in attempts to distinguish an intimate experience from an intimate relationship. It is often noted that an intimate experience is limited in time, scope, predictability, and repetition. An intimate relationship, in contrast, displays recurring intimate experiences in several dimensions; intimate relationships also require greater effort, time, and proximity (Schaefer & Olsen, 1981). However, defining an intimate relationship as one in which there are satisfyingly frequent intimate experiences offers little to the clinician; what does one do with a once-happy couple trying to recapture or exceed their prior level of intimacy? Consider instances in which marital difficulties result from intolerance of the increased intimacy (potentially) available as relationship duration increases. What makes a relationship intimate or not involves more than the pattern of interaction.

A thorough review of the professional literature leaves a striking picture of people desperately seeking someone to reassure them that they are worth loving. If the undertone of this material is any indication, the quest for intimacy is not about the trials of knowing and being known; it's about the quest for a reflected sense of self.

This theme underlies almost all of the literature, including the most extensive segment which concerns *self-disclosure*. Superficially, self-disclosure emphasizes partners' knowing and being known by each other (e.g., Altman & Taylor, 1973; Berscheid & Walster, 1978; Hatfield, 1982). Patterson (1984) even considered the role of nonverbal self-disclosure.

Self-disclosure is often conceptualized as serving the purpose of acceptance-seeking (gaining acceptance for one's self-concept).[1] Authors emphasize gaining external validation of one's self-worth and identity as the major goal of self-disclosure (Altman, 1973; Jourard, 1971; Kelvin, 1977). Derlega (1984) went so far as to suggest that gaining acceptance from one's partner is a major *task* in intimate relationships.

However, few authors consider the *politics* of self-disclosure when intimacy is pursued to validate one's self-image and self-worth. The assumption that what is "disclosed" is honest, forthright, and innermost to the individual underlies the extensive literature on self-disclosure.

Chambliss (1965) considered the manipulation of self-presentation according to the situation and individuals involved, suggesting that an individual experiences self-disclosure as validating when he perceives that others see him

---

[1]Other motivations for intimate self-disclosure have also been proposed: the development of a "we-feeling" (Archer & Earle, 1983; Levinger & Snoek, 1972), relationship maintenance (Derlega & Grzelak, 1979), function-regulation (coordination of actions and reducing ambiguity about expectations and intentions) (Derlega, 1984), meeting mutual needs, and creating the opportunity to protect (Kelvin, 1977). McAdams (1984) considered power motives (control, self-assertion and self display) and "communal" orientation (self-surrender, communication, and union).

as he has attempted to *present* himself. Derlega and Grzelak (1979) and Schlenker (1984) recognized that self-disclosure shifts to self-presentation when the affirmative response of the audience becomes more important than "being known" or defining oneself. Derlega (1984) referred to this as the difference between "selective" and "honest" self-disclosure.

Validation derived from self-disclosure requires (a) that the information presented is a core reflection of the true self and (b) that the individual has a relatively stable self-concept. Paradoxically, neither of these requirements is likely to be fulfilled when an individual seeks validation from others to improve his/her low self-esteem or poorly defined self-image; such an individual is more likely to give superficial disclosure, edit content to elicit a positive response and pander to the perceived preferences of the audience. Successful *selective* self-presentation has the paradoxical impact of increasing fears of rejection about the remaining undisclosed aspects of self.

The quest for a reflected sense of self becomes more evident in the second largest segment of the literature, which concerns *reciprocity* and reciprocal self-disclosure (e.g., Levinger & Snoek, 1972; Lowenthal & Haven, 1968; Walster, Walster, & Berscheid, 1978). The concept of "disclosure reciprocity" (Derlega & Grzelak, 1979) highlights the widespread expectation that one partner's disclosure *should* elicit acceptance or validation, as well as self-disclosure, from the other. The expectation of accommodation and reciprocity is further underscored by the view that self-disclosure serves to announce one's expectations for individual and joint outcomes (Archer & Earle, 1983).

Professional legitimation of expectations for reciprocity (which we will track throughout the literature) is an expression of people's widespread desire for someone to help carry the burden of a dissatisfying relationship with themselves. Attempts to *enforce* this wish surface in the invocation of *equity* regarding self-disclosure.

A number of authors utilize *equity theory* to explain (and validate) the expectation of reciprocity in self-disclosure (e.g., Chaikin & Derlega, 1974; Derlega, Harris, & Chaikin, 1973). Equity theory has its roots in the work of Thibaut and Kelly (1959), Homans (1961), and Blau (1964). According to reciprocity expectations underlying equity theory, the recipient of another's self-disclosure is obligated to disclose information of comparable intimate "value." Some writers have paused briefly to consider whether exchange theory is applicable to the processes of intensely intimate or loving relationships (Hatfield, Utne, & Traupmann, 1979; Miller & Berg, 1984; Walster, Berscheid, & Walster, 1973); by and large they assume it is.

According to equity theory, the "recipient" of self-disclosure is considered the "benefited party"; reciprocal disclosure of similar "goods and services" is expected. Derlega's (1984) articulation of self-disclosure equity highlights the clinical naivete that dominates cognitive- and social-psychological descriptions of intimacy:

> If one individual always reveals something personal and the second person never does, the high discloser may see this arrangement as unfair. The benefited party may also perceive that this arrangement is unfair, because the discloser has invested more in the relationship in the form of high self-disclosure than has the listener. . . . (Derlega, 1984, p. 8)

The calculator view of self-disclosure reciprocity is as firmly entrenched in the professional literature as it is in the self-presentation exchanges of many couples.

> The internalization of the principle of equity should be one factor leading a person to reciprocate or return benefits he or she received from an exchange partner. To the extent that the individual subscribes to the principle of equity, he or she feels a greater urgency to repay the other. Also, this sense of urgency should increase as the degree to which he or she has been benefited increases. Other factors that will affect the sense of urgency a person feels to benefit another who has previously helped him or her may include the type of benefit received and the attributions made for the benefactor's behavior. (Miller & Berg, 1984, p. 163)

In actuality, the listener who understands the expectation of reciprocity often feels pressured to disclose and wishes that the partner was not so "beneficent." Since needy, dependent people are more likely to seek out validation through (selective) self-disclosure, and (theoretically) derive the most benefit, both equity theory and clinical experience suggest that they readily feel obligated to reciprocate; they also become the most resentful.

In real life, couples develop strategies that are less altruistic than equity theory anticipates: The recipient of repeated disclosure learns to not "receive" or to negate the benefit of what is received. (Subsequent consideration of existential perspectives of intimacy will suggest an alternative paradigm: the primary benefit of self-disclosure accrues to the discloser.)

If the literature is any indication, prevailing views of intimacy are quite narrow. What might be considered other-validated intimacy is mistakenly perceived as reflecting the breadth and depth of intimacy itself. It might not be immediately clear what the alternative to other-validated intimacy is; however, introducing this concept begins to illustrate the difference between academic and clinical ways of thinking.

Descriptive vs. Clinical Models of Intimacy

There is a marked difference between *descriptive* and *clinical* models of intimacy. Descriptive models tend to arise from observations of: (a) social exchanges involving relatively low levels of intimacy, (b) couples in the early stages of relationship formation, and (c) couples who have successfully maintained high levels of intimacy over a period of years.

Descriptive models tend to consider relatively minor fluctuations in intensity of intimacy. While intimacy is recognized to be episodic, and "intimate relationships" vary in intimacy over time, extreme levels of marital conflict are almost never addressed.

Relationships tend to be discussed dichotomously with regard to intimacy, as if they were either "intimate" or not—rather than occurring along a continuum. There is little recognition that the same relationship can (and does) occupy drastically different positions on that continuum at different points in its evolution. Little attention is devoted to a common occurrence: relationships often develop some initial level of intimacy, or sustain a significant level for some period, and then go astray.

Descriptive approaches tend to draw on the literature of social and cognitive psychology and emphasize rationality and altruism. Rarely is there consideration of nonconscious factors surrounding intimacy or integration with the vast clinical literature regarding individual and systemic processes in general.

A *clinical* model of intimacy, in contrast, is based on an understanding of the fundamental dynamic processes necessary for intimate experiences. In addition, a clinical model attempts to explain the process by which intimate experiences develop into an intimate relationship; it involves both a molecular and molar view.

However, it is insufficient to consider the conditions under which intimacy blooms. *A clinical model must address the processes of intimacy under the circumstances of stress and conflict (commonly presented by couples seeking treatment).*

In practice, the difference between descriptive and clinical models involves a shift from the usual questions of, "What is the nature of intimacy?" and "What are couples, who have sustained ongoing intimate relationships, like?" The question becomes, "How do you help a couple become more intimate than they are currently?" Kerr and Bowen (1988) highlight the distinction between description and explanation in their discussion of the difference between a relationship system and an emotional system:

> The relationship system was a description of what happened, and the emotional system was an explanation for what happened. Saying that people function in

reciprocal relationship to one another is a description of a phenomenon, not an explanation. This description of what happens is contained in the concept of the family relationships system. Saying that the human relationship process is rooted in instincts, has much in common with what occurs in other forms of life, and has a function in evolutionary terms is a step toward accounting for what occurs. This way of thinking about what "energizes" the phenomenon being described is contained in the concept of the family emotional system. (p. 11)

The contribution by Chelune, Robison, and Kommor (1984) represents one of the rare attempts to develop a functional model of intimacy. They write:

Almost everyone *knows* what intimacy is, but as soon as one must point to specifics, the concept becomes either elusive or bogged down in idiosyncratic trivialities. The rub appears to lie in the attempt to define intimacy as something specific—a particular class of behavior—rather than a quality—a cognitive appraisal of certain behaviors. (p. 13)

Chelune et al. (1984) define intimacy as a subjective appraisal of interactive behaviors that leads to relational expectations regarding knowing and being known at "innermost" levels. They propose a model combining cognitive psychology and systems theory in which interactive behaviors are considered to have connotative (metacommunication) meanings beyond their content. These metameanings develop and change over time, modifying and modified by the evolution of the relationship and the individuals involved. In Chelune et al.'s view, intimacy is a relational and individual process in which mutuality, self-differentiation, and prior history play a significant role in the evaluation of current experiences.

Many authors use the terms "self-disclosure" and "intimacy" interchangeably (e.g., Altman & Taylor, 1973; Derlega & Chaikin, 1975; Derlega & Grzelak, 1979; Hatfield & Walster, 1981; Jourard, 1971). Chelune (Chelune, 1979; Chelune, Robison, & Kommor, 1984) suggests that these terms are not the same, and that the difference is not just semantic:

While self-disclosures (both verbal and nonverbal) may be the major interactive behavior upon which subjective appraisals and relational expectations for intimacy are based, they do not, in themselves, constitute intimacy. Because of the nature of human communication, the same self-disclosure in one social-situational context may have entirely different intended and perceived meanings in another. To understand the process by which individuals come to know and have known the innermost, subjective aspects of self, we must shift our attention away from merely *what* is shared to those factors that influence the *meanings* of what is shared. (Chelune, Robison, & Kommor, 1984, pp. 14–15)

Following the reasoning advanced by Perlmutter and Hatfield (1980), Chelune et al. (1984) propose that self-disclosure becomes intimate when metacommunication is intentional and congruent with ideation, sensation, affect and behavior. Reciprocal self-disclosure per se and self-disclosure without intentional "honest" metacommunication fall short of their notion of intimacy.

> However, when the interactants begin to metacommunicate intentionally, they enter the immediacy of their relationship and share on a literal level their subjective meaning, unbound by implicit social rules. This is a ruleless domain where the interactants employ novel and spontaneous strategies and tactics in which the outcomes cannot be known until after the change has occurred. (Chelune, Robison, & Kommor, 1984, p. 17)

Intentional metacommunication about intended meanings differs from typical social communication; it entails greater risk of rejection. Intentional metacommunication, for example, might involve disclosing one's reactions to interactions as they are unfolding or removing any ambiguity regarding intentions behind one's own behavior.

In retrospect, it becomes clear that disclosure reciprocity is more applicable to casual or short-term relationships (in which intentional metacommunication is absent) than it is for marriage. In brief relationships, participants disclose personal information on the basis of reciprocity and implicit social rules; each individual is left to infer the meaning of the messages. When self-disclosure is a vehicle of reciprocity, rather than metacommunication, intimacy is diminished.

In marriage, self-disclosure is more determined by metacommunication than it is by reciprocity expectations. Moreover, it is veritably impossible to avoid disclosure metacommunication within marriage (including metacommunication regarding reciprocity expectations). Marital difficulties often lead to sexual difficulties (and vice versa) because of the difficulty of *precluding* metacommunication during sexual contact. In fact, Helen Singer Kaplan's "bypass" approach attempted to circumvent the impact of metacommunication.[2] Sexual behavior (in its broadest conceptualization) is the

---

[2]From this vantage point, one can see that sexual and marital difficulties might result from an intolerably *high* level of intimacy rather than the *lack* of it. Common clinical assumptions that all sexual and marital difficulties can be solved by *increased* intimacy become a questionable proposition. In actuality, this observation portends the model of intimacy to be proposed shortly.

literal embodiment of intentional (and non-intentional) metacommunication.

Although Chelune et al.'s (1984) sophisticated model offers a systemic alternative to reciprocity theories of intimate relationships, it fails to consider realistic clinical processes that become problematic in long-term intimate relationships. The authors suggest, for example, that intimacy breaks down when metacommunication and interpersonal attributions remain solely at an implicit level or are not periodically updated (via intentional metacommunication); what causes this to happen is not directly addressed.[3]

Chelune et al. (1984) do describe the processes of ongoing "positive" intimate interactions. If one reads their description imagining a progressively *deteriorating* relationship, it becomes apparent that the metacommunication processes that facilitate and debilitate relationships are the same:

> Communications become increasingly interpersonal in nature in that they are designed not only to convey information, but to elicit a response (command aspect) from the other (Satir, 1967). "In this effort, an explanation of why the communication was sent is important, both for purposes of understanding as well as for responding" (Newman, 1981, p. 60). Thus, the metamessage (meaning) begins to have precedence over the literal message. (Chelune, Robison, & Kommor, 1984, p. 26)

Contributions from Sexual Therapy

Intimacy has received relatively little attention in the professional sexuality literature.[4] This may stem from tendencies to divorce intimacy from sexuality,

---

[3]There are numerous ways to account for individual differences in ability to engage in intentional metacommunication. Chelune et al. (1984) utilize Mischel's (1973, 1977) five social-learning variables to explain individual differences in intimate relationships: (a) cognitive and behavioral construction competencies; (b) encoding strategies and personal constructs; (c) behavior- and stimulus-outcome expectancies; (d) subjective values; and (e) self-regulatory systems and plans. For this last factor, Chelune et al. (1984) advance a predominantly cognitive psychological model of self-regulation. In contrast, the sexual crucible model utilizes Bowen's concept of differentiation as a primary self-regulatory process; this will be discussed shortly in this chapter.

[4]A casual review of basic sexuality texts fails to find *any* mention of the topic of intimacy in such books as *Marital and Sexual Counseling in Medical Practice* (Abse, Nash, & Louden, 1974), *Taking a Sexual History* (Pomeroy, Flax, & Wheeler, 1982), *Sexuality: The Human Experience* (Gotwald & Golden, 1981), *Human Sexuality* (Rosen & Rosen, 1981), *Human Sexualities* (Gagnon, 1977), and *Handbook of Human Sexuality* (Wolman & Money, 1980). Katchadourian and Lunde (1972) mentioned that intimacy "requires expressing (and exposing) oneself, giving and sharing, and both sexual and more general union." Sandler, Myerson, and Kinder (1980) briefly mentioned intimacy as a common euphemism for coitus and added that "letting down our barriers and moving towards openness is often accompanied by fears" (p. 221).

and conversely, to equate physical contact with intimacy (obviating the need to examine the latter in detail). Within the field of sexuality, even a luminary like Barbach (1982) (who discussed fear of intimacy, and power conflicts and fantasies in intimacy) failed to critically consider the concept of intimacy per se. L'Abate and Talmadge (1987) used the term to refer to a relationship characteristic, the foundation of a marriage, a component of other emotions (e.g., love), an individual phenomenological experience, and a personal need.

Within the field of human sexuality, perhaps the most prolific (and best known) authors on the topic of intimacy have been William Masters and Virginia Johnson (e.g., *The Pleasure Bond*, 1976). In 1982, Masters, Johnson, and Kolodny defined intimacy as follows:

> Intimacy can be defined as a close, trusting relationship between two people who are both willing to be emotionally open with each other in spite of the risks that may be involved. Intimacy differs most specifically from love in that the happiness of the other person is not its principal concern. Under some circumstances, intimacy includes a sexual component (whether or not love is present), while in other relationships there may be great intimacy without any sexual contact. Intimate partners usually reach an early understanding about the boundaries of their closeness, permitting their relationship to continue under a mutually agreeable set of expectations. (pp. 236–7)

This definition has several strengths. It clearly differentiates love from intimacy and points out that intimacy is neither necessarily pleasant nor focused on the happiness of the partner. At times, self-disclosure may be crucial to the development of a relationship, although it does not bring a warm glow between partners. Many couples who complain of a "lack of intimacy in the relationship" are referring to the absence of warmth, acceptance, and mutual agreement they anticipate and demand from self-disclosure. Rarely do couples consider that intimacy may be disquieting and uncomfortable at times.

Many authors have emphasized fears and realities of vulnerability and deprivation, and underscore the sharing of hurt and fear of being hurt as the hallmark of intimacy (e.g., Kelvin, 1977; L'Abate, 1977, 1986; L'Abate & Talmadge, 1987; Waring & Reddon, 1983). Derlega (1984) discussed vulnerability in intimacy with regard to: rejection of self-concept, partner indifference or disinterest, manipulation through disclosed information, secondhand disclosure and betrayal of relationship boundaries, and inequity of self-disclosure. Hatfield (1984) similarly mentioned fears of exposure, abandonment, loss of control, or engulfment; fear of the partner's anger or one's own destructive impulses; and fear of losing one's individuality.

At this point, two threads of our discussion resurface. First, the literature as a whole suggests a "solution" to the vulnerability of intimacy: expectation of disclosure reciprocity, "trust," and validation from the partner. Second, what is the clinical utility of a description of intimacy such as that of Masters, Johnson, and Kolodny (1982)?

Does intimacy require a close, trusting relationship? Do *both* people have to be emotionally open? Do they need to agree about the level of intimacy? If so, are these realistic expectations for couples in troubled relationships?

If people "share hurt" and fear being hurt, are they being intimate? More importantly, will it give them the feelings they crave? When the couple is emotionally estranged, should the clinician encourage sharing hurt and exposing vulnerabilities?

The clinical implications of these questions are far-reaching. While Masters et al. hit upon several salient aspects of intimacy, they also embrace the same ineffective strategies that drive patients into treatment (i.e., the expectation of reciprocity).

Contributions from Marriage and Family Therapy

The topics of sexuality and intimacy are also relatively rare in the marriage and family therapy literature.[5] Kerr and Bowen (1988) address the fundamental dynamics of marital intimacy, although they don't focus on the topic of intimacy per se and never define the term. Wynne and Wynne (1986) found it confusing to use the label "intimate" to refer to a temporal subjective experience and a relationship in which that experience occurs frequently; they chose the term "mutuality" to refer to the relationship characteristic.

Beavers (1977, 1985) is one of the few figures within family therapy to address the topic of intimacy. In *Successful Marriage*, he defined intimacy as "the experience of being open, vulnerable, and able to share one's innermost feelings and thoughts" (p. 76) and as "the joy of being known and accepted by another who is loved" (p. 52). While seemingly compatible at first glance,

---

[5]The topic of intimacy is totally absent in the texts of *Family Therapy Concepts and Methods* (Nichols, 1984), *Strategic Family Therapy* (Madanes, 1981), *Family Therapy Techniques* (Minuchin & Fishman, 1981), *Family Counseling: Theory and Practice* (Perez, 1979), *Family Therapy* (Erickson & Hogan, 1981), *Couples in Collusion* (Willi, 1982), and *Family Therapy in Clinical Practice* (Bowen, 1978). More recently, the topic of intimacy has emerged as a legitimate area of interest in the work of L'Abate (1986; L'Abate & Talmadge, 1987; Sloan & L'Abate, 1985), Kantor and Okun (1989), and Patton and Waring (1984).

these definitions address two very different processes: The former focuses on the temporal, unilateral, experience of the discloser, while the latter focuses upon the response of the discloser to the response of the listener.

While Beavers' second definition is a restatement of the predominant other-validated view of intimacy, the first is more equivocal. If the specified open self-disclosure and "vulnerability" are predicated on the expectation of acceptance and validation from the partner, then Beavers' viewpoint is nothing more than a reflection of the quest for a reflected sense of self.

However, is it "intimacy" when core disclosure does not meet with joyous acceptance from the partner? Beavers (1985) seems to suggest it is: " . . . the old rule 'loving means thinking and feeling just alike' can be replaced with 'You have to be separate to be close'" (p. 208).

In contrast to the concept of other-validated intimacy, we can call this type self-validated intimacy. Models of self-validated intimacy are exceedingly rare.

For example, Wynne and Wynne (1986) emphasize other-validated intimacy:

> Intimacy is a *subjective relational experience* in which the core components are *trusting self-disclosure* to which the response is *communicated empathy*. Intimacy may be asymmetrically complementary, with one person disclosing more than the other. It is important to recognize that self-disclosure, in itself, does not necessarily generate intimacy—for example, when divorcing couples use self-disclosure to "prove" how little they care for one another. Rather, a key component is the willingness to share, verbally and nonverbally, personal feelings, fantasies, and emotionally meaningful experiences and actions, positive or negative, with the expectation and trust that the other person will emotionally comprehend, accept what has been revealed, and will not betray or exploit this trust. (pp. 384–5)

Wynne and Wynne suggest that self-disclosure per se does *not* create intimacy; the *expectation and fulfillment of trust* and the *response of communicated empathy* make self-disclosure intimate. Their approach highlights the politics of "acceptance" that surround intimacy. Wynne and Wynne emphasize the asymmetric aspects of expected complementarity, in contrast to the symmetrical aspects of Masters, Johnson, and Kolodny's approach; *both* are similar in the clear expectation of reciprocity. As we shall see, however, reciprocity and acceptance by the partner are not inherent to a view of intimacy as a relational experience.

Expectations of Trust and Empathy Interfere With Intimacy

Although clinicians differ with regard to the content of the response, the expectation of reciprocity is probably the greatest commonality in contemporary views of intimacy. Wynne and Wynne (1986) suggest the partner's necessary response involves *empathy* and *approval*. Chelune, Robison, and Kommor (1984) state the response is *trust, commitment* and *caring*.

Likewise, Masters, Johnson, and Kolodny (1986) make the common error of assuming that intimacy involves *trust*. After defining intimacy as "a process in which two caring people share as freely as possible in the exchange of feelings, thoughts and actions" (p. 234), they state:

> In order to understand the process of intimacy, we will examine its basic components: caring, sharing (self-disclosure), trust, commitment, honesty, empathy, and tenderness. (p. 236)

Masters et. al (1986) go on to clarify:

> The process of self-disclosure we mentioned above doesn't occur in a vacuum but depends on the degree to which you trust the person to whom you are making disclosures about yourself. Thus, trust [of the partner] is another necessary ingredient for intimacy, and, like caring and sharing, trust develops over time. (p. 238)

Does a relationship require all these facets to be "intimate"? Are trust and commitment necessary precursors or results of an intimate relationship?

Trusting one's partner involves a dependency on the partner's perceived trustworthiness. This raises the rarely asked question: Trust him/her about or for what? Common notions of "trust" involve the expectation that one's partner will provide security, acceptance, commitment, caretaking, and (most of all) not challenge one's sense of identity. Popular expectations of "trust" reflect the widespread quest for a reflected sense of self.

However, expecting to have one's feelings "taken care of" by one's partner is often a direct impediment to intimacy (Malone & Malone, 1987). The responsibility to protect a partner's feelings limits disclosure that might potentially "hurt." Malone and Malone (1987) note that truly knowing ourselves is sometimes quite unpleasant. We are not always overjoyed with those whose honesty brings us to an awareness that confronts our pre-established mythology:

It seems to be easier to "like" a mistress or casual lover whose ways of loving suit our personal mythology; that, after all, is why we picked them. But the struggle of the primary relationship *does* have real importance. All of us need to learn to be loved in ways we have never been willing or able to be loved before. This need is where the critical importance of intimacy becomes clear. Love forces us to grow, and humans grow with extreme reluctance. We often resent those whose love forces our growth. The intimate experience is the only opportunity we have to resolve this dilemma. . . . The primary relationship is where we can relearn most profoundly. (Malone & Malone, 1987, p. 16)

In many relationships "*taking care of*" is confused with "*caring for.*" Although the Malones and the Wynnes represent divergent theoretical perspectives, all agree that "taking care of" someone is close, but it is not intimate. *Caretaking is a necessary affirming and sustaining part of a relationship; it maintains the status quo. Intimacy facilitates change, but not necessarily short-term stability.* Perhaps this is why marriage and family therapists (e.g., Wynne & Wynne, 1986) devote considerable attention to caretaking (as an essential cornerstone of the family unit), while intimacy has received limited clinical attention.[6]

The Leap From Description to Prescription

One of the main problems of descriptive approaches to intimacy involves the unwitting confusion of symptoms and systems. Such misunderstandings guide clinicians, as well as the general public, in hot pursuit of intimacy—but in the wrong direction.

If *other* processes underlie the ability to disclose core personal information, then confusing prerequisites with the results of repeated intimate disclosure tends to obfuscate matters. The core issue is the discrimination of the *fundamental requisites* of intimacy from its *long-term effects*. It is equivalent to the distinction between the process of achieving and the impact of achievement; this is not merely a question of semantic labeling.

Herein lies the critical difference in definitions and descriptions vs. a clinical model of intimacy. As Kerr and Bowen note:

This distinction between "describing" and "accounting for" a phenomenon may seem academic, but it is quite important in the conduct of psychotherapy. The way a therapist thinks about what energizes or drives the process he observes in a family will govern what he addresses in therapy. (1988, p. 11)

---

[6]See page 140 (Chapter Five) for further discussion on the relevance of intimacy to a "good" relationship.

Clinicians often point out that reciprocal disclosure, trust, honesty, and caring recursively[7] perpetuate and reward further disclosure (e.g., Jourard, 1968; Rubin, 1973). One might argue that the recursive manner in which these factors facilitate further intimacy renders the distinction between cause and effect moot. This viewpoint does not, however, address the clinical question of how to get the cycle started. While there is little doubt that trust, caring, honesty, empathy, tenderness, and commitment facilitate intimate exchange, this information does not help couples whose relationship is on a downward slide.

Is it realistic to expect that the partner or "the relationship" should provide a nourishing and facilitative environment before or during intimate self-disclosure? While reciprocity is characteristic of the early "commitment" stage of mutual acceptance, it tends to vanish during the developmentally important "disenchantment" stage that follows thereafter. During this latter period, when other-validated intimacy declines, many couples seek professional help for intimacy problems. Thus, a clear clinical distinction between *outcomes* of repeated intimate exchange and the *pathway* to getting there becomes particularly vital.

It is one thing to describe the spontaneous patterns couples exhibit early in their relationship as they explore the rudiments of intimacy; it is quite another thing to prescribe such patterns to couples who have already proceeded through that stage and are having difficulty "later" in their relationship.

As an example of the leap from description to prescription, consider the discussion of intimacy in *On Sex and Human Loving*. Here, Masters, Johnson, and Kolodny (1986) conceptualize effective communication skill as a basic capacity for intimacy and present a cognitive-behavioral approach for treating intimacy difficulties. They suggest "sending signals more clearly" verbally and nonverbally, risking vulnerability, using "I" language, expressing affection and anger, and listening effectively.

Therapists who see intimacy as the behaviors observed in couples who appear to be intimate tend to encourage patients to perform these same behaviors. Unfortunately, telling people with dysfunctional relationships to copy the systemic patterns of "good relationships" often does not work. Damaged relationships cannot always be repaired by reverting to prior roles and "good" styles of interaction (assuming they existed previously).

The repair process often requires going through unfamiliar interactions so that the

---

[7]"Recursive" refers to a process that operates on the product of its own operation (Maturana & Varela, 1987).

requisite individual and systemic dynamics can be developed to create and sustain patterns observed in "intimate relationships."[8]

Treatment often deteriorates when therapists attempt to "improve communication" in couples who complain of "poor communication." Partners may actually be referring to their expectation of *consensus* as the criterion of "good communication." Naively focusing on "communication skills" only fuels the conflagration.

Intimacy is not *in* a behavior, although behavior *is* generally the vehicle of intimacy. Intimacy *is* a skill or ability, but a skill approach to intimacy is like practicing for the Superbowl by throwing a football at a swinging tire.

Therapists are tempted to suggest "I messages" to jump-start the engine of a stalled relationship when there is no gas in the tank. Patient compliance is often poor because the behavior feels "phony." The stylized language of long-term intimate partners does not survive between patients with chronic relationship problems, since it doesn't emanate from the same individual and systemic dynamics. *The distinction between other-validated and self-validated intimacy is a critical factor that has been totally overlooked in the professional literature.*

Sometimes therapists induce partners to "be reasonable" and stroke each other emotionally, hoping that "effective" behaviors might be maintained by positive reinforcement and reciprocity. Unfortunately, things don't often work that nicely in damaged relationships. Partners in hostile-dependent marriages function at far too low a level of emotional development to implement these suggestions. Moreover, such approaches create the inherent paradox of *increasing* dependency, triggering *more* withholding from both individuals. The common lack of clarity about requisites in descriptive approaches to intimacy leads to erroneous conclusions, groundless expectations, ineffective treatment, and increased likelihood of divorce among couples who wish to become (more) intimate.

INTIMACY AND EXISTENTIAL SEPARATENESS[9]

We now shift our focus to a smaller segment of the professional literature, offering a vastly different viewpoint than the foregoing. Important contributions regarding the nature of intimacy come from existential psychology, with

---

[8]This does not negate cognitive-behavioral theory or the notion that acting and thinking a particular way lead to feeling that way. However, a considerable level of emotional autonomy is often required to implement and maintain prescribed patterns of communication in dysfunctional relationships.

[9]The reader should regard this section as a prelude to the clinical model of intimacy to be proposed shortly.

its focus on existential loneliness. This school of thought suggests that people must grapple with the immutable separateness and aloneness of being human if they are to come to terms with the meaning of life and to understand and appreciate intimacy. While seeming steeped in philosophy, this approach offers a surprising degree of clinical utility.

According to Moustakas (1961, 1972), loneliness is a basic condition of human existence which, when correctly handled, enables individuals to deepen and extend their fundamental humanity and capacity to love. Loneliness is neither good nor bad, but rather creates an acute self-awareness that enhances one's appreciation for the finite points of engagement with others.

There are two different categories of loneliness in modern society: (a) *existential loneliness*, which is an inevitable part of human existence, and (b) common but unnecessary *loneliness anxiety* that results from self-alienation and self-rejection. On the latter topic, Moustakas writes:

> Loneliness anxiety results from a fundamental breach between what one is and what one pretends to be, a basic alienation between man and man and between man and his nature.
>
> Insidious fears of loneliness exist everywhere, nourished and fed by a sense of values and standards, by a way of life, which centers on acquisition and control. The emphasis on conformity, following directions, imitation, being like others, striving for power and status, increasingly alienates man from himself. The search for safety, order, and lack of anxiety through prediction and mastery eventually arouses inward feelings of despair and fears of loneliness. Unable to experience life in a genuine way, unable to relate authentically to his own nature and to other selves, the individual in Western culture often suffers from a dread of nothingness. (1961, p. 24)

Widespread loneliness anxiety is not the psychiatric loneliness Bowlby (1960, 1969, 1973) studied that results from childhood abandonment and rejection. It results, instead, from a manifestation of *adult* life:

> It is possible to live too much in the world, to try to escape loneliness by constant talk, by surrounding one's self with others, by modeling one's life from people in authority or with high status. Alienated from his own self, the individual does not mean what he says and does not do what he believes and feels. He learns to respond with surface or approved thoughts. He learns to use devious and indirect ways, and to base his behavior on the standards and expectations of others. (Moustakas, 1961, p. 31)

Although he did not label it as such, Moustakas graphically describes the manifestations of low levels of differentiation[10] that people generally never mature beyond. Lack of differentiation forces people to make adaptive, anxiety-modulating responses to each other. Differentiation is the substance of what Moustakas refers to as the "inner fortitude" and "creative courage" to openly and honestly accept the inevitable, existential loneliness of life.

> To love is to be lonely. Every love is broken by illness, separation, or death. The exquisite nature of love, the unique quality or dimension in its highest peak, is threatened by change and termination, and by the fact that the loved one does not always feel or know or understand. In the absence of the loved one, in solitude and loneliness, a new self emerges, in solitary thought. The loneliness quickens love and brings to it new perceptions and sensitivities, and new experience of mutual depth and beauty. (Moustakas, 1961, p. 101)

The pervasive "never be lonely" theme in modern society is a manifestation of man's estrangement from himself, which stems from avoidance of existential loneliness. Helmuth Kaiser (in Fierman, 1965) writes that popular fascination with precision military drill teams, synchronized swimming, chorus-line dance shows, and other group activities executed in unison gratifies a ubiquitous "fusion-delusion"—the appearance of individuals functioning as if they have one mind rather than wholly separate personalities. The result of this fusion-delusion is diminished capacity to love, inability to be empathic, and difficulty establishing fundamental social ties.

Yalom (1980) suggests that compulsive sexual behavior (recently mislabeled "sexual addiction") is a common response to avoidance of existential isolation. Yalom's premise questions the wisdom of "addiction" and "co-dependency" "support groups," while also explaining their widespread popularity: the group itself becomes a further denial of one's separateness.

It is the acute awareness of one's isolation and finiteness as a living entity that motivates intensely intimate contact. Fromm's (1941) notion of intimacy as an escape from "the prison of one's separateness" involves an *acceptance* of existential loneliness rather than a denial of it. Both Fromm and Moustakas assert that the ability to be alone is a crucial precondition to the ability to love.

---

[10]In its most basic terms, differentiation concerns people's hyper-reactivity to one another and their ability to function autonomously in the face of pressures for togetherness. See page 124 for a brief definition of differentiation. Also see Chapter Seven for a more detailed discussion of this topic by Kerr and Bowen (1988) and Papero (1990).

It is not loneliness that separates the person from others but the terror of loneliness and the constant efforts to escape it. We must learn to care for our own loneliness and suffering and the loneliness and suffering of others, for within pain and isolation and loneliness one can find courage and hope and what is brave and lovely and true in life. Serving loneliness is a way to self-identity and to love and faith in the wonder of living. (Moustakas, 1961, p. 103)

At its very essence, existential loneliness is inherently paradoxical:

Strange as it may seem, the individual in being lonely, if let be, will realize himself in loneliness and create a bond or sense of fundamental relatedness with others. Loneliness, rather than separating the individual or causing a break or division of self, expands the individual's wholeness, perceptiveness, sensitivity, and humanity. (Moustakas, 1961, p. 47)

Part of the therapist's task involves helping patients confront isolation, thereby generating anxiety and catalyzing personal growth (Yalom, 1980). The hallmark of maturity is comfort and peace (rather than mere tolerance) in being alone. *This advance in one's relationship with oneself empowers the transition from dependence on other-validated intimacy to self-validated intimacy.*

Existential View of Closeness vs. Intimacy

As mentioned previously, many clinicians use the concepts of closeness and intimacy interchangeably (e.g., Hatfield, 1984; L'Abate & Talmadge, 1987; Lowen, 1965; Masters, Johnson, & Kolodny, 1986). Authors of more existential orientation make a significant distinction between the two.

Malone and Malone (1987) state that *closeness* is the experience of contact with another, characterized by the qualities of being "together with," "part of," or "at one with" that other person. In contrast, *intimacy is the process of being in touch with or knowing* oneself *in the presence of a partner*. Intimacy differs from meditation or introspection, which are ways of looking *at* oneself.

Said differently, closeness is the experience of contact with the partner; intimacy is the recursive experience and disclosure of self in the presence of the partner.

Learning more about closeness (*the "being part of"*) is easy. Just study systems: large, small, independent, dependent, functional, non-functional, real, imagined. There are a myriad of well-structured, detailed systems. The how-to literature of counseling, management, religion, friendship, warfare, supervision, on adjusting, coping, fixing, maintaining, on psychological stratagems, and so on ad infinitum, are all discourses about closeness. Most of the many concepts of relationships that we mentioned earlier (supportiveness, commitment, etc.) are also aspects of closeness. We are as imbalanced in our literature as we are in our living. Read the scholarly treatises in psychiatry and psychology, and in the vast majority you will see a preoccupation with the ego (the engineer of closeness) and an ignoring of the unconscious (the source of intimacy). Go to the popular-psychology section at a bookstore. You will be overwhelmed by the number of books on how to be close. . . . To learn more about *intimacy* is much more difficult. (Malone & Malone, 1987, pp. 5–6)

To see the clinical utility and sophistication of the existential view of intimacy, one must step outside that body of literature and look elsewhere; relevant material emerges from the most unlikely places. Consider, for example, the central importance of *self-awareness* in the existential view, in relation to Maturana and Varela's (1987) view of cognition.

Maturana and Varela (1987) regard cognition as an active process rooted in human biology (evolution), in which we *create* our world of experience (rather than merely developing an internal mirror image of an objective "out there" reality). They suggest that cognition permits an awareness of "self" to emerge only when we know that we are seeing ourselves.

For instance, self-awareness comes when one realizes that all sides of a situation have not been perceived; one recognizes that one's reality is *a* reality but not the *only* reality. At such a point, there is the (1) acute awareness of self, and (2) realization of one's inherent inability to perceive Reality.[11] In the process, we experience our immutable isolation from even our most intimate partners.

This awareness creates an inherent paradox: We are dependent on interaction with other people to expand our knowledge of ourselves and the surrounding world, but this simultaneously reinforces our awareness of our immutable aloneness. This exacerbation of existential loneliness and self-awareness, however, also potentiates our capacity and motivation for intimate union with another human being.

The relationship between interpersonal systems and intimacy is not as simple as it might appear. Maturana and Varela (1987) state there is no "self" outside of relationships with others, and yet the concepts of "self" and "others" reveal the existential separateness of human existence.

---

[11]See R. D. Laing's (1967) classic *Politics of Experience* for further discussion of this topic.

Communication is a form of coordinated social behavior, in which people contribute their individual neurological capacities to bring forth a higher-order system (e.g., the development of complex language). The emergence of language, a manifestation of the recursion between evolution and social contact, is a crucial step in the emergence of the capacity for self-observation and *self-consciousness*.

> . . . there is no self-consciousness without language as a phenomenon of linguistic recursion. Self-consciousness, awareness, mind—these are phenomena that take place in language. Therefore, as such, they take place only in the social domain. (Maturana & Varela, 1987, p. 230)

> . . . it is in language that the self, the *I*, arises as the social singularity defined by the operational intersection in the human body of the recursive linguistic distinctions in which it is distinguished. This tells us that in the network of linguistic interactions in which we move, we maintain an ongoing descriptive recursion which we call the "I." It enables us to conserve our linguistic operational coherence and our adaptation in the domain of language. (Maturana & Varela, 1987, p. 231)

To underscore their point, Maturana and Varela cite "split brain" research with epileptic humans. When the connections between the sides of the brain are severed (isolating language functions to one side of the brain), people are not able to perform self-reflective operations when functions located on the other side of the brain are utilized.

Language facilitates intimacy because, beyond permitting verbal disclosure, language permits emergence of *self*-concept. Without the concept of self, there is no possibility of intimacy, since the ability to maintain the distinction of an "I" in the context of "you" is fundamental to the existential view.

On the other hand, while the very structure of language facilitates certain thoughts, it excludes others; language limits intimacy, because it is inherently exclusive rather than inclusive. The result is that language leads to rigidity of self-definition (and self-presentation), which presents barriers to intimacy.

As if anticipating our quandary, Maturana and Varela (1987) state:

> Doing that [seeing the world as brought forth in coexistence], of course, will put us in a circular situation. It might leave us a bit dizzy, as though following the hands drawn by Escher. This dizziness results from our not having a *fixed point of reference* to which we can anchor our descriptions in order to affirm and defend their validity. In effect, if we presuppose the existence of an objective world, independent of us as observers and accessible to our knowledge through

our nervous system, we cannot understand how our nervous system functions in its structural dynamics and still produces a representation of this independent world. But if we do *not* presuppose an objective world independent of us as observers, it seems we are accepting that everything is relative and anything is possible in the denial of all lawfulness. Thus we confront the problem of understanding how our experience—the praxis of our living—is coupled to a surrounding world which appears filled with regularities that are at every instant the result of our biological and social histories.

Again, we must walk the razor's edge. . . . Indeed, the whole mechanism of generating ourselves as describers and observers tells us that our world, as the world which we bring forth in our coexistence with others, will always have precisely that mixture of regularity and mutability, that combination of solidity and shifting sand, so typical of human experience when we look at it up close. (Maturana & Varela, 1987, pp. 240–241)

While the relationship between constructivism and intimacy might have been heretofore easily overlooked, the inextricable connection between self-awareness, subjectivity, and participation in relationships should now be rather obvious. In experiencing our inability to experience Reality (including all aspects of the partner's reality), one becomes both self-aware and aware of the partner. *Many couples who complain of "lack of intimacy" are actually intolerant of the intense awareness of self and other created by the recognition of existing in two separate but congruent realities.*

We are left with our inherent paradox: Participation in social systems (which gives rise to language) is fundamental to the capacity for intimacy; at the same time, such involvement quickly tends to limit intimacy.

In regard to the latter point, the notion of *capture by the system* underscores how membership in a system tends to rigidify an individual's self-definition and public role. When partners' identities are primarily relationally defined, the relationship inhibits display of *novel* aspects of self (the antithesis of intensely intimate experiences).

When we become captured by our systems, we lose connection as *I-other* and embroil ourselves in closeness: in fixed systems. In this closeness, we are no longer *I-other* but instead are a "part of" something—a marriage, an office, a company, a country. Our desire for systems reflects our concern with maintenance and familiarity, and our neglect of creativity and energizing connections. Closeness is certainly important and necessary, but it has become a neurotic, obsessive preoccupation, and a destructive over-concern in current human societies. . . . Cyclic, as is the case in all of nature, the pendulum needs now to swing back the other way. (Malone & Malone, 1987, p. 3)

Other authors concur with this emphasis on autonomous self-definition. Putney and Putney (1964) recognize the legitimate need for other people to function at various times as one's mirror, as models for one's goals and as the recipients of one's actions. However, they also note the societally promulgated distortions of intimacy that commonly occur in the quest for a reflected sense of self:

- the quest for a flattering, rather than honest, "mirror" in a *mutual admiration society*;
- *reciprocal rationalization* of behaviors or beliefs about which either individual may be extremely dubious;
- *unrecognized self-discovery* in which self-development is erroneously attributed to the influence of the partner, rather than to oneself, laying the seeds of discord;
- *localized self-acceptance*, similar to the last concept, in which positive self-worth is experienced sporadically and attributed to favorable circumstances and particular behaviors.

Putney and Putney (1964) note that Americans seldom question the assumption that emotions have an external explanation. When someone feels angry he looks around to see what provoked him; when he feels happy he looks around to see who delighted him. This, they suggest, stems from a lifetime of *indirect self-acceptance* that we are socialized to pursue in lieu of the more difficult and painful development of autonomous self-worth. Their observation goes to the heart of the existential view of loneliness anxiety. Autonomous self-acceptance develops from the courageous exploration of self-doubts.

Putney and Putney's belief in the ubiquity of indirect self-acceptance is reflected in their suggestion that it lies at the core of the American *normal neurosis*:

It is the abnormal (i.e., nontypical) neuroses which invite attention and analysis because of their novelty; the normal neuroses are generally endured, precisely because of their prevalence in a society. (Putney & Putney, 1964, p. 11)

The normal neurosis and its underlying indirect self-acceptance are enshrined in the numerous professional publications on intimacy that specify reciprocity as a primary feature. This quest for an acceptable reflected self-image fuels the rush toward, and away from, intensely intimate relationships.

Reliance on a reflected sense of self has wide-reaching implications for intimacy and sexual potential (as we shall see in the next section). It will even surface when we address the integration of sexual desire and spirituality in our last chapter.

By way of summary, we can integrate several main points by beginning to explore the relationship between capacity for intimacy and level of *differentiation*. Murray Bowen's concept of differentiation refers to people's degree of emotional reactivity to one another and their ability to function autonomously in the face of pressure for consensus, reciprocity, and conformity. Although it will be discussed more fully in Chapters Five and Seven, it is useful at this point to outline what differentiation implies:

- the ability to maintain one's sense of separate self in close proximity to a partner;
- nonreactivity to other people's reactivity;
- self-regulation of emotionality so that judgment can be used;
- the ability to tolerate pain for growth (Friedman, 1990).

Kerr and Bowen offer a clear description of the relationship between levels of differentiation and patterns of intimacy:

> Well differentiated people can tolerate and enjoy intimacy and aloneness. Less differentiated people, when intimate, tend toward enmeshment (fusion) in which they eventually experience a terror of engulfment that compels them to take flight. When they are alone, they tend to suffer an unbearable sense of abandonment and long for fusion. (When undifferentiated people are seen from an interactional perspective, their intimate relationships are usually characterized by cycles of enmeshment and flight.) (1988, p. 9)

The capacity for intimacy is directly linked to the ability to tolerate existential loneliness and the relativity of one's perceptions. Differentiation is what permits an individual to participate in a system—whether a marriage, a family, or a society—without being captured by it. Indirect self-acceptance is the driving force in the lives of individuals at low levels of differentiation; other-validated intimacy is the hallmark of their relationships.

Putney and Putney's (1964) *reflected sense of self* is the analogue of Kerr and Bowen's *pseudo-self*. When individuals with little solid ego receive a reflected sense of self, they function at a higher level than they are capable of sustaining unilaterally; in the absence of such responses, their level of functioning deteriorates. The ubiquity of reciprocity models of intimacy is not coincidence: It reflects the normal neurosis of indirect self-acceptance that is pandemic among health-care professionals and the general public.

Disparity Between Reciprocity and Existential Models of Intimacy: Emergence of a Metamodel

A fundamental contradiction exists between popular definitions and descriptions of intimacy and the existential viewpoint. *The contradiction concerns the expectation of reciprocity and dependence on the partner's response.* Why hasn't anybody noticed? The oversight is indicative of our failure to develop an effective clinical model of intimacy.

The unnoticed contradiction is not merely academic: It reflects the professional and lay communities' expectations for achieving an intimate marriage. Training as a health-care professional provides no prophylaxis for the normal neurosis. Many clinicians admire the philosophy of the existential view, blissfully unaware that their clinical approaches are rooted in symptom prescription and reciprocity.

The situation is like the "Wizard of Id" cartoon strip in which the king renders a judgment on the correctness of his advisors, who are debating whether the world is flat or round. The king sagely decrees that the world is both flat and round, bringing forth his "Pizza Pie Theory of the World"! Within the world of professional literature and practice, intimacy is flat and round.

However, there is also a way of resolving this contradiction: *It requires a developmental metamodel of intimacy.*

The professional literature actually contains two different models of intimacy, each appropriate for a particular developmental epoch. The more common viewpoint emphasizes the expectation of reciprocity and validation of one's self-image and self-worth; we will refer to such approaches as *level 1* models.

While developmentally appropriate for infancy, childhood, and adolescence, this model is mistakenly promoted as efficacious for *adult* intimate relationships. It is not that intimacy based on a reflected sense of self is "wrong"—indeed, it is an absolutely appropriate and necessary . . . in childhood and adolescence. *The fundamental paradigm of level-1 intimacy is mother-infant symbiosis and fusion.*

Response reciprocity is vital in early mother-infant bonding. When the mutually reinforcing aspects of eye-gazing, cooing, burbling, and smiling are absent, decreased maternal care and infant failure-to-thrive often result. Response synchrony is a powerful determinant of object relations capacities, which become more apparent in later life.

In infancy, the internalization of a reflected sense of self[12] (resulting from response reciprocity) is critical to the eventual emergence of *self*-awareness. It provides the basis for the prototype of existential separateness: the infant's awareness of self as separate from the mother.

Young children and adolescents *need* to internalize parents' reflections, thereby mutually validating each other's intrinsic self-worth and accomplishments. The expectation of reciprocity encourages age-appropriate dependency and denial of separateness. It buffers, for example, the ambivalent struggles of adolescent individuation (which are often truncated if awareness of existential separateness becomes overwhelming).

It is one thing, however, to note that mother-infant response synchrony is the prototype of later adult intimacy, and quite another to suggest this as a strategy for adults.

New trends in developmental pediatric research challenge the glorified image of level-1 models of intimacy: Emphasis is shifting from response synchrony and internalization of parental response, to the importance of "time-out" and the infant's ability to self-repair inaccurate reflections from ineffective caretakers (Brazelton, 1978; Tronick, 1989). Other research demonstrates that the infant leads the mother in the dance of response synchrony rather than vice versa (Lester, Hoffman, & Brazelton, 1985). *Synchrony* and *dissynchrony* are considered healthy developments, while *symbiosis* is not.

Level-2 models of intimacy emphasize acceptance of existential separateness and little expectation of reciprocity from the partner.[13] Level-2 intimate relationships are based on differentiation rather than the quest for a reflected sense of self. Level-2 intimate relationships more readily sustain long-term marital intimacy and the adult developmental task of ego integration (both of which rarely occur): They rely on self-validated, rather than other-validated, intimacy.

The existential view of intimacy is a prime example of a level-2 approach. Expectation of reciprocity is antithetical to acceptance of existential separateness. Such expectations encourage a "we" mind set that promotes emotional fusion; it is alien to the acute experience of *self* and partner as related but separate entities.

---

[12]E.g., indirect self-acceptance, although it is hard to conceptualize it this way regarding an infant.

[13]This model of two levels of intimacy will return when we discuss Sebastian Moore's two-level model of *desire* in Chapter Seventeen.

Many people are reluctant to renounce the fantasy of obtaining (and *demanding*) their sense of self from their partner. Other permutations involve relinquishing the notion that spouses are "meant for each other" or obliged to make each other happy.[14] Accomplishing this developmental task makes the crucial difference in Wile's (1988) observation that talking about not feeling intimate can, itself, be an intimate act. *Talking about feeling "unconnected" can be "connecting" (to use his terms) if the individuals can tolerate recognizing separateness as a fact of life rather than an indication of a problematic relationship.*

The Transition to Level-2

What happens when "adult children" fail to make the age-appropriate transition and pursue level-1 intimate relationships to compensate for (real or imagined) childhood deprivations? Level-1 relationships have an entirely different impact:

- Regression and "return to the womb" mother-infant fusion become glorified as the peak intimate experience. Behind such idealizations lurk fears of "being swallowed alive," which make intense intimacy anxiety-provoking. Reciprocity models encourage infantile emotionality, fuel narcissism, and reassure "adult children" that unsatisfied IOU's of childhood need not be relinquished.
- Low levels of differentiation are perpetuated. These often surface as extreme emotional reactivity within the marriage, constant demands for reassurance, distancer-pursuer oscillations, and inability to deal with the (eventual) death of the partner.
- Exploration of sexual potential and intense forms of *adult* intimacy are impeded; both require an autonomous sense of self-worth. A high level of differentiation permits an appreciation of separateness that *enriches* the experience; at a low level of differentiation, the same awareness is an intolerable threat to fusion-fantasies.

In marriage, prolonging level-1 styles of intimacy until partners become engorged with a reflected sense of self does not guarantee a smooth transition to level-2. It insures, if anything, future marital instability: Spouses eventually play out the final stages of adolescent individuation with each other.

---

[14]The difference in level-1 and level-2 paradigms is apparent in a quote attributed to Goethe, the great German poet. According to one story, Goethe was asked by someone, "Do you love me?" to which he responded, "What possible business could that be of yours!"

What the refusal to relinquish the expectation of reciprocity *does* lead to is "*I will if you will*." The attitude that one derives from the reciprocity models of intimacy might read:

> I will tell you about me, but only if you then tell me about you. If you don't, I won't either. But I want to, so you have to. I'll go first and then you are obligated to disclose too; it's only fair. If I go first, you have to make me feel secure. I need to be able to *trust* you.

"I will if you will" is an attempt to avoid rejection by forcing reciprocal disclosure of insecurities from the partner. This strategy fosters a relative sense of adequacy rather than autonomous identity and self-worth. Self-disclosure based on the consolation that the partner has flaws involves a mental interpersonal tally system (that is itself a denial of existential separateness). In the name of intimacy, each partner hopes the other has something about which he or she is defensive. Understanding this level-1 strategy clarifies why many attempts at intimacy limit partners' development rather than foster it.

Many individuals never emerge from an equity model of caring to explore the depths of adult intimacy (Fromm, 1956). Many who attempt it are incapable of commitment without guarantees that love will be returned. Keifer (1977) wondered if we are so much a product of our capitalistic society that it is impossible to transcend the utilitarian "self" of exchange theory.[15]

When people come to terms with existential loneliness, they approach intimacy with a markedly different attitude; they might think:

> I am so happy to have you in my life, to share with you my days which would otherwise be filled with emptiness and meaninglessness. My fears of your rejection are only a defense against the greater fears of my own separateness and mortality. Come let me show myself to you, and in so doing, let me transcend my aloneness. I celebrate knowing you and give thanks for this opportunity during my turn on earth.

In level-2 relationships, the bittersweet awareness of immutable separateness heightens the salience of intimacy. It yields a sense of knowing oneself, one's

---

[15]One often unnoticed aspect of equity models of intimacy is the implied strategy of each partner attempting to derive maximal affective rewards at minimal cost (Thibaut & Kelly, 1959). Later versions of equity theory included the possibility that "benefit to the partner" might become an additional personal goal and lead to a deviation from a "minimal cost" strategy (Kelly & Thibaut, 1978). This revision makes reference to personal development akin to increased differentiation.

partner, and the nature of human existence. At level-2, intense intimacy and sexuality have several qualities:

- It is profound, but not infantile.
- It is primal but not regressive (except in the sense of regression in the service of the ego).
- It is the embodiment of the archetypal man and woman—essence of maleness meets essence of femaleness.
- It has the sense of fathomless separateness, the exaltation of *self*, and inviolable connectedness with all other humans.

How does one finally make the transition to level 2? What if, for example, an individual failed to "get his/her needs met" as a child?

Many issues of childhood are *not* resolvable in adulthood through styles of intimacy appropriate for an earlier age. Level-1 relationships inherently involve low levels of differentiation, which *fuel* neediness, insecurity, and anxiety. Relinquishing fantasies of "compensation" for one's childhood is one of the "necessary losses" of adulthood; forsaking them and attempting a level-2 intimate relationship often provide the sought-after relief. One cannot "take care of one's (or each other's) wounded child" to the extent that the wounds are no longer problematic; such attempts only *perpetuate* the problem.

It is in the struggle to maintain oneself unilaterally in marriage that the final resolution of childhood occurs.

This is not simply a matter of renegotiating the style of one's marriage. It involves a complete paradigm shift in the way we see ourselves, our spouse and children, the nature of marriage and life itself.

What enhances differentiation sufficiently to permit intimacy based on autonomy and separateness, rather than fusion? Bowen wasn't particularly optimistic about people raising their basic level of differentiation—but then again, he never considered intimacy-based therapy as a vehicle for this process. Bowen *did* think it was possible with concerted effort. This is what the sexual crucible is all about.

The sexual crucible is a treatment approach utilizing the recursive relationship between intimacy, sexuality, and differentiation to facilitate all three. In the next two chapters we will explore a cure for the normal neurosis of indirect self-acceptance and the widespread quest for intimacy. We will encounter a level-2 clinical model of intimacy (Chapter Five) and our first real look at the sexual crucible (Chapter Six).

A Clinical Model of Intimacy

Our focus on intimacy continues: a clinically useful model is proposed. Capacity for self-validated intimacy is crucial to developing and maintaining a long-term intimate marriage; this capacity is determined by one's level of differentiation. Folks need realistic expectations about intimacy: It isn't automatic, "normal" people find it hard to tolerate at profound levels (especially in combination with sexuality), and conventional suggestions about how to improve it generally don't help.

Popular views of intimacy are no more than our preferred archetypes. *They reflect our hopes and ideals, rather than a real appreciation and examination of the nature of intimacy per se.*

Can "bad sex" be intimate? Many individuals' initial sexual experiences are brief, anxiety-provoking, and disappointing. Such experiences, like intensely pleasurable sex, often contain an acute awareness of *self* in the presence of the partner.

Can casual sex be intimate? Obviously so. It is the only context that many people (who are unable to maintain their sense of self in the context of an ongoing relationship) are able to reveal their eroticism. Desire for chance sexual encounters involves more than curiosity about how a stranger might look or act with his/her clothes off; there is the heart-thumping thrill (and anxiety) of experiencing *oneself* sharply defined in relationship to the new person. "Trying the other person on for size" means more than just intertwining bodies.

Intimacy depends on my ability to experience being *me* and *I* simultaneously; being who I am in relationships, sensitively aware of the other person. The prototype of this experience is, oddly, not personal but sexual. Whereas the prototype of closeness is the personal experience (in which I am more aware of the other person than I am of myself), in the sexual experience both persons are much more aware of themselves than they are of the other. The commonality of intimacy and sexuality is not surprising. . . . Intimacy, of course may be genital, but genitality is not at its essence. The essence of intimacy is the awareness one has of one's *self* in the immediate presence of another person to whom one is closely related. And that is profoundly sexual. (Malone & Malone, 1987, p. 64)

Why is there a continual parade of famous characters (e.g., Jim Bakker, Gary Hart, Jimmy Swaggart, and Donald Trump) risking public humiliation and their livelihood for sexual experiences? Whether pursuing "power," "excitement," or "forbidden fruit," their goal is not simply to *do* something; they want to experience *themselves* doing it, revealing a secret aspect of their makeup in the process. While this is not the "essence of intimacy" the Malones refer to, it is probably an intimate experience nonetheless.

Rape is despicable violence, but can it be "intimate"? By our definition as an acute awareness and disclosure of self in the presence of "the partner," unfortunately, yes—unfortunate, in the sense of possibly seeming to condone an atrocity. Such an answer skirts close to the edge of many readers' sensibilities. However, backing away from the unpleasant implications of our discussion does little to further our understanding of interpersonal behavior.

Shortsighted clinical considerations which stipulate that intimacy must involve trust, caring, acceptance, commitment, and tenderness promulgate the quest for comfort and soothing from others. When all facts are known, folks are often quite unprepared for the rigors of intimacy and pass up the opportunity.

It is hard to know what upsets couples more: the assumption that they are doing something wrong when intimacy is disquieting (as it often is) or the realization that, indeed, they are doing it right!

The professional literature lacks a clinical model of intimacy—one that takes into account the process of human development and the praxis of human relationships. The following is offered to fill that void:

- *Intimacy* is the recursive process of open self-confrontation and disclosure of core aspects of self in the presence of a partner. The salience of an intimate experience increases as the significance of the relationship and the depth of self-confrontation increases.
- Intimacy is a multisystemic process—intrapersonal and interpersonal—involving both the discloser's relationship with the partner and his/her relationship with himself/herself.
- When the response of the partner is acceptance and reciprocal disclo-

sure, intimacy is experienced as loving and validating (*i.e., other-validated intimacy*). When intimacy occurs in the absence of trust or affirmation from the partner, the threat to one's sense of self increases in proportion to the salience of the experience. When the discloser's relationship-with-self enables him/her to self-soothe and master the resultant anxiety, the experience is self-validating and enhances differentiation (*i.e., self-validated intimacy*).

- While other-validated intimacy is the widespread ideal and expectation, self-validated intimacy is the bedrock of long-term marital intimacy.

- *Sexual intimacy* is the self-confrontation and expression of one's eroticism, or the use of sexuality as the vehicle for disclosure of other aspects of core self. Eroticism[1] is a core aspect of self, disclosed to varying degrees during sexual and nonsexual contact with others.

Intimacy is the ability to display one's inner life in the relationship with one's partner. Pursuit of the latter to compensate for deficits in the former is a commonplace prescription for failure. The common proclivity to seek a partner to escape or "find" oneself underlies the widespread pursuit for a long-term intimate relationship and the rarity with which it occurs.

Other-validated and self-validated intimacy are characteristic of people whose identity is primarily composed of *pseudo-self* and *solid-self*, respectively. Briefly, solid-self is the core view of oneself and one's world that develops slowly over time and is only changed from within; it is the part of self that is disclosed in self-validated intimacy. Pseudo-self is comprised of the aspects of identity that are molded and shaped by attempts to reduce anxiety and accommodate others; presentation of pseudo-self can improve the apparent level of emotional functioning, even when edited and manipulated to insure positive reactions. (These Bowenian concepts are discussed further in Chapter Seven.)

"Being in touch with oneself" is the process of self-confrontation (of solid-

---

[1]In the current context, eroticism refers to that which is depicted in an individual's lovemap, a term coined by John Money (1986):

> It is a developmental representation or template in your mind/brain, and is dependent on input through the special senses. It depicts your idealized lover and what, as a pair, you do together in the idealized, romantic, erotic, and sexualized relationship. A lovemap exists in mental imagery first, in dreams and fantasies, and then may be translated into action with a partner or partners. (p. xvi)

Eroticism is not simply limited to idealized depictions; it refers to all manifestations of polymorphous pleasure seeking. Money also talks about lovemap "pathology" in which love and "lust" are cleaved, giving rise to a continuum of hyperphilia (erotomania) and paraphilias ("perversions" in the legal sense).

self) in engagement of a partner. It is not merely self-disclosure; disclosure of familiar, mundane aspects of self does not evoke the sense of aliveness and personal growth common to intimate experiences. Malone and Malone describe the subjective experience of intimacy eloquently:

> Few of us could sit in a closet with another person for any length of time without learning a great deal about that person. . . . In the closet our own awareness is focused on the other while we are close. But in some rare moments, in that shared space of our closet and in the presence of the other, we may experience ourselves in some new, different, and more profound way. This is *intimacy*. When I am close, I know you; when I am intimate, I know myself. When I am close, I know you in your presence; when I am intimate I know myself in your presence. Intimacy is a remarkable experience. Usually I know myself only in my aloneness, my dreams, my personal space. But to feel and know myself in the presence of another is enlivening, enlightening, joyful, and most of all, freeing. I can be who I am freely and fully in the presence of another. It is the only true freedom we have as human beings. . . . (Malone & Malone, 1987, p. 29)

Pseudo-intimate experiences often mark the outset and the conclusion of relationships. Some occur during early courtship when partners "reveal" information in an over-trumped aura of risk-taking and "trusting"; the actual information is well-digested and has relatively minor significance to the discloser. Rancorous couples in mid-divorce who disclose negative feelings for one another are similarly pseudo-intimate because of the absence of self-confrontation.

The true level of self-confrontation, as well as metacommunication regarding the discloser's experience of his/her own discomfort, create the sense of immediate presence and risk-taking which characterize intensely intimate experiences.

DEVELOPMENTAL ASPECTS

Other-validated and self-validated intimacy reflect level 1 and level 2, respectively, of the developmental model of intimacy presented in Chapter Four. The clinical model described above considers both level-1 and level-2 types of intimacy, and explains the ebb and flow of intimacy in marriage. Accordingly, the occurrence and style of intimacy are a function of:

- each individual's level of self-development (i.e., level of differentiation); and
- the prior and current nature of their relationship.

Table 5.1
Intimacy Dynamics at Different Levels
of Differentiation

High Differentiation	Low Differentiation
Some capacity for self-validated intimacy. Self-disclosure is relatively independent of partner's behavior or dynamics in the relationship; low need for reciprocity.	*Dependence on other-validated intimacy.* Self-disclosure is dependent on partner's behavior or dynamics in the relationship; high need for reciprocity.
High intimacy tolerance.[3] Partner's tolerance sets upper limits of relationship norms for frequency and intensity of intimacy. The individual is capable of unilaterally pushing norms.	*Low intimacy tolerance.* The individual's tolerance sets upper limits of relationship norms for frequency and intensity of intimacy. Partner's pushing of norm creates considerable anxiety.

Level of personal development determines the degree to which one affects (and is affected by) normative patterns of intimacy in the relationship. Said differently, level of differentiation determines whether the predominant style is self-validated or other-validated intimacy; degree of expected reciprocity is inversely proportional to level of differentiation (see Table 5.1).[2] Kerr and Bowen summed it up this way:

> The individuality of very well differentiated people is developed to the point that they can be responsible for themselves and not fault others for their own discontents. Togetherness needs are such that, while people are attracted to and interested in one another, their functioning is not dependent on each other's acceptance and approval. This degree of self-containment, coupled with the fact that expectations of one another are governed far less by infantile need than by the realities of cooperation, results in the relationship spawning little anxiety. In addition, any anxiety that is spawned does not escalate through a series of actions and reactions. Unconstrained by fears about how one another might respond to moves toward increased or decreased involvement, the relationship has remarkable freedom. (1988, pp. 74–75)

---

[2]The role of individual and relationship dynamics in intimacy and sexuality will be considered at length in Chapters Seven and Eight, respectively.

[3]*Intimacy tolerance* is an aspect of differentiation which refers to the ability to maintain a clear individual identity and modulate one's anxiety as one (and one's partner) discloses increasingly core aspects of self. It can be thought of as a relative measure that differs between partners; it can also be considered relative to one's sexual potential. Intimacy tolerance is discussed further in Chapter Seven.

To the degree that there is discrepancy in intimacy tolerance, the lesser of the partners' tolerance tends to become the relationship norm. When level of differentiation is high, partners are capable of (unilaterally) violating the norm when desired and are better able to drive that norm higher.

Discrepancy in intimacy tolerance is lower than appearances often suggest (even in highly polarized relationships). Given that people tend to pick partners at the same level of differentiation as themselves, partners tend to have roughly the same level of intimacy tolerance. Apparent discrepancy in intimacy tolerance is often the result of *borrowed functioning* (Kerr & Bowen, 1988): One spouse appears to function at a higher level than the other (i.e., have more intimacy tolerance)—*as long as the partner remains relatively avoidant.* When the partner raises his/her level of intimacy tolerance (i.e., differentiation), the individual withdraws to a level of intimacy capable of being self-validated (which is lower than that supportable through other-validation).

Intimacy is not simply autistic self-confrontation in front of the partner; the partner and the nature of the relationship *are* important. It is the partner's importance that increases the salience of intimacy and heightens the threat to self and the requisite ability to self-validate. *In fact, our clinical model predicts that intimacy tends to diminish simply because one's partner becomes more important as time evolves.*

The notion of intimacy as a relational process, however, does not automatically sanction dependency on the partner's response—on the partner's instilling confidence, trust, security, and caring in the disclosing spouse. As we shall see, the notion that intimacy is a relational process doesn't even necessitate that both partners feel "intimate" at the same time.

HOW DOES A RELATIONSHIP DEVELOP (OR RESTORE) INTIMACY?

Conventional wisdom assumes that intimate relationships develop linearly. For example, Masters, Johnson, and Kolodny (1982, pp. 236–7) suggest that couples negotiate expectations for depth of intimacy and privacy at the outset of the relationship; once agreed upon, they set out toward this goal. In reality, however, expectations (and abilities) for intimacy ebb and flow *throughout* the relationship, in recursion with the evolution of the relationship, the partners' individual development, and the broader family system. Verbalizations during courting often bear little resemblance to the pattern of intimate transactions (negotiated outside of conscious awareness) that emerges later.

Other-validated models of intimacy suggest that, barring discontinuity in reciprocity, relationships proceed to progressively deeper (core) levels of disclosure. The untoward acceptance of social relationships as a paradigm for marital intimacy overlooks that *this pattern stops at a certain point*. Several factors at multiple levels are involved:

- Couples expect the initial emotional honeymoon to continue forever. When partners eventually become disenchanted, however, they are unable to maintain the same level of (other-validated) intimacy.
- When intimacy is predominantly other-validated, progressive disclosure of core information generates increasing levels of anxiety; dependence on a reflected sense of self, along with the fear of not receiving it, increases.

Other-validated intimacy usually deteriorates as time progresses. After several years of marriage, a level of intimacy is reached that is not capable of being supported by a reflected sense of self. At this point, the style of intimacy that facilitated relationship development thus far is exactly what keeps it stuck. An equilibrium is reached in which dependence on validation is equal to fears of rejection, and both attain critical levels. When this asymptote is reached, intimacy becomes non-linear and discontinuous. Further progress requires greater differentiation, and corresponding increased capacity for self-validated intimacy.[4]

Many people mistakenly assume there is something "wrong" when this happens. Some jettison their partner (rather than their idealized image of intimacy) and repeat the process with someone else. Others adapt by reducing intimate exchanges. Fewer still use this natural stage in relationships as a crucible for their own emotional development; increased intrapsychic and dyadic conflict leads to requisite increments in differentiation.

If we now shift our focus to the level of behavioral exchange, the nonlinear evolution of intimacy (and intimacy expectations) becomes readily apparent. Relationships that eventually sustain long-term intimacy often start out in a nonreciprocal vein. At low levels of differentiation, one partner commonly has higher intimacy *need* than the other.[5]

---

[4]For sake of clarity, we have discussed other-validated and self-validated intimacy as if they were invariant and mutually exclusive events in a relationship. Actually, both occur to varying degrees in any relationship, including highly differentiated ones. However, it is useful to use these labels to identify the predominant patterns in a relationship and the degree of dependency on a reflected sense of self. Other-validated intimacy is not the determining factor in highly differentiated couples—it is *lagniappe* (a New Orleans colloquialism meaning *a little something extra*).

[5]*Intimacy need* refers to the degree of hunger or desire for intimacy, which, unlike intimacy *tolerance*, may *not* reflect one's level of differentiation. Well-differentiated individuals (capable of level-2 styles)

Marriages often develop by one partner dragging, cajoling and or threatening (to leave) the other into progressive levels of intimacy. The reluctant partner unconsciously picks a mate more comfortable with and/or hungrier for intimacy, whose pushing allows him/her to move in that direction while still resisting. The comic strip "Cathy" captured it best: A young man proclaimed his commitment stating, "I'm ready to have a woman drag me into a serious relationship."

At the outset of this common arrangement, both partners enjoy the respective benefits. The "pursuing" partner feels "needed" and valued for the ability to self-disclose; it is assumed the partner will eventually "change." The "pursued" partner enjoys being "wanted." Fogarty's (1979) classic paper on "distancer-pursuer" dynamics offers a full description of this pattern.

The reciprocal validation and other-dependent quality of this period are often unrecognized; this intimacy is *not* necessarily self-validated on the pursuer's part. Expected reciprocity for self-disclosure or emotional validation eventually takes its toll. The requirement of empathic affirmation in every encounter places a stifling burden on the listener and encourages emotional dependency in the discloser.

> One response to the pressure to adapt, however, is a feature of *all* relationships. This response is *emotional distance.* (Kerr & Bowen, 1988, p. 81)

After several years, amplification and polarization cause the *original* pattern of intimacy to be the source of gridlock and resentment. The pursuer becomes frustrated by the distancer's lack of self-disclosure; s/he presses for "more communication." The distancer experiences the other as demanding and feels threatened and diminished by the other's ability to self-disclose; he/she discourages further intimacy. When tolerance for self-validated intimacy is exceeded, further self-disclosure paradoxically limits subsequent depth of engagement in the relationship.

When such a point is reached, the distancer is often mistakenly described as "non-communicative," rather than less self-disclosing. *More accurately, he/she is quite communicative (on a meta level) about the refusal to verbally self-disclose.* This

---

actively seek intimacy and miss it when not available; they can self-soothe, maintain an intact sense of self, and retain a high degree of partner selectivity in the interim. Poorly differentiated individuals are *driven* to either seek others or avoid them, in order to maintain a sense of self; functional level diminishes (and anxiety increases) when deviating from customary levels of other-validated intimacy. Intimacy-seeking behavior of poorly differentiated people is highly dependent on (a) the behavior of the partner, and (b) modulating physical or emotional proximity to control emotional reactivity.

presents an inherent paradox: The distancer repeatedly self-discloses about a core aspect of self: the refusal to self-disclose.

The pursuer (of other-validated intimacy) avoids the dilemma by creating another interlocking paradox: S/He withholds validation of the distancer's meta-disclosure by *refusal to accept the message*. The pursuer commonly complains that the distancer is "won't communicate"! More succinctly, the pursuer sends a reciprocal meta-message indicating that s/he only believes her/his ears, not her/his eyes.

At this point, the pursuer embraces a reciprocity model, self-disclosing in a "give-to-get" fashion; the goal of being better "known" quickly fades. The distancer attempts to avoid real or imagined obligations to validate or reciprocate, ignoring the event or content of the partner's disclosure.

The pursuer, often pursuing out of his/her neediness and insecurity, seeks to elicit approval for his/her insecurities. *Conversely, the distancer actively seeks to elicit insecurities in the pursuer — insecure people don't self-disclose very long.*

Troubled marriages face another inherent paradox: The path to other-validation is through self-validated intimacy. When validation from the partner is not needed or demanded, it is more likely to be forthcoming.

The Importance of Self-Validated Intimacy

The path to a long-term intimate marriage is arduous and circuitous. The initial steps can be accomplished using other-validated styles; the abrupt, steep assents (and descents) of the slippery peaks of intense marital intimacy require the traction of self-validation.

Self-validated intimacy is the "bottom line" in marriage, particularly troubled ones; without the ability to persevere when validation from the partner is not forthcoming, couples bog down. In fact, it requires the ability to do so *especially* when a less-than-favorable response is anticipated. A couple in which at least one partner is capable of sustained unilateral disclosure is more likely to successfully weather the missed opportunities and poorly phrased responses that often accompany rebuilding a relationship.

Lacking this, couples become locked in a paralysis of defensiveness and withholding from which neither partner is strong enough to extricate him/herself. Marriages mired in "exchange theory" expectations have difficulty sustaining intimacy (and other aspects of their relationship) through life's realities, which preclude lock-step *quid pro quo*. Such couples experience the sexual boredom and emotional indifference presumed to be inherent in married life.

A person may lack sufficient differentiation to support unilateral disclosure in an ongoing relationship, although he/she is able to do so at the outset or in an isolated experience. This point underlies Wynne and Wynne's observation:

> Indeed, as most persons can testify, intimacy occurs surprisingly often in encounters with relative strangers. Such highly sporadic, intimate disclosures in "one-time-only" relationships seem possible *because* of the unlikelihood of a further relationship and the attendant opportunities for betrayal. (Wynne & Wynne, 1986, p. 385)

High level of differentiation is a requirement for, and a result of, intense self-validated intimacy as a marriage increases in importance and longevity. Erikson (1959) said that an individual is available for an intimate relationship only after he or she has achieved a core sense of identity. Kerr and Bowen (1988) suggest that "know thyself" is the first step for those aspiring to attain intimacy. Keifer (1977) wrote:

> Unfortunately, for many of us the need to "have someone to call our own" represents a very basic problem of needing to depend upon and cling to another person. The individual who comes to an intimate relationship with the need to "find" him- or herself in another person has very little to offer or to gain in the relationship. Once again, we must realize that the ability to be alone is one of the most important characteristics in a potential intimate. As Fromm (1956, p. 94) has stated, "If I am attached to another person because I cannot stand on my own feet, he or she may be a lifesaver, but the relationship is not one of love."
>
> Mature intimate relationships are not the proper home for dependent people! . . .
>
> Of all of our personal and nonbiological human needs, it would seem that the need for intimacy and the complementary need for self-hood and autonomy comprise our most basic and most unheralded needs. The need to be alone and the ability to be intimate are two challenges facing modern individuals and modern societies. (p. 293)

But Kahlil Gibran said it best in *The Prophet* (boldface added for emphasis):

And what of Marriage? . . .

Let there be spaces in your togetherness, And let the winds of the heavens dance between you.

Love one another, **but make not a bond of love**: Let it rather be a moving sea between the shores of your souls.

Fill each other's cup, but drink not from one cup. Give one another of your bread, but eat not from the same loaf.

Sing and dance together and be joyous, but let each one of you be alone,
Even as the strings of a lute are alone though they quiver with the same music.
    Give your hearts, **but not into each other's keeping**. For only the hand of
Life can contain your hearts.
    And stand together, yet not too near together: for the pillars of the temple
stand apart, and the oak tree and the cypress grow not in each other's shadow.
(1923/1982, pp. 16–17)

It is striking that these suggestions, the antithesis of how most people live
their lives, are coupled with the outcome they crave:

You were born together, and together you will be forevermore. You shall be
together when the white wings of death scatter your days. And you shall be
together even in the silent memory of God. (p. 16)

Intense self-validated intimacy produces an enhanced sense of self. Jourard
(1968) and others have written about the self-validating and ego-strengthening
impact of "authentic self-disclosure" in the presence of the partner.

In this level of sharing, the individuals experience the state of intimacy even
more existentially than has been described thus far. In a relationship that is
characterized by intense depth, the self of each of the partners is able in a truly
mystical sense to be even more purely him- or herself, as s/he partakes of an
egoless fusion with another person. (Keifer, 1977, p. 276)

*If the relationship between autonomous sense of self and intense intimacy is
recursive, how does one break into this heavenly cycle?*
    Other-validated intimacy does not explain the emergence of extremely
intense intimacy or novel additions to sexual repertoire (both of which are
generally anxiety-provoking). Hammering out progressively higher levels of
intimacy and eroticism in marriage requires repeated self-confrontation, self-
validation, and unilateral self-disclosure. Keeping sex alive constitutes a crucible for differentiation.
    The internal conflict and queasy insecurity that follow unilateral disclosure
of core personal information (if not truncated by "support" from the partner)
eventually give rise to integration and self-validation. The increased sense of
self derived from self-confrontation increases the likelihood of subsequent
disclosure in the face of questionable responses from the partner.
    We will demonstrate this in the sexual crucible (next chapter). Eventually,
intimacy ceases to be just a vehicle for "closeness," validation, or orgasmic

release; it becomes the arena in which individuals confront the issues of *integrity* and *cowardice*. These are highly charged, value-laden words—and this is exactly what Bowen's notion of solid-self development specifies: the emergence of self-defined value and meaning.

Truisms about marriage and relationships abound: "Intimate relationships take work," and "Intimacy requires trust." *Work* in intimate relationships is seldom specified beyond "spending time together" and "communicating"; *trust* always implicitly refers to one's partner. *In actuality, the work of intimate relationships is self-maintenance in the face of fears of betrayal and abandonment (i.e., self-validated intimacy). The most important "trusting relationship" is the relationship one has with oneself.* As existential theory, this makes wonderful contemplation. As a praxis for living, it becomes a crucible for human development.

Can One Person Have an Intimate Experience?

The implications of this viewpoint are quite striking. Differentiation, the ability to maintain a non-anxious presence in the face of others' anxiety, is not the same as being uninvolved or indifferent. Differentiation is what (a) *permits* intense involvement without becoming infected with other people's anxiety, and (b) obviates the need to withdraw or interfere with the partner to modulate one's own emotionality. However, this lack of emotional reactivity is often misinterpreted by others as a lack of involvement or "caring." *The general public (and the therapeutic community) are so firmly, yet unknowingly, entrenched in an other-validated model of intimacy that the absence of the side effects of this style of relating are taken as indicative of the absence of intimacy itself!*

When patients achieve a significant increment in their level of differentiation (and capacity for self-validated intimacy), the absence of reactivity, discomfort, or defensiveness during intensely intimate moments commonly causes couples to wonder if they are, indeed, becoming indifferent or uninvolved. As they achieve the very goals they sought through treatment, growth tends to be reinterpreted in ways consistent with conventional reciprocity paradigms. *If the therapist also happens to ascribe to this model, he or she then becomes an impediment to further growth.*

For example, consider common expectations for knowledgeable acceptance and communicated empathy which clinicians promote:

> An intimate experience has not taken place, in our definition, until there is empathic feedback, that is, until acceptance and acknowledgment are communi-

cated, verbally or nonverbally, as an indication that this trust is justified. (Wynne & Wynne, 1986, pp. 384–5)

Again we are confronted with the lack of clinical utility of popular views of intimacy. The expectation/demand of empathy or reciprocal disclosure allows the listener to define the partner's disclosure as "intimate" or not, depending on the response given. Moreover, it encourages partners to tamper with each other's "reality," permitting prior events to be retroactively redefined!

Consider, for example, a situation where a couple awakens having had sex the night before. The wife casually remarks on the wonderfully intimate time they shared. The husband comments that he didn't find it wonderfully intimate *or* sexually satisfying. The wife, shocked and wounded, responds that she must have been mistaken about the night before. Until her husband spoke, however, there was no doubt in her mind that it was intimate and satisfying to *her* (and to him too for that matter). The wife is now faced with a dilemma:

(a) If she remains reliant on other-validated intimacy, she must actually stop trusting her own phenomenological experience, and "trust" her husband instead. In the process, she must give up what *has* been a gratifying intimate experience, as a distortion or misperception.

(b) If she does not allow her husband's response to retroactively redefine her reality, she must rely on self-validation and trust her relationship with *herself*. In that case, she might make a simple nondefensive statement like, "I'm really sorry to hear that. I, and the man *I* was with last night, had a wonderful time! What was the woman you were with like?!"

Notice that this vignette brings us right to a clinical dilemma often seen in treatment. It is quite possible that such an exchange might precipitate some troubled couple's request for treatment. If the wife selects option (a), the couple is likely to present with issues that reflect their fusion: validation and "reality" fights. If she selects option (b), the presenting issues will reflect concerns about individuation: communication, distance and "caring."

Thus, the question of whether or not one person can have an intimate experience is not simply an intellectual exercise. It strikes right at the core of our understanding of intimate processes and merits an answer: *It takes two people for there to be an intimate experience, because there has to be the "other,"*[6] *but*

---

[6]E.g., open self-confrontation and self-disclosure in the context of the partner.

each "one" has his/her own experience of it. Intimate experiences are like coital orgasms: it takes two, but only one might "have it."

It is entirely possible for one spouse to have a self-validated intimate experience while the other does not. There are times when the speaker has an intensely intimate experience of self-disclosure, while the listener regards the information as mundane. Dependence on the listener for validation and unwillingness to accept one's existential separateness often lead to fights about the meaning and salience of what has transpired.

By its nature, intimacy is a highly individual and idiosyncratic experience. Psychotherapy is a prime example of unilateral intimacy. Many experiences that are particularly intimate for the patient are not correspondingly experienced by the therapist. Psychotherapy *can* be an extremely intimate experience for the therapist (without indulging in reciprocal self-disclosure); therapeutic impact is often at its zenith when patient and therapist have this experience simultaneously.

The unilateral quality of intimacy is not unlike other interpersonal phenomena; *autonomy* is constructed unilaterally, although it occurs in a relational framework. *Insight* also occurs unilaterally, although, as Maturana and Varela (1987) pointed out, it occurs in some dyadic context. But simply "knowing oneself thoroughly" is not intimacy. Insight without self-disclosure is not intimate, although intimacy involves some degree of insight. Through intimacy we gain new awareness of ourselves; profoundly intense intimate experiences involve disclosure of insights *as they occur*, leading to further insights (and continued disclosure, *ad infinitum*).

The viewpoint of intimacy as a fundamentally unilateral experience is not unique. Other authors have perceived *loving* in much the same way:

> . . . to love is to be alone, at least initially and momentarily, since it is unilateral and not dependent on response from the loved one. And since the fear of being separated makes us concerned with the response of the other, and so keeps us from loving, the very fear of aloneness and separation oddly enough results in our awful aloneness and deadly separation. (Malone & Malone, 1987, pp. 10–11)

HELPING PEOPLE TOLERATE INCREASED INTIMACY

Many individuals remain stuck at low levels of differentiation (Kerr & Bowen, 1988). Moreover, most relationships persevere at the level of projective identification and splitting (Johnson, 1987). Is it any wonder that most views of intimacy, written by professionals at the same level of differentiation as the public, contain the expectation of validation reciprocity?

Modern sex therapy encourages clinicians to "focus on the relationship"; the systemic focus of marriage and family therapy does likewise. Unfortunately, "focusing on the relationship" of spouses at low levels of differentiation doesn't offer a long-term solution for intimacy problems: It reinforces dependence on other-validated intimacy. Couples seeking treatment are almost inevitably poorly differentiated; highly differentiated individuals tend to resolve their difficulties spontaneously.

Sadly, few individuals *ever* achieve levels of differentiation sufficient for intimacy and eroticism at the limits of human sexual potential. Many couples maintain their equilibrium of emotional proximity by reducing communication and emotional availability during sexual activity.

> Norma's husband is close but has problems with being intimate. He cannot be sexual with her. He has sex with her, but cannot be sexual with her. These are different experiences. Although he goes through the physical motions, he is not having a sexual experience. (Malone & Malone, 1987, p. 195)

> Gary sees his sexuality with his lover almost as a job. Not quite a chore, but very much a service. He knows he feels little joy himself in their "sexuality." He accepts this loss of desire, somewhat sadly, as an inevitable part of a long-term "relationship." . . . The sadness is that when his wife comes in to see us with him, it is apparent that she is more than willing and able to be as sexual as he appears to so passionately desire. He is simply not ready and able to accept and enjoy her sexuality. He is so afraid of mixing closeness (the personal) with intimacy (the sexual) that he lives in a sexual limbo. (Malone & Malone, 1987, p. 196)

Kaplan (1987) touched on the topic of intimacy tolerance in the etiology of sexual aversion:

> Patients with intimacy and commitment conflicts make love without difficulty during the beginning phases of a relationship, but develop "emotional claustrophobia" which frequently goes along with sexual aversions and the avoidance of sex when the partner demands a deeper level of commitment.
>
> There are considerable individual differences in the tolerance level for emotional closeness. Normal individuals can meld erotic desire and intimacy and are able to enjoy a gratifying sexual relationship with the partners to whom they are committed. But the "emotional comfort zone" of a person with intimacy conflicts is exceeded at a certain point of increasing commitment. . . .

An emotional crisis is created when the level of closeness exceeds the patient's defensive threshold and taps into his latent fears of rejection and abandonment. He loses his sexual interest and/or begins to panic when he senses that he is becoming vulnerable and emotionally dependent on his partner. (p. 65)

"Aversion" to intimacy and sexuality is simply a matter of degree — Kaplan's comments are no less applicable to the general population. Like many clinicians, Kaplan overestimates the intimacy tolerance of "normal" people with normal neuroses; such distortions, however, reinforce the view that intimacy problems necessarily reflect psychopathology. The concept of *sexual potential*, in contrast, is asset-based: *"Normal" people are "aversive" to very intense intimacy and capable of vastly increased intimacy tolerance.*

Popular wisdom suggests that women are, by and large, more interested in intimacy then men. However, it is often overlooked that such notions concern *moderate* (but important) levels of intimacy (e.g., daily communication about joint tasks, reflections on the day, etc). However, "sharing feelings" is not the same as open self-confrontation in the presence of the partner. *When the focus is intense intimacy, there is no consistent gender difference in intimacy tolerance: almost no one wants it.*

Contemporary sex and marital therapy does not facilitate intense intimacy any better than it promotes eroticism; worse yet, it doesn't help link the two.

Traditional norms of "good" sexual behavior (driven by reciprocity expectations and fears of being "selfish") suggest one should focus on the partner's needs during sex. Yet, patients are often living demonstrations that it is possible to focus on "satisfying the partner" in a manner that actually *precludes* intimacy or eroticism.

Taking turns receiving "non-demand pleasuring" *does* redirect exclusive focus to one's own sensations; in many circumstances it facilitates sexual response, but at the expense of diminished awareness of the partner. Sensate-focus *can* be prescribed as an intimacy-based activity (i.e., awareness of self in the context of awareness of the partner).[7] More often, however, it is promoted as a *bypass* in which one's focus on kinesthetic cues is used to *remove* awareness of the partner (or of one's *self*, for that matter).

Glib acceptance of the notion that focusing on the partner interferes with one's own arousal reflects widespread lack of intimacy during sex: Focusing on the partner is a "turn-off" when partners are not deeply involved; focusing on

---

[7]Intimacy-based sensate-focus prescriptions are detailed in *The Intimacy Paradigm*.

the partner is a "turn-on" in the context of a shared alternative sexual reality involving profound depth of partner-engagement and role-enactment.

When partners have difficulty being sexual and intimate at the same time, they develop sexual styles that emphasize either intimacy or eroticism, but maintain the separation of the two. The style of a couple's sexual interaction (including location, behaviors, techniques, and sequencing) contains this meta-communication.

When we examine the sexual crucible (Chapter Six) we will encounter the notion of *elicitation*, which highlights meta-messages embedded in sexual styles. "Reading" sexual styles permits cross-modality interpretations of how couples handle intimacy (in general, and during sexual activity in specific); in so doing, the therapist implicitly re-integrates intimacy and eroticism.

Helping people experience enhanced awareness of self and partner by tolerating separateness is often a step towards resolving ambivalence toward intimacy. When this is done in a sexual context, the impact is particularly powerful. For example, people avoid intensely intimate erotic play because it makes them feel self-conscious and "exposed"; curiously, this is what intimacy is all about. Intense intimacy and sexuality are difficult to generate; once accomplished, they are hard to tolerate as well.

People often become defensive as they recognize their reluctance; pointing out that they are no different from others in this regard seems to help them. Understanding that intense self-validated intimacy is an important foundation for profound marital sexuality helps explain why people don't often experience it — accepting this understanding is a developmental milestone.

Putting the Expectation of Intimacy into Context

Is intimacy a "natural function"? Couples' expectation that they *should* have become intimate only adds guilt and recrimination to disappointment when it doesn't occur.

Malone and Malone's (1987) position that intimacy is a natural function contains the same two flaws as Masters and Johnson's "natural" view of sexual function: (a) it isn't true, and (b) it promotes response anxiety which further diminishes the likelihood of the predicted event occurring.

The notion that marriage *should* be intimate confuses the human *potential* for intimacy with the expectation of its fulfillment. There are many behaviors humans share in common with non-human species by virtue of evolution of the brain (e.g., some aspects of mother-infant nursing behavior, pair-bonding, and communal development). However, such biologically encoded scripts are not the same thing as intimacy; some notion of volition underlies the special status intimate partners accord each other. Some animals cohabitate for life; many humans do too, but neither are necessarily intimate.

How Long Has Intimacy Been a Possibility?

In their natural systems theory of family functioning, Kerr and Bowen (1988) note that the universe was created some 10–20 billion years ago, gradually cooling for 5–10 billion years. The solar system subsequently formed 4.6 billion years ago. Prokaryotes, the first form of life on earth, appeared approximately 3.5–4 billion years ago. Complex animals such as plants, fish, and vertebrates, developed only 500 million years ago.

"Lucy," the earliest known "human," dates back only 3.5 million years. A million years after "Lucy," the human brain underwent significant evolution, finally stabilizing in its present size in the last million years. *Homo erectus* first used fire half a million years ago and developed hearths and houses in another 100,000 years. *Homo sapiens* emerged 200,000 years ago and within 100,000 years was displaying the first rudiments of culture (e.g., sophisticated tools, rituals, and burying the dead).

It is only within the last 100,000 years that mankind has demonstrated critical cognitive functioning reflecting the capacity for self-concept and intimacy. The prefrontal neocortex, evolved in the transition from *Neanderthal* to *Cro-Magnon*, is the structure permitting a "inner world" of self-reflective emotions, goal formulation, and extended concentration.[8]

Kerr and Bowen point out, "If one uses the figure 15 billion years for the period of time since the cosmic 'big bang' and the figure 35,000 years for the time since Cro-Magnon has been on Earth, then Cro-Magnon has existed only 0.0002% of cosmic time" (p. 26). *Even assuming homo sapiens developed the biological capacity for intimacy 100,000 years ago, intimacy has been a possibility for only 0.0007% of cosmic time!* Putting couples' expectation that "intimacy is a given" into proper perspective assuages their disappointment; we are just beginning to explore the parameters of this relatively "recent" phenomena.

---

[8]The limbic system controls emotions in non-human mammals. Bowen's concept of differentiation involves the capacity for neocortex-modulated response rather than highly reactive (reflexive) limbic-type response to provocation. Kerr and Bowen (1988) offer an example distinguishing limbic and neocortical responses:

> . . . someone reacts to disapproval by withdrawing (an emotionally rooted response observed in all forms of life), feeling sad (a feeling experienced only by higher forms of life), and by becoming preoccupied with a sense of inadequacy (a subjectively determined attitude of self that is undoubtedly unique to humans). (p. 33)

How Far Down the Phylogenetic Scale Can You Go?

Our prior discussion of *self*-awareness as an inherent requisite of intimacy now takes on other significance: How widespread is intimacy? "Eye-gazing," preening, collaborative child-rearing, and lifetime pair-bonding are not necessarily intimate; intimacy involves a concept of self. The mainspring driving proximity reactions in other species (e.g., territoriality and dominance) is not clear; animals forced into species- and situation-specific abnormal proximity seek distance by hiding or avoiding eye contact (Wilson, 1975).

Humans may *not* be the only species capable of intimacy—what of other highly sophisticated mammals (e.g., great apes and dolphins)? Cortical development and linguistic ability suggest that humans have greater potential for intimacy than other mammals. However, the manner in which some members of our own species live their lives makes one pause to wonder.

Several studies suggest that great apes have self-concept; their use of language suggests the capacity for the notion of "I." The chimp "Lucy" (trained by Gardner and Gardner) was able to "make linguistic distinctions of linguistic distinctions" when signing "*Lucy cry*" in response to seeing her human parents leave (Maturana & Varela, 1987, p. 215). Gallup's (1979) research also suggests that gorillas have an internalized concept of *self*:

> A colored dot was painted between his [an anesthetized gorilla's] eyes—a place that could be seen only in a mirror. After awakening from the anesthesia, he was given a mirror. What a surprise! He put his hand to his forehead to touch the colored dot. Perhaps we expected the animal to stretch his hand and touch the dot in the mirror where it could be seen. A macaque would not do what the gorilla did. Whatever the case with other animals, this experiment suggests that the gorilla can generate a domain of self through social distinctions. In that domain there is a possibility of reflection, as with a mirror or with language. (Maturana & Varela, 1987, p. 224)

Our discussion brings us to the cutting edge of neuroanatomy, neurophysiology, developmental and evolutionary biology, and cognitive psychology. Nobel laureate Gerald M. Edelman's (1989) comprehensive theory of consciousness, *The Remembered Present*, offers a unified neurobiological explanation of self-awareness. Apropos to the question at hand, Edelman states:

> . . . we will distinguish between higher-order consciousness and primary consciousness. Higher-order consciousness (including self-consciousness) is based on direct awareness in a human having language and a reportable subjective life. The more basic primary consciousness is present in all humans and is perhaps

also present in some animals as biological individuals. Primary consciousness may be considered to be composed of certain phenomenological experiences, such as mental images, but in contrast to higher-order consciousness, it is supposed to be bound to a time around the measurable present, to lack a concept of self and a concept of past and future, and to be beyond *direct* individual report.

. . . normal humans have self-consciousness and subjective experience, while certain animals at best have primary consciousness. . . . (p. 24)

According to Edelman, only humans demonstrate higher-order consciousness, "a state that requires the construction through language and social interactions of a concept of the self and the ability to model the past, present, and future" (p. 166). As if anticipating the example of the gorilla and the mirror, Edelman states:

An animal may have phenomenological experience, and that experience may have an individual, historical character that can affect future behavior, but it is not *subjective* experience—there is no subject or person to make discriminations or reports of that phenomenological experience over time. This is not a denial of the possibility of phenomenological experience. (pp. 167–168)

So . . . humans may be alone in their capacity for intimacy; if not, it is still a rather exclusive club. When couples perceive the gift of intimacy as an *opportunity* rather than a "given," they tend to approach marriage with the respect it warrants.[9]

Reconsideration of the Quantum Model

Our discussion offers another perspective on the quantum model (Chapter Two), which conceptualizes *total stimulus level* as a function of *physical stimulation* and *the receiver's psychological processes*. In other species, total stimulus level is more directly a function of tactile input. The capacity for *self*-awareness

---

[9]Our clinical model focuses on cognitive and emotional *self*-awareness rather than the more commonly emphasized "caring" side of intimacy; it is similar to the orientation of Chelune et al. (1984) and Malone and Malone (1987). One result of its resultant emphasis on cortical capacity for higher order consciousness may be an underestimation of primates' and other complex mammals' capacity for intimacy.

On the other hand, this orientation is consonant with differentiation-based theory and therapy (which emphasizes *neocortical modulation of emotionality*). A *"self-awareness"* emphasis does not negate the role of caring in marriage; rather, it suggests that caring based on the ability to self-validate is fundamental to the ability to (unilaterally) love. Relationships which mask lack of differentiation behind intimacy-as-caring tend to disintegrate in times of stress.

represents a nonreducible increment in complexity of sexual functioning: Psychological processes play a increasing role in human sexual functioning and variations in behavior, compared to non-human mammals.

- Human copulatory behavior is more controlled by thoughts and feelings and less by hormonal factors.
- Human mate selection is more idiosyncratic.
- Human sexual behavior is (potentially) more capable of highly refined nuances of meaning.
- Mother-infant bonding, family cohesiveness, and social learning are particularly important determinants of capacity for intimacy in adult life and erotic "love maps" (Money, 1986).
- *The same psychological processes in humans that make sexuality (potentially) meaningful and intimate also increase the possibility (and likelihood) of sexual dysfunctions.*

Adequate genital performance is a "natural function" in other species. With the introduction of the capacity for self-awareness and intimacy, human sexual functioning traded mechanistic, programmed regularity and invulnerability to sexual dysfunctions for increased subtlety and richness of experience—and increased vulnerability to performance difficulties from these same psychological capacities. Sexual interest and depth of involvement became susceptible to the positive and negative effects of intrapsychic and interpersonal processes.

As sexuality became something more than reproduction by virtue of the evolution of human neuroanatomy, emergence of the capacity for intimacy established the biological basis for profound sexual experiences for which there is no physiological counterpart (e.g., erection, lubrication, orgasm or ejaculation).

Social learning plays a pivotal role in the fulfillment of the human potential, including the ability to combine intimacy with sexuality. Sexual potential is rooted in our biological evolution, nurtured in the formative years of childhood and adolescence, and fulfilled in the emotional differentiation and development of later adult life.

Is Intimacy Even Necessary for a Good Relationship?

Numerous authors consider intimacy to be a basic human need (e.g., Fromm, 1956; Maslow, 1971; Schutz, 1966). Some suggest the ability to establish an "intimate foundation" is one of three necessary and sufficient conditions for a fulfilling marital and sexual relationship (sharing love and negotiating power being the other two) (L'Abate & Talmadge, 1987). Others state the potential for sexual problems increases dramatically when core intimacy needs are not satisfactorily addressed (Hof, 1987).

In contrast, Wynne et al. (1958) argue that intimacy is a nonessential aspect of a relationship; they exclude intimacy from their four cornerstones of a healthy family unit:

- *attachment/caregiving:* "complementary affectional bonding, prototypically manifest in parent infant relatedness,"
- *communication:* "the sharing of foci of attention and continuing with exchange of meanings and messages,"
- *joint problem-solving:* "renewable sharing of the day-to-day tasks, interests, and recreational activities,"
- *mutuality:* "the flexible, selective integration of the preceding processes into an enduring, super ordinate pattern of relatedness. There is a shared commitment to one another to shape the relationship as the life cycle unfolds, as unexpected events take place, as new interests and aspirations emerge. . . . Mutuality incorporates both distancing, or disengagement, and constructive re-engagement. Divergence and conflict, growth and aging, and transitions in the life cycle generate many outcomes for relational systems other than mutuality." (p. 385)[10]

Wynne and Wynne (1986) suggest common marital complaints about "lack of intimacy" reflect couples' misdiagnosis of difficulties with attachment, communication, joint problem-solving, and mutuality. As family therapists, Wynne and Wynne primarily focus on marriage as a means to facilitate family functioning, rather than on marital satisfaction. They suggest that relationship maintenance as a whole—rather than the quest for intimacy per se—is more likely to facilitate repeated intimate experiences.

If couples give primary or continual attention to maintaining intimacy, they paradoxically will achieve it less; their expectations will be illusory and their efforts misdirected. Maintenance of continual intimacy even if possible feels

---

[10]Wynne and Wynne's concept of mutuality is somewhat antithetical to their reciprocity expectations for intimacy. While some expectation of reciprocity underlies mutuality, its hallmark is the ability to *deviate* from an invariant, ever-balanced quid pro quo; equity occurs in a long-term framework.

stiflingly symbiotic to us and would impose a continual burden on each partner
to deny his or her own selfhood in the effort to support the other. Relationships
thrive when the distance between the couple waxes and wanes as different
relational or individuating processes come into play. (p. 392)

No doubt Wynne and Wynne have in mind the many adults preoccupied
with satisfying their own emotional needs, ignoring their vital functions as
parents and spouses. These authors give a much needed balance to the epidem-
ic quest for intimacy in our society.

However, there is a legitimate place for marital intimacy in family therapy — promoting overall family functioning and effective modeling for children's
future marriages. Enhancing parents' capacity for emotional and physical intimacy facilitates (a) bonding with children, (b) acceptance of appropriate intergenerational boundaries, and (c) increased differentiation (which permits
the continual evolution of family processes throughout the life span). The
crucible of sexual-marital therapy provides an effective vehicle for that pursuit.

Wynne and Wynne assume that intimacy surely flows from effectiveness in
their four key dimensions. However, such an assumption is erroneous, particularly with regard to sexual intimacy. While intimate sex doesn't often last
when a marriage is troubled, *mutuality* doesn't guarantee intensely intimate or
erotic sexuality. Some spouses are eager to establish a basic utilitarian relationship in order to *avoid* more personal, intimate exchange.

To paraphrase Wynne and Wynne, a good relationship is a necessary, but
often insufficient, ingredient in long-term marital sexuality and intimacy. And
this awareness helps people keep their disappointment in perspective.

Why Popular Articles on "Improving Your Marriage and Keeping Intimacy and Sex Alive" Don't Work

The plethora of popular magazine articles promising to improve intimacy and
keep sex vibrant highlight the frequency with which these problems occur.
Their solutions, however, are misguided: *If they really worked, there would be no
need for next month's article.*

"Lack of communication," lack of "private time," repetitive and invariant
sexual styles, women's discomfort with being sexually aggressive, and men's
discomfort with romance and emotional involvement are often cited as common causes. And, indeed, these *are* factors in some (but not all) couples'
mediocre sex and low levels of intimacy. However, simple-minded suggestions

to "communicate honestly," spend more time together, schedule time in advance, and surprise your partner with new apparel or techniques don't work. They skirt the obvious questions: If these are such common problems, what is causing them? If these problems continue, is it because people are too foolish to adopt these trivial suggestions, even after reading them month after month?

Perhaps solutions go unimplemented because there are underlying issues that predispose dysfunctional patterns and maintain them once they occur. *Disclosure of intimate information (e.g., sexual preferences, fantasies, masturbatory activity), increased emotional contact, and expansion of sexual style require more autonomy and ego strength than many individuals possess.* There are reasons why people do not have extremely good marriages or equally good sex; these have nothing to do with sexual technique per se (but do, in fact, determine the sexual technique of choice).

Spouses may hide dissatisfactions for years because they lack the differentiation to cope with their own (and their partner's) emotional reactions. Many spouses want their partner to be more aggressive, *but only when that aggression conveys a reflected sense of desirability.* Sexual aggression is not welcomed when it is feels like a demand, when it threatens one's ability to "keep up," or when one wonders about the source of this newfound aggressiveness (e.g., feeling competitive with a partner's prior lovers, or fears of infidelity).

Magazine articles suggest that the difference between a facilitative and nonfacilitative initiation is one's timing and tone of voice. In reality, the difference is equally dependent on the partner's mind-set and emotional stability. Although the listener's negative reaction is often displaced onto the speaker ("If you had just said it in another way at another time, I would have had an entirely different reaction"), this is often not the case.

People have boring, monotonous sex because intense sex and intimacy (and change itself) are more threatening than many people realize. Although spouses complain of boredom and lack of sexual variety, they get quite upset when their partners display new sexual behavior. *Sexual boredom is a systemic defense against intimacy and eroticism.*[11] Until partners develop resilience to intense sexual expression and persist through the disequilibrium it often creates, sexuality generally remains bland.

"Pop" articles reflect contemporary social "reality" about intimacy and sexuality. People enjoy thinking that intense sexuality and profound intimacy are like mother's milk: easy to digest. The notion that many people lack the

---

[11]We will discuss the systemic aspects of sexuality in Chapters Eight, Nine, and Ten.

differentiation necessary to sustain intense sex and intimacy in marriage is a relatively unpalatable idea. Suggestions in magazines will continue to appear, not because they are useful in changing the problem, but because they perpetuate the fantasy that wonderful sex and profound intimacy are only a garterbelt away.

In Chapter Six, we will examine a way in which people *can* achieve wonderful sex and profound intimacy: the sexual crucible. It is not easy—but then, little of value in life is. And if, in the process, someone wants to put on a garterbelt, that is fine too.

Constructing the Sexual Crucible

First, we encounter the notion of elicitation: Sexual style and content offer a window into partners' individual and dyadic functioning; there is greater predictive reliability extrapolating from sexual styles to the broader aspects of patients' lives than vice versa.

Second, we examine the sexual crucible from two perspectives: (a) a highly nonreactive treatment alliance in which metamorphic reactions occur, and (b) a severe test or trial, as in the crucifixion of Christ. The latter view addresses patients' subjective experiences and their trials of integrity; the former focuses on clinical process and the therapist's integrity.

Third, we consider three crucial topics: (a) Does sex take work?; (b) development of begrudging respect; and (c) the need for simultaneous multidimensional (isomorphic) interventions.

There is considerable peril in discussing differences in clinicians' approaches and insights based on their writings. Clinicians write to convey their intent, but the reader only infers the author's meaning by interpreting his/her words. Moreover, a good clinician's approach is refined by new insights, but the public image of his/her work remains frozen in the static depictions of prior publications. Is it appropriate to refer to such publications even though the clinicians may have "moved on"?

The actual clinical and conceptual processes of the leaders in the sex therapy field have been available only to the small group of clinicians who interact directly with them on an ongoing basis. For example, William Masters has said on many occasions that *Human Sexual Inadequacy* does not accurately depict the Masters and Johnson treatment approach. However, interpretation of this publication constitutes the sum total of most therapists' knowledge of their clinical work. So too with other clinicians.

Treatment approaches developed by other clinicians (e.g., Masters and Johnson, Kaplan, and Apfelbaum) provide a backdrop to highlight some of the subtle features of the sexual crucible model. The work of these authors comprises some of the most significant contributions to the field of sex therapy; this analysis is in no way meant to minimize their significance. Quite the contrary—the intent is to clarify important points of sexual-marital therapy for the reader, using publications of well-known clinicians as reference points. If my interpretation of a particular author's work is in error, it may well reflect a widely held distortion. It is just such distortions that have shaped the practice of modern sex therapy.

There has been little access to the actual data of what sex therapists *do* in treatment, as opposed to how they conceptualize and describe it. In 1990 and 1991, AASECT,[1] the largest sexological organization in the United States, if not in the world, conducted live clinical demonstrations by three different sex therapists. I am proud to say that I was instrumental in organizing this development. One can only hope for live demonstrations of sexual-marital therapy to become commonplace.

ELICITATION MODELS IN SEXUAL-MARITAL THERAPY

The sexual crucible is an elicitation approach to sexual-marital therapy. In an elicitation approach, couples' sexual behaviors (including the style and content included and excluded in their repertoire) become a window into the whole of the partners' individual functioning and their relationship. The notion that "sexual problems are a reflection of relationship problems" is overly simplistic. The relationship between sexual and non-sexual problems is complex: (a) each can be a manifestation of the other, (b) each can have relatively unique etiology, and (c) the interaction of the two often creates such an enmeshed system that "chicken and egg" distinctions become a moot point. The therapist must be able to intervene in all dimensions *simultaneously*—and an elicitation approach evokes the exquisite multidimensional display of the entire system.

Considering sexual style in the absence of sexual *problems* provides one of the most powerful ways of ascertaining the details of each partner's development. Exploration of sexual style in couples having *utilitarian* sexual functioning is the very essence of the sexual potential approach. The experienced sexual-marital therapist can become adept at cross-modality evaluation and intervention, shifting back and forth between sexual and nonsexual behaviors for an enhanced perspective.

Couples' sexual relationships contain a literal depiction of their lives, a metaphorical construction not unlike dreams. The analogy to dream interpretation is an apt one. As with dream interpretation, there are many differences

---

[1]The American Association of Sex Educators, Counselors, and Therapists.

in therapists' ability to interpret couples' sexual behavior and many perspectives from which the interpretations can be made. Just as the therapist never sees the actual dream content, it is neither necessary nor appropriate for the therapist to observe patients' sexual behavior. It *is* necessary that the therapist obtain a graphically detailed report of the behavior (or nonbehavior) and that he/she listen to the style and phrasing of the patients' report.

As with dreams, there are no inherent meanings or purposes to human sexuality; in fact, human beings use sexuality to express every emotion and motivation of which the species is capable. Moreover, since touch accesses determinants of behavior outside of verbally mediated (conscious) *explanations*, issues that patients are unable/unwilling to articulate are inevitably displayed in sexual style.

An elicitation approach also implies that latent unresolved problems of the individual, the dyad, or the extended emotional system can be deliberately evoked and resolved through selective prescription and proscription of sexual and nonsexual interactions. All couples follow the therapist's suggestions in ways that reflect their own beliefs, fears, and perceptions—perceptions, that is, about themselves, the partner, gender roles, the nature of sexuality, and even the therapist and the therapeutic process. In the hands of a skilled therapist, behavioral suggestions become a vehicle for eliciting and resolving the complex meanings and agendas that have precluded satisfying sexual-marital functioning and exploration of sexual potential. In the sexual crucible of sexual-marital therapy, profound personal growth in nonsexual areas is a fundamental goal.

The notion of an elicitation approach to sexual and marital difficulties is not new; it has been mentioned in the literature for some time. But the degree to which it has been consistently implemented is far from clear: The ways in which clinicians conceptualize their work, the therapeutic interventions they utilize, and the intended uses of these interventions vary greatly. For instance, "sensate focus" prescriptions may be far more complex than perhaps even the inventors of these activities dared imagine. Did Masters and Johnson use prescriptions for elicitation? They make no explicit mention of such use in their publications, and there is little in their cognitive-behavioral orientation to suggest this was their intent. Moreover, their focus on performance anxiety as the cause of sexual dysfunction, their explicit use of sensate focus prescriptions to reduce performance anxiety, and their focus on the treatment of sexual dysfunction per se all suggest to the contrary.

One clinician who thinks otherwise is Apfelbaum (1985, 1988), who suggests that widespread failure to recognize the full subtlety of Masters and Johnson's view of performance anxiety and implementation of sensate focus prescriptions has led to an underappreciation of the magnitude of their contribution. This misinterpretation, he suggests, has led others to think that they are using, integrating, or "progressing beyond" Masters and Johnson's clinical approach. He notes the main source of this possible oversight:

> Much of the difficulty in even recognizing that there is an alternative view arises from Masters and Johnson's way of presenting their work. Outside of participation in their full-time training program or attendance at their training seminars, there is no way to become familiar with many of the essentials of their model, a novel and perhaps questionable method of presentation in a scientific field. As a consequence, their contribution has been evaluated, even by their peers in the field, on the basis of a reading of *Human Sexual Inadequacy*. This is what makes it all too easy to subsume their contribution under the work of others. (p. 6)

Apfelbaum (1985), who apparently had firsthand knowledge of Masters and Johnson's approach, states that their usage of sensate focus prescriptions was not merely desensitization and training, but also diagnostic. He states that in the Masters and Johnson approach, "the sensate focus activities cannot fail, or at least when they fail they also succeed—succeed that is in pinpointing the anxiety that should be the target of treatment" (p. 7). Apfelbaum, however, does not make clear what therapeutic approach Masters and Johnson utilize once the problematic anxiety is elicited; the absence of this elaboration in their own writing casts further doubt on Masters and Johnson's use of an elicitation approach in their original clinical approach. In 1985, Masters and Johnson presented an address to the Annual Meeting of the Society for Sex Therapy and Research, in which they stated:

> The judicious use of sensate focus exercises has multiple clinical applications. For example, sensate focus exercises are now initially used to identify and evaluate levels of inhibited sexual desire and/or states of sexual aversion. Thus, sensate focus techniques are employed both as diagnostic and as therapeutic modalities. (1985, cited by Apfelbaum, 1985, p. 7)

From the wording of their statement, it is not clear whether diagnostic utilization was part of their original clinical approach at the time of the publication of *Human Sexual Inadequacy* or an evolution in keeping with subsequent developments of the field. Moreover, evaluation of *levels* of inhibition is not the same as elicitation of the *content* or nature of the inhibition. There was actually little need for an elicitation of *content* in Masters and Johnson's original clinical approach, since they believed they already knew what the problem was: performance anxiety. At best, Masters and Johnson's use of an elicitation approach concerned the narrow purview of genital dysfunctions (and later, sexual desire), rather than the broader focus of the sexual crucible approach as a vehicle for individual and relationship development.

The role of elicitation in Helen Singer Kaplan's treatment model requires more complex discussion. Kaplan clearly recognized the use of behavioral prescriptions for the resolution of unresolved personal issues. In *The New Sex Therapy*, Kaplan (1974) noted the contribution of sensate-focus behavioral prescriptions to the resolution of previously avoided sexual conflicts. *Sexual Aversion, Sexual Phobias, and Panic Disorder* (Kaplan, 1987) offers a more current elaboration of her views:

> The sexual interactions that are prescribed in sex therapy are not simply mechanical exercises. They are highly charged erotic and intimate experiences which the patient has previously avoided because they are too threatening to him. Although they are used by behavior therapists for the sole purpose of extinguishing the unwanted phobic response, in integrated sex therapy we also exploit the dynamic potential of the exposure assignments. (p. 104)

Moreover, Apfelbaum wrote of her work:

> In *The New Sex Therapy* Helen Kaplan has been the first to show how Masters and Johnson's set-breaking behavioral assignment, designed to bypass the conditions that create sexual dysfunctions, can also be used to uncover and resolve them. Kaplan's integration of this analytic approach into the behavioral sex therapy model has broadened the range of applications of sex therapy, taking it out of the province of the adjunctive technician. The therapeutic objective of our (own) group has been to further this development by finding ways to use assignments consistently for the purpose of uncovering without losing the opportunity for rapid symptom resolution. . . .
>
> This simple behavioral bypassing strategy was developed on the assumption that the use of an uncovering approach would precipitate either an impasse or an inconclusive long-term therapy, losing the opportunity for rapid symptom resolution. Kaplan has shown how, contrary to this assumption, the use of assignments and the consistent symptom focus of the behavioral sex therapy model has created an unexploited opportunity for rapid analytic therapy if the therapist is receptive to whatever the couple does with an assignment rather than dependent on having the couple do assignments in the prescribed manner. (Apfelbaum, 1977a, pp. 128–129).

However, Kaplan's notion of elicitation is far different from what this means in the sexual crucible. In the sexual crucible, elicitation refers to broader issues that limit sexual potential; the scope of treatment extends far beyond sexual *function* and concerns depth and salience of intimacy and eroticism.

"Elicitation" in Kaplan's model is limited to those factors that interfere with minimal sexual function and desire; Kaplan recognized that factors directly causing sexual problems could be made manifest through Masters and Johnson's sensate focus activities. In Kaplan's bypass model, evocation of unresolved issues was kept to the minimum necessary to obtain symptomatic sexual and marital improvement; even volatile relationship discord and other problems were ignored if they did not directly interfere with sexual function or interest. To the degree that Kaplan was concerned with sexual potential, she thought that only long-term psychoanalysis and resolution of oedipal conflicts offered that option:

> Our therapeutic approach to resistance generated by relationship problems is a conjoint version of the brief dynamic method we use for intrapsychic neurotic resistance, and based on similar premises. We actively support both partners and their commitment to the relationship. First we attempt to modify the immediate sources of friction between them, "bypassing" hidden, threatening relationship issues as much as possible. Therefore, the partner's individual problems are *not* confronted, reconceptualized or interpreted, no matter how blatant these seem, if they are not causing problems in the couple's relationship nor mobilizing resistances to treatment. (Kaplan, 1987, p. 126, italics original)

Apfelbaum's assumption about elicitation involving the acceptance of whatever the couple does rather than expectations of behavioral compliance seems rather straightforward; it is the same approach that is used in the sexual crucible. However, Kaplan's subsequent clarification of her notion of treatment "resistance" suggests that her approach is not consistent with Apfelbaum's assumption:

> Resistance has several meanings in the context of dynamic sex therapy. Resistance refers to the reluctance or refusal of patients or their partners to carry out their assignments. The term is also used when a patient is not open with the therapist during the sessions and withholds or distorts information. In the language of behaviorists, resistance denotes the failure of the patient's anxiety to diminish despite the fact that he has carried out the assigned desensitization tasks. And to the psychodynamically oriented clinician, the patient is resisting when he blocks or fails to remember significant dreams, memories, and associations, or when he "acts out" destructively outside the therapeutic setting. (Kaplan, 1987, p. 108)

Kaplan's (1987) notion of prescriptions for elicitation is further clouded by her discussion of the typical manifestations of resistance by patients with sexual panic states. In this she notes that doing the wrong assignment ("misunderstanding" directions), "overdoing" or "underdoing" the assignment, stopping the assignment "prematurely," putting oneself in a negative mental state, and trivializing gains constitute ways that the patient can "sabotage" prescribed activities. This construct of "resistance" is antithetical to the elicitation viewpoint that in doing things in a way that reflects some aspect of themselves, patients *facilitate* rather than defeat the purpose of the activities. Kaplan's conceptualization of resistance, her notion of patients' "defeating" behavioral suggestions, and her conceptualization of therapist suggestions as "assignments" imply the expectation of behavioral compliance with the therapist suggestions as "ordered."

> Resistances that express the patient's neurotic sexual conflicts and/or characterologic defenses are actively and relentlessly confronted as soon as they emerge. These confrontations and interpretations follow a progressively "deeper" course until the resistances are resolved.
> We begin by interrupting the immediately operating surface defenses against sexual gratification which the patient consciously recognizes and then proceed to confront increasingly more threatening and deeply buried unconscious material until treatment moves forward again. (Kaplan, 1987, p. 114)

Another curious aspect of Kaplan's view of elicitation concerns the most often cited characteristic of the approach: the notion of *bypassing*. Kaplan's treatment approach integrated prescribed behavioral exercises with psychotherapeutic exploration of intrapsychic defenses and resistances. Initially (Kaplan, 1974), her treatment of sexual dysfunctions involved relatively straightforward, cognitive-behavioral oriented interventions (sensate focus activities, as outlined by Masters and Johnson, and a ban on intercourse); psychoanalytically-oriented, insight-focused interpretations were used to deal with noncompliance. Over time, Kaplan (1979) modified her "psychosexual therapy" approach to deal with problems of sexual desire; treatment duration was lengthened and insight through brief psychoanalytic psychotherapy was given greater emphasis. However, Kaplan's intent to bypass all difficulties nonessential to rapid symptomatic improvement remained.

We can understand why Kaplan would propose a bypass model by looking at the state of the profession in the early 1970s, when *The New Sex Therapy* was written. For Kaplan, there already was a therapeutic crucible: psychoanalysis. Her intent was to broaden Masters and Johnson's cognitive-behavioral paradigm, adding conceptual depth and refocusing attention on underlying personality processes that had been ignored in the first blush of behavioral sex therapy. Kaplan was also educating her psychoanalytic colleagues about alternatives to long-term treatment and resolution of unconscious conflicts—while still honoring psychoanalytic doctrine. This latter focus is evident in the arguments she advanced in her initial publication:

> The concept of oedipal conflict and return of the repressed infantile conflicts is highly useful in clarifying otherwise puzzling clinical phenomena seen in cases like the one described. However, one may take issue with the contention that unresolved oedipal issues are the *only* cause of sexual conflict. Moreover, unre-solved oedipal material, even when present, does not always result in sexual symptoms. There is compelling clinical evidence that many persons who are burdened by unresolved infantile conflicts and oedipal neuroses are nevertheless able to function well sexually. (Kaplan, 1974, p. 143)

Kaplan's proposal that oedipal conflicts did not cause all sexual dysfunction was a remarkable notion at the time. Her work was a considerable step forward, and a rereading offers some perspective on how far the sex therapy field has come in the past 16 years:

> The first difference [of her *New Sex Therapy*] with the traditional viewpoint lies in the fact that the new approaches operate on the premise that it is primarily the "here and now" conflicts which require resolution and that basic personality conflicts that derive from childhood do not need to be resolved in order to cure the patient's sexual dysfunction. . . . Although, of course, we give recognition to the deeper source of the conflict, sex therapy does *not* ordinarily deal with this deeper structure unless this proves to be specifically necessary. . . . Thus, the therapist will *not* interpret and work with the patient's unconscious oedipal material even if this should be in evidence, unless such material cannot be "bypassed" and it presents palpable obstacles to sexual functioning or to the treatment procedure. (Kaplan, 1974, pp. 150–1)

Kaplan's unique implementation of elicitation and bypass derived from her attempts to contend with psychoanalytic concepts of "deep" unconscious con-flicts and repressed impulses. Her notion of bypassing oedipal conflicts is not surprising by contemporary practice in sexual and marital therapy; the vast majority of practitioners "bypass" oedipal issues with alacrity. On the other hand, bypassing individual, dyadic, or broader systemic issues that do not directly create sexual panic, disinterest, or dysfunction is the *antithesis* of sexual-marital therapy as a vehicle for human development. Kaplan was trying to bridge the gap between the options as she saw them at the time: intensive psychoanalysis or behavioral sex therapy. An intensive, broadly focused thera-py rooted in sexuality and intimacy, such as the sexual crucible, did not exist. It is no longer necessary to choose between working on issues of individual and relationship development vs. (utilitarian) sexuality. Moreover, bypassing has other often-overlooked implications.

In our previous discussion of sexual potential (Chapter Three), we pointed out that Kaplan's bypass approach and the sexual crucible differ with regard to the topic of intimacy. Kaplan taught patients to tune out their partner and focus on genital sensations and sexual fantasies. Her notion, "sex is composed of friction and fantasy" (1974, p. 122), is itself antithetical to notions of intimacy (and sexual potential). On the one hand, this is understandable considering that her position was formulated at a time when sex therapy was focused on dysfunction rather than intimacy; "bypass" was consistent with Masters and Johnson's emphasis on sensory awareness (rather than intimacy) in prescribing taking "turns" during sensate focus exercises. On the other hand, "bypassing" seems somewhat incompatible with awareness that intimacy intolerance was a common factor in inhibited sexual desire and sexual aversion, that is, unless Kaplan's intent was to bypass the intimacy intolerance as well.

Although these contradictions in Kaplan's approach have generally gone unnoticed, other pitfalls have not. Apfelbaum was one of the few clinicians who took issue with Kaplan's bypass approach, pointing out that her approach emphasized "functioning over feeling" (1983, p. 227). Apfelbaum also noted that Kaplan's bypass approach didn't take patients' preexisting sexual styles into account. Many patients had previously used a bypass approach to avoid intimacy during sex or to function sexually when the relationship was conflictual and stressed. By the time they sought treatment, their partner was intolerant of being bypassed further during sex. Moreover, patients who were sensitive to "context" during sex could not be taught to bypass; for those people, bypassing caused guilt and vulnerability to distractions.

Apfelbaum (1977a, 1983) suggested an alternative: *counter-bypassing*. Counter-bypassing is an alternative sexual script which involves broadening rather then narrowing awareness; it encourages patients to focus on the same experiences that the good bypasser can successfully tune out. Obviously, counter-bypassing is more compatible with our own focus on intimacy and sexual potential.

Apfelbaum (1977a, 1983) referred to Kaplan's theoretical orientation as *depth analysis*. Apfelbaum contended that "depth" interpretations of unconscious conflicts (e.g., retarded ejaculation as a defense against urges to "soil" the woman with semen and the fear of usurping and castrating other men) missed the cause of sexual dysfunctions. Apfelbaum didn't dispute that an individual might have such impulses; instead, he disagreed with the utility of impulse-level conceptualization and intervention in sex therapy. Moreover, Apfelbaum took issue with the view of ego defenses:

> To say that you *repress* disowned parts of yourself causes all kinds of mystification because it represents the ego as being *able* to handle these experiences, i.e., to control them and keep them selectively out of awareness. It seems more appropriate to represent the ego as unable to cope rather than as capable of deviousness and subtlety. (1983, p. 91)

Apfelbaum proposed that sexual dysfunctions weren't caused by repressed impulses. Fears of castration or performance anxiety per se were not the problem, he thought; the problem was the sense that one was wrong to feel these things. Apfelbaum was concerned about the absence of a sense of "entitlement" to one's difficulties. Apfelbaum perceived two causes of sexual dysfunction: an inability to bypass existing interferences combined with performance-anxiety anxiety. He developed a treatment approach that emphasized ego deficits in validating oneself, rather than unconscious impulses per se; he described his approach as *ego-analysis*:

> When the depth therapist arrives at the idea that the retarded ejaculator is intimidated by other men, the treatment strategy is to work on that problem. But, to the ego analyst the problem is not that the patient is intimidated by other men, but that he is *afraid* of being intimidated by other men. That's what *repression* means. If he could allow himself to be intimidated by other men, he would simply experience this directly. He would not be inhibited in competition or dream of losing his teeth.
>
> This is often a hard idea to grasp because it just seems like this man must be helped to *not* feel vulnerable and intimidated. But this idea plays right into *his own* belief that he should not have such "weaknesses." To help someone accept feeling scared of the opposite sex runs into mental health norms that most therapists share. According to these norms you shouldn't be afraid of people. The trouble is that this is that very belief that causes these fears to be experienced indirectly. (1983, p. 89)

Apfelbaum's point was that, even if the clinician correctly identified the fear of women as a cause of difficulty, the "pathologizing" of this very factor caused the man to self-reject and alienate himself from his own experience. Some clinicians might suggest that the man would have fewer problems if he could not feel what he feels. While commonsensical, this position is paradoxically counterproductive. Even if the goal *were* to reduce his fear of women, the more appropriate strategy might be to first help normalize these dynamics. Although there are exceedingly few men who do *not* harbor fears of women (many of whom have utilitarian *genital* functioning), clinicians don't often normalize what they believe to be pathogenic.

Apfelbaum pointed out the important difference between "accepting the patient's feelings" (to use the popular jargon of the day) and believing in their *validity*. He noted:

> When we say that our goal is to help patients to accept or to "have" a feeling, we mean that our goal is to help them to see that it has its validity. This contrasts with the depth therapist's interest in proving that a feeling is invalid—that it is inappropriate. (1983, p. 92)

Apfelbaum noted the similarity between his "entitlement" approach and that of the Mental Research Institute in prescribing the symptom. However, he made the important distinction that the MRI approach is a paradoxical injunction to double bind the individual to abandon the performance anxiety, whereas his approach does *not* try to remove that feeling from the patient. Apfelbaum discussed the reaction of therapists who attend his workshops in this regard:

> In talking to the whole range of psychotherapists we discovered that we could think that we were talking about the context of sex, about relationships, about the motivations for sex, and about sexual systems, only to find that there were therapists in the audience who didn't think we were talking about these things at all. I also said that we found the opposite reaction . . . some therapists would think that they got the idea right away and that we were just belaboring a simple point. They would say: "You help people to accept their feelings, to believe that their feelings are OK. And that's good. But *then* what do you do? Suppose the impotent man does learn that it is OK to be afraid of women or to hate women? What do you do next? How do you help him to feel less afraid or angry?"
>
> At first we found this response puzzling. Then we realized that we were being heard from within the depth analytic paradigm. Helping the patient to feel OK about a feeling is a limited goal for the depth therapist because for the depth therapist the feeling is likely to be *ultimately* not OK. (1983, p. 91)

For Apfelbaum, the sense of entitlement is the *whole* of the treatment. The role of elicitation in Apfelbaum's model is to determine the aspect of self the patient has difficulty validating; it does not extend to a growth model of intimacy and eroticism. Counter-bypassing focuses on sexual dysfunction rather than broad-band personal development. In fact, Apfelbaum (1990) suggested that one-session treatment was his ideal.

Apfelbaum encouraged people to "be themselves" in order to avoid encouraging change out of self-rejection. Although his points are cogent in regard to the common practice of sexual and marital therapy, there is a potential pitfall in this approach; focusing therapy on entitlement alone can be shortsighted. A sense of entitlement can easily stem from narcissism, defiance, and immaturity. *Differentiation*, rather than entitlement, is necessary to face the adversities of living and loving.

THE VIEW THROUGH THE WINDOW

Sexology, as it applies to humans, is generally defined as the study of human sexuality. Even studying the sexual behavior of lower species is thought ultimately to shed light on human behavior. But perhaps sexology should be thought of as the study of human beings (in the broader sense) *through* their sexuality. One patient couple remarked after several sessions:

> Now we understand how you *use* sex in therapy. You are looking at our sexuality to understand us and see us in ways we didn't even realize existed and couldn't articulate. It makes sense since sex is so personal; looking at sexual styles and attitudes gives you a very personal view of us.

A couple's (and an individual's) sexual style is a naturally occurring window into current adjustment, contemporary life concerns, and unresolved emotional development. There is greater predictive reliability in extrapolating about the broader aspects of patients' lives from their sexual styles than vice versa. Herein lies one of the great inherent contradictions between modern sexual and marital therapy approaches and an elicitation paradigm. If the couple's sexual and nonsexual activities are routinely channeled into stereotypic "homework assignments," there is little possibility of seeing the more subtle aspects of their lives when looking through the window of their sexuality.

In an elicitation framework the therapist does not teach patients behavioral "techniques." Rather, patients teach themselves, as well as the therapist, through their own sexual behavior. Suggestions may be given, but later in treatment than in behaviorally oriented approaches and with the anticipation that the couple will modify the suggestions in salient ways that reflect the broader aspects of their lives. The distinction between a "homework assignment" and a suggestion is crucial in this regard.

The sexual crucible is not merely a paradigm for organizing the therapist's experience and behavior. It is a *patient* paradigm as well. The therapist must *demonstrate the use* of the elicitation window of sexual behavior and invite patients to collaborate in watching and using it. The first inklings of this process begin in the debriefing and interpretation of explicit descriptions of patients' sexual behavior. Eventually, patients learn how to use this window into themselves, producing insight without therapist interpretation. Treatment is less likely to lapse into intellectualizations and interpretations of "why" and "what" if the "how" of patient's emotional experience is used.

The development of a personally significant context for sexual activities is fundamental to construction of the sexual crucible. This is the antithesis of the position that one's sexual behavior is merely an adaptation to expectations from one's partner, one's culture, biology, or "normality." In accepting one's sexual behavior and experience as a reflection of oneself (even if contrary to conscious intent) one begins to "see" oneself. In the process of conjoint sexual-marital therapy, one is also "seen" by one's partner.

You may begin to note the growing relevance of the distinction between level-1 and level-2 intimacy (Chapters Four and Five) to constructing the sexual crucible. Level 2 is a "crucible model of intimacy": the ability to self-disclose and self-validate in the absence of validation or presence of disconfirmation from the partner. It is a disquieting and challenging task for most people.

Level-2 intimacy fits quite nicely—much better in fact than level-1—with an elicitation model of sexuality. The use of sexual behavior as a window—the *knowing* participation in the inherent self-disclosure of sexual behavior—is obviously consistent with the expectation that one had best be able to take care of oneself. Ironically, what is often elicited in the crucible is the reality that the spouses ascribe to level-1 expectations of validation and reciprocity and do not want to be known, sexually or otherwise.

For the masses of people who quest for a reflected sense of self (i.e., level-1 intimacy), establishing preferred sexual behaviors and styles as a significant self-reflection is a powerful framework. This develops from judicious collaboration in which spouses learn not only "what" the therapist looks at, but also "how" the therapist looks at them. Herein lies the issue of the therapist's utilization of an asset or deficit model of treatment (a point we will return to shortly). The development of a personally significant context (i.e., an elicitation approach) accomplishes several goals:

- Within the treatment alliance, it creates a paradigm shift that redefines "success" in physical contact and reduces performance anxiety about genital functioning.

- On the dyadic level, it facilitates the use of the couple's sexual activities as a collaborative laboratory in which significant data (other than "pass" or "fail") emerge.
- On the individual level, it facilitates the development of an observing ego.
- Redefining sexuality as a process in which spouses see (and change) themselves establishes a framework that inherently involves self-confrontation and self-disclosure in the presence of the partner (i.e., our working definition of intimacy, developed in Chapter Five).
- An elicitation approach defines marital sexuality (and sexual-marital therapy) as an intimacy-based process, setting the stage for struggles of differentiation and the emergence of level-2 intimacy.

Teaching patients the concept of differentiation often has minimal utility; framing it as *personal integrity*, however, is often intensely impactful. Patients are often shocked when therapists raise the issue of integrity. For one thing, sex therapists are always suspect of placing the importance of sexual gratification above personal integrity and values; marital therapists are similarly suspect of valuing compromise and marital continuity above integrity. For another thing, integrity in the sexual domain is often misperceived as concerning what one *won't* do; rarely is it perceived as the willingness to look at oneself through the style and content of what one *currently* does, or the struggle to *expand* one's repertoire.

Often patients ask, "What does integrity have to do with sexuality and intimacy?"; upon reflection, they are shocked by their own question. It is exactly such an attitude that they expect a sex therapist to have.

The use of sexuality as a vehicle of self-discovery in the presence of the partner is a matter of personal integrity. Integrity is the fundamental determinant of level-2 marital intimacy. An elicitation approach to sexual-marital therapy challenges spouses' integrity; it is the pathway into the sexual crucible.

THE SEXUAL CRUCIBLE DEFINED

There are two meanings to the term "crucible," each surprisingly relevant to the processes of treatment to be described. The first, more obvious meaning is derived from chemistry and metallurgy. A crucible is a highly nonreactive ("refractory") vessel in which a transfiguring reaction takes place. Raw materials are placed in the crucible, to which heat, pressure, or some other catalyst is added. Crucibles are used when the final desired result is not merely an additive mixture of ingredients; there is a catalytic process that creates a *qualitatively* different final product. In industry, crucibles are commonly used in the creation of high grade steel and alloys of unusual strength, which actually differ in quality from the raw ingredients themselves.

The crucible participates in the metamorphosis of the ingredients by *containing* the reaction so that the qualitative changes can occur. The crucible must have a lower coefficient of reactivity (e.g., a higher melting point) than the ingredients placed in it; moreover, its degree of inertness must be higher than that required for the intended reaction. Said differently, the crucible must be nonreactive to the specific ingredients it will contain as well as to the process itself. Depending on the nature of these two variables and their unique interaction, a particular crucible might be appropriate for some uses and not for others.

The second meaning of a crucible is that of a severe test or hard trial. *Webster's* dictionary gives the example of "His probity was tried in the *crucible* of temptation and poverty" (p. 437). This secondary meaning is closely associated with the crucifixion of Christ, both in the act of crucifixion and the notion of a test. It refers to the experience of Christ on the cross, feeling forsaken by God (e.g., experiencing "fears of abandonment" and existential loneliness), and enduring unbearable pain. Ultimately, Christ transcends his separateness, forging a new relationship with God and with himself.

The story of Christ's crucible is an apt metaphor for the transition from level-1 to level-2 intimacy. You may remember from our prior discussion of intimacy (Chapter Four), that one definition of differentiation was the ability to tolerate pain for growth. People often feel their partner is out to crucify them, that the marriage is a trial designed to test their breaking point, and that the decisions they face are absolutely untenable, overwhelmingly anxiety-producing, and excruciating.

Both views of the crucible involve the notion of *metamorphosis*. The spiritual view addresses patients' subjective experience, and their trials of integrity. The metallurgical view focuses on clinical purpose and process and the therapists' integrity. A crucible is often baked or tempered prior to its use, in order to attain the necessary degree of nonreactivity. If the crucible reacts or participates in the metamorphosis, the final product is contaminated; the result contains unique properties of the crucible's flaws in *reaction* to the specific qualities of the intended ingredients.

Nonreactivity is only one necessary quality of the crucible. The other requisite is structural integrity. When some aspect of the process is lost due to the crucible's lack of structural integrity, the "leak" determines, in part, the properties of the (unintended) outcome. The therapist's integrity, like patients' integrity, is a vital aspect of treatment in the sexual crucible.

The sexual crucible is an approach to sexual-marital therapy in which the therapist and the therapeutic alliance function as the nonreactive container for patients' transformation. The clinician participates in the therapeutic process by being highly involved and invested, but also by *not* participating in highly specific ways. The therapist's capacity to be nonreactive while remaining highly involved is another manifestation of a high degree of differentiation. From this perspective, it becomes obvious that therapists cannot help patients achieve a higher degree of differentiation than they themselves have reached.[2]

A Brief Example of a Sexual Crucible

A perfect example surfaces through the auspices of Bell Telephone. Recently, I have been consulted by men who spend considerable amounts of time and money on commercial "sex-talk" telephone services. The consultation is often occasioned by an angry and upset wife, who is disturbed and threatened by this practice. Characteristically, the calls are made from the home telephone, making eventual discovery of the calls inevitable.

Consider the typical case of Mike and Virginia, both age 36. Virginia starts off the session with the premise that she is open to any reasonable, healthy form of sexual contact; she cannot understand the need for her husband's "kinky" or "sneaky" behavior. Mike tends to agree with this premise, stating that their sexual relationship is "fine," and looks confused about his own motivations. Mike suggests that he might be a "sex addict," to which the wife eagerly agrees. When asked what a "sex addict" is, he states that he doesn't know, but his wife suggested he might be one and he thought it might be true.

Both Mike and Virginia, in their own ways, promote the notion that the problem is *inside* him (i.e., the telephone behavior and a hypothetical disease process that motivates it). Nothing in this observation, or in the following paragraphs, should suggest that Mike's sexuality is organized in a way that ultimately facilitates his sexual potential. Indeed, there is much to suggest it isn't. However, the couple promotes the view that *all* their problems, individually and conjointly, revolve around Mike's telephone calls.

Just a little probing reveals that Mike has great difficulty disclosing and maintaining himself with his spouse, particularly regarding (but not limited to) his erotic prefer-

---

[2]This will be discussed further when the therapist's role in treatment is considered in detail in Chapters Thirteen and Sixteen.

ences. For her own part, Virginia is defensive about her husband's behavior, demonstrating her general proclivity to take what other people think and do (particularly her husband) as a reflection upon *her*. Her prototypic solution has been to control the superficial construct of their marriage, while Mike's has been to maintain a hidden identity they have tacitly agreed not to acknowledge. They communicate about not communicating: Mike generally doesn't say what Virginia doesn't want to hear. He can do more or less what he wants as long as he doesn't talk about it. In return, Virginia complains that Mike doesn't "communicate" with her, referring to the verbal dimension of their exchanges.

Mike and Virginia's sexual relationship is merely *functional*; neither have overt genital dysfunctions. The sexual style is romantic but at a less-than-profound depth. The permissible dimensions of sexual expression within the relationship are not those most salient to Mike. He is thoroughly bored with their sexual relationship; he prefers more role enactment and experimentation, and masturbates to fantasies of erotically aggressive women.

However, Mike has a hard time validating his preferences with Virginia. Verbal aggressiveness during sex "offends" her, and she is uncomfortable with both giving and receiving oral sex. Mike has pushed for oral sex several times over the course of their marriage, but her passivity and anxiety are so antithetical to the style of partner he craves that he has given up in anger and frustration. As far as Virginia is concerned, she has given it a good try, doesn't like it, and is entitled to her preferences.

Mike acknowledges fantasies about sex with other women. Virginia suspects he may have had casual sexual encounters during the course of their 12-year marriage, but he denies it. They have sex about three times a month, at Virginia's initiation, which is all the sexual release she desires.

Mike masturbates three to four times a week, using a *Playboy* from the collection he "hides" in a shelf in the garage. When Virginia confronted Mike about why he "needed pornography," Mike folded: he "could not explain it." Virginia finds it upsetting when Mike masturbates, so he does it surreptitiously. She does not understand why he "needs it" so often, and reiterates that she doesn't think Mike's interest in sex is healthy.

Virginia is also upset when she finds new copies of *Penthouse* tucked in a bookcase near their bathroom. When confronted, Mike says he will stop bringing such material into the home, but doesn't. Virginia sees this as "disrespectful": Mike knows that she does not approve of such material and does not want it in the house. Virginia agrees to let him keep the magazines in the garage, high on a shelf where no one is likely to see it accidently. Virginia is afraid that her 13-year-old niece, who visits her about four times a year, might be traumatized by it.

While it is easy to see that Virginia plays the overt role of the controlling mother to Mike's behavior as a defiant little boy, it is harder to see that she also functions like a pseudo-mature, overresponsible little girl. Virginia complains that Mike is emotionally unavailable, secretive, and untrustworthy. Mike complains that Virginia is emotionally labile, in need of constant reassurance, and extremely controlling. Both seem to see some of the other's limitations, but neither sees him/herself.

It rapidly becomes clear that, although Mike's phone sex may be an avoidance of intimacy with Virginia, she also wishes to avoid an escalation of eroticism and broadening of intimacy in the bedroom. Virginia has a style of talking about "intimacy" and "tenderness" that makes Mike's blood boil: He can intuit the death knell of intense eroticism in her requests. His preoccupation with his anger and fantasies leave him unaware that Virginia is no more available to him during sex than he is to her.

While Virginia may be accurate that Mike likes his sex "dirty" and "base," her notion of "making love" is pristine and disinfected of any hint of aggression or "fucking." Mike has not been able to integrate his heart with his genitals; Virginia has not reconciled her genitals with her heart.

Every time Mike expresses a sexual interest, Virginia confronts him about why he "needs it." This puts Mike on the defensive, and allows Virginia to avoid what she has difficulty with. Virginia wants Mike to stop the telephone behavior. She also wants him to give up the preferences that push her to the uncomfortable limits of her own sexual repertoire. Virginia wants *two* choices where, at best, she might be able to get *one*.

There is no passion, no wallop in their sexual transactions. Virginia is uncomfortable with eroticism and intense desire; she wants romance, but doesn't want sex to be wet or noisy. She says she wants intercourse to be "something personal between them"; she doesn't, however, want Mike seeing her while they copulate. Mike is more comfortable with eroticism, but only if he keeps it separate from salient attachment. It is questionable if he would really let Virginia participate in the sex games he fantasizes about.

Neither spouse wants the other "looking inside his/her head" during sex. Mike still maintains the whore/madonna split, and for her part, Virginia does too. Ironically, it is not only where they differ that gives them trouble, as where they implicitly *agree*.

Before going further, a comment regarding the description of Mike and Virginia's sexual styles is in order. Some readers may find the characterizations to be moralistic and value laden. The point is not whether or not such terms are value laden—they are. The *real* question is whether or not this is "bad."

These are the terms that exist in the spouses' thoughts, although they are not often uttered openly (e.g., dirty, prissy, sleazy, disinfected); they have significant unique secondary meanings beyond social gender politics. In the parlance of Ericksonian hypnosis, these labels are anchored in patient's preexisting reality. It is exactly this value-laden quality that give the terms therapeutic utility.

The reflexive demand for "politically correct" phraseology illustrates an important point. For the therapist, walking headlong into the maelstrom of competing accusations and counter-claims is an act of clinical integrity. When therapists become more concerned with "political correctness" than pursuing the couple into the recesses of their metacommunication, treatment develops blind spots in both content and process. Clinicians' efforts to be "value free," moreover, epitomize the common complaint that therapists promote sexuality lacking value (or common sense). This does not, however, license disparaging attitudes on the therapist's part.

In point of fact, Mike *did* like his sex "dirty" and "base" — part of the problem was that he was *defensive* about it (e.g., lacking the feeling of *entitlement*, to use Apfelbaum's terminology). Mike's defensiveness about liking "naughty" sex kept him from pursuing a change in the style of sex he had with Virginia. It also kept him from recognizing his fear of women and his unwillingness to make peace with their eroticism.

Neither spouse's sexual style is inherently problematic; from Mosher's discussion of three dimensions of sexual styles, one might argue that the ability to use *both styles* is indicative of sexual development (Chapter Three). It is the *rigidity* and *narrowness* of each spouse's sexual style, rather than the style per se, that reflects immaturity.

Some therapists might think that the description of Virginia is pejorative, suggesting she is merely trying to cope with feeling "used" by her husband. Such readers are referred back to the prior discussion regarding complaints of usury (Chapter Three). Mike lacks the nerve to use her *well* (like he imagines he could do with a Playboy centerfold); if anything, he uses Virginia poorly. Virginia doesn't want to be used poorly *or* well; she objects to the very notion that she might want to be used at all: She is afraid to enter the mind set in which the concept of using a sexual partner well brings an appreciative smile to many men and women; she defends herself by framing the situation as an issue of women's equality, self-respect, and social exploitation and sexualization. When Virginia points to these very salient and pressing problems, she wields them like a cudgel to keep Mike (and the therapist) on the defense to ward off being confronted.

Construction of the Crucible

So much for background material on the case, which demonstrates the use of the elicitation "window" of sexuality. How does this become a sexual crucible? In two ways:

- introducing the couple to the notion of sexuality as a window and,
- the formulation of two separate but interlocking individual conflicts (crucibles).

In this case, I declared my willingness to see the couple for another session but refused to treat the man as an "addict." If they wanted Mike to be treated as a "addict," I was happy to refer him to another therapist who advertised this type of therapy. I also declined to take a stand on the degree of pathology inherent in calling a telephone sex-talk service or looking at erotica, per se. Beyond the strategic advantage of such an initial position, I simply could not ascertain, at the outset, the degree of compulsive erotic motivation to engage in the phone calls. At least some of the motivation for the calls was nongenital in nature:

- defiance of his wife's control,
- expression of anger at being "deprived" of the sexual style he wanted in his marriage,
- enjoyment of his wife's discomfort, and
- gratification of playing "hide and seek" and "getting away with something" with his wife.

Until these factors were removed, it was hard to tell how much desire there was for the purely erotic gratification derived from the telephone calls.

I offered to help Mike stop buying printed or auditory erotica if he so desired or, alternatively, to help him stop sneaking around about it. For Virginia, I agreed that she was entitled to not be exposed to this material or to such problems in her life. Neither person had to give himself/herself up to meet the preferences of the partner.

Later in the first session, I deliberately made an out-of-context statement. I looked at Mike and stated that it was clear he was used to dealing with people who, he felt, wanted to control him. Mike acknowledged that this was true of his parents; he felt his mother was particularly intrusive and controlling. But Mike was startled and wanted to know how I figured this out. I said that it was clear from looking at his sexual style. The passive-aggressive sadism involved in using his phone calls to upset his wife was mirrored in his sexual fantasies, in which he openly dominated and manipulated women into having sex with him. Mike was pretty much a coward in other aspects of his life, including (and especially) with his parents. Mike was surprised and impressed that sex could have some value other than "good or bad."

It was clear that the *style* emerging around the general area of sexuality also reflected Virginia's restricted development; her defensiveness and extreme reactivity, however, suggested that timing and pacing were of the utmost importance. The problem here was that the elicitation window was *too* revealing. Virginia would simply not tolerate, at present, seeing herself through her sexual relationship with Mike. She was presenting herself in treatment as the betrayed party—and as a resource for Mike's treatment. If she were to enter into an alliance as a patient, it would not be to work on her own immaturity and lack of differentiation. It would first occur by focusing on problems in her life presented by her husband's behavior.

In what way, I asked, did it make a difference to her that her husband looked at pictures of women or called phone services? He seemingly spent income he had earned and in about the same amount as she spent on her own separate activities. He did not deprive her of sex, and made his phone calls or looked at his pictures outside of her physical presence. The point of the question was not to validate or defend the husband's behavior, but rather to address its relevance to *her*.

I suggested that she was, in general, always working to uphold the image that others might have of her and that she took her husband's behavior as a reflection upon herself. At first Virginia agreed with the former statement and disagreed with the latter. But then she recognized that they were one and the same, and asked how I figured that out when she had not. It was inherent in their overall sexual style, I pointed out. Virginia was curious about what else I saw in their sexual style.

I suggested that it was understandable that she was frequently wondering what Mike was doing, since she allowed him to control her feelings of adequacy by simply picking up the phone and calling someone else. I pointed out the paradox in Virginia's complaint that Mike was acting in what she considered to be a deviant, untrustworthy, and possibly "sick" way. If that were the case, then why was she overtly and deliberately putting her adequacy and sense of well-being in the hands (and the phone) of a (from her perspective) deviant, sick, and untrustworthy person? Moreover, why did she act as though she would be helpless to take care of her feelings until he was "cured"?[3]

Virginia was immediately on the defensive. However, rather than suggesting that she was contradicting herself (as she anticipated), I suggested that there was a *good* explanation for this. Moreover, I stated that although we didn't know exactly what it was (yet), she would know a very powerful piece of information about herself when she understood the answer to this question. In point of fact, I was laying the groundwork for the family-of-origin work that I knew would surface for her in the near future.

This mollified Virginia for the moment. I shifted my attention back to Mike, indicating my willingness to support his right to look at erotica or make phone calls to commercial telephone sex services. That is to say, if Mike thought there was something problematic to address with his sexual preferences, I would be glad to assist. But if the issue was whether or not Mike would superficially agree to use his penis only in ways that his wife permitted and then use it surreptitiously in other ways, then he would have little foundation to stand on (phallic pun intended) if he wanted to renegotiate his sexual relationship with his wife.

---

[3]This is an example of inherent paradox, to be discussed shortly.

I suggested, moreover, that Mike would continue to be afraid that someone would try to control him, as long as he failed to demonstrate openly that he was in control of himself. To conclude on a positive note, I opined that, since Mike seemed smart enough to know that Virginia would find out about the phone calls if he made them from home, then he was either incredibly lazy or ready to use the inevitable confrontation as a way of precipitating a very necessary and long-overdue crisis that would help them grow—that is, a crisis in the marriage and an individual crisis for both of them.

As I anticipated, this brought forth threats from Virginia that she was thinking of leaving Mike. Moreover, she suggested that there was little point in her remaining in treatment with him.

I suggested I would help her get control of his behavior, his impulses, or control him to control his impulses, if she thought that was the solution. However, I was openly offering the same type of choices and assistance to her husband; so, while I would help her to control him (or help her help him to help himself, as she might prefer to label it), I would also help Mike get over the sense that she could control him. On the other hand, I would be glad to help her get control of herself, directly, and not have to control him to modulate her own reactivity.[4]

Moreover, I suggested that the possibility of divorce actually seemed to argue *for* conjoint treatment. That was to say, she would be able to either leave or stay more comfortably when Mike's behavior was no longer a personal reflection upon her, but rather just a matter of preference on which they might still disagree. The very dynamic that made her need to control his behavior also made it impossible for her to truly consider divorce: the negative reflection it might cast upon her. While she thought that he was an "addict," she was similarly trapped by her inability to function in anything more than a reflected sense of herself, and was subject to control by those whose validation she sought.

Once again, I suggested, the problem was not where the spouses disagreed, but rather, where they implicitly agreed: the confusion of issues of "privacy" with *hiding*. Both Mike and Virginia were highly fused with each other, as well as with their respective families of origin. There is no privacy for individuals of low differentiation—only hiding from partners, parents, and the world.

Both spouses feared that the price of maintaining personal integrity was the demise of the marriage. They didn't realize that without it, there would be no true marriage at all. Mike and Virginia began to feel the emotional impact

---

[4]The reader should note that one aspect of this multi-dimensional intervention focuses on enhancing differentiation.

of rapid construction of the sexual crucible. The lid of the crucible snapped tight when I refused to let them depend on me. I suggested that they not trust what I had deciphered from the little they had told me about their sexuality. Each could hold onto himself/herself by looking through the elicitation window: I encouraged them to go home and watch their interactions around the topic of sex in general, and with regard to the phone calls and magazines in particular. If there was validity to my interpretations, they would probably see it for themselves. If so, that might not change their behavior or their feelings yet. Alternatively, it might allow them to begin to see their respective dilemmas and possibly figure out a new way for each to get control of himself/herself. On the other hand, the supporting data might not be there, or they might miss it. In any event, Mike and Virginia were free to make or postpone any decisions they wanted; they would have to live with the outcome.

Constructing the Crucible, But Not the Bind

Construction of a sexual crucible is a differentiation-enhancing multidimensional intervention, combining the best elements of systemic rituals and object relations issues within the present-day context. In the initial stages of treatment, the crucible effect is first experienced in the therapist's office through in-session interactions with the couple. Soon the sexual crucible expands to the emotional boundaries of the therapist's alliance with the couple. It progressively permeates patients' interactions at home (including the bedroom and living room), eventually encompassing all aspects of patient's interactions with extended family and friends.

Notice that the telephone service is not the crucible, although it might appear to be the catalyst. The catalytic situation is always there, but a nonproductive one up to and including the time that patients initially seek out a therapist. It is only when the therapist redefines the two interlocking but individual conflicts that the crucible begins to emerge. Heretofore, each partner attempted to avoid his/her crucible by insisting that the partner modify himself/herself, thereby modulating the situation below critical mass for a metamorphic reaction.[5] If the therapist attempts to defuse the escalating situa-

---

[5]The reader may wonder about the distinction between conceptualizing two separate crucibles vs. two individuals coming togther in a single crucible. Clinically, the notion of two *interlocking* crucibles seems to be the most helpful. The disadvantage of conceptualizing one crucible lies in reinforcing patients' common notion of "we are in the same boat"; two interlocking crucibles reinforce the differentiation-enhancing awareness that each spouse enters marriage with his/her own conflicts which cannot be resolved through accommodation by the partner. The two-crucible mode, moreover,

tion by encouraging negotiation, the result is a *mixture* or fusion rather than a personal metamorphosis. If either spouse attempts to maintain his or her structural (emotional) integrity by removing himself/herself from the relationship, the potential reactivity continues into the future. This is not to suggest that it is never appropriate to divorce – sometimes it is. However, the utility of divorce is a function of dynamic history and timing. (This latter point will be considered more fully in Chapters Twelve, Thirteen, and Sixteen.)

At this point, our crucible metaphor of psychotherapy requires a more sophisticated distinction between metallurgy and psychotherapy. In metallurgy, the end product is an alloy involving a fusion of the ingredients, wherein each loses its separate identity and characteristics. In the therapeutic crucible, each of the ingredients (i.e., the two individuals) actually undergoes a metamorphic reaction in which one or both modify their respective identities and properties, but *they do not fuse.* At the outset of treatment, the problem is often that the couple is *thoroughly* fused; attempts at negotiation lead to greater fusion. As the crucible process continues the couple becomes *un*fused, each individual reducing his/her reactivity to the other. The couple's relationship itself becomes the crucible for further development, now and in the future.

The therapist is not the catalytic agent. There is no need for this, since the patients' current life situation contains a far better catalyst. The therapist and the therapy simply become the container in which the reaction takes place. The catalyst is usually a naturally occurring reality of adult life that most people "pathologize." In containing the preexisting players and working within the dynamics of the patients' presenting complaints, the therapist and the therapeutic alliance incorporate the necessary ingredients for developmental alchemy.

Sometimes patients suggest that the therapist is the *crucifier*. While that notion is upsetting to patients (and often, to the therapist), it is less upsetting than the notion that the dynamics of the patient's life (condensed over time), rather than the therapist, constitute the crucible. If the therapist were the crucifier, it would be a simple matter to just fire him or her. But there is still the crucible of the praxis of their lives.

The sexual crucible approach is not an educational model in which the therapist explains or "educates" the patient. Instead, it is a somewhat Zen-like

---

underscores the need to construct a personally relevant context for each spouse connecting family-of-origin and contemporary issues.

Having said this, conceptualizing a single crucible sometimes helps therapists recognize the interlocking (systemic) aspects of spouses' individual dilemmas.

approach involving the use of the current situation to focus on an *experience* that patients have actually spent a considerable portion of their lives building for themselves. It is the experience, *not the therapist*, that "teaches."

Constructing a sexual crucible does not involve the therapist's constructing paradoxical binds or giving prescriptive or proscriptive "homework assignments" in the manner of modern sex or marital therapy. The requisite custom-tailored conundrums that patients both need and avoid preexist in their presenting situation. *Inherent paradox* (Chapter Fifteen) is far more elegant and useful than any paradox the therapist could construct. In the sexual crucible, what is required of the therapist is detailed examination of, and respect for, patients' presenting complaints and the details of their sexual style. Generally, the critical developmental tasks reflected in both are one and the same.

Herein lies another irony of the sexual crucible. In containing the current presenting problem and not venting pressure or heat, treatment permits patients' developmental processes to reach critical mass. *Yet, the reason patients most often enter therapy is to reduce the heat or pressure in their situation.* The request for "treatment" is often just another attempt to *avoid* or diffuse the situation, rather than a request for assistance in going *through* it. When therapists fail to recognize this common motivation, they are surprised when patients abruptly terminate treatment with the complaint that the therapist "is not helping" or "is making them worse."

Couples generally do not enter therapy until the anticipated negatives of treatment appear less than the experienced and anticipated negatives of their current situation. One role of the therapist is to help patients stay in the crucible of their own situations, not out of masochism or fusion, but rather to help them "cook themselves" until they have accomplished the developmental metamorphosis at hand. The crucible is "constructed" when patients see the possibility that the solution to their dilemma is to *use* the dilemma instead of looking for a way around it.

The inability or unwillingness to deal with anxiety is one of the major *meta-problems* that transcend specific situation or symptomatology. This hallmark of low differentiation often takes two relevant forms: the inability to remain non-anxious in the presence of the anxiety in significant others and the unwillingness to tolerate anxiety for personal growth.

People attempt to avoid the crucible of their lives by acting as if they have the choice of tolerating anxiety or not. In reality, the choice is not between anxiety vs. no anxiety, but rather between the anxiety that things will change vs. the anxiety they will stay the same. One can choose not to choose, but then other people will usually make choices that directly affect one's life.

People want *two* choices at one time, but all they get is *one*. Often they attempt to make one decision to follow their desires and another to avoid the ramifications of that decision. Or they try to exercise one option for themselves, and to prevent their partner from exercising his/her option.

Well, what if the patient doesn't want to be under heat and pressure? Does anyone? It is not the therapist's job to make the patient choose. The patient is welcome to continue trying to find a way around it. (Sometimes the patient does find a new, previously unrecognized option.) The nonreactive but involved therapist in the sexual crucible might respond:

> Well, you don't have to have the pressure or anxiety of therapy, but take a look at your situation and the inability to get beyond it. While you have been avoiding doing things that make you feel pressured, you haven't been exactly anxiety or pressure free. Moreover, you are also feeling the anxiety that, if you don't move ahead, things will stay the same, and that is becoming more worrisome.
>
> If you think the solution is to find some new way around the situation, I will be glad to help if I can. But that assumes that I am smarter or "more objective" than you are, and that your dilemma is a function of insufficient intelligence or objectivity.
>
> On the other hand, there is nothing wrong with subjectivity, because you are going to have to live with whatever decision you make, and you will experience it subjectively. And I am not sure that there is a way around this, because you haven't found one yet. Perhaps you might want my assistance in going *through* your dilemma. So take your choice . . . or not, as you choose. . . .

There is a truism familiar to many therapists: people would rather fight with their partner than fight with themselves. However, the corollary that underlies this observation is even more telling: A spouse would rather believe that it is his/her partner who is depriving him/her than recognize that he/she is banging his/her head against reality. In the latter case, the individual realizes that the partner is often as trapped as he/she is, and *can't* offer a way out; each person is in a struggle with himself/herself. That is the crucible of human relationships. Being progressively confronted with such a truth stimulates increased differentiation and relationship with self.

Does Sex Take Work?

For some people, climbing a mountain is unthinkable work; for others it is a vacation. Sometimes therapists tell people to fantasize in advance "to prime the pump" for having sex with their partner; this is fun for some, and burdensome and ineffective for others. "Work" is not inherent in a behavior, and a behavior is not work simply because it requires effort. Work for the workaholic is play, and *not* working takes work.

The man whose wife refuses to wear a negligee because "her body should be beautiful enough as it is" often wants her to work more at sex. The woman whose husband goes to sleep after he quickly ejaculates often wishes he would work more at sex. When we think of a romantic interlude with food, beverage, nice music, and surroundings, we are fantasizing about sex that takes work. People watch sex on TV soap operas because it depicts sexual settings that require considerable effort to set up, while gratifying fantasies that sex involves no work at all.

Inherent paradoxes about "working at sex" often result from half-truths embedded in contemporary culture. Masters and Johnson revolutionized prevailing emphasis on toilsome foreplay by suggesting that working at *genital response* is ineffective. That message has been beneficial to many people – working at what is a natural biological response is paradoxically counterproductive. And yet, there are others who are able to function genitally *because* they work at it. Working at responding to what one regards as sufficient conditions for sexual response creates functional sex and response anxiety. This *type* of working at sex is ineffective, whether it accomplishes the goal of genital response or not. At best, it results in utilitarian sex that reinforces belief in required performance.

Modern sex therapy is rife with inherent paradox about the role of work in sex. Therapists warn that working at sex kills sex, and yet they ask patients to do things that patients don't really want to do (and which many therapists haven't done either). Contemporary practice encourages people to not work at sex by working at not working at it. Therapists perpetuate a boondoggle, mouthing this phrase on the one hand, advocating sensate focus activities on the other, and issuing interpretations of resistance when patients don't progress in treatment.

The notion that sex should *not* involve work continues to claim its own casualties. It coincides with common views of sex as an "automatic" function. While Masters and Johnson did not advocate many of these distortions, neither did they recognize how their pronouncements would reinforce preexisting problem-promulgating beliefs about sex and marriage in contemporary society.

One such belief is the idealized, *romantic* view of sex. This view suggests that if you love your partner (enough), and if your partner loves you (enough), desire and performance follow. This confusion of love, sex, and fusion sets up a painful corollary by couples who experience sexual difficulties: They begin to wonder if this indicates they aren't loved by, or don't love, the partner.

Other beliefs surface in the view that nature perpetuates the species by making desire and performance the "natural" result of exposure to naked bodies. The biological drive/function model causes couples with sexual dysfunction or disinterest to generate painful but erroneous theories to explain their difficulties. One is that they reflect massive sexual "hang-ups" and religious prohibitions (a notion with which Masters and Johnson actually agreed). Another is that sufficient unattractiveness will override the biological imperative.

Working at *desiring* sex is trickier. Pushing oneself to desire when one is not desirous is often self-defeating. Working at the things that might effectively increase desire for sexual contact often requires *advance* preparation. This might involve scheduling appropriate time with one's partner, disclosing one's sexual dissatisfactions, demonstrating what one really wants, and struggling through one's attendant anxiety and embarrassment. It might involve losing (or gaining) 30 pounds. It might involve keeping one's integrity intact.

Addressing latent sexual and nonsexual issues threatens the stability of a relationship; expending effort for sex often upsets the existing relationship system. Shifting and broadening sexual repertoires require work. Developing one's ability to utilize all three dimensions of psychological experience at profound depth (Mosher, 1980) requires work. Discarding pathogenic gender-roles takes work, as does introducing sexual novelty into established relationships. Ironically, patients often *don't* want to work at sex, because it feels like work. Expending effort to have sex worth wanting offends the infantile and narcissistic "shouldn't have to work at sex" ethic embraced by contemporary society. It challenges Erica Jong's deified "zipless fuck," the notion that sex involves just "doing what comes naturally." Contemporary slogans against working at sex validate the belief that life is or should be easy, or that there is something wrong if life is hard. Anything labeled "work" is immediately considered antithetical to sexual pleasure, and therefore an inappropriate expectation. And yet the entire perfume and lingerie industry is predicated on people putting effort into sex.

There is nothing inherently ineffective about working at sex; it is a matter of *how, what,* and *why* one is doing it. All sex takes effort, even if it is only the effort to hump—the concept of *flow* (Csikszentmihalyi, 1990) epitomizes effort and behavioral mastery transcending into self-celebration. Work and play are subjectively defined by the degree to which behaviors are ego-syntonic, compatible with current enjoyable proclivities, and portend satisfaction from the expenditure of effort. When treatment focuses on sexual *fulfillment,* rather than *sexual function*, the concept of working at sex is more clearly seen for the boondoggle it is.

Our subsequent discussion of inherent paradox (Chapter Fifteen) will distinguish *reproductive sex* (as a natural function) from *intimate sex* (as an acquired taste and developed skill). The notion of intimate sex as a developed skill differs markedly from mechanical techniques promulgated by Van de Velde (1930) and the myriad marriage manuals that emerged over the decades (e.g., Comfort, 1972; Ellis, 1960). Performance-anxiety-provoking emphasis on technique in general, and laborious "foreplay" in particular, the hallmark of the sexual work ethic, actually interferes with intimate sex: One tends to focus on *doing*, rather than the person being *done*.

Intensely intimate marital sex takes effort. Effort in intense sex doesn't feel like work; in mediocre sex it does. Intense sex and profound intimacy take more effort than people generally want to invest. It takes a lot of work to grow enough to tolerate intense intimacy and eroticism, and accept that life is both hard and sweet. The notion that intense sex takes work is both philosophically consistent and emotionally acceptable to highly differentiated people.

If one understands that the capacity for intimacy during sex is a function of personal development, then focus on sexual technique becomes secondary. The skill of intimate sex cannot be learned through "intimacy skills" such as "I messages" and "communication" exercises. It is not a function of routinized behaviors; it is a developed personal capacity.

Intimate sex is not a skill in the sense of learning to look in your partner's eyes while monitoring how you rub his/her genitals. Granted, this is no small feat when it is taught as a technique. And yet couples who have the capacity for intense sexual intimacy do this all the time. When one reaches a metalevel at which one focuses on the erotic connection, it allows one to see and be seen *behind the eyeballs*. One stops staring at eyeballs and genitals and yet is able to see both at the same time.

What if people turned this into a new performance anxiety about not being "personally developed" enough for intimate sex? While that might be counterproductive in the short run, it would not be the worst thing in the world—that is, as long as therapists are up to the task of helping patients accomplish that goal. In part, this requires not offering simplistic solutions and patchwork "techniques" that only interfere with the desired end.

SHIFT FROM A GENITAL MODEL TO AN INTIMACY MODEL

The sexual crucible provides a means to work directly on intimacy disorders, utilizing the following line of reasoning:

- Intense intimate contact elicits unresolved issues in one or both partners, which reciprocally preclude or shape intimacy.
- An individual's "intimacy tolerance" is a function of his/her particular unresolved issues, which can be triggered by varying situations, partners, and modalities of expression.
- Disparity in partners' "intimacy need" is likely to trigger disparities in "intimacy tolerance."
- Sexual activities that increase the intensity of intimacy are often avoided or eliminated from "normal" repertoire to the degree that they conflict with unresolved issues or intimacy tolerance.
- Sexual activities suggested by the therapist can be used to *elicit* unresolved issues and construct a crucible for resolution.
- Depending on one's view of treatment, the emergence of increased anxiety and refusal to participate are either resistance to treatment or the actual context of the treatment.
- If the therapist triggers this process unwittingly or is unprepared to proceed in an elicitation model of treatment, the therapist and patients are more likely to view the surfacing of preexisting underlying individual and systemic defenses as "resistance" rather than as an important stage of progress.

Sex therapy has been trapped in a deficit model by its inherent focus on sexual dysfunction. The inherent deficit focus of modern sex therapy stimulates feelings of sexual inadequacy, potentiating early terminations and homeostatic pitfalls throughout the course of treatment. Sex therapy that focuses on genital performance circumvents the most powerful, the most avoided, and perhaps the most therapeutically useful aspects of sexual contact: profound emotional intimacy.

An *asset model* of treatment, with the concept of sexual potential as a central feature, greatly reduces patients' defensiveness in treatment, reduces embarrassment about treatment, reduces tendencies towards stasis, and increases patients' self-esteem. This asset model is inherent in the shift to focusing on enhancement of intimacy and eroticism. Success in symptomatic improvement often provides the momentum for focusing on broader individual and systemic issues. This requires that the therapist develop comfort shifting back and forth in seamless fashion between the relationship system and the individuals within it.

Casting sexual-marital difficulties and their treatment as a crucible for personal and emotional development (rather than merely ameliorating genital performance difficulties) is more than clever reframing. It is an approach designed to enhance differentiation. Certainly this could be approached by addressing nongenital issues in a nonsexual framework. But it is particularly powerful to work with nongenital issues in a sexual framework, since they quietly surface in this dimension. Moreover, addressing patients' physical contact (even in the absence of overt sexual dysfunction) offers several powerful advantages:

- Deepening the potential for, and realization of, greater intimacy and eroticism; increasing overall marital satisfaction.
- Enhancing individual development in the context of marital or sexual therapy, thereby reducing recidivism.
- Introducing a strategic intervention into an otherwise stalled, homeostatic marital or family therapy.
- Strengthening the resilience of the family unit, enhancing the capacity for relatedness, bonding and caregiving, and promoting differentiation throughout the nuclear family.
- Shifting depth and directions of alliances in the marriage to create shifts throughout the extended family.

This paradigm shift is not merely a strategic position. The sexual crucible is an integrated clinical paradigm offering:

- an interface between individual and interpersonal processes as viewed within the sexual arena;
- an interface between individual, marital, and sexual therapies;
- an interface between object relations and systemic theories; and
- a very powerful intervention strategy for change.

The Role of "Pathology"

Processes that inevitably seem to arise in marriage are often seen as expressions of pathology. Apfelbaum (1983) astutely observed that clinicians tend to idealize relationships, wherein "what could be" becomes "what should be":

> Nowadays these simple interpretations have become highly elaborated and the idealized sexual relationship they refer back to is even harder to notice. Nevertheless, present-day interpretations still preserve much of the innocence of the classical conception and the fact remains that our sexual relations are supposed

to be *smooth*. When it comes to sex, the contemporary analyst (and psychody-namic therapist) is still, at heart, a lyric poet. We still are supposed to fit together effortlessly, and the more awkward and inhibited we are the more we find ourselves the target of interpretations about unconscious motives and fears, all based on what sex is thought to *require*. Sex now requires, not just ability to lose control and to surrender, it also is a test of our ability to regress and to relax our ego boundaries. It is a test of our ego functions, of the "goodness" of our internal objects, and of our skill at separation-individuation. What actually goes on in sexual relationships is ignored, as I've said. It is *dismissed as aberrant*, as merely diagnostic signs of a variety of immaturities and of unfinished business. (1983, p. 7)

An example of this is evident in L'Abate and Talmadge's (1987) overestimate of the level of intimacy achieved by most couples, wherein they state, "Only disturbed couples are able to fulfill each other without intimacy. For most couples, satisfactory and enjoyable sexual expression is not an option without intimacy" (p. 29). Moreover, their view of intercourse confuses the way it *can* be with the way it is for most couples:

Sexual expression, especially the act of intercourse, is one of the most vulnera-ble interactions that a couple undertakes. The experience of lying nude with one's partner in the process of giving and receiving pleasure is a most vulnerable and dependent state. At no other ordinary time in the life of the couple are they more vulnerable. (L'Abate & Talmadge, 1987, p. 25)

The vulnerability that most couples experience during intercourse is, unfor-tunately, a function of their lack of differentiation (which limits intimacy) rather than a high degree of intimacy per se. And yet, by confusing vulnerabil-ity with intimacy and suggesting that sexual behavior is generally intimate, L'Abate and Talmadge perpetuate the pathologizing of those who do not experience ideal sexual intimacy.

The sexual crucible approach does not pathologize patients based on some theoretical ideal, nor does it suggest that psychopathology necessarily under-lies sexual dysfunction or disinterest. Just as sexual dysfunctions are not neces-sarily indicative of underlying "psychopathology," the absence of such symp-toms is not indicative of healthy or satisfying sexual adjustment. The notion of sexual *functionals* conceptualizes nonsymptomatic but limited sexual experi-ence, which is more the norm than the exception.

Although the vast masses of people reach only a utilitarian (functional, nonsymptomatic) state of emotional/sexual development, this is not pathologi-cal. There is nothing "wrong" with this state of affairs; the world is as it is.

Although one might wish it to be different, it is the only show in town and there is little benefit in pathologizing the masses. Normal sexual adjustment is simply incredibly painful, and most adults and therapists are reluctant to abandon their idealism and use their own experience as a reflection of reality. There is nothing wrong with believing in the possibility of the highest levels of human development, as long as one does not establish this as a norm by which all others are then held in contempt.

Begrudging Respect

By the time that couples enter treatment, they are usually thoroughly enmeshed. One or both individuals usually lapse into fights about some gender-appropriate variant of:

- "I am not your mother."
- "You are just like my mother."
- "You are just like your mother."

Haunted by uncomfortable visions of Oedipus Rex, spouses often think they made a terrible mistake in partner selection. Moreover, they assume this reflects serious latent psychopathology on their part. Sometimes it does, but more often it simply reflects the universal struggle for differentiation.

It is hard for people to accept that this pattern of development is not a negative reflection on the relationship. While not particularly gratifying, it indicates that the relationship is serving one of its primary but often misunderstood purposes. Given cultural norms, people don't usually achieve a high level of differentiation by the time of marriage. One purpose of marriage is the selection of a partner having the requisite personality characteristics such that, stability permitting, spouses can complete that process. Whatever important characteristics one overlooks in partner selection are provided by the processes of introjection and projective identification, polarization and amplification, and behavioral shaping.

It is paradoxical that what many couples take as an indication of a bad relationship is actually the potential hallmark of a good one. If the couple can weather the storm, it paves the way for profound and relatively stable levels of intimacy not possible until projective identifications are withdrawn from the partner and "owned" as a part of oneself.

Living through the head-butting, the threats and ultimatums, the yelling and crying, partners develop *begrudging* respect for each other. Begrudging respect develops from watching one's partner master him/herself and not knuckle under to one's demands. *Begrudging respect — rather than "unconditional positive regard" — is the foundation of interpersonal trust and "fighting fair."*

The remaining chapters of this book on *normal* individual, dyadic, and broader systemic processes suggest that relationships should be anything but *smooth* — not because people are aberrant but because a relationship is the framework in which people grow themselves up. If anything is to be regarded as aberrant, it is the expectation that relationships should be smooth and that normal sexuality should be intense. The sexual crucible model suggests that intimacy and intense sexuality should be anything but effortless.

Multiple Dimensions of Existence and Isomorphic Interventions

Many clinicians, and the training programs that spawn them, tend to practice a unidimensional treatment approach. Perhaps this is necessary in order that students learn at least one avenue of conceptualization and intervention in the unrealistically brief period of graduate training we expect to produce a therapist. But some clinicians take *pride* in being a "systemic therapist," a "behavior therapist," or a "psychodynamically-oriented therapist," as if any single approach was sufficient to conceptualize and intervene in the complex dynamics in which human beings operate. Therapy format is little more than the initial point of departure through which patients select their way into treatment. Identifying oneself to the general public as a *marriage therapist, individual therapist,* or *sex therapist* is a good way to attract patients with the particular presenting problems that one might wish to deal with. However, when such designations represent the *limits* of the therapist's clinical acumen, the old adage that everything looks like a nail to someone with only a hammer becomes an increasing possibility.

While the clinician may wish to limit him/herself to a particular dimension of emotional interaction, human experience is eclectic. Increased attention to the problem of inhibited sexual desire (Chapter Nine) has led many prominent therapists to recognize the need for a treatment approach that combines individual therapy, systemic marital therapy, and sex therapy. For instance, Lief (1988) noted that clinicians are pretty much in agreement that marital conflict is the major cause of hypoactive sexual desire; Lief himself articulated the inextricable link between the processes of the individual and the system:

> One cannot easily separate intrapsychic from interpersonal events, even if a person enters a relationship with a well-defined neurotic conflict like the ma-

donna-prostitute complex (Lief, 1985). Transference to the partner changes the relationship, and the response to and from the partner may modify the original neurotic conflict so that interpersonal behavior is changed. The schema one partner develops about the other not only influences perception through a process of selective attention and inattention, but also augments and perpetuates itself by modifying behavior. (1988, pp. xi-xii)

It is easiest to appreciate the "grand circularity" of cases which appear to be moving well in treatment. In more problematic cases of sexual and marital difficulty, even systemic therapists tend to regress to linear thinking; the tendency is to think that another school of therapy or a different therapy format might be more effective.

An integrated model of sexual-marital therapy is not as easy to conceptualize or actualize as one might like to think. This is commonly reflected in the tendency to conceptualize sexual therapy and marital therapy as separate and independent forms of treatment, as if one could or should be done independently of the other. This is evident in the writing of even such an important contributor to the field as Harold Lief.

In 1980 Harold Lief was honored by AASECT for his lifetime contributions to sex therapy, sex counseling, and medical school sex education. In receiving this well-deserved award, Dr. Lief stated that certification as an AASECT sex therapist, and clinical membership in the American Association for Marriage and Family Therapy should be *mandatory co-requisites* for the other. Although he challenged both organizations to face the need for integration, subsequent publication suggests he envisioned it occurring within the clinician (i.e., dual certification) rather than on the level of core conceptualization and professional practice:

> The clinician is often faced with the problem of attempting to weight differentially the intrapsychic and the interpersonal, as has been suggested earlier. This has important ramifications because the choice of individual therapy versus marital therapy, or as a third alternative, some combination of the two, has practical significance. (Lief, 1988, p. xii)

Likewise, David Scharff demonstrates a similar conceptualization of sexual and marital therapy as distinctly different processes. Scharff (1988, p. 59) considered sex therapy, couples therapy, intensive individual therapy (including psychoanalysis), and "combined" approaches (including family therapy) as treatment options for desire disorders. While the point being made may seem nit-picking, it is one vital to recognizing the subtle legacy of distinct boundaries in professional identity and therapeutic orientation which shapes clinical practice. Both Lief and Scharff mentioned a "combined" approach which had yet to be systematically developed and articulated.

When one looks closely, there are very few clinicians who have developed a holistic systemic approach to sexual-marital therapy. In *Integrating Sexual and Marital Therapy*, Hof (1987) stated regarding conflict resolution, that "without the ability to manage conflict effectively, angry and resentful feelings have a way of remaining unresolved and ever-present, serving as effective means for undermining sex therapy" (p. 14). Hof cited Feldman's (1982) suggestions for emotional awareness training, dream work, empathy training, cognitive awareness training, relationship strength specification, self-instruction training, problem-solving training, and behavioral contracting as methods to resolve these problems. This piecemeal concoction of solutions for problems to be resolved *prior to* rather than *through* sex therapy hardly reflects an integration of marital and sexual therapy.

In advocating fairly restrictive patient selection criterion, LoPiccolo and Friedman (1988) also take a narrow view of sex therapy, distinct from marital or individual therapy:

> We tend to defer sex therapy and suggest other forms of treatment if assessment indicates any of the following major issues: depression, severe psychopathology, alcohol or drug dependence, spouse abuse, active extramarital affairs, and severe marital distress with imminent separation/divorce. (LoPiccolo & Friedman, 1988, p. 114)

Putting aside for the moment the advantages of holistic intervention, there are many circumstances in which a linear progression of narrow-band treatment modalities is not possible. Consider, for example, the inclination to terminate marital therapy with an enmeshed, combative couple and refer one or both partners for individual treatment. There are many cases in which one partner is not agreeable to, or capable of handling, the overt self-focus of individual treatment. In couples who have been battling over culpability for marital or sexual problems, entering individual treatment has implications for power hierarchies in the family. Sometimes, the couple's relationship is too tenuous to tolerate the strain of one or both partners' undergoing individual treatment without ongoing attention to dyadic processes. The notion of patients' "putting the relationship on hold" while they resolve their individual issues is a convenient conceptualization for therapists who are unable to work with such difficulties as distinct but simultaneous and interactive processes.

Archaic therapeutic guidelines suggesting that sex therapy is contraindicated by the presence of severe marital conflict imply such couples should first undergo marital therapy; a conceptualization of sexual and marital therapy as discrete forms of treatment is implicit. What of sex therapy as the arena for the marital work?

The sexual crucible utilizes common, necessary, and expectable conflict as a medium of treatment. It provides a crucial answer to the question: "When should the couple receive sex therapy, and when is marital therapy more appropriate?" The answer befitting this vitally important question is "YES!" If couples are to ever relinquish the expectation that relationships progress "smoothly" without extreme conflict, perhaps therapists have to relinquish the same expectations about sexual-marital therapy.

Isomorphic Intervention

The sexual crucible is a multisystemic application offering simultaneous frames of reference. It should be particularly attractive to the increasing numbers of therapists who recognize multiple causation and the need for multidimensional interventions.

Kaplan (1974) introduced the dimension of time to sexual therapy through her distinction of immediate and long-range *causes* of sexual dysfunction. The sexual crucible provides a *present-day context for resolving contemporary and past developmental tasks*. However, since sex therapy has traditionally been thought of as a brief form of treatment, little has emerged in the professional literature in terms of *stages of treatment*. If the goal is optimal speed in symptom reversal, as well as utilization of sexual and marital difficulties as a crucible for personal development, the sexual-marital therapist must conceptualize both immediate and long-range *interventions* in treatment. Ideally, these are one and the same.

A change in the interpersonal system often upsets the internal equilibrium of one or more individuals in the system. Interventions designed to modify interpersonal systems have an impact on individuals' object-relations capacity. Interventions aimed at object relations problems of one or both individuals have a systemic impact. A complex meta-system of these dimensions develops, creating interlocking, multidetermined sources for the difficulties that the therapist is asked to modify. It is often impossible to bring about the desired change in sexual functioning, while also keeping all other aspects of individual and relationship equilibrium the same. The ecological complex of individual, dyadic, and extended family systems that confronts the therapist is capable of exquisitely subtle cross-system compensation. In this process, a disequilibrium in one system (e.g., the marital dyad) is quickly compensated by a shift in another system (e.g., individual or extended family system) such that overall homeostasis is preserved.

In dealing with multidetermined difficulties, the greater the degree to which any given intervention simultaneously addresses *each* of the relevant dimensions of difficulty, the more likely that the intervention will result in change. A therapeutic intervention that is appropriate to the intrapsychic issues of both partners, the systemic patterns between them, and the broader family system is more likely to succeed in treatment than one that addresses a single dimension. Interventions that are simultaneously congruent on multiple levels of causation are more difficult to develop, and more effective, than several "unidimensional" linear interventions given simultaneously or sequentially. Abandoning one unidimensional intervention in lieu of another unidimensional intervention (from an alternative school of treatment) overlooks the possibility that the initial intervention was accurate, but insufficient.

Some unidimensional strategies *are* effective with some patients, fueling the debate on the superiority of one approach over others. Clinicians' tendency to explain colleagues' success by reinterpreting interventions into their preferred school of thought reflects the tenacity with which we cling to our own limited vantage point. On the other hand, the therapist who is able to conceptualize and intervene on *several* simultaneous dimensions with a *single* intervention is more likely to be successful with any given couple and with a wider range of couples.

Couples' erotic and intimate behavior (in all its subtle and blatant manifestations) is (a) a vantage point for eliciting multiple levels of reality, (b) an arena for direct therapeutic intervention, and (c) a measure of the efficacy of those interventions. Humans use sexuality to express every human emotion and drive our species is capable of: boredom, insecurity, anger, lust, dominance, avoidance of intimacy (among others)—as well as love. Understanding the meaning of sex in a given encounter requires considering the relationship system in which it occurs. This system is composed of the ongoing pattern of reciprocal interaction, the prior history of the couple as well as the anticipated future, the legacy each individual brings from his/her family of origin, and the larger context within which the relationship and specific sexual encounter occur. In the subsequent six chapters, we will consider each of these dimensions. Each will be considered sequentially in order to focus on each in sufficient depth, and because books, unlike relationships, are a linear medium. However, we will stop periodically to appreciate the grand recursiveness of it all.

CHAPTER SEVEN

Individual Dimensions of Intimacy and Sexuality

In this chapter, we consider the individual dimension of intimacy and sexuality by way of object relations theory and Bowen's model of differentiation. We will examine self-soothing, needing to be needed, denial of hatred, the politics of sexual abandon, and the unconscious connection between people who "can't communicate."

Intimacy is a relative experience. Each individual's *intimacy need* and *intimacy tolerance*[1] determine when and what interactions will be experienced as satisfyingly intimate. What is intimate to one person may be stifling and uncomfortably self-revealing to another; a third person might find the same interaction mundane and impersonal. Discrepancies in intimacy need and intimacy tolerance play a crucial role in the interplay of individual and dyadic issues, creating conflict and determining the ebb and flow of relationships over time.

Intimacy need is the degree of desire to engage and disclose core aspects of oneself to one's partner. *Intimacy tolerance* is the unilateral ability to maintain a comfortable and clearly defined identity as one (and one's partner) discloses core aspects of self. Intimacy tolerance has several components:

- The ability to modulate one's dependency strivings in the face of intensely pleasurable or frustrating interactions.
- The willingness to be guided by one's own perceptions of reality, while accepting it is a subjective view.
- The capacity to maintain an internalized sense of self-worth.
- The ability to *self-soothe* in the face of inevitable emotional nicks and

---

[1]The concepts of intimacy need and intimacy tolerance were introduced in Chapter Five.

abrasions that occur in ongoing intense involvement with a valued partner.

The ability to self-soothe increases the range of enjoyable and tolerable interactions, flexibility and adaptability to the marital bond, and overall family stability. Hatfield (1984) discussed how intimacy is commonly impeded by fears of exposure, abandonment, angry attack, engulfment, loss of control, and one's own destructive impulses; the real problem, however, is the inability to soothe such fears and not the ubiquitous fears themselves.

SEXUAL INTIMACY, SELF-SOOTHING, AND EROTICISM

Many couples with satisfying relationships find sexual intimacy is a relaxing, exciting exchange that leaves them feeling soothed and secure. However, couples with marital discord or sexual difficulties lose the ability to use physical contact similarly. Contact that was once a source of joy becomes anxiety provoking. In the context of repeated fights or failures, relaxed sex rapidly ceases to exist.

It is gratifying when one's partner responds affirmatively to self-disclosure of extremely personal information or displays of eroticism. But individuals who seek intimate relationships cannot rely on this when disclosing information unsettling to the partner. At least one individual must be able to self-soothe when couples challenge and expand their normative level of intimacy.

We approached this point in our discussion of self-validated intimacy (Chapter Five). "Self-validation" involves more than resilience or "knowing one is right"—highly defensive people can be quite self-righteous, but intimacy generally ceases at such points. *Self-validated intimacy also requires the ability to self-soothe.* Soothing oneself involves assuaging pain, mollifying anger, softening shock, pacifying fears, and comforting sorrow and disappointment.

The degree to which partners can unilaterally detoxify hostility and conflict greatly determines the extent to which their relationship can tolerate stress without fracturing. Self-soothing is the antithesis of "holding feelings in" or repressing feelings that surface at a later date. The ability to self-soothe is a critical component of the elastic attachment Wynne and Wynne (1986) refer to as "mutuality."

People with low intimacy need and tolerance often have little difficulty as long as they remain relatively emotionally uninvolved. They pair comfortably with a partner having similar low tolerance and need.

People with high intimacy need but *low* intimacy tolerance often find themselves oscillating in and out of close emotional and/or physical proximity with their partners. They simply cannot buffer, by themselves, the intense connection they seek with others. They hunger for connectedness as a means of soothing their own fears and anxieties. Such individuals create an inherent paradox for themselves: their motivations for intense bonding preclude tolerating and maintaining it.

L'Abate and Talmadge (1987) state, "In order for intimacy to progress, we must make room for the regression of the childlike and often scared needy selves" (p. 29). However, notions of a "capacity for dependency" can be misleading; dependency that results from an inability to maintain oneself limits a relationship to other-validated intimacy. Douvan (1977) considers the abilities to be dependent *and* maintain oneself during conflict resolution to be critical to intimacy. Dependency derived from adequate self-maintenance and self-soothing is entirely different; there is less anxiety about rejection and "abandonment," less resentment when caretaking is not offered, and less anger when it is terminated. Ego strength permits *regression in the service of the ego* (where the ability to resume autonomous functioning remains ever-present), rather than regression per se (where infantile emotionality predominates).

People with low intimacy tolerance become anxious and avoidant when the current or anticipated levels of intimacy exceed their ability to self-soothe. This often occurs during sexual intimacy, given folks' extreme sensitivity regarding erotic preferences, practices, and performance. *An individual's ability to self-soothe is crucial to maintaining and expanding displays of eroticism in the face of discordant messages from the partner.*

People who are highly dependent on their partner for soothing can have intermittently intense erotic experiences (if the appropriate responses from the partner are present); they have little resilience when the partner is frustrating or merely inattentive. In other words, their sexual style is more reactive than proactive or creative. Their first solution is to request/demand reassurance. Their second solution is to limit intimacy and eroticism to a level they can maintain unilaterally (which may be quite minimal). Unfortunately, either strategy forstalls developing greater ability to self-soothe.

The ability to self-soothe is also a critical variable in the etiology of overt sexual dysfunction. Occasional situational fluctuations in genital performance are a common and normal occurrence. Unfortunately, they also create anxiety and distract from pleasure—and thus, interfere with threshold levels of stimulation in current and subsequent sexual encounters. The less able individuals are to self-soothe their own (and their partner's) reactions, the greater the likelihood that a negative feedback loop around sexual performance will develop.

While moderate (functional) levels of desire can be maintained through reliance on the partner for one's soothing, the ability and willingness to self-soothe are fundamental requisites for reaching one's sexual potential.

Later we will discuss how the ability to self-soothe is as critical to tolerating *high* levels of intimacy and eroticism as it is to resolving marital discord and sexual difficulties. Profound desire is not safe without the corresponding ability to self-soothe.

Self-soothing is one aspect of autonomous, adult functioning. Its roots lie in the vicissitudes of infancy and are modified by successful resolution of the developmental tasks of later childhood, adolescence, and adulthood. As we will see, two major schools of thought offer useful theoretical perspectives on the development of the capacity to self-soothe: the psychoanalytic school of object relations theory (which emphasizes parent-child interaction in the first years of life) and Bowen's theory of differentiation (which emphasizes general family processes and adult functioning).

THE INFLUENCE OF EARLY EXPERIENCE

Quality of childhood contact with parents, grandparents, and other primary caretakers is a determinant of ability to self-soothe as an adult. But what determines the requisite quality? Theorists and therapists differ in the degree to which they focus on the "actual" characteristics of the caregiver vs. distortions in the infant's phenomenological experience. Therapists working from an object relations perspective emphasize proprioceptive distortions due to primitive perceptual/conceptual abilities, limited reality testing, and the impact of wishes and fears. Family systems therapists, in contrast, consider the infant to be highly perceptive of parents' unresolved emotional needs, unconscious feelings, and overt behavior.

Therapists also differ regarding the immutability of early childhood experiences. Family therapy recognizes the importance of the first years of life, but emphasizes childhood, adolescence, and adulthood as modifiers of earliest experiences. Object relations theory, in contrast, emphasizes the relative impermeability of intrapsychic representations of early childhood experience.

Object relations[2] refers to the organization of mental representations of the self and significant people (the objects) that constitute one's ego (Horner, 1979). *Objects* are the residue of the child's interactions with people upon whom he/she is dependent during infancy and early stages of maturation (Phillipson, 1955). Sometimes referred to as *introjects*, these internalized images of parents are the building blocks of the infant's self-image and ego structure, his/her overall view of the world, and anticipations of emotional commerce in later relationships.

In a simplistic sense, introjects are evident in the self-talk of young children who, while struggling to cope with a current event, often parrot the phrasing and intonation of a parent who has been effective in comforting them. Likewise, the introject of a critical, disapproving, or anxiety-inducing parent is apparent in the child's self-scolding. According to object relations theory, internalized objects (representations and expectations) from childhood are a critical determinant of the ability to organize conflict and self-soothe anxiety and sorrow in adulthood.

Object relations capacities (i.e., the capacity to sustain resilient and meaningful emotional attachments in later adult life) emerge during the first three to four years of life. This involves the capacities to tolerate loving and hating the same person and to value others for attributes beyond their need-satisfying functions (Burgner & Edgcumbe, 1972). Good experiences with primary figures result in the emergence of a unified central ego having (a) the capacity for creativity, sexual involvement, and self-assertion, and (b) a residual of "good" objects which increase the individual's "relational potential" (Dicks, 1963).

Less fortunate experiences result in (a) difficulty tolerating ambivalence towards partners and inability to relate to them as separate individuals, and (b) self-rejection, defensiveness, anxiety and/or depression. Horner (1979) offers a

---

[2]Ego psychology and object relations theory emerged from the roots of Sigmund Freud's work. Fairbairn (1963) rejected Freud's (1915/1949) emphasis on instinctual processes (e.g., "id," death instinct), and moved the ego to a central position interacting with the outside world (rather than as arbiter between inner and outer realities).

Object relations theory emphasizes that human behavior is fundamentally oriented around seeking (and managing) relationships, rather than modulating impulses. The most concise summary of Fairbairn's seminal contributions to object relations theory is contained in his own brief synopsis (Fairbairn, 1963) and that of Sutherland (1963).

Melanie Klein (1932, 1935, 1946) and Margaret Mahler (1952, 1968; Mahler, Pine, & Bergman, 1975) have written extensively on the various phases of object relations development. Other significant contributors to object relations theory are Balint (1952), Beres (1956), Dicks (1963), Sutherland (1963), and Winnicott (1953).

graphic summary of the pathologies associated with disruption of various stages of object relations development (see Figure 7.1).

Splitting, Repression and Projective Identification

According to object relations theory, an infant in the early stages of *individuation* experiences the parent or caretaker as a collection of discrete, absolute "good" and "bad" functions (i.e., as multiple utilitarian objects), rather than as a single person with diverse qualities. Portions of the infant's experience are repressed in order to love the parent despite inevitable frustrating experiences. The result is:

- *Conscious* "part objects," which constitute idealized expectations for an adult marital partner in later life, and
- *Repressed* "part objects," denied aspects of parents and oneself, which emerge in the form of projections, attributions, anticipations, and distortions of significant others.

Fairbairn (1963) suggested that the schizoid quality of people's relationships (and of human personality, itself) reflected the manner in which non-ideal

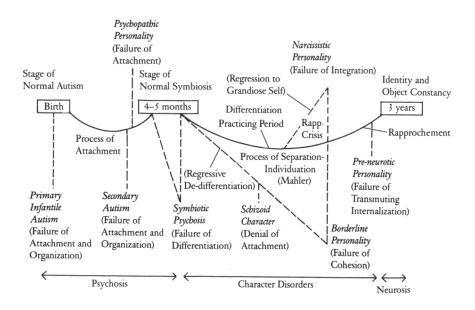

Figure 7.1 Horner's (1979) model of object relations development and associated pathologies

aspects of parents and self are handled. He conceptualized the ego as composed of three separate but interactive "structures": a central organizing ego in which consciousness resides, and two repressed ego segments (which he referred to as the *libidinal and antilibidinal* egos). Fairbairn hypothesized that the overly-exciting and overly-frustrating aspects of parents are split off, resulting in two repressed internal objects (i.e., exciting "libidinal" and rejecting "antilibidinal" objects). In addition, less-than-ideal portions of self are repressed in conjunction with the repressed frustrating and gratifying aspects of parents.

In a relationship, each partner's needs constantly affect and are affected by the other. Unconscious anticipations are increasingly expressed in those relationships whose importance approximates the prototype with parents. In marriage, conscious and unconscious communication shapes each partner into the embodiment of the spouse's unresolved object attachments and the denied aspects of self. Object relations theory refers to this process as *projective identification*.

> A particularly important feature of these needs is that, though there is a defensive tendency for the person to take them to other people than those he wishes to maintain his close good relationships with, nevertheless, there is an even more powerful trend for them to come back in any close relationship with one person. That is to say, *the repressed not only returns, but it tends to return to the representative of the more comprehensive relationships from which it was originally split off.* (Sutherland, 1963, p. 118)

Marriage is one of the primary theaters in which the drama of projective identification unfolds; Dicks (1963, 1967) notes that people can manifest extreme dysfunction in sexual and marital relationships, while remaining highly successful in worldly activities.

Spouses unconsciously shape each other into the necessary form, which they rail against to emancipate themselves from their conscious and unconscious fears. As partners are "shaped," they begin to experience the corresponding impulses and fantasies being projected onto them. The partner may or may not be aware that he/she is receiving and internalizing this projected image from the spouse. *Sometimes partners have the sense that the other sees them in a way that is "not me"; oftentimes, however, this awareness is lacking because the projected image lies uncomfortably close to some denied personal characteristic.* Because of the role of projective identification in partner selection, some congruence between the partner's true characteristics and the projected image always occurs.

Partner Selection and Transference "Storms"

It is commonly accepted that experience with one's parents subsequently affects selection of a mate. Object relations theory suggests that partner selection and relationship interactions involve attempts to experience and reintegrate repressed aspects of parents and oneself. This is an intrapsychic view of resolving family-of-origin issues. Object relations theory explains it this way:

> I visualize the obscure process of mate selection (i.e., the person one decides to *marry* and not merely have a flirtation or affair with) as largely based on unconscious signals or cues by which the partners recognize in a more-or-less central ego-syntonic person the other's "fitness" for joint working-through or repeating of still unresolved splits or conflicts inside each other's personalities, while at the same time, paradoxically, also sensing a guarantee that with that person they will not be worked-through. Thus, they both hope for integration of the lost parts by finding them in the other, and also hope that by collusive "joint resistance" or mutual defence this painful growth can be by-passed. . . .
>
> Teleologically, such marriages continue because of the real need for growth and integration. The marriage—the dyad—here represents a total personality with each partner playing the role of "one half" of the unrecognized conflicting polarization, instead of a complementary growth towards individual completeness and enhancement such as is possible in the healthy marriage by acceptance of the ambivalence of a "mixed" person. (Dicks, 1967, p. 128)

During courtship, partners project onto each other an image of the gratifying person he/she wishes for (and wishes to be); each becomes the embodiment of the promise of gratification. Each partner shapes the behavior of the other to correspond to these projected images.

As the relationship progresses and attachments become increasingly meaningful, however, responses are progressively determined by each partner's unconscious (negative) introjects. As one's partner is shaped to be congruent to these expectations, he/she eventually becomes the embodiment of one's worst nightmares (literally and figuratively). Recognizing one's own projections becomes increasingly difficult, since the partner's behavior appears to validate the notion that the problem is external (i.e., in the partner).

By the time a relationship is troubled, any thought of reciprocal validation has long since vanished. *The couple is often living in the midst of a transference storm of projections and counter-projections, which overwhelms the ability of either partner to maintain a stable identity.*

Treatment of marital and sexual difficulties can provide a vehicle for the resolution of underlying object relations difficulties, and a testing ground for enhanced abilities to self-soothe.

Fear of the "Gratifying Partner"

By this point, the importance of the ability to self-soothe in the face of deprivation and frustration becomes clear. However, object relations theory offers an understanding of a common but little-understood phenomenon that has crucial relevance for sexual-marital issues.

Some individuals find themselves angry with their partner for no apparent reason; the partner is loving, generous, and available for repeated experiences of intimacy and sex. The individual avoids the partner, when time is available and everything seems ideal. He/she may pick a fight to rationalize reluctance for intimacy or sex, while secretly wondering if this indicates not loving the partner or being unlovable. What causes this?

One possible answer lies in the distinction between a "soothing object" and a "libidinal object." The unfortunate common usage of "good" and "bad" as descriptors of part-objects, rather than the more accurate "*libidinal*" (impulse gratifying) and "*antilibidinal*" (impulse frustrating) labels, leads to an erroneous assumption: Unsoothing antilibidinal objects are presumed "bad," gratifying libidinal objects presumed "good," and the ability to self-soothe is mistakenly thought to develop from libidinal (as opposed to antilibidinal) objects. This is not the case.

According to Fairbairn (1954), impulse-gratifying aspects of the parent give rise to "bad" objects as well. The "exciting" parent who tantalizes and creates desire in the child gives rise to a "bad" object (just as a "frustrating" parent does). This understanding of object relations theory highlights *(a) the pain and sorrow of unfulfilled hunger and longing for the parent, and (b) the fear of losing autonomy through one's own desire to be gratified and indulged.* The gratifying aspects of the parent/partner are, themselves, an unconscious source of threat.

It is easy to understand that a frustrating, indifferent, ungratifying parent often yields a child who expects to be frustrated and devises corresponding strategies to cope. Such a child/adult might become rebellious, defiant, and demand immediate gratification; on the other hand, the child might simply become depressed. The child does not anticipate (eventual) gratification or comfort, and is unable to self-soothe in the absence of immediate gratification.

But family and marital therapists have witnessed all too often the "overly gratifying" parent who interferes with the child's evolution (and the family's evolution, for that matter). The parent is intrusive, seductive of the child's attempts to individuate, and intolerant of the child experiencing growth-stimulating frustration.

The child of such a parent anticipates being controlled and manipulated by the parent's covert demand for gratification. Such a child (or adult) might attempt to reduce his/her desire to be gratified, to combat the needfulness the parent induces. Said differently, the child of an exploitive parent who selfishly manipulates in the name of "caring" might attempt to *not want*. As adults, such children appear indifferent and shallow. As children, they are often labeled "spoiled," although "ruined" is a more apt description of their intimate relationships in later life.

Beyond the role of early childhood in adult self-soothing, our sojourn into object relations theory offers three additional observations. *First*, an "all-gratifying" spouse can be ungratifying. Of course, no spouse is *all* gratifying; but one who seeks validation and security by "sacrificing" for others often comes close enough to someone with the corresponding fear of becoming a "prisoner of indulgence." Object relations theory explains the inevitable: These two types of people seem to find each other to play out their mutual dramas.

Second, our discussion brings up the question of what is a "soothing" spouse. According to object relations theory, a really "good" parent is only "good enough" (Winnicott, 1960). He/she is available for core-level bonding with the infant, without indulging in undue intrusiveness or symbiosis: he/she delivers (sufficient) frustration and gratification, which the child eventually integrates into a view of a single whole individual ("whole object attachment").

The ability to tolerate the simultaneous gratifying and frustrating aspects of a parent (or partner) is the substance of self-soothing. A parent who is able to tolerate the frustrations of parenthood (and other exigencies of life) provides the raw material for a soothing introject. In marriage, a "soothing" spouse is gratifying and accommodating, but maintains his/her autonomy and self interest. Unfortunately, this is hardly the behavior spouses utilize seeking a reflected sense of self-worth.

Third, the repressed pain and sorrow triggered by being gratified are often overlooked. Recently, *not wanting to want* has received attention via growing interest in problems of inhibited sexual desire (see Chapter Ten). *However, the most common instance of this has been totally overlooked in sexual and marital therapy, because its own moderate results do not bring it to the surface.*

When couples far exceed their wildest imaginations of increased intimacy and sexual pleasure, the resulting increased desire for the partner triggers physical pain and sorrow.

Some patients experience it as "bittersweet" melancholy, while others report it as chest-bursting heartache; by and large *all* patients identify it this way: "I know this is the pain of what I have always been missing."

It is not the pain of past hurts from the partner; this pain is far more profound. It is not a fear of being hurt by the partner, but rather a fear of what already has been: the pain is already inside.

Sexuality and intimacy that approach the limits of human sexual potential trigger what one patient referred to as "a bottomless pit of past disappointment about things that *didn't happen.*" What "didn't happen" isn't the pain of things not received; *it is the pain of the child who longed to admire and love his/her mother or father, when that proved to be unsafe.*

This pain, which almost *everyone* carries, is an impediment to the ultimate level of marital satisfaction and sexual intensity achieved in life. It is finally experienced (and resolved) when spouses, having attained a high level of differentiation and a wonderful marriage, dare themselves to unabashedly want their partner. In so doing, there is an isomorphic integration of existential loneliness and "whole object attachment." (Note that our discussion has implicitly integrated the role of self-soothing in both high and low sexual desire.)

Practitioners of contemporary sexual and marital therapy may mistake this for the more pedestrian outcomes facilitated by such approaches; in general, most couples never get far enough to trigger the phenomena described above. The sexual crucible, however, provides an "abnormal" solution for a "normal" problem that affects "normal" people with "normal neuroses." The "normal solution" is obvious: *Most people would rather live with a pain in the ass than a pain in the heart.*

People have to work long and hard for the *"privilege"* of having this type of pain. Another patient stated, "I am not overjoyed about feeling this pain, but at least it has purpose and *meaning.*"

Modulating pain of this calibre requires well-developed capacities to self-soothe; without this, patients reduce the intensity of their marriage just as other people do. The elicitation window (described in Chapter Six) permits the therapist to start addressing object relations issues (and systemic issues) long before patients are ready to address that level of pain (and pleasure). Patients prepare themselves through lower-level manifestations of self-soothing such as self-validated intimacy, increased levels of sexual gratification, and displays of eroticism.

Helping people learn to self-soothe is not a "technique" or an "exercise"—it is a complex task of some intensity and duration. General orientation and case examples of the sexual crucible are presented throughout this book; more specific discussion regarding clinical implementation occurs in *The Intimacy Paradigm.*

Intimacy and Ego-Structure

Ego boundaries involve the ability to maintain a sense of emotional intactness in relation to other people's wishes and projections. It also involves the modulation of one's own impulses and the recognition that they emanate from within. These abilities become increasingly difficult to maintain as physical proximity and emotional importance of one's partner increase.

Ego-strength, reflected in the ability to modulate ego boundaries, is a determinant of the depth, frequency and salience of marital sexual contact. Ego-strength involves resiliency; but resiliency without flexibility leaves only rigidity and brittleness.

The ability to relinquish an external focus (discussed by Harry Stack Sullivan [1953] as *termination of security operations*) and engage in sensate focus and erotic enactments, is sometimes called "regression in the service of the ego." Such "regression," however, requires a *strong* core sense of self; it requires a solidity that permits variation in roles and behaviors, loss of time awareness, and self-absorbed engagement in an alternative sexual reality.

When ego boundaries seem compromised, the relationship between intimacy and self-soothing becomes evident. There are two options: (a) increased self-soothing which permits continued close proximity, or (b) compensatory modulation of physical and emotional involvement. When people feel their ego boundaries being breached, the slightest assertion by the spouse is experienced as if "the bad guys are coming over the walls of the fort." People need "oscillating skin thickness" to function in marriage: thin skin for sensitivity, and thick skin for sanity and self-protection (Nordine, 1987).

Unresolved object relations issues impose an upper boundary on level of intimacy in terms of tolerance for self-soothed (self-validated) intimacy during troubled times, and for the intense pain of profound sex and intimacy during good ones.

Scharff (1982) has taken a more extreme view, suggesting sexual dysfunctions are fundamentally object relations disorders given expression in bodily processes. While noting that sexual dysfunctions may also denote relationship difficulties, Scharff suggests "its 'pathology' resides in the vicissitudes of internalized object life" (p. 13).

Object relations theory embraces two aspects of idealism (much like we observed with regard to theories of intimacy): (a) It is based on the child's quest for the *perfect* parent (and subsequent [ineffective] attempts to self-soothe disappointment), and (b) it embraces a vision of the perfectly adjusted individual and pathologizes all who deviate from this standard. (One might say that there is little that is soothing about object relations theory!)

Bowen, in contrast, starts with *natural family processes* and ends with an emphasis *on normality*. Bowen's theory of differentiation offers an alternative viewpoint on self-soothing and proximity modulation.

BOWEN'S THEORY OF DIFFERENTIATION

Bowenian theory represents a less subjective, personalized picture of human behavior than does object relations theory. Object relations theory depicts individual functioning as an autistic distortion of external reality. Individual responses, according to Bowen, are adaptations (albeit sometimes ineffective ones) to actual external conditions.

Bowen's notion of the individual is inextricably tied to awareness of the system in which the individual operates. His model explains "normal" difficulties with intimacy, sexuality, and long-term relationships in ways vastly different from (and yet somewhat compatible with) object relations theory.[3]

Bowen, like Freud, based his theory on an understanding of biological instincts and evolutionary processes; both believed biology is destiny, although this meant vastly different things to each man. Bowen's thinking was greatly influenced by MacLean's work (1958, 1972, 1982) on the relationship of brain structure/function to emotion in animals at various levels of evolutionary sophistication. Basically, MacLean was interested in three structures of the human brain shared in common with lower species: the *reptilian* (R-complex), the more primitive *mammalian* (limbic) and the evolutionarily newer mammalian neocortex systems. MacLean's experiments with neural functioning were consistent with Bowen's concept of emotion, suggesting that much of human behavior is outside conscious awareness or control (i.e., limbic rather than neocortical in nature).

---

[3]The attempt to integrate Bowen's view of differentiation with object relations theory leads to an interesting awareness of differences in "directionality" of focus. Both approaches focus on the impact of anxiety on individual functioning; differentiation can be thought of as the degree of resilience to interpersonal contagion of anxiety. Object relations theory predicts that as anxiety increases in the system, one's expectations, perceptions, and responses are more determined by one's fears and prior unhappy experiences (unresolved objects) than by the immediate "external" situation; likewise, Bowenian theory predicts that as anxiety rises, feelings and reactions are more determined by compliance pressures of others.

On the one hand, the former view involves the ability to be "inner-" rather than "outer-determined"; on the other hand, the latter view involves the ability to be "outer-" rather than "inner-determined" (i.e., by an accurate perception of external reality). Although the models seem to be pointing in two opposite directions, the emphasis is actually the same: the ability for self-reflective rational (neocortical) processes to modulate reflexive (limbic) emotionality.

The difference between Freud and Bowen is evident in Bowen's use of the term *emotional illness* instead of *mental illness* (Papero, 1990). Bowen uses the term *emotion* to refer to automatic responses that govern the functioning of all life forms. These automatic responses include instinct, reproduction, automatic activity controlled by the autonomic nervous system, subjective emotional and feeling states, and relationship processes (Bowen, 1975).

Bowen's notion of emotion fits quite nicely with Calhoun's (1956) extensive studies of natural systems in rat colonies. Calhoun (1971) defines pathological behavior as the inability to adjust to ongoing or changing conditions. Calhoun's studies on the effects of proximity in rats (e.g., population density, environmental conditions, and resulting social and individual behavior) are consistent with Bowen's interest in the family as a naturally occurring human system.

Bowen started by exploring attachment and symbiosis between dysfunctional children and their mothers, later studying clinical application with schizophrenogenic families. Bowen eventually suggested that psychological symbiosis has the same type and degree of impact on organisms as does biological symbiosis (Bowen, Dysinger, Brady, & Basmania, 1978).

Obviously, a theory that addresses diminished cortical functioning in response to decreasing physical distance and "pressure to adapt" has relevance to understanding human intimacy. Papero (1990) (whom Bowen described as an important participant in the development of his theory) recently wrote:

> In a sense Bowen Theory addresses the interplay of different levels of brain development as expressed in the behavior of the individual. The limbic functions, presumably an evolutionary development providing greater adaptive response and flexibility to the early mammal, can inhibit the functioning of a later evolutionary development, the neocortex. A key variable is the level of demand to adapt to a changing environment. The more pressure to adapt, the greater the likelihood of the operation of automatic behaviors or mechanisms that hinder the full potential of neocortical functioning. (p. 15)

Kerr and Bowen (1988) postulate the operation of two counterbalancing life forces—*individuality* and *togetherness*—in the family emotional system. *Individuality* propels an organism to follow its own directives, to be an independent and distinct entity. *Togetherness* propels an organism to follow the directives of others, to be a dependent, connected, and indistinct entity. It is the balance of these two forces, and not merely diffuse uncoordinated actions and reactions between individuals, that shape the nature of relationships.

Noting that man lives in the densest populations of any primate (Wilson,

1975), Kerr and Bowen point out that *individuality* in highly social species, such as humans, must be integrated into a tight-knit relationship system. Whereas sociobiologists consider individuality to be "the instinctually rooted capacity of an animal to be a separate and competent individual, capable of independent functioning and not governed by the needs of the group," Kerr and Bowen considered it to be the ability to function as "an individual *while [being] part of the group*" (p. 63).

To paraphrase Kerr and Bowen (1988), individuality and togetherness are biologically rooted life forces, but the extent to which either or both develop is largely a function of learning (p. 63).

Kerr and Bowen distinguish their concept of individuality from the American stereotype of "rugged individualism," pointing out that the latter term implies the quality of "counter-dependence." The "rugged individualist" has trouble being an individual without permanently disrupting relationships—the flip side of the "compliant" individual who has difficulty maintaining individuality in the context of ongoing relationships.

The forces of individuality and togetherness coexist in dynamic equilibrium. While all relationships exist in a state of balance, the balance point in various relationships differs. The difference is in the degree of energy that is *bound* (obligatorily invested) in the relationship. Papero (1990) suggests that the developmental path of the family unit is characterized by the increasing ability of each member to be responsible for him/herself. Incomplete caretaker–child differentiation creates dependencies that handicap the adaptability of everyone involved, because maneuvers are developed to manage difficulties generated by the attachment without addressing the incomplete development.

Differentiation of Self

Eight concepts comprise Bowen's family system theory. Seven of them concern broader systemic processes (triangles, sibling position, nuclear family emotional processes, family projection, emotional cutoff, multigenerational transmission, and societal emotional process). However, the eighth concept, which concerns the *individual*—the concept of differentiation of self—is at the core of Bowen's work. Differentiation "addresses how people differ from one another in terms of their sensitivity to one another and their varying abilities to preserve a degree of autonomy in the face of pressures for togetherness" (Papero, 1990, p. 45). Differentiation accounts for individual variations in (genetically rooted) reactivity to others.

The term differentiation is borrowed from biology and suggests an analogy to cellular development. From essentially the same material cells develop, or differentiate, to perform separate yet related functions in the organism. The comparison with the development of the individual in the family is illustrative of the goal of remaining in viable emotional contact with the family yet retaining the ability to function with responsible autonomy.

The basic level of differentiation of self is manifested in the degree to which an individual manages across life to keep thinking and emotional systems separate, to retain choice between behavior governed by thinking and by emotional reactivity, and to set a life course based on carefully thought out principles and goals. (Papero, 1990, p. 47)

Differentiation is the process by which a person manages individuality and togetherness in a relationship. According to Kerr and Bowen, the degree of differentiation achieved is determined by the nature of one's relationship with one's parents and significant caretakers, and the degree to which one's parents achieved emotional separation from their own families of origin.

Parents function in ways that result in their children achieving *about* the same degree of emotional separation from them that they achieved from their parents. However, not all children of one set of parents separate emotionally to the same degree. This is because the characteristics of the parents' relationship with each child are not the same. Their relationship with one child may foster more separation than their relationship with another. (Kerr & Bowen, 1988, p. 95)

The degree of emotional separation between a developing child and his family influences the child's ability to differentiate a self from the family. . . . He can view parents, siblings, and others not just as people with roles in his life, but as distinct and separate individuals. His self-image is not formed in reaction to the anxieties and emotional neediness of others; nor do others define the child through their own emotionally distorted perceptions. . . .

In a poorly differentiated family, emotionality and subjectivity have a strong influence on family relationships. The high intensity of emotionality or togetherness pressure does not permit a child to grow to think, feel, and act for himself. The child functions *in reaction* to others. A good example is a rebellious adolescent. (Kerr & Bowen, 1988, p. 96)

Differentiation permits a person to function individually and yet be emotionally involved with others, and to do both simultaneously at profound depth. Differentiation of self is a critical task that ideally precedes adult attempts at intimacy, for it is differentiation that permits one to be intimate rather than "close" or fused. More realistically, the emergence of differentiation sufficient to maintain an intimate marriage *coincides* with the attempt to have it. Said differently, marriage is the natural crucible of adult differentiation (if properly used).

> The togetherness needs of a very poorly differentiated person, which are over-riding in their influence, are felt as deep yearnings to be loved, accepted and guided through life. . . . [In well differentiated people] the togetherness force is felt not as deep yearnings and needs, but as a basic attraction and interest in one's fellow man. . . .
>
> A very poorly differentiated person has *no capacity for autonomous function-ing*. . . . When involved in a relationship, his functioning becomes totally gov-erned by what transpires between him and the other person. (Kerr & Bowen, 1988, p. 69)

The "divorce-busting" (Weiner-Davis, 1990) side-effect of getting control of oneself in the midst of a marriage is rivalled by its value as a crucible for differentiation. And, as Kerr and Bowen point out, spouses always bring the right partner with them into the crucible: *people tend to pick partners with similar levels of differentiation*. Partners' level of differentiation is correlated with the amount of energy available for individual development and inversely correlated with rigid investment in the relationship. Two well-differentiated people can remain fairly separate in their emotional functioning; individuality among poorly differentiated people is almost nonexistent.

Differentiation, Autonomous Functioning, and Capacity for Intimacy

The lower the level of differentiation, the more prone people are to engage in highly dependent relationships—while also having the chronic urge to escape from each other (Kerr & Bowen, 1988). The more differentiated the individu-al, the more he/she can function autonomously while in meaningful contact with others. Given our prior discussion of self-validated intimacy, the role of differentiation in the development, maintenance, and enhancement of marital intimacy should be obvious.

> If a well differentiated person is not involved in a relationship, he can manage his life effectively and retain a sense of emotional well-being. . . . At the very highest levels of differentiation, no matter what the intensity of emotional, feeling, and subjectively determined pressure from others to operate in other than a self-determined direction, the person can retain his autonomy. Autono-my does not mean selfishly following one's own directive; it means the ability to be self-determined. Self-determination could result in a *choice* to be guided by the best interests of the group.
>
> The capacity for autonomous functioning does not mean a person lacks emotions and feelings. It means that while the person may respond to input

from others on an emotional, feeling and subjective level, *he has the capacity to process these responses on a objective level*. (Kerr & Bowen, 1988, p. 70)

Kerr and Bowen (1988) propose a conceptual scale of differentiation, ranging from 0 to 100. They suggest that a completely differentiated person has fully resolved emotional attachments to his/her family. His/her sense of self is sufficiently developed to permit him/her to be an individual in the group whenever it is important to do so. He/she is responsible for himself/herself and neither fosters nor participates in others' irresponsibility. At the other end of the scale, a completely undifferentiated person has achieved no emotional separation from his family. He has "no-self" and is incapable of being an individual in the group.

Little credence is given to notions of unconscious determinism, picturing humans as being capable of not being governed by irrational conflicts. On the other hand, since no one fully resolves issues of family attachment, the notion of reaching 100 on their scale is more theoretical than realistic.

Kerr and Bowen roughly categorize individual functioning into four quadrants on their scale. People at the lowest level are so emotionally needy and reactive to others, so driven by feelings, and so avoidant of anxiety that they are unable to increase their basic level of differentiation. At the second level, individuals are still highly emotionally reactive and display the same general behavior but have the potential to improve themselves. However, individuals at both levels display the same characteristics (including difficulty self-soothing) to varying degrees:

> Bowen observed that people vary greatly in their ability to manage reactivity. As anxiety increases, so does the tendency to react emotionally and to lose sight of a broader, more objective picture. Some people appear to function with continued emotional reactivity. Life for them is primarily a matter of feeling good or feeling poorly. Such individuals are generally either highly involved with important others or withdrawn. Life's troubles affect people with this level of automatic emotional response frequently and severely. (Papero, 1990, p. 46)

Individuals achieving the third quadrant on the differentiation scale (a) have intellectual systems sufficiently developed to make a few independent decisions and (b) are freer to choose between being governed by intellect or feelings. They have greater intimacy tolerance and more freedom to move back and forth between intimacy and other goal-directed activities.

> . . . there are people who appear to have greater control of their reactive responses. While they react emotionally at times, their major life decisions appear to be based more on careful thought and clearly defined principles than on

reactivity. They can enter into intimate relationships with other people and not have life governed solely by those relationships. They do not deny, however, the importance of the relationship. Such people have a degree of choice. They can respond to a situation emotionally or in a less emotional, more thoughtful manner. And they have less reactivity to anxiety in other people. (Papero, 1990, p. 46)

At the highest level of differentiation, the individual is sure of his/her beliefs, convictions, and self-assessment—but capable of hearing others' viewpoints and discarding old beliefs in favor of new ones. He/she can listen without reacting, tolerate intense feelings, and not act automatically to alleviate them. Individuals at this stage of differentiation can respect the identity of others without becoming critical or involved in trying to modify others' life course. He/she is realistically aware of his/her dependence on others and is free to enjoy relationships.

Despite Kerr and Bowen's attempts to articulate the characteristics of individuals at different points on their continuum of differentiation, it is difficult to accurately assign people a place on the scale. One reason is the difference between *basic* and *functional* levels of differentiation. *Basic differentiation* refers to core internalized development of the individual, which can be maintained independent of shifting circumstances in the relationship. *Functional differentiation* is highly dependent on the current status of the relationship.

The scale of differentiation refers to basic differentiation, which is largely determined by emotional separation from family of origin. Kerr and Bowen suggest that basic differentiation is established by the time of adolescence and usually remains fixed for life. It can be modified through crisis or structured effort (such as therapy) in later life, but such attempts involve more than insight regarding one's situation:

> The level of reactivity of an individual and of a group is believed to be the product of several factors. The internal guidance system of any organism and any species is the result of millions of years of evolutionary development. It is the outcome of the endless struggles of countless individuals within a species to survive and to mate. More immediately it is the product of the experiences of recent generations in the organism's immediate line of decent, in human terms the extended family. Finally, the history of the organism or group of organisms interacting with one another in the immediate past plays a role. (Papero, 1990, p. 46)

Functional differentiation can appear higher or lower than the level of basic differentiation, depending on the current status of the relationship. When anxiety is high, people become more reactive and less thoughtful, and functional differentiation declines. Thus, it is possible for two people in different relationships to appear to operate at the same functional level, although they have achieved different levels of *basic* differentiation. The difference is that the individual with the higher level of *basic* differentiation will more *consistently* display a high functional level because he/she is not very emotionally dependent on others.

Sexual dysfunctions (and attendant anxiety and disruption in the marital system) tend to reveal partners' level of basic differentiation. The result is often rapid and drastic shifts in the functional level of the relationship. Individuals whose functional level characteristically exceeds their basic differentiation are particularly prone to sexual dysfunctions, which rapidly become chronic problems.

Basic differentiation determines the ability of the receiver to maintain an efficacious mind set during sex in the presence of minor disruptions in relationship equilibrium. Likewise, basic differentiation is a significant determinant of the individual's (and the couple's) response to treatment for sexual-marital difficulties. Proscriptions and prescriptions used in treating sexual dysfunctions and/or marital discord require abandoning ineffective beliefs and values and modifying behavior patterns. Such changes often lead to diminished (functional) differentiation in one or both partners—a response often mislabeled by therapists and patients as a "negative treatment response."

Solid Self and Pseudo-self

Closely related to the notions of basic and functional differentiation are the concepts of *solid self* and *pseudo-self*. Solid self is an important component of basic differentiation, while pseudo-self relates to functional differentiation.

> Lacking beliefs and convictions of their own, they [people at low levels of differentiation] adapt quickly to the prevailing ideology. . . . Conviction is so fused with feeling that it becomes a cause. When comprised of beliefs and opinions that are comforting or provide direction, pseudo-self can reduce anxiety and enhance emotional and physical functioning. This can be so even if the beliefs conflict with facts. (Kerr & Bowen, 1988, pp. 102–103)[4]

People with mostly pseudo-self have difficulty abandoning culturally prescribed and relationship-negotiated mores and folkways about sex and intimacy. They have difficulty establishing a view of sexuality (or a style of sexual

---

[4]Herein lies an explanation of the phenomenon of "sexual addictionology."

behavior) that differs from their expectations of others' expectations. Given the tendency to establish norms during adolescence that are often ineffective in later life, such individuals are ripe for sexual problems and can be difficult therapy patients.

Solid self is central to one's capacity for intimacy, since it is at the core of intense experiences of self. Solid self is what is disclosed during intimacy, and what allows one spouse to encourage the other to "be who he/she is." *Said differently, the degree of solid self (as opposed to pseudo-self) revealed in an individual's disclosure is a major determinant of the saliency of intimacy. Solid self is vital to relinquishing expectations of reciprocity and tolerating existential separateness. Solid self determines the individual's upper limit for intense intimacy.*

> While pseudo-self is always vulnerable to being molded and changed by others, it is most vulnerable in emotionally intense relationships. That is where people have the most difficulty permitting each other to be what they are. Each reacts to the beliefs, attitudes, values and way of being of the other and tries to reshape them. If one person gets the upper hand, that person's beliefs, attitudes, and values become dominant in the relationship. The dominant one gains strength and confidence in what he thinks and feels. He is sure his compass (what he believes, values and thinks) is pointing in the "right" direction. Meanwhile, his partner loses confidence in her compass. One becomes the "strong" self (really pseudo-self) and the other the "weak" self. Solid self is not negotiable in any relationship system and little "borrowing" and "trading" of "self" occurs in well differentiated relationships. (Kerr & Bowen, 1988, p. 104)

One patient, to his own discomfort and credit, recently understood the difference between pseudo-self and solid self. He suddenly realized that he had a "good image" (i.e., an idealized image) of himself, but little *identity*. For many people, "good self-image" really means "power-of-positive-thinking" self-talk designed to maintain an idealized or artificial picture of oneself. This is actually a reflected sense of self, seeing the result of one's actions as though through another's eyes.

Functional differentiation is the artificial inflation or deflation of functioning based on "exchanging" pseudo-self in a relationship system. Spouses engaged in such exchange often present for treatment complaining of lack of "intimacy" and sexual intensity, although intimacy is often the last thing they can tolerate. *Unresolved individual issues of differentiation are not negotiable; pursuit of intimacy in quest of a transfusion of "self" ultimately leads to frustration, disillusionment, and alienation.*

Kerr and Bowen (1988) point out: "In contrast to pseudo-self, solid self is made up of firmly held convictions and beliefs that are formed slowly and can be changed *only from within self*. They are never changed by coercion or by persuasion from others" (p. 105). A partner's (or therapist's) attempts to change an individual's core self are doomed to failure. While the desired pseudo-self compliance may occur, such effort actually backfires: It weakens the crucible of solid self development.

Effective treatment often involves encouraging one or both partners to maintain their own beliefs, even if they are antithetical to effective sexual and marital functioning. As Kerr and Bowen state: "The person who stands firm does not have to be 'right' to be of benefit to the group. . . . He is not attempting to influence or change others, but simply stating, 'This is who I am; this is what I believe'" (p. 105). The emergence of greater solid self in at least one partner often has a catalytic impact on the development of both individuals and enhances intimacy and sexual intensity. Sexual and marital therapies that "teach" "proper" technique and attitudes often fail to demonstrate long-term generalized gains.

It is important to note that Bowen's theory does not focus on "pathology"; it embraces a rather accepting, asset-based outlook. Bowen did not regard low levels of differentiation as inherently pathological (although many clinicians might).

> The concept of differentiation eliminates the need for a concept of normalcy. Any level on the continuum is both natural and normal. Nor is any level particularly concerned with pathology. People and families at any point on the scale can appear to function very well with little overt difficulty. As long as a family can maintain a tolerable level of emotional equilibrium, it can function very well indeed. However the level of differentiation of a family or individual plays an important role in the family's ability to adapt to changing conditions. Said slightly differently, the level of differentiation plays a role in the ability of the family to absorb and manage tension produced by changing conditions. (Papero, 1990, p. 47)

Likewise, emotional gridlock in the marital dyad and intergenerational triangle are natural, inevitable, and circular results of each other:

> A marriage could be thought of as a union of two transferences. The emotional "fit" in a marriage results from each spouse's having been groomed by his or her own growing up experience to act out the reciprocal side of his spouse's transference. This interlocking of transferences is *not pathological*. It seems inappropriate to regard a phenomenon as pathological when it is a universal feature of human relationships. (Kerr & Bowen, 1988, pp. 169–170)

UNRESOLVED INDIVIDUAL ISSUES SURFACE IN RELATIONSHIPS

Privacy, Intimacy, Exclusivity, and Boundaries

Intimacy is an inherently exclusive experience. On the individual level, awareness of self in the context of another involves awareness of the boundary between self and other. In the dyadic alternative sexual reality of profound intimate sex, nothing exists beyond the immediate presence of the two partners: Awareness of the room (or even the bed) may cease to exist, creating an exclusive phenomenological adventure. On the macro level, the entire notion of a social *happening* is the experiential distinction between those who participated and those who did not.

Recognizing this phenomenon on individual, dyadic, and group levels helps crystallize the essence of *exclusivity* and *boundaries*. Exclusivity develops through the *experience* of the moment, not the content. The same thoughts, sexual behaviors, and self-disclosure may be repeated with others, but the experience is not the same; exclusivity is the feeling, *"you had to be there at the time."*

Unfortunately, some people (especially men) mistakenly expect exclusivity about the event, rather than the experience, when they disclose. Issues of confidentiality aside, expectations of exclusivity often generalize to any reaction by the listener to the disclosed information or the discloser. In effect, self-disclosure often occurs with the sense of boundary around the couple in relation to the outside world.

There *is* a need for boundaries and exclusivity in marital intimacy. However, the boundary is not "you and me against the world," implicitly taking the partner as an extension of oneself. Instead, the necessary boundary is provided by the discloser's relationship with him/herself: self-soothing and solid self permit flexible partner engagement without restrictive demands on the partner's contacts or confidences with others.

Many men are threatened by their female partner's conversations with other women. Given his low propensity to self-disclose to his own friends, the man experiences the woman's behavior as an information leak. The notion that she is talking about what is happening in her *life (of which he is an important but nonexclusive focus) is sometimes quite beyond him. Attaining a view of his partner as a related but independent entity may require more ability to look beyond his self-centeredness than he possesses. Once he self-discloses, she is seen only as a part of himself. She is his Achilles' heel, his vulnerability. Denial of separateness has its price.*

Unfortunately, this common occurrence perpetuates the inaccurate conclusion that women are more interested in intimacy than men. Gender differences in intimacy need or tolerance are often stated without regard for the *level* of intimacy in question. Low to moderate levels of intimacy are most often considered, whether in women's non-sexual friendship or research (e.g., college students, randomly selected couples or patients). At low to moderate levels of intimacy, women may be more interested than men. *There is little gender difference, however, in tolerance for the intense levels of intimacy that can occur in "eyeball to eyeball" marital sexuality. When intimacy is distinguished from dependency, codependency, and fusion, many women don't want it either.*

The distortion of gender differences in intimacy need and tolerance also carry over to understanding affairs. When men have affairs, it is often assumed they want sex and are avoiding intimacy. When women have affairs, it is assumed they seek intimacy their husbands are unable to tolerate. Both stereotypes diminish recognition that women's desire for sex and their aversion to *intense* intimacy does not differ from that of men.

Affairs can sometimes be understood as refusal to relinquish the fantasy of "becoming one with the partner." The individual retains the fusion fantasy through an intense affair, attributing the failure to attain "unity" to the spouse. Improved functional differentiation based on *borrowed functioning* in the affair is often mistaken as indication of having found a more appropriate partner. By its very structure and time limitations, however, an affair is a part-object relationship. Brief intensity is gratefully confused with depth.

Expecting to Be the "One and Only"

The common unresolved infantile wish to relive the symbiotic fusion and narcissistic gratification originally experienced (or missed) with parents during childhood can be called the desire to be the *"one and only."* The demand to be the "one and only" surfaces in the belief that marriage is an implicit promise by one's spouse to make one happy, and moreover, to remain ever vigilant to accomplish this. Individuals who are unable to relinquish the desire to be the "one and only" relate to the partner as an extension of him/herself, and cannot accept the partner as a separate individual with priorities and agendas of his/her own.

The demand to be the "one and only" makes all the spouse's personal goals, outside interests, and private relationships a source of threat. Sometimes it surfaces in competition with one's own child for the spouse's attention; other times it manifests in narcissistic anguish over a partner's prior lovers, even though contact may have terminated long before the current marriage.

When the fantasy of being the "one and only" is gratified, the individual demonstrates higher functional differentiation than can be maintained unilaterally. Sometimes one spouse willingly assumes responsibility for making the other happy, as the first step in establishing a *quid pro quo*. However, offering each person the opportunity to be the "one and only" to the partner usually fails: There can only be one *"one and only."*

Denial of the Partner's "Separate Life"

While there may be useful reasons for monogamy (see Chapter Twelve), gratifying the demand to be the "one and only" is not one of them; when this is the motivation, the result is further attempts to deny the partner is a separate individual with his/her separate life. Denial of the partner's separateness surfaces in the belief that one's spouse "belongs to" or "reflects upon" oneself in some proprietary way. In the quest for an acceptable reflected sense of self, the individual must control his/her spouse in order to control how he/she is perceived by others.

Common reluctance to "teach" or "ask" one's partner about preferred forms of sexual stimulation is another manifestation. While "embarrassment" and fears of rejection are sometimes cited as the source of the hesitancy, deeper origins often lie in refusal to relinquish the fusion fantasy that a good partner should "read one's mind."

Many couples would rather divorce than relinquish the fantasy of finding the "perfect partner." Differentiation permits spouses to tolerate disparate goals, interests, and emotional investments in others.

"You Can't Love and Hate the Same Person at the Same Time"

The complexity of human emotion is nowhere more apparent than around the topic of *hatred*. Framing the issue as "hostility" or "anger" simply does not elicit the same visceral impact, as witnessed by the common side-step, "Yes, I am angry with you, but I don't *hate* you." Acknowledging hatred is like crossing an emotional threshold; it is qualitatively different from acknowledging "lots of anger."

Acknowledging anger rather than one's hatred towards a partner reminds us of the difference between "having sex" and really *fucking* (in the most wholesome sense of the term). The reluctance to openly acknowledge one's hatred for a loved one often equals (or exceeds) common resistance to integrating eroticism and intimacy.

Although often initially unpleasant, the unilateral self-validated disclosure of hatred for a spouse (in the context of a relatively uncombative conversation) is one of the more profound intimate experiences; it often has an unanticipated settling impact on the discloser. Many people still carry the idealized split-object parental introject they adopted to cope with the childhood dilemma of parental and personal hatred. Often this was encouraged by parents who, themselves, failed to integrate hatred and love towards the same cherished individual. Part-object attachment around the topic of hostility often surfaces in such "beliefs" as:

- "If you love me, you can't hate me."
- "If you hate me, you can't love me."
- "If I hate you, I must not love you."
- "If I love you, then I can't hate you."

Mature adults have the self-soothing capacity to tolerate loving and hating the same person at the same time, and to recognize this same ambivalence in one's partner. It involves recognizing that feelings of love and hate do not "cancel out" or mitigate each other. Rather, they sit side by side, often of equal intensity.

The ability to tolerate this disparity is referred to (in object relations terms) as the capacity for whole-object attachments. The adaptive utility of part-objects (for children) becomes obvious: Recognizing hatred towards a loved one challenges fusion fantasies, because of possibly having one's hatred exposed or encountering the same feeling in the partner. Whole-object attachments involve relinquishing infantile fantasies of a totally gratifying partner and recognizing one's ambivalence towards the most cherished people.

Recognition that one hates and loves a cherished partner threatens infantile hopes of being "*unconditionally loved*." The concept of unconditional love, the darling of the Rogerian-dominated 1960s and 1970s, reflects the unresolved issues of both health professionals and the lay public. Artificial distinctions such as "loving a person but hating his/her behavior" (although totally contrary to contemporary understanding of unconscious processes) exemplify attempts to avoid the tension of ambivalence. The notion of unconditional love denies hating one's partner and keeps the fusion fantasy alive.

An individual who can maintain a whole-object attachment has a different understanding of "unconditional love": Loving "unconditionally" is not the same as being totally loving. Cherishing a beloved partner (or child) need not vacillate—if one does not deny hating the person for transgressions or disappointments.

A marriage in which hatred is not tolerated generates major distortions and impediments to intimacy. Spouses can be "close" and "caring," but not intimate, when neither is able to recognize or acknowledge what he/she is feeling: Being "known" stimulates fears of being unloving and unlovable.

Denying the coexistence of hate and love does not prevent expression of hostility; it creates difficulty modulating and buffering hostility without hurting others. Hatred surfaces suddenly in dramatic and obsequious ways, followed by periods of collusive denial. Exploitive and hurtful outbursts create a "dirty little secret" that binds partners together and enhances an "us vs. them" attitude towards the rest of the world. Paradoxically, this draws the couple together in pseudo-intimacy and pseudo-mutuality.

Boldly confronting the fact that partners hate each other, and questioning why they attempt to deny it, is a powerful intervention with embittered couples. The therapist's calm acceptance of the couple's mutual hatred often creates a paradigm shift from the preexisting view that it is the hatred itself that threatens their relationship. It can be pointed out that both individuals are operating in a reality that says hatred negates the possibility of being loved or loving. In so doing, the therapist reframes "communication difficulties" more accurately as *intolerance for what is communicated* — in this case, both individuals' infantile intolerance of their partner's (and their own) hatred. Therapeutic interventions of this nature are a working demonstration of intimacy, just as such interactions are the crucible for, and the result of, higher levels of differentiation.

Needing to Be Needed and Not Settling for Being Wanted

Many people lack the differentiation to settle for being *wanted*; they only feel secure when they are needed. Spouses who rely on borrowed functioning from their position in a relationship seek enmeshment and perpetuate their partner's neediness. Such individuals function at artificially inflated levels by virtue of being needed; they maintain the veneer of encouraging the partner's autonomous functioning, while they suppress the "helped" partner on a daily and long-term basis.

The prototype for needing to be needed lies in the separation-individuation phase of child development. For insecure children and adults, being needed and valued (albeit as a service provider, rather than as a person having intrinsic worth) is a gratifying but pseudo-secure position. Their difficulty relinquishing control and allowing themselves to be openly nurtured often interferes with sensate focusing and acceptance of effective sexual stimulation. People who *need to be needed* satisfy themselves by creating incongruous power hierarchies (see Chapter Eight).

Fears of Engulfment, Entrapment, and Exploitation

To the degree that marital difficulties reflect unresolved individual issues, resolving marital conflict often feels like a descent into one's nightmares with attendant fears of never awakening. At the height of this process, the ability to buffer one's fears of engulfment, entrapment, and exploitation become paramount.

At first glance, this may present a very dismal picture of relationships doomed to frustration and failure; however, exactly the opposite is true. In the process of selecting a partner and untangling the web of interlocking unresolved individual issues, each of us creates the crucible for our personal development and the vehicle for achieving our freedom from our past.

Having Sex, Getting Sex, and Getting Gotten

Early in their sexual careers, people learn to equate sexual contact with "getting" and "getting gotten." These themes are institutionalized in common adolescent male and female sex roles, particularly around losing one's virginity. It can be both gratifying and frightening to believe that one has turned over some irretrievable aspect of oneself, conveying an irrefutable position of importance to the partner. In one respect, it reflects an inflated estimate of the intimacy inherent in sexual contact; in another, it involves a sense that core psychological boundaries and physical integrity have been compromised.

Adults with an unstable sense of solid self replay such issues in subsequent relationships. Such individuals act like having sex gives away a special secret, just like a four-year-old child playing "doctor" or some variant of "I'll show you mine if you show me yours." "Giving oneself to one's partner" is vastly different from the notion of generously *sharing oneself* during sex. The former notion reflects some gain or loss of pseudo-self; the latter requires flexible and resilient ego boundaries.

Consider, for example, an imaginary couple named Sally and Bill:

- When Sally "gave herself" to Bill, what did he get?
- When Sally feels she "lost herself" when she married Bill, has he "had her" all these years? What if Bill feels they have grown apart and he no longer "has her"? If he has "had her," how does he "return her," when he doesn't "know where she's at"?
- Does Sally have to get away from Bill, so she can "get herself back"?
- What if Bill *believes* he has "gotten" Sally (sexually and otherwise), even though Sally feels good about her own participation?

While such questions may seem absurd, articulating them helps expose the trading of pseudo-self that often permeates couples' sex and intimacy. *The spectre of "equity theory" (Chapter Four) and borrowed functioning suddenly rears its head, and the realization occurs that these are two sides of the same well-worn coin.*

The notion of *having been gotten* sexually has diverse impacts on relationships. Sometimes, it precludes further emotional and physical contact; other times, it forges an inflexible attachment based on low self-esteem and an inflated sense of investment. When the latter case precipitates marriage early in adulthood, there is often a residual feeling of restricted sexual experimentation, lack of personal freedom, and resentment in later years. While this results in an intense period of struggle for differentiation in some couples, conflict simply reflects a continuation of displacement, projection, and pseudo-autonomous functioning in others. Part of what complicates resolving fears of *being scored* or *"gotten"* is the myriad partners who are well equipped to consensually validate this distortion.

The Vampire Model of Sexual Intimacy

Many people approach sex (and relationships in general) as a means to emotionally incorporate and feed off their partner. This involves a common but unwarranted equation of sexual contact with validation, nurturance, and love. The prototype of the vampire model of intimacy is evident in Klein's (1946) description of an infant's experience nursing at its mother's breast in the first half year of life.

Widespread fascination with vampire themes celebrates the pursuit of borrowed functioning. In vampire movies, relationships are depicted in which personal need (i.e., for blood) outweighs everything else, including the rights and needs of the partner. This fascination reflects the ambivalent fear and desire to be both the feeder and the food in a relationship.

For example, during her childhood and adolescence, Barbara's father flagrantly flaunted his affairs with many women, many young girls her own age. In fact, Barbara's father often requested that she solicit girls for him to date from among her own friends. For the most part he was emotionally distant and often absent during her childhood, spending major holidays with his lovers instead of the family. Barbara was often sent by her mother to beg her father for grocery money.

Yet, Barbara's father was incredibly puritanical about her contact with boys. Early in her adolescence Barbara was caught kissing a boy in the livingroom; her father chased her for blocks until she hid in some hedges in fear.

Barbara developed an elaborate prepubertal bedtime ritual in which, after donning a sheer nightgown that her mother provided, she would arrange her long hair on her pillow to display her neck. She would then masturbate to the fantasy of a frightening but charming and seductive Dracula biting her neck. In adulthood, she developed a repetitive masturbatory fantasy of being humiliated by a group of abusive men who forced her to masturbate to orgasm in front of them.

Symbiotic relationships can be very gratifying at the outset; later in the relationship, however, the equation of sex and love can be a frustrating source of contention. Even spouses who initially have a healthy appetite for sex eventually resent being used to feed a partner's self-esteem and dependency.

What turns people into vampires? Object relations theory suggests that repressed split-objects are largely destructive and hateful in content. Our prior discussion of *libidinal bad objects* and "overgratifying" parents who instill hatred comes to mind. Children of emotionally seductive overgratifying parents are trapped in a negative double bind: they experience hatred when their demands are not met and fear further deprivation and dependency when they are.

Whirlwind Relationships and Transference Storms

Individuals who have difficulty self-soothing and maintaining ego boundaries rely on physical proximity to control emotional reactivity. In *long-distance relationships*, for example, partners spend time together in sporadic, but intense, bursts. During periods of contact, lovers are totally consumed with each other and cut off from realistic interaction with their day-to-day routines. They avoid the internal and interpersonal conflicts involved in maintaining boundaries within a relationship and balancing other aspirations, friends, and agendas. Crucial autonomy struggles are postponed until they have made the commitment to cohabitate or marry. Part-object attachments become apparent as the time draws near to shift to common living space: off-and-on again wedding plans, changes in sexual patterns, refusal to respect privacy, and triangulation with parents.

In *"whirlwind" relationships*, there is a powerful press for immediate consummation. "Consummation" is an apt pun that foretells the dynamics of the relationship: Very shortly, the couple becomes locked in fights about decision-making and attempts to control each other (and themselves) in the fusion they have created. *Each has the feeling he/she is seeing a previously unnoticed side of the partner, which in a certain sense is true; each partner's behavior and perception of the other is dependent on proximity.* Although the fights may look like autonomy struggles, it is likely that neither partner is truly interested in the pleasures and responsibilities of autonomy. *They are merely struggling over which of them will determine the direction of the fusion.*

Fear of Abandonment and the Politics of "Sexual Abandon"

The ubiquity of "fears of abandonment" is a fitting counterpart to societal preoccupation with "sexual abandon." In healthy individuals, sexual abandon can be an extremely gratifying intimate exchange; it is only rewarding, however, in the context of solid self and high differentiation. In such a context, sexual abandon is the equivalent of "a tight grip on a loose rein." A person can then really let himself/herself "go," indulging in the uninhibited expression of eroticism.

Total abandon, however, does not provide gratification in itself. In individuals with mostly pseudo-self, it gives rise to fears of "losing oneself."

Many people have experienced "losing themselves" where sex was good but the relationship was destructive and demeaning. Although there may have been wildly erotic sexual contact, the individual may not be able to maintain the same level of eroticism or self-soothing with a "loving" partner. In fact, the true extent of sexual (and personal) abandon in the prior destructive relationship may be hidden from the current partner. In some cases, the person manifests "self-control" during sex with the spouse, while simultaneously engaging in a highly erotic affair.

When a husband accuses his wife of not "abandoning herself" during sex, for example, the wife may claim that he is not "trustworthy"; she implies that she would be more spontaneous and involved if he *made* her trust him. Unfortunately, this misguided approach makes the "untrusting" wife dependent upon her husband, thus increasing the likelihood of suspicion and distrust. Once again, the importance of self-validated intimacy and one's relationship with oneself becomes evident.

"Pop" therapies emphasizing "the needy child within" give credence to the notion of "fears of abandonment" in adults. While this conceptualization often speaks to people's feelings, it also *validates* the fusion fantasy of normal neuroses: "Fears of abandonment" in an adult reflect a denial of existential separateness. Adults do not have the same physical and emotional vulnerability to abandonment that children do. Aside from the rare case where one spouse drains the bank accounts and suddenly departs, leaving the other as a destitute single parent, fears of "abandonment" are a misnomer.

It is like an adult, thrashing about in 3 feet of water several yards from the shoreline, complaining he/she will drown. A child in the same situation has more basis for such fears; in adulthood, the solution is to put one's feet in the "muck" and walk to shore!

Some poorly differentiated people revel in the temporary fusion of sexual abandonment—their difficulty is intolerance for resuming "separateness" and self-maintenance following intense sexual contact. *Sequential affairs are a haven for people who resent the differentiated functioning required to balance marriage, family, careers, and outside friendships. The intermittent nature of affairs permits the fantasy that a full-time relationship with that person would always be as intense as it is during clandestine meetings.*

There is a difference between healthy dependency needs that all people have and "a dependency relationship"; the latter is primarily organized to gratify, rather than improve, low levels of differentiation. A high level of differentiation permits the intermittent gratification of being taken care of; the ability to self-soothe buffers the shock of having it end. Counter-dependent people, in contrast, overreact to their underlying impulse to lose themselves in a relationship. Their tenuous pseudo-self cannot permit the slightest reliance on another person. Counter-dependency is a parody of autonomy and independence.

Dependency and Distortion in Intimate Communication

When relatively undifferentiated couples are beset with struggles for gratification and validation, the fusillade of projections in the subsequent transference storm creates distortions in partners' perceptions and subsequent behavior. Such distortions include:

- distortion of what should be (and has been) disclosed;
- distortion of the meta-meanings of what has (and has not) been disclosed;
- failure to recognize encouraging responses;
- failure to recognize superficial responses and lack of true interest;
- fears of being controlled and engulfed by listening attentively; and
- assumption of responsibility to "fix" the partner's dissatisfactions.

Part-objects and Half-truths

Devotees of inherent paradox appreciate the subtle ways in which couples fight over "who has the truth" to collusively deny they exist in two separate (parallel) realities. The common marital premise that "we are in the same boat" sets the stage for the conflict over who will be captain of the ship. This "control" fight denies that spouses are forever in two separate boats whether they like it or not. They can sail them side by side on the same course, but they will never become one (fused) boat: The reality of death makes that clear.

However, spouses' views of their problems, and their theories of causation provide excellent information on their system of distortions and projections; the ineffective solutions reflect their interlocking realities. Like the pseudo-logic of paranoid thinking, a dysfunctional couple's interpretations and counter-interpretations *almost* make sense.

Partners' interpretations invariably have truth. Whether or not the interpretations are accurate views of the partner, they are always accurate reflections of the dynamics, distortions, and phenomenological experience of the perceiver.

Fights about truth are quite complex. Each partner uses his/her truth to avoid the partner's truth. Ironically, the core dynamic is collusive rather than adversarial: Both partners are denying the *simultaneous* validity of *all* the statements (i.e., the existence of separate realities).

Truths in a relationship are invariably *half-truths*; half-truths are true as far as they go, but they don't encompass the whole truth. Half-truths are difficult to perceive because it requires looking beyond one truth to find another truth. For example (if the reader is a thoroughly *normal* clinician), the foregoing has probably been interpreted as a discussion of *abnormality* (i.e., *pathology*). Moreover, the above descriptions have been interpreted as explanations why people have sexual dysfunctions, intimacy problems, and mediocre sex. While the discussion *is* applicable in this way, *these very same issues surface (resurface) as the salience and intensity of intimacy and eroticism approach the upper limits of human sexual potential.* One does not see one's assumptions until they are disconfirmed.

Intense intimacy and eroticism in marriage are very difficult to tolerate: Unresolved object relations conflicts reemerge. This is not "regression," but rather elicitation at a higher level of complexity offering further refinement in differentiation and personal development. When treatment stops prematurely (as it often does), sufficient resolution occurs to permit minimal levels of intimacy and sexual desire, and completion of the sexual response cycle. Residual aspects of these issues lie dormant and unnoticed until the meaningfulness of sex and intimacy becomes sufficient to evoke them.

Many therapists and patients never observe the process of elicitation at high levels of salience. Intense eroticism and intimacy create a sexual crucible of pleasure, offering a vehicle for further personal development.

It becomes increasingly obvious that discussion of individual dynamics offers *one* way of understanding dyadic processes. Interlocking individual con-

flicts offer a clinical truth about relationships. Yet, that view is a half-truth—
not because it is part false, but because it is an incomplete way of understanding intimacy and sexuality in marriage. In the next chapter, we will address the
same phenomena from a more systemic perspective.

Personal separateness and the indelible unity of living things constitute a
fundamental inherent paradox of sexuality (and of life). Early in the exploration of sexual potential, patients ask logical questions like, "Won't we drift
apart if we both learn to fulfill our own needs?" or, "Won't focusing on our
own physical sensations during sex draw us in opposite and separate dimensions?" Such questions touch on the differentiation necessary for intense intimacy, profound bonding, and intense sex.

In the exploration of sexual intimacy, a peculiar duality repeatedly emerges:
the acute experience of self as the center of one's phenomenological universe,
and the equally acute experience of self as finite, inextricably separate, and on
the periphery of a much larger whole. John Muir recognized this by simply
walking in the mountains. "When we try to pick out anything by itself," he
said, "we find it hitched to everything else in the universe" (Spring & Manning,
1988, p. 131). This delicious sense of self that comes in relinquishing one's
narcissism drives the mystic transcendence of sexual experiences.

CHAPTER EIGHT

The Dyadic System in Intimacy and Sexuality

This chapter reexamines the treatment alliance from a systemic perspective, considering (a) reasons why couples need or seek treatment, (b) hidden agendas in treatment requests, and (c) couples who report an otherwise "good relationship." Understanding the marital-sexual system allows the therapist to mitigate the tendency for treatment progress to trigger attempts at homeostasis. Detailed consideration of incongruous power hierarchies and power issues surrounding sexuality (and sexual-marital therapy) leads to two systemic facts of marriage:

- *A couple's sexual repertoire is more determined by the unresolved issues either spouse is avoiding than by efficacious technique.*
- *The partner who wants sex the least always controls sex in the dyad.*

WHY DO SOME COUPLES "NEED" TREATMENT?

If informal shoptalk among colleagues at professional conferences is any indication, sex therapy cases are becoming increasingly difficult to treat. Some couples with sexual difficulties appear able to take care of them through the resources available in the relationship. Sometimes serendipitous partner selection permits spontaneous curative interaction, and such couples may never present for treatment.

Consider, for instance, a man with premature ejaculation whose partner is experienced and proficient in performing fellatio. Over the course of time, Dirk recognizes that Monica really enjoys "doing" him, and allows himself to passively receive. They spontaneously create what is formally prescribed in sex therapy as nondemand genital pleasuring. When Dirk finally realizes that fellatio is *distinctly* pleasurable for her (she prefers oral sex over coitus), it creates a context that facilitates sensate focusing: Dirk begins to think of his penis as something Monica likes, rather than a defective organ that embarrasses him.

Monica can establish a profound depth of role enactment and partner engagement with fellatio—she knows guys like it, and she gets off on feeling sexy and powerful by

217

actively making them come. Monica often likes to bring men right to the point of inevitability and keep them there. Dirk unwittingly receives patterns of stimulation therapists describe as "stop-start," and he gets the best version possible: Monica doesn't do it like a "technique," and she feels erotic (rather than anxious) when she pauses.

Perhaps most importantly, Dirk can *feel* the erotic connection with her when she is sucking his penis. Gradually, he stops feeling isolated like when he "tunes her out" during coitus (to delay his ejaculation). For the first time in his life, Dirk makes erotic contact with a woman during sex.

After numerous repetitions, Dirk has significantly reduced anxiety during sexual contact, has greater awareness of his cues of ejaculatory inevitability, and has more tolerance for high levels of sexual stimulation. Dirk and Monica experience more than just a spontaneous cure; they enjoy a profound sense of immediate self-presence (i.e., intimacy) in their erotic connection that makes them like being with each other.

Most couples, however, do not live under the banner of splendid serendipity. There are many couples for whom the match of individual and systemic dynamics triggers, maintains, and exacerbates sexual difficulties. In such cases, sexual and marital difficulties are multiply determined and reinforced, making treatment necessary as well as difficult.

Most times, partner selection is a compromise solution of unresolved issues. It is not uncommon for individuals to pick partners with whom they can have adequate genital functioning, but little passion. Such couples may present for treatment if the issue of eroticism and intimacy is important enough that the partner with systemic clout will pursue it all the way to the therapist's office.

Allison is afraid of being exploited by men and fearful of male aggression. She picks Alvin, who is "understanding and gentle," and who is afraid of his own aggression. Allison has no difficulty with the style of sex that spontaneously evolves in their relationship. While it may not be the height of eroticism and sexual inventiveness, they have "tender" sex that is enjoyable and satisfying. They define themselves as having a "good" sexual relationship and do not present as a clinical treatment case — that is, until Allison discovers Alvin's hot sexual affair with her best friend.

Many, if not most, people pick partners who hold the promise of personal completion, and thus become involved in the picker's unresolved individual issues. A significant degree of this process occurs unconsciously, wherein the partner is intuitively picked for exactly the personality characteristics that later "crunch" and block the relationship. Whether this is regarded as human perversity or normal developmental reconstruction and resolution depends upon the therapist's theoretical orientation and success at treating such problems.

Rigid Response Patterns of the Individual and System

Kerr and Bowen (1988) pointed out that the emotional fit of a relationship can be just as complementary in a poorly differentiated relationship as in a well differentiated one. The lower the level of differentiation, however, the more likely that anxiety-driven "togetherness pressure" in the relationship will transform the couple's compatibility into the very source of their "incompatibility":

> Ways of thinking, feeling, and acting that promote an emotional fit between people in the beginning of their relationship become exaggerated in response to pressures that develop later in the relationship. Qualities that are attractive in moderation become unattractive when they are more extreme—charm becomes irresponsibility and decisiveness becomes overbearingness. At higher levels of differentiation, people function less in automatic reaction to one another and so compatible qualities are less likely to be driven to the polarized extremes that generate incompatibility. (pp. 170–171)

This "incompatibility" gives rise to the marital crises which David Kantor (1980) sees as normal developmental processes of relationships and the individuals therein. His concept of *psychopolitics* refers to the attitudinal posturing and systemic positioning characteristically adopted by individuals in a relationship or family. Kantor states there are only four possible psychopolitical roles:

- *mover*, who defines or initiates action;
- *follower*, who agrees with, supports, or continues the action;
- *opposer*, who challenges or goes against the action; and
- *bystander*, who witnesses the action, but remains outside of it, and neutral.

Kantor suggests that a system's psychopolitical configuration is like its signature, showing some variation around a preferred pattern based on the participants' early family experience. *Ritualized developmental crises* occur when individuals take predictable, self-defeating, system-disabling positions at critical moments. Under such circumstances, many couples require treatment to free the resources of the relationship for critical tasks of decision-making, crisis resolution, and problem-solving.

Kantor suggests that the mark of developmentally healthy and necessary identity struggles is the surfacing of competing claims about reality: how things are and how they ought to be. It is through these ritualistic struggles that partners complete their transformation into adults. Kantor states, "intimate relationships then become both context and occasion for completion. Where this fails, the job may be passed onto a therapist" (p. 150).

When sexual difficulties coincide with simmering developmental crisis in the relationship (as often occurs), couples need sexual-marital therapy to free their blocked creative resources. At such times, the purpose of treatment is not simply to "cure" the genital difficulty, but also to facilitate the development of the individuals and stimulate the inherent formative growth processes within the relationship.

Situations Beyond the Range of Adaptive Behaviors

Couples encounter situations that require resources and adaptive approaches that lie outside their own development, including options beyond their preexisting ways of handling sexuality. The determinants of such crises are the nature of the specific event or situational challenge, the functional level of the relationship, and the individuals' adaptive resources.

Normal sexual attitudes, behavior and beliefs are ineffective, if not totally debilitating, in coping with such realities of adult life as stress, illness and physical trauma. Their impact on the sexual and marital functioning of "normal" adults is predictably overwhelming. While the residual effects and attempts at resolution are partially determined by the specific nature of the stressor, pre-trauma functioning is the major determinant of its significance and impact. Long-dormant individual and family issues triggered by the illness are generally overlooked. Sexual-marital therapy can offer new options of adaptation and an opportunity for enhanced sexuality and personal development.

For some people, the precipitating event is the diagnosis of cancer or a spinal cord injury. For others, the event might be a rape or the surfacing of unresolved childhood incestuous experience. In other cases, the situational challenges are anticipatable developmental shifts in the family life cycle. In some households, the apparent stressor may be *decreased* partner access due to the birth of a child or *increased* access when the spouses retire from work. For others it may be the death of a parent, bringing sudden awareness of personal mortality and vulnerability to loss of the spouse. In yet other marriages, it is the revelation of a spouse's illicit affair and the threat of divorce. In all these cases, the ultimate impact of the events is in large measure a function of individual and systemic inflexibility in adapting to new circumstances.

A couple's traditional sexual repertoire is determined more by the unresolved personal issues either individual attempts to avoid than by effective and pleasurable technique. Both individuals generally reserve the right to refuse disquieting behaviors; their traditional sexual repertoire is simply a function of engaging in the remaining sexual options for a period of time. From this perspective it is easy to recognize how the couple's construction of "sexual normality" restricts sexual behaviors and attitudes and limits the spontaneous construction of corrective and healing sexual experiences. Sexual-marital therapy is required in many cases to provide the novel input, unavailable within the existing system, required to modify the system itself.

Differentiation is a major determinant of individual and systemic adaptability to shifting sexual and marital circumstances. As emotional boundaries between the partners blur, anxiety becomes more infectious. People become more intolerant of anxiety in themselves and the partner, and experience pressure to feel and act only in ways that reduce each other's discomfort. In the process, responses to problems become more impulsive and immediate, consequently reducing adaptation (and intimacy). Both the magnitude of problems and the rate of deterioration in the relationship increase at lower levels of differentiation. Relatively undifferentiated couples are thus more likely to require sexual-marital therapy due to (a) the fertile conditions for the creation of sexual and marital difficulties, (b) the relative poverty of effective problem-solving resources, and (c) the rapid deterioration of secondary aspects of the relationship.

Stuart Johnson (1987), former director of family therapy at the Yale Psychiatric Institute, developed a five-stage conceptual hierarchy of relationship styles based on the degree of separation and individuation achieved by the partners. Although the numerical rating system is somewhat confusing (lower numerical values reflect higher development), the scale does an elegant job of integrating intrapsychic defense mechanisms, relational coping style, and level of development:

- *Level 5: paradox.* At this lowest level of differentiation, the two driving needs—for a separate self and emotional connection—cannot be met. Relationships at this level are characterized by the paradoxical double-binds of satisfying both needs. Partners are constantly threatened by fears of engulfment and abandonment. Stable intimacy at this level is not possible.
- *Level 4: projective identification.* This is the level at which most relationships remain. Although the issues are the same as at the previous level,

some dilemmas are partially worked out by the defense mechanisms of splitting and projective identification. Autonomy and intimacy are seen as mutually exclusive polarities, and one or the other of these needs is met. (In level 5 relationships, neither need is met.) Partners in level 4 relationships are polarized, with each partner embodying one-half of the partner's rejected conflict. One partner becomes the embodiment of affiliative needs, and the other, of autonomy needs. Distancer-pursuer conflicts are characteristic. There is no tolerance for recognizing internal ambivalence or complex views of self or the partner. Subsequent levels on this scale represent a quantum leap in developmental complexity.

- *Level 3: conscious splitting.* This is similar to level 4 in that projection still takes place. However, partners are eventually able to comprehend it, own the projected side of themselves, and recognize their displacement onto the partner. Each can begin to acknowledge his/her own ambivalence at quieter and more rational times.
- *Level 2: tolerating ambivalence.* Partners in level 2 relationships can take conscious ownership of *both* sides of their inner conflicts regarding competing needs of autonomy and intimacy. Conflict in the relationship increasingly takes place intrapsychically rather than interpersonally. Awareness of internal conflict is not as readily confused with the partner's being the source of the frustration. There is greater appreciation of complexity of self and the partner.
- *Level 1: integration.* Individuals at this level of development no longer conceive of the needs for independence and togetherness as conflicting forces, either intrapsychically or interpersonally. Intimacy at this level involves an intense appreciation for togetherness and existential separateness, rather than fusion and merger. This represents the highest levels of individuation and separation of human development, which few individuals attain.

There are two aspects in Johnson's developmental model of relationships of particular relevance to the sexual crucible approach. The first is the focus on resolution of splitting and increasing tolerance of ambivalence as the couple moves from projective identification to integration (i.e., whole object attachment). Illustrative case examples of the crucible approach offered thus far have clearly illustrated the nonreactive therapeutic focus on both sides of each individual's ambivalence, such that he/she is isolated in it as a *personal* dilemma. In the process, spouses become more resolved and more tolerant of their own (and the partner's) ambivalence.

The second point of interest concerns the subtle *shift in the significance of paradox* as one moves from the lowest to the highest levels in Johnson's model. At low levels of differentiation, paradox is experienced as indicative of systemic or individual pathology. Paradox still exists at high levels of differentiation, but its previous toxicity disappears through appreciation and acceptance of one's own (and one's partner's) competing needs. In this sense, spouses become tolerant of the paradox of life.

It is useful to note that (a) Johnson has actually offered a developmental model of paradox; and (b) the use of inherent paradox is a fundamental aspect of the sexual crucible approach to sexual-marital therapy, a point to be pursued in Chapter Fifteen.

The Desire for Something Better Than "Normal" Sex

Contemporary society provides people with lots of *musts* or *shoulds* about sexuality. Common *musts* include the implicit assumptions that all people must want sex, that they should find it pleasurable, that it must occur in the context of intercourse, and that there must be erections, orgasms, etc. Albert Ellis refers to this pattern of intrinsic sexual expectations as *must-erbation* (Ellis & Harper, 1977). Sex therapists are often unwitting purveyors of such pressure-generating expectations (Szasz, 1980).

Sometimes couples enter treatment not so much because their functioning differs from that of their contemporaries but because they think it does. Society makes little provision for education and experiences to facilitate the achievement of commonly accepted *musts*. Few of us have a history and interpersonal experiences that would lead us to seek sexual and marital excellence out of positive motivations; more commonly the motive and goal involve compensating for feelings of inadequacy.

Sometimes couples enter treatment in pursuit of better sexual adjustment and more intense experiences than are supported and facilitated by contemporary society. Often this involves increasing resilience to the *musts*. Sexual-marital therapy, as it is presented in this book, can help people (a) abandon the feelings of inadequacy that drove them into therapy in the first place and (b) achieve a greater degree of intimacy and sexual intensity than is supported by "normal" approaches.

SEXUAL DYSFUNCTION IS NOT A DISEASE PROCESS

Despite diligent efforts by the committee that developed the most recent diagnostic criteria for sexual difficulties, *DSM-III-R* perpetuates the misguided notion that the etiology of sexual dysfunction and disinterest resides within a single individual. That perpetuation occurs in the form of a diagnostic system that emphasizes individuals and diseases rather than systems and processes. Alternative diagnostic systems specifically addressing this problem, such as the multi-axial diagnostic scale proposed by Schover et al. (1982), have not been widely adopted. Ironically, the few *DSM-III-R* diagnoses that address systemic processes, such as marital discord, are "V codes" which are generally not reimbursable by insurance companies.

Some cases involving lifelong invariant psychogenic erectile or orgasmic dysfunctions, sexual aversion secondary to sexual trauma, or childhood abuse can be thought of as primarily intrapsychic in origin. However, the particular successive partners of such individuals often participate through their own reactions, broadening the dynamics into interpersonal dimensions. The absence of spontaneous improvement in sexual functioning is not always attributable to "deep-seated" intrapsychic problems; sometimes it results from the subtle, continual reinforcement and maintenance of the identified patient's difficulty by interaction with his/her regular sexual partner.

The sexual relationship system sometimes *creates* the problem. As illustrated in Chapter Two, the same "identified patient" with a different partner might not have the same sexual difficulty. In other cases, the same physical symptoms might occur but would not be considered problematic and would not present as a "clinical problem." The relationship system provides the frame of reference from which arises the particular significance spouses attribute to their situation.

Contrary to popular stereotypes, women who present with inhibited sexual desire are not invariably "frigid" or aversive to sex; many have histories of reliable multiple orgasms and high desire. One such case involved a young woman whose husband was intimidated by her sexual aggressiveness, her preference for provocative boudoir clothing, and her explicit language during sex. By accepting sex only at his own initiation and thoroughly embarrassing her when she engaged in any of her preferred behaviors, the husband eventually conditioned his wife into hating sex and losing her ability to reach orgasm during coitus.

The labeling of behavioral events (or non-events) as sexual "problems" occurs as a function of the relationship context, rather than quantification according to the clock or calendar. Peter thrusts for 45 minutes of coitus before ejaculating and is the "cock of the rock" to himself and his partner. Right next door his neighbor, Barney, starts and stops the same behavior at the same moment; he and his wife are disappointed with their inability to resolve their problem of delayed ejaculation.

On one level it is obvious that the system *defines* the behavior as problematic or not (a) through the phenomenological experience of each individual during the behavior and (b) through its significance in the history of the relationship. On another level, the system *may create* or perpetuate the problem. Peter's wife loves long, prolonged thrusting, which produces a series of multiple orgasms; Barney's wife loves having problems and only a single orgasm. She also happens to have endometriosis, and between their mutual anticipation of her coital pain, his fears of failure, and the awareness that she just wants him to hurry up and finish, Barney can't get a total stimulus level sufficient to reach orgasmic threshold (Chapter Two).

Likewise, the concept of "inhibited sexual desire" is a relative term. The identified "low sex drive" partner in one relationship might be the comparatively more desirous partner in another. The actual level of the "low sex drive" partner's desire might increase with a different partner and might well have been higher with the current partner at a prior time.

Many sexually dysfunctional people treat their difficulties situationally. Some don't date at all, some maintain relationships only until sexual expectations arise, and some pick partners who don't stress them beyond the limits of their unresolved issues. The particular relationship system determines *what*, *when*, and *if* a couple will present for treatment. It is a significant clinical error to consider sexual and marital difficulties out of context, although this is exactly the way that many clinicians conceptualize problems and interview patients.

Consider a case in which the husband qualifies for the diagnosis of primary (lifelong) inhibited sexual desire. In this particular couple, the wife happens to be using this as a "reason" for flaunting her own multiple sexual affairs. These affairs would likely have occurred anyway, given her own prior history of difficulty with intimacy and compulsive sexual behavior. On the surface, the sexual difficulties of the identified patient mask and legitimize other difficulties of the wife. What is considered foreground and background in the couple's presentation of their problems is a function of the relationship system.

Systemic adaptation to dysfunctions of purely organic etiology can make reversal of original symptomatology quite difficult. For instance, spouses who become alienated and combative during a period when the husband has erectile difficulty due to medication often develop a secondary psychogenic erectile dysfunction that remains after the medication ceases. Likewise, spouses whose relationship has deteriorated during a husband's chronic alcoholism and resultant neurologically impaired erectile functioning often develop magical expectations for implantation with a penile prosthesis. However, insertion of the device confronts the realities of their marriage, precipitating rapid dissolution of the fantasy and a lurch forward into divorce.

There is a need for a simultaneous multisystemic viewpoint in understanding complex sexual-marital difficulties. Developing such a viewpoint is not easy because of a tendency to confuse *causation* of sexual and marital problems with *secondary impact*. On the one hand, systemically-oriented marital therapists often attempt to reframe a spouse's negative interpretations of dysfunctional interaction into something more "positive" and "treatable." "Benevolent" reframes reflect a schizoid view of the role of individual dynamics in dyadic processes, and a simplistic conception that ignores the role of competition, greed, insecurity, and hostility in individuals, couples, families (and family therapy). While sexual and marital problems may provide some benevolent secondary gain for someone in the system, suggesting that this is the sole reason for the symptom's existence defies logic and blocks the pursuit of multisystemic intervention.

Conversely, we are equally mistaken if we jump to the conclusion that symptomatology exists *because* of the existence of hostility or for the purpose of its expression. In some cases, there is little doubt that some gratification is derived from depriving the partner. Sometimes people are simply angry about their symptom or their position in a system and take it out on their partner. The sexual or marital problem, which may derive from other sources, becomes a convenient vehicle for this. The simultaneous appearance of affect and symptomatology does not prove directional causation, because causation can at the least occur in both directions and is, in fact, usually circular.

Relationship duration also has a systemic impact on sexual functioning. The pattern of declining sexual interest and satisfaction over a period of five to seven years of marriage is so endemic to our society it has been nicknamed "the seven-year itch." While the actual nature of this phenomenon will be considered in Chapter Ten, it is sufficient to note here that the underlying concept behind the seven-year itch is one of systemic, rather than individual, etiology.

In spite of people's best efforts to maintain stability through rigidity, ebb and flow of the life cycle inevitably change sexual commerce in marriage. Early in the cycle, one partner's initial hesitation to respond to sexual invitations may have a mutually gratifying quality for both. For the initiator, the pattern creates a sense of conquest and prowess in overcoming the partner's hesitancy. For the hesitant spouse, it conveys the feeling of being truly sexually desired. However, the same behavior may have a distinctly negative attribution five years hence, when it is interpreted by the initiator as withholding and frustrating laziness. The initiator's persistence, once appreciated, is now experienced by the hesitant partner as demanding.

Much to our chagrin and dismay, we sometimes recognize how we condition successive partners (each chosen specifically because he/she seemed different from the last) to function *and dysfunction* in exactly the same way. It is far more convenient to conclude that "all men (or women) are alike," than to admit, "I function the same with all men (and they, with me), given sufficient time."

Attribution theory highlights that all couples assign meaning to the events that transpire in their lives. The particular meaning assigned derives from their collective individual and systemic histories. The meaning that couples with sexual-marital dysfunction assign can both create and perpetuate the dysfunction. These attributions are neither accessible nor modifiable through direct appeal to reason, observation, and intellectual examination, because their source is illogical, unconscious, and systemic in nature.

At the outset of relationships, partners tend to agree that certain events have occurred; they fight over the meaning of the events and the intent of their actions. Once thoroughly enmeshed, partners fight over whether or not the event itself has occurred. This ensues because the attributional meaning and psychopolitical posturing surrounding similar events has been established through prior interaction. The meaning of the event is more or less fixed; what is debated is whether or not the event in question occurred. For instance, the statement "We never have sex" really means "You don't find me desirable and you think I'm oversexed"; the listener hears it as "You are so inadequate, and I think you're nuts to pass me up." The result leads to debates about how long it has been since they had intercourse. In this fashion, the system becomes a significant contributor to the attributional connotation of daily events.

INCONGRUOUS POWER HIERARCHIES

All natural complex systems (e.g., dyadic relationships, families, and institutions) organize along hierarchies. Within families, for instance, numerous simultaneous hierarchies exist around such issues as decision-making about money, vacations, discipline of children, nurturance displays, physical prowess, and housekeeping responsibilities.

Studies of healthy and troubled families (Beavers & Hampson, 1990; Lewis, Beavers, Gossett, & Phillips, 1976) indicate that hierarchies in healthy families are characterized by fluidity and flexibility over time, both within a given dimension and across dimensions of influence. Hierarchies in troubled families, in contrast, are characterized by rigid inflexible structure, unresponsive to shifting situational demands and maturational development of the individuals involved. To maintain this unstable order, the family or couple ascribes to a manufactured reality that precludes change or growth for its members.

In troubled families and relationships, power consists of the ability to dominate, control, and deprive others, or to enhance one's own status and prowess at the expense of stifling development of other family members. In healthy families, power has a positive connotation, involving the ability to provide nurturance, support, achievement, and leadership in a way that facilitates the functioning and development of other family members. Sometimes, these are conceptualized as *control*-oriented and *empowerment*-oriented families respectively.

Power hierarchies in the sexual arena have existed in every generation in every society, perpetuating various versions of "the natural order." Sexuality in early Catholic dogma was the province of male power; women submitted but did not participate as equals. By the early part of this century, the updated version promoted a virginal woman who was to be "educated" by her "experienced" husband. Coitus-focused sexuality, with its inherent emphasis on male erectile functioning, invariably perpetuates male insecurity and fear of female sexuality and elicits corresponding attempts to subjugate and control women.

Inflexible hierarchies are perpetuated at the expense of the participants' development. In male-dominated inflexible systems, restriction of women's development is relatively obvious; reciprocal inhibition of men's development is less apparent (except to many women). As the pre-Civil War phrase *"The slave knows the master better than the master knows himself"* indicates, inflexible hierarchies also facilitate *incongruous* structure as well.

Congruity, an important aspect of power hierarchies (Haley, 1976), concerns relationships among status, ability, power, control, and responsibility in a hierarchy. Healthy families display *congruous power hierarchies*: The person most senior in the hierarchy has the most power, control, and responsibility, and is openly respected for his/her ability. Individuals lower in the hierarchy have proportionate and mutually congruent amounts of power, control, responsibility, and status. Position within the hierarchy is proportional to ability and interest and shifts over the course of time. Positions in the numerous hierarchies that exist within a single relationship display variability.

Congruous power hierarchies are relatively stable, with periodic reorganization regarded as a healthy, anticipated process. Although there may be some anxiety for the participants during the process of change, it quickly recedes as people adapt to their new roles, prerogatives, and responsibilities. Congruity keeps tension low between the overt structure and the underlying ways people function. There are opportunities for individuals to develop new abilities, display them openly, and have them duly recognized. Beavers (1985), L'Abate & Talmadge (1987), and Stock (1985) emphasize that ongoing intimate relationships require equality in overt power and the absence of intimidation between the partners. Congruous hierarchies, unlike incongruous ones, demonstrate mutuality.

Incongruous power hierarchies, on the other hand, are inherently unstable and exist only as long as the dynamics of the system remain covert. There is a disparity between the apparent structure of reality and the actual interactional dynamics. In incongruous power hierarchies, one individual is designated as having the highest overt status, but some other individual has more control, responsibility, or capability in the relevant dimension. Moreover, individuals' control and responsibility for steering the system are inconsistent. Incongruous power hierarchies tend to generate a constant state of tension in the participants, even though it develops from maladaptive attempts to avoid anxiety.

One of the most salient contributions of systems theory is the notion of the *identified patient* and the *asymptomatic partner*. This view looks at symptomatology both as the result of systemic processes and as a way of regulating them. In these terms, incongruous power hierarchies are the cause and result of symptomatology in the identified patient. It is quite possible for a husband to be the identified patient in one incongruous power hierarchy, while his wife is simultaneously the identified patient in another. Both may be symptomatic in the same hierarchy, but one will have higher status than the other.

Partner selection often represents an attempt (a) to compensate for self-perceived deficits, (b) to meet hopes for gratification, and (c) to quell fears from prior experience. One common strategy is to pick a partner to whom one feels superior, which unfortunately builds an inherent competition into the system. At the outset of the relationship the "superior" partner is constantly "supportive" and "encouraging" of the other's development. However, this is done more for the status enhancement of the expert than for the partner; it requires subtly pointing out the shortcomings of the partner in the name of "constructive criticism." "Encouragement" lasts only as long as the partner does not appear to be developing. The underdog's development and increasing autonomy trigger more open competition and an embarrassingly clear vision of the "expert's" insecurity. Incongruous power hierarchies and relationship homeostasis are inextricably intertwined.

Couples with sexual problems often display incongruous power hierarchies. The identified patient with overt sexual dysfunction or low sexual desire generally has lower status in the hierarchies of sexual ability, desirability, and initiative experience. The asymptomatic partner is generally regarded as the *sex expert* and the sexually healthier of the two. Unfortunately, this leads to increased efforts on the part of the "expert" to effect a change in the problem and cure the partner. Kerr and Bowen note:

> People become overinvolved in trying to fix problems in the name of helping others and on the basis of a belief that what is happening should not be happening. Fixers try to "correct" the situation and put it on the "right" track. The fixer's Achilles heel is underestimating the resources of the people he intends to "help." In the process he can create a dependence in others that undermines their functioning. (1988, p. 109)

The common response, as in all incongruous power hierarchies, is an exaggeration of respective roles. The sex expert attempts to exercise more overt control over the situation, while the identified patient controls the actual process by doing progressively less. In effect, the identified patient gains more control by looking helpless; he/she diminishes the apparently greater status of the expert by not responding.

The almost inevitable failure to fix the identified patient further threatens the tenuous competency of the expert and exacerbates the incongruity of the situation. To reestablish a relative sense of competency, the expert may attack the identified patient's adequacy with greater frequency. However, the identified patient has already abdicated his/her sexual competency and has little overt status left to lose. In cases of chronic sexual difficulty, the identified patient may adopt a superficial passive acceptance of inadequacy, although he/she secretly smolders for years. This further frustrates the expert, who then escalates by becoming (a) more passively indifferent than the identified patient, or (b) more insistent about the growing sexual-marital difficulty.

Given the extreme vulnerability people have in regard to their desirability and performance, the sexual arena is exceedingly ripe for developing incongruous power hierarchies. For example, *the socially endorsed proclivity of a man to take his partner's orgasm as a testimony to his own prowess readily sets up the situation wherein the woman controls his sense of adequacy whether she wants to or not.* The result is both paradoxical and incongruous. The man is responsible for something that he, at best, has relatively little control over, and moreover, his attempts to control it make its occurrence less likely. Women generally recognize this, consciously or not, and sometimes respond in a variety of ways: faking orgasms, "withholding" her orgasm from him, or having the orgasm but faking *not* having it.

For another example, consider a couple in which the man has difficulty ejaculating intravaginally during coitus. Although the wife may not actually feel the ejaculation or the ejaculate inside her, the idea that her husband is "depriving" her of something increasingly bothers her. For his part, the husband feels inadequate as well. However, he is content to let the wife, who has begun to question her own desirability, carry the manifest "blame" for the problem ("Maybe I don't excite him enough").

Numerous variations of incongruous power hierarchies occur around sexual desire and initiation. This can occur around the diminished desire that commonly develops secondary to overt genital dysfunction, or when sexual desire is a problem in its own right. The partner designated the sex expert initiates sexual invitations more frequently, gaining status simply for having the "higher sex drive." However, the person with the lower sex drive always controls when sex occurs, through the acceptance or rejection of the various invitations. This dynamic underlies common relationship issues around disparate sexual drive and is strikingly evident in cases of inhibited sexual desire. This point, which will be considered subsequently (Chapter Ten), is significant enough to warrant repeating: *The partner who wants sex the least always controls sex in the dyad.*

Notice that this does not necessarily reflect malicious intent; incongruous power hierarchies often arise out of attempts at self-protection and accommodation to the partner's difficulties and weakness. Unfortunately, such adaptation generally cripples both individuals, and problems become more chronic. The resulting anger perpetuates the system as both stimulus and secondary gain, although it might not have been inherent in the origination of the system.

Differentiation plays several significant roles in the establishment and operation of incongruous power hierarchies. The lower the level of differentiation, the greater the likelihood that the individual will attempt to modulate his/her emotional reactivity by controlling the behavior and proximity of the partner. As level of differentiation increases, the individual is better able to unilaterally control his/her emotional reactivity and stability; it is thus less likely that incongruous power hierarchies will emerge.

Moreover, level of differentiation determines the degree of perceived openness/closedness of the relationship system and the way in which competition, power, and negotiation strategies will be handled. At low levels of differentiation, "togetherness" pressure increases and partners are more likely to perceive their relationship as a *closed* system. One aspect of a closed system is the notion that power and prerogative are finite in quantity, and that one partner must lose what the other gains. This is commonly played out not only between spouses, but also intergenerationally as "one-penis systems" between fathers and adolescent sons (and in institutions as well): Fathers feel challenged and usurped by their sons' growing masculinity and prowess; women have their own gender-appropriate variation.

Attempts to create a "closed" system manifest themselves in the politics surrounding sexual fantasies and seductive public behavior. Couples often play out differentiation struggles in their intolerance for the partner's sexual fantasies about other people, whether during partnered monogamous sex, during masturbation, or even while walking down the street. Flirting and exaggerated leering at "other people" in the presence of the partner challenge the fantasy of controlling the content of the other's thoughts, and serve as an infantile but effective demonstration of the immutable separateness of the partners' two realities. On the level of object relations issues, such behavior triggers the narcissistic trauma of not being the *one and only*. On the systemic level, it reflects more than toying with the boundaries of the relationship with regard to monogamy: It concerns whether that relationship is an open or closed system with regard to power and status.

Sexuality, power, and competition are handled differently in open and closed systems. Consider the model of two business people trying to negotiate the best terms of a deal. First, imagine the strategic position of a salesman trying to get a monopolistic buyer (closed system) to recognize the value of his product. The buyer starts out by negating the value of the product and emphasizing that the salesman has no other option but to take what he can get. In an open system, if either the buyer or seller does not like the terms, he or she can take his/her business elsewhere. Negotiations generally include a significant period of economic "foreplay" involving the admiration of the other's product and emphasis on the merits of one's own position. In a relationship, this is commonly observed in the period just prior to emotional "commitment"; the subsequent shift to a closed system is often strikingly apparent. The issue here is not monogamy or the importance of honoring "till death do us part" commitments, but rather the systemic impact of such commitments in couples at low levels of differentiation.

It is ironic that the process of getting where the partners *think* they want to go is circular, rather than linear (as was also true in regard to the topic of intimacy, Chapter Four). While the problem may be that they are only capable of functioning on an equity/reciprocity basis, partners do not achieve altruism by mimicking or modeling such behaviors. Individuals at low levels of differentiation need to become *better* business people, which involves monopoly-busting and tolerating the recognition of a free marketplace (antithetical to "togetherness" pressure). It is inherently paradoxical that the way people develop the high level of differentiation necessary for mutuality, altruism and caring for the beloved (without sacrifice of *core* self) involves the hardball-playing, head-banging, begrudging respect that emerges from the sexual crucible.

HOMEOSTASIS (NONPRODUCTIVE EQUILIBRIUM)

All relationships exist in a delicate dynamic balance. In healthy relationships, there is an ever-changing flow that permits evaluation and resolution of spouses' age-appropriate developmental tasks. There are consequential shifts in the multiple alliances between family members, including shifts in the marital dyad; at the same time, there is a tendency to return to a more-or-less recognizable family system.

In *Paradox and Counterparadox*, Palazzoli, Boscolo, Cecchin, and Prata (1978) point out that every living system is characterized by two apparently contradictory functions: the homeostatic tendency and the capacity for transformation. In healthy relationships, the interplay of these seemingly antithetical functions creates a provisional equilibrium whose instability guarantees evolution and change. Pathological systems maintain homeostasis through compulsive repetition of solutions that were previously effective in dissimilar situations.

Some degree of homeostasis is required in all relationships and organizations for stability and growth. However, in some cases homeostasis is nonproductive, as, for instance, when the role of the symptom bearer in a family shifts to another individual although the family's overall style and level of functioning remain pathologically symptom-producing. Many couples that request treatment for sexual-marital difficulties (and their extended families) are in a state of nonproductive homeostasis.

Anyone who has lived in an ongoing relationship has experienced nonproductive homeostasis. For instance:

You and your partner have been together long enough to develop a pattern of interaction that is noxious for both of you. Your respective behaviors and responses are both predictable and unwanted. Your partner always complains that you yell to get your way. You think your partner attacks your style of talking because he wants to avoid the topic under discussion, and does not want to admit that you are correct. You promise yourself that next time you will make some new response to avoid the old frustrating pattern—and prove that you are right.

Your partner soon makes a provocative opening remark, just as you expect. You are frustrated but decide you will not raise your voice at any cost, hoping that he will listen if you do it "right." You take a deep breath to relax, and then ask your partner why he is doing what he is. Your partner looks at you for a moment, and tells you that you don't have to sigh and act so burdened. You reply that you are not sighing, you are trying to relax and not raise your voice.

Your partner then makes a quick series of statements, each of which seems designed to incite riot in you. You start to get angry because your partner responds to your attempts to change the pattern of interaction with no similar attempt of his own. Initially your partner does not acknowledge that you are trying to change; then he interprets your change as admission that you were wrong all along. You make every effort to monitor the decibel level of your voice. Your partner says that you are acting condescending. He also warns that if you raise your voice like you usually do, he will not talk to you.

With your anger choking in your throat, you point out as calmly as you can that you are not raising your voice. Your partner responds that he is just telling you in case you do. You feel absolutely unappreciated and frustrated. Your partner points out that you are getting angry.

Your words come quickly now. You point out that you weren't angry until he started telling you not to raise your voice. You point out that you weren't sighing, you were trying to keep your cool. You weren't acting condescending, you were trying to avoid the same old frustrations and do something to help the relationship. You look over as you speak, and your partner is wearing a smug smile. You suddenly listen to your voice and you realize that you are yelling. *You want to strangle him.*

Homeostasis and Individual Dynamics

The forces of individuality and togetherness are in a constantly adjusting, dynamic equilibrium. According to Kerr and Bowen (1988), people tend to pick partners who are willing to make similar investments of energies in these two dimensions:

> When a relationship is calm and in fairly comfortable balance, the interplay of individuality and togetherness may be barely visible. The adjustments people are making to one another are so subtle and automatic that they are not

obvious. When the relationship moves toward a significant imbalance, however, the pressure for adjustment is more intense and more easily observed. At times of high anxiety and serious imbalance, statements people make about the situation range from the one extreme of, "I can't survive unless you respond the way I want you to," to the other extreme of, "I can't survive if I do what you want." (p. 66)

While all relationships exist in a state of balance, the balance point within relationships differs. The difference is in the degree of energy that is "bound" or obligatorily invested in the relationship. At lower levels of differentiation, the degree of rigid investment in the relationship increases and the energy available for individual functioning and development decreases. In other words, the lower the degree of differentiation, the higher the potential for nonproductive homeostasis. Spouses in such marriages may adopt highly polarized positions, but remain undifferentiated. Since partners generally interpret their experience of marital interactions consistent with their unfinished family-of-origin issues, the resilience of nonproductive marital homeostasis results not only from the multiple alliances within an extended family, but also from the individuals' unresolved developmental issues.

All relationships have an elaborate prenuptial agreement, albeit unwritten and often unconscious (Sager, 1976). Written financial/property agreements compose only a minor segment. The actual prenuptial agreement, established in the dynamics of the early courtship, involves the implicit promises, fears, hopes, and wishes of both people. In the early years, the prenuptial agreement is instrumental in getting and keeping the couple together. The same rules embodied in this unconscious contract block effective management of shifting agendas, situations, and personal development issues that arise later in the relationship. One or both partners cling resolutely to some cherished aspect of the initial marriage contract, as if it offered protection against the very fears they avoided facing at the outset of the relationship. Ironically, relinquishing the unconscious marital agreement allows spouses to confront and rid themselves of the internal conflicts harbored all these years:

For instance, John and his wife presented for treatment after years of marriage. John's one-year affair with a younger woman had recently been discovered. At the time of the initial session, John reported loving his wife, and she likewise loved him. They agreed that his wife's role in the relationship was to be "the steady, unflappable one"; at the same time, John felt that he was "suffocating" because his wife was trying to live vicariously through him. Together, they presented a picture of two people heavily dependent on each other for validation, and angry at each other for withholding soothing for their respective wounded feelings of inadequacy and undesirability. John reported that he was sexually satisfied with his wife. In fact, he volunteered, he could not keep up with his wife sexually if she got any more aggressive. John reported that sex in his affair had not been as good as it was with his wife.

John revealed his attraction to the young girl was in her needing him. She appeared respectful and in awe of his financial and emotional resources. He related this back to his own family of origin, in which his father played the role of the patriarch who controlled everything and around whom everyone and everything centered.

John soon realized that he was emotionally "wired" to have a relationship that lasted no more than five years. The aspects that attracted him to the young girl in the affair were the same characteristics that had led him to pick his current wife. However, after a number of years of playing out this dynamic with his wife, he had a distinctly different experience of it with her. John felt his wife depended on him for everything, financial and otherwise. He felt stifled, burdened, trapped, and angry about his life rapidly slipping by him. His feelings about his wife and his feelings about his girlfriend reflected the same dynamic that drove him in relationships with all women, only differing by elapsed time in the relationship.

In seeing this, John realized that his reactions to his wife were predictable; he was likely to feel the same way towards his girlfriend in several years. He recognized that his freedom lay not in escaping from his wife, but rather in resolving the unrealistic gender-role expectation he carried within himself. This served as powerful stimulus for his wife to persevere in her own struggles for self-validation and establishing an independent identity outside of John's sphere of influence.

INCONGRUOUS POWER HIERARCHIES AND TREATMENT HOMEOSTASIS

When a sexual problem exists for sufficient duration, spouses' roles, rules, and self-concepts adapt and interactional patterns and power hierarchies absorb the dysfunction; it becomes a purposeful entity in the system. The time required for this process to occur can be as brief as a matter of weeks or as long as several years.

The hope of positive change embodied by the therapist does not mitigate the anxiety of giving up painful but familiar patterns. Although the individuals may be capable of more economical and pleasant styles of coping, the relationship system in which the sexual problem is spawned or perpetuated is their best attempt (to date) at coping with the complex situation.

When couples become firmly entrenched in patterns of sexual dysfunction, the identified patient develops multiple levels of resistance to treatment. At the individual level, there is the fear of being inadequate, not to mention "incurable." At the dyadic level, the incongruous power hierarchy gives the identified patient control over the partner's feelings of adequacy and desirability, which he or she is not about to relinquish. Covert control over the spouse's feelings of sexual competency may be the only power the other feels him/herself to have. This is painfully true in relationships that ascribe to traditional sex roles. The man controls all aspects of the relationship and finds it threatening to acknowledge his wife's competency in any significant way.

Within the preexisting dyadic system, the identified patient may have relatively little to gain, and more to lose, if he/she is "cured" (especially prior to treatment). If the identified patient has successfully avoided sexual contact on the basis of the sexual dysfunction, the legitimacy of refusing sex with the partner is diminished once the "problem" is removed. Resolution of the sexual-marital difficulty may be taken as implicit validation that the problem existed *within* the identified patient. Credit for the "cure" may be attributed to the spouse's efforts. In the typical incongruous sexual power hierarchy, resolution of sexual difficulties offers the identified patient little change in status or power. If the treatment alliance does not embrace a significant shift in the couple's power hierarchy, then these same dynamics are replayed with the therapist.

When the husband is the identified patient, traditional machismo results in the adequacy threats taking a particular form. There is the possible sense of being one-down to the therapist (whether male or female), and moreover, feeling chagrined about not being able to "handle his own problems." Feeling humbled in front of the spouse, sexually competitive with (or attracted to) the therapist's imagined prowess, and fearful of the spouse's possible sexual attraction to the therapist, the husband is primed to reconstruct the incongruous power hierarchy in treatment.

Cases where the husband is the asymptomatic partner have different dynamics. Treatment offers a variety of adequacy threats when culturally-prescribed sex expert meets professionally-trained sex expert (whether the therapist is male or not). Husbands enter treatment having been unable to fix, satisfy, or turn on their partner. Husbands lose their status as top gun in the sex department when they enter the therapist's office. Some men get angry at having to "negotiate" with the therapist about how they touch their wives. There is the matter of making room for the therapist's input in the relationship hierarchy, not to mention in the bedroom.

When the asymptomatic partner is the wife, she may be more willing to permit the therapist to enter the marital system in a manner congruent with the therapist's abilities and status. In cases where the wife fears the loss of a desired overdependence on (or dominance over) the husband or fears being blamed by the therapist for the sexual and marital difficulties, she will often "reserve judgment" about the therapist. The attempt is to retain control by leaving the question of hierarchical organization in the treatment alliance undefined.

With all the threats to establishing a suitable working alliance with the couple, it seems somewhat remarkable that movement does occur in treatment. Therapists often complain about the many "unmotivated" couples who soon terminate in "modern" approaches to sex or marital therapy. The real skill of a therapist is often seen in the initial sessions, when the terms of engagement are indirectly negotiated. One aspect of "skill" is the therapist's nonreactivity to the numerous invitations to enter into incongruous power hierarchies with patients; the sexual crucible approach helps position the clinician optimally.

Ambivalence

When I received my training in the mid 1960s, budding therapists were encouraged to weed out "unmotivated" patients. "Sexual desire" was considered to be a selection criterion. Twenty years later, low sexual desire has become a treatable disorder in its own right.

Ambivalence in individuals or couples seeking treatment is often overlooked by the therapist eager to find "highly motivated" patients. Therapists are often blind to conceptual distortions that stem from linear thinking: We implicitly assume that "highly motivated" means "positively disposed to change." Patients may be "highly motivated," (i.e., having multiple motives) but not eager to change.

On the one hand, patients desperately want to change in order to feel "normal" and happy. They would like to have the marriages they fantasize others have and feel inadequate because they don't. They often think their lives would be far better if their sex and their marriage would improve. They are frustrated with the way they are living and often cannot think of anything new to resolve their situation. They are afraid that their situation will never change and life will be a deteriorating series of unpleasant experiences.

On the other hand, these same patients may be feeling very inadequate, embarrassed, and inclined not to "air dirty laundry in public." They are afraid they will look foolish or stupid in front of the therapist. They are terrified to finally try sexual-marital therapy—and fail. They are nervous that their partner will "tattle" their secrets, or worse, reveal previously undisclosed feelings about them during the session. There is the dark fear that their marriage is fatally flawed.

What is the sum total or equilibrium of these numerous, powerful competing and contradictory motivations? *Patients who look unmotivated.*

Hidden Agendas in Treatment Requests

The reasons why couples seek treatment are complex, as is the ambivalent balance permitting the referral at any particular time. Some of these motivations are incompatible with a successful resolution of the sexual and marital problems; others are incompatible with treatment continuing beyond the first session:

- "We (I) have tried everything, now we can separate."
- "I'll get you, you bastard."
- "*You* (the therapist) look after him (her)."
- "Let's make a career of marital therapy."
- "Obviously, I am the innocent party."
- "We can take the heat off decisions by coming into treatment."
- "Let's get out without fighting." (adapted from Miles, 1980)

Andolfi (1980) pointed out three common hidden agendas in treatment requests:

- "Help us stay the same."
- "Change the symptom without changing anything else."
- "Help the identified patient, but leave me alone."

It is wise to assume that all patients have multiple complex motivations. Reasonable patients will approach treatment with a fair degree of skepticism and ambivalence. If anxiety and insecurity produce a premature "commitment" to treatment, the other side of their ambivalence will surface once treatment is underway.

Therapists often collude in eagerness to have "highly motivated" patients—a collusion encouraged by the narrow conceptualization of sex therapy that subtly permeates professional practice (discussed in Chapter Six). This circumscribed view has promulgated patient screening criteria which have seemingly not changed in the last decade, although practitioners increasingly address more distressed relationships (see Table 8.1). When clinicians accept criteria (at least in principle) that exclude a majority of patients from sexual (and mari-

Table 8.1
Chapman's Criteria for Diagnosing When to Do Sex Therapy
in the Primary Relationship

1. Absence of physical problems (e.g., infection, drug side-effects).
2. Absence of other "primary" problems (e.g., drug abuse, depression).
3. Presence of bona fide sexual dysfunction in one or both partners (as defined by *DSM-III*).
4. Presence of "therapy-positive" factors (e.g., believe therapy "works").
5. Absence of interfering situational events (e.g., crisis, death in family).
6. Presence of basic relationship requirements:
    a. Absence of or arrest of significant individual pathology.
    b. A commitment agreement is established and clear.
    c. A basic repertoire of communication skills is present.
    d. "Relationship relevant" material is not being withheld to excess.
    e. Mutually compatible life and relatioship goals are present.

From Chapman, 1982.

tal) therapy, it fuels collusion with patients' overly positive initial presentations.

"Highly motivated" patients need to be approached with a little caution, since even they have alternative motivations as well. If the therapist has naively made an alliance with only the *therapy-positive* side of the patient's ambivalence, the patient feels obligated to mask the *therapy-negative* side of his/her feelings. It is the systemic equivalent of a part-object attachment, which might be overlooked until (and perhaps even during the time) the couple announces a firm decision to terminate treatment.

An unbalanced alliance with the "treatment positive" side of one partner's ambivalence often requires the spouse to adopt a compensatory position weighted against investment in treatment. Moreover, this occurs along the same rigid scripts that preexisted in the couple's individual and interactional dynamics. The result further polarizes the partners' roles regarding motivation for intimacy, investment in the relationship, and control/dominance issues. This is often "simply" perceived as the unfolding of the couple's dynamics, without recognition of the therapist's own contribution to this process.

The Problem of the "Good Relationship"
The net result of this motivational soup is that patients report, "We have a good relationship, we just have this problem with sex." The report of a "good relationship" can be an anathema to treatment. Patients want to please their therapist and be accepted for treatment. No one wants to be told he/she is "untreatable" or hopeless. Spouses do not want to violate the accepted facade

of the relationship. No one wants to be punished on the way home from the session.

Sometimes the report of a "good relationship" is obtained from deeply troubled couples who are afraid to crack the veneer of their "model marriage." They may have gained status with their peers for the external appearance of their marriage and fear losing it. They may have very low tolerance for anxiety, instability, and anger, and cling to traditional gender roles as a way of maintaining stability. Couples who report "we don't fight" are often referring to their notion that fights must be physical, verbally hostile, or violent.

Kerr and Bowen (1988) point out that "good relationships" can be as dysfunctional as those displaying overt conflict:

> An "emotional cocoon" and a conflictual relationship can be at the same level of differentiation. . . . The intensity of attachment and degree of problem in a harmonious relationship, in other words, can be just as great as in a conflictual relationship. In one instance the problem has been bound in harmony and in the other it has been bound in disharmony. (p. 84)

Both "harmonious" and openly conflictual relationships have difficulty changing their sexual styles and level of intimacy if underlying anxiety drives and controls the relationship. One response to the pressure to adapt in all types of relationships, Kerr and Bowen point out, is *emotional distance.*

The label of "good" or "bad," when applied to relationships, may be more indicative of the partners' expectations than of the absolute quality of the interaction. At best, it is a statement of how the individuals see themselves or wish to be seen. It is often a clue to the level of intimacy tolerance and intimacy need of the individuals involved.

For instance, consider the case of Jennie, the wife of a long-haul truck driver with erectile dysfunction. Jennie was the daughter of a cruel and abusive coal miner. In the initial evaluation session, the spouses were asked what they would do if treatment were not successful. Jennie replied that very little, if anything, would change. She said, "He is a good man, and we have a good relationship. He doesn't beat the kids or me; he don't cheat on me as far as I know; he don't get too dirty drunk; and he gives me his paycheck every payday." For her, this was a "good" relationship.

Report of a "good relationship" often represents negotiation regarding the potential scope of treatment. In the case of treatment of sexual problems, "We have a good relationship" means, "All you can look at is the sex. This is the area we are willing to acknowledge as problematic." If the therapist limits the scope of examination to the boundaries defined by the couple, treatment is likely to be no more successful than the couple's prior efforts. The task of the therapist is to titrate the anxiety by examining the "off-limits" material in a manner and pace that the couple can tolerate.

Progress Makes the Threat of "Success" Outweigh the Threat of "Failure"

Some couples exist for years in a stable ambivalent attachment of hostile dependency, in which the sexual dysfunction is pivotal in their pendulum-like oscillations of closeness and distance. Requests for treatment, which often emerge during exacerbation of one of these oscillations, are often followed by a swing towards homeostasis.

Sometimes, the precipitant for treatment is the asymptomatic partner's announcement that he/she is leaving if sex does not improve immediately. However, the ultimatum may stem from the expectation that sex will *not* improve, providing a "legitimate" opportunity to leave the relationship. The ultimatum is an attempt to disown responsibility for the decision to leave, placing it squarely on the identified patient's anticipated lack of progress. It allows the asymptomatic partner to act as if he/she truly regrets leaving, but has no choice in the face of deprivation created by the identified patient's difficulty.

Progress in the treatment of such couples creates a shift in dilemmas. At the outset of treatment, the manifest threat to both individuals is that they will be forced to separate. The implication of the threat to leave if the sex doesn't improve is this: *They will stay together if the sex is improved, and the only reason for the separation will be the sexual dysfunction.* When treatment starts to succeed, the fear of separation is replaced by the fear of having to stay together. Ambivalent partners oscillate in a cycle of "I don't want to be without him, but I also don't really want to be with him either." Fears of giving up the partner are quickly replaced by fears of losing the opportunity to experiment with other partners and lifestyles. As the sexual functioning and self-worth of the identified patient improve, the asymptomatic partner loses the powerful hierarchical position of being the undecided "chooser" regarding continuity of the relationship.

When one partner grows in his/her capacity or ability to be intimate, there is usually a fundamental disruption in the homeostasis in the relationship. Depending on how the couple uses this destabilization, the outcome can be extremely beneficial. It can be a trigger for both partners' development, albeit an anxiety-provoking one at times. It can also be disabling and disappointing, particularly if the other spouse responds defensively and rigidly with attempts to reinstate an equilibrium that is no longer possible.

Cindy's increasing self-esteem from her new job, along with her increased sense of adequacy and self-acceptance, led to her desiring and initiating sex more frequently. Although her husband, Benson, had pushed this for years, he was not pleased or receptive to the new approaches. Benson wanted sex when it was an indication of Cindy's desire for him. He did not like it when her initiation was based on her self-acceptance and sense of prowess. Benson liked sex when he felt that it was his domain of expertise, unwittingly fueled by Cindy's inhibitions and feelings of inadequacy.

Benson tried to reestablish his sense of power and control in the relationship by adopting the exact opposite strategy: He expressed disinterest in sex. Indeed, his desire for sex *had* lessened. Under the new circumstances, he struggled with feelings of threat. Seeing himself as a "liberated" male, Benson was particularly defensive and guarded about feeling insecure over his wife's development. As time continued, he became a perfect candidate for overt sexual dysfunction, experiencing decreased enjoyment and intensity when they did have sex.

The dyadic system determines the sexual implications and elicitation value of a given behavior at different times in the relationship. *Couples rarely understand that they simply cannot be "doing it the same old way," as they report in the midst of their discord and unhappiness, because the same old way no longer exists.*

It is almost impossible to improve sexual function and sexual style without affecting other aspects of the relationship. Partners who demand change in the sexual arena while simultaneously demanding status quo in other dimensions usually manifest resistance as progress occurs. The asymptomatic partner may suddenly produce sexual and nonsexual symptomatology in response to progress in the identified patient (Strauss & Dickes, 1980). Consider the fairly common situation of the husband who is eager for his wife to become orgasmic:

Denise and Craig presented for treatment with Craig stating the altruistic motivation of "wanting Denise to enjoy it as much as I do, so we can share it together." He had been her only sex partner, and her "teacher" in sexual matters. Secretly, Craig was hurting about his own sense of sexual adequacy. Like many men, he took Denise's lack of orgasm as a reflection on his sexual skill and needed her to reach orgasm to validate him.

As treatment progressed, Denise learned to have orgasms during masturbation. Craig was threatened by this development, wanting "to be the one to do it for her." Inherent in the use of masturbation was the recognition that Denise's orgasms accrued to her own competency, and not his. Craig voiced concern that masturbation might become her only successful sexual outlet, fearing that Denise would become less responsive to his demands for intercourse. Likewise, Craig feared Denise becoming less dependent on him, which indeed she was.

Denise soon became orgasmic during sexual contact with Craig, first with manual and oral stimulation and eventually during intercourse. However, it was clear from the process of treatment that Craig was not "giving her" an orgasm. Rather, treatment had made it clear that he "helped" Denise have orgasms, but played a secondary role in the process.

Denise taught Craig her sexual preferences, but he never received the validation of his masculinity that underlay his desire to bring his wife into treatment. Craig was surprised, embarrassed, and defensive about his own response. He became somewhat fearful about Denise's new adventuresome attitude and sexual appetite. He began to fear she might fantasize about sex with other men.

If Craig possesses sufficient ego strength, he will be able to master this challenge to his emotional equilibrium. If not, he may attempt a quick termination to reestablish the prior equilibrium, stating, "We can finish up from here, Doc."

A similar interplay of systemic variables and fears of engulfment is common in cases of male retarded ejaculation. In one such case, a young couple decided that the future of the marriage depended on the man's ability to overcome his ejaculatory difficulty and impregnate his wife. The wife wanted to have children, but not as unequivocally as did her husband. It soon became apparent that he was pushing this contingency, overtly posturing as though it were unfair of him to remain married to his wife in view of her desire to have children. The "barren relationship" was thus the husband's escape hatch from the marriage; he actually had little desire to become a parent.

In another case, a middle-aged man presented for treatment with his new bride. He reported a history of inhibited sexual desire in each of his three prior marriages. In each case, sexual disinterest started on the wedding night. In contrast, he reported being "sexually carnivorous and promiscuous" between each marriage. He had told his current bride about his prior difficulties, and they agreed to marry and enter treatment. The husband announced at the initial evaluation that he had already decided to divorce his new bride if he could not learn to want sex with her.

In the preceding two cases, both men were highly ambivalent about treatment success. Both hoped to use a treatment *failure* as a *successful* way to terminate their relationships. Treatment must be structured such that progress in target symptoms is not automatically determinant of other unresolved individual and dyadic agendas. In the former case of retarded ejaculation, for instance, the therapist refused to accept the couple into treatment unless they were willing to tackle the problems of sexual functioning and reproduction separately. The couple accepted this alternative and used birth control for the duration of treatment.

The latter case of inhibited sexual desire required reframing the "meaning" of progress and the basis for commitment to treatment: Progress in sexual functioning did not signify an inherent commitment to continuity or deepening of the relationship. The therapist maintained the viewpoint that the husband might become interested in sex and *still* want to get divorced. Moreover, the therapist encouraged the young wife not to be so sure that she would be willing to give up having sex for the rest of her life if treatment failed.

Unlinking sexual functioning from relationship permanence reduced the secondary agendas that disrupted both men's internal processes during sex and minimized the construction of incongruous power hierarchies in treatment. Therapists who attempt to establish treatment alliances based on negotiated commitment to the relationship unwittingly build in sources of resistance to treatment, which are bound to emerge later. This is particularly important when one spouse demands a "commitment to the relationship" from the other in return for agreeing to enter sex therapy.

Clandestine affairs, justified on the basis of a partner's sexual dysfunction, are threatened by progress in treatment. The unfaithful spouse's intrinsic desire for an affair becomes manifest, as well as his/her unwillingness to terminate it. Moreover, the identified patient's tolerance for affairs, previously maintained out of his/her own feelings of inadequacy, often drops markedly.

Treatment progress also threatens the pseudo-autonomy of infantile, dependent spouses who rationalize affairs as being the result of their having gotten married "too early." They are not unlike children who, while exploring their surroundings, frequently glance at mother from across the room to reassure themselves that they can retreat to security if necessary. If the partner, like mother, exercises his/her own autonomy, the unfaithful spouse often becomes insecure and rageful.

Thus far, we have considered treatment homeostasis in response to improvements in the identified patient. This view of homeostasis surrounding the removal of symptomatology is relatively familiar to many therapists. It involves the notion that the family or marriage functions to maintain the symptomatology of one individual so that the system itself retains its current equilibrium. Homeostatic efforts do not often appear until the systemic equilibrium is disrupted by the identified patient's improvement.

However, there is another time at which homeostatic efforts become strikingly apparent, although many sexual and marital therapists never encounter it (because therapy terminates prior to that point). This occurs when the partners approach the farther limits of their own sexual potential. At these relatively extreme levels of gratification, there is a recoiling and spontaneous downward cycling.

Marital therapists often abandon the topic of sexuality when the couple gives the vague report that they are "satisfied." *The problem is that most people are satisfied only being partially satisfied.*

When satisfaction gets either too intensely good or bad, couples mobilize to modulate it. Having "better than we ever thought it could be" sex and intimacy (and maybe better than the *therapist* thought it could be) generally triggers extreme discomfort. We will consider this point subsequently in Chapter Fourteen, when we return to consideration of the sexual crucible and sexual potential.

CHAPTER NINE

The Problem of "Problems of Sexual Desire"

This chapter challenges the contemporary view of "inhibited sexual desire." Modern sex therapy, unwittingly captivated by the notion of a desire "phase," has (a) been preoccupied with desire-as-initiatory-eagerness for sexual behavior, and (b) ignored any focus on desire-as-passion and craving for the partner during sex.

A conceptual paradigm shift in sexual desire "problems" is proposed (in preparation for our focus on clinical treatment in Chapter Ten); a three-dimensional model of sexual desire is presented, focusing on desire during sexual activity (i.e., desire-as-passion).

There is a growing shift away from Kaplan's disease model of individual etiology and increasing interest in systemic approaches. We encounter a reflection of growing pains: Approaches whose systemic conceptualizations mask their non-systemic interventions lead us to believe we have come farther than we have.

Examining one's clinical approach to desire problems recapitulates the triumphs and tribulations of our developing field. Some widely accepted theoretical constructs quickly lose their luster. For example, are *boredom*, *lack of novelty*, and the *"seven year itch"* basic phenomena in their own right, to be treated with cognitive-behavioral suggestions for variety, creativity, and communication? Or is boredom itself a systemic defense against intimacy and intense eroticism that arises when spouses' level of differentiation is insufficient? How many patients (and therapists) would trade the comfortable label of being a seven-year "itcher" for a self-perception as being dependent, anxiety- and intimacy-avoidant, and aversive to intense eroticism and personal growth?

Is absence of "seduction rituals" a *cause* of low desire? Exhortations from therapists and women's magazines promote the linear view that lack of seduction is an omission in sexual repertoire resulting from skill deficits, ignorance, frustration, or relationship duration. Is it *also* the *end result* of systemic processes? That is, does it result from repeated attempts by one partner to evoke desire in the other, wherein the latter *doesn't want to want*, and the former is culturally predisposed to take this as a reflection of personal inadequacy?

Levine (1988a) offers some words on what awaits the clinician with intellectual integrity:

> Finally, in some ultimate sense, understanding sexual desire requires coming to grips with a more basic question: "What is the nature of any kind of desire?" This philosophical issue is so fundamental that I have been avoiding it for fear that some of the seemingly useful notions about sexual desire will evaporate in uncertainty and confusion. (p. 43)

Interest in sexual desire simultaneously reflects the increasing maturity and the youth of modern sexual science. Longitudinal research on initially successful treatment cases presents a somewhat dismal picture of the long-term stability of therapeutic progress and raises questions about the ability of existing treatments to modify sexual desire in meaningful ways (DeAmicis, Goldberg, LoPiccolo, Friedman, & Davies, 1985; LoPiccolo, Heiman, Hogan, & Roberts, 1985). But modifying sexual desire in treatment implicitly embraces a view of what sexual desire "problems" are (e.g., *Disorders of Sexual Desire*, Kaplan, 1979; *Sexual Desire Disorders*, Leiblum & Rosen, 1988); it implies a conceptualization of sexual desire per se. Diagnosing and treating "inhibited" sexual desire presumes an understanding of "uninhibited" desire. As was noted in our discussion of sexual potential (Chapter Three), such an understanding has itself been inhibited to date.

Clinical attention to problems of sexual desire is one of the newest developments in the history of modern sex therapy. Low sexual desire was not even mentioned in the initial contributions from Masters and Johnson (1970) or Kaplan (1974). It was only in 1977 that Lief introduced the concept of *inhibited sexual desire* (*ISD*) to refer to a chronic lack of sexual initiation or responsiveness; he suggested that ISD was rapidly becoming the most common sexual complaint of the day. At approximately the same time, Kaplan (1977) suggested the addition of a desire (initiation) phase to the sexual response cycle originally suggested by Masters and Johnson, giving birth to the notion of *desire phase disorders*.

Publication of Kaplan's *Disorders of Sexual Desire* in 1979 reflected and stimulated growing clinical interest in problems of sexual desire. Her contribution was quickly followed by others such as Zilbergeld and Ellison (1980), who offered a less pathology-based viewpoint. Problems of sexual desire soon attracted attention from other perspectives. Addressing the question of sexual desire from a bio-anthropological viewpoint, Money (1980) considered it as an appetitive response for copulatory behavior; he coined the term *proception* to refer to the phase of attraction, invitation, solicitation, and seduction observed in all species that reproduce by mating. More recently, Levine proposed a somewhat similar viewpoint: "Sexual desire is that which precedes and accompanies arousal. Sexual desire is the psychobiological propensity to engage in sexual behavior. Sexual desire is the energy brought to sexual behavior" (1988, p. 23).

Clinicians who develop diagnostic criteria (e.g., *DSM-III-R*) or who conduct epidemiological research often find a clear definition of desire phase disorders an elusive goal. Therapists, however, approach inhibited sexual desire the same way that Supreme Court Justice Stewart[1] approached "hard-core" pornography: They "know it when they see it." For example, LoPiccolo and Friedman (1988) state, "most clinical cases are so clearly beyond the lower end of the normal curve that definitional issues become moot" (p. 100); the many clinicians who profess to treat desire phase disorders appear to concur.

Other clinicians attempt to sidestep diagnostic issues by noting pragmatically that patients define themselves as having desire disorders at the outset of treatment. In couples where desire discrepancy coincides with power discrepancy, however, it is not uncommon for one spouse to browbeat the other into believing he/she is either "frigid" or "sexually addicted." The problem remains to distinguish "intrapsychic" desire phase disorders from desire discrepancy, system-driven ISD, and other problems that reflect nonspecific relational distress. When one spouse reports preexisting inhibited sexual desire, clinicians often adopt a historical perspective and overlook contemporary contributing (or replicating) factors beyond the patient's awareness.

For the clinician, conceptualization of desire phase disorders determines the diagnosis, the treatment, and the "clinical meaning" attributed to patients' response. For patients, conceptualization has immediate impact on self-image and existing power hierarchies within the relationship.

Now, if the foregoing paragraphs sound reasonable to you, this is *exactly* the problem I wish to address. It is not that our discussion is faulty; rather, the problem is that it is a *half-truth*.

The phrase "desire *phase* disorders" has so thoroughly permeated the professional lexicon that its impact on the conceptualization of "sexual desire" has become invisible. The notion of a desire "phase" and desire "phase" disorders sounds familiar to the clinician's ear. It involves the view of sexual desire as limited to the time *immediately preceding* sexual behavior; *one might suggest (tongue in cheek) that clinicians think sexual desire is only a passing phase.*

---

[1]*Jacobellis v. Ohio*, 378 U. S. 184, 197 (1964) (Steward, P., concurring).

The phraseology of desire "phase" disorders does more than immortalize the conceptualization of those clinicians who first addressed the phenomenon of human sexual desire—it has captured the conceptualization and focus of sexual desire of the rank-and-file clinicians who followed them. In many respects, the view of human sexual desire that permeates the fields of sexual and marital therapy is much closer to Money's animal husbandry notion of *proception* than anything involving human phenomenology and intimacy. Levine's definition begins to move beyond the notion of a desire "phase" and address emotional responses that *accompany* arousal.

The lexicon of modern clinical practice rapidly and imperceptibly narrows conceptualization of sexual desire to "problems" at the lower end of the continuum; nonpathological high desire and its role in personal development and sexual potential quickly cease to be self-evident or of interest. The early viewpoint of sexual desire was enshrined in the *DSM-III* diagnostic criteria for *inhibited* sexual desire:

> Persistent and pervasive inhibition of sexual desire. The judgment of inhibition is made by the clinician's taking into account factors that affect sexual desire such as age, sex, health, intensity and frequency of sexual desire, and the context of the individual's life. In actual practice, this diagnosis will rarely be made unless the lack of desire is a source of distress to either the individual or to his or her partner. Frequently this category will be used in conjunction with one or more of the other Psychosexual Dysfunction categories. (American Psychiatric Association, 1980, p. 278)

These criteria follow quite closely those Kaplan used in *Disorders of Sexual Desire* (1979), although she noted using the diagnosis more often than indicated in the *DSM-III* incidence guidelines. The more recent revision of *DSM-III-R* replaced "inhibited sexual desire" with the term "hypoactive sexual desire disorder" and more clearly stated the "phase" connotation: "persistently or recurrently deficient or absent sexual fantasies and desire *for* sexual activity" (American Psychiatric Association, 1987, p. 293, emphasis added). Kaplan (1987) further elaborated on the appetitive phase of sexual initiation, emphasizing the distinction between inhibited sexual desire and "sexual aversion." Sexual aversion is defined in *DSM-III-R* as "a persistent or recurrent extreme aversion to, and avoidance of, all or almost all, genital sexual contact with a sexual partner" (p. 293).

In keeping with her notion of a discrete desire "phase," Kaplan also considered disorders of this phase discrete clinical syndromes as well. In 1979, she wrote:

Inhibited sexual desire is a distinct clinical entity. It is related to the other sexual dysfunctions in that it involves sexual anxieties, but it also differs in many important respects. Specifically, as a group, patients suffering from blocked desire have deeper and more intense sexual anxieties, greater hostility towards their partners, and more tenacious defenses than those patients whose sexual dysfunctions are associated with erection and orgasm difficulties. (p. 55)

Like all significant advances, however, Kaplan's work contained its own inherent limitations and roadblocks to new ways of thinking; like all advances, the limitations were difficult to see at the time. These roadblocks lie in her medical model focus on the individual, her emphasis on psychopathology, the notion of sexual desire as a "phase" which ends when sexual behavior begins, and her conceptualization of sexual desire as appetitive *hunger* and "inhibited" desire as sexual *anorexia*:

The concept of inhibited sexual desire gains clarity when it is compared with anorexia nervosa, with which it has some interesting similarities and analogies, both with respect to the nature of the pathological structure and the clinical course and treatment response for the two disorders. In both syndromes, a biological drive which is the expression of specific neurophysiologic activity of the brain is inhibited by unconscious psychological factors. Also, both disorders have a poor prognosis for spontaneous recovery. (Kaplan, 1979, p. 55)

However, it is increasingly clear that inhibited sexual desire is *not* a distinct clinical entity, and moreover, the sexual "anorexia" metaphor has distinct iatrogenic implications.

Low sexual desire—like many other conditions that seem to fall outside the classical medical model—is a complaint with different meanings and is the endpoint of a pathway of dysregulations, failed attempts at integration, or the incapacity to reach a consistent interactional fit. (Verhulst & Heiman, 1988, p. 266)

Kaplan recognized that contemporary treatment remained to be fine-tuned when she wrote, "One factor in the high failure rate may be related to the fact that the immediate causes of the suppression of sexual appetite have not yet been clearly delineated" (1979, p. 56). However, she implicitly viewed the problem as reflecting limited understanding of the syndrome rather than the limits of her paradigm. Simon (1989) articulately addresses the "naturalized" viewpoint embraced in Kaplan's "drive" models of desire. His own view of sexual desire is consistent with the diverse vantage points of object relations and systemic theory, Bowen's concept of differentiation, and Maturana and Varela's sociobiological approach:

The denaturalization of the sexual does not require an abandonment of all we have learned about the constancies and varieties of the biological substratum, but it does require the effort of going beyond that and examining that which can only be understood in terms of individual situations in specific points of social space and specific points of time; individuals with and within history. (p. 23)

The reverse [of the naturalized] position, that for all practical purposes the sexual is constructed, must be considered: that the origins of sexual desire can only be found in social life and its variable presence in the lives of specific individuals is predominantly dependent upon their experience in and with social life. In other words, a view of sexual desire as the continuously evolving product of human cultures; transmitted not through our genes but either through language or through the behavior of others that, in turn, reflects the impact of language upon their behavior. The difficulty with this position is that it requires that we accept the possibly superficial nature of that which many of us experience as emerging from our deepest and sometimes most compelling sense of our own beings. (p. 25)

PREOCCUPATION WITH BEHAVIOR AND APPETITIVE RESPONSE

In Chapter One, we first noted the curious inattention to sexual salience and profoundness in the seminal works of modern sexual therapy (Figures 1.1 and 1.2). The extraordinary impact of Masters and Johnson's sexual response model encouraged conceptualizing desire as another "phase," when the topic was first addressed in the mid 1970s. Zilbergeld and Ellison noted a portion of the problem:

> Of course, in clinical work Masters and Johnson and most other therapists have dealt with the subjective—with how clients felt and how they interpreted their experiences. But because of the powerful influence of the Masters and Johnson paradigm, the sexual response cycle—which, to repeat, consists almost entirely of physiological data—we have been slow to recognize the tremendous importance of subjective factors like interest and excitement, despite the fact that both desire and arousal problems are quite common (Kaplan, 1977; Zilbergeld, 1978). (Zilbergeld & Ellison, 1980, p. 70)

Another factor encouraging the "phase" view was the attempt to establish sexual desire as a topic of legitimate inquiry. It was only a short time before that Masters and Johnson dared to study physiological response; they did so by stripping it of all eroticism and draping it chastely in a medical model. In addressing sexual desire, clinicians treaded on thinner ice; they were nearing the phenomena of *eroticism* in people's bedrooms (i.e., what people actually do). In viewing sexual desire as copulatory initiation, clinicians (a) borrowed credibility from animal research, and (b) sidestepped uniquely *human* capacities for intimacy and phenomenological nuance *during* sexual behavior. Investigating *proception* is one thing; examining how people deal with *lust* and *ecstasy* is quite another.

Once the animal husbandry model of sexual desire was firmly in place, the likelihood of considering sexual desire during *sex quietly disappeared. MacLean's (1972, 1982) model of the triune brain makes it clear (in retrospect) that modern sex therapy has pursued the aspects of sexual desire deriving from limbic brain functions (shared in common with all other mammals).* Sexual desire-as-eroticism, in contrast, is more dependent on neocortical functions. Given that neocortical (rather than limbic) emotional response is also the hallmark of highly differentiated people, the potential for conceptually integrating human development with a *new* sexual desire paradigm becomes obvious. Conversely, the failure of the contemporary sexual desire paradigm to do likewise becomes understandable.

Early sexological researchers were more focused on sexual behavior than sexual experience (Kinsey, Pomeroy, & Martin, 1948; Kinsey, Pomeroy, Martin, & Gebhard, 1953); they assumed that sexual activity reflected levels of sexual desire. The "phase" model of sexual desire addresses functional, utilitarian desire, similar to the focus of modern sex therapy on functional genital response. Some clinicians are becoming aware that coital connection does not necessarily reflect subjective feelings of desire; unfortunately the importance of phenomenological desire is conceptualized within the modern sex therapy paradigm *which focuses on desire as an appetitive response to sexual behavior. Discussion of an "emotional component" within an appetitive response paradigm obfuscates the reality that one is still focusing on "doing it"; the success of treatment is assessed in terms of frequency of behavior and not the profoundness of experience.*

Kaplan's (1979) original formulations epitomize this pitfall; it has been embraced more recently by Schwartz and Masters (1988). While the latter clinicians maintain that frequency of sexual behavior is a poor criterion for diagnosing inhibited sexual desire, they clearly consider sexual desire within the confines of *initiatory* behavior: "low initiatory behavior and/or a persistently negative receptivity to sexual approaches by an established sexual partner" (Schwartz & Masters, 1988, p. 232).

Therapists' attempts to free themselves from the "phase" paradigm of sexual desire (and its inherent focus on behavioral frequency) has led to some interesting conceptual positions. For example, the notion of desire *discrepancy*— disparity between partners in desired frequency for sex—introduces the relationship rather than the calendar or the adding machine as the reference point. Its asset lies in the introduction of a systemic context to complaints; its deficit is that the implicit focus is still on *frequency*. Yes, discrepant desire can, and often does, stem from differences in sexual arousal and satisfaction during sex. However, behavioral frequency remains the most common conceptual focus of discrepant desire.

SEEING THE PROBLEM IN ACTION

To see the inherent focus on behavior in another context, consider how clinical histories are taken. *The question is commonly posed, "How often do you want sex?" as opposed to, "How often do you want* during *sex?"* The later orientation is such a paradigm shift that it sounds awkward to the ear; it immediately connotes something negative (e.g., one should not *want* during sex, one should be *satisfied*). The former question of "desire *for* sex" addresses desire *to have* or *to do* something rather than a subjective emotional experience *during* that involvement; it reflects the very objectification and depersonalization of sex that make some people feel exploited. The latter question of "desire *during* sex" is more akin to popular notions of *longing* and *passion*, reflecting salience and intensity; it addresses the "heartache" aspects of desire that consume adolescents and most married couples wish they could rekindle.

There is nothing wrong and something nice about helping people experience spontaneous desire *for* sex; it becomes problematic, however, when this is confused with desire *in* sex. More exacting distinctions within the desire "phase" model do *not* yield a paradigm shift to the notion of sexual potential. The notion of sexual potential includes a continuum of both low and high sexual desire, without pathologizing either end of the spectrum. If desire-as-passion were the focus of attention, epidemiological estimates of desire "problems" would be *significantly* greater.

For another example, consider a very plausible therapeutic intervention in a case of low sexual desire. In this case, the frustrated husband develops the pattern of initiating sex by asking his wife, "Are we going to do it or not?" Instead, the therapist recommends alternative approach of asking, "Do you want to do it?" or "I would like to do it, would you?"; the therapist feels these latter approaches sound more personal, display more subjective emotional eagerness, and involve "I" messages.

This vignette illustrates the paradigmatic problem in conceptualizing sexual desire. The therapist's suggestions recognize the importance of an emotional component in sexual desire. However, the problem is that these alternatives primarily focus *on behavior*. Problems arise in the bedroom (and the clinician's office) from unwillingness to make the quantum leap in intimacy to, "What's it like for you right this moment (now that we're doing or not doing whatever)? This is what it's like for me!" In this paradigm shift, the doing of behavior recedes into the background and the phenomenological exploration of two separate realities becomes paramount.

The reader might ask, *"What framework besides appetitive responses to sexual behavior would you expect, given the current approach of DSM-III-R to the issues of sexual desire?"* The question itself targets the problem. The point is not to criticize the experienced and dedicated clinicians who invested time and energy to advance the field. Recognizing the importance of desire in *human* sexuality and "legitimizing" sexual desire problems through a diagnostic classification in *DSM-III* was a significant step in the development of the sexual health-care field. On the other hand, it also concretized a viewpoint of a broader phenomenon that was only *beginning* to be explored, enshrining its narrow focus without awareness of its inherent biases.

The *DSM-III-R* conceptualization of desire has confined subsequent development by (a) focusing on "problems" of sexual desire at only the "lower-than-normal" end of the continuum, and preempting consideration of developmental tasks and issues at "higher-than-normal" levels of desire and arousal; and (b) focusing attention on sexual desire as a precursor rather than a concomitant to sexual behavior and physiological response. The efforts of authors to clarify the importance of subjective eagerness in the clinical application of *DSM-III-R* criteria for hypoactive sexual desire *underscores* this point. The solution is neither abolition of the DSMs nor construction of ever more terminology or diagnostic categories; the solution is understanding what we have already wrought and what we mean when we say what we say.

Zilbergeld and Ellison (1980) point out that Master and Johnson's (1966) use of the term "excitement" to describe the first stage of physiological response (rather than subjective experience) obscured the absence of phenomenology in their sexual response model. They also note that their own use of the term "arousal" to refer to subjective evaluation of physiological reactivity (Zilbergeld & Ellison, 1980) can easily be confused with the common use of the term to refer to nonspecific physiological response. Given this, and the fact that the different processes referred to as *excitement* or *arousal* can occur independently of the other, clinicians practice in a professional environment ripe for fuzzy thinking and ambiguous communication. Said differently, it is easy to think that we mean more than we say, and that we know more than we think.

Surfacing momentarily from the professional lexicon to consider popular usage of the concept of "desire" further clarifies the point being made. Table

9.1 contains the views of the desire that people kill themselves (and each other) for.

Sex therapy's notion of desire is mainly limited to the first two meanings in Table 9.1: request and hunger. The remaining four meanings refer to desire in the way that people actually *want* (or want to think they want). The former deal with appetitive response for behavior; the latter addresses issues of partner selection and engagement, and interpersonal processes such as intimacy, love, and romance. Notice the subtle but salient differences elicited by *longing* or *craving* when they refer to *hunger* as opposed to *coveting* one's partner. More-over, notice that the latter meanings of desire in Table 9.1 are often the most problematic; one might say that difficulty with aspiration, devotion, coveting, and lust creates problems with request and hunger (i.e., appetitive responses) for sexual behavior. It is these meanings that are also the most relevant at extreme heights of sexual salience and pleasure.

A THREE-DIMENSIONAL MODEL OF SEXUAL DESIRE

Reconsidering Kaplan's desire phase model from the forgoing perspective highlights several shortcomings (the diagram which appeared in Chapter One is reproduced below for convenience; see Figure 9.1). Perhaps the most glaring problem is the impossibility of considering the *degree* of desire preceding the sexual encounter; there is no dimension on which it can be scaled! The vertical axis displays level of physiological arousal, not desire.

A three-dimensional model, however, permits scaling the level of desire preceding and during sexual behavior (see Figure 9.2). Level of desire is plotted along the vertical (z-axis); physiological arousal is plotted along the y-axis, and the x-axis denotes the passage of time.

Comprehending a three-dimensional model takes a little adjustment, since the stereotypic sexual (physiological) response cycle is two-dimensional and usually depicted "vertically." In Figure 9.2, however, the sexual response curve

Table 9.1
Notions of Desire

Request:	ask, seek, solicit
Hunger:	appetite, motive, craving, urge, will, longing
Aspiration:	mind, hope, want, wish
Devotion:	rapture, admiration
Covet:	choose, pant, crave, fancy, long for
Lust:	greed, fervor, passion, carnality, pleasure

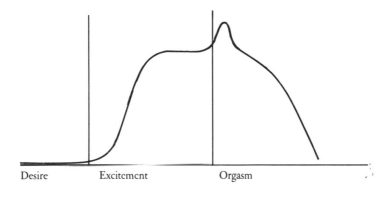

**Figure 9.1 A Common Understanding of Kaplan's Triphasic
Concept of Human Sexuality**

is displayed as if laid flat on a tabletop (i.e., on the horizontal (x-y) plane). A
vertical surface like a fence (corresponding to the z-axis) has been constructed
along the outline of the sexual response curve, on which level of desire can be
plotted at any given point; points higher up on the fence indicate higher levels
of desire: Onset of physical stimulation is assumed to occur where the y-axis

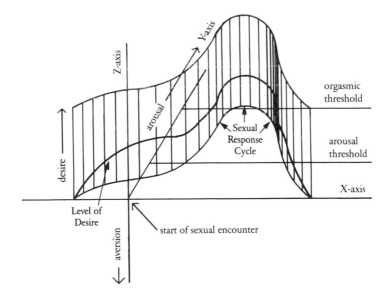

Figure 9.2 A Three Dimensional Model of Sexual Response and Desire

intersects the x-axis; the area to the left of the y-axis represents the time preceding the start of the sexual encounter.

Figure 9.2 has actually been drawn to take Kaplan's "hunger" model of sexual desire into account. *As in eating, level of desire diminishes as soon as consumption commences.* A utilitarian level of sexual desire is depicted overall; there is a minor increase in desire as orgasm becomes imminent, followed by a rapid and total reduction in desire.

The three-dimensional perspective also highlights another flaw in Masters and Johnson's model: level of physiological arousal is usually indicated as nonexistent at the outset of the encounter. Figure 9.2 is more consistent with clinical reality. People with moderate levels of desire often enter the sexual encounter with some level of physiological arousal; some women are known to achieve orgasm simply through fantasy.

The three-dimensional model of arousal and desire is also useful in illustrating some of the points made in previous discussion. Figure 9.3 depicts Apfelbaum's notion of a sexually *functional* individual; his/her body completes the physiological response cycle with minimal subjective desire.

The next figure illustrates the relative independence of profoundness of sexuality and physiological response (Figure 9.4). This individual is having a profound sexual experience although he/she has not had an orgasm. Note that the sexual response cycle does not cross the orgasmic threshold, although the level of desire-as-passion is high. This occurrence is quite common in initial

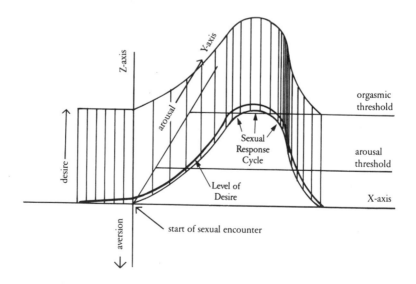

Figure 9.3 "Adequate" Sexual Function with Minimal Desire

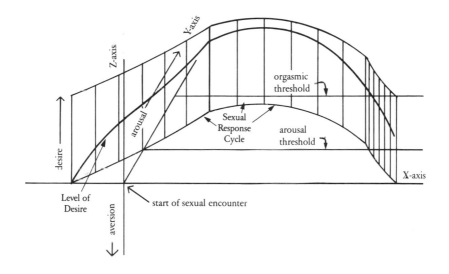

Figure 9.4 Profound Levels of Desire Below the Orgasmic Threshold

experiences of "wall-socket" sex and in the pursuit of sexual potential. In Taoist teachings, this is the *ideal* sexual experience (referred to as *Transforming the True*) and the object of dedicated practice (Douglas & Slinger, 1979).

The final figure depicts sexual aversion (negative desire) in an individual who also fails to demonstrate clinical manifestations of arousal (e.g., lubrication or erection) (see Figure 9.5). The sexual response cycle is still plotted horizontally on the x-y plane (i.e., on the "table top"). Note that the level of arousal does not cross the arousal threshold. Reading the level of desire requires a minor shift in visualization: The surface on which arousal is plotted (the z-axis) extends *below* the x-y plane (i.e., the "fence" starts at the "table top" and projects *downward*).

In Figure 9.5, the individual's minimal level of arousal begins only after some period of direct stimulation; level of aversion increases as the individual becomes aware of proprioceptive cues of (sub-clinical) arousal. Moreover, the individual exits at a higher level of aversion than he/she entered with. The reader should note that all of these illustrations are consonant with the quantum model outlined in Chapter Two.

DESIRE-AS-PASSION

Returning to the issue of sex therapy's focus on desire as an initiatory phase, it *is* important to recognize that physical diseases, chronic illnesses, hormonal

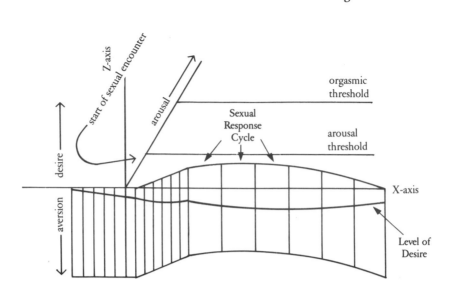

Figure 9.5 Sexual Aversion with Minimal Clinical Arousal

imbalance, and drugs can affect appetitive responsiveness. Moreover, it is good to know that androgen augmentation has been successful in some cases of low desire (Bancroft & Wu, 1983; Sherwin, Gelfand, & Brender, 1985). However, it is *also* important to recognize that this is still the libido, desire-as-initiation, paradigm.

Yes, it is true that "organic" sources may also cause desire-as-passion problems, and moreover, that people who lack desire-as-passion very often experience initiatory indifference. However, the millions of dollars that pharmaceutical companies will reap from marketing (currently experimental) dopamine-antagonist and anti-depressant drugs that may enhance desire (Segraves, 1988) will stem from the pursuit of desire-as-*intensity* and salience, and not merely the pursuit of *frequency*.

Traditional sexual and marital therapy does not address desire-as-passion. Table

Table 9.2
Notions of Passion

Emotion:	ardor, enthusiasm, fire, outburst
Desire:	craving, lust, love, amorousness, infatuation, affection, attachment, fancy, fondness
Anger:	fury, rage, wrath, vehemence, resentment, ire, indignation

9.2 presents popular notions of passion; they have only cursory similiarity to the *DSM-III-R* view of desire.[3] *Passion* (as an aspect of sexual desire) has two qualities: (a) extreme intensity that tests the individual's self-soothing abilities (e.g., the *passion* of Christ—and its association to the crucible) and (b) the focus of desire in one's *partner* (as opposed to desire for sexual behavior per se).[4]

What the desire "phase" paradigm *does* do well is pressure people to want sex. It shapes therapists into unwitting purveyors of the same pressure (to have or want sex) that patients experience prior to entering treatment. Matters become more complicated yet when therapists believe their interventions (e.g., non-demand pleasuring; ban on intercourse) are intrinsically *pressure-free*.

The hunger (sexual *drive*) model of desire is a part of the *normal neurosis* of Western culture. Its roots lie in Freud's libido theory (1905/1986), which pictured adult sexuality like a perpetual adolescent: a biologically-driven cistern of sexual impulses constantly demanding expression (constructive or otherwise). However, a hormonally driven, biologically mediated sexual "drive" has not been borne out in recent research (Leiblum & Rosen, 1988).

Despite this, the drive model of sexual desire prevails: Widespread expectations for unceasing sexual interest live on, although almost no one's personal experience validates it (those who do qualify as "sex addicts").

STEPPING OUTSIDE THE PREVAILING PARADIGM

Not all therapists have been captured by the prevailing "phase" (drive) model of sexual desire. Shortly after Kaplan published *Disorders of Sexual Desire* (1979), Zilbergeld and Ellison (1980) wrote a chapter on this topic; the subtle aspects of the latter authors' approach were lost in the overwhelming attention that Kaplan's received. The notion of subjective desire *during* sex is imbedded in Zilbergeld and Ellison's (1980) concept of *arousal*, in the same way it permeated Apfelbaum's (1977c) concept of sexually *functional* people (who respond physiologically without concomitant pleasure or desire). Zilbergeld and

---

[3]Although most people don't think of *anger* when they contemplate sexual passion, its inclusion in Table 9.2 is instructive: *Healthy sexual aggression* has never enjoyed a place of honor in contemporary sexual and marital therapy. In the glare of the *victim advocacy* (vs. *systemic*) approach to sexual abuse treatment, it has fared worse.

The topic of healthy sexual aggression is very intimate (or embarrassing, depending on one's personal reaction). It is eagerly overlooked by therapists and the lay public; it fares far better dressed in the Eastern religious trappings of "sexual energy." If a therapist doesn't appreciate the utility of a sexual crucible or its output (i.e., fulfillment of sexual potential), he/she also usually overlooks the requisite "raw" ingredients that go into it: *Sexual aggression is a component of sexual potential.*

[4]*Eroticism*, the desire for engaging the partner *through particular behaviors*, is discussed in Chapter Eleven.

Ellison (1980) distinguished *desire* (interest; initiation and receptivity to initiations; "horniness") from *arousal* (subjective excitement, "turn-on," cognitive attribution of positive sexual feelings to physiological response). Their notion of subjective arousal is noteworthy in two respects: (a) attributional labeling of physiological response is often ignored in drive models of desire (which assume that sex is inherently pleasing); and (b) from the standpoint of sexual potential, it connotes a subjective experience conceptually unbound by the limits of orgasm.

Walster (1971) previously proposed an attributional model of desire similar to Zilbergeld and Ellison's, offering some utility for understanding desire during sex. Walster suggested that an individual experiences passion when two conditions are met: (a) the individual is physiologically aroused, and (b) the arousal is attributed to positively experienced passion or love for the partner. She cited as empirical support Schacter and Singer's (1962) experiment utilizing epinephrine injections in conjunction with varying attributional conditions; under particular conditions, unpleasant states of physiological arousal (e.g., fear, pain, frustration, and challenge) can enhance passion. Rejection, for example, is often an antecedent of ardor.

Walster's attributional theory of passionate arousal is similar to our prior discussion of anxiety in the quantum model (Chapter Two). She writes:

> We would suggest that perhaps it does not really matter how one produces an agitated state in an individual. Stimuli that usually produce sexual arousal, gratitude, anxiety, guilt, loneliness, hatred, jealousy, or confusion may all increase one's physiological arousal, and thus increase the intensity of his emotional experience. As long as one attributes his agitated state to passion, he should experience true passionate love. As soon as he ceases to attribute his tumultuous feelings of passion, love should die. (1971, pp. 90–91)

Leiblum and Rosen's (1988) sexual "scripting" approach addresses subjective desire during sex in several ways. First, they consider sexual desire to be a subjective feeling state primarily determined by intrapsychic and interpersonal processes (in the context of intact neuroendocrine functioning), which *may* result in overt sexual behavior. Second, their view that variations in sexual desire are a *result* as much as a *cause* of sexual behavior introduces a recursive view of subjective desire and satisfaction during sex. Third, this "result" is not merely a function of "drive reduction"; it is a function of *script satisfaction*. Rosen and Leiblum's (1988) concept of sexual script satisfaction further addresses phenomenological experience during sex.

Steven Levine (1988a, 1988b) offers a clinically useful model in which sexual desire is divided into three basic components: *drive, wish,* and *motive.*

Sexual *drive* refers to genetically programmed, neuroendocrine-mediated processes manifesting themselves in genital response, "horniness," perceptual narrowing towards erotic stimuli, erotic fantasies, and partnered or solitary sexual behavior. Sexual drive is the quintessential embodiment of the appetitive response model of desire.

Many therapists who treat sexual disinterest believe sexual drive to be a factor in relatively few cases. True cases of low sex drive usually involve biochemical abnormalities in dopamine, serotonin, norepinephrine, or testosterone blood levels (Kaplan, 1979; Lief, 1988). Levine astutely notes that many individuals who report inhibited desire present manifestations of intact drive.

Sexual wish refers to ideations, cognitive aspirations of desire (i.e., the wish to have or not have sex). Sexual wish is often misrepresented by patients and misinterpreted by therapists. Many patients who secretly lack the willingness to be sexually active prefer to represent themselves as wishing to have sex but lacking drive. Levine shrewdly points out that relationship politics surrounding sexual desire have implications for clinical evaluation: "Clinicians must beware of equating the aspiration to be sexual with sexual desire. As patients represent themselves to a therapist, the truth told about sexual wishes is often only a partial truth" (p. 27).

Levine's notion of sexual *motivation,* the *willingness* to have sex, has multiple facets. Most clearly, it refers to the subjective *willingness* to engage in sexual behavior (i.e., as an initiatory variable). More subtly, it refers to the subjective degree of eagerness *during* sex. Levine is not particularly concerned with this distinction, although he perceives sexual desire as something preceding *and accompanying* physiological arousal; instead, he devotes his attention to articulating a sophisticated analysis of willingness in general.

According to Levine (1988a), the major determinants of sexual willingness are intrapsychic (i.e., sexual identity and object relations issues) and interpersonal (i.e., quality of the nonsexual relationship, and regulation of one's own and one's partner's sexual tension and nonsexual agendas). Interpersonal factors are the most important determinant of sexual willingness, and willingness is the major determinant of sexual desire. It is here that Levine comes closest to addressing the matter of sexual desire *during* sex.

Although not rooted in systems theory, Levine's complex topography of sexual desire represents a conceptual step forward towards a dynamic model that facilitates treatment; he clearly perceives sexual desire as existing in a sexual "system":

The intrapsychic and interpersonal aspects exist in interactive dynamic equilibrium. The study of this equilibrium during therapy occasionally suggests how an individual's sexual desire was organized and how, once it was mentally programmed, it has determined subsequent experience. (Levine, 1988, p. 23)

STEPPING BACKWARDS: CONFUSING CONCEPTUALIZATION WITH CLINICAL INTERVENTION

As clinicians become increasing aware of problems of low sexual desire, the need for broad-band conceptualization and intervention has been more frequently articulated. Some mixture of psychoanalytic psychotherapy and behavior therapy, the early foundations of modern sex therapy, constitutes the predominant clinical strategies in contemporary practice. More recently, however, the thrust has been towards integrating social and systemic approaches. Zilbergeld and Ellison's (1980) use of the brief therapy frameworks of Milton Erickson and the Mental Research Institute was an early forerunner of this trend. Fish, Fish, and Sprenkle (1984) reported a case study of one couple treated with a combination of structural family therapy and traditional sex therapy.

However, development of more effective multi-systemic treatment approaches has been impeded because (a) clinicians' conceptualizations are often more systemic than their interventions, and (b) the distinction between the two is often overlooked. This confusion of conceptualization with clinical implementation is not unlike what we encountered regarding the absence of clinical models of intimacy (Chapters Four and Five).

For example, Kaplan's integration of behaviorism with psychoanalysis (borrowing heavily on Masters and Johnson's sensate focus activities) is perhaps the most widely known treatment approach for desire inhibition. In her view, inhibited sexual desire, like sexual dysfunction, is the result of intrapsychic conflicts and anxiety about sexuality, intimacy, and impulse control; individuals with desire "phase" disorders are more pathological and deeply conflicted.

Kaplan (1979) briefly discusses relationship systems: "But when issues in the couple's relationship raise obstacles to treatment, the focus of intervention shifts to problems in the *marital system*. This method of dealing with intrapsychic and interactional issues in a fluid manner that is responsive to the constantly shifting patterns of the couple's resistance is illustrated . . . " (p. 116, italics original). Unfortunately, this is interpreted by some readers as reflecting a "systemic approach," obfuscating its actual absence and creating an erroneous impression that stifles them from looking further. Kaplan's treatment approach emphasizes insight in conjunction with desensitization (i.e., a lengthier version of her psychodynamically-oriented sex therapy for genital dysfunctions); her examples of "interpersonal interventions" don't deviate from this approach. In her more recent "integrated approach" (1987) for sexual aversion, the integration concerns the addition of psychopharmacology; systemic intervention still receives only perfunctory consideration.

For a more blatant example, LoPiccolo and Friedman (1988) characterize their treatment approach to low sexual desire as an integration of cognitive, behavioral and systemic therapy; they cite a variety of causes of desire phase problems (Table 9.3). However, systemic aspects are not apparent in their four "key" treatment assumptions: (a) Many patients are more sexually aversive than they recognize; (b) insight is necessary; (c) treatment must be couples-based because individuals with desire problems rarely request help; and (d) Masters and Johnson's sensate activities are an integral part of treatment. Moreover, a systemic approach is not apparent in the four main aspects of their brief (15–25 session) therapy: (a) experiential/sensory awareness; (b) insight; (c) cognitive restructuring (including taking "fantasy breaks"); and (d) behavioral interventions. From their own description, LoPiccolo and Friedman's *treatment* approach appears to be cognitive-behavioral, although they attempt to *conceptualize* systemic etiological processes.

This impression is borne out in LoPiccolo's more recent articulation of his approach (LoPiccolo, 1991). One might expect his intervention strategy to be congruent with his proposition that sexual symptoms have systemic signifi-

Table 9.3
Causes of Inhibited Sexual Desire

INDIVIDUAL CAUSES	RELATIONSHIP CAUSES
(a) religious orthodoxy	(a) lack of attraction to partner
(b) anhedonic or obsessive-compulsive personality	(b) partner's poor sexual skills
(c) gender identity or choice object issues	(c) marital conflict
(d) specific sexual phobias or aversions	(d) fear of closeness and vulnerability
(e) fear of loss of control over sexual urges	(e) disparity in point of optimal closeness
(f) masked sexual deviation (paraphilias)	(f) passive-aggressive solution to power imbalance
(g) fear of pregnancy	(g) inability to fuse feelings of love and sexual desire
(h) "widower's syndrome"	
(i) depression	
(j) hormonal issues	
(k) medication side effects	
(l) aging-related concerns	

Derived from LoPiccolo & Friedman, 1988

cance and "utility." However, his implementation involves asking patients what benefit they derive from their symptom.[5] Although the conceptualization *sounds* like systemic thinking, the intervention betrays LoPiccolo's background in cognitive-behavioral approaches: *If the symptom is, indeed, systemically driven, (a) insight into secondary gain doesn't usually change a system, and (b) the therapist might do better to ask the identified patient what secondary benefit the* spouse *derives from the symptom.*

While many authors state the need for integrated approaches, the conceptualizations and treatments they offer are merely multilinear rather than multisystemic and isomorphic; for example, there is little consideration of systemic and object relations issues in LoPiccolo's analysis of partner selection:

> As psychologists, we often tend to look for complicated psychodynamic or relationship system causes of low sexual desire, and sometimes overlook the obvious. If a person simply does not find his or her spouse physically attractive, low sex drive is hardly a surprising result. (LoPiccolo & Friedman, 1988, p. 125)

A final example of the confusion of conceptualization and intervention occurs in Schwartz and Masters' (1988) characterization of their treatment approach as addressing systemic issues and intimacy problems. Their basic etiological model is summarized in Table 9.4.

The casual reader might think their approach addresses object relations and systemic dimensions, since the authors state their recognition of "'deeper levels' of contributing factors in desire disorders, which often require intervention. . . . Successful treatment of the couple's sexual disorders usually requires realignment of the entire interactive system" (p. 235). However, like many clinicians who *conceptualize* systemic and ego-deficit factors, Schwartz and Masters' *treatment* approach (1988) emphasizes cognitive-behavioral and social-skill-building interventions:

---

[5]Joseph LoPiccolo is a noted figure in the sex therapy field who has made significant contributions in treatment and outcome research. Focusing on the clinical approach of such a luminary highlights the ease with which average therapists can mistakenly think they have integrated a new paradigm when indeed they have not.

LoPiccolo's intervention raises several points addressed in previous chapters. Asking patients what they "get" out of their symptoms suggests (a) that secondary gain is the *reason* for the symptom, (b) that the secondary gain was deliberately sought (consciously or unconsciously), and (c) that recognizing the secondary gain or being willing to give it up will make things change. LoPiccolo's intervention is actually more similar to Kaplan's depth-analysis than to a systemic approach. The reader may also wish to refer back to the discussion of Apfelbaum's concepts of *response anxiety* and *lack of entitlement* (Chapters Three and Six) or his own publication (Apfelbaum, 1983) for a thorough analysis of this intervention.

Table 9.4
Additional Causes of Inhibited Sexual Desire

Spiral effect of false beliefs and hurt feelings between partners
Secondary impacts of sexual dysfunctions.
Attentional and labeling deficits.
Poor relational transactions.
Intimacy issues.
Ambivalent attachment.
Enmeshment between the partners.

(derived from Schwartz & Masters, 1988)

If a couple is placed in social isolation and seen on a daily basis for 14 days, with as few interruptions from work and family as possible, deep-seated roadblocks to the ISD partner's sexual desire will manifest themselves or will be catalyzed by therapeutic intervention. Controlled therapeutic situations allow the therapist to increase the couple's skills in intimate exchange. These skills include sending and hearing each other's messages; problem solving; demonstrativeness; responsiveness to each other's needs; creativity in socializing; ways of dealing with long-term hostilities; and ways of handling ambivalence regarding closeness, vulnerability, trust, and bonding. . . .

If a couple manifests transactions that are destructive to feelings of intimacy and sexual desire, the therapist actively directs the couple to their mutually stated goals in several ways: (1) by confronting the transaction; (2) by pointing out its potentially destructive consequences; (3) by offering skills to improve the couple's interactions; and (4) by providing specific suggestions on ways and means to practice the new skills. . . . (1988, pp. 238–239)

Although Schwartz and Masters recognize the potential use of sex therapy to elicit unresolved individual issues, their interventions emphasize permission-giving, education, support, and insight. They state that their treatment approach is basically similar to the original Masters and Johnson (1966) program for overt sexual dysfunction. Kaplan (1979), however, reported that results with this approach for sexual desire problems were disappointing. Verhulst and Heiman (1988) concur with Kaplan, attributing this outcome to Masters and Johnson's focus on coordinating sensory stimulation and decreasing inhibitions, rather than addressing the broader multifaceted problems in the dyadic system.

A STEP FORWARD

Other well-recognized clinicians have proposed clinical approaches to desire problems that address systemic issues at increasing levels of sophistication.

Rosen and Leiblum's (1988) sexual-scripting approach, derived from social learning theory, emphasizes the contextual character of sexual interaction. They distinguish between *performance scripts* (overt sequence and range of sexual behaviors that people actually do) and *cognitive scripts* (preferred or idealized sexual styles, behaviors, and goals). They write, "In emphasizing independent assessment of performance and ideal script elements for both partners, we are also clearly highlighting the importance of understanding the *interpersonal context* of sexual choices and conduct generally" (p. 179, italics original).

Rosen and Leiblum hypothesize that low sexual desire often stems from intrapsychic or interpersonal incongruity between ideal scripts and behavioral repertoire, and differences in script complexity, rigidity, conventionality, and satisfaction. Sexual script rigidity surfaces in difficulties adapting to shifting circumstances like those presented by parenthood, illness, and aging.[6] These clinicians depart from the common focus on sexual frequency and consider factors occurring *during* sex (e.g., degree of variety and spontaneity). Rosen and Leiblum note their approach is ineffective as an exclusive intervention in cases where inhibited sexual desire is long-standing, or the result of intrapsychic conflict or marital discord.

Verhulst and Heiman (1988) offer an even more sophisticated systemic viewpoint on low sexual desire. They distinguish their approach from Kaplan's formulations by emphasizing that inhibited sexual desire reflects *distress* rather than *disease*. Their definition of low sexual desire is inherently systemic, "a subjective complaint about the absence of sexual feelings, voiced by one or both sexual partners, indicating unsatisfactory individual coordination and/or interpersonal synchronization" (p. 245).

Verhulst and Heiman propose that synchronization of desire is a function of multiple, interdependent levels of regulation, including *symbolic interactions, affect-regulating interactions,* and *sensate exchanges*. Symbolic interactions refer to " . . . formal exchanges of words, ideas, symbolic gestures and other representations" (1988, p. 246) through sensate exchanges. To the degree that sexual behavior elicits congruous focus and content of emotional reactions, a mutual emotional context of meaning can be constructed (successful affect regulation). Partners with incongruity in these dimensions fail to maintain a sexual context in their physical contact; they become bogged down in other individual and systemic issues (e.g., attachments, territoriality, boundaries, and hierarchies). The authors suggest that therapists monitor these latter dimensions in

---

[6]Script flexibility is analogous to Wynne and Wynne's (1986) concept of *mutuality*.

the course of observing patients' in-session behavior and debriefing sexual (and nonsexual) activities that occur at home.

Sensate exchange, affect regulation, and symbolic interactions are simultaneous, interdependent aspects of actual or anticipated sexual encounters which determine their outcome and meaning. Verhulst and Heiman write, "As for the clinician, the major advantage of this model may be that it imposes a dialectical way of thinking: clinical findings and statements about one structure or one level immediately call forth questions about other structures and levels" (1988, p. 266).

While most authors mention relationship interaction as one of many causes of low sexual desire, Verhulst and Heiman (1988) exemplify a true systemic clinical approach to sexual desire disorders. The reader may wish to refer back to Figure 2.7 for a graphic depiction of the multi-systemic nature of their approach.

Verhulst and Heiman's contribution provides a good reentry point to our prior discussion of individual and dyadic issues in Chapters Seven and Eight. As we leave we might ask, "What allows couples to re-establish and modulate successful affect regulation?"; the answer will return us to the importance of differentiation.

In the subsequent chapter we continue our focus on problems of low sexual desire, turning our attention to details of clinical treatment. There we will encounter the sexual crucible as an isomorphic integration of systemic and object relations interventions, having additional utility in enhancing personal development.

CHAPTER TEN

Politics of Sexual Desire and the Nature of Wanting

This chapter offers a multidimensional analysis of problems of low sexual desire. Common object relations issues create psychopolitical stances around sexual desire (e.g., not wanting to want, wanting to be wanted, and not wanting to reciprocate). Incongruous power hierarchies surrounding low sexual desire are inevitable: The partner with the lower sexual desire always controls sex. Culturally promulgated views of sexual "normality" encourage inhibited sexual desire; prevailing treatment paradigms compound matters by inherently pressuring patients to want sex and inducing iatrogenic resistance.

A paradigm shift in the treatment of inhibited sexual desire is proposed: We construct a sexual crucible by seamlessly integrating object relations and systemic interventions, and enhancing differentiation and capacity for level-2 intimacy. Details of the therapeutic alliance, establishment of the elicitation window, and vectors of intervention are presented.

Problems of sexual desire come in different manifestations (e.g., initiatory willingness, passion during sex) and intensities (e.g., aversion, disinterest, functional/utilitarian desire, lack of fulfillment of sexual potential). Each can be seen as a strategic attempt to achieve nonsexual intrapsychic and relational equilibrium, played out in the sexual arena.

Changes in physical proximity and emotional commitment often upset individual and dyadic homeostasis, even though the couple may have lived together for years. Suddenly each partner finds he or she is cohabitating with the living embodiment of their manipulative, withholding, or intrusive childhood parent. Individuals who seek marriage as a defense against unresolved issues of individuation and bonding invariably are in for a disappointing but necessary experience as their relationship evolves.

People are often able to bypass such difficulties in relationships with close friends; they may, in fact, use this as "proof" that marital problems stem from their mate's unique characteristics. However, difficulties with intense emotional contact often become evident only in the intimate confines of marriage.

Critical mass for the brewing transference storm often requires that both partners' dynamics be brought together in the crucible of increased emotional proximity, intensity, and commitment.

The fact that an individual has a history of inhibited sexual desire predating the current relationship does not negate the simultaneous realities of mutual impact and reciprocal maintenance. In discussing object relations, the clinician must avoid the tendency to see causation as a closed system of intrapsychic functioning.[1] Moreover, the politics of *wanting* (to be discussed subsequently) are common to *all* individuals; they become more prominent in one partner or the other at various points in the shifting equilibrium of the relationship.

The prudent therapist will pay attention to the politics of wanting if he or she has any thought of helping couples reach a *high* level of sexual desire and salience. At the outset of sexual-marital therapy, each partner often sees the other as the embodiment of his/her frustration and deprivation. Conflict escalates when spouses feel *unwanted* by each other. As treatment progresses, the relationship improves and partners become more emotionally attractive to each other. Predominant transferences shift, triggering anger, fear, and frustration of *wanting* the partner. A second cycle of fighting often ensues at this point, confusing an unknowing therapist. This second level of conflict cannot be resolved in the same way as the first; such fights are a defense against the growing intimacy and the fear of *wanting*.

Not Wanting to Want

The manner in which couples modulate their desire *for* sex and their desire *in* sex reflects the painful and crucial issues of *not wanting to want* and *wanting to be wanted*. At one level, these represent two polarized positions adopted by the identified patient and the spouse, respectively. At another level, these two positions reflect the multiple agendas within each person, often split off and projected onto one's partner.

In marriage, however, each partner is not merely the recipient of the other's projections; rather, each is the other's required stage, prop, and participant.

---

[1] The term *identified patient* will refer to the partner with the manifest lower sexual desire; the term *asymptomatic partner* will refer to the other spouse. No assumption is necessarily made regarding the relative health or intrinsic sexual interest of either partner. These terms highlight (a) the systemic manner in which object relations issues modulate sexual desire (and vice versa), (b) the common psychopolitical positions partners adopt when they present for treatment, and (c) the relative nature of complaints of low sexual desire. It is quite common for the respective positions of the partners to alternate in the course of treatment.

Usually the asymptomatic partner is well selected: He or she possesses a corresponding set of dynamic issues and projections to fuel construction of the system. He or she may also be particularly vulnerable to the partner's projections. Spouses unwittingly create the very situation they fear (and need). The resulting developments are the creation (and reflection) of patients' expectation of inevitable individual and dyadic outcomes (i.e., their introjects). For instance, in couples that develop inhibited sexual desire, the asymptomatic partner has his/her own reasons to be fearful of being withheld from (sexually or otherwise), and to respond with increasing rage, demands, or some other response that amplifies the pattern. It is through the construction of this living prototype that partners devise the opportunity to resolve family-of-origin issues and individual long-term developmental/existential conflicts.

The notion of the overly gratifying object, as discussed in Chapter Seven and outlined by Scharff (1982, 1988), is a crucial element in understanding the politics of sexual desire.[2] Increasing levels of intimacy and pleasure can elicit the perception of the partner as a tantalizing, cunning, manipulative creator of needfulness. It is often easier to grasp the gut-wrenching and crushing pain of intense *wanting* by thinking in terms of personal experience than imagining some theoretical infant's fear of dying for want of a caretaker. Most of us have experienced, at some time, the feeling that *we* might burst from the pain of *longing* and the anxious vulnerability of *caring*.

The notions of desire and passion in Tables 9.1 and 9.2 (e.g., aspiration, devotion, coveting, lust, ardor, fire, outburst, and craving) fit quite nicely with this view of *wanting*. For example, *choosing* a partner (exercising options and committing resources, unilaterally declaring desire for increased emotional/physical contact, announcing the other's personal importance) is sufficiently anxiety-provoking and deprivation–inviting that many people simply do not *want to want*. As the pleasure derived from the partner (and his/her uniqueness) grows, the attendant anxiety elicits expectations based on prior successes and failures in significant relationships. The result sometimes triggers an attempt to deprive the partner of being wanted, as well as an indirect refusal to *want*.

Not wanting to want sometimes surfaces as an attempt at maintenance of ego boundaries; inhibited sexual desire can be created (and maintained) when *wanting* becomes integrated into either partner's difficulty accepting emotional boundaries. Some individuals would rather be frustrated with a tolerable level of deprivation than cope with the vulnerability of valuing and the hunger of

---

[2]It is easy to assume that discussing wanting (hungering for a partner) in an object relations context implies acceptance of a hunger/drive model of sexual desire; in this case it does not.

longing. A thorough evaluation of people reporting low sexual desire some-times reveals a prior relationship in which the identified patient exhibited both high desire and a serious impairment of functioning. Sometimes this was punctuated by severe depression, substance abuse, and suicidal ideation. The current partner is picked precisely for the *lack* of desire he/she stimulates.

For instance, consultation was requested for a case of female inhibited sexual desire in which a bisexual woman chose to marry a male "friend" who was her confidant through her scorching sexual relationship with another woman. He had nursed her through the period of severe depression and suicidal episodes that followed the break-up of the homosexual relationship. His prior contact with her had been strictly platonic, and their initial sexual encounters after marriage were bland. However, the inept and inexperienced young man hoped she would eventually learn to desire him. After a year of marriage marked by sporadic sexual contact, she announced that she had no sexual interest in him and wanted to resume sex with women. Issues of sexual orientation aside, the woman had picked a partner who offered her safety, including safety from frustrated desire.

Wanting to be wanted and *not wanting to want* are not simply polarized positions that spouses adopt; people struggle ambivalently with both posi-tions. Sometimes the individual reporting low sexual desire also attempts to keep the spouse wanting him/her. In *wanting to be wanted*, common quests for a reflected sense of self surface repeatedly in treatment:

- "He (or she) doesn't love me, he just loves my body" (i.e., he loves the gratification rather than me).
- "He doesn't love my body, he loves the lace and garterbelt" (i.e., the source of gratification is not even me).

The desire to withhold stems from the fact that any gratification derived by the asymptomatic partner stimulates the identified patient's doubts about being loved for his/her intrinsic self. The identified patient withholds gratifica-tion in an attempt to reassure himself that he, and not the gratification he provides, is the object of the partner's interest. This stance obviates the oppor-tunity for the asymptomatic partner to express any preferences whatsoever, and frustrates legitimate pursuit of personal pleasure and welfare. Sexual agendas often embody the script, "If you are willing to go *without* having sex, then you must really love *me*."

A variant of this is the individual who *wants to be wanted and gratified* by the partner but *does not want to reciprocate*. Individuals who are insecure about exploitation and "abandonment" are also usually hypersensitive to their partner's expectations. Expression of even mild preferences by the partner can be experienced as demands that threaten the emotional and territorial integrity of the individual's sense of self. *Wanting to be wanted but not wanting to reciprocate* represents a narcissistic demand for unilateral gratification. Any expectation of reciprocity is experienced as an intrusion on personal freedom.

In one case, a man in his sixties refused to have sex with his wife. The wife was a very attractive and youthful woman and an enthusiastic sexual partner. The husband fancied himself something of a "cocksman" with women, but never experienced any interest or pleasure in sex with his wife. One striking element of the marital relationship was the husband's insistence that his wife maintain a copious supply of toilet paper in the house. His daily use of a small rectal syringe filled with water to start his bowel movements had left him unable to evacuate without it (i.e., "lazy bowel syndrome"). He reported deriving a certain sense of enjoyment at an abundance of toilet paper in the house. At the same time, he bitterly resented his wife's expectation for sexual contact, even when it had not occurred for a month or more. He was thoroughly outraged when his wife suggested that they trade toilet paper for sexual contact.

Not wanting to be wanted represents the ultimate avoidance of reciprocity; not wanting to be wanted reflects the extent of the individual's fears of being "gotten."

In another case, for instance, a socially prominent businessman sought consultation to help handle an affair that went awry. The man had a long history of exploitive relationships with women, expecting sexual gratification upon his demand while avoiding any consideration of his partner's emotional or sexual needs. In his most recent liaison the woman would not tolerate being put off or rejected by him. Her oxymoronic statement of "loving him so much she was going to get him" was consistent with his own unconscious expectations of women.

Wanting to be wanted and gratified, but competing with the partner's gratification is another variant. It is an old theme, best embodied in Goethe's story of Faust. As part of trading his soul to the Devil for knowledge and power, Faust has a young girl fall hopelessly in love with him. Faust saw the girl's previous indifference to him as one source of his dissatisfaction with life. If only he was wanted by her, he thought, he would be happier. In the end, Faust is miserable and jealous of her being in love when he is not, even though she awaits death in jail. Ironically, he is jealous of her fulfillment in desiring him, even though he is the object of her desire. Never would Faust have asked the Devil to fill him with longing for the girl; that would only have exposed him to greater longing and pain of unfulfilled desire (although it was the source of the girl's fulfillment).

Beyond the phenomenological experience of *wanting* lies the dyadic politics of open declarations of desire. *For someone at a low level of differentiation, there is little capacity to buffer the anxiety and vulnerability of openly longing and wanting; it triggers further increments in fears of manipulation and deprivation. The more common solution is to modulate the anxiety by withholding the display of desire,* and moreover, titrating it in reference to the partner's display as well. Low levels of differentiation require a rather tricky balance:

- On the one hand, it is only safe to want the partner to the degree that the partner wants you.
- On the other hand, it is only safe *not* to want your partner as long as the partner wants you.

If the partner stops demanding sex, it becomes unsafe not to want—at the least, it becomes necessary to express a wish to want or to find some other means to stimulate desire in the partner. When the asymptomatic partner starts to go through extinction conditioning, fear of the partner's *not wanting* drives the identified patient to offer periodic sexual contact. This intermittent reinforcement schedule keeps the partner both desirous and frustrated.

Case Example: "Over-exciting Objects" and Intrapsychic-Systemic Interaction

Elliot displayed the pattern of not wanting to want his wife sexually. He had grown up with an erratic and unstable alcoholic mother. When his parents divorced around the time he reached adolescence, Elliot assumed responsibility for keeping his mother sober enough to keep her job; he took over paying the bills and running the house. Elliot's mother was flirtatious and exciting when she had a drink or two, but these times were overshadowed by her deep depressions, drunken angry outbursts, and sudden crying jags.

Elliot couldn't stand to be with his mother, seeing her stumble drunkenly around the house or embarrassing him in public; he was often terrified, however, when she was out of his sight. Elliot lived in fear of her driving off the road on the way home from a bar, and his suddenly being "all alone." After many disappointments and heartaches, Elliot tried to protect himself by "giving up hope" that she would change; it hurt (somewhat) less when he didn't *want* his mother to be any different.

Unfortunately, and as might be expected, Elliot selected a woman who needed to please others to feel lovable and worthy. Kari's own mother was an erratic woman who thrived on receiving attention as a prominent socialite and hostess, but who was chronically depressed and neglectful of her family at most other times. Years of trying to please her mother were yet to bring Kari the sense of acceptance and security she craved.

Once married, Elliot repeatedly insisted that Kari do things to please him. However, the underlying purpose was for Elliot to prove to himself that Kari did not love him as much as she professed, and that she was not as considerate and selfless as she appeared. Kari was "too good to be true" as far as Elliot was concerned: When he enjoyed her, he became afraid of losing her. Eliott almost felt disloyal to his mother by how badly she measured up in comparison.

Kari readily responded to Elliot's ever-escalating demands out of her need to please and secure his favor. Unfortunately, this made things worse; Elliot's "tests" of her were designed to be *failed*. Well, not *really* failed: Desiring his wife made him feel vulnerable to disappointment and loss; as before, Elliot's "defense" was not to *want*. Kari's compliance with his outrageous demands reinforced Elliot's anger at his wife's overly gratifying presentation of herself; he was increasingly angered by his own pleasure derived from her emotional seductiveness. And yet, he sort of wanted Kari to "convince" him it was safe to want her, and rid him of his fears and doubts.

Elliot's solution was typical: escalation of demands in the attempt to find something that Kari would not do to please him. Elliot was vaguely aware that the paradoxical goal of his demands was to elicit a refusal. Kari's compliance with his increasing demands fueled his feelings of grandiosity and dependency, as well as his need to find some flaw in her to counterbalance his own feelings of defectiveness. For her part, complying with his demands made Kari feel more secure. Subsequently, however, Elliot's demands were accompanied by increasingly frequent barrages of insults and attacks on her adequacy.

In such cases, several paths of resolution occur. For instance, the individual who *doesn't want to want* may totally dominate the partner who needs to be wanted. In such a development intimacy is inhibited, as is both partners' growth, in that:

- Elliot has no respect for Kari for tolerating and complying with his outrageous demands.
- Elliot is perfectly aware of his own destructiveness and selfishness, and is not about to let Kari close to him in such a way that these traits might be openly disclosed and confronted. Elliot's demands increase in an attempt to keep Kari at an emotional distance, and to reduce Kari to the level of his own low self-worth.
- Elliot perceives his wife as a "sweet-natured, good person" who is often referred to as "the saint" by their friends. He lacks any awareness of Kari's angry and punitive impulses to withhold from him.

In an alternative common outcome, the partner who *needs to be needed* becomes more independent and resilient in the face of demands and attacks on her adequacy. This path can lead to growth for both people, although short-term relationship stability is often challenged; this process is characteristic of the sexual crucible:

- Elliot, who has been angry at his wife's compliance, is suddenly threatened by her autonomy and noncompliance. He shifts, interpreting his wife's resilience to his demands as his "not being loved." Elliot's demands increase.
- Elliot's complaints strike a resonant chord with Kari, stimulating internal conflict regarding the validity and utility of her previous attempts to validate herself by gratifying others. Repeated self-confrontation, stimulated by Elliot's demands, enhances Kari's growing sense of autonomy.
- Elliot is threatened and chagrined by the seeming irrationality of getting what he said he always wanted and not being able to handle it—Kari is not taking his crap.
- Elliot becomes increasingly afraid of losing Kari. He fears the loss of her indulgence of his infantile demands and the possibility that she will be attracted to others. Elliot begins to make new demands to reassure himself that Kari does, indeed, still love him.

This systemic model of interaction, full of inherent paradoxes and multidetermined behaviors, is derived from an understanding of the intrapsychic functioning of a single individual and the partner he is likely to pick. This is not to suggest that intrapsychic processes are the primary determinant of behavior or systems. To do so would be to fall prey to linear thinking. Instead, it points out the seamless integration and interaction of intrapsychic and systemic processes. To conclude, here are some final ramifications to this crucible:

- If Kari is able to maintain her new-found sense of self, Elliot will have the opportunity to experience not having his demands met and to develop a "begrudging respect" for his partner.
- Elliot will have the opportunity to struggle with his own narcissism and to see the links between his demands to be gratified, his dependency on Kari, and his fears of loss of autonomy.
- Kari will have the opportunity to confront her confusion of deference

and compliance with "loving and caring," and ultimately, the failure of her attempts to earn her mother's praise.

- Kari will have the opportunity to recognize her anger at being a parentified child for her mother and the replay of these dynamics with her husband. The contemporary relationship difficulties with Elliot could become the vehicle for *resolution of problems of the past in the present-day context*. Interpretations should avoid theoretical constructs and focus on observation of the unfolding processes in current time.

- Elliot's sexual (and nonsexual) attractiveness will probably diminish for Kari as she perceives his selfishness and insecurity more clearly. At first she will hide this to spare his feelings, although Elliot will sense it nonetheless; eventually she will be more open about it. Elliot will become more insecure and have to master himself without making the same types of demands on Kari that further diminish her desire for him.

- Kari will have the opportunity to change and improve day-to-day interactions with Elliot, modifying fundamental hierarchies and the nature of "reality" as they have seen it in their house. While some portion of this process involves interpersonal confrontation, a significant segment involves self-confrontation.

- As either partner emerges successful from the crucible of self-confrontation, his or her resultant increased nonreactivity (differentiation) to the demands and anxieties of the spouse provides a stronger and more resilient crucible for the further development of the spouse.

- This process of self-confrontation in the context of the partner is the basis for a profound sense of intimacy. As one learns more about him/herself, that new knowledge provides the substance of what is shared with the partner. As one becomes more self-accepting through open self-confrontation, he or she is better able to maintain a sense of adequacy in the process of revealing him/herself to the partner (i.e., increased capacity for level-2 intimacy).

- From the shared experience of open self-confrontation, and confrontations between them, Kari and Elliot develop a "begrudging respect" based on strength rather than on insecurity. Each spouse will have observed the other master him/herself, each will have stood up to the manipulations of the other. Together they will have redefined the relationship on the basis of "desire" and "wanting," rather than dependency and need.

INCONGRUOUS POWER HIERARCHIES IN
INHIBITED SEXUAL DESIRE

There is always an incongruous power hierarchy in a sexual relationship involving wide disparity in levels of sexual desire. The identified patient has less overt status in the sexual hierarchy than does the asymptomatic partner. The asymptomatic partner, who is usually regarded as the de facto sex expert in the relationship, appears to have greater sexual desire and a healthier attitude toward sex and sexiness. The identified patient, on the other hand, is perceived as being sexually incompetent, "hung-up," and "less sexual" than the asymptomatic partner.

The Partner With the Lower Sexual
Desire Always Controls Sex

In the incongruous power hierarchy surrounding inhibited sexual desire, the person who wants sex the least always controls frequency and specific timing of dyadic sexual contact. Often he/she controls the content and style of sexual contact as well.

Given that robust sexual performance and unflagging sexual desire are common self-expectations, patients with inhibited sexual desire secondary to sexual dysfunctions are in the paradoxical position of feeling extremely inadequate while simultaneously feeling baffled and burdened by the power and control they inherit.

Other incongruous hierarchies exist within the sexual sphere. The individual with the least desire is often the partner more desired. When the identified patient is also the more physically desirable of the two, defined either by contemporary social values or by partner preference, the effect is heightened. In effect, the symptomatic partner, overtly regarded as the less sexual or sexually competent, is also the more sexually powerful, the more physically attractive, and the more desired of the two.

Cases of partner-specific low desire present additional incongruous power hierarchies. The identified patient may have previously been far more sexually active and erotically inclined than the asymptomatic partner. In prior or ongoing sexual affairs, sex and the identified patient's sexual presentation may be far "hotter" than what occurs at home with the spouse. While the asymptomatic partner is flaunting his or her superior status, the identified patient has a very different view of reality.

Laboratory research indicates that monkeys develop ulcers when manipulated into believing they can make some response to successfully avoid being shocked, while cohorts who have no illusion of control over outcome remain ulcer-free (Washburn, Hopkins, & Rumbaugh, in press). In inhibited sexual desire, the asymptomatic partner has sexual status to lose and the fantasy of sexual control to maintain. Like the "executive" monkey, he/she makes furious efforts to exercise the fantasy of control. In contrast, the identified patient gains relative status by diminishing the status of the partner or by increasing his/her manifest level of sexual functioning. The asymptomatic partner must be willing to trade a relative loss of status as the "sex expert" for the identified patient's improved sexual desire.

While explicit pressure is on the identified patient (let us say, in this case, the wife) to become aroused, massive implicit pressure rests on the sex expert (the husband) to be arousing. Incongruity results from the fact that this is something over which the sex expert has only limited *positive* control. At best, the sex expert can cease ineffective behaviors and attempt more facilitative ones. The more passive the identified patient becomes, the more control (albeit negative control) she exerts. The asymptomatic partner's attempts to arouse the identified patient paradoxically increase the safety of the identified patient's position in remaining unmotivated for change.

As we shall discuss subsequently, these dynamics result not only from the inherent processes of natural systems, but from prevailing culturally prescribed sex-role behaviors. Loomer (1976) offers a useful view of power in this regard. He distinguishes *unilateral* power (the ability to produce an effect, bring something into being, or maintain what has been actualized against the threat of non-being) from *relational power* (the capacity to absorb an influence from a partner, without losing his/her identity or freedom). Unilateral power is a traditionally masculine conception of power, whereas relational power is a traditionally feminine view: Relational power is what a wife develops in accommodating a husband who must control everything in order to control himself; it is the woman's relational power that makes him both seek her out *and fear her*.

Although the sex expert generally sees himself/herself as having to take *action*, sexual power can be thought of as being acted upon or affected by the spouse *without losing his/her preferences and priorities. Relational power is a function of differentiation*. The sex expert loses relational power by his/her unwillingness to let the identified patient have an "impact" on him/her. Granted, the sex expert's redoubled efforts to arouse desire in the spouse result from the latter's impact—more accurately, it is the attempt to *mitigate* this impact. It is as if, both concretely and metaphorically, the sex expert won't take "no" for an answer. If the sex expert *allows* the identifed patient to impact him/her (i.e., to *invite*, rather than combat, the other's "input"), the system often shifts markedly. Unfortunately, this doesn't often happen.

What is not immediately obvious, however, is that these same problematic incongruous dynamics are perfectly consistent with prevailing physiological models of human sexual response. Masters and Johnson's and Kaplan's models of sexual response, which do not include the receiver's internal processes as a crucial factor, promote the notion that sexual response is simply a function of quality and quantity of stimulation supplied by the giver. That is to say, their physiological models suggest that whether or not the receiver becomes aroused and orgasmic is a reflection on the adequacy of the giver.[3] Contemporary sex therapy paradigms based on such models subtly perpetuate common incongruous power hierarchies, despite verbal encouragements to the contrary.

Returning to our example, increasing polarization of the sex expert and identified patient roles reciprocally interacts with the frequency and timing of sexual initiation. Until a new strategy is adopted, the sex expert usually increases the frequency of sexual initiations as sexual desire becomes more inhibited. Although the sex expert becomes angry when his initiatives are repeatedly rejected, each repetition is used as "proof" that he is ready, willing—and blameless. Such refusals raise the manifest status of the asymptomatic partner, while simultaneously diminishing his underlying feelings of adequacy. Moreover, such refusals diminish the manifest status of the identified patient, thereby actually increasing her control.

The end result is a fairly typical system of interaction. The identified patient's response, "You never give me chance to initiate," is a complex half-truth. It *is* true that the expert makes frequent initiations, in a "shotgun" approach controlled by anger and anxiety. Moreover, the identified patient's receptivity to sexual initiations shifts from desire to accumulated guilt, based on the number of approaches declined. Recognizing this, the sex expert has additional motivation to increase the frequency of initiations and complaints.

However, decreasing the frequency of initiations to create a vacuum for the identified patient to fill also creates a double-bind. The identified patient is well aware of being expected to initiate. This engenders resentment, as if the expert can now dictate when the identified patient is supposed to have sex by

---

[3]The implications of the sexual response models of these clinicians are quite in contrast to their stated therapeutic emphases. Kaplan's accent on individual psychopathology clearly "indicts" the receiver's internal processes. Masters and Johnson's promotion of "sex as a natural function" was an attempt to deviate from obsessive focus on the giver's technique, pervasive in the "marriage manuals" that preceded their work.

not initiating. The identified patient still feels pressured, and both partners become calendar watchers.

The expert's retort, "Well, if I didn't initiate we would *never* have sex because you won't," is another half-truth. The identified patient has learned that if she waits out her partner, he will initiate. This allows her to have the *sex* she might desire without desiring the partner. When the identified patient complains of "being tested" by the asymptomatic partner, the knot of double-binds is tightly drawn.

In a less common script, incongruous power hierarchies are established by the identified patient's assumption of total responsibility for inhibited sexual desire. When the couple agrees that lack of desire is a personal characteristic of the identified patient, the asymptomatic partner is both absolved and rendered powerless. The corresponding defense requires the asymptomatic partner to adopt a pseudo-egalitarian position, claiming that sexual difficulties cannot be totally one person's fault and involving him/herself in the cure. In the ensuing struggle over who has the problem, the identified patient may attempt to isolate her/himself from the asymptomatic partner by claiming both full responsibility and total helplessness in dealing with the problem.

In an alternative strategy, the asymptomatic partner may attempt to regain some control by refusing to have sex unless the identified patient gets aroused. The position, "It is too frustrating to make love to someone who won't get turned on," creates another arousal double-bind for the identified patient. Pressure to become aroused makes it less likely that it will happen.

In another strategic maneuver, the sex expert may start an affair, using it to remove his/her dependency on the partner for sex and validation. Although it merely transfers this dependency to someone else, the affair serves to state, "See, it is not me—someone else does want me. It is you." Subsequently, the couple must fight over the meaning to be attributed to the affair, as well as the allocation of blame.

Sometimes the asymptomatic partner in the sexual hierarchy is the symptomatic partner in another incongruous hierarchy. Alternative hierarchies might involve financial resources, achievement, substance abuse, education, or social status outside the home. Multiple incongruous power hierarchies do not really "balance out"; instead they create two simultaneous interlocking incongruous systems. When the slightest contributing factor of the asymptomatic partner is revealed in treatment, he/she feels highly vulnerable to attack by the identified patient. The identified patient may keep the asymptomatic partner from acknowledging the slightest personal insecurity or vulnerability by attacking his/her prior blaming and disowning of responsibility, thus furthering the incongruous systems that fuel inhibited sexual desire.

When the identified sex expert is the wife, there is often further incongruity between the partners' sex-role behavior and their respective internalized gender role. Increased sexual initiation or aggressiveness by the woman can lead to greater anxiety for both partners. Such behavior might have been welcomed by the man at the outset of a relationship, when he felt sexually competent and desirable. However, the same behavior is often experienced as "pressure" and an opportunity to fail when he is feeling threatened.

In some cases of male sexual dysfunction, the man may respond by *increasing* his frequency of initiation. Such a pattern is not uncommon, given the male tendency to try again to "redeem" himself. However, each attempt may be punctuated by a rapid cessation of sexual and emotional contact, and withdrawal into narcissistic self-flagellation after "failing." Oftentimes, the woman, who is also frustrated and angry, feels drawn to comfort him. Over the course of time, the wife trains herself to minimize arousal, hope, and desire, so as not to be more frustrated. Unfortunately, her husband feels more rejected and further internalizes this as a demonstration of his inadequacy.

Sometimes this leads to further increments in sexual demands by the husband. Fights over frequency of sex, covertly aimed at equalizing status and power, begin. Superficially, it appears that he wants sex more than she, and that he is the more sexually frustrated of the two. In fact, the wife may be more erotically inclined, but she restrains herself (a) to protect herself against frustration, (b) to avoid his repeated initiations, and (c) to reduce the level of threat and anxiety he is experiencing. Caught in a double-bind, she is furious when accused of being withholding or undesirous of sex. Very rapidly such accusations become self-fulfilling prophecies.

ISD, Incongruous Power Hierarchies, and Differentiation

In the etiology of inhibited sexual desire, spouses' level of differentiation and the ensuing incongruous power hierarchies are extremely important but rarely considered. This is particularly true in cases where both partners display inhibited sexual desire.

Consider the case in which Judy believed she sold out her future, her freedom, and her integrity by marrying her husband, Vaughn. Although increasingly ambivalent as her wedding approached, Judy "caved in" to the pressure and expectations she perceived from her parents, friends, and most of all, her fiance. Never having achieved a significant degree of differentiation from her intrusive mother or her infantilizing father, she felt she lacked the "courage" to redefine herself in the context of the mounting social expectations and financial commitments. Judy never lived on her own before marriage, something that she both longed for and feared. Judy married as a default option, never having taken responsibility for her action; she never actually chose Vaughn, and lost respect for his willingness to take her on that basis.

Actually, Judy felt superior to Vaughn in many ways, and secretly she had little respect for him from the outset. Their courtship was marked by numerous "tests" to make him "prove" his love. Judy's lack of solid self required constant reinforcement, as well as diminishing Vaughn down to her own low level of self-esteem. Judy felt she made Vaughn "crawl" to earn her sexual favors during their engagement. The result was that by the time of the wedding Judy looked down on her husband and had also lost respect for herself.

If one starts with the recognition that Judy's behavior reflects a low level of differentiation, and remembers Bowen's hypothesis that individuals tend to pick partners at similar levels of differentiation, then Vaughn's characteristics come as no surprise.

Vaughn was a very insecure man whose job in the marriage, at his place of employment, and in his family of origin was to make other people happy (with him). Like Judy, his sense of self was dependent on what others thought of him. He was also extremely uncomfortable with anger and confrontations, and went to great lengths to avoid them.

Judy's smoldering resentment was fueled by her feeling of being trapped in her marriage. She was able to feign mild interest in sex with Vaughn, but it was short-lived. Judy liked orgasms, but became increasingly intolerant of her husband, angered by his every mannerism and shortcoming, real and imagined. Her increasingly domineering and demeaning behavior increased when he sheepishly accepted it; although embarrassed by her own behavior, she felt her responses to him were almost automatic. It was as if seeing what she could get away with was more exciting than their sex.

Judy began to withhold from Vaughn in a myriad of ways, sexual and nonsexual. Herein lay the inherent paradox that continued both in and out of the bedroom. She blamed him for her lack of contentment and wanted him similarly uncontented. Judy didn't want Vaughn to be satisfied; in her infantile way, she wanted him punished. Living with her would be the punishment. In the process, however, Judy, who felt she had sold out her integrity by marrying Vaughn, felt that she sold herself out further: Her war with Vaughn was a covert war of attrition and she felt increasingly like "a withholding bitch."

When Vaughn tolerated the diminishing quality and quantity of sexual encounters, Judy's loss of respect for him continued. She lost all desire for sex with him and thought of him as a nauseating "little puppy dog." And yet, Judy curiously felt that he was "a better person" than she, especially when he was undemanding and kind to her. This made her feel more insecure, ironically triggering even more of the same demeaning sexual style.

Judy struggled with the simultaneous perception of Vaughn as both unmanly and kind. She told herself that she thought of him as a friend but not as a lover. She desired him sexually less than ever before, and yet did not want to give him up. She wished to be "rid" of him, but actually divorcing Vaughn required more differentiation than she possessed. She fantasized that she could "do much better" in the selection of another mate, and yet she wondered if someone would want the "bitch" she seemed to be. She also didn't want her jettisoned husband to become another woman's gem. She enjoyed the joke: "My husband is an asshole, but he is *my* asshole."

Judy's sexual withholding was often cloaked under the veil of "confusion," depression, or illness. She feared open withholding might lead to a precipitous end of his patience and an end of the marriage. At the same time that she demanded his "understanding" and patience, she lost respect and punished him for his compliance. She secretly thought of him as a "coward," and yet her "cowardice" originated at the outset of the marriage, and grew in the covert sexual withholding. Judy simply lacked sufficient differentiation to divorce Vaughn, and his accommodation of her only kept her stuck.

Finally, the dynamics in the relationship shifted. For many years Vaughn took his wife's lack of sexual desire personally. He pursued her, wanting the chance to "do better" and prove himself in her eyes and thighs. He permitted himself little conscious awareness of her withholding and disrespect for him, or their growing mutual anger.

Another man, no more differentiated but more narcissistic and demanding than Vaughn, might have embarked on a series of affairs to get both his sexual enjoyment and emotional stroking from someone else. He might have even displayed a brief infusion of pseudo-self from the affair.

However, Vaughn began to differentiate himself sufficiently to permit some increasing awareness of Judy's anger, although he stopped taking it personally. He gradually stopped trying to please her and sullenly withdrew. Unwilling to go through the inconvenience, cost, and "stigma" of divorce, Vaughn launched into a war of attrition similar to his wife's.

Had this couple presented for treatment prior to this time, Judy would have been the identified patient with inhibited sexual desire. However, at this point, both Vaughn and Judy became identified patients: dual ISD with a pattern of sex only several times annually, and none in the last six months. The only thing Judy hated more than the thought of having sex with Vaughn was the thought that he didn't want to have sex with her.

At the time that Judy and Vaughn entered treatment, she reported that she did not desire her husband. This was true—one of the few truths that could be acknowledged in their marriage. But it was also a half-truth. Part of the half-truth was that Judy enjoyed telling the therapist that she didn't find Vaughn appealing; she felt that it further humiliated him. Other far more volatile half-truths await the couple in treatment:

- Judy is secretly less depressed, ill or confused, and more rageful at Vaughn and at herself, than her anxiety tolerance will permit acknowledging. Vaughn's anger is more openly acknowledged and explainable.

- Judy does not *want* to want Vaughn. She has always toyed with fantasies of leaving him, and *wanting* him is a threat to that plan. She only wants to give up something that has no redeeming value to her.

- Judy does not want to want Vaughn, because then he will have what he wants, and she wants to deprive him of it. If Vaughn becomes happy with her when she is not, she will be filled with rage and jealousy.

- If Vaughn becomes happy with minor progress in treatment, she will be angry and disrespectful because she knows that she is offering him so little. She will think that he either doesn't expect very much from sex or is too stupid to know what he is missing.

- If, on the other hand, Vaughn's contentment reflects that all he wants is what she is giving, then Judy will be even more rageful for his willingness to use her (since all she offers him is the use of her) and his lack of interest in the "more" she knows/hopes she has to offer.

- And yet, ironically, it is Vaughn's increasing nonreactivity to Judy's sexual withholding that actually offers her the crucible she needs for her own emotional development.

In other cases, low levels of differentiation and multiple incongruous power hierarchies combine to create a complex background for inhibited sexual desire.

Ted and Suzie's background revealed an intense covert competition for adequacy and dominance. Several years prior to their referral for treatment, Suzie was enthralled with her rapidly advancing career. Ted, meanwhile, labored as a lab technician, unappreciated and lacking advancement opportunities. Knowing that any shift of his own might conflict with his wife's well established career, Ted secretly applied to law school.

Upon being accepted, he demanded that she give up her job and relocate with him. Feeling forced to choose between her career and her marriage, and afraid to stand on her own and either fight or separate, Suzie chose to give up her career. As Ted buried himself in his studies, Suzie threw herself into 18-hour workdays in her new, unsatisfying job. Their schedules insured that they would have little overlapping time at home.

At the time of the initial evaluation for sexual-marital therapy, Suzie presented a pattern of inhibited sexual desire and dyspareunia. She reported a long history of frequent pain during intercourse, which led to her packing her vagina with Vaseline prior to penetration.

At the outset of treatment, Suzie refused all forms of sex on the grounds that she found intercourse painful. I was initially confused by her unwillingness to consider a mutual agreement to forgo intercourse, until I realized that Suzie created an excuse to avoid *all* sexual activity with Ted by keeping the possibility of intercourse alive.

Subsequently, Suzie complained that she could not consider having intercourse while she was so angry with her husband. She presented this as a refusal to sell herself out sexually. Moreover, she belittled her husband by noting that she differed from him in not being able to ignore the hostility between them. After several months of therapy, a brief period of reduced hostility was followed by further exacerbations Suzie revealed that she felt Ted would "win" in their competitive relationship if she became less angry and regained her desire for sex. She felt he would "get what he wants" without having responded to her marked dissatisfactions with their relationship. Moreover, Suzie was angry at her husband for her self-prescribed need to remain angry.

In one particularly revealing session, Ted and Suzie agreed that her lack of sexual desire was a negative reflection on Ted's adequacy. Ted, who had always been unsure of his competency in relation to his wife's prior achievements, was ripe for feeling inadequate about Suzie's pain and lack of arousal during intercourse. The session uncovered another incongruous power hierarchy: Although Suzie took Ted's emotional discomfort and anxiety as a reflection on her own abilities as a partner, she resented having to take care of his ego in bed.

Suzie was in the throes of differentiating herself from her parents' troubled marriage and her mother's emotional dependency on her. She feared ending up like her mother, nursemaid to an inadequate husband. Inhibited sexual desire attempted to force Ted to take greater responsibility for her, but backfired because it made him feel more inadequate. Actually, Suzie had achieved a higher degree of differentiation than had Ted, who was thoroughly fused with his mother since his father's early death.

Suzie was torn between wanting a competent husband and wanting to toy with Ted's feelings of adequacy. As was mentioned previously, sometimes the sexual crucible involves the tantrum over wanting *two* choices simultaneously, when only one choice between several options is available.

CULTURAL SHAPING OF INHIBITED SEXUAL DESIRE

Contemporary western culture predisposes construction of particular incongruous sexual hierarchies. In young couples, the male traditionally is the aggressor and culturally prescribed female inhibitions about expressing sexual desire insure that the woman controls the style and timing of sex. On the other hand, there is often a role reversal in the fifth and sixth decades of life. With higher male mortality rates and the relative shortage of single men, single women are more likely to be the aggressors in dating relationships. Moreover, increasing concern about reduced erectile speed (due to organic, situational, and emotional factors) makes men less eager to initiate sex. When a married couple ceases having sexual contact, spouses often agree that the cessation is the man's choice (Pfeiffer et al., 1972; Pfeiffer & Davis, 1972).

The rule that the partner with the lower sexual desire controls the timing and frequency of sex still applies, although the position of control may change as the relationship and the partners age; men are more likely to control sexual contact during senescence. Inhibited sexual desire is more incongruent with contemporary gender roles when the male is the identified patient, since most gender roles are age-insensitive and established around adolescent norms.

The socially prescribed gender-role double standard of a sexually naive woman who is educated by a sexually experienced male is another predisposition for inherent paradox. The woman's demonstration of sexual knowledge becomes a threat to the man's gender role, since whatever the woman knows "must" have been taught to her by his competitors, her prior or current sexual partners; the woman is encouraged to present herself as less knowledgeable and experienced than she may be. Moreover, the very notion of a man's teaching a woman what she should like sexually is a setup for (a) increased incongruity in the sexual knowledge hierarchy and (b) feelings of inadequacy on the man's part. How can a man not feel threatened by the expectation that he should base his sexual adequacy on knowledge of something he could not possibly know? Given that the lack of consideration of the receiver's internal processes in contemporary physiological sexual response models also parallels traditional male-female gender-role scripts, there is fertile ground for the development of incongruous power hierarchies and inhibited desire.

Sexual "Normality" Encourages Inhibited Sexual Desire

Desire-inhibiting standards and anticipations are transmitted from generation to generation through humor, traditional sex roles, mass media, and couples' own behavior in the bedroom. Prevailing sexual attitudes and beliefs are conveyed so totally that they become the very fabric of contemporary society and hence invisible to those who operate within that society.

Since contemporary definitions of sexual normality potentiate inhibited sexual desire and sexual dysfunction, the politics of sexual normality are crucial in the diagnosis, research, and treatment of sexual problems. Leiblum and Rosen (1988) highlight the temporal nature of societal definitions of normal sexual desire:

> Given the ever-changing attitudes toward sexual expression from one historical time or place to another, our views of what constitute "normal" levels of sexual desire are in a constant state of flux. Clearly, what are deemed acceptable and appropriate levels of sexual interest today may not have been similarly viewed in the recent past or may not be so viewed in the foreseeable future. (p. 2)

Lazarus (1988) refers to several "myths" (cognitions) that potentiate desire disorders:

- "If he really loved me, he would want to have sex with me as often as I wish to have it with him."
- "If she was truly turned on to me, she would become aroused as soon as I started kissing and caressing her."
- "Before I let my husband make love to me, I must be sure the he wants *me* and not just my body."
- "My wife wanted me to have intercourse with her last night. How could I, when only three days ago she accused me of being stingy?" (p. 153)

The relationship mythology of a given culture encapsulates the socially prescribed and proscribed relationship expectations of that time and place. The examples above reflect the lack of differentiation in relationships endemic to contemporary Western society, which surface in the characteristic relationship difficulties of our time, including problems of sexual desire.

Understanding the role of sexual normality is vital to comprehending the creation and perpetuation of inhibited sexual desire. Lacking such understanding, the clinician may unwittingly validate contemporary assumptions antithetical to maintaining sexual desire. *Contemporary views of sexual normality are uncritically assumed to be synonymous with health and happiness.* The philosophical position "sex is a natural function" is often cited to validate the expectation that healthy individuals desire sex. Apfelbaum (1988) suggests that sexual oppression is masked in maxims about sex being a natural function, an expression of beauty, or a form of communication. He astutely observes that contemporary sexual oppression is most evident in such common behaviors as faking orgasms.

Belief that sexual disinterest is a reflection of psychopathology makes treatment of inhibited sexual desire particularly difficult. Such cognitions by the patient create internal pressure and a self-sustaining negative reinforcement loop; such beliefs in the therapist lead to unwitting reinforcement of similar beliefs in the patient. Often this reinforcement occurs within moments of initial therapeutic contact: If the therapist, in his/her eagerness to help the patient, accepts the patient's implicit assumption that he/she *should* want sex, treatment is established on a premise antithetical to successful outcome and maximum desire.

Apfelbaum points out that "giving permission for pleasure" has the paradoxical effect of increasing pressure for desire. He suggests this creates iatrogenic *response anxiety* ("performance anxiety about desire" [1988, p. 81]). Apfelbaum also refers to *performance-anxiety anxiety*, as " . . . the anxiety about feeling performance anxiety after being told (in treatment) that it is not only unnecessary to feel it but perhaps foolish as well" (p. 91). Social ideals of invariant sexual desire actually create an inherent paradox that contributes to the creation of low sexual desire:

> I propose that, in these cases, what looks either like simple apathy or like a case of unconscious resistance is in actuality a state of *withdrawal* from negative reactions. This withdrawal is a consequence of the pressure that everyone is under in sex to respond positively (of course, excluding those whose culture prohibits sexual response). This pressure is created by the expectation that in all relationships one should respond positively and not cause friction—a pressure that is intensified in sex by the belief that sexual response should be automatic, since it represents a biological drive. (Apfelbaum, 1988, pp. 76–77)

According to Apfelbaum, the etiology of inhibited sexual desire most often lies in inherent social pressure to desire sex and injunctions against declining invitations to become aroused. He discounts the notion that patients' fears of intimacy are a source of inhibited sexual desire, adroitly noting that in most sexual encounters there is very little intimacy to be avoided. The pressure to want sex is often overlooked in the haze of modern liberalism towards sex.

In his thorough review of cultural and historical definitions of sexual desire, Apfelbaum (1983, 1988) concluded that marriage manuals in the 1920s and '30s promoted a biological drive model of sexual desire, as well as a work-ethic approach to sexuality. He credits Masters and Johnson as ushering in the era of the nonperformance therapeutic paradigm—something that has been so thoroughly accomplished that many clinicians fail to recognize Masters and Johnson's contribution in this regard. Apfelbaum suggests:

> Many contemporary sex therapists find the technique approach to be just as inevitable as did Van de Velde. They rely on sexual enhancement techniques, professional sex films (for a critique, see Apfelbaum, 1984), pornography, fantasy assignments, vibrators, and instruction in techniques of stroking and massage (especially self-stroking and self-message). Sex therapists who use these techniques will also use Masters and Johnson assignments without regard to the incompatibility between the demand quality of direct efforts to manipulate level of arousal and the nondemand Masters and Johnson assignments (Apfelbaum, 1985). Masters and Johnson's comparatively abstinent approach is typically seen by these sex therapists as an expression of a personal preference rather than as an inevitable consequence of Masters and Johnson's theoretical and therapeutic model.
>
>   . . . Missing is the Masters and Johnson insight that the "sex-positive" reaction against what we can call the "sexual drive phobia" represents a new tyranny. Just as the fear of being dysfunctional can create a dysfunction, so the fear of lacking a "yes" response to sex can create a desire disorder. (1988, pp. 89–90)

However, in defining their approach to inhibited sexual desire, Schwartz and Masters (1988) offer the most recent articulation of "sex as a natural function." They begin, "All humans are born with the natural functions of sexual desire and sexual response" and continue:

> *Sex as a natural function* means that an individual's ability to function as a sexual being is congenitally established. Sexual functioning is in the same category as other natural biological functions, such as respiratory, bowel or bladder activity. Erection, lubrication, [and] desire develop spontaneously in healthy individuals. . . .
>
>   The hunger for food, for sex, for affection, and for intimacy are all expressions of natural appetites that vary according to time, place and circumstances. (1988, p. 240)

Such statements embody the very biological-drive model Apfelbaum indicts as creating response anxiety. Is it any wonder that professional and lay consumers of Masters and Johnson's approach come away with an interpretation of their message that reinforces pressure for sexual desire? It is common for patients with desire disorders, as well as ubiquitous dyadic desire discrepancy, to use Masters and Johnson's own phrase to construct an inherent paradox for themselves: *"If sexual response is natural response, then why am I not responding or even wanting to respond?"* Like psychoanalytic theory, the Masters and Johnson approach has become so acculturated into contemporary society that it is imperceptibly accepted as fact, rather than as a paradigm.

Although Masters and Johnson's sensate focus activities were obviously intended as non-goal-directed activities to reduce performance anxiety, the "sex as a normal function" stratagem obfuscates their conceptual and clinical intent and leads to contextual messages that stimulate response anxiety. Apfelbaum's insights into the paradigm shift Masters and Johnson attempted, as well as the deleterious and paradoxical way in which sensate focus activities are used by the rank-and-file of clinicians, seem both accurate and profound. At the same time, Apfelbaum's insights also point out the lack of integration and strategic conceptualization of the various tenets of Masters and Johnson's approach—obscuring their insight and clinical intent from the vast majority of clinicians.

Leiblum and Rosen (1989) question the utility of sensate focus techniques in treatment of inhibited desire, noting that Schwartz and Masters (1988) advocate them in all cases and LoPiccolo and Friedman (1988) in most. Rosen and Leiblum (1987) themselves recommend such techniques only when genital performance difficulties are also present. In contrast, I believe that the issue is not *whether* to use them, but rather, *in what paradigm* to use them. In the prevailing paradigm—that in the absence of organic or psychological pathology the individual *should* want sex—sensate focus "exercises" place implicit pressure on patients. Therapists' attempts to remove pressure not only place *more pressure* on patients, but also lead clinicians to assume that continuing performance expectations do not stem from the treatment paradigm.

AN ALTERNATIVE PARADIGM FOR TREATMENT OF INHIBITED SEXUAL DESIRE[4]

The Alliance

Construction of the therapeutic alliance is particularly crucial in the treatment of inhibited sexual desire. Impediments to successful treatment can be estab-

---

[4]In preparation for this section, the reader may wish to note that treatment of low sexual desire is often regarded as more difficult than that of overt genital dysfunctions. However, some clinicians report that inhibited sexual desire poses no greater therapeutic challenge than other sexual problems (e.g., Apfelbaum, 1988). Using the approach described here, my clinical experience concurs with Apfelbaum's. As you read on, the reason will become evident: Many clinicians regard the sexual crucible as "industrial strength" treatment.

Drs. Linda Stone Fish and Dean Busby of the Department of Child and Family Studies (Syracuse University) are currently completing a unique research study of the efficacy of a structural/strategic family therapy approach to treating couples with inhibited sexual desire (personal communication, 1991).

lished in the initial moments of contact with the couple using contemporary sex therapy paradigms. Fortunately, the sexual crucible paradigm offers a strategic posture that can sidestep these pitfalls-in-the-making and restructure the treatment alliance and the couple's hierarchies in and out of the bedroom.

Couples often enter treatment offering an alliance that is antithetical to the positive outcome they request. On a brighter note, this alliance contains the same inherent paradoxes and unworkable hierarchies contained in the marital relationship. It can be used by the alert therapist to recognize problems in the existing dyadic relationship system, as it is realigned into a more workable format.

It is all too easy for therapist and patients alike to adopt the implicit assumption that the purpose of treatment is to make the identified patient have, and want to have, sex. Moreover, it is easy to slip into the trap that this "sex" should be in the form of intercourse. When this occurs, treatment embodies the same response pressure that inhibits sexual desire.

There is a "natural" temptation for the therapist to align with the asymptomatic partner as a junior therapist. This unworkable alliance situates the therapist as a "bigger hammer" to force the identified patient to have sex more frequently or with more enthusiasm. Moreover, such an alliance recreates the same incongruous power hierarchy between therapist and identified patient as exists between the partners. Once this is established, the identified patient may attempt to neutralize the therapist's input in exactly the same way that has been successful with the spouse.

Establishment of the Elicitation Window

As many other authors have pointed out, the treatment of inhibited sexual desire must be multimodal and custom-tailored to each couple. Since the requisite inherent paradoxes and conflicts are preexisting in the couple's presenting situation, the sexual crucible approach offers the ideal form of custom-tailoring. In constructing their unique style of sexual and relationship interaction, the spouses have tailored the vestments that suit them perfectly. What is required is a *detailed* look in the elicitation window of their own sexual behavior.

Kaplan and others anticipate seeing psychopathology in the window. Sometimes one sees psychosis, and other times one sees a failure in differentiation. In many cases one or both patients seem to have difficulty tolerating their own eroticism, but the etiology does not necessarily stem from repression; it may be more determined by the disruptive implications of presenting oneself as a mature, responsible adult to one's family of origin and the spouse. Yet in other cases, eroticism is hardly the problem at all. The answer always lies in the details of the elicitation window.

In the previously discussed case of Judy and Vaughn, Judy came in by herself for a session that had been scheduled for both. Vaughn had been called out of town on business. She reported that she didn't see how treatment could help—she simply didn't like sex with her husband. She casually mentioned that they had sex the night before, and I inquired about it.

Initially, Judy's report was vague and uninformative. When I stated that I needed more detail, she emphasized that she was "afraid and embarrassed to talk to a stranger about such personal things." I suggested that she was free to disclose or withhold any degree of detail she chose, but that I would not be of much use to her without more specificity. I mentioned that I was interested, not in the behavioral details per se, but rather in the information they contained about her, her husband, and the rest of their relationship. Intrigued, she continued.

Judy described herself initiating sex with her husband. Her stated motivation was to "feel close" and have an orgasm. She described lying on the bed with her eyes closed, tuning out Vaughn. Judy said she found the way that he french-kissed disgusting, with his pointy little tongue darting from side to side in her mouth. However, she had never taught him how she liked to do it, ostensibly because she didn't want to hurt his feelings.

Judy went on to report suddenly pushing Vaughn away while he kissed her breasts. Judy initially suggested she "didn't know why" she did it, but laughed as she reported that she found him repulsive. She subsequently let Vaughn continue to kiss her breasts, uninterrupted, deriving a moderate degree of pleasure from his caresses.

Judy was surprised when I asked where her hands were at this point in her scenario. They were lying flat on the bed beside her, palms down. She kept her legs tightly together while Vaughn straddled her with his knees apart by her thighs. Judy then described Vaughn shifting to lie beside her in order to touch her vagina. She kept her legs straight out and together, deliberately making it difficult for him to touch her. At best he was able to reach her pubic hair and labia. Judy reported being able to lubricate spontaneously simply by thinking about something erotic; she did not require additional stimulation before penetration.

After several minutes, Judy reached down and touched Vaughn's penis for a minute or so in a careless and indifferent manner. This was usually sufficient for him to develop an erection, which angered her.

Judy always determined when coitus began. She deliberately spread her legs with her knees bent, raising her heels in the air to give herself the opportunity for deep penetration. However, she told him, "Just go ahead and get it over with." Although Vaughn could voluntarily delay his ejaculation for eight or nine minutes, he did as he was told and ejaculated in three. Vaughn then jumped out of bed to "wash up," as was his custom, although Judy reported she was fairly comfortable with ejaculate and did not require this.

Judy used to be capable of reaching orgasm with five or six minutes of coital thrusting; she had been experiencing difficulty doing so with Vaughn in recent months, ever since she noticed he was not as eager for sex as before. On this particular occasion, she announced that she was going to masturbate to orgasm as her husband left to clean up. Vaughn left without further response, and Judy brought herself to orgasm with her vibrator while he was in the adjoining bathroom.

In relating her story, the ease with which Judy reported masturbating, and moreover, the apparent invitation she offered her husband to watch, was in striking contrast to her apparent "discomfort and embarrassment" telling me about her sexual behavior. In point of fact, what was embarrassing Judy was not the disclosure of her eroticism and sexual behavior, but rather the disclosure of her sexual style, which she knew displayed her as a lousy sexual partner. When I pointed this out, Judy's demeanor changed: she became more forthright and less child-like. Judy stated that her sexual partner in her 10-year affair would never have tolerated similar behavior. In fact, she reported, she had generally engaged in lusty, eyes-opened sex with this partner, and considered herself to be a "good fuck."

As the reader can ascertain, the elicitation window of Judy's sexual style speaks volumes about the content and dynamics of her relationship with her husband and offers the prerequisite details for custom-tailoring the sexual crucible.

Vectors of Intervention

One of the most common therapeutic pitfalls lies in conceptualizing interventions only within a single vector, consistent with the ineffective one already attempted by the spouses. *A single multidetermined intervention, simultaneously congruent in all relevant dimensions of causation, is preferred for multidetermined problems such as inhibited sexual desire.*

Object relations theory can predict and explain the complex system of projections and introjections surrounding problems of sexual desire. Beyond *explaining* both individuals' behavior, however, the therapist needs to understand *how* the pattern of inhibited sexual desire is enacted, and then interrupt it and turn it back on the individuals, as a mirror and vehicle for their own development. Each repetition of the negative interactional style and sexual symptomatology revalidates the couple's distortions as an accurate construction of reality; each break in the pattern opens up the possibility of change. Systemic change allows individuals to function in patterns antithetical to the projected image/role they have been playing in the relationship and increases the possibility that each person will look within him/herself to find the explanation of his/her own motives and behavior.

Object relations and systemic interventions can be thought of as facilitating long-term and short-term change, respectively. Systems can shift relatively quickly, but swing back the other way just as fast (especially after the therapist is out of the picture). Long-term systemic change is supported when it coincides with stable intrapsychic development in one or more members of the system. Increasing awareness of discontinuity between the internal state of the individual and the state of the system facilitates that process.

It is possible to err by focusing on either dimension to the exclusion of the other. However, all interventions obviously have simultaneous meaning in both dimensions. And focusing on differentiation seems to permit this process to move forward with exquisite elegance.

The therapist should intervene in directions and dimensions different from what is anticipated by the couple. This includes not being drawn into being or appearing to be the agent of pressure on the identified patient. The problem in cases of inhibited sexual desire is not just the pressure for sexual behavior per se, but moreover, intolerance for the pressures inherent in nonsymbiotic marriage wherein couples remain together out of *choice* rather than out of *need*.[5] Both of these elements are inherent in the sexual crucible approach.

If the therapist does not explicitly reframe the meaning of treatment and realign with both patients, the prospect of "successful treatment" can trigger unnecessary scrambles for systemic and individual equilibrium that work against positive results. While the threat of divorce may appear to be the major motivation for change, *the threat that the relationship will remain the same is far more powerful.* Patients expect therapists to be "pro-sex" and encourage sexual activity. The therapist who fulfills this expectation severely diminishes his/her own clinical mobility and impact.

The therapist's declaration that he/she is unable and unwilling to force sexual desire upon the identified patient and, moreover, that lack of sexual desire is a

---

[5]Recognition of existential separateness (inherent in relationships based on *choice*) has multiple impacts: (a) reinforcement of the legitimacy of one's own (and one's partner's) preferences, and (b) realization of the inability to force one's preferences upon the spouse, given the ultimate potential for separation. These two realizations have a paradoxical impact; the former reduces pressure to relinquish one's preferences, while the latter creates the internal motivation (pressure) to induce the partner to remain.

Although the focus at hand is inhibited sexual desire, the concept of existential separateness indicates that the topic of intimacy (*particularly level-2 intimacy*) hovers close by. Indeed, level-2 intimacy (i.e., the capacity for self-validated disclosure of personal preferences) is a critical co-requisite in constructing a sexual crucible and resolving sexual desire problems.

reasonable and often healthy response to one's actual experiences creates a systemic and intrapsychic shift. The identified patient is no longer safe to remain passive, content in the expectation that the therapist will provide the counterbalancing motivation and input to make him or her desire sex. The therapist's position drives the identified patient into his/her own fear of relationship dissolution if no progress is forthcoming.

One might argue that, based on evolution and neuro-hormonal physiology, humans *should* want sex, and hence, a treatment paradigm that similarly expects people to want sex is reasonable. One might even bolster this position using Maturana and Varela's (1987) notion of structural coupling, which states that a species evolves physiological and emotional capacities in response to recurrent social interactions (i.e., the couple should couple because couples developed the capacity to couple because couples coupled frequently). However, from a *clinical* perspective, that very premise is what makes such a treatment paradigm entirely *unreasonable*. Said differently, given the genetic heritage and psychophysiological predisposition to want sex, lack of desire for sex in the absence of physiological disease is generally indicative of something salient in the individual's life. It is strategically wiser and eminently more logical to approach individuals from the perspective that if they *don't* want sex, given their prior and current life experiences, they probably *shouldn't* want it.

The question, *"What makes you both think you should want sex and that it should be great?"* addresses and soothes implicit expectations that fuel feelings of guilt, deprivation, and pressure. This question elicits the couple's expectations and misconceptions regarding sexual desire, intimacy, and intense sex, and paves the way for a more realistic view of human sexual potential throughout the life span. It also raises the issue of the identified patient's intrinsic motivations for sex and removes projections of "other people's expectations" as acceptable incentives. Moreover, it removes the convenience of a defiant alliance between the identified patient and the therapist and, in fact, permits the pursuit of *positive* personal motivations for sexual contact. It creates the opportunity for the identified patient to voice the most difficult position of all: to *want* sex, and to *want* to want sex, for oneself.

The question stated above removes the therapist from the position of being the unequivocal ally of the asymptomatic partner's demands for sex, and (given the prior history of ISD in the relationship) focuses on the actual basis for his or her desire for sexual contact. However, this must be done in a way that searches for meaning, rather than implying encouragement for the asymptomatic partner to relinquish his/her desire for sex in accommodation to the identified patient's preferences. Aligning with the identified patient's lack of desire without also aligning with the asymptomatic partner's desire for sex triggers an unbalanced alliance that is in *neither* patient's best interest. While an unbalanced alliance with the identified patient obviously makes the asymptomatic partner fearful of losing his/her preferences and options, *it also removes the identified patient from the sexual crucible.* The therapist's alignment with both the identified patient (not to force sex) and with the asymptomatic patient (not to abandon sex) has a systemic impact of increasing motivation for change. It maintains pressure on *both partners* to find a new equilibrium point with regard to both sexual behavior and differentiation.

The sexual crucible approach takes full advantage of the multidimensional impact of any given intervention. While it may appear that an intervention is being delivered to one spouse, the simultaneous impact on the other, as well as on their dyadic system, is always in mind. For example, depending on whether covert control of the sex expert's adequacy is a outcome desired or an unfortunate systemic reality for the identified patient, the therapist can compliment or commiserate with him/her. By openly acknowledging the identified patient's covert control in the sexual monopoly, the therapist accomplishes the *separation and equalization of partners' adequacy and competency*, necessary for a workable treatment alliance. Moreover, incongruous power hierarchies do not work as well when they are no longer covert. This can be accomplished by pointing out that the identified patient knows that the asymptomatic partner's emotional vulnerabilities and dependencies, including his/her need to feel competent and desirable, are expressed in the dynamics surrounding the sexual problems. This tends to (a) elevate the status of the identified patient, (b) bring forth his/her hidden understanding of the situation, and (c) alleviate the blustering strong arm tactics of the asymptomatic partner. References to the experience of the United States in Vietnam often require no further explanation for the couple.

This leads to the next intervention, seemly directed to the asymptomatic partner. In the case of dual ISD, this intervention is addressed to the partner who is more seeking of reassurance from the other, or who is more upset about the current state of events. Repeatedly addressing the identified patient only increases the incongruous power hierarchy between the spouses and encourages a replay with the therapist. Instead, the intervention in the office (and in the subsequent sessions) is to enhance the differentiation of the asymptomatic partner, (a) encouraging the development of a more internalized sense of self and (b) diminishing the tendency to take the identified patient's lack of sexual desire as a reflection on him/herself. This actually does several things:

- It reduces the identified patient's control over the adequacy of the asymptomatic partner, as well as the power of withholding sexual interest or behavior in that regard.
- It paradoxically reduces the pseudo-self level of functioning in the asymptomatic partner, while also offering the challenge for enhanced solid-self development. This shift occurs both in the eyes of the asymptomatic partner and in those of the identified patient. It is an act of intimacy for the asymptomatic partner to openly acknowledge his/her tendency to seek validation from others, master his/her insecurities, and earn his/her own (begrudging) self-respect in the process.
- After a suitable period, subsequent sexual approaches from the asymptomatic partner to the identified patient are acknowledged to be made on the basis of desire rather than neediness. This destroys both one of the primary defenses and one source of anger of the identified patient: the needy and impersonal nature of the asymptomatic partner's approach.

This shift in the nature of sexual initiation is usually the perfect systemic move. In cases where the asymptomatic partner has been falling over himself/herself to please the identified patient, the frequency of initiations diminishes. In cases where the asymptomatic partner has withdrawn to sullenly lick his/her wounded ego, approaches start to increase. In either case, the approaches stem from a *sense of self as more desirable*, not out of neediness for validation from the spouse. That is to say, the change in desirability focuses around *oneself*, not the spouse.

Usually, there is a subtle but unmistakable shift in the dynamic balance of the relationship. The asymptomatic partner becomes more differentiated, using the ISD as a crucible for personal development. Moreover, the identified patient has the unmistakable sense of losing control of the situation: He/she can withhold sexual contact, but no longer can withhold validation and adequacy. Moreover, the *basis* of power shifts; the locus of control is *one's relationship with himself/herself, rather than one's relationship with the spouse.*

But equally importantly, an interesting and unanticipated shift emerges in the issues of "pressure." Heretofore, the identified patient has been able to control the asymptomatic partner by feeling "pressured." In our age where "modern" sex therapy has been thoroughly acculturated, any claim to feeling pressured by one partner generally elicits an immediate cessation and withdrawal of agendas by the other. No one ever bothers to ask, "Is the problem that the identified patient is feeling pressured, or that the identified patient is *intolerant* of feeling pressure?"

The increasing differentiation of the asymptomatic partner reduces the pressure on the identified patient to offer sex and validation. Ironically, this *increases* the pressure on the spouse from another vector, and this pressure is not going to go away. When the asymptomatic partner places less pressure on the identified patient to provide sex, the position of the identified patient is less secure. The very thing that makes the asymptomatic partner less needy for sex also makes him less willing to wait indefinitely for the identified patient to get around to dealing with himself/herself. The asymptomatic partner is better able to leave the relationship (walking not running away) and find someone whom he/she *does not need* but may find more to his/her liking.

The increasing differentiation of the asymptomatic partner creates more pressure on the identified patient to deal with his/her own lack of desire for sex, or lack of desire for the asymptomatic partner. *This is the pressure inherent in the realization that they are two separate people. The therapist does not seek to dissipate the pressure.* Instead:

- The therapist openly points out that the identified patient's feeling of being "pressured" is not the problem and is not going to diminish, unless the identified patient seduces the asymptomatic partner into abandoning his/her recent development.
- The therapist encourages the identified patient not to cave into perceived "threat," "demand," or "pressure" at any price. As with the asymptomatic partner, the therapist offers support to the identified patient's sense of self. Somehow, the identified patient can't quite figure out how he/she is feeling increasing anxiety and pressure, when the therapist is being supportive of "no change" and the asymptomatic partner is becoming increasingly less demanding. *The crucible is starting to cook*.
- Increasingly, the identified patient is confronted with the option of struggling with *him/herself*, as the therapist and the spouse become less reactive.
- Most of the prior defensive postures no longer work. The identified patient's feeling, "I can't be amorous when I feel angry or pressured," is more a problem for him/her than it is for the partner. And that is as it should be.
- Suggestions that the asymptomatic partner's personality or characteristics are the source of the identified patient's lack of desire allow the therapist to encourage the asymptomatic partner not to sell him/herself

out by internalizing these complaints (unless asymptomatic partner perceives them to be accurate). The therapist can point out that, if the asymptomatic partner leaves, the identified patient won't be giving up something he/she really wants anyhow.

During this process, the asymptomatic partner generally becomes more stabilized, less anxious, and as a result, more perceptive of the identified patient. The identified patient's prior covert agendas and manipulations are no longer taken by the asymptomatic partner as a reflection on his/her lack of "lovability." Prior rationalizations that the identified patient did not discuss problematic aspects of the sexual relationship in order to "spare" the asymptomatic partner are no longer credible: The asymptomatic partner has openly demonstrated his/her resilience and increasing self-worth. It now becomes clear that the identified patient has remained silent because he/she does not *want* to want and does not *want* the spouse to be pleased. *The crucible intensifies.*

This does not involve a Pollyanna view of the asymptomatic partner as either uninvolved or noncontributory. Remember that we started from the point of two individuals at relatively similar levels of differentiation, who selected each other because of their particular unresolved issues and interlocking dynamics. The increasing differentiation of the asymptomatic partner actually increases the pressure for further self-evaluation and growth. Moreover, the differentiation of the identified patient, stimulated by the differentiation of the asymptomatic partner, now places subsequent pressure on the asymptomatic partner for further development (and so on, hopefully, *ad infinitum*).

- The therapist states that he/she is willing to take the asymptomatic partner's view of him/herself as noncontributory at face value, defining the problem as existing solely within the identified patient. However, to the degree that the asymptomatic partner has both participatory responsibility and the power to change the system, he/she will be culpable to him/herself if treatment fails or if he/she is regretful about the subsequent future of the relationship.
- Moreover, the therapist points out the obvious truth to both partners: If treatment is successful in improving the sexual desire and desirability of the identified patient, it will produce and result from a corollary increase in the identified patient's level of differentiation. In that case, it is more likely that the identified patient will be able to *live* comfortably with the asymptomatic partner's personal idiosyncrasies, but also able to *leave* comfortably. Treatment that is successful at increasing

sexual desire in the dyad will also shift the fundamental basis for the relationship from dependency to desire.

• There is increasing pressure for each spouse to be the person he or she *really* wants to be, because, should the relationship end, the solace will be that the spouse did not truly want him/her as he or she was intimately known and increasingly became the person he/she desired to be.

The sexual crucible approach is not consumed solely with a focus on enhancing differentiation. What has been outlined above are the "hardball" aspects of the paradigm, which are perhaps the most alien to many clinicians. At any point, including the first session, the therapist must be prepared to work on modifications in behavioral and emotional aspects of the couple's intimate exchanges. However, several caveats are in order:

• The identified patient must be sufficiently motivated for symptomatic improvement to be more than a ploy to reduce the tension produced by construction of the crucible.

• Particularly at the outset, the therapist should not be too eager to begin the utilization of physical touch for therapeutic purposes. Errors in pacing made in this direction can result in the couple demanding that the therapist address only their sexual exchanges. Such "errors" still permit the therapist to deepen the alliance with the identified patient (not pushing him/her to have sex), as well as with the asymptomatic partner (encouraging the development of an internalized sense of self and resilience to being withheld from).

• The therapist's interest in physical exchanges between the spouses is framed in terms of the elicitation window and the use of touch for increasing personal development, *not* on specific gratifications and physiological responses (e.g., erection, orgasm) per se.

The details of sexual crucible techniques used in modifying the couple's behavioral exchanges are fairly complex. Several innovative interventions, as well as a new paradigm in which they are given, have been developed. In all, these details are beyond the scope of what can be contained in this single book. However, they will be published in a companion volume: *The Intimacy Paradigm: An Elicitation Approach to Sexual-Marital Therapy*.

Increasing Differentiation via the Sexual Crucible

The therapist using the sexual crucible paradigm establishes a treatment alliance with *each* individual, with the goal of helping him/her be as happy as possible and reaching his/her sexual potential, in whatever form that should take. This is decidedly *not* an alliance with "the relationship," nor is it "therapeutic neutrality" as an end in itself. It is the stance from which the sexual crucible emerges. Patients' refusal to accept that it makes no difference to the therapist whether or not they stay together (or have sex) is a reflection of their unwillingness to relinquish the therapist as a source of pressure and commitment.

The therapist who positions him/herself as an ally to both individuals is situated to support the differentiation and ego boundaries of both parties. This includes assistance in building resilience to the projective identifications of the partner. One reason for conducting most, if not all, treatment of inhibited sexual desire in a conjoint context is to have therapy embody one of the major developmental tasks involved: the ability to maintain oneself in close emotional proximity to the partner (i.e., level-2 intimacy). In contrast to Scharff's focus on increasing the couple's ability to provide a "mutual holding environment" (Scharff & Scharff, 1987), the sexual crucible approach encourages each partner to increase his/her ability to "hold" or soothe him/herself.

Paradoxically, the therapist's disinterest in negotiation often promotes a softening of emotional positions between the partners. But this is a softening that emerges out of conflict-with-self, not capitulation to the partner or to one's fear. Since the spouses have previously attempted to negotiate a solution surrounding sexual frequency and style, it is somewhat curious that they expect the therapist to encourage negotiation. In taking the position that negotiation is often confused with subtle forms of selling oneself out, the therapist supports the self of both individuals.

Negotiation at low levels of differentiation is no virtue; it encourages dependency, fuels incongruous power hierarchies, and perpetuates emotional fusion. By not encouraging negotiation, the therapist strengthens the crucible: Treatment can either work directly on the sexual relationship or use the sexual arena to focus on greater differentiation. No relationship contracts or commitments are required or encouraged, and no obligations or debts are incurred.

The sexual crucible's attention to differentiation provides an interesting vantage point on prior treatment paradigms for low sexual desire. Zilbergeld and Ellison's (1980) attempts to *reduce* desire of the asymptomatic partner in order to resolve desire discrepancy is the antithesis of differentiation. While the "give-to-get" philosophy that Schwartz and Masters (1988) encourage is no doubt attractive to patients who would rather negotiate than differentiate, it is the therapeutic embodiment of an exchange theory approach to intimacy with all the attendant limitations (see Chapters Four and Five). Moreover, the "lending of self in sex" they advocate (1988, p. 240) is imprudent for people at low levels of differentiation who are unable to maintain interpersonal boundaries and lack much solid-self to begin with.

Rosen and Leiblum (1989) encourage "a process of compromise and renegotiation toward a more mutually acceptable and satisfying repertoire of sexual exchange" (p. 30) and highlight that "harmony" is a common general approach in the treatment of sexual desire problems. This has several important implications:

- There is no room for compromise in couples at low levels of differentiation, without compromising the sense of *self*. Couples seeking treatment are invariably at low levels of differentiation, in part because highly differentiated couples are likely to experience spontaneous resolution of their difficulties.
- Compromise seeks the lowest mutually acceptable level of sexual desire.
- Compromise *compromises* the use of the crucible for enhancing the personal development and sexual potential of the person with the relatively higher desire. Treatment stops at the point of acceptable absence of conflict and harmony.
- Traditional treatment approaches to desire problems focusing on compromise are generally antithetical to a sexual crucible approach.

Where Does It Lead?

But what of increasing the intensity of sex to the point that *both* individuals experience the limits of their own tolerance and development, and no longer desire it? That is the point where treatment shifts from a deficit model to an asset model. Further treatment challenges the self-soothing ability of *both* individuals and pushes the envelope of their capacity for intimacy and eroticism forward. Such use of sexual potential is absent in prevailing treatments for "problems of low sexual desire."

Perhaps you ask, "Why would the spouses stay in treatment if neither desires more sexual intensity than they are currently experiencing, and in fact, may find the current intensity disquieting?"

Couples usually stay in treatment because their own personal reality is now (a) antithetical to their prior experience, (b) antithetical to their prior picture of themselves, and (c) antithetical to the prevailing societal expectations that one necessarily wants sex to always be intense and always getting more so. This experience is so surprising and startling that folks become curious to "look further into the looking glass" of their own sexual experience: The reflection they see is no longer the reflection they expect. These are also some of the most rewarding times in treatment, for both the couples and the therapist.[6]

Moreover, changes in the broader family system of both spouses are often occurring. Changes across three generations in both families often begin to emerge; shifts with children, parents, friends, and business relationships appear. The relationship between the couple and the broader emotional network will be examined in the subsequent chapter; suffice it to say that spouses who have made progress often want to look into improving relationships with children and parents through the curious vehicle of improving profoundness of sexuality and intimacy in the marital dyad.

---

[6]We will return to this topic with a lengthy care example of such use of the sexual crucible in Chapter Fourteen (*In Pursuit of Sexual Potential*). It will be preceded by additional discussion of the sexual crucible approach in cases of extreme marital conflict in Chapter Thirteen.

CHAPTER ELEVEN

The Extended Emotional System: Eroticism and Families of Origin

This chapter presents a rare detailed discussion of the nature of eroticism: the pursuit and delight in sensual pleasure. The family system shapes children's eroticism through (a) daily interaction, (b) the impact of parental sexual-marital adjustment, and (c) multi-generational impact of triangulation and differentiation. Conversely, children affect marital eroticism variously, including "border skirmishes" over parents' bedroom door. Families have other systemic impacts on sexuality, including (a) children's symptomatic reflection of the extended system, and (b) the meaning of "normal" sexuality, (c) which shift as the system ages. These factors and their impact on erotic "maps" are illustrated in an extensive case example highlighting one couple's triumphant exploration of eroticism.

Although all therapists obviously don't use the same framework, most recognize the importance of considering the families from which troubled marriages emerge.

To some clinicians, the influence of the extended family system is not directly germane to sex therapy (as commonly practiced); for them, the extended system is simply a given within (and against) which the marital bond must sustain itself. Marriage and family therapists, on the other hand, emphasize unconscious family loyalties and replication of dysfunctional scripts in the etiology of sexual and marital difficulties. *Sometimes* sexual dysfunction can be alleviated by recognition of intergenerationally transmitted predispositions for failure and modification of the extended family system. *More often,* well established sexual dysfunctions require additional direct intervention into the moment-to-moment behavioral exchange occurring during sexual activity.

Even in the latter circumstances, the extended family system's long-term global contribution to sexual dysfunction and marital discord merits consideration. Such an enterprise highlights contemporary forces exerted on the couple from outside the dyad and the broader subsystems that are reciprocally maintained by the marital difficulties. It reveals the spouses' level of differentiation, their unresolved developmental issues, and their competing metamodels of marital and family interaction.

Why is it, however, that "family-of-origin issues" implicitly refer to negative legacies but do not include positive ones? Families seem to pass down a residual from one generation to the next, each taking its turn neutralizing the toxicity of some unmastered developmental task. As dysfunctional as one's parents might seem, they often improved on what they inherited.

While touting the supremacy of the family unit, family therapy perversely intimates that each succeeding generation creates itself anew in *spite* of the previous one; the genogram seems to be a tool for tracking the lineage of negative legacies in families. It is as if, had we been born to better parents, we too would be more than we are; parental triumphs rarely make it into the view of our intergenerational legacy. We resentfully clean up our parents' unfinished mess in the infantile belief that, had our parents done *their* job, ours would be easy.

All families contribute legacies that facilitate some developmental tasks and hamper others. Accepting that life is hard (but sweet) and taking our turn in the family process is a major milestone in maturation; as Carrie Fisher (1990) sardonically suggests, the mark of adulthood is the stoic acceptance of endless realism.

FAMILY DETERMINATION OF EROTICISM

Why should discussion of eroticism occur in a chapter on family of origin? Because it is the birthplace of eroticism with regard to (a) its first expression, and (b) the inextricable shaping of further expression throughout one's life.

Parents have considerable impact on their children's sexuality (and vice versa), albeit not always in intended, desired, or recognized ways. Generally, consideration focuses on the transmission of family "values," referring to consciously held beliefs that affect sexual behavior: what is imagined is a series of "go/no-go" decisions. But family values and history are encoded, like a rich metaphor, in the child's *eroticism*. As we have discussed previously (i.e., the elicitation window), eroticism (as reflected in inclusions and exclusions in sexual repertoire) displays one's personal, marital, and familial history.

Transmission of Sexuality and Intimacy Attitudes

When the general public refers to a person's *sex*, there are generally two frames of reference: sexual behavior and gender. However, homosexuality, transsexualism, and transvestism demand a more complex conceptual model of "sex." Health-care and educational professionals respond with a four-part conceptualization: (a) *gender* (genetically determined primary and secondary physical characteristics differentiating males and females), (b) *gender identity* (self-concept as male or female), (c) *gender-role* (the behavioral repertoire through which gender identity is expressed), and (d) *gender object choice*, which is more commonly called *sexual orientation* (the preferred gender of sexual partners in fantasy or reality).

The above sexual schema is useful in understanding the family's role in determining an individual's sexuality:

- Parents' genes define the child's *gender* and general physical appearance. Family history defines the attributional meaning particular characteristics receive.
- Early family experiences have a significant impact on the *gender identity*, which is thought to be permanently determined by the age of two or three. Although the relative contribution of genetics, uterine hormones, and subsequent socialization are not yet established, clarity of gender identity (and how one feels about being male or female) is strongly influenced by one's family.
- Male and female *gender-roles* are learned first within the family, and then subsequently reinforced and broadened by schools and mass media.
- *Sexual orientation* (i.e., heterosexuality, homosexuality, or bisexuality) is well established prior to latency age. While there is still debate about the determinants of sexual orientation, most clinicians agree that one's family plays some significant role.

One topic remains, however, that both involves and transcends these four dimensions—that is the topic of *eroticism*. In all the above, *eroticism*, the most idiosyncratic (and often problematic) aspect of people's sexuality, is generally ignored. At best it receives cursory attention within the concept of sexual orientation.

People are fascinated and repulsed by patterns commonly labeled as "perversions" (formally known as *paraphilias*). Paraphilias raise the question, "How could he/she like doing *that*?! I sure don't (and hope I don't)." That "question" is the issue of eroticism.

Paraphilias involve unusual inclusions, distortions, and omissions in erotic patterning. Money (1985) defines six categories of paraphilias: *sacrificial/expiatory* (e.g., sadism, masochism); *marauding/predatory* (e.g., rape, necrophilia, theft); *mercantile/venal* (e.g., prostitution, telephone sex, obscene phone calls); *fetishistic/talismanic* (e.g., touching shoes, smelling dirty underwear, smearing feces, wearing diapers); *stigmatic/eligibilic* (e.g., amputated limbs, pedophilia, sex with animals); and *solicitational/allurative* (exhibitionism, voyeurism, frottage).

At best, the topic of eroticism is glossed over by health-care and educational professionals. Beyond the topic of paraphilias, discussion of eroticism per se is almost non-existent in the sex therapy and educational literature. One is hard-pressed to find a major text in which the topic appears in the index or receives substantive coverage; eroticism generally incurs the same treatment sexual desire originally endured: it is subsumed under (and confused with) sexual behavior. "Our society is overly sexual but withered in its erotic sensibilities . . . " (Feuerstein, 1989, p. 97).

Byrne and Schulte's (1990) articulation of *erotophobia* and *erotophilia* is instructive about how eroticism is handled in the professional literature. First, their use of standard research language and techniques lends scientific legitimacy to the examination of eroticism, while also stripping it of its very nature: their discussion of eroticism is thoroughly a-erotic. Second (as was true of Masters and Johnson and Kaplan), Byrne and Schulte's (1990) discussion of individual differences in a self-motivating "imagination-arousal subsystem" is not integrated into their otherwise-interesting conceptual model (see Figure 11.1). Although the authors state that the six internal dispositions depicted in Figure 11.1 can initiate behavior, the thrust of Figure 11.1 accords this secondary importance (in keeping with their research on response to external erotic stimuli). The *recursive* self-stimulating, self-initiating aspect of eroticism—what many people miss and others fear—is only depicted obliquely as "rewards."[1] One is hard-pressed to specifically locate eroticism within their six dispositions—until one realizes the eroticism encompasses them all!

We will digress briefly to consider the nature of eroticism for two reasons: (a) discussion of the nature of eroticism is sorely lacking, and (b) it will provide a backdrop for our discussion of eroticism in the family. As we shall see, it is difficult to establish a simple, clear definition of eroticism.

---

[1]The reader who experiments with revamping Byrne and Schulte's (1990) diagram will discover the tremendous difficulty of developing a graphic model and appreciate what they *did* accomplish: models highlight the *limits* of our conceptualizations.

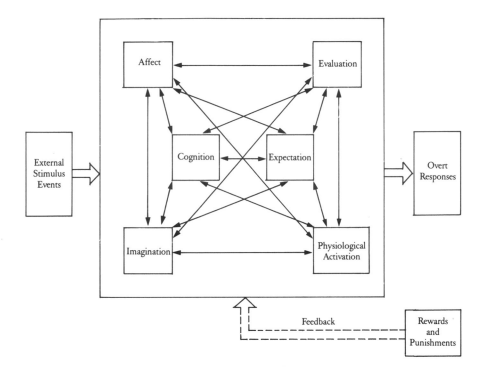

Figure 11.1. The Human Behavior Sequence
(Byrne & Schulte, 1990, p. 95)

What Is Eroticism?

Thus far, we have critically examined two crucial concepts of sexual and marital therapy: *intimacy* and *sexual desire*. How does eroticism relate to both concepts? (a) *Far* less is written about eroticism than either of the other two topics;[2] (b) if the absence of *any* attempt to define the term clinically is an indication, authors are *more* willing to assume a common understanding

---

[2]It is noteworthy that several wonderfully "articulate" books on eroticism actually contain almost no text discussion of the topic. *Eros in Antiquity* (Mondadori, 1978) presents beautiful photographs of Greek and Roman erotic art and ruins of temples devoted to the deities of sex. One is left with the clear impression that eroticism was held in high regard and thrived in the fantasies of the people who commissioned and created these works. *Erotic by Nature* (Steinberg, 1988) contains contemporary photographs and poetry; it lives up to its subtitle: a celebration of life, of love, and of our wonderful bodies.

Table 11.1
Notions of Eroticism

Amorous:	passionate, romantic, ardent, devoted, tender
Lewd:	indecent, prurient, off-color, racy, ribald, risqué, suggestive
Carnal:	sensual, lustful, libidinous, lascivious, lecherous
Debauched:	licentious, depraved, dissolute, wanton

regarding the meaning of eroticism; (c) eroticism is the aspect of self that is disclosed in sexual intimacy and displayed in sexual behavior; (d) eroticism is a crucial aspect of sexual desire, but not identical with it. As many marriages sadly reflect, it is possible to have sexual desire (and sexual function) without eroticism.[3]

Table 11.1 presents four different vantage points on aspects of eroticism.

Several observations about Table 11.1 are in order. First, each dimension displays internal gradations in tonality; gradations across successive dimensions are more obvious. Secondly, the preponderance of terms are negative in valence; interest in eroticism per se has always been presumed inappropriate or unhealthy.[4] Third, and most importantly, the particular label an individual selects from Table 11.1 to describe any of the innumerable variations of human sexual expression is significantly influenced by his/her family of origin. With Table 11.1 in mind, the following points are offered regarding the meaning of *eroticism*.

- Eroticism is a component of the psychological *energy* that drives sexual behavior.
- Eroticism constitutes the component of sexual desire in which the

---

[3]Our discussion of eroticism as a self-stimulating, self-initiating component of sexual desire is consistent with the quantum model (Chapter Two): eroticism is part of the receiver's internal processes and a determinant of total stimulus level.

[4]John Money's work stands alone in the professional literature for his attention to the topic of eroticism. In *The Destroying Angel: Sex, Fitness and Food in the Legacy of Degeneracy Theory, Graham Crackers, Kellogg's Corn Flakes and American Health History*, Money (1985) documents the anti-eroticism of American medicine and social/legal policies in the 19th and 20th centuries (e.g, Anthony Comstock's sexual dictatorship as special agent to the U.S. Post Office), and the origins of common breakfast cereals as anti-masturbation foods. In *Lovemaps* (Money, 1986), he points out that *eroto-*

focus is not simply contact with one's partner; it concerns engagement of the partner in a particular way (*i.e.*, particular *behaviors* or *styles* of interaction). The term *passion* has been used thus far to refer to desire *for the partner* (see Chapters Nine and Ten). *Eroticism and passion are components of sexual desire.*

Eroticism is subjectively experienced as (a) the vibrant flow of *primal energy* coursing through one's veins, and (b) *specific intent* which creates a unique enjoyment of increasing tension, involving the ambivalent experience of desiring more tension and resolution at the same time.

Eroticism is not so much in one's genitals or loins as in one's *head* and *soul*. Herein lies the inherent paradox: When one is really experiencing one's eroticism, one is not aware of one's head at all.

Eroticism need not include a partner except perhaps in fantasy (i.e., during masturbation); even then, one may take *oneself* as the object of one's eroticism. Eroticism involves the script in one's head, as John Money (1986) discusses in his concept of a *lovemap*.[5]

- Eroticism contains an element of sexual aggression (discussed in Chapter Nine), although it differs from sexual aggression per se. Negative aspects of sexual aggression are evident in many views of eroticism in Table 11.1.[6]

---

graphy (a Greek word meaning erotic writing) does not appear in Webster's dictionary: the substitute term, *pornography* (meaning harlot writing), appears instead:

> By implication, they [harlots] alone are entitled to be erotic and to be imbued with the sin of carnal passion. By contrast, respectable women — wives, sisters and mothers — are saintly and undefiled by the depravity of the flesh. Their husband, sons, and fathers are the depraved ones who keep the harlots in business, and read and look at pornography. This is the stereotype that has shaped Western sexual ideals for centuries. The ideal, of course, does not always correspond with practice. An uncounted proportion of men are sexuoerotically apathetic and inert. Conversely, not all women who are not harlots agree that they are lacking in eroticism and carnal passion. They know better. (Money, 1986, p. 161)

For a scholarly study and collection of sexual euphenisms, curses, proverbs and similes in all languages, see *Maledicta: The International Journal of Verbal Aggression* ("The Journal the World Swears By").

[5]Money's description of a lovemap was previously presented in Chapter Five, p. 122, footnote 1.

[6]It is probably worth restating that the sexual aggression discussed here addresses consenting partners; the context of our discussion of eroticism concerns marital sexuality. *Nothing* should be construed herein as condoning or encouraging violence or hostility expressed through sexual dimensions (e.g., rape, physical assault, or sexual harassment).

Eroticism is a core component of sexual intimacy, often the most anxiety-provoking part of self-disclosure during sexual contact. Eroticism is the "dirty" part of sexuality (particularly if you are doing it right, according to sex expert Woody Allen). As the French novelist Marcel Proust observed at the turn of the century, eroticism seemingly makes folks cortically dysfunctional and interpersonally manipulative: "There is nothing like sexual desire to keep our words from having anything to do with our thoughts."

- Eroticism is not inherent *in* behavior or depictions of behavior. Eroticism is a subtle but all-important qualitative characteristic transmitted *through* behavior, innuendo, or gesture, and perceived by the observer.
- Eroticism pertains more to *qualitative* aspects of the execution of behavior—particularly those instilling *desire* in oneself or others.[7]

Eroticism is not the same as sexuality or sexual behavior—many people have sexual behavior (and orgasms) that are totally devoid of eroticism. Eroticism and passion are the missing ingredients for the vast masses of sexually *functional* people who never experience the full impact of their sexual potential.

---

[7]Many terms in Table 11.1 reflect negative views of the inducement of desire. These include (a) unrestrained sexual indulgence in disregard for social standards, and (b) leading others to sexual excess, lustfulness and moral turpitude (e.g., depraved, dissolute, lecherous, lascivious, licentious). This "dangerous" view of eroticism permeates the rationale underlying obscenity laws: It is a matter of public interest to (a) protect society from people bent on aggressively discharging their sexual impulses, and (b) remove depraving materials from the access of those "vulnerable" to such influences. The famous case in obscenity law, *Roth v. United States*, addressed this aspect by defining *prurient interest* (in part) as *itching, longing, uneasy with desire*, and *lecherous*; "itching" is analogous to "itchy palms" or "horniness." Patrick Carnes (1983) writes: "Sexual addiction has been described as "the athlete's foot of the mind." It never goes away. It always is asking to be scratched, promising relief. To scratch, however, is to cause pain and to intensify the itch (p. vii)."

The common complaint of low sexual desire indicates that many people find it *difficult* to induce lasciviousness and licentiousness in their spouses. Marcel Proust opined, "Nothing is more limited than sexual pleasure and vice. By changing the meaning of the phrase, it can truly be said that we move in the same vicious circle."

According to a national *Newsweek*/Gallup poll (1985), the general public recognizes the value of sexually explicit videotapes in (hopefully) stimulating eroticism in marital sexuality. Based in part on the advent of the home video cassette player, a two-tier community standard of obscenity is developing: a liberal one for VCR tapes used at home (still barring materials involving children and sexual violence), and a more restrictive one for materials displayed in public.

- Eroticism is what people are revelling in (and revealing) as they become submerged in, for example, the minute details of their partner's
  genitalia, or the *style* of licking or sucking (which is not reducible to
  technique issues of speed or firmness). *There is a vast difference when a
  man stops trying to "do" his wife with his penis, and uses his penis to "do" her
  with his eroticism.*

For many people, eroticism is a *mystery*. Whether we turn to the Taoist and
Tantric studies of eroticism as a means of transcendence, or American jurispru-
dence, the topic of mystery surfaces repeatedly:

> Desire, which is known as Kama or "love," is dangerous only when it is consid-
> ered as the end. In truth Kama is only the beginning. *When the mind is satisfied
> with the culture of Kama*, only then can the right knowledge of love arise.
> (Translation from *Rasakadamvakalika* by Douglas & Slinger, 1979, p. 169,
> italics added)

> However, sex and obscenity are not synonymous. . . . The portrayal of sex, *e.g.*,
> in art, literature and scientific works, is not itself sufficient reason to deny
> material the constitutional protection of freedom of speech and press. Sex, a
> great and mysterious force in human life, has indisputably been a subject of
> absorbing interest to mankind through the ages; it is one of the vital problems
> of human interest and public concern. (Supreme Court Justice Brennan's opin-
> ion in *Roth v. United States*, 354 U.S. 476, 487 (1957))

Likewise, eroticism retains its mystery for many families:

- "How *do* you maintain eroticism in a long-term marriage?"
- "Did my parents *really* do it this way?"
- "How can I stop my child from touching himself/herself (at least in
  public)? It makes me uncomfortable when I see him/her enjoying it so
  much."

In our discussion, we will use the following definition: *Eroticism is the
pursuit and delight in sensual pleasure*. As we shall see, it is the aspect of
acknowledging one's *delight* that is the most denied and problematic aspect of
sexuality in marriage and in the family.

Eroticism in the Family

Eroticism is one of the most powerful driving forces behind family dynamics
and individual behavior—*it is also the aspect most denied*. Indoctrination about

eroticism is a powerful, invisible, substratum of family sex education. Some parents address sexual plumbing; fewer still discuss copulatory mechanics. Most often, sex information is handled like any "top secret": on a "need to know" basis. Although the question of who needs to know what at what age is debatable, what is *never* discussed, however, is the topic of *eroticism*: Talking about sex being "pleasurable" or "feeling good" doesn't address the same issues as when a parent acknowledges his/her *delight* in sexual gratification (or lack thereof).

Denial of eroticism runs deep. Dealing with parents' eroticism is easy: *they never had any.* While some adult children accept that their parents copulated (or still copulate), it is quite another matter to picture one's mother with her heels in the air screaming "Oh God, Oh God!" With denial this thick, is it any wonder that homes with adolescents sometimes have a scantily-clad pubescent girl or boy prancing through the house while everyone relives the fairy tale of "The Emperor's New Clothes?"

The politics surrounding children's eroticism surface in the issue of sex play and sex education. *"There's time enough to tell them, when they become sexual"* really means, *"Let's deny their (and our) eroticism as long as we can."* Ultrasound intrauterine photography, however, regularly detects erection in 17-week-old male fetuses; female fetuses probably undergo corresponding vaginal lubrication. This pattern continues after birth, wherein male infants exhibit nocturnal penile tumescence (associated with REM sleep) approximately three times per night; the pattern continues throughout childhood, peaking at puberty, and continuing through senescence (Money, 1985). While a 17-week-old fetus probably lacks sufficient physiological development to *delight* in sexual arousal, one look at a healthy infant leaves little doubt.

Contemporary sexology has developed only a preliminary understanding of human erotic development. Prenatal hormonal environment appears to be a fundamental stage in preparation for programming an erotic template into the brain. Money (1985) refers to the many mammalian species in which adult sexual behavior is totally governed by prenatal hormonal programming as "hormonal robots."

Primates (particularly humans), in contrast, require postnatal programming to complete their erotic training. Programming of erotic turn-ons occurs during childhood, although it is not fully manifest until puberty and later; early childhood imprinting of native language is a counterpart process. Research suggests that early physical contact (erotic, in the best sense of the term) is not only crucial for development of healthy object relations, but also requisite for the ability to accurately perceive and respond to the intangibles of interpersonal communication (Bowlby, 1960, 1969, 1973; Harlow, 1976).

Very young children don't know anything about sexuality in the sexuopolitical sense, but they know everything *about eroticism. That is what* innocence *is all about:* eroticism without sophistication. Children have to learn about the sexualization of everyday life, and in the process, develop an erotic *map*. This lovemap evolves from interactions with the family (and later, through television and the schools).

Sexual rehearsal play in monkeys is an essential prerequisite for male-female breeding in adulthood; Money (1985) points out it is similarly crucial in humans:

> Age-concordant, gender-different, sexuoerotic rehearsal play in infancy and childhood is a prerequisite for healthy lovemap formation. Deprivation and neglect of such play may induce pathology of lovemap formation, as also may prohibition, prevention, and abusive punishment and discipline. (p. xvi)

Money (1985) provides a thorough description of spontaneous demonstrations of children's eroticism and normal rehearsal play:

> By age three or four, at nap time or bed time, if children are in close proximity, side by side, rhythmic pelvic thrusting may be observed, perhaps in association with rhythmic thumb sucking. . . .
> Three or four is also the age at which children may be seen to engage in flirtatious rehearsal play. A parent or other older child of the opposite sex is often the recipient of their flirtatious attention, which is fairly obviously patterned after models in the social environment, including those seen on television.
> By age five, or thereabouts, as the number of agemates increases at kindergarten or school, flirtatious play becomes boyfriend-girlfriend playmate romance. This also is the age when pelvic rocking or thrusting movements against the body of a partner while lying side by side gives way to the rehearsal play for coitus. . . . (pp. 16–17)

While this is *normal* behavior, Money (1985) observes the inherent paradox predisposing sexual problems and inhibitions of eroticism in adulthood:

> The taboo in our society condemns in childhood the very heterosexuality that it prescribes in adulthood. It condemns any genital manifestation of juvenile sexual rehearsal play as a sin that requires absolution or expiation. It defines some manifestations of eroticism, regardless of the age, as perversions or, in lurid legalese, as abominable and unspeakable crimes against nature. . . .
> Just as they absorb their society's native language, children absorb also its

sexual precepts, negative as well as positive. Even as precepts of antisexu-
alism are in the process of vandalizing a child's lovemap, they continue to be absorbed. . . . (p. 18)

Lack of effective sex education augments the deleterious impact of parents'
denial of, and interference with, children's healthy sexuoerotic rehearsal. Since
children's eroticism is constantly evident, focusing instead on reproductive
capacity provides the "out." Delaying sex education until reproductive capacity
itself becomes problematic stokes the struggles surrounding childhood masturbation and increases the realistic problems of (a) adolescent copulatory behavior without responsible contraceptive planning, and (b) increased childhood
vulnerability to the inappropriate erotic motivations of others. Beyond pro-
hibiting erotic behavior with self or others and instructing girls about menstrual hygiene, discussion of eroticism *never* occurs.

It is not uncommon for parents to blush when talking to their children
about sex; *blushing* is a much overlooked indication of what is really tran-
spiring. Systematically, the blushing is occasioned by the parent's embarrassed
awareness of his/her own eroticism (*i.e., delight in sensual pleasure*) while also
attempting to skirt that topic with the child. The embarrassment actually
occurs on two levels; the intrapsychic level has actually received a great deal of
attention, the systemic level almost none. The former level concerns intrapsychic conflict, involving battles with one's superego or object relations introjects.

The latter, systemic level of embarrassment in this case occurs from *hidden
joy*; hidden joy is the link to the phenomenon of blushing (Robertson, 1991).
Blushing is the unaccepted *heat of hidden joy* that is consciously suppressed and
experienced on a physiological level; our emphasis here is psychophysiological
and systemic, not psychodynamic.[8] Blushing doesn't betray our hidden joy of
sensual delight (i.e., our eroticism) as much as it betrays our *discomfort with
acknowledging that delight, particularly to those with whom we are the closest.*
Discomfort with eroticism is the cause of parental embarrassment and silence;
talking about sex treads uncomfortably close to acknowledging the child's *and*
the parents' eroticism.

Byrne and Schulte (1990) suggest that individual differences in comfort
with eroticism stem from early family environment. They define *erotophobia-
erotophilia* as "the predisposition to respond to sexual cues along a negative-
positive dimension of affect and evaluation."

---

[8]Blushing is not unique in being a psychophysiological response with systemic features; another such
reaction is discussed in detail in *The Intimacy Paradigm*.

Erotophobia-erotophilia is presumably learned in childhood and adolescence through experiences associating sexual cues with negative emotional states (Byrne, 1983). As a result of such emotional conditioning, erotophobes report relatively negative emotional reactions to sexuality, including guilt and anxiety (Kelly, 1979, 1983). In various retrospective investigations, erotophobes (in contrast to erotophiles) report more parental strictness about sexual matters (Fisher et al., 1988) [and] greater religiosity (Fisher et al., 1983; Fisher & Byrne, 1978a). Verbally or nonverbally, purposefully or inadvertently, children can be taught that sex is something bad, embarrassing, and shameful that should not be discussed except in negative terms. (p. 96)

Every model of human development credits childhood experiences as having considerable import for adult sexual functioning; what is often overlooked is the impact of *silence*. Silence suggests that eroticism is dirty, inherently embarrassing, dangerous, inappropriate, or vulgar; silence is an education in sexual attitudes and gender role.

Silence, of course, can only be *verbal*; everything else speaks volumes. Like it or not, the family is always the predominant purveyor of the child's erotic map *and* attitudes towards eroticism. Control of the prevailing image of eroticism is the unstated turf in community debates over sex education in schools; people's discomfort with eroticism is what brings riches to television evangelists who make eroticism an abomination. The former implies that the responsibility and prerogative of providing education about eroticism *might* be wrestled away from the family; the later is willing to "exorcise" it from the family (for a price). Both are misguided: Those who fear classroom sex education might provide untoward influence on children's developing erotic map *would do better to wish that it were possible*; only the brainwashing of television can begin to compete with the impact of day-to-day family interaction.

Families start the healthy process of giving shape and meaning to children's innate sexuality; when this process goes astray children become *de*-eroticized or *over*-eroticized. Only recently has the topic of *healthy* family sexuality received due professional attention (e.g., Maddock, 1991).

Parents aren't always grateful when helped to recognize their children's eroticism (or their erotic interest in their children).[9] Some parents can't stand

---

[9]*Child Magazine* published a courageous first-person account (Leonard, 1991) about a father's shock at becoming erect in response to normal touching and rehearsal behavior with his 7-year-old daughter. The resulting letters-to-the-editor reflect the point being made here. Four letters were published: a breast-feeding mother honestly acknowledged becoming aroused, the only *anonymous* writer appreciated the reassurance s/he was normal in spite of knowing it intellectually, a woman thought this would scare children about their parents and encourage child molesters, and a husband and wife declared the author was abnormal.

the inherent sexual tension; and yet, it is parents' tolerance for this tension that makes the entire household safe for children's erotic maturation.

Unfortunately, many families never successfully negotiate the tension inherent in establishing even rudimentary interpersonal boundaries. When privacy and personal space are not respected, acknowledging eroticism within the household presents too many emotional and physical risks: Children are forced to maintain the family equilibrium by restricting their own eroticism.

For instance, early in my training, Janice, a young college coed, sought treatment with the question, "Is it possible for a woman to like someone without it being sexual?" Janice reported extreme confusion and fear about signals of sexual interest and seductiveness she might unwittingly be giving to others.

In the process of treatment, she revealed that her parents often had drunken fights about sex. More than once these spilled over into the hallway, where the father raped the mother while she called out to the children for help. Janice was often chased around the livingroom couch by her uncle in plain view of her mother, who laughed while it occurred but later blamed her for "leading her uncle on." She reported being beaten by her father whenever she set her hair, apparently because it was sufficient to identify her as a female and strained her father's limited sexual self-control.

After a very productive course of individual therapy, Janice entered the final termination session with the request for a "goodbye kiss" from me. It would be an understatement to say that I had developed a warm affection and admiration for her: I was fully cognizant of her attractiveness and of my own erotic impulses toward her. I knew that I could rationalize a "goodbye kiss" if I kept it semi-chaste; I also sensed that this one interaction could retrospectively redefine all our prior interactions. After deliberating for a minute I declined, whereupon Janice responded with a heartfelt "thank you," and therapy proceeded to a successful conclusion.

Sexual abuse results from the inability to tolerate both the awareness of eroticism and the resulting sexual tension: some parents simply act it out. Abuse may be emotional and/or physical, and need not be specifically sexual in focus: Repeated inappropriate verbalizations, exhibitionism, touching, or sexual intrusiveness affect expression of eroticism and capacity for intimacy in later life.

Impairment [in erotic lovemaps] may also be secondary to being introduced precipitously, and without prior preparation, to one of the erotosexual practices that both exist in society, and are morally or criminally condemned by it. In consequence, the practice is experienced as traumatizing. . . .

Vandalism of the developing lovemap under the aforesaid circumstances is effected because the experience constitutes entrapment of a catch-22. That is to

say, the children are damned if they do, and damned if they don't disclose what
has happened. The penalty of nondisclosure is continued entrapment with no
escape possible. (Money, 1985, p. 18)

A child's erotic template is most vulnerable to vandalism between the ages
of five and eight, and fairly rigidified by the age of puberty; once formed, it is
extremely resistant to modification (Money, 1985).

IMPACT OF PARENTAL SEXUAL-MARITAL ADJUSTMENT

Parents' sexual relationship, especially when marked by discord, has an impact
on children's erotic maps. Many patients are themselves the children of couples who never resolved their own sexual-marital difficulties. Parental marital
and sexual maladjustment has negative effects at *multiple* levels.

The absence of positive modeling is an obvious problem: Prolonged marital
conflict produces ineffective modeling regarding (a) gender role, (b) public
displays of affection, eroticism, and modesty, and (c) privacy both within the
marital dyad and between parents and children.

When the marital bond of intimacy and eroticism is severely ruptured (or
fails to materialize), everyone in the family is aware. Children become acutely
mindful that parents do not share the same bed or sleeping quarters. Subtle
reflections of parents' sexual and intimate behavior become preoccupations for
children and adolescents. Violations of monogamy generate intense childhood
curosity and anxiety, subtly oversexualizing the child.

Errors arise from children's misinterpretations (and parents' deliberate mis-
representation) of the household reality. For instance, difficulty with intimacy
is often misrepresented as family rules about privacy. Perceptions of parents'
marriage create expectancies for sexual behavior and marital difficulties in later
life, including distortions of the normal effects of aging on sexual functioning
and satisfaction.

Relationship Geometry: Triangulation

Kerr and Bowen (1988) offer a model of intergenerational transmission of
parents' marital legacy which reintroduces the topic of differentiation. According to these authors, a triangle is the smallest stable relationship unit of an
emotional system. Triangular relationships appear to be universal in both
human and subhuman species, such as monkeys, mice, and hens (Wilson,
1975).

The triangle describes the dynamic equilibrium of a three-person system. The major influence on the activity of a triangle is anxiety. When it is low, a relationship between two people can be calm and comfortable. However, since a relationship is easily disturbed by emotional forces within it and from outside, it usually does not remain completely comfortable very long. Invariably, there is some increase in anxiety that disturbs the relationship equilibrium. A two-person system may be stable as long as it is calm, but since that level of calm is very difficult to maintain, a two-person system is more accurately characterized as unstable. When anxiety increases, a third person becomes involved in the tension of the twosome, creating a triangle . . . the formation of three *interconnected* relationships can contain more anxiety than is possible in three separate relationships because the pathways are in place that allow the shifting of anxiety around the system. (p. 135)

Triangulation describes (a) a model of fluid relationship dynamics at any given point in time, and (b) transmission of the same dynamics across generations, transcending time and location. According to Kerr and Bowen, triangular dynamics function like intergenerational "DNA."

Triangles are forever, at least in families. Once the emotional circuitry of a triangle is in place, it usually outlives the people who participate in it. If one member of a triangle dies, another person usually replaces him. (p. 135)

The interlocking multiple triangles that exist in any nuclear family, and those in the spouses' families of origin, determine the capacity, style, and depth of eroticism and intimacy within the marital dyad. Kerr and Bowen give a clear example of how one generation bequeaths this legacy to the next:

While the mother-child relationship usually has the most direct influence on the level of differentiation developed by the child, his differentiation from the family is also influenced by other relationships. The degree of anxiety and level of maturity of the father and other family members have effects both on the child and on the relationship between the mother and the child. A mother-child relationship is influenced through the process of interlocking triangles by other relationships in the nuclear and extended families. The marital relationship is an example. Emotional distance between the parents increases a mother's vulnerability to overinvolvement with her children. Or, if a mother is prone to overinvolvement with the children and the father reacts passively to that involvement and distances from his wife, the marital distance makes it more difficult for mother and child to separate emotionally from one another. A father may actively promote his wife's overinvolvement with the children because it reduces pressure on him to deal with her emotional needs. Another way a father may undermine his child's separation from the mother is by holding his wife responsible for changing some aspect of the child *he* is anxious about. He may do this by repeatedly telling his wife what worries him about the child. (1988, pp. 196–197)

Hinman also noted that dysfunctional parenting styles are the vehicle by which marital difficulties take on intergenerational power. Some of these manifestations include overprotection ("smotherlove"), perfectionism, overt rejection, neglect, and abuse.

> An upset mother who has had an unplanned and relatively unwanted child may use him as a highly effective contraceptive. How can the husband expect her to be sexually available when "he can see she has to sleep with the baby in order to get the baby to sleep"? The father who finds sexual relationships unrewarding or has relative impotence may be the one who sleeps with the baby. It is all so rational and socially acceptable that it is easily defended. To tell such parents authoritatively that the baby must have a room of his own is not going to be very helpful. (Hinman, 1974, pp. 276–277)

DIFFERENTIATION, TRIANGULATION, AND EROTICISM IN THE FAMILY

The result of this process is a multisystemic recursion of low differentiation, difficulty with eroticism and intimacy, and increased potential for marital difficulties. Intergenerational emotional legacies — modulated by the degree of differentiation — determine the likelihood of marital crisis and emergence of sexual and nonsexual symptoms within the family. We will address each of these in turn, considering how children are shaped to be the parents of tomorrow, and the subsequent impact on their own children's eroticism.

Childhood Development

Bringing our discussion of the topics of eroticism and differentiation to a head, low level of differentiation within the family of origin potentiates interference in the healthy development of children's eroticism.

- In poorly differentiated families, parents are more likely to be upset by children's erotic rehearsals or by acknowledgment of their own eroticism; they are more prone to intervene in the child's eroticism in order to maintain their own self-regulation. In well-differentiated families, conversely, members have the ability to handle eroticism-related anxiety as separate individuals (without attempting to diffuse it dyadically or through triangulation).

- Triangulation increases the likelihood of interference in the child's erotic development. Such interference may be a general outcome of systemic attempts to modulate overall level of anxiety in the family; likewise, it may be a specific and deliberate incursion occasioned by the way eroticism is handled in the family.

At the same time that the child's *eroticism* is modulated and shaped for consistency with parents' individual and marital dynamics, the child's overall attempts at *differentiation* are similarly regulated.

- In the triangulation that often results from attempts to stabilize a poorly differentiated marriage, differentiation of the child is inhibited.

When the child is exploited as a confidante by one or both parents and subject to inappropriate parental disclosure (e.g., intimate details of marital conflicts, sexual dysfunctions, and affairs), he/she is likely to feel responsible for providing compensatory gratification for the parent and maintaining family stability. In the process, the child often becomes an emotional consort and object of affection (and eroticism), encouraging underfunctioning in both parents. In addition to the other negative impacts on the child's developing eroticism, the child's own physical maturation and emotional differentiation trigger guilt about "abandoning" an unhappy dependent parent and upsetting the family system.

- As the child moves towards dating (and eventually, marriage), his/her fairly concretized erotic script and anticipations (introjects) shape (and are reconfirmed through) erotic rehearsal and sexual experimentation in adolescence.
- If and when the child begins to differentiate himself/herself from being triangulated, the resulting anxiety in the marital dyad manifests in such a way as to draw the child back in (e.g., parental symptomatology, destabilized family functioning, inducements, threats, etc).

A young woman about to graduate from college came home to announce her engagement, expecting parental blessings and acceptance as an adult: "Don't tell your father," Mother counseled, "It will kill him!" Father's blatant disapproval masked his attempts to induce insecurity. "Well, I just hope you have thought this through," he said. "Just remember, you are on your own; no financial aid from us, pay for your own graduate education. How are you kids going to survive?"

- Entering marriage with a pejorative set of expectations, the individual is particularly prone to anxiety from events both occurring and anticipated. His/her relatively low level of differentiation (a) decreases the likelihood of success in coping (unilaterally) with the resultant anxiety, and (b) determines the pattern of eroticism, intimacy, and triangulation in his/her own marriage.

Marital Eroticism and Symptom Production

Differentiation plays multiple specific roles in the erotic aspects of marriage:

- Differentiation is requisite for disclosure and long-term maintenance of eroticism in a marital relationship. Said differently, differentiation is the foundation for self-validated (level-2) *sexual* intimacy.
- Differentiation provides the self-validation and self-soothing ability required to hammer out a sexual relationship in which one's eroticism can be gratified within marriage.
- Highly differentiated parents are less likely to have difficulty setting and maintaining appropriate interpersonal boundaries within the family, thereby increasing the safety and opportunity for each member to develop and gratify his/her respective eroticism in an age-appropriate fashion.

Lack of differentiation predisposes (a) marital tension and dissatisfaction, (b) minimal eroticism and intimacy during sexuality, and (c) sexual affairs (to be discussed in Chapter Twelve).

- At low levels of differentiation, each partner's need for emotional validation from the other increases, making it likely that the marital system will develop symptoms of distress.

Traits that initially comprised an emotional complementarity become polarized and exaggerated, evolving into the source of contention between the spouses. Kerr and Bowen (1988) suggest that the *pattern* of exaggerated traits determines whether the symptom emerges in one or more of three areas: marital conflict, spouse dysfunction, or child dysfunction. The pattern of traits in the family system, moreover, determines the likelihood and way in which the child's erotic development will be affected.

The forgoing discussion integrates differentiation in the development of adult eroticism, from healthy to inhibited or "kinky" (i.e., paraphilias). In the process, we have actually explained (a) the widespread inhibition of sexual potential,

(b) the common predisposition for sexual/marital difficulties, and (c) the need for broad-band sexual/marital therapy. The relationship between triangulation, differentiation, and capacity for intense intimacy and eroticism clarifies why *normal sex is mediocre sex.* Precious few individuals persevere to explore the limits of their sexual potential, of which eroticism is a significant and obvious component.

The concept of triangulation, however, does not automatically dictate multigenerational family therapy as the approach of choice. Although family therapy suggests itself when problems of the extended system surface through a symptomatic child, long-range symptom reduction (and marital satisfaction) lies in differentiation of the marital dyad (and the child). The sexual crucible offers a powerful approach to help couples (a) achieve the differentiation necessary to soothe intergenerational contagion, and (b) permit the healthy development (and gratification) of eroticism within the family.

Sexual-marital therapy must be conceptualized and practiced in sufficiently broad scope: Narrow-band therapy is more likely to fail in modifying genital symptomatology and to miss a powerful opportunity for personal development and restructuring of the family system. The latter goals are accomplished by repeatedly shifting back and forth between (a) focusing on the concrete issues of sexuality and eroticism in marital interactions, and (b) utilizing cross-modality interventions based on an elicitation approach to address issues of differentiation.

The following section presents a sexual crucible case example illustrating:

- problems of eroticism and differentiation (and their etiology) discussed above;
- use of sexual-marital therapy for their resolution;
- exploration of sexual potential; and
- broad facilitation of individual growth, resolution of family-of-origin issues, and systemic family intervention.

CASE EXAMPLE OF MULTIGENERATIONAL TRANSMISSION AND TRIANGULATION

A middle-aged couple, Paul and Sarah, came to me by way of referral from Sarah's therapist. Having made gains with her depression in individual treatment, Sarah was apparently ready to deal with a "lack of communication" in her marriage and her lack of desire for sex. Aside from a lack of desire attributable to being depressed, Sarah was resentful of Paul's expectations for coitus. Sarah had previously given up her job to become a full-time homemaker for their four children (three boys, ages 22, 17, 15, and a daughter, age 20). Now, when she increasingly wanted to return to work, she was angered by a lack of "support" from her husband.

Paul, on the other hand, was uncomfortable with Sarah's increasing autonomy and assertiveness. She had always been soft-spoken and amenable. His career as a physician reinforced the patriarchal family model he (and Sarah) had grown up with: He was used to having other people accommodating to his schedule and priorities. Paul was uneasy about being in treatment; however, Sarah seemed to benefit from her prior individual therapy and he was willing to give conjoint treatment a somewhat reluctant try.

At the outset, the presenting problems were disparate levels of sexual desire and overall lack of sexual desire on Sarah's part. The marriage was acknowledged to have some tensions around "communication" and common problems of daily living, but the main tension concerned sexual frequency and the pressure Sarah felt to satisfy her husband's needs (sexual and otherwise). Sarah offered that she had been brought up with very conservative views about sex; she had struggled throughout adolescence with the sense that sex was dangerous and sinful. She had received almost no education regarding sex; she perceived her mother to be uncomfortable with the topic and reported a strict religious upbringing. Paul reported a similar religious background; in fact, he and Sarah were very active in their church. As a couple to whom religion and ethics were of focal importance, Paul and Sarah expressed some desire to find ways to integrate their sexuality with their spirituality. The initial presentation fit nicely into a stereotypic case of inhibited sexual desire secondary to strict religious upbringing.

Treatment was initially structured along the approach outlined in the preceding chapter concerning inhibited sexual desire. It was an anxious time for both partners. Both were highly committed to continuing the marriage; both were thinking how awful it would be if nothing changed. Sarah felt both guilty and angry about Paul's dissatisfaction with her. Paul felt defensive and righteous about his desire for sex. I resisted Paul's repeated requests to get them started on something "tangible" that would improve their sexual relationship. After about five sessions, Sarah seemed ready to give some type of physical contact a try.

Paul and Sarah's initial experience with nongenital touch was a shocker: Sarah came to orgasm while her husband touched her back! It was immediately clear that she was, indeed, highly sexually arousable—much more so than she could tolerate. She had spent much of her adolescence thinking about going to hell, readily experiencing her own arousal and desire in early dating from simply kissing boys. By sheer avoidance, fear, and willpower, Sarah remained a virgin until she married; she was age 22 and Paul was 25.

The presenting problem clearly reflected an incongruous power hierarchy: Sarah was actually far more arousable, responsive, and capable of desire than was Paul. Both spouses struggled with this awareness, which challenged their respective traditional gender roles around sexual aggressiveness and desire. Paul's sexual demands diminished somewhat. Swallowing his pride, he became more open to Sarah's opinions in the livingroom and her preferences in the bedroom.

In the ensuing weeks of treatment, Sarah became increasingly sexually responsive, and the couple entered what they experienced as the most wonderful honeymoon of their lives. Treatment progressively shifted to Paul's sexual inhibitions and truncated development, which prevented a display of erotic depth similar to his wife's. It turned out that Paul was only comfortable with "polite" sex; Sarah, who became increasingly radiant and emotionally and physically vivacious in her daily life, was capable of deeper intimacy and sexual abandonment.

After one or two sessions with this new focus, Paul remembered something during debriefing of their sexual activities that he had thought about several times between sessions but always "forgot" to mention. He reported that he slept in his parents' bedroom until the age of 13. Another "guest" bedroom had been vacant in the house, but he was forbidden by his mother to sleep in the antique bed it contained. At the age of 13, the family moved to another city and Paul was then permitted to sleep in the antique bed in another room. The reason for the change was never explained to him. Paul reported having no memory of his parents' sexual behavior or any sense that he interfered with his parents' privacy or sexual exchange in any way. He also reported no awareness of nocturnal emissions, no sexual curiosity or experimentation, and no desire for privacy on his own part.

This information confirmed my growing impression that Paul's sexual style reflected "adequate" genital functioning in the context of restricted eroticism and differentiation. Sexual activities were redefined as a window of elicitation and designed to construct a crucible to resolve these and other developmental tasks; the couple progressed in shifting their focus from orgasm to eroticism and developing increased tolerance of profound levels of contact.

Over the next several sessions, the couple's intimacy deepened and their sex became more delightful. Paul looked forward to having sex with Sarah more than he ever had. The couple was acutely aware of developing an entirely new sexual reality and set of expectancies surrounding their physical exchanges. And to think that this started off with Sarah's not wanting to have sex!

During a subsequent session, Paul and Sarah mentioned that their time for themselves had been preempted by trouble with their 15-year-old son. However, the emotional intimacy and working alliance between the spouses had remained during this difficult time. They reported being called to school by the son's counselor, who informed them that their son was threatening suicide. I was quite surprised; nothing in their modest presentation had cued me to serious problems with the son. In the process of reporting this to me, Paul mentioned anecdotally that their older son (now age 17) had also threatened suicide at the age of 15.

Paul reported that the younger son's difficulty seemed to be primarily between the son and himself; in desperation, Paul had offered to move out of the house until things quieted down. Sarah saw this as regression and was disappointed in Paul for contemplating the abdication of his rightful place and responsibility. Actually, Paul felt that the father was supposed to be the center from which all power in the family emanated. He clearly functioned as if he had grown up in a household that believed in a "closed" power system. At the time, I thought Paul had come very close to playing out the oedipal triangle of the son who usurps the father. Had Paul left the house, it would have encouraged his son to fear being replaced by another man, just as Paul was now.

The details of the threatened "suicide" appeared definitely nonlethal. The dynamics behind the symptom appeared to reflect the son's difficulty in differentiating from the family, particularly his father. The son was reportedly "afraid" of Paul's punishing him harshly. Ironically, Paul had difficulty with aggression and, if anything, tended towards intellectualized displays of power and modulated anger. The son constructed the image of his father, as in all mythological quests for manhood, as the overbearing monster whom the hero must vanquish.

Reporting his subsequent dialogue with his son, Paul said that he had told him that they would have to work out their difficulties together and that he, the father, could not be expected to have all the answers. Paul looked upon this last statement somewhat defensively, like an admission of inadequacy; as he related the story in therapy, Paul was talking about sharing the "blame" when he "laid some of the responsibility for the problem and the solution on my son." To Paul's surprise, the son seemed delighted with this prospect.

Paul's previous defensiveness about not having all the answers kept him from recognizing his son's need to have some answers too, in demonstration of his own masculine prowess. However, in a family where "head of the house" was defined as the person with all the answers, there was little room for adolescent sons to demonstrate their soon-to-be manhood without entering into a competition with father that threatened to diminish one or both. Although unaware of it at the time, Paul had set up a situation where there would be room for two penises (an open power system), that is to say, two men under the same roof. Apparently, the same issue had arisen with the older son as well. Paul and Sarah recognized this was not significantly different from Paul's having slept in his parents' bedroom until age 13, requiring the denial and restriction of his parents' eroticism and self-assertion, as well as his own.

The quality of Paul and Sarah's relationship in subsequent months, in and out of the bedroom, exceeded all their prior experience. Sexual contact was frequent, satisfying, and varied. Conflicts arose, but there was a marked absence of hostility and these were resolved to both their satisfaction. Mutual respect became the hallmark of their interaction. Sarah took pride in her ability to maintain herself in the face of her anxieties; Paul prided himself on his ability to tolerate an increasingly strong partner.

All of this provided additional stimulus for Sarah's own level of differentiation. She began to confront previously unrecognized aspects of her mother's control of her through guilt induction and manipulation via childhood views of self-sacrifice and consideration for others. Sarah also regained control of her volunteer time at her church, where she continued to maintain a significant personal commitment. Eventually, she had her first orgasm with her eyes open throughout their lovemaking.

Soon, however, this led to complaints from Sarah about Paul's sexual inhibitions. Initially, Paul had a hard time understanding what Sarah was talking about. He had no sexual dysfunctions, he was eager to please her, and he was a gentle and considerate lover. For several sessions, Paul's "emotional armor" and his inability to truly abandon himself to receiving pleasure from his wife was the topic of treatment. Paul acted as though he didn't know what his wife and I were referring to; eventually he acknowledged that *no one* got too far inside him and he wasn't sure that he wanted to change that. For a while, it was uncertain whether he was willing to risk a further increment in the level of intimacy and eroticism. For her part, Sarah was increasingly frustrated that Paul would not let her "put him into orbit" during their sexual interactions. She struggled in the crucible, knowing that making demands would only exacerbate the situation; her best move was to hold onto herself and hope that Paul mastered himself.

Eventually, Paul and Sarah entered one session with four pieces of "good news." First, Paul commented on his ability to recognize other couples who had marital difficulties or who were embarrassed to be in treatment, simply by observing their interactions. His comment reflected his increasing perceptiveness of interpersonal dynamics, as well as his lack of defensiveness about being in treatment himself.

Next, Paul reported a conversation with several male friends in which someone commented on an apparent contradiction in an issue under discussion. Paul mentioned, "That's not a contradiction, that's just two sides of the same thing that drives you forward to a better understanding of the whole issue." Only two of his friends had an inkling of what he meant, but Paul was clearly delighted with the development reflected in his insightful, differentiated stance.

The third news item was that Paul had finally permitted himself to be truly abandoned in receiving Sarah's sexual attentions. Sarah reported it was the most intense sexual encounter she had ever experienced, and spoke of her husband with respect and amazement. For his part, Paul was somewhat surprised, since he had actually found it quite easy to do once he allowed himself a different role in bed.

However, the best had been saved for last. Their son had asked to be placed in a boarding school of outstanding reputation in a nearby community. The other siblings and even Paul and Sarah had attended a local private school. Although the son's requests started when he was unhappy at this local school, his desire for boarding school remained even after his grades and social life improved markedly in the last few months. After visiting the boarding school and reviewing their financial situation, Paul and Sarah realized that sending this son away for high school would limit the range of options he would have for college. Paul and Sarah decided that even though he was only 16, the son should be allowed to make the choice! This was an extremely salient step for Paul, who only months before had insisted on retaining all manifest power and control, and for his son who contemplated suicide as the only way to resolve the barriers to differentiation and his own sense of masculinity.

Together, Paul and Sarah explained the options to their son. They reported that he was delighted and almost stunned that they would trust him to make his own decision and support him in it. Although the son looked somewhat frightened by the prospect of making his decision, Paul chuckled, "You would have thought we had handed him a check for a million dollars." Paul, Sarah, and their son were all immensely proud of themselves and each other. Sarah's respect for her son's decision subsequently provided a stimulus for further recognition and confrontation of her own mother's manipulation and control, enhancing her own differentiation.

In this respect, the family could be seen to be functioning as a living dynamic organism, extending over several generations, composed of multiple people. Over the course of treatment, differentiation in one family member stimulated parallel development in others. Along the way core individual, dyadic, and intergenerational issues were addressed and resolved. The process was sometimes pleasurable and sometimes poignant, but never linear or tranquil:

- Sarah and Paul took a vacation together, one of their first without their children. The youngest son stayed with a family friend and attended school during their absence. As Paul and Sarah were returning from the airport, the son "ran away from home" with their car and was picked up by the police. It was the first time the son had ever given them any "trouble."
- On the way back from a mid-day out-of-town automobile trip with Sarah, Paul suddenly stopped at a motel a short way from their home. He knew they would be passing by and had previously made a reservation.
- Both Sarah and Paul engaged in a number of skirmishes with their older children. Sarah's refusal to remain in her former role as the sacrificial mother exacerbated the college-bound children's ambivalence about leaving home. Boundaries appropriate to their increasing maturation were established and revamped regarding personal responsibility and autonomy. Sarah relished her own sense of mastery and self-respect as she saw the shock in her children's eyes when she no longer let them take her for granted.
- Intimacy, both sexual and otherwise, continued to deepen for the couple. Initially, keeping their eyes open had been a daring event (and a challenge for increased differentiation) during any aspect of sexual contact; later it advanced to "eyes-open" orgasms. Now, Sarah and Paul experimented with eye-gazing and letting each other see him/her "*behind* the eyeballs." They began to experiment with the subtle and almost imperceptible levels of emotional armor people maintain even during "good" sex. Both spouses concurred: Sarah allowed Paul to really "see" her, in a way that Paul couldn't. Paul could feel that some level of guardedness remained. He talked about it openly, with minor reactivity from Sarah; it was his problem, not hers. Eventually, they

accomplished it, in a memorable sexual experience that was independent of orgasms and in which "time stopped."

- Sarah and Paul recognized a previously unnoticed level of sexism within their religious group. Sarah openly questioned the inconsistencies with the stated spiritual philosophies, and maintained herself in the face of considerable pressure and anxiety from the group. Paul fully concurred with Sarah's position, and did not undermine her by becoming overly helpful.

- Paul began to deal with sexual fantasies towards other women, prompted by seeing a group of young women dashing around the beach in bikinis. Sarah was feeling "used" and furious about the idea of Paul subsequently having sex with her while probably thinking about the younger women. Previously guilty about such thoughts, he began to struggle with the fundamental nature of his own eroticism. Masturbation, previously a topic dispensed with by biblical injunctions, became a focal point for issues of differentiation, morality, and spirituality. The result was a significant increment in Paul's ability to access a healthy level of aggression in his eroticism with Sarah. The counter-result was the triggering of heretofore untapped issues for her. Whereas she was previously frustrated by her husband's restricted eroticism, Sarah could feel herself pull back as he became more unabashedly erotic outside the bedroom.

Subsequently, Paul requested an individual session "to discuss some ideas and issues." At the outset, he mentioned that he still felt somewhat inadequate and "replaced" when using a vibrator with Sarah for sexual purposes; he suggested that we discuss this topic later in the session. First, however, he wanted to outline other topics for discussion.

Sarah's diminishing need for validation from him and others (i.e., her differentiation) had triggered Paul's recognition of his own unresolved longing for validation from his father. Painfully, Paul described how his father had never complimented him nor displayed any pride in Paul's noteworthy accomplishments. As he spoke, it became clear that Paul had taken the absence of his father's acknowledgment as a reflection on himself. Paul assumed that either he had not accomplished enough to gain his father's recognition, or perhaps his father had not really loved him. Paul's father had died several years earlier, always having provided for the family financially but never saying the words Paul craved. He felt forever precluded from getting the acknowledgment he sought for so long.

I pointed out that Paul had never said much about his father. He related that his father had gotten into a fight with his high school teacher only two days prior to graduation, and left school never having completed his degree. Interestingly enough, Paul and his brother both completed high school and earned several advanced degrees. Paul went on to relate one of the highlights of his career as a physician: he diagnosed a significant medical condition his father was overlooking, and provided the treatment himself. Paul's father said, "Thank you," but never offered a word of praise. Subsequently, however, Paul found out that his father had bragged to all his cronies about the fantastic job that *his* son had done.

What Paul presented was not simply an opportunity to resolve an old personal wound; it was another crucible for enhancing his level of differentiation. In effect, Paul felt that his father's behavior—or actually the lack of behavior (the lack of acknowledgment of Paul's abilities and achievement)—was a reflection on him. That is to say, Paul took his father's behavior as a reflection of how Dad felt about *him* (an undifferentiated stance). Paul was confused about how it could be anything else. I suggested that maybe Paul's father's behavior was a reflection of his feelings about *himself*.

In a rhetorical question I raised the possibility that the dilemma of how a father made room for his son to become a man, without feeling himself diminished in the process, had been a problem that traversed several generations in his family. Perhaps Paul might be able to piece together the family history to understand why his father could not afford to graduate from high school. Had his father committed the ritual suicide that his own sons had struggled with? The story about sleeping in his parents' bedroom was relevant once again. Had Paul, his father, and perhaps his father before him struggled with this issue, some more successfully than the next, and passed it on?

I opined that Paul's father might indeed have been extremely proud of him, but unable to conquer his own feelings of inadequacy and lack of accomplishments enough to acknowledge Paul's achievements. While his father may have loved him deeply, giving Paul the acknowledgment he wanted may have involved more anxiety (in confronting his own self-defeating behavior and abandoned dreams) than his father could tolerate. From the sound of Paul's story, his father actually rode on Paul's coattails, using his son's adequacy to compensate for his own feelings of low self-worth, gaining status with his cronies.

While these events were a loss for Paul, they also told a very sad story about his father who died never having mastered himself. If one sees the adequacy of the father, I suggested, by the way in which the son is allowed to surpass his own achievements, then Paul was actually a better reflection upon his father's ability than his own father had been upon Paul's grandfather.

Paul was moved by our discussion. Actually, we never returned to the other topics he mentioned at the outset. Instead, we discussed the interplay between Paul and his own sons, his daughter's conflicts with Sarah, and their crucial importance in his children's eventual freedom to use themselves fully in ways that would, he hoped, surpass their parents' accomplishments. We talked about Paul's participation in a family developmental task that spanned an unknown number of generations, passed down through the process of triangulation. Each generation did its best to detoxify it and pass down a less virulent condition. Together, we hoped that, through the differentiation occurring throughout the family, it would be worked through sufficiently in this generation that it would stop there. If it didn't, Paul was willing to let his children take their turn in finishing what was left. Moreover, the experience Paul's children might receive in watching their parents master themselves around such anxiety-provoking issues would constitute a powerful positive legacy as well.

The next session Paul returned with his wife, happy and smiling. Paul reported that they had discovered a new way to use the vibrator, qualitatively different from anything we had discussed in our sessions. At his own initiation, Paul suggested using the vibrator on his wife, not as a replacement for himself, but as another way of adding to their mutual pleasure. Paul held the vibrator in a more balanced way, offering him greater sensitivity to movement and pressure on his wife's vagina. He imagined using it as an extension of his hand, rather than something he was holding. I smiled, acknowledging my pleasure in his pleasure and success, and stated that I was glad we found a way not to discuss technique in our last session. Puzzled, Paul inquired what I meant. This way, I suggested, we were both clear that this was his innovation and not mine. Moreover, I thanked Paul for his compliment; he obviously thought I was secure enough to tolerate his innovating and exceeding what he had learned from me.

A *lot* transpired in the many sessions since that day. Additional clinical vignettes appear elsewhere in this book; others will be found in *The Intimacy Paradigm*. Sarah returned to college to pursue an advanced degree in ministerial counseling, much to their mutual delight. Actually, to my delight as well. Her readings became an ongoing stimulus in our sessions for integrating their spirituality and sexuality; it stimulated my own thinking on this topic (some of which appears in this book).

At our final session, Paul and Sarah had just returned from a vacation (just the two of them). Their eyes shone with pride as they talked about themselves and each other. Sarah laughingly mentioned that Paul wasn't interested in the young women on the beach anymore. "I watched him looking at them occasionally," she said with a smile, "but his heart wasn't in it." Paul had realized two things while girl-watching. "I have the *real* erotic woman, right here," he said, "I'm married to her." His other observation surprised him: As he looked at the girls, Paul realized he was no longer fantasizing "scoring" one of them; he was thinking of *himself* as the sex object. "If they had a chance with me, they would be amazed," Paul thought, "Too bad girls, you don't know what you're missing!"

Paul then told me about having read a book on his vacation, *Iron John: A Book about Men* by Robert Bly (1990). He related the metaphorical story of every boy's developmental struggle to integrate his masculinity and phallicness (i.e, his caged *Wild Man*); the boy must retrieve the key to his Wild Man's cage from under his mother's pillow. "I now understand your approach to therapy," he said, "You don't let anyone slip their key under your pillow."

I sat there as my eyes filled, *stunned*. Paul, Sarah, and I silently looked into each other for about 20 seconds, a smile on my face, as I slowly nodded my admiration and appreciation. *Paul and Sarah each had their key.*

While non-reactivity is a principal asset of the therapist in the sexual crucible, it is useless if it does not coincide with the ability to feel. Sometimes the joy and the pain of patients' successes are quite as much as I think I can bear. And yet, the integrity of folks like Paul and Sarah, who honor me by entering into the crucible I offer them, drives my own differentiation forward in my respect for their efforts.

THE IMPACT OF CHILDREN ON THE MARITAL DYAD

Who of us is mature enough for offspring before the offspring themselves arrive? The value of marriage is not that adults produce children but that children produce adults. (Peter De Vries in Augarde, 1991)

Children *can* have a positive impact on parents' marital and sexual relationship. The sharing of commitment as life mates, watching the unfolding of human development, joining the life-cycle, and tasting the sweet joys and pains of parenthood can add depth and meaning to marital intimacy. At its best, the process of good parenting builds character in the parents as well as the child. And at its best, good parenting is demanding and stressful. The birth of a child has immediate and broad systemic reverberations that challenge the individual and dyadic stability of the marital partners. When these stresses and challenges exceed the adaptive capacities of the parents, as commonly happens, marital intimacy and eroticism are affected.

The physical requirements of caring for a healthy happy baby demand a shift in exclusive time available within the marital dyad, and test maturation, mutuality, and differentiation; the special needs of a handicapped or chronically ill child amplify this. There are definite shifts in sexual availability and interest, coupled with possible fears in the husband about the wife's priorities. In some couples, this stimulates competition for attention and increasing demands for sex from the husband; his neediness decreases his attractiveness to his fatigued wife. For her part, the wife may be simultaneously comforted and alienated by her husband's demands; fears about attractiveness regarding genital and more global physical changes of pregnancy and delivery are common. Women often report a decline in sexual interest, activity, and desire, both during and after pregnancy (Tolor & Di Grozia, 1976).

Children challenge the family's anxiety tolerance around the recognition of *ambivalent* attachments. Highly differentiated couples can accept ambivalence as a *normal* facet of life and relationships, even within marriage; such couples find it easier to tolerate the recognition of ambivalent attachment towards the child. Couples at lower levels of differentiation find recognition of ambivalent attachment highly anxiety-provoking. They attempt to circumvent this by experiencing both sides of their ambivalence sequentially, giving rise to double messages and double-binds within the marriage and the family.

Children's Symptomatic Reflection
of the Extended System

Children embody multiple levels of significance for marital intimacy:

- shifts in distribution of time, emotion, and physical access;
- increase in stress and requirements for self-soothing;
- intrusion of the extended family; and
- attainment of social identity as an "adult."

Children are a challenge that commonly exceeds the adaptive capacities of parents' level of differentiation, making the emergence of symptoms likely. Given the physical and emotional changes involved in pregnancy, and the very close association of pregnancy and progeny to sexuality, it is particularly likely that the symptomatology occurs within the sexual arena (although it need not be an inherently sexual issue). It may be in the form of an affair, marital conflict about sexuality and intimacy, or arousal, desire, or performance difficulties in either spouse.

Children often become symptomatic when parents' level of differentiation is insufficient to modulate the degree of anxiety in the marital dyad or in the extended family system. Certainly, children can become symptomatic as a manifestation of difficulties in their unique individual adjustment. However, given the tendency for triangulation together with a child's de facto low level of differentiation, children are particularly ripe for becoming the identified patient in a troubled family system.

Children's symptomatology emerges in myriad forms, some more obviously related to sexuality than others (see Table 11.2). The dichotomized classification in Table 11.2 is approximate and nonexclusive: Precocious sexuality, for example, often becomes the focus of power struggles and alliances within the family; encopresis and eating disorders can have an associated erotic component. As mentioned earlier in this chapter, the relationship between familial level of differentiation, triangulation, and interference in children's developing eroticism is complex.

Table 11.2
Children's Symptomatic Reflection of the Family System

Disruption of Erotic Development	Disruption of Differentiation and Object Relations
(a) precocious sexuality or flaunting of sexual interest	(a) breaching boundaries of marital bedroom
(b) minimization/denial of pubertal body changes	(b) school phobias and separation problems
(c) lack of age-appropriate sexual curiosity	(c) childhood sleeping disturbances
(d) excessive childhood masturbation	(d) enuresis of encopresis
(e) sibling incest	(e) eating disorders
(f) premature pregnancy	
(g) deliberate interference in parental erotic/intimate encounters	
(h) rigid or absent gender-appropriate behavior (e.g., cross-dressing in boys)	

Politics of the Bedroom Door: Border Patrol

Patients joke that children seem to know the exact moment to get sick or bang on the door to interrupt parents' most pleasurable sexual encounters. While children are often traumatized by unstable marriages, it is equally true that a happy marriage is a great inconvenience for children. At best, the relationship between children and their parents is marked by ambivalence on both sides.

Few parents or children are eager to go through the anxiety of establishing a boundary indicating that parents have a relationship into which the child is not invited. Quarrelsome parents are much easier for children to manipulate for their own immediate preferences than are harmonious ones, although children also desire the security of firm parental boundaries. No child likes to recognize that parents were not put on the face of the earth to serve the child's needs. While a happy marriage offers significant pleasures to the child, indulgence and immediate gratification of attention are not two of them.

There are few, if any, secrets between family members. Although the awareness is often unspoken, everyone usually knows about parents' intimate/erotic life. An adolescent daughter can sense subtle improvements in the marital relationship and manifest anorexia in a manner inviting parental attention; while not exactly pleasant, the focus on her reduces her growing anxiety about individuation. The fact that the same symptomatology might have, at another time, reflected triangulation with the parents' unstable marriage does not negate the same symptomatology's utility in maintaining the daughter's own equilibrium.

Improvements in marital satisfaction are often met with anger and sabotage by children in families where triangulation has previously been an important source of marital stability. An adolescent who has played a substitutive role for one parent (or merely served to diffuse marital tensions) may be furious when parents assume their appropriate roles and the adolescent is replaced. Should this occur when the adolescent is embroiled with fears of assuming adult autonomous self-responsibility, he/she may feel both rejected from the previous triangulation and ill-equipped to cope due to the restricted differentiation it created. The child who storms the parental bedroom, interrupting his parents' coupling with complaints of "nightmares" exemplifies these dynamics. Others are more creative and less obvious.

In one case, an adolescent son chose to run off with the family car on a joyride while his parents tentatively explored each other's bodies. The household had been organized around an inappropriate triangulation of mother and son against dad. Mother had initially expressed some fears of the son's feeling "neglected" if she sat with father instead of helping with the son's homework. Mother felt she was betraying the son's alliance and feared the loss of the son's support against her husband. The initial weeks of treatment were punctuated by a marked reduction in marital combat and some tentative hugging and kissing at the kitchen sink. Just prior to the joyride, the son had asked, "What is going on?"

In another family, the parents' alcoholism, emotional instability, and marital discord precluded an age-appropriate intergenerational boundary about nudity and sexuality when their daughter was a young teenager. Sexual contact between the spouses was nonexistent, and the wife's alcoholism removed her as a reliable bulwark against the husband's rather typical[10] sexual impulses for his daughter. The daughter embarked on a series of casual sexual encounters and drinking sprees. A number of years later (after considerable treatment for both spouses) they were shocked and angered when their then college-aged

---

[10]"Typical" in the sense of common and healthy, as resulting from awareness of the daughter's (and his own) eroticism. One might call it *normal*, if one also recognized that most men will tell you that it is *abnormal*; actually, claiming that it would be abnormal to feel that way towards one's daughter is *normal*, in the same way that a man who had a healthy comfortableness with this reality would be thoroughly *abnormal*.

daughter walked essentially bare-chested in front of them. In treatment, they recognized that the daughter was actually signaling her awareness of their improved level of functioning. They were ready to deal with the intergenerational sexual issues that could not be handled earlier. The daughter's challenge reflected appropriate ambivalence from one whose own sexual escapades had become the substitute focus of her parents' eroticism.

In marriages blessed with children, the *bedroom door* takes on a significance and complexity reserved for war maneuvers. Perhaps no single landmark in the home more clearly delineates the complex triadic interactions that mark progressive intimate/erotic bonding in the marital dyad. The multiple alliances and hierarchies that pervade families are often expressed by the degree and manner in which parents maintain control of their bedroom door.

Couples muster extreme creativity in rationalizing why their bedroom door must remain open or unlocked. The bottom line is *whoever controls the bedroom door controls the timing and style of marital sexuality*.

Most couples have sex when their children permit it; when children reach puberty, couples accord them even *greater* control of parental sexuality. Some couples engage sexually only when their adolescent daughter is safely out of the house, lest she take her parents' sexual activity as consent for her own experimentation.

Parents report fearing their children will feel "rejected" and "not wanted" if confronted with a closed and locked marital bedroom door. However, lack of differentiation in the marital dyad encourages collusion to avoid an important reality: the child (and the spouse) is *not* always wanted. *Both* generations collude to erode the appropriate intergenerational boundaries, hierarchies, and alliances necessary for developmental progress on *both* sides of the bedroom door.

In many families, *closing* the bedroom door destabilizes maladaptive alliances. It is not "safe" to close the doors in families where one or more children are triangulated pillars in the parents' marriage. *Locking* the door establishes whether parents or children are in control of the boundary.

While the bedroom door is the tangible battlefield of differentiation, the human mind is capable of even greater subtlety: the more sophisticated level of auditory privacy. Fears of being "heard," waiting until children are asleep, and anticipating a child's knock at the closed bedroom door are but a few of the ways that family dynamics supersede mere sheetrock and plywood. In another version, adults suspend sexual behavior while temporarily lodging with either spouse's parents.

BROADER SYSTEMIC IMPACT OF FAMILIES OF ORIGIN
Constructing "Normal" Sexuality

It was stated previously that parents are the primary sex educators of their children. More accurately, the *family teaches itself* about sexuality, each member contributing his/her unique information about his/her stage of life. Within each generation, the family recreates sexuality in its own image. Whether or not it labels itself as "normal" or deviant, the family creates a vision of human sexual potential through shared life experiences.

In the extended family emotional system, collective memories of long-past experiences and deceased family members from spouses' families of origin constitute an emotional dowry each brings to marriage. Family "secrets" and mythology from prior generations' sexual transgressions affect the vision of human sexuality in later decades. Such history can often be elicited through the use of the family genogram (Berman & Hof, 1987; Bowen, 1978; Guerin & Pendagast, 1976; Wachtel, 1982).

For instance, Gwen, the first of three daughters, was the illegitimate product of an adolescent affair known only by the mother and a different man she subsequently married. The other two daughters were the product of this marital union, although the husband raised all three daughters as his own. Gwen's mother became controlling and sexually puritanical during Gwen's adolescence, fearing Gwen might repeat her own sexual transgressions.

Gwen felt "different" and discriminated against by her mother's controlling behavior. This accusation came close to the underlying family secret; in her anxiety, Gwen's mother became more restrictive. Gwen responded with rebellious defiance, including outrageous displays of unconventional clothing. She turned to boys for acceptance and approval, heightening her mother's fear of genetically transmitted promiscuity and prompting increased prohibitions. Gwen soon became pregnant. Later in life, Gwen remained as sexually unresponsive as her mother had been (and wanted Gwen to be).

The impact of family functioning did not end in transmission between mother and daughter. The family's response to Gwen's pregnancy affected her sisters, as well as other members in the extended family system. Gwen's parents' marriage destabilized as mother became preoccupied with Gwen and withdrew from her husband; shared parental authority over children's privileges became a marital battleground. A palpable feeling of anxiety and alienation permeated their home. Other relatives unearthed stories from prior generations and fueled Gwen's mother's sense of shame and estrangement from the surrounding community. Gwen's pregnancy influenced her peers' developing view of sexuality and intimacy, through their own perceptions (and their parents' admonitions) of the luckless girl's example.

Finally, there was education about the nature of sexuality for Gwen and her child. Teen motherhood imposes severe limits on educational, employment, economic, and marital opportunities. These factors and attendant situational pressures predisposed Gwen's child to abuse, neglect, and failure to thrive. A process had been set in motion that echoed through succeeding generations.

In 1982, 48% of teenagers (ages 15–19) used no contraception in their initial experience with intercourse. Although this number decreased by 1988 (to 35%), the percentage of sexually active girls (between 15 and 17) increased by 18% (Forrest & Singh, 1990). Economically and socially disadvantaged teenagers are particularly prone to attempt raising their babies and are further economically, educationally, and socially deprived. Imagine what a pregnant teenager teaches herself about sexuality and life, and the myriad ways this is passed on to her child, who is similarly deprived. Ripples trickle down to the educational system, affect national productivity, increase demands on welfare and child care systems, and polarize the political left and right on sex education and abortion access. The link between adolescent copulation and family crisis is a societal problem of epic proportions.

Teenage pregnancy is a complex social problem, the etiology of which extends far beyond lack of sexual information. However, prevailing models of human sexual response do little to contravene in that problem and reduce pregnancy. If education and health-care professionals promote a model which presumes sexual desire is a given and a simple function of physical gratification, do we really expect teenagers to delay initial coitus or stop copulating once the issues about virginity are out of the way? If our models of human sexual response have no component for *intimacy* or *salience*, how do we expect to talk to children about sex having "meaning" without it sounding like proselytizing, religious moralizing, or conservatism? If we have no clinical models to show children the dynamics of sexual desire or eroticism, how do we explain the advantages of age and maturity in these dimensions? Do we really expect them not to leap into the hormonal floods of adolescence that teenagers correctly see adults lusting for? Education and health-care professionals face an important role in helping families construct a "normal" view of human sexuality that also happens to be *healthy*.

Aging of the System

As the intergenerational family system ages, there is a consequential shift regarding sexuality and intimacy. Grandparents enter retirement, with its own differential effect on their marriages. Men whose sense of masculinity and competency has depended on gainful employment doubt their desirability; women whose identity was dependent on their reproductive capacity fare similarly. Marriages of convenience become contentious in the face of increased time together at home. Rising anxiety in the grandparents' marriage, coupled with increasing requests for financial, physical, and emotional assistance, often rekindles old triangles with adult children.

Adult children confronted by custodial responsibility for parents and their parents' inevitable death find previously established levels of differentiation challenged. Adult children's marriages are often rocked by the shifting pressures in the family system. Placing one's parents in custodial living facilities destroys traditional boundaries of economic and physical privacy. The intimate relationships of married, widowed, or divorced parents are often disproportionately affected by the preferences and opinions of middle-aged children and vice versa. Improvements in marital intimacy and satisfaction of middle-aged children often trigger insecurity in parents who fear abandonment at a time of increasing dependency.

Consider Mrs. Adano,[11] a wife in her late fifties who called her 74-year-old mother at least daily. Mrs. Adano was worn out by the demands of caring for her mother, involving numerous trips to numerous doctors and midnight calls about physical preoccupations. She felt stifled by the strain of being both dutiful child and mother to her infantile mother. Mrs. Adano had been thoroughly enmeshed in her parents' inadequate relationship, further draining her energy and vitality. This was a constant source of conflict between Mrs. Adano and her husband regarding loyalties and priorities.

It happened that Mr. Adano was also constantly belittled by *his* mother, even while trying to please her. This paralleled Mrs. Adano's behavior—attacking him for not being more considerate and helpful in her struggles with her own mother, and criticizing him when he supported her against her mother's demands. In the daily wear and tear of caring for parents and the struggles for differentiation, Mr. and Mrs. Adano found little energy or interest for sex. Mr. Adano developed a variety of hobbies to fill his time, which his wife also criticized.

---

[11]Since the use of formal surnames in this and subsequent vignettes may capture the reader's attention, some additional comment is in order. I refer to *all* patients formally for many months into treatment, regardless of their age. In many cases, for varying reasons, this continues throughout treatment. It has systemic advantages in some cases (discussed in *The Intimacy Paradigm*), and is a matter of mutual comfort and deference in others. Some readers may not see this as anything other than ageism; to me, writing this other than I have feels uncomfortable to my ear and uncharacteristic of my professional style. Consider this an act of personal differentiation.

Couples' level of differentiation is a crucial determinant of success in coping with the time demands, priority conflicts, and normal sadness and grieving that follow shifts in the life cycle.

Mr. and Mrs. Klein, parents of two grown children, entered treatment for long-term difficulties with intimacy and sexual dysfunction. Both spouses were in their early sixties and both remained highly fused with their respective widowed mothers, who took turns dominating the couple. Mrs. Klein's mother's sister, who had functioned as a surrogate parent during Mrs. Klein's childhood, also dominated her with her mother's tacit approval. The mother and her sister fought constantly, triangling Mrs. Klein as the referee in their arguments. The aging sisters' relationship was no more differentiated than was Mrs. Klein's relationship with either of them.

Treatment was fairly protracted, extending over the course of several years. Mr. Klein's mother died, after which time he showed marked improvement in his own level of functioning. He began to stand up to his wife's verbal abuse and accusations. Where he had previously offered his wife control of their daughter as replacement for his own emotional unavailability, he now supported his daughter in her efforts to differentiate from her mother.

Mrs. Klein, however, entered into a protracted period of slavishly tending to her mother's and her aunt's medical problems and domestic needs. Unfortunately, attempts to satisfy the demands of both "mothers" only fueled the competition and rivalry between the aged sisters. Mrs. Klein terminated treatment as it became evident that her husband was becoming more independent of her. She became more accusatory and demanding. Mr. Klein's sexual functioning failed to improve, which his wife cited as the basis for her own chronic lack of sexual desire. Mrs. Klein denied any need for treatment on her own part, blaming all the marital problems on her husband's "unemotionality" and "spinelessness." However, he continued in treatment and proceeded to become more differentiated from his wife, as did his daughter.

Eventually the aunt died after a long illness, and Mrs. Klein entered intensive individual treatment with another therapist some months later. She became more resilient to her mother's attempts to control her through guilt induction and threats of her own impending demise. Mr. Klein recognized this as a significant shift in his wife's level of functioning. He also began to show marked improvement in sexual interest, although his erectile difficulties did not improve.

Gradually, Mr. Klein began to report that his wife's acceptance of his initiations were less condescending and ambivalent, although she remained highly inhibited in her sexual response. Mrs. Klein continued to have difficulty becoming aroused, although she refused his offers of prolonged foreplay. Gradually, Mr. Klein became sufficiently differentiated to introduce and sustain effective modifications in foreplay technique that his wife had adamantly refused previously. Eventually, Mrs. Klein's increasing sexual arousal and slight demonstrations of enjoyment permitted him to relax sufficiently for his own sexual functioning to improve. Mr. Klein became able to *feel* the ever-shifting level of emotional connectedness between them. The couple progressed to being able to look at each other during sexual activity, whereas Mrs. Klein had previously insisted on staring at the ceiling or closing her eyes.

In this case, the reasons why both spouses demonstrated improved sexual and emotional functioning upon the death of their parents were complex and multisystemic. There was the removal of a "spectator" in their bedroom, and greater freedom from parental expectations; death sometimes offers emotional boundaries that adult children are otherwise unable to establish. Similarly, death of a parent heightens awareness of mortality, paradoxically underscoring discontinuity and separateness while reinforcing family lineage and appreciation of one's partner.

THE TEMPTATION OF HALF-TRUTHS

Recent years have witnessed a dramatic increase in public and professional awareness of the high frequency and negative impact of child sexual abuse, exploitation, and neglect (Bass & Davis, 1988; Courtois, 1988; Maltz & Holman, 1987). This is long overdue and to be applauded.

Reports of prior sexual exploitation and neglect should be taken seriously. Patients' verbalization of previously concealed abuse can be productive, in and of itself. However, the current focus on childhood victimization may also weigh against a thorough understanding of how a particular individual comes to have sexual dysfunctions and interpersonal difficulties.

"Addiction counselors," "abuse counselors" — *any* therapist who develops a professional identity based on an a priori approach to a particular problem — may see their patients (and the world) through a myopic lens. Family therapists may become so enamored with reports of family history that intergenerational *similarity* is confused with *causality*. Sex therapists may similarly be guilty of explaining all contemporary marital distress as the result of sexual difficulties. Clinicians can and *must* look for the rich mélange of factors underlying particular difficulties, being flexible in assigning the pivotal position around which all other factors will be conceptually and therapeutically arranged.

On the other hand, causation can be commonplace, perhaps even pedestrian in simplicity. Precipitious acceptance of the prevailing view of "sexual normality" often precludes recognition of problem-maintaining patterns. What is normal and endemic may be invisibly pathogenic to an individual, a society, and to treatment. Clinicians enamored with pathology, trauma, and family history may confuse *potential* causes of sexual and relationship difficulties with *actual* causes in a particular case. Distinguishing causal factors of *sexual dysfunction* and factors contributing to restricted *sexual potential* helps maintain perspective.

What we have here is another of the pitfalls of believing half-truths — half-truths not in the sense of falsehoods, but in the literal sense: They are true as far as they go, but block understanding of alternative, equally valid, simultaneous realities. Recognition of a significant contributing factor often satisfies clinicians enamored of their own pet conceptualizations and simple solutions; however, acceptance of such half-truths as *truth* inhibits exploration of other factors contributing to causation and maintenance of clinical problems and restricted development.

The question is not whether the therapist can "trust" the patient's report. *The patient's report is always accurate. It is the therapist's job to figure out what it is accurate about.* That job involves a tolerance for multiple causation, multiple realities, and a steadfast unwillingness to settle for simple answers to complexities like eroticism, sexual behavior, and relationship dynamics.

Childhood experiences, positive and negative, *do* have an affect on adult intimate functioning. And one cannot make it to adulthood without childhood experiences. On the other hand, patients attribute current difficulties to past experiences, in avoidance or ignorance of contemporary, age-appropriate, contributory adult issues. Effective clinical approach does not involve doubting the veracity of reported childhood experiences, but rather, remaining open to their significance in the etiology of particular difficulties. Attribution of causation to childhood experiences can maintain ineffective solutions: Adult intimacy and eroticism, particularly at high levels of intensity, are fraught with traumas and struggles.

Contemporary dyadic issues commonly replicate and stimulate prior childhood difficulties, creating a complex situation. A common case example illustrates this situation:

A young couple, Phyllis and Morgan, presented with problems of female inhibited sexual desire and marital discord. At the outset Phyllis reported that her problems predated the marriage: She had been sexually fondled by her stepfather for over five years, starting at the age of six. She reported she never liked sex, and felt she needed individual treatment to resolve her sexual trauma. Defending his own demands for sex, Morgan said he never realized his wife was so affected by this childhood trauma. Had Phyllis been more obviously disturbed and upset, Morgan suggested, he would have been more considerate. Morgan was supportive of Phyllis's request for individual treatment.

The above conceptualization was palatable to the anxious couple, although it perpetuated their problem. Morgan was only too happy to see himself as the secondary victim of his wife's prior sexual abuse. However, this conceptualization – that the current situation was only the manifestation of prior sexual abuse – overlooked (a) the complexity of what was occurring and (b) the need for multidimensional intervention.

While the couple saw the increasing awareness of prior childhood sexual abuse as a problem in itself, it reflected Phyllis's readiness to address and resolve this long-hidden issue. Phyllis's suggestion of individual treatment as a necessary precursor to dyadic work might be the approach of choice in some cases, but not in all – and not in this one. Such a program would have validated the couple's prior conceptualization. Phyllis appeared to possess sufficient ego strength to work concurrently on the childhood abuse and the marital "pushing and shoving" occurring around sexual and nonsexual issues. Since many of the childhood issues actually paralleled the current marital sexual dynamics and styles of interaction, the latter could be used as an arena in which the former could be resolved without encouraging regression in Phyllis's functioning.

Since Phyllis and Morgan were all too ready to attribute everything to sexual abuse problems, I used this framework to introduce a more realistic focus on their contemporary marital and sexual dynamics. Phyllis and Morgan's current style of sexual interaction had its own deleterious impact, both in its immediate effects and in replicating and reinforcing more remote issues. First I asked the couple to describe the style of their most recent sexual encounters. Then I suggested that "sexual abuse" consisted not only of inappropriate sexual contact, but also of the use of sexuality to abuse oneself or one's partner.

I suggested that Morgan was sexually abusing his wife by "mind fucking" her: Statements of "wanting to please" her were only manipulations to gain physical access to her for self-gratification. Like her childhood stepfather, Morgan chose to overlook obvious cues of Phyllis' unwilling and coerced participation. He reinforced what his wife had "learned" previously: Men want sex only for their own selfish desire and care little about the feelings of their female partners. Moreover, Morgan encouraged her to act irresponsibly by (a) having sex with her when it was clear that she did not want to; (b) allowing her to have sex when she said she wanted to even though she remained passive or issued ambiguous signals; and (c) pestering her to the point that acting hysterical or gravely disabled was the only way she could effectively dodge his demands.

Similarly, I suggested to Phyllis that she was abusing herself and her partner. She revictimized herself, making her prior difficulty the apparent cause of her (and their) problems. On the one hand, Phyllis seemed to be taking all the responsibility upon herself; on the other hand, doing so was thoroughly irresponsible. Moreover, Phyllis was abusive to her husband through her subtle withholding and passive participation, diminishing Morgan's pleasure both in and out of bed. She, too, misrepresented her intent towards her husband: Her sexual disinterest partially stemmed from her anger at his selfishness and immaturity, and not merely from childhood sexual abuse.

Phyllis and Morgan were initially embarrassed and stunned by the more realistic conceptualization of their situation; they were also relieved by it. It confirmed what each spouse had been perceiving about the other and established a secure footing for treatment. The success of the intervention demonstrated that both the marital relationship and the treatment alliance could tolerate a workable level of intimacy and anxiety. Phyllis and Morgan accepted the increased tension in acknowledging their current interpersonal conflicts in "exchange" for some hope that their difficulty was not totally locked up in the past.

The point of this vignette is *not* that almost all sexually abused women replicate their childhood abuse with their partners (although this is true). *Our discussion is about half-truths.* Recognizing the replay of old events causes some clinicians to precipitously declare the historical events to be the primary determinants of contemporary difficulties, and hence, the de facto focus of treatment. Focusing on broader conceptualization and multisystemic intervention (a) increases the likelihood of treatment success, and (b) permits the resolution of "problems of the past" through *utilization* of present day dilemmas. In *openly* maintaining herself in the face of her husband's demands (and her own sexual desires), Phyllis was able to rework the damage of her erotic lovemap and restricted level of differentiation from long ago.

All attributions of "negative childhood experience" as the basis for adult difficulties with eroticism and intimacy can be taken at face value. The appropriate question becomes: What is the meaning of face value? At the very least, face value means the patient's attributions reflect a perfectly accurate picture of how he/she conceptualizes his/her own predicament. On the other hand, it may reflect a perfectly accurate picture of how the patient invites the therapist to see it; either way, it is an important piece of information about the patient. The therapist's response to the patient's presentation is an important piece of information about the therapist.

As another example, consider the ubiquitous report of "strict religious upbringing." Such reports should not be disregarded, but neither should they be automatically accepted as the root cause of inhibited eroticism or passion. It is wiser to *simultaneously* consider contributory contemporary factors, such as having picked a partner well equipped to play out the power and gender role issues inherent in strict religious upbringing. Contemporary life-stage issues replicating and stimulating unresolved childhood issues are not simply the "expression" of prior experience, as a unidimensional/unidirectional conceptualization would suggest. *Process* is missed if one only looks to the past or present for *facts*. As Maturana and Varela (1987) note, one needs to walk the razor's edge.

If one hypothesizes that a particular factor is implicated in sexual dysfunction or lack of sexual desire, one must develop a complete and plausible explanation of the manner in which such factors exert their influence on genital functioning and phenomenological experience. Once this is developed and cross-validated against other known information, one has only established that it is a *plausible contributing* factor.

Whether one accepts inhibited sexual desire to be caused by "unconscious hatred and desire to deprive men," "unconscious loyalty to stabilize a parent's marriage," "flashbacks to childhood sexual trauma," or "distracting mind-wandering during sex regarding the partner's affair," the manner in which such processes actually affect sexual functioning must also be stipulated. The absence of such delineation creates a situation reminiscent of psychoanalysis in the mid 1950s, from which modern sex therapy revolted. Therapists must think through the specific dynamics of sexual functioning and phenomenological intensity, from "loyalty" to mother to lack of physical response, and all the complex intervening steps in between. This is no simple task.

In the subsequent chapter, we will continue our focus on eroticism and systemic processes. There we will find the need for multisystemic conceptualization and intervention applicable as well. The topic of *extramarital affairs* often meets with smiles, scowls, and some genuinely unsystematic clinical thinking.

CHAPTER TWELVE

The Extended Emotional System: Lovers and Friends

This chapter addresses the poignant and (sometimes) humorous sides of marriage, monogamy, and extramarital affairs. Human noncyclical sexual interest and pair-bounding, which emerged over four million years ago, create an inevitable tension between two opposing impulses: the desire for multiple sexual partners and the desire for sexual exclusivity. Level of differentiation is a multifaceted determinant of the likelihood that this tension will emerge in extramarital sex; given common low levels of differentiation, the frequency of affairs is not surprising. Monogamy offers a number of strategic advantages as a crucible for personal development.

Contemporary clinical conceptualizations of affairs leave a lot to be desired; the intervention strategies they foster, even more so. Incongruous power hierarchies that permeate affairs play havoc with couples and therapists. An alternative (differentiation-based) treatment approach, stressing isomorphic multisystemic intervention, is proposed. Capacity for self-validated (level-2) intimacy is a critical factor in the resolution of affairs.

Extramarital affairs are something almost no one is neutral about, most are conflicted about, and everyone has an opinion about. Adultery is probably the aspect of sex most written about, by people who seemingly possess firsthand knowledge of the topic; quips and quotes offer a collective reflection of what was perhaps the first (and by some accounts, the most delicious) sexual crucible since humans developed the capacity for pair-bonding.

Depending on culture, politics, psychological theory, and need to validate personal behavior, affairs are variously seen as (a) the height of sophistication or depravity, (b) the pursuit or avoidance of intimacy, or (c) healthy or pathological sexual expression. Some argue that adultery is the *savoire faire* of a mature adult; others find it to be the antithesis of adulthood. One has only to review the shifts in sexual values within the United States during the mid 1800s (or the 1960s) to recognize their temporal nature (D'Emilio & Freedman, 1988), and the way they have often been promoted by health-care providers as "scientific knowledge" (Duffy, 1987).

Over the ages our views of affairs, and who should have them, have changed greatly in some ways and little in others. In some generations it was almost expected that men would have extramarital dalliances. However, they still had their *propriety* to consider: *cuckoldry* has always been unseemly, particularly involving a lower caste Romeo. Modern folks erroneously conclude "heathens" had *no* standards when it came to monogamy, when, in fact, they had *two*.

> When a woman commits adultery with a man of a caste inferior to her husband's she shall be torn to pieces by dogs, and in some public place. (The Mahabharata (c. 350 B.C.), in Seldes, 1985)

> If thou findest thy wife in adultery, thou art free to kill her without trial, and canst not be punished. If, on the other hand, thou committest adultery, she durst not, and she has no right to, so much as lay a finger on thee. (Marcus Poricus Cato (234–149 B.C), in Seldes, 1985)

There have always been those, however, less sexist and more discerning in values: With the advent of Catholicism, *everyone* became an adulterer. Before long, give or take a couple of centuries, you could have an affair if you weren't careful how you looked or thought. Some folks had affairs and didn't even know it; some did and enjoyed them (until publicly acknowledged).

> Passion is the evil in adultery. If a man has no opportunity of living with another man's wife, but if it is obvious for some reason that he would like to do so, and would do so if he could, he is no less guilty than if he was caught in the act. (Saint Augustine (354–430 A.D.), in Seldes, 1985)

> I've looked on a lot of women with lust. I've committed adultery in my heart many times. This is something that God recognizes I will do—and I have done it—and God forgives me for it. (Jimmy Carter (1924–), in Augarde, 1991)

Sanctions against affairs often vary with duration, deception, disclosure, gender, and circumstance. "Friendships" during long-term separation, or a spouse's protracted terminal illness, are received with greater equanimity than are (a) a long-term history of business trip one-night stands, (b) cavorting with your best friend's spouse, or (c) frolicking with one half of a couple you and your spouse see regularly.

Are humans capable of monogamy? If it's possible, is it natural? Does it require men and women to fight their basic nature? There are those who have always argued that monogamy is *unnatural*. Conversely, there are those who argue that all that is natural is neither wise nor healthy. Concerned citizens of every generation have argued against the evils of "promiscuity" and "inconstancy":

> As concerning lust or incontinency, it is a short pleasure bought with a long pain, a honeyed poison, a gulf of shame, a pickpurse, a breeder of disease, a gall to the conscience, a corrosive to the heart, turning man's wit into foolish madness, the body's bane, and the soul's perdition. (John Taylor (1580–1653), in Seldes, 1985)

> Accursed from birth they be
> who seek to find monogamy,
> Pursuing it from bed to bed
> I think they would be better dead.
> (Dorothy Parker, in Tripp, 1970)

While morality *is* important, it is problematic when it surfaces (as it has recently) in the guise of modern psychology and mental health science:

> Because our sexuality is one of our most fundamental life processes, sexual compulsiveness is extremely threatening to all of us. The intensity of our fears can be easily measured by the complex mosaic of proscriptions, laws, taboos we use to guide our sexual behavior. This mosaic is the real expression of our values and cultural wisdom. When someone breaks a sexual taboo, i.e., goes beyond the socially acceptable limit, everyone's trust is shaken in our most fundamental social bonds—those "rules," written or commonly understood, which allow us as individuals to live comfortably with each other as a society. (Carnes, 1983)

There have always been proselytizers who position themselves as the champions of morality vs. amorality. Likewise, there are others who correctly recognize that pseudo-morality is the banner of fascism; they argue that the "moralists" have duped us all.[1]

What is pornography to one man is the laughter of genius to another. If a woman hasn't got a tiny streak of harlot in her, she's a dry stick as a rule. . . .

---

[1]The following two remarks are relevant to contemporary controversies over other sexual health-care issues (i.e., access to birth control/condoms and abortion) and *some* sexually explicit materials.

And there are, of course, many people who are genuinely repelled by the simplest and most natural stirrings of sexual feeling. But these people are perverts who have fallen into hatred of their fellow man: thwarted, disappointed, unfulfilled people, of whom, alas, our civilization contains so many. (D. H. Lawrence (1885–1930), in Seldes, 1985)

I never came across someone in whom the moral sense was dominant who was not heartless, cruel, vindictive, log-stupid, and entirely lacking in the smallest sense of humanity. Moral people, as they are termed, are simply beasts. I would sooner have fifty unnatural vices than one unnatural virtue. (Oscar Wilde (1854–1900), in Seldes, 1985)

The psychology of adultery has been falsified by conventional morals, which assume, in monogamous countries, that attraction for one person cannot coexist with a serious affection for another. Everybody knows that this is untrue. (Bertrand Russell (1872–1970), in Seldes, 1985)

But who is there to save us from those who would save us from sexual excess? In avoiding "petty bourgeois morality" about multiple couplings, they miss the point that only a *therapist* would address. The question is not, *"Can you feel eroticism and passion for more than one person at a time (particularly when you are married)?"* Certainly everyone does. Nor is the question, *"If humans are inherently capable of feeling such things, isn't it also 'natural' to act on them?"* Such feelings are inherent in (a) reaching one's sexual potential, and (b) membership in a gregarious species, but neither requires acting them out. The question is, *"What is the impact of married people acting or not acting upon such feelings, and what causes them to do so or not?"*

SWIMMING IN THE MARITAL SOUP

What causes extramarital affairs? Without being overly flippant, some think the cause is marriage itself. It just might be that sexually *normal* marriages (i.e., the exigencies of normal marital sexuality) cause affairs. Given the rarity of people doing much to explore their sexual potential, it is no wonder: Marriage and marital sex are often a disappointment.

Niagara Falls is only the second biggest disappointment of the standard honeymoon. (Oscar Wilde, in Peter, 1980)

A man marries to have a home, but also because he doesn't want to be bothered with sex and all that sort of thing. (Somerset Maugham, in Peter, 1980)

It would be misguided, however, to suggest that affairs stem mainly from mediocre sex. Some argue that the marital bed remains the hot bed of sex; people report greater variety of sexual behavior in marriage than in extracurricular assignations (Zilbergeld, 1991). So, are marriage and monogamy inherently mutually exclusive? Is monogamy antithetical to our basic nature? Monogamy is often accepted ambivalently, if not begrudgingly. One clergyman boldly admitted, "The vow of fidelity is an absurd commitment, but it is the heart of marriage" (Father Robert Capon).

Is it the quest for romance that propels affairs? Many couples' personal experience suggests that romantic long-term marriage is an oxymoron. Marriage often starts out with poetry and shifts into prose; forgetting to send cards on special occasions (and no occasion at all) is not far behind.[2]

Marriage encourages adultery when we forget that our partner is a separate person, and not a personal convenience. Once we think of our spouse as just another set of hands, marital sex becomes nothing more than masturbation.[3] Once this has happened, the ignored and the ignorer often wander. The right hand stops knowing what the left hand is doing; sometimes *both* are "doing," but not each other.

> No matter how happily a woman may be married, it always pleases her to discover that there is a nice man who wishes she were not. (H. L. Mencken (1880–1956), in Peter, 1980)

Even when romance remains in the marital bed, convenience and opportunity often suffice instead. Stephen Stills' song *"If you can't be with the one you love, love the one you're with"* was a paean to the casual sex "revolution" of the 1960s. Herein lies the common pattern of romance in marriage and affairs: It seems easier to love the one you're *not* with. Its better-said counterpart from a century ago suggests this is nothing new.

> 'Tis sweet to think, that, where'er we rove,
> We are sure to find something blissful and dear,
> And that, when we're far from the lips we love,
> We've but to make love to the lips we are near.
> (Thomas Moore (1779–1852), in Tripp, 1970)

---

[2]Chapters Thirteen and Fourteen will illustrate the utility of the sexual crucible in keeping romance alive within long-term marriages.

[3]This is not to slur the good name of masturbation, but rather, to indicate that people's experiences cause them to look upon masturbation pejoratively: *when most people have sex by themselves, there is* no one *there*. A positive view and a positive *use* of masturbation (far beyond cranking out orgasms) are detailed in *The Intimacy Paradigm*.

"If you stray, should you tell?" The problem in even a mediocre long-term marriage is that your spouse knows you well enough that *not* finding out takes effort. If it takes no effort at all, the marriage that preceded was probably worse than you wanted to know.

Coming Up for Air

The foregoing analysis of marriage as the cause of extramarital trysts is offered (somewhat) tongue-in-cheek. However, it is poignant how badly couples *want* to be satisfied with their marriage. For those who develop the requisite maturity, marriage is the place were the partner's hair still smells like *home, comfort,* and *sex,* all in one, after 30 years together.

> Marriage is the result of the longing for the deep, deep peace of the double bed after the hurly-burly of the chaise-longue. (Mrs. Patrick Campbell (1865–1940), in *Concise Oxford,* 1981)

> My definition of marriage: It resembles a pair of shears, so joined that they cannot be separated; often moving in opposite directions, yet always punishing anyone who comes between them. (Rev. Sydney Smith (1771–1845), in *Concise Oxford,* 1981)

To the degree that affairs predispose divorce, helping people reach their sexual potential is not merely "optional." In the face of AIDS, divorce, single parent families, and other social ills spread by extramarital affairs, improving the quality of married life might be the single greatest boon to national economic, social and emotional health (see Table 12.1).

Some clinicians ride the crest of this problem, promoting the notion of "sexual addiction." In defining the parameters of this new "disease," they indict the common behavior of (a) young adults, (b) single and divorced middle-aged men and women, and (c) the average person in a normal marriage who values eroticism more than his or her partner, but who lacks the differentiation to propel the relationship forward:

> Think of . . . the partnered woman who remains technically monogamous, yet spends hours in a dream world of romance and sexual trysts with other men; the woman who destroys her relationship through her compulsion to flirt and have affairs; the woman who frequents singles bars and picks up men, risking disease and violence; the woman who wants a long-term relationship but feels compelled to leave her partners when sex loses its high. . . . (Kasl, 1989, p. 5)

Others consider this same pattern to be a personality trait. Kinsey et al. (1948, 1953) noted a subcategory of individuals they labeled "sociosexual,"

Table 12.1
Incidence of Extramarital Affairs

Kinsey (1948)	50% of married men
Kinsey (1952)	25% of women under age 40
Athanasiou et al. (1970)	40% of married men; 36% of married women (*Psychology Today readers*)
Hunt (1974)	47% of married men under age 40
Tavris & Sadd (1977)	39% of married women age 40 and over (*Redbook readers*)
Wolfe (1980)	69% of married women over age 35 (*Cosmopolitan readers*)

characterized by numerous sexual partners in uncommitted relationships, extramarital sex, and partner-replacement sexual fantasies. Byrne and Schulte (1990) suggest low sociosexuality is more common among women than men (e.g., preferring committed, close relationships as prerequisites to sexual involvement); within-sex differences, however, exceed those between the sexes. They postulate multiple underpinnings of this "trait": "the desire for diversity and novelty, a sociopathic inability to become emotionally close to a romantic partner, and (especially among females) using uncommitted sex instrumentally as a way to attract and retain desirable partners" (p. 108).

Are men and women fundamentally promiscuous? Are affairs a sign of illness, a personality trait, a lack of morality, or an expression of humans' basic "animal" nature? To the average person, such hard questions lack even provisional answers. The common solution is to approach the problem as strictly a matter of personal values (or one in which values and behavior expectedly differ); many clinicians do likewise.

Therapists approach the problem as if (a) science offers little clinically useful information in this area, and (b) continual concern for "laying one's values on the patient" is the best strategy one might hope for. While the latter vigilance *is* important, the former assumption is unfounded. *Two* sources of information are useful, one anthropological, and the other clinical. We will consider both in turn.

A SOCIOBIOLOGICAL VIEW

Monogamy is often presupposed to be an artificial social convention, alien to people's basic nature. Helen Fisher (1982) points out that anthropologists of the 19th and 20th century (like those since the first century A.D.) have promoted the notion that humans have always been promiscuous. An anthropologist herself, Fisher finds this assumption to be half-true: chimpanzees, gorillas, orangutans, and every other higher primate except gibbons (and their close relative, the siamang) are promiscuous.[4] She writes:

> So there is every reason to think we were promiscuous in the dim days of our first beginnings. That we have not yet totally shed this habit is obvious. (p. 87)

However, the other half of the truth concerns the evolutionary transition of female sexual functioning, which Fisher refers to as the most spectacular sexual revolution the world has ever witnessed. She offers a picture of our basic sexual "nature" which is both compelling and different from common simplistic viewpoints.

Fisher presents a sociobiological narrative, detailing the evolution of human eroticism as a recursive response to the *interpersonal environment*, as well as an adaptation to the general physical habitat. Her approach is consistent with that of Maturana and Varela (1987), compatible with Kerr and Bowen's (1988) conceptualization of natural systems theory, and remarkably similar to our previous discussion of neocortical evolution in the emergent capacity for intimacy (Chapter Four). Fisher's focus pertains to a major evolutionary advance *immediately preceding* the period in which the neocortex evolved.

In *The Sex Contract: The Evolution of Human Behavior* (1982), Fisher details the evolution of protohominid females from estrus-controlled to noncyclical patterns of sexual interest and behavior, and the corresponding emergence of *pair-bonding*. Prior to this transition, female protohominid sexual interest was (as in many other animals) confined to a (ten-day) period surrounding ovulation. During this time, females engaged in multiple sexual couplings. Outside of this period (or from pregnancy through the subsequent two years of infant nursing), sexual behavior ceased.

During her periods of sexual interest, a female was the center of attention of a small band of lovers who traveled with her, protecting and feeding her; once pregnant or nursing, she and her child tagged along, fending for them-

---

[4]John Money (1985) states: "Among the great apes . . . gorillas and chimpanzees are troopbonding species. Orangutans in the wild are not. Pairs meet in the jungle. When the female is in heat, they mate, and then separate until their next encounter. Gibbons, like siamang, are pairbonders. They do not form extended kinship troops, but families of two parents and children. Among nonhuman primates, they are said to most closely approximate the nuclear family of human beings" (p. 10).

selves as best they could. Tired from the demands of childcare, she was less able to feed and protect herself and her offspring.

Fisher describes the beginning of the transition:

> And so it was among the female protohominids—some were sexier than others. A few females had unusually long monthly cycles, remaining in heat for as long as two or three weeks. Some had the outstanding ability and inclination to copulate during much of their pregnancy. A few resumed sexual behavior months or even years before they weaned their young.
>
> In former days, these females had no particular advantages. They simply engaged in sex more often than did normal females. But by 8 million years ago, the more amorous females acquired enormous benefits—particularly as new mothers. Why? Because this was a crucial time in human evolution—a time when the complications of walking had selected for protohominid females who bore their young too soon. Now all the females had to carry and feed their young for longer and longer periods of time. But those females who came back into heat soon after delivering their young received the attentions of an entourage of suitors. Everywhere they went they were in the middle of the group. This had tremendous gains.
>
> Thus the new mother who came into heat soon after parturition received extra meat and protection for the part of every month she provided sex. These profits she shared with her infant. And because of these special benefits, her baby had a better chance to live into adulthood than did the infants of nonestrus mothers. More of the infants of sexier mothers did live, grow up, and breed—passing this genetic anomaly to a greater percentage of the next generation. Selection had begun to favor those unusual females who resumed sexual activity soon after delivering their young.
>
> Like these females, those who offered sex during pregnancy received the benefits of male attention too. . . . And with time, females who engaged in sex during pregnancy proliferated in the protohominid population.
>
> Among them were a few who had a slightly longer period of heat each month. Because they were in estrus longer, they acquired more meat and more protection than females with shorter cycles. . . .
>
> As generation passed, selection gradually produced more and more female protohominids who copulated for a longer period of their monthly cycle; who made love during pregnancy; who had sex sooner after parturition. Protohominid females were beginning to lose their period of heat. With this, daily life began to change again. (pp. 89–91)

Fisher personifies the 8 million year old transition through a saucy little protohominid named "Hoot" who predated "Lucy," the prototypic hominid, by some 4 million years. One couldn't say Hoot didn't give a hoot; according to Fisher she did, repeatedly. Hoot's sexual interest made her a celebrity with the local men ever since her adolescence. Hoot reconfirmed her stardom through her unique interest in sex during pregnancy. Hoot's next claim to fame, however, was her transition to wanting sex while still nursing her child:

> As the dry season became monotonous, Hoot yearned for her old life, her carousing, her wandering with the males. She wanted some meat too. Then one morning she woke up feeling strange. She nursed her infant and then reached for a sleeping comrade and pulled him to his feet. He woke up blinking, but in moments his haziness had moved to astonishment. Hoot was rubbing against him, enticing him to make love to her. He was happy to oblige and the commotion roused the others. Hoot's old lovers were overjoyed. They had not expected Hoot to start making love until her infant was walking and eating vegetables. But here she was, up to her old tricks months before her daughter was even weaned.

As Hoot continued to be receptive on a daily basis, her male friends returned, following and feeding her although she had not returned to estrus.

> There had been other ladies like Hoot in the prairie. Her mother had attracted a coterie of suitors and there were two well-known females who distracted everyone at the annual rendezvous near the lake. But none would do what Hoot did next.

Fisher suggests that constantly available sex provided the stimulus for a profound sociobiological recursion: pairbonding. Hoot selected one male (who was unusually good with infants) and copulated only with him. They shared food and gradually divided labor according to ability; they moved together across the savannah during the changing seasons.

Over successive generations, females developed other sexual traits that increased their survival (and hence, genetic selection) because men liked them; this included more complex erotic "maps" (as discussed in Chapter Eleven). In the process, males were picked (i.e., genetically selected) for the tendency to *bond*.

> Other sexual cement helped too. Some females were capable of intense sexual pleasure during copulation. A few had the physiological equipment for multiple orgasm. Others orgasmed continually during intercourse. Some experienced satiation-insatiation, the female physiological response during copulation in which the more orgasms she has the more she can have and the stronger they become. Some females experienced the premenstrual tension syndrome—a period of heightened sexual desire at the end of their monthly cycles. A few females

retained a high sex drive way past their youth, experiencing a peak in sexual activity in middle life. Finally some females had the anatomy to enjoy sex even more after childbirth than before.

Not only regular, intense sex attracted the males—so did intimate sex. And for this, face-to-face copulation was necessary. Unlike all other female primates, the human female today possesses a forward-tilting vaginal canal, one designed for frontal copulation. . . . sex was intensely pleasurable in this position [due to the location of the clitoris being massaged by the male's pubic region]. But frontal copulation had another advantage. Each partner could see the other's face, observe nuances of expression, and express his own. Face-to-face copulation nurtured intimacy, communication, and understanding. It strengthened the ties between sexual partners. (pp. 94–95)

Selection for loss of estrus periodicity, copulation during pregnancy, and rapid resumption after parturition eventually had profound impacts (see Table 12.2). By the time Lucy came along, hominids had developed centripetal extended families, nuclear families in dry season, bonding, serial monogamy, evolution of social emotions, and incipient kinship and language.

So . . . what has all this got to do with monogamy and extramarital affairs?

Fisher states that pair-bonding evolved more than 4 million years ago, cemented by frequent sex. This bond was not permanent—pairings often lasted only through the offspring's infancy. While it is no longer necessary to keep the young alive, *bonding* is like other evolutionarily acquired behavior patterns: It is deeply engraved in the human psyche.

Upon this primate pattern man developed bonding—and with it all the basic human emotions that kept bonds intact. Like our other primitive fears and

Table 12.2
Impact of Protohominid Noncyclical Sexual Desire

1. Increased female fertility

2. Females overburdened with more premature births

3. Extended consorts and incipient bonding

4. Male/female sharing and division of labor

5. Sexual selection for male/female secondary sexual characteristics

6. Incorporation of male into nuclear family/matricentric extended family

7. Selection for individuals with tendency to bond

Derived from Fisher (1982), pp. 227–228.

habits, these emotions have not been shed. We still flirt. We still feel infatuation at the beginning of our bond, allegiance during it, and often sorrow when it is over. We feel guilty when we are promiscuous, jealous or vengeful when our bond is sexually betrayed. Men still worry about being cuckolded. Women still worry about being deserted. We don't need these emotions in our industrial world. We don't need the bond—yet we continue to do it.

To bond is human. It began long ago with the sex contract, and though the rules of the contract will change with the changing times, the instinct to make a contract will prevail. (p. 224, italics added)

Fisher's point is that, by and large, we are not as monogamous as we think, but more prone to pair-bonding than the frequency of adultery might suggest:

Promiscuity and adultery are found in every society ever studied—probably because we are naturally promiscuous, as are our ape relatives. (p. 222)[5]

We practice "serial monogamy," bonding first with one mate, breaking up, and bonding with another. So do people in all other societies. Divorce is permitted everywhere. Yet most individuals around the world who do divorce will proceed to bond again. (p. 223)

There are several principal versions of monogamy:

- (a) "You can mate with one partner in your life, and never take another partner, regardless" (*strict monogamy*);
- (b) "You can mate with another if this one dies" (*digamy*); and
- (c) "You can mate for extended periods with other partners, but only one at a time" (*serial monogamy*).

Digamy (the traditional marital vow) and serial monogamy are the versions most commonly ascribed to these days; strict monogamy was more common in prior generations and still surfaces in the musings of young lovers. Serial monogamy represents common bottom-line concerns about boundaries and functional exclusivity. Some cynics suggest serial monogamy is merely socially condoned promiscuity stretched over time—laying the groundwork for arguing that adultery is inevitable.

---

[5]The dictionary defines *promiscuous* as the quality of being mixed, mingled, confused, or undistinguished. In scientific application, it is a value-neutral term referring to multiple couplings with different partners. In common sexual parlance, it implies varying degrees of pejorative value-laden connotation. Most commonly, it refers to "casual" sexual intercourse, engaged in with many people, as an end in itself. In its most negative sense, it refers to immoral, lewd, and licentious behavior. Fisher's use of the term is scientifically accurate, but does not denote the highly negative view of sex and the base view of humankind promoted by some religious fundamentalists.

Does this mean that adultery is inherent in the nature of our species? Fisher suggests that the *impulse* is inherent, but what about the *behavior?* Having arrived at this point by way of Fisher's work, we will venture a tentative answer that continues her sociobiological view of human development (i.e., evolution).

The critical question is often formulated incorrectly. The issue is not (a) "Aren't men and women naturally promiscuous?" or (b) "Isn't it natural to want sexual exclusivity of one's partner?" The answer seems to be yes . . . *to both questions*. Long-term monogamy involves a conflict between *two* basic natures: Humans have the simultaneous desire for multiple partners and sexual exclusivity. Whether or not affairs occur is not a question of people fighting their basic nature; it is, rather, a battle between *two* impulses.

The conclusion *isn't* that affairs are "normal" or that monogamy is like putting a tuxedo on a gorilla (or more accurately, on a gibbon); it *is*, however, that marriage and monogamy are more likely to be short term (and affairs more common) when people lack the capacity to tolerate the tension.

From this perspective, the problem is *not* unique: It is the fight of wanting two choices at the same time, when only one is available. It involves wanting sexual diversity for *oneself* and monogamy for *one's partner*. Inherent paradox exists at the very core of development of the individual and of the species. The solution to the two-choice problem is a familiar one: *differentiation.*[6]

How does one approach the sexual crucible? Does one vent the pressure or let it build up? If it builds (rather than being vented via an affair), the evolutionary pressures for pair-bonding and promiscuity remain; such tension may be just the ticket to drive our species, as individuals and as a whole, to a higher higher level of differentiation. We all participate in the continuation of human evolution.[7]

How does one accomplish this in one's lifetime? An alternative to common life-long struggles with impulse control involves undergoing a differentiation-based multisystemic paradigm shift, in which:

---

[6]The "two-choice" dilemma, previously discussed in Chapter Six, will be referred to repeatedly in this chapter. This problem can be approached (intellectually) from another direction: the study of *ethics* regarding contracts and obligations. Fisher refers to the sex *contract* in this sense. We will address the topic of sexual ethics at the conclusion of this chapter.

[7]If one jumps to a meta-level at this point, it becomes apparent that we have developed a "process" view of evolution, rather than a autocratic one: We, our children, and the generations of *families* participate in bringing forth the nature of humankind, as opposed to "merely" playing out Hoot's genetics. If that sounds a little spiritual, it should. In our quest for a single isomorphic intervention (simultaneously congruent on multiple dimensions), it is a *very* short conceptual bridge to the core of *process theology* (to be discussed in Chapter Seventeen). However, our focus is not merely philosophical; shortly we will detail the utility of monogamy in driving *individual* development forward.

- monogamy is no longer based on exchange or reciprocity;
- monogamy results from a unilateral vow *to oneself*;
- one no longer feels controlled sexually by one's spouse;
- one's spouse is relinquished as an extension of oneself;
- one has all the sexual intimacy and eroticism, mystery, and novelty one can handle, right at home.

Our description of differentiation in previous chapters now sounds like a prescription for dealing with the urge for multiple couplings: (a) the ability to shift from limbic to neocortical emotional responses, (b) dampening of reflexive emotionality, (c) increased ability to modulate tension and frustration, (d) non-reactivity to other people's reactivity, and (e) the ability to tolerate pain for growth.

The route to this outcome is simple to articulate and hard to traverse. Strengthening marital bonding through increased differentiation (and level-2 intimacy) has several impacts: (a) increased neocortical control of emotionality and impulsiveness which disinclines one to affairs; (b) increased capacity for sexual intimacy, curiosity, and novelty with one's spouse; and (c) increased erotic display and gratification.

Sex itself might be *different* but probably no *better* with someone else; it lacks the custom tailored fit of knowledgeable partners and the clean wallop of wall-socket eroticism that stems from one's *integrity*.[8] Making a commitment to oneself as a matter of integrity is easier when one really *wants* and *prefers* sex with one's spouse; dealing with the existential crisis of finite options is *much* easier when one is not choosing monogamy and sexual martyrdom at the same time.

CLINICAL VIEW OF EXTRAMARITAL SEX

No doubt some readers will take issue with some aspect of the foregoing analysis. There are few topics that cause more disagreements among therapists than affairs or that raise more concern about confusing personal values and therapeutic strategy. Discussion of affairs tends to trigger therapists' own conflicts, prompting a remarkable degree of attention in the professional literature (Atwater, 1982; Bernard, 1977; Block, 1987; Cuber & Harroff, 1965; Glass

---

[8]Although integrity has everything to do with personal morality, our focus here is *clinical* not moral. Integrity is not mentioned here as an end in itself; integrity, integration, and differentiation are actually one and the same. The *utility* of integrity in facilitating intense intimacy and sexuality will be discussed in subsequent chapters.

& Wright, 1977; Glenn & Weaver, 1979; Humphrey, 1987; Hunt, 1969; Lampe, 1987; Leigh, 1985; Libby, 1977; Lusterman, 1989; Maykovich, 1976; Myers & Leggitt, 1975; Neubeck, 1969; Spanier & Margolis, 1983; Sprenkle & Weiss, 1978; Strean, 1980; Thompson, 1983, 1984a, 1984b; Walster, Traupmann & Walster, 1978; Weil, 1975; Whitehurst, 1971).

In an effort to avoid appearing "judgmental," some clinicians abandon any discerning clinical judgment; others approach the topic contritely. Scharff (1982), for example, attempted to circumvent the problem of therapist values by limiting the applicability of his analysis of affairs to *patients*; by virtue of seeking treatment, he argued, extramarital affairs are self-defined as failures in the marriage and therefore open to critical comment. Scharff's caveat evades the issue, however, since his analysis pertains to *the nature of affairs per se* and not simply to those couples who seek treatment.

Subtle but salient inconsistencies have gone unnoticed in the contemporary clinical literature concerning affairs. If one suggests (as I do) that affairs are a reflection of low levels of differentiation, and notes the anxiety engendered in therapists by the topic of affairs, then the lack of critical thinking might reflect a lack of differentiation about a lack of differentiation. The discussion contained within this chapter addresses common systemic dynamics that may not apply to all couples in all situations, but which are applicable to a large number of couples, patients and nonpatients alike.

A Look at Two Contemporary Approaches

Frank Pittman's (1987) chapter on marital infidelity and his subsequent book on the topic, *Private Lies: Infidelity and the Betrayal of Intimacy* (1989) offer a remarkable blend of humor and insight on the topic. Pittman (1987) talks about "why people screw around" (p. 98) and refers to the three positions involved as the "infidel," the "cuckold," and the "mistress" or "mister."

Pittman, however, uses the concepts of infidelity and affairs interchangeably—a common practice for many clinicians. Unfortunately, the two concepts shape one's thinking in different directions. The concept of adultery leads to examination of intrapsychic, dyadic, and systemic politics; it addresses behavior or function. *Infidelity*, on the other hand, concerns patients' phenomenological experience; it addresses the pain of the cuckold and the guilt of the infidel. As the subtitle of Pittman's book suggests, the notion of infidelity immediately leads to thinking in terms of betrayal.[9]

---

[9]In the subsequent discussion of affairs, labels for both spouses have been selected which emphasize the violation of personal commitment, rather than violation of the partner's expectations; the clinical

Approaching the discussion from the vantage point of infidelity and betrayal is an invitation for infusing the politics of low-level differentiation in the guise of "love" and "ethics." One need not ignore adultery, betrayal of "trust," or the pain and anguish that such abrogations bring. The point is simply that such concepts take on different meanings at varying levels of differentiation. Most people never reach a sufficient level of differentiation wherein fidelity reflects strength rather than fear and betrayal refers to the violation of self rather than the institutionalization of dependency.

For example, Pittman (1989) identified seven "myths" about extramarital affairs (see Table 12.3). Note that each of these reflects some aspect of low-level differentiation. Contemporary clinical approaches embrace low levels of differentiation and reciprocity (level-1) models of intimacy (discussed in Chapters Four and Five).

The occurrence of affairs and the nonoccurrence of intimacy are two of the most common complaints presented to therapists. Is it possible that prevailing fusion-potentiating treatment approaches for intimacy problems actually predispose the occurrence of affairs, and vice versa? If this clinical conundrum reflects an unnoticed inherent paradox in common social values (and I suggest it does), then it is little wonder that only half of all marriages survive—and the survivors are often not blissful.

It is easy to lose sight of issues of differentiation in the midst of conceptualizing treatment of affairs. For example, Pittman (1989) conceptualizes a topology of infidelity consisting of four categories: *unique, in love, structural,* and *philandering* (habitual infidelity). Pittman's topology is not merely descriptive; he offers different therapeutic strategies for each type. He even suggests ten subcategories of philandering: charming, friendly, heroic, psychopathic, hostile, hobbyists, borderline (attitudinal), impersonal, gay, and female. While

---

reasoning behind this will become clear in the differentiation-based clinical approach to be proposed shortly. *Perfidy* (i.e., the deliberate act of violating a faith or vow) is much closer to the intended focus than *infidelity* or *betrayal* (which emphasize the impact on the spouse.) The term *adulterer* (a married person having sexual contact with someone other than the spouse) will be used because it tends to focus on behavior rather than impact. While this label once had profound social stigma (*e.g., The Scarlet Letter*), the arcaneness of the term has diminished its emotional wallop. Terms such as *cheater, liar, deceiver, philanderer,* and *infidel* have more moralistic and pejorative connotations.

Finding an appropriate label for the other spouse is even *more* difficult. *Cuckold* has the connotations of being outsmarted by the spouse's lover, and of the spouse as one's possession (i.e., someone putting their "eggs" in *your* nest). The term *resolute spouse* (i.e., one who maintains his/her commitment or belief; unwavering, persevering in monogamy) has been selected. In some cases, the resolute spouse may also be resolute in resisting attempts to improve the sexual and/or nonsexual relationship. Nothing more is implied than the fact that he or she has remained monogamous; often the resolute spouse is *not* resolute in the sense of a solid sense of self.

Table 12.3
Foregone Conclusions If Cheatin's on Your Mind*
(*Analysis of Differentiation in Italics*)

1. Everybody is unfaithful; it is normal, expectable behavior.
   (*Low ability to tolerate tension*)
   (*Lack of autonomous values*)
   (*Acts irresponsibly; participates in the irresponsibility of others*)

2. Affairs are good for you; an affair may even revive a dull marriage.
   (*Insufficient capacity for self-validation to drive [sexual] relationship forward*)

3. The adulterer must not love the resolute spouse; the affair proves it.
   (*Reactivity to other's reactivity*)
   (*Need for reflected sense of self*)
   (*Willingness to take partner's behavior as a reflection on self*)

4. The lover must be sexier than the resolute spouse.
   (*same as #3*)

5. The affair is the fault of the resolute spouse, proof that he/she has failed the adulterer in some way that made the affair necessary.
   (*same as #3*)

6. The best approach to the discovery of a spouse's affair is to pretend not to know and thereby avoid a crisis.
   (*same as #1, #2 and #3*)

7. If the affair occurs, the marriage must end in a divorce.
   (*same as #3*)

*Seven "myths" derived from Pittman, 1989, p. 34.

the list is both provocative and entertaining, Pittman's clinical approach to treatment is antithetical to increased differentiation. He writes:

> Philandering is addictive behavior, and, like all addictive behavior, is difficult to change without great honesty and the willingness to put yourself under someone else's control. (p. 181)

Pittman's approach suggests that the philanderer put him/herself under the control of a hospital, a therapist, a 12-step program, or a "higher power"—and dodges the underlying problem. The philanderer is *constantly* organizing life around who will temporarily control him/her (e.g., his/her latest paramour or therapist) and who never will (e.g., his/her spouse and former conquests). Pittman (1990) himself recognizes that the philanderer is often driven by fears of being controlled by someone else. However, the one control the philanderer most categorically refuses is self-control (which is the operational definition of low-level differentiation).

David Moultrup's (1990) approach offers another backdrop upon which these subtle and complex conceptual and clinical issues can be seen. To the casual reader, Moultrup's approach to affairs might appear somewhat similar to some aspects of this book. He couches his conceptual framework in Bowenian concepts now familiar to the reader: differentiation, triangulation, multigenerational patterns, and systemic regulation of anxiety. The similarities, however, are only superficial.

Moultrup's approach is interesting in that it offers a conceptual framework emphasizing the importance of differentiation, together with a clinical approach that emanates from an undifferentiated position. On the one hand, Moultrup conceptualizes the systemic and strategic significance of an affair and discusses the importance of incongruous power hierarchies in the treatment alliance (e.g., the decision to demand that the infidel terminate the affair). On the other hand, his actual intervention strategy is anything but focused on enhancing differentiation; it is thoroughly rooted in the reciprocity/fusion paradigm of level-1 intimacy. As we have seen repeatedly in previous chapters, it is quite common for a clinician to develop a sophisticated conceptual approach, only to abandon its application in actual clinical work with patients.

For example, Moultrup suggests that the outset of treatment should focus on the couple's commitment to continuance of the marriage, "Since the therapist cannot begin to establish the goal of saving the marriage if the couple is not willing to do so . . ." (p. 135). In traditional marriage and family therapy fashion, Moultrup encourages the therapist to make an alliance with *the marriage*, rather than joining with each individual to explore his/her own future options in whatever form they take. Moultrup's stance not only encourages a lack of differentiation in a time of crisis but also reinforces the "togetherness pressure" characteristic of poorly differentiated spouses (which often was the impetus for the affair). Such couples are often totally preoccupied with the question of whether to continue or terminate the relationship; they cannot decide because neither option resolves the stuckness they feel.

A similar problem is apparent in Pittman's approach. Regarding the decision to reveal the affair to the resolute spouse, Pittman (1987) suggests, "The secret does not belong to the adulterer or to the therapist but is the property of the marriage. The couple can and must decide what to do about it" (p. 121). Aside from the problem of the therapist's commitment to the marriage as an entity, the notion of the resolute spouse's proprietary rights to details of the affair is a very poor stratagem from the vantage point of differentiation or systemic politics:

First and foremost, it encourages the resolute spouse to take the fact of the affair as a reflection upon him/herself. Granted, the affair will have an impact *on* the spouse (in terms of subsequent decision-making), but this is quite different from the notion that the affair is something *about* or *done to* the spouse (even if this was the adulterer's intent). Second, Pittman's notion suggests that the therapist should encourage the adulterer (who has already demonstrated an unwillingness to"play by the rules") to act in a way possibly contrary to his/her perceived personal interests. Third, it encourages an undifferentiated alliance between the therapist and the adulterer. Fourth, and finally, Pittman's position fuels the incongruous power hierarchy inherent in the affair, perpetuating it in the treatment alliance.

Moultrup's attempt to "establish the systemic nature of the crisis" is a further example of a clinical approach antithetical to the goal of enhancing differentiation. The problem stems from confusing *therapist* paradigms with patient paradigms. While the systemic nature of affairs is a good concept for the therapist to consider, it is of little benefit to patients *if the goal is differentiation and the development of an effective treatment strategy*. Introduction of the concept of systemic involvement at the outset of treatment only fuels the fusion; it offers the adulterer an opening to disown responsibility for his/her behavior.

Moultrup's attempt to teach patients systems theory while their world destabilizes may actually involve a feeble effort to mollify the rage of the "uninvolved spouse." In effect, Moultrup attempts to get spouses to share the *blame*. Moultrup's nomenclature of "the uninvolved spouse" is a contradiction, not simply because it is antithetical to the systemic conceptualization he espouses, but also because it contradicts his *clinical* approach:

> The assumption underlying this treatment goal is that both partners had some part to contribute in the evolution of the crisis of the affair. If in fact the contribution of either one of them is hidden or unacknowledged initially, the treatment strategy is to comment on the lack of understanding of that person's contribution to the problem. (p. 137)

Pittman's (1987) approach in this regard is similar but more subtle. He suggests defining the problem within therapy in a way that provides the adulterer with an opportunity to demonstrate willingness to make changes for the sake of the marriage. Whether "making amends" to the partner or "for the relationship," the approach is an inherently undifferentiated one that encourages the resolute spouse to "trust the adulterer" and restart the cycle of dependency, vulnerability, and control.

One final aspect, totally antithetical to the enhancement of differentiation, is Moultrup's inclusion of the lover in treatment. Surprisingly, Pittman (1987) concurs with this approach. Moultrup rationalizes that the lover is a significant component of the emotional system, that affairs are systemic problems, and that he is a systems therapist. However, such a treatment approach flies in the face of good judgment and conceptualization of affairs as a failure in differentiation. Moultrup's approach *reinforces* the very dynamics that may have caused the affair: triangulation in lieu of differentiation.

DIFFERENTIATION IN ACTION: AN ALTERNATIVE CLINICAL STRATEGY

The impact of a clandestine affair is usually multisystemic; think of it as a "multiple orgasm" offering the adulterer (a) defiance of feeling controlled and dominated by the resolute spouse; (b) gratification of the desire to punish, deprive, hurt, or "get one up" on the spouse; (c) avoidance of intimacy in the marriage while appearing to seek (or find) it in the affair; and (d) use of the affair as a strategic buffer in the marriage, and vice versa.

Incongruous Power Hierarchies in Affairs

The common quest for a reflected sense of self sets the stage for constructing powerful incongruous power hierarchies through an affair. Emotional fusion—which surfaces in the belief that an affair is a negative reflection on the competency and adequacy of the resolute spouse—creates a host of systemic complications. Society's undifferentiated view of affairs (i.e., as something done *to* the resolute spouse) just fuels the problem.

The spouse who strays appears paradoxically "validated" by having found "acceptance" with someone else; marital problems are "therefore" the fault of the other. In the resulting incongruous power hierarchy, the adulterer (a) attains higher systemic status than the spouse, and (b) is able to "diminish," "embarrass," "betray," or "do something to" the other. *When one person can control the adequacy of another simply by undressing with a third, the stage is set for a control fight.*

These "normal" assumptions encourage affairs as an expression of hostility, of which there is usually an abundance. In spite of ingenuous disclaimers of "not wanting to hurt anyone," affairs are ubiquitous as a vehicle for hostility, dependency, and power struggles. The clinician's failure to intervene in the resultant incongruous power hierarchies severely diminishes the prognosis and degree of personal development achieved in treatment.

The need for multisystemic *isomorphic* intervention (mentioned in earlier chapters) is highlighted in Pittman's and Moultrup's approaches. Both lack integration of two simultaneous viewpoints of causation: The notion of spousal involvement (i.e., the systemic view), and the problem of low-level differentiation (e.g., high reactivity to others, togetherness pressure, and quest for a reflected sense of self). *The question of isomorphism centers around which dimension to lead from. The more core issue is that of differentiation; when that is addressed, the others fall into place.*

Incongruous power hierarchies *do* require immediate attention at the outset of treatment; they are best addressed initially as issues of differentiation rather than as systemic processes. When handled properly, spouses' participation in the development of their current state of affairs surfaces relatively rapidly. But when this occurs, it does so in the paradigm of "responsibility to self" rather than conjoint culpability; the latter unfortunately reinforces fusion.

When this approach is followed, common problems such as (a) dealing with the resolute spouse's anger and (b) "insisting" that the affair be terminated and/or announced simply fail to become stumbling blocks in treatment. Such "treatment problems" are generated by the treatment approach, and not simply by patients' characteristics or the inherent nature of affairs.

The Shift in Paradigm

Contemporary clinical approaches to affairs *amplify* the problem of the pervasive quest for a reflected sense of self. Therapists seem at their empathic best when reinforcing the resolute spouse's wail, "How could he/she have done this to *me?*" In the name of support and commiseration, however, the therapist's stance undermines differentiation by reinforcing the patient's belief that something *has* been done to him/her. The result is perpetuation and exacerbation of the very pain which the patient seeks to ameliorate.

As was noted previously, a paradigm shift is heralded by the sudden emergence of new questions. In treating affairs, the efficacious lead from a highly differentiated position accomplishes exactly that:

- Why does the resolute spouse assume the adulterer's behavior is a reflection on him/her? Why does he/she take it "personally"?
- What does the resolute spouse think the adulterer has actually *"done"* to him/her?

- Why does the resolute spouse think the adulterer's behavior was *aimed* at him/her?
- Why, in fact, does the resolute spouse think that the adulterer's behavior had *anything* to do with him/her at all?
- Why won't the resolute spouse allow the adulterer's behavior to be a reflection on the adulterer, aimed at and having damaged himself/herself?
- Why, if the resolute spouse believes that the adulterer was out to "get" him/her, does he/she gratify that hostility by acting as if he/she has been "gotten"?

Progress will occur regardless of the direction the resolute spouse takes the questions: Taken one way, they enhance differentiation; taken another, they tap the role of participation in the system. For example, (a) What does the issue of revealing the affair reveal? (b) Why does the resolute spouse feel diminished by what the adulterer has done, while denying any culpability in the affair? (c) What is the nature of the *trust* that the resolute spouse complains has been destroyed? and (d) Why does the resolute spouse keep insisting that he/she cannot trust the adulterer, when this is the only rational position?

Examining the notion of "trust" is a portal into the individual and dyadic dynamics of the system. The resolute spouse's anger and the adulterer's hesitancy stem (in part) from feeling compelled to look *into* the affair as a elicitation window.

Either way these questions are taken, the crucible starts to heat up. At first the questions may sound preposterous, being so alien to the reciprocity/fusion paradigms of clinical practice and contemporary society. If reading these questions produces a somewhat awkward feeling, don't be too surprised. When therapists start to work in the crucible paradigm, patients aren't the only ones who feel the heat.

Notice the isomorphic multisystemic impact of the above interventions:

- reduction of the resolute spouse's pain and anger,
- increased differentiation in the dyad,
- circumvention of incongruous power and control hierarchies with the adulterer,
- circumvention of the need to issue ultimatums to the adulterer to terminate the affair, and
- construction of a crucible for the resolute spouse and (indirectly) the adulterer.

Intervening through the avenue of differentiation creates a simultaneous *systemic* impact. Enhancing the differentiation of the resolute spouse does more than alleviate some pain in the midst of tumultuous marital destabilization; it gives the pain *utility* as a vehicle for personal development. The interventions mentioned on the previous page don't immediately stop the pain — but they give it direction and meaning.[10]

Construction of the sexual crucible for the resolute spouse creates a simultaneous crucible for the adulterer as well.[11] For all the glib comments about the positive impact of affairs on marriage, the adulterer is often *not* pleased when the affair has unintended benefit for the resolute spouse. When the resolute spouse is *not* hurt or diminished by the affair, (a) the affair often ends, and (b) the adulterer's underlying anger, dependency, and insecurity surface. When the resolute spouse *stops* hurting, the adulterer *starts* to.

> Those who are faithful know only the trivial side of love; it is the faithless who know love's tragedies. (Oscar Wilde, in Tripp, 1970)

Reworking the incongruous power hierarchy by increasing differentiation causes the adulterer to take his/her own behavior as a reflection of *him/herself*, not necessarily in a moral sense but rather as a elicitation window. The end result is that the adulterer is often in crisis. If the therapist is intent on fostering differentiation of *both* partners, it is important that the adulterer's pain *not* be considered expiation to the resolute spouse; the more significant frame is each spouse's relationship with him/herself.

Differentiation, Intimacy, and Affairs

In marriage, we find out who we really are — which makes affairs all the more attractive. At times we don't like *what* we see; other times, the onerous part is *how* we find out. *The struggle of marriage is to find out who you are, while maintaining your boundaries with a partner who is only too eager to tell you.* "A man may be a fool and not know it," said H. L. Mencken, "but not if he is married (in Peter, 1980)."

There is a basic problem with intimacy in long-term marriage: It is often

---

[10]Couples can (and often do) make "a full recovery" — often far exceeding their prior level of individual and relationship development. It would be gratuitous, however, to suggest that this was the intent or benefit of the affair.

[11]Examples of constructing simultaneous interlocking crucibles have been presented in Chapters Six and Ten.

abundant in uncomfortable ways, and paltry in those we believe we crave. Sometimes it is the *presence* rather than the *absence* of intimacy in marriage which stimulates desire for "meaningful secondary relationships." *When the goal is to be seen as you want, but not known as you are, marriage can never compete with part-time romance.* How ironic that, "My wife (husband) doesn't understand me," is the adulterer's battle cry. Familiarity doesn't always breed contempt, but by common reckoning, it doesn't breed lust either. *What does breed eroticism and passion (i.e., sexual desire) is differentiation.*

Differentiation is the backstop of sustained eroticism in long-term marriage. What else can survive the very *necessary* pushing and shoving that arise in the course of marriage? What else can help marriage compete with intoxicating "instant attraction" to people who seem perfect just the way they (and we) are? Home holds the spouse who takes our good points as due compensation for our bad, who never stops trying to change the latter, and often has to be reminded of the former.

In an affair, the lover receives the positive attributions from borrowed functioning. Affairs are easier to sustain than a marriage, and it is easier to handle interpersonal challenges in them, as well. The wayward spouse may superficially function "better" in the affair and erroneously attribute this to the lover's "bringing out the best in me." The result, however, perpetuates the quest for a reflected sense of self common to level-1 intimacy. Constant reciprocal validation *is* common in affairs, and level-2 intimacy is less threatening if it occurs. Intimacy in affairs is more likely to *look like* level-2, however, although it is almost always *level-1*. Self-validated marital intimacy and eroticism require a greater level of differentiation.

Do some people "grow" from having an affair? Do married people with limited prior sexual experience learn something new about eroticism and intimacy in a secret rendezvous? While a secret liaison might raise one's motivation to improve one's sex life, motivation without differentiation leads to more affairs rather than marital reconstruction. The unilateral capacity for self-validated (i.e., level-2) intimacy is the requisite footing for forging and sustaining increased eroticism and romance in marriage.

Considering an affair might be a significant growth step for some; open declaration of interest in an affair can *productively* destabilize an individual or a relationship.[12] *Terminating* an ongoing affair often has the same impact; it can

---

[12]Ironically, fidelity and commitment mean *nothing* without the ability to even think of having an affair; without the existence of the possibility, there is no *choice*. Some people take pride that they "can't even imagine" having an affair: This is fusion, *not love*, and/or avoidance of internal conflict over options declined. Such proclamations have an untoward impact on the marital system which leads to being taken for granted.

require (and produce) as much (if not more) differentiation to stop an affair as it does not to get into one in the first place.

At low levels of differentiation, monogamy results from reciprocal extortion of sexual exclusivity (*i.e.*, *exchange theory*). This "lose-lose" marital contract fertilizes common unresolved autonomy issues that bloom into control fights and "rebellious" affairs. This is the common outcome to the "two-choice dilemma" between promiscuity and pairbonding discussed earlier.

In highly differentiated couples, in contrast, monogamy is based on two unilateral commitments for which partners owe each other *nothing* (except perhaps respect). That is, the covenant is not made to *the partner* but rather *to oneself*, with the partner as witness and secondary beneficiary. Folks at high levels of differentiation are (a) more likely to successfully handle situations of adultery or "open relationships," and (b) more likely *not* to start them.

This requires a higher state of differentiation than many people ever achieve, and certainly higher than most have at the outset of marriage. If people *remain* monogamous, the basis on which they do so generally changes from quid pro quo to differentiation over the course of the relationship. *Patients are often surprised to recognize that this transformation of monogamous commitment occurs spontaneously in the sexual crucible approach to treatment.* They feel little craving to have an affair, although they can admire an attractive man or woman; often they can (and do) feel friends' and strangers' eroticism, and enjoy the *infamity*[13] of it all.

MOTIVATIONS OF THE "OTHER PERSON"

The triangulated relationship of an affair often exists in the context of a triangulated extended family system. The preceding chapter considered the role of intergenerational triangulation in the development of erotic "maps." The extended family is affected by the emergence of an affair. Likewise, affairs may be encouraged by the family's core unresolved problems which are transmitted intergenerationally through the childhood experiences of the succeeding generation, ongoing interactions, and current family circumstances. Like-

---

[13]*Infamity* is a mnemonic word describing those moments where one shares the mutual awareness of mutual attraction, recognizes that sexual encounters often occur best in fantasy, and doesn't need to make physical contact to gain the complement of selection. *I.n.f.a.m.i.t.y.* stands for *If not for AIDS Ms./Mr., I'd take you.* Obviously, much more than fear of AIDS is involved in the ability to not go beyond window shopping—such as personal integrity and the belief that one is desirable to others. Although many folks pay lip service to the notion that eroticism is located between the ears and eyes (and not the thighs), common behavior suggests that they don't believe it.

wise, the extended family may be reciprocally affected by the emergence of the affair. Prather (Prather, 1970; Prather & Prather, 1990) offers an unusually clear illustration of intergenerational and systemic inducement of affairs:

> Perhaps the material that was the most difficult for us to include was our anguish over infidelity during the first fifteen years of marriage. Gayle grew up in a home that had its share of problems, but a lack of loyalty was not among them, whereas on both sides of Hugh's family infidelity and divorce were a deep and long-standing pattern. Hugh's father was married four times, his mother three, and as a boy his father frequently instructed him by word and example on the "proper" way to carry on an affair. That a real man had them was never questioned.
>
> The year we were married (1965) was the beginning of an unfortunate string of antimonogamous movements in this country ("wife-swapping," "free love," "swinging," "open marriage," etc.) that continues to this day. It was not only Hugh's boyhood indoctrination but the ideals of many of the couples who were close friends that Gayle had to outendure and that Hugh had to see through and overcome. (Prather & Prather, 1990, introduction)

All that has been discussed thus far regarding affairs' maintaining intrapsychic and interpersonal equilibrium of the spouses also holds true for the "lover." Obviously, the "lover" stands to lose a variety of privileges and gratifications if the marriage improves and/or becomes monogamous. The film "Fatal Attraction" presented a powerful illustration of marital reinvestment triggering a psychotic episode in a borderline "other woman." More often, however, the "lover" is ambivalent regarding the continuation of the marriage. The existence of the marriage provides the safety to indulge in an "all-consuming" affair; the marriage embodies one side of the "lover's" ambivalence (e.g., fears of engulfment), permitting him/her to embrace the other side (e.g., fusion with the married partner). Many single women who have affairs prefer married men because they don't want someone around all the time (Richardson, 1985).

The same ambivalent response holds true of friends. While friends may often wish us well, they don't wish us *too* well. Alliances and emotional investments with friends made to compensate for conjugal deficits often change when the marriage improves. This doesn't mean that highly differentiated couples disinvest from outside interests—quite the contrary. But the shifts in priorities, power hierarchies, boundaries, and confidences that result from increased marital satisfaction and investment generally trigger anxiety throughout the extended system of friends and family. "Significant others" often resent the loss of ready access to one or both spouses. Friends who play shuttle diplomacy between the spouses lose their powerful pivotal position in the triangle.

Estranged and bored couples often develop a clique of close friends who provide reciprocal triangulation as their children might have done in prior years. Each couple helps the others ignore the fact that the partners have little to say to each other when they are alone. One couple's improved marriage triggers unpleasant self-reflection in the others: "We can't get together with you tonight, we'd like to spend the night alone," confronts the barrenness of couples who require the constant contact of others. Couples who enter sexual-marital therapy often disappoint friends to gain more time together.

An "emotional" affair need not require physical contact or sexual overtones. Sometimes the triangulation is played out with the family pet (Zussman, 1985). In one memorable case, the pet became more than the object of alienated affection within the marital dyad:

Mr. and Mrs. Cole had a 13-year-old dog, who had been with the family since birth. The husband and wife, both in their late sixties, were unable to bring themselves to put their beloved dog to sleep.

Now blind and unable to negotiate the steps to the bedroom on the second floor of the home, the dog was carried into the bedroom every night. The dog cried repeatedly and jumped between them when they caressed in bed. When outside the door, the dog's cries distracted Mrs. Cole's attention; she could not focus on her husband's touch or feel erotically involved. They agreed that the dog could not be put downstairs out of earshot, because she might hurt herself in her stumbling blindness. Although the dog was not the initial cause of the couple's long-term marital discord or Mr. Cole's sexual difficulty, the dog's own agendas presented barriers to treatment and deeper intimate involvement.

The pain and heartache involved in the imminent loss of the dog had additional significance for Mr. and Mrs. Cole. Each was acutely aware of the inevitable loss of the other through death. Both were attempting to "protect" themselves by modulating the depth and salience of the marital bond. Mrs. Cole, in particular, had refused to participate in financial planning of their estate and insurance death benefits, refusing to accept her husband's mortality. Their attempts to grapple with these issues surfaced in their intense but ambivalent involvement with their beloved pet. In the final stages of treatment, Mr. and Mrs. Cole were able to permit their long-suffering pet to be gently put to sleep.

In this age of workaholism, jobs and careers have increasingly become the quasi-legitimate "other person" in triangular relationships. People who otherwise pride themselves on "being their own boss" or "conquering the business world" frequently present themselves as being controlled by their job in order to control, or avoid being controlled, by the spouse:

Another couple in their sixties, Mr. and Mrs. Johnson, requested treatment for problems of erectile dysfunction. They had been married only several months. Mr. Johnson was recently divorced for the second time, and Mrs. Johnson's first husband had died a year ago. Mr. Johnson reported prior erectile difficulty with his prior wife, but attributed this to her unfaithfulness and the ensuing marital discord.

The new Mrs. Johnson was also upset by the lack of time Mr. Johnson spent at home. He claimed he was merely trying to keep his small business partnership afloat during difficult economic times. Mrs. Johnson volunteered information that her husband felt was "inconsequential": his business partner was a woman he had been dating seriously until the time of their recent wedding.

Mr. Johnson appeared in a panic about being controlled by his current wife and being forced to confront his sexual difficulties. He resisted making any shifts in his alliance with his former girlfriend/business partner. Mr. Johnson presented his work as an insurmountable barrier to scheduling therapy appointments. He terminated after two sessions, professing sorrow that continued treatment was not feasible.

THE BENEFITS OF MONOGAMY FOR
HUMAN DEVELOPMENT

Nothing in the foregoing discussion argues against close friendships, robust careers, and salient family ties. In fact, highly differentiated couples are able to establish the true mutuality that facilitates significant outside attachments without triggering affairs or anxiety.

When all is said and done, monogamy is a powerful vehicle for increased differentiation. Monogamy facilitates construction of a sexual crucible for personal development, which affairs often preclude. In fact, affairs often start in order to circumvent the spontaneous construction of a sexual crucible.

In contrast to the notion that an affair may help an individual "grow," monogamy (and the inevitable sexual boredom that results from low levels of differentiation) prods individuals to push themselves, the partner, and the relationship to confront a critical developmental task: elicitation of defenses against eroticism and intimacy and development of the requisite differentiation to sustain both.

Consider four assumptions regarding partner selection:

- Partner selection tends to identify individuals at similar levels of differentiation.

- The partner selected contains some element of one's unresolved object-relations conflicts.
- The partner selected embodies some element of one's unresolved issues about eroticism.
- Personal growth of marital partners is generally sequential rather than simultaneous.

With these notions in mind, it becomes relevant to consider *how a relationship expands the depth and breadth of its sexual repertoire*. Once again we arrive at the sexual crucible. *It occurs through conflict rather than negotiation and consensus.* One partner's growth makes the partners' prior adjustment and development an untenable match, creating the stimulus for the other's development. It involves systemic jujitsu utilizing common emotional gridlock; resolution in one spouse triggers the interlocking issues of the other. "Sexual negotiation" tends to be superficial since (a) negotiation creates "regressions towards the mean" rather than self-exploration and confrontation, and (b) the requisite target often lies outside one's comfort range. This dynamic underlies the notion that one "works on the relationship by working on oneself." *When applied to sexuality, "disparate desire" can be seen as a normal situation – not simply because of its ubiquitousness, but also because it reflects an inherent developmental growth process potentially available within relationships.*

Consider a common scenario in which, like the "distancer-pursuer" dynamics of intimacy struggles, the partner with lower sexual desire and less access to eroticism picks someone with more. The intent of the selection is to find someone to drag him/her into an area he/she would like to go, albeit in an ambivalent manner. This dynamic allows the "low eroticism" partner to resist and avoid the anxiety generated by owning his/her impulses and preferences and "wanting," while still having sex and maintaining the opportunity for his/her own future development. The "high eroticism" partner enjoys the status of being the "sexier" and "more knowledgeable" one in the relationship.

At the outset of the relationship, the couple plays out a mutually gratifying scenario in which the eroticism, desirability, and prowess of the "high eroticism" partner overcome the inhibitions of the spouse. Both partners enjoy the fantasy that this will eventually be absorbed by the "low eroticism" partner, who will then become equally aggressive. They do not recognize that the underlying dynamic itself tends to preclude this. Several years later, when the "high eroticism" and "low eroticism" positions amplify and polarize into the "sex fiend" and "frigid" stereotypes, the resulting positions are redefined as "sexual incompatibility."

At that point, the couple predictably faces the choice between entering the sexual crucible, divorcing, or diffusing the anxiety through one or both partners' having an affair. Properly managed, disparate desire can reflect having picked the "right" partner rather than the "wrong" one. *Perhaps sexual compatibility can be redefined as the willingness to utilize disparate desire and preferences, rather than reciprocal willingness to accept each other's current sexual development.* Although it is gratifying to find a partner similar in sexual style and preference, the willingness and ability to struggle through the *differences* that inevitably emerge in a long-term relationship are crucial to increased differentiation, enhanced sexual potential, and freedom from boredom.

Monogamy provides the boundaries of the sexual crucible for human development. Like a pressure cooker, it prevents the dissipation of energy and tension necessary to forge two highly differentiated individuals capable of intense intimacy and eroticism:[14]

- The absence of alternative relationships for sexual gratification forces the "high eroticism" partner to validate his/her erotic preferences and interest, in the face of contrary pressure from the partner.
- The anxiety generated by this necessary confrontation (a monogamous relationship) forces the "low eroticism" partner into one of two conflicts: (a) self-confrontation, driving his/her own development forward, or (b) outward deflection into fights with the spouse and attempts to undercut the other's ability to validate his/her erotic preferences. Either way, (at least) one partner's capacity for self-validated (level-2) intimacy and eroticism is challenged and potentially enhanced.
- Commensurate with the lack of differentiation, anxiety and anger will diffuse to other unresolved issues in the relationship. Negotiated resolution of these other issues, without corresponding increased level of differentiation, generally does not lead to subsequent improvement in the unresolved sexual issues.

The diffusion of anxiety into nonsexual relationship issues is complex: The "low eroticism" partner often seizes upon substantive preexisting problems outside the bedroom, insisting that resolution of these problems is necessary

---

[14]*Terminating* an affair and making a commitment to monogamy can create a crucible for object relations development, mastery of narcissism, and acceptance of existential finiteness, and can increase one's resolve to hammer out a more effective marital contract.

for resolution of the sexual difficulties. Sometimes it is implied that the nonsexual problems *cause* his/her lack of eroticism or diminish his/her motivation to tackle whatever sexual difficulties exist.

In some cases the linkage actually reflects the dynamics of low desire; in many others it simply represents a strategic defense against self-confrontation by the "low eroticism" spouse. Many of the nonsexual issues seized upon by the "low eroticism" partner are ones that *both* partners were content to let slide in a quid pro quo of avoided individual conflicts. The solution is to not deny the legitimacy of the nonsexual issues raised, but rather to question the implied necessary linkage of issues and its exchange-theory basis.

The requisite process of resolution involves less negotiation and more differentiation (less fusion), and hence increased capacity for intimacy (in which display of eroticism plays a large part). If the "high eroticism" partner hasn't achieved sufficient differentiation to maintain the confrontation, the ensuing anxiety dissipates into an affair, other forms of triangulation, and/or other symptomatology. *Increased differentiation transforms monogamy from a sexual monopoly (that encourages withholding) into a sexual crucible in which masturbation, the possibility of separation, and other displays of autonomy surface.*

Self-confrontation involves those issues related to intense eroticism and profound levels of intimacy. Such issues are not confined to specifically sexual content. However, at increasing levels of eroticism, the process involves confronting ambivalence about one's own eroticism, that of the partner, and what one regards as "dirty" sex. Although many people like some degree of "naughtiness" in their sexuality, sharing "naughtiness" with one's spouse is a level of self-integration that few individuals achieve.

This is a crucible for both spouses. While the "high eroticism" partner may appear to have resolved this issue, selection of a partner who has not suggests some stages of development yet undone. The defensive issues seized upon by the "low eroticism" partner often provide further clues regarding the unresolved issues of the "high eroticism" partner. Moreover, the "low eroticism" partner's progress in confronting sexual inhibitions triggers anxiety, disequilibrium, and possible further development in the "high drive" partner.

In contrast, relationships in which one or both partners are having affairs have quite different dynamics:

- The "high eroticism" partner has less motivation to confront the spouse and establish an unavoidable ongoing focal issue that may take years of head-butting to resolve.

- The "high eroticism" partner may have a mistaken notion that he/she possesses "more" eroticism than the partner, when in fact the difference may not be as great as it appears. "Irreparable" differences are distorted when behavior in affairs is used as the measure of eroticism. Lack of sufficient differentiation to either leave the marriage or drive it forward is generally overlooked.
- When the "high eroticism" partner having an affair *does* confront the spouse, the motivation and style are subtly different from those in monogamous relationships. The purpose of the confrontation is to validate prior or current extramarital sex, rather than to seek resolution and growth. Confrontations often consist of attacks on the "low eroticism" spouse's adequacy, rather than statements of one's own legitimate preferences. There is less motivation to facilitate the "low eroticism" spouse's growth, lest this progress threaten the continuity of the affair.
- Clear and continued display of the "high eroticism" partner's sexual repertoire and preferences implicitly raises both the threat and actuality of the affair (which both partners would rather not have come to the forefront). Erotic display by the "high eroticism" partner diminishes in the case of covert affairs. Conversely, flaunting of sexual interest and "prowess" occurs in cases of blatant philandering in order to further polarize and diminish the adequacy of the spouse.

The preceding discussion presents the prototypic ways in which the "high eroticism" partner avoids the sexual crucible. *Sometimes, it is the "low eroticism" partner who is having the affair.* In such cases, all the preceding dynamics hold true for the "low eroticism" partner instead. Such individuals may be highly erotic in extramarital sex, while presenting their lack of eroticism with their spouse as pervasive rather than situational. Such a presentation offers the "low eroticism" partner several strategic "advantages":

- a cover for passive-aggressive noncompliance with the spouse's sexual overtures;
- creation of an incongruous power hierarchy, breeding anger and contempt for the spouse;
- avoidance of open confrontation of both partners' dissatisfactions;
- maintenance of dependency and circumvention of the sexual crucible which would foster increased differentiation;

- abrogation of the partner's opportunity to make free and informed choices about continued participation in the marriage; and
- confusion of "privacy" with lack of self-integration and differentiation.

And what of the argument that the "high eroticism" partner has *tried* in vain to push the partner and him/herself to higher levels of eroticism and intimacy? In such cases, is the "high eroticism" partner required to sacrifice his/her own needs for intimacy and sexual gratification for the rest of his/her days? Any decent systemic therapist would recognize the paradoxical improbability of such a "till death do us part" commitment ever producing change. Such a position increases resentment, fueling the "low eroticism" partner's resistance. Moreover, an unswerving commitment embodies one-half of the "low eroticism" partner's ambivalence, making it safer for him/her to oppose change.

So, at what point has the "high eroticism" partner fulfilled his/her responsibilities to him/herself and the partner, not having bailed out prematurely into a convenient affair? At what point has he/she actually been *too* patient? The best answer I can offer has two parts:

First, this "point" is more a function of differentiation than of time, degree of self-sacrifice, or amount of pain. Differentiation is what permits the person to persevere when necessary and healthy emotional "pushing and shoving" get intense, and likewise, what permits him/her to leave when staying represents a denial or fear of being two separate people. That evaluation is itself another aspect of the sexual crucible: *Guidelines never obviate the responsibility of making a decision that shapes one's life. Often it is in the crucible of openly making that decision that one reaches a higher level of differentiation.*

The second part of the answer involves the role of the therapist. *Answering this question presupposes that therapists know when couples should get divorced.* Some years ago my comment in a *McCall's* magazine article about selecting a therapist was picked up and widely quoted in national newspapers. I suggested that one way to check out a therapist was to ask what he/she does when he/she knows that a couple should divorce. I went on to suggest that if the therapist offers *any* plan of action, *implicitly presupposing that he/she knew when a couple should divorce*, the couple should quickly find another therapist. Therapists do *not* know when one or both spouses "should" leave the marriage. If the patient has not made this decision independently of the therapist's encouragement, then he/she is not ready to carry out this life step independently; leaning on the therapist to do so only interferes with the necessary personal development.

The foregoing discussion of affairs does not argue for *lifelong* monogamy. That is a different but related topic. The foregoing analysis suggests that a certain level of differentiation and aspect of development is facilitated by at least a *period* of monogamy. The reader is left to wrestle with the larger issue: Are people more *likely* to remain monogamous after reaching a greater fulfillment of sexual potential, a higher tolerance for intimacy and eroticism, and a better relationship with self?

Has "the Fling" Flung?

Writing this book occasioned a rereading of *Marriage and Alternatives* (Libby & Whitehurst, 1977), a product of the pre-AIDS 1960s free love/open marriage heyday. The arguments presented by the various contributors provide an interesting commentary on the implicit assumptions of the time. The oft-repeated phrase, "It's unrealistic to expect one partner to meet all of one's needs," embodies the assumption that one *should* expect to have all of one's needs met one way or another. Little thought was given to the notion that the "good life" comes, not from getting what one wants, but rather from being able to master the realistic frustrations of living and loving.

The sexual crucible is the antithesis of Erica Jong's *zipless fuck*. The 1970s focused on human potential and "growth," assuming that one grew through experimentation and exposure, rather than through self-mastery and a relationship with *oneself*. The narcissistic self-gratification of *me* produced the backlash focus on *us* and the emphasis on intimacy in the early 1980s. *Us* begat the problems of too-much-*us*: codependency and "sexual addiction." Perhaps now, at the threshold of the 1990s, we can return to *me*, but from a more mature adult position of *self*. The sexual crucible offers an adult *me*: the *me* of self-discipline, self-mastery, and self-development.

And what of the "two-choice" dilemma between the desire for multiple couplings *and* pair-bonding? Helen Fisher (1982) ventures an answer:

> Is the family an endangered species? I think not.
>
> Orgies, mate-swapping, illicit love affairs, adultery, rape, abortion, incest, "living together," and homosexuality have been going on for thousands if not millions of years. And none of this has endangered the status of the family. Nor are these sexual patterns likely to change dramatically. As long as females are continually sexually receptive—which undoubtedly will be for the duration of our existence as a species—people will continue to experiment with sex.
>
> But bonding is a much more complicated matter than sexual affairs. It is a

contract, a commitment made between individuals to accept mutual duties, obligations and responsibilities. (p. 222)

Fisher (1982) leaves off at the threshold of the other (previously mentioned) approach to the two-choice problem: sexual ethics. Tristam Engelhardt addresses this issue, discussing *friendship* and inner conflict as inevitable aspects of the crucible that yields an individual capable of transcending conventional sexual values. Engelhardt (1987) writes:

As Nietzsche has argued, nihilism does not destroy the world of values. It may preclude the discovery of a ready formed constellation of values. However, individuals can still fashion meaning, structure a world. The superman (and superwoman—the German is *Uebermensch*) is able to look at the abyss and laugh because the superman still has the courage to create values in the absence of enduring standards. Friends create a common history, an enduring bond, a meaning to their sexuality. Their sexuality finds its "higher truth," to use a Hegelian phrase, within the embrace of their commitments. They create a world of the mind, an objective place for their spirits, which place sustains, interprets, and gives moral and other significance to the pleasures and urges of sexuality. . . . In this sense, friendship, including sexual friendship, is an accomplishment, a work of art.

It is also a sacrifice. Since humans are not gods or goddesses, friendship entails the abandonment of other possibilities. Humans have limited resources of energy and time. The person who has a hundred friends has none, or is a god. To develop a sexual friendship with one person is not to be able to have a sexual friendship with someone else (I do not mean to exclude polygamy or polyandry, but only to suggest that King Solomon did not know all of his thousand wives as friends). . . . To choose to be a friend to one, two, three, or four individuals is an exclusion of other possibilities and a commitment to making certain common worlds of friendship and not others. . . .

Making love, *making* a friendship, *making* a family are tasks of constant commitment and of sacrificing some possibilities on behalf of others. (pp. 59–60)

Engelhardt concludes:

The difficulties involved in sustaining commitments are significant. Sexuality is marked by passions, and passions are not reasonable. They tear at reason, undermine values, and strain the structure of commitment. As Lawrence Durrell had Justine summarize the confusions of passion, "Who invented the human heart, I wonder? Tell me, and then show me the place where he was hanged." One comes to lust after those whom one does not love, and to be driven to love sexually against prior commitments of exclusivity. Because of passion's challenge to constancy and purpose, it is often said that one may hold others accountable for their friends but not their lovers. It is against such difficulties that love is made in the serious sense of a sexual friendship. (1987, p. 61)

Engelhardt's discomfort at arriving at a position that could be characterized as "bourgeois sexual morality" caused him to reflect on the *value* of bourgeois sexual morality. His thoughts may comfort those therapists who might abandon clinically useful positions out of fear of seeming "bourgeois," or worse, "judgmental":

> Some may complain that this approach to sexuality supports much of the classic bourgeois sentiments regarding the family and sexual morality. But this fact may provide additional support rather than a criticism. The bourgeois family developed as an institution focused on creating and sustaining resources. Insofar as the aristocracy is free of such need and the proletariat too impoverished to aspire to them, the bourgeois develop and sustain societal resources. Both within and outside of socialist countries such families meet the challenge of sustaining meaning and of husbanding resources, intellectual, moral and financial. (1987, p. 61)

Although it now sounds derisive, *bourgeois* originally referred to a medieval freeman—how many of us are *really* free? The ultimate freedom to explore our sexual potential comes from *self*-control and integrity, not the absence of commitment.

The conclusion of this chapter brings us to the doorstep of the next, where we examine the sexual crucible from the inside. Our discussion of affairs leads us back into the sexual crucible. The quest for the perfect partner reflects our self-rejection; the crucible is where we find the dear partner we crave most: ourself.

> Did I pick the right person? This question inverts the starting and ending points. We do not pick our perfect match because we ourselves are not perfect. The universe hands us a flawless diamond—in the rough. Only if we are willing to polish off every part of *ourselves* that cannot join do we end up with a soul mate. (Prather & Prather, 1990, p. 10)

CHAPTER THIRTEEN

Inside the Sexual Crucible

There is a dark and a light side to eroticism and marriage. This chapter addresses the former (including "normal marital sadism"); the next chapter explores the latter. The sexual crucible is particularly useful in treating "stuck" relationships, and extreme marital discord. Part of its impact stems from the therapist's refusal to "push" patients.

Anxiety and anxiety tolerance are concomitants of personal (and particularly sexual) development. Anxiety-reduction treatment paradigms ignore that effective modulation of anxiety isn't the same as keeping anxiety (a) as low as possible or (b) "comfortable." Providing patients with a "safe, secure environment," clarifying their "confusion," and habitually offering empathy reduces motivation for treatment and interferes with personal growth. Although standard sex therapy "exercises" are sometimes thought to create "pleasure anxiety," this is rarely the case—until couples can endow such activities with their own eroticism.

Think about how people actually develop a sexual repertoire: People grow sexually by mastering anxiety. They do *not* refrain from intercourse until they have intellectualized, educated, and fantasized their way to a comfortable, relaxed, and anxiety-free experience. After some period of ambivalence, intercourse is attempted in an atmosphere of excitement, fear, curiosity, and "the unknown."

Initial coitus is generally anxiety-provoking. Many people are cortically dysfunctional with anxiety, sexual dysfunctions are rife, and acute awkwardness and embarrassment are the norm. For those fortunate enough to have an arousing (and not-too-brief) experience, there is still considerable anxiety.

But this doesn't stop subsequent attempts. Coitus is repeated, each time (hopefully) bringing expertise, increased sense of mastery, and reduced anxiety. When the anxiety of missionary-position intercourse is sufficiently reduced, folks go on to do something *else* they always thought was so disgusting, perverted, and revolting that *they* would never do it.

Remember first hearing about french kissing as a child on the school playground? Hard to understand why you might want someone to stick his/

her tongue down your throat and slobber, wasn't it? But you didn't wait until it no longer scared you. You did it feeling uncomfortable, awkward, and inadequate. Eventually you mastered it and went on to repeat this pattern with other behaviors that now you would miss not doing.

French kissing? Oral sex? Not really very different from this perspective. What about religious prohibitions? Doesn't everyone grow up with religious prohibitions about intercourse? That prohibition doesn't stop most folks from converting the ultimate no-no into the one-and-only way most people have sex.

Parental and religious prohibitions are overestimated as deterrents to adult sexual behavior; this is because (a) these are readily identified in patients' histories, (b) people hide behind this convenient rationalization, and (c) the contributing role of *unresolved contemporary adult issues* is vastly overlooked. Sometimes folks choose which sexual anxieties and prohibitions they want to be "controlled" by (i.e., which fears we don't want to confront).

ANXIETY INTOLERANCE

Anxiety is both a precursor and a concomitant to sexual development; mastery of sexual anxiety is at the root of sexual development. Anxiety indicates the way into areas previously precluded from personal experience. Arrested emotional development (and sexual immaturity in particular) results from intolerance for the anxiety of maturational tasks.

It isn't only sexually immature people, however, who experience sexual anxiety; people with a high degree of sexual development have anxiety during extremely intense erotic experiences. The difference is that the latter group also have (a) high anxiety tolerance which permits them to experience the situation as arousing and growth enhancing, (b) prior success in mastering similar situations, and (c) the opportunity to use the process to *deliberately* enhance personal growth.

It is no coincidence that people who have nonsexual disorders associated with anxiety modulation problems often have sexual difficulties as well. Anorexia, for example, is often conceptualized as an individual (or family) failure to master the anxiety of individuation and assume adult responsibilities and activities, including sexual interactions.[1] Anxiety controls the life movements

---

[1] This doesn't mean that one must be sexually active and emotionally intimate to be an adult; emotional development makes this an *option*.

of poorly differentiated people like the light-aversion response of an amoeba, ever moving away from what frightens them (rather than approaching what interests them or offers a richer life).

Many people live their lives as if something is wrong if anxiety increases; anything that increases anxiety is also "wrong." When it comes to broadening marital sexuality, most folks don't seem to "believe" in being anxious. Sebastian Moore (1985) writes, in contrast:

> Perhaps there is a notion of God that lies at the root of all false notions of God and consequently of the self. It is the notion of an all-knowing one whose serene omniscience would float above our self-aware existence and leave no trace in it. If God is not pressing on me to know myself, God does not know me. (p. 62)

Friedman (1990) uses the character of Cassandra (doomed by the gods to speak the truth and never be believed) to address common anxiety intolerance that surfaces in the form of *the quest for certainty*. In his brilliant fable, Friedman has her tell us why people are unable to control their destiny (and why therapists often aren't helpful):

> It is our undying quest for *certainty* and the resulting reductionism which inevitably follows that allows the Furies to spin out our fate. (p. 102)

> The real molder of denial, I came to see, was not the absence of something, such as courage, but the presence of something, the pursuit of certainty to be exact. . . . We pursue it [truth] in a way that prevents us from accepting responsibility for our fate. In short, civilization is not the result of repression; rather it takes shape out of the manifestations of denial. . . . The quest for certainty has produced a fascination with reducing everything to its basic components; everything must have an answer. Only the poets are unafraid of ambiguity. Everyone else goes to experts. It is true that in my day we sought oracles, but today people still want the oracular, whether from their therapist, their physician, their minister or their politician. The helping professions have turned into certaintizers. At least in my day at Delphi they had the good sense not to be too specific. (pp. 104–105)

> And we gave our fate over into their [the gods] imaginary hands rather than take responsibility for the fact that the hostility of most environments depends less on the toxic elements within them than on the response of the organism to challenge. (p. 105)

> . . . [today's] gods have merely changed their names. Now they are known as *genes, gender, class, race, symptoms, the age, peer groups, statistics* (which doubles as a Trojan Horse), and Zeus, all-powerful king of the gods, is now called *a*

dysfunctional family of origin. I think it was Euripides (who said) . . . "we are continually molding our character and calling it fate." (p. 106)

Causes are notorious for the way they allow their champions to deny responsibility for their own personal destiny. Spirituality is not implanted; it is freed. Salvation depends on the struggle for clarity, not certainty, and that means *preserving* the ambiguity of the human condition and the perplexing paradoxes of protoplasm. (p. 107)

Marital problems often result from intolerance for the anxiety inherent in normal developmental tasks and ongoing differentiation throughout the life cycle. Anxiety spills over into the sexual relationship, where it interferes with intimacy and eroticism and may create overt dsyfunction; conversely, the anxiety of avoided sexual development can spill over into nonsexual systems. The intolerance for (and susceptibility to) anxiety which occurs at low levels of differentiation provides a ripe foundation for the development of treatment-resistant sexual dysfunctions and desire problems. Kerr and Bowen write:

The greater the emotional interdependence of a relationship, therefore, the more easily people are threatened, the more anxiety they experience, and the more energy is invested in actions aimed at reducing that anxiety. The more actions people feel compelled to take to reduce anxiety and to avoid triggering anxiety, the less the flexibility of a relationship. (1988, p. 74)

An important consequence of anxiety is that it creates pressure on people to adapt to one another in ways that will reduce each other's anxiety. (1988, p. 78)

Low differentiation blocks the couple's spontaneous efforts and the therapist's suggested modifications. People at low levels of differentiation have little resilience to anxiety induced by others and limited ability to calm their own fears and insecurities once "infected."[2]

The Various Faces of "Pleasure Anxiety"

The common problem of anxiety intolerance[3] is compounded when couples visit a therapist using a contemporary sex therapy approach. The notoriety of

---

[2]Kerr and Bowen (1988) discussed contagion of anxiety (see Chapter Seven); Chapter Fourteen presents a similar discussion of the "contagion of eroticism."

[3]The reader may recall Apfelbaum's (1977b) case example (Chapter Three, page 74) of the young man who could *function* sexually in spite of incredible obstacles (and then couldn't) as a good example of extreme anxiety tolerance in a relatively dysfunctional individual.

the *performance anxiety* concept reinforces the widespread assumption that sexual problems result from *anxiety* rather than *anxiety intolerance*. Common attempts to reduce patients' anxiety in modern sex therapy validate this erroneous assumption.

The behavior-modification *anxiety-desensitization* paradigm of modern sex therapy is evident in the organization and timing of new prescriptions. Prescriptions are ordered in hierarchy, from least anxiety provoking (e.g., non-genital touch or showering together) to most so (e.g., coitus). Anxiety is presumed to peak at the original prescription of an activity; the goal is to extinguish anxiety with repetition of the sensate focus activity. A new step in the anxiety-provoking hierarchy is prescribed when the couple is able to do the activity *without difficulty. It is often overlooked that prevailing models of sexual (and marital) therapy focus on the absence of anxiety, not the presence of pleasure.*

The situation deteriorates when therapists (who think *anxiety* is the problem) *prescribe* "non-demand" non-genital sensate focus exercises and *proscribe* customary sexual behavior (i.e., intercourse), assuming this will inherently reduce patients' anxiety. *Such prescriptions commonly exacerbate anxiety by undercutting behaviors people use to validate themselves.* The fact that standard sex therapy prescriptions create anxiety isn't the problem; this is advantageous in the sexual crucible approach. *The problem is that therapists have erroneous assumptions about the nature of common behavioral prescriptions and proscriptions: Therapists convey the expectancy to patients that these activities should be relaxing (if not downright pleasurable).* Framed rationally as easy and nonstressful, common sex therapy interventions can be particularly anxiety-provoking because they undercut any expectation that one might feel as much (albeit different) anxiety as one usually does. Apfelbaum (1983) referred to this as *response anxiety* (Chapter Three).

The problem is further compounded when therapists, blind to the impact of their own interventions, advance theories of "pleasure anxiety" when patients fail to obtain the results that therapists think their methods should evoke. Although Kaplan (1974, 1979) clearly recognizes the anxiety-provoking potential of common sex therapy interventions, her discussion of "pleasure anxiety" and treatment resistance encourages therapists (sex therapists and non-) to fall into the hidden boondoggle of modern sex therapy. She wrote:

> When the sensate focus exercises fail to elicit a positive response, we make the assumption that the patient may have a conflict about his affectionate and erotic needs and has therefore erected defenses against the emergence of sexual and sensuous feelings. (1974, p. 212)

Apfelbaum (1983) critiqued Kaplan's notion of pleasure anxiety, pointing out that it conveyed the expectation that sensate focus activities *should* be arousing. *Response anxiety*, not pleasure anxiety, was the more common cause of sexual dysfunction, he suggested; moreover, response anxiety was exacerbated by Kaplan's approach. Response-anxiety models encouraged explanations based on "sexual reality" and validated patients' phenomenological experience; pleasure-anxiety models led to idealized conceptualizations of sexuality and violated patients' experience. The expectation that sensate focus activities *should* be arousing merely produces anxious patients, combative therapists, and an erroneous perception of "pleasure anxiety."

"Pleasure anxiety" is not triggered by the low-level arousal created through initial experimentation with sex therapy prescriptions except in extremely emotionally damaged individuals. Kaplan's suggestion that "pleasure anxiety" is related to more severe psychopathology happens to be true, *if one recognizes the limited scope of pleasure she implicitly was using as a screening device*; her subsequent work with highly uncommon "sexual phobias" requiring anti-anxiety medications (Kaplan, 1987) is consistent with this viewpoint.

There are many reasons why couples don't do sensate focus behavioral "assignments"; the avoidance of pleasure, unfortunately, isn't usually one of them.

The most common pattern in treatment is one in which couples find the sensate focus activities to be "OK" and then quickly become bored. Boredom is a much greater source of resistance to sensate focus activities than pleasure anxiety. Is this boredom actually a defense against pleasure anxiety? No doubt it is for a very small segment of patients. The idea itself isn't novel: The notion of boredom as a defense against intense forms of intimacy was advanced in Chapter Eight; sensate focus prescriptions as commonly used, however, don't require a defense against pleasure anxiety.

Differing approaches to sensate focus activities and pleasure anxiety distinguish the sexual crucible from modern sex therapy approaches. The "pleasure anxiety" mentioned in previous chapters concerns avoidance of *intense* eroticism and intimacy at the limits of sexual potential. This *normative* pleasure anxiety isn't often reached in dysfunction-focused treatment.

Keep in mind the concepts of *response thresholds* and *total stimulus level* outlined in the quantum model (Chapter Two). If the level of total stimulation required to achieve arousal and orgasm lies within the couple's preexisting tolerance range, conventional approaches may reverse the problem; the couple never experiences pleasure anxiety during treatment.

Pleasure anxiety is often unknown (and unbelievable) to people whose experience has been limited to the intensity of intimacy and eroticism available within traditional sex roles; they know a lot more about boredom. Sexual boredom and shallow depth of intimacy are the systemic results of "success" in modulating anxiety; couples' sexual repertoires consist of the residuals of these efforts.

> People begin to feel bored and dissatisfied with many aspects of the relationship while simultaneously feeling bound to it. Actions are taken in an attempt to fill this void, but these actions rarely provide more than temporary relief. The more the stuck togetherness, the more constraining the attachment between people, but, paradoxically, the more sterile the quality of that attachment. (Kerr & Bowen, 1988, p. 77)

In the sexual crucible approach, sensate focus activities are a focal point through which couples attempt to access and invest their sensual and sexual feelings; these feelings are by no means inherent in sensate focus prescriptions themselves. Although pleasure anxiety is a fundamental part of the asset-based approach of the sexual crucible, it doesn't set in when activities are first done. It occurs when the particular style of physical contact is mastered and couples infuse the activity with their own eroticism. Some effort is often required to make the activities erotic. *Eroticism is in the people, not in the assignment per se.*

Why is the point so important? Because patients and therapists (particularly those not specializing in sexual therapy) need realistic expectations and accurate understanding of the tools they attempt to use. Couples have to break out of a "laboratory" mentality and endow the activity with their own eroticism; it is not so much a function of learning to use the activity as learning to use *themselves*. When folks becomes "bored" after the activities have become *highly erotic*, when the therapist is tempted to prescribe another activity to keep the couple from complaining, *that* is the point at which pleasure anxiety starts to surface. Most don't experience pleasure anxiety *until they develop the ability to attain high levels of sexual arousal, eroticism, and intimacy. It is incumbent on the therapist to help couples reach a level of intensity which permits the personal experience of pleasure anxiety.*

Having said all this, is there much clinical utility to the concept of pleasure anxiety? Not in the direct symptomatic treatment of sexual dysfunction. Apfelbaum correctly notes that a response-anxiety model is the approach of choice for direct symptomatic resolution of sexual dysfunctions. Exploration of pleasure anxiety at the outset of treatment is strategically unwise because it delays symptom resolution and undermines credibility for further work (particularly with patients near panic about repeated sexual failures.)

Ironically, multiple uses for the concept of pleasure anxiety arise at the outset of treatment in the sexual crucible.

- It explains the lack of spontaneous progress thus far; it reduces patients' expectation that their sexual and marital relationship *should* have been better than it was. It lends respect to the couples' prior efforts.
- It predicts avoidance of future progress. The notion of having intolerably powerful sex and intimacy is unbelievable to everyone, a challenge to some, and lends respect to the process of treatment.
- It provides a context for helping patients understand their own reports of prior "good" sexual experiences: "good" is a relative judgment based on one's tolerance and expectation. A "good" sexual relationship is nothing more than the absence of sexual dysfunctions, utilitarian interest and as much emotional intensity as one expects and can tolerate (which often isn't much).

ISOMORPHIC CROSS-MODALITY INTERVENTIONS

The foregoing three levels of impact from a single statement actually demonstrate a fundamental type of intervention in the sexual crucible: *cross-modality intervention*. Multidimensional cross-modality interventions, based on the multidimensional perspective developed throughout this book, offer advantages in the course of treating couples with marital difficulties and/or sexual problems: (a) pacing and enhancing differentiation, and (b) developing interventions for treatment-resistant problems. When a single intervention is planned so that the multidimensional impacts are isomorphic, the result is a multi-determined intervention that is congruent on all multiple dimensions that create and maintain the system of problems facing the couple. The effectiveness of such an intervention far exceeds a conglomerate of unidimensional interventions covering the same range of dimensions; an hour of therapy becomes very rich when packed with such interventions.

The importance of isomorphism in selecting the dimensions and order of interventions was illustrated previously in dealing with extramarital affairs (Chapter Twelve). An isomorphic cross-modality intervention involves effecting dimension "A" in a manner optimal for that dimension and in the process deliberately causing an impact on dimension "B" that is optimal for it as well. When an intervention in dimension "A" impacts dimensions "B" through "Z" in a way that makes them fall into place like the tumblers in a lock, one understands the system. This often occurs on a lesser scale, for example, in working with incongruous power hierarchies—an intervention in one hierarchy also has simultaneous congruent impact on another, because all hierarchies in the marriage ultimately exist within a common system.

The concept of isomorphic cross-modality intervention brings us to the conceptual and clinical issues of applying systems theory to sex therapy. There are many ways this can be done: (a) making an intervention in the nonsexual system to create an impact in the sexual system, or (b) making an intervention in the sexual system to create an impact in a nonsexual system. The former strategy is the way marriage and family therapists commonly think of applying systems theory to sexual problems: focusing on the "purpose" that the sexual "symptom" serves in the nonsexual systems—thereby obviating the need to deal directly with the sexual system (and eroticism).

This common "systemic" approach (i.e., sexual problems as "merely" system-caused and system-maintaining symptoms, without any independent etiology of their own) is much less sophisticated than it appears, and far less than it needs to be. Part of the problem is that it doesn't accurately account for the facts:

- It doesn't account for the large number of *functional* people who have the ability to *bypass (the most common sexual style)*. Lots of people have utilitarian genital function during mediocre sex in troubled marriages.
- *It is not necessarily true* that improving sex will improve the marriage—improving the sex after a point will often trigger new fights and emotional withdrawal (see Chapter Fourteen).
- It isn't necessarily true that improving the marriage will improve the sex.

This last point of the "simple" systemic approach is never really scrutinized. The notion that, "One can improve sex by improving the relationship," is based on the "circular" reasoning that relationship problems cause low quality/quantity of sex (and sexual dysfunctions). On the surface, it *sounds* good—unfortunately, it doesn't *look* good.

Figure 13.1 presents a graphic conceptualization of this relationship. Although the conceptualization *is* systemic, its superficial circularity stems simply from the idea that quality of sex and quality of relationship are *correlated*.

If one moves from point A to point B in Figure 13.1 and monitors the

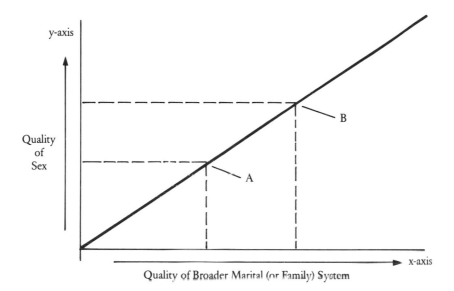

Figure 13.1 Quality of Sex as a Symptom of Broader Systemic Processes

corresponding values on the x and y axes, the quality of sex increases as the quality of the marriage (or family) increases (like a symptom of the system should). Moving from point B to point A, likewise, sexual quality diminishes as the quality of the system declines.

However, there is a flaw in the model: Improving the marriage as a whole will improve the sex just so far. An upper ceiling (i.e., an *asymptote*) is imposed from dimensions not displayed in this model, but which have an impact nonetheless (e.g., levels of differentiation, anxiety intolerance, sexual repertoire, sexual abuse, etc.). The half-truth of the common systemic conceptualization becomes *graphically* obvious; it isn't very different from the simplistic notion that *loving, caring*, and *compromise* lead to good sex.

Figure 13.2 offers a more realistic (and more sophisticated) view of sexuality as a symptom of the broader system.[4] Note that the upper ranges of pat-

---

[4]The micro details in patterns C and D note a minor curvilinear relationship as the marriage runs its course. In pattern C, the relationship improves, with relatively little improvement in the sex; eventually there is a minor regression in the quality of sex as the marriage settles in to its point of long-term equilibrium. In pattern D, the sex improves rapidly, without a corresponding improvement in the quality of the relationship; as it gets clear that little additional improvement in the nonsexual aspects

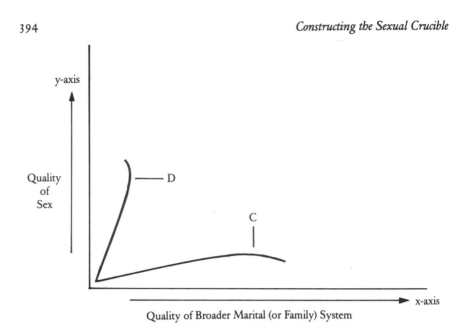

Figure 13.2 Realistic View of Interaction Between Sexual and Nonsexual Systems

terns C and D are truncated. Other aspects of the *sexual system*, not reducible to simple manifestations of the broader system, present an upper limit on how far sex can improve without being directly addressed.

An Example of Isomorphic Intervention: The Sexual Crucible

Sexuality is rarely approached as a (sub)system in its own right to which systems theory can be applied.[5] Notice, however, that Figure 13.1 can be read "backwards" along the same lines that couples in conflict over discrepant desire generate in their arguments: The quality of the marriage increases as the quality of the sex increases.

Therapists rarely think about intervening isomorphically in the sexual domain to create a nonsexual impact (except in mundane ways). This doesn't

---

of the marriage will occur, there is a regression in the relationship, and a cessation of improvement in the sex. In some variants of pattern D, both spouses' sexual interest (even with the relationship problems) can sustain the quality of sex over the long haul; in other cases, there is significant regression in both quality of sex and the broader relationship which often ends in divorce.

[5]Chapter Ten offered an example of such an application to low sexual desire.

imply that better sex cures everything; it suggests, rather, that the elicitation approach allows the sexual domain to be used to work on nonsexual issues.

There is a subtle but important difference between "sex is a symptom of the system" and an elicitation approach: The difference is between primarily intervening in the nonsexual dimension (while monitoring the general characteristics of sex as an outcome measure) vs. looking *into* the sex. In the latter approach, moment to moment interactions (e.g., content, style, subjective experience, interpersonal reaction and counter-reaction) are taken as the *embodiment* of nonsexual issues (both systemic and intrapsychic), and used to intervene in the *sexual* arena to create isomorphic impact; knowledge gained in the elicitation window is used to plan direct interventions in the nonsexual systems as well. *This* is what *integrated* sexual-marital therapy is about.

The "simple" systemic approach to sexuality does involve a cross-modality intervention, but only in the most superficial sense that interventions are made in the nonsexual dimension with the specific intent to evoke a new response in the sexual dimension. However, the sexual crucible focuses on the sexual elicitation window to increase differentation, thus creating a *profound isomorphic impact throughout the system of subsystems.*

Intervening in the sexual domain where isomorphic impact in a *nonsexual* system is the *primary* goal is particularly powerful because (a) it circumvents defenses prepared for a frontal assault on nonsexual topics, (b) it circumvents common defenses to sexual topics by its oblique interest in sex per se, and (c) it enters through the avenue of a *powerful* lynch pin in people's equilibrium (i.e., sex). This type of intervention is possible because the sexual and nonsexual dynamics are interlocking parts of the overall marital system.

Using *emotional hydraulics* one can, for example, (a) intervene in an incongruous power hierarchy in order to (b) change the bedroom interaction, so as to (c) reverse a sexual problem, which (d) dramatically increases awareness of eroticism, so that (e) the desired intrapsychic impact occurs, necessary for creating the requisite (f) self-confrontation, the avoidance of which was perpetuating the incongruous power hierarchy which perpetuated the sexual problem (et cetera, ad infinitum). Most therapists would consider such an intervention to be isormorphic.

THERAPIST MODULATION OF ANXIETY

Our prior discussions of anxiety intolerance and isomorphic intervention come together around the clinical task of modulating patients' anxiety level.

Therapy, like life, is inherently flavored with anxiety; a "good enough" level of anxiety in the sexual crucible implicitly involves activities that make patients somewhat uncomfortable. Little is accomplished by restricting suggestions to those things that the couple can accomplish without anxiety or accepting patients' self-assessed anxiety tolerance as anything more than a self-assessment.

This doesn't mean, however, that the focus of the sexual crucible is on anxiety per se. Anxiety is neither inherently therapeutic nor growth producing; treatment is not as simple as imploding patients with anxiety. What's at issue is the therapist's ability to help patients maintain an *effective* level of anxiety. Therapists differ, however, in the level of anxiety they regard as optimal; these differences show up in the varying emphasis placed on treatment being an anxiety-free "safe haven" where patients are free to do (or not do) or say anything without fear of rejection or reaction from the spouse (or the therapist).

"Safety and Security" Treatment Paradigms

The importance of "safety and security" and the degree to which they can actually be provided is vastly overestimated. While some therapists emphasize a "secure ambiance created by sex therapy [which] provides the couple with the opportunity to learn to make love in freer and more enjoyable ways" (Kaplan, 1974, p. 206), all too often one spouse is punished by the other at home for things said in-session. As pointed out previously, poorly differentiated couples' obsessive anxiety-reducing activities often stifle the emergence of new adaptive responses.

"Safety/security" treatment models reinforce couples' erroneous belief that commitment, interpersonal stability, and "love" will lead to intense forms of eroticism and intimacy. (The widespread occurrence of affairs would suggest that the opposite is true.) "Safety/security" treatment paradigms fuel preexisting distancer-pursuer dynamics, commitment struggles, and fears of engulfment/abandonment.

Safety in therapy is illusive and a matter of perspective. What safe haven do therapy and the therapist offer in the broader framework of patients' lives if treatment is ineffective? What brings most couples into treatment—*lack* of safety in the current situation. Therapists who validate the expectation of safety encourage patients to go nowhere. Life is not free from anxiety; the tasks one faces often disturb one's womb-like comfort—and so does the sexual crucible. The sexual crucible approach focuses on (and develops) the anxiety *tolerance* required for intense intimacy and eroticism.

Treatment paradigms emphasizing reduced anxiety and increased safety are antithetical to enhancing differentiation and exploring sexual potential. Safety and security ultimately come from one's willingness and ability to stand alone and take care of oneself. Anxiety is always present when "being alive and facing the moment," and tolerating higher levels of intimacy and eroticism. "Safety/security" treatment paradigms reinforce anxiety intolerance and reduce motivation for continued treatment beyond that required to quiet the anxiety of "no-change" because change itself is anxiety-provoking.

This discussion raises questions about (a) optimal levels of anxiety and conflict and (b) the fragility of patients' egos. *Any* treatment approach requires a therapist possessing the practical skill and conceptual depth to evaluate a wide range of personal adjustment and personality structure; no purpose is served in overwhelming the tolerances of psychotic individuals or those with severe borderline personality structure. "Borderline" features run the entire gamut of severity, however, and people with long histories of psychiatric treatment have often found the sexual crucible to be the one most helpful and most rewarding.[6]

For instance, one couple presented a long history of inhibited sexual desire. Both spouses demonstrated numerous features of borderline personality; the wife, in particular, presented herself as extremely infantile and psychologically fragile.

After some months of conjoint treatment, Connie, the identified patient, was seen for several individual sessions when her husband went out of town on business. These sessions were marked by her constant tears and complaints of harsh treatment from me. After one individual sessions, I felt punitive, insensitive, and hesitant to discuss anything that might upset her. I ruminated on this all the way home from work,

---

[6]Many people who benefited from prior long-term psychotherapy but continued to view themselves as psychologically fragile have done quite well in the sexual crucible. Such people are often *not* as fragile as they have convinced themselves, their partner, and prior therapists through lengthy treatment (and sometimes, hospitalization). A particularly notable subgroup are patients in their mid fifties and older who are capable of functioning at a far higher level of integration than previously demonstrated. They have not been challenged to function that way, and their relationships have evolved correspondingly low expectations for both spouses. These individuals emerge from treatment with a vibrant sense of self and an intense sexual-marital relationship they thought they missed out on forever. Such patients have taught me to stop limiting my own estimations of what people can do in their struggles for integrity.

feeling emotionally drained and unappreciated. As I debriefed myself, licking my wounds, first I felt bruised, and then I felt abused. Suddenly it occurred to me that Connie had been emotionally punishing me while she used her tears to make it look like the converse was occurring. I suddenly felt refreshed and renewed.

As Connie launched into her tearful stance at the subsequent session, I inquired as to her reaction to the prior meeting. She replied that she felt like I had "beaten her up." I smiled and thanked the puzzled wife. "You taught me something last session I have never realized before," I said. "It took me several hours to recognize that *you* beat *me* up last time. Your tears made me think that it was the other way around. I think you just helped me as a therapist, but you've ruined it for future patients who want to beat me up with tears. If you want to beat me up, however, you are welcome to try. Let's just do it openly."

At this point Connie who had stopped crying, leaned forward in her chair. Clear-eyed and anything but fragile, she said, "I don't want to fight fair. When I want to get you, I'll do it *my* way."

This was the most intimate contact between Connie and me up to that point. Rather than "poisoning" the relationship, this interaction strengthened it. What was most notable about her at that moment was not her anger or her malevolence, not her negative transference, her introjects or her projective identifications; what was most noteworthy was that she actually started functioning in a more adult and less regressive fashion. In fact, it focused the discussion on her strengths, resilience, and ability to take care of herself.

More and more, I am impressed by people's strengths rather than their weaknesses; as I increasingly dwell on the former rather than on the latter, people seem to rise to the level of their abilities rather than sink to the level of their anxieties.[7] When individuals with blatant psychoses are excluded from consideration, competent clinicians' assessment of optimal levels of anxiety and conflict will differ. One therapist's "constructive crisis" is another's "invitation for psychosis" and a third's "insufficient intervention." Approaches that emphasize sensate focus prescriptions for desensitization will tend to modulate anxiety at lower levels, as will those emphasizing safety/security in the treatment relationship.

---

[7]This point is particularly relevant for maintaining perspective when reading the lovely results in the case example presented in the subsequent chapter. The reader may mistakenly assume that the approaches outlined in this book are applicable only to an elite patient subgroup (e.g., intelligent, psychologically minded, treatment-positive, highly verbal, etc.). Be aware that *many* couples that look primitive, embittered, and fused at the outset of treatment quite often obtain the extensive gains to be described; the therapist's role in creating "easy" and "difficult" cases will be discussed in Chapter Sixteen.

The well-differentiated therapist working in an elicitation model of integrated sexual-marital therapy is neither intent on precipitating crisis or "stripping defenses" nor fearful of relationship disequilibrium. Maintaining a "good enough" anxiety level does not mean that the therapist *creates* anxiety. The therapist's task, instead, is anxiety *modulation*: using anxiety that is already present. *Couples who enter treatment are de facto already in crisis and often seek therapy to avoid it rather than resolve it.*

When anxiety is managed effectively, construction of *additional* crises of the therapist's design is not required. *Utilizing* inherent paradoxes to arrive at a new level of individual and systemic resolution (rather than constructing additional crises) is often sufficient.[8] For example, the crucible offers the opportunity to develop *anatomy-independent* eroticism and self-worth. Suggestions might involve daring oneself to be held or receive pleasure when one is *not* performing as one expects, and mastering the feelings elicited. Treatment can utilize current sexual difficulties to develop increased tolerance of intimacy rather than reinforcing a panicked pursuit for genital functioning that actually limits it.

The foregoing discussions may lead to the erroneous assumption that the therapist deliberately tries to make patients anxious by "pushing" them to face their problems, or to do (or not do) certain activities; nothing could be farther from the goal. "Pushing" patients to engage or not engage in particular styles of behavior destroys the possibility of increased differentiation and the power of the sexual crucible. Patients' current level of sexual and marital discomfort often stems from attempts to get *around* rather than *through* personal conflicts and life decisions. Intense but subtle negotiations occur in regard to who will be responsible for supplying the motivation for patients to do the work of growing. Patients both fear and *wish* the therapist *will* push them forward: Patients attempt to maneuver the therapist into thinking that s/he *is* pushing (too hard) and/or *should* push (harder). Either way, the notion that the therapist can't/won't push for growth highlights uncomfortable recognitions:

- The problem doesn't have to change. The therapist is unwilling to pander to the patient's performance anxiety or concern about the relationship's future "if nothing happens."
- In "pushing" patients, the therapist destroys the anxiety and gratification of the patient's mastering himself/herself, even if the patient complies.

---

[8]The therapeutic use of inherent paradox is discussed in detail in Chapter Fifteen.

- The very notion of "compliance" or "defiance" of the therapist destroys the work of differentiation.
- Anger that the therapist *won't* push defends against the more frightening recognition that the therapist *couldn't* push the patient into "progress"; personal development involves a *willingness*.

The therapist's deportment conveys a troubling reality: The unwillingness to push the patient into compliance stems from neither lack of caring nor lack of activity. The therapist is quite active and involved rather than passive and detached; *he/she is invested but differentiated*. This involves manifesting no greater level of investment than the patients, and willingness to "let go" when necessary. When a patient confronts his/her fear of change, fear of no change, and recognition that he/she is all alone, it creates a *powerful* crucible for differentiation and resolution of individual and systemic issues.

Inside the sexual crucible, the therapist offers discussion, interpretations, challenges, and suggestions, and monitors the style of his/her self-presentation; the result creates tension for change. The therapist's behavior conveys an alternative vision of "caring": holding onto him/herself in order to permit each spouse to fight with him/herself for resolution. This involves actively resisting the easier alternative of "getting helpful," reducing both partners' anxieties, truncating their struggle-with-self and encouraging fusion and dependency. *The therapist's own level of differentiation (demonstrated through detriangulation)[9] has a paradoxical impact: it escalates patients' conflicts while reducing their overall anxiety.*

Part of the requisite paradigm shift can be staged around "trusting one's own feelings." Different therapists draw different implications from this phrase; the one that creates differentiation (rather than dependency and irresponsibility) involves the therapeutic stance that *encouraging patients to trust their own feelings and perceptions does not imply that their perceptions are accurate or "approved of" by the therapist.* Part of "standing on your own two feet" involves taking responsibility for determining the accuracy of your perceptions, making your own mistakes, and paying the consequences; personal responsibility is still required when accepting the suggestions of others (e.g., even from the therapist).

Except in cases where a patient's judgment is sufficiently impaired to rep-

---

[9]Detriangulation is a therapeutic stance involving the therapist's personal development; it is discussed in Chapter Sixteen.

resent a clear and imminent physical danger to him/herself or others, the therapist takes no stand on the accuracy of the patient's perceptions.

- The therapist is not omniscient.
- The patient (and not the therapist) will have to live with the consequences of the patient's decisions.
- Attempting to "save" patients from their distortions only makes it "safer" for them to *not* confront themselves. The couple's prior history demonstrates that arguing with either spouse about projective distortions is ineffective.
- Statements regarding the accuracy of the patient's perceptions undermine his/her responsibility and opportunity to self-soothe and self-validate, and undermine the process of differentiation.

Patients need to be alone in their struggles with their own ambivalence. Given that spouses' struggles are often parallel and interlocking, the therapist intervenes to stave off partners' fighting with each other rather than themselves, operationalizing the dilemma of existential separateness and triggering increased differentiation.

THE PATHOLOGY OF EMPATHY

Many therapists have been trained as professional anxiety reducers, able to empathize and "accept" almost anything. Like the lay public, they believe that anything that can be understood, ventilated, and "accepted" is thereby resolved; one does not have to *do* anything for resolution, one simply has to *be*. Such therapists are overly ready to offer "nurturance," without due consideration for what they are "nurturing" or whether it actually serves its intended therapeutic purpose. Kerr and Bowen (1988) commented:

The process of trying to be more differentiated requires more awareness of the influence of anxiety and emotional reactivity on one's actions and inactions, and it requires some reexamination of one's basic assumptions about behavior and the origin of human problems. A common assumption about people with emotional problems, for example, is that they did not receive enough "love" and support from their families. Many people have an attitude that if only they could get more "love" and attention, they would feel and function better. The concept of differentiation places this assumption in a broader context, namely, that the most needy people have achieved the least emotional separation from their families. The broader context can provide a guiding principle for an approach to human problems that runs counter to the feeling and subjective process. An approach based on the feeling process is one that says, "People who feel unloved need more love." An approach based on a systems principle is one that says, "People who feel unloved are addicted to love." An intense and nonthreatening relationship may relieve the person's symptoms, but it does so by replicating what once existed in the early parent-child relationship (in reality or fantasy), not by supplying a need that was never met.

Many dedicated mental health professionals have tried to give patients the "love" and "caring" both the professional and the patient are sure the patient never had. Many therapists have then found themselves in a hopelessly ensnared transference in which the patient perceived the therapist to be as "ungiving" as the mother. When a therapist's remarks to a patient are guided by the assumption that people who feel rejected and unloved are the product of an intense emotional attachment to their families, the remarks may not "sound" or "feel" right to the patient or the therapist. Regardless of how they feel, the remarks usually open up communication and reduce tension in the therapist-patient relationship. The constructiveness of the remarks appears to be based on a "collision" of different ways of thinking, different basic assumptions. (Kerr & Bowen, 1988, p. 109)

Empathy is not necessarily nurturant; both empathy and nurturance are therapeutic tools rather than ends in themselves. Nurturance is best defined by its intended outcome (rather than a stereotypic behavior)—enhanced development of the nurturee. Sometimes nurturance is a firm, well-timed, benevolent provocation to face the issues of one's existence, like Minuchin's "stroke and nudge." Validating patients' view of nurturance as something soothing only perpetuates their inability to self-soothe. It is all too easy to "soothe" (rather than confront) patients who rule their bed and their household through their emotional volatility.

Poorly differentiated therapists who gratify their own needs to soothe and stroke at the patients' expense *induce* regression and transference storms. Therapists operating in the safety-security treatment paradigm sometimes attempt to circumvent this problem by avoiding "personal involvement" (i.e., utilization of transferences that arise) with patients (e.g., Kaplan, 1974, p. 242). When the "safety/security" paradigm falls apart, however, the ensuing mess is usually blamed on patients' "personality characteristics"; Kerr and Bowen's theory of *detriangulation* offers an alternative perspective: The therapist *must* become personally involved but remain differentiated. This stance is more consistent with the goals and orientation of the sexual crucible.

Apfelbaum's treatment emphasis on *entitlement*, which involves more active engagement between therapist and patient, has its own pitfalls. Entitlement, like empathy, is a wonderful therapeutic approach that can just as easily end up immobilizing patients as empowering them. A sense of entitlement offers little when it reflects narcissism rather than ego strength; the difference is the ability to support oneself emotionally through the quest for that which one feels entitled.

Apfelbaum operationalizes entitlement within treatment by focusing on sharing *feeling* during sexual interaction. He suggests that in sharing rather than hiding one's anxieties and fears (including the fear of negative reactions to sharing) the patient transcends sexual performing. However, "sharing" does not necessarily create the ego strength or differentiation required for intense intimacy. The process of being understood by the partner (and the assumption that being understood implies acceptance and compliance with what is transmitted) is gratifying and performance-anxiety-reducing. But the willingness and ability to unilaterally share oneself (i.e., level-2 intimacy), including maintaining oneself in the face of anticipated or actual reactions from the partner, are the bedrock of marital intimacy and the ultimate performance-anxiety reducer.

Confusion About "Confusion"

"Confusion" is one arena in which the politics of anxiety management are often played out in treatment. The ability to tolerate confusion, like tolerance of anxiety, is a developmental step: (a) it involves recognizing the limits of one's "factual" knowledge, and (b) it requires holding onto a core sense of adequacy and competency. Confusion is the *awareness* that one does not know one's solution or direction, *rather than the absence of all information*. Knowing what one does not know is a very powerful form of knowledge, and generally one of the hardest to come by.

Patients sometimes respond to confusion by suggesting:

- that confusion is negative,
- that it is the therapist's responsibility to "unconfuse" them,
- that confusion has immobilized them, and nothing can be done until they "understand," and
- that the therapist's personal answers will help them.

Confusion is either an inherent problem or a therapeutic opportunity, depending on the treatment paradigm. As Friedman (1990) has Cassandra point out, confusion is rarely recognized as an opportunity to confront oneself about the *need* to know, the intolerance of anxiety and ambiguity, and the anticipation of dissatisfaction. In a world without doubt, what does faith mean?

Integrity is the ability to enter into confusion. When the topic of *integrity* was introduced in Chapter Twelve, it was emphasized that the focus of discussion was clinical rather than moral; how one handles "confusion" is just such an example. Issues of integrity are commonly involved in (a) avoiding anxiety and confusion, (b) feigning confusion to avoid confronting anxieties, and (c) hiding behind one's real confusion to avoid one's fears.

Confusion is an initial response to inherent paradox. In Ericksonian hypnosis, confusion is one way patients drive themselves inward. From confusion springs belief in oneself and the ability to master new, unknown, and apparently insurmountable tasks. The *quality* of patients' confusion determines whether the appropriate response from the therapist is clarification or a compliment for becoming confused.

Some traditionally trained therapists may find the shift to the sexual crucible's use of inherent paradox as confusing as do most patients. While therapists' confusion is not very comfortable, it is not problematic; resolution requires that the therapist go through the same process as patients do to make the paradigm shift. This is as it should be, since therapists and patients generally differ only by professional training rather than level of development. Therapists' intolerance for confusion restricts the development of alternative paradigms for sexual-marital therapy, and their own personal abilities.

THE SELF IN THE SYSTEM VS.
"TREATING THE RELATIONSHIP"

The orientation of the sexual crucible is contained in the phrase "relationship with self in the context of relationship with partner." The therapist aligns with each spouse as a separate individual, reinforcing development of *self*-control and obviating the need to control the partner to control one's emotionality.

At the time it was put forth, Masters and Johnson's notion of "the relationship is the patient" was as uncritically accepted as was "sex is a natural function." Granted, "treating the relationship" was a vast improvement over the exclusively individual focus of psychoanalytic psychotherapy; it was readily accepted by therapists who treated sexual problems and the growing ranks of marriage and family therapists.

However, there is nothing magic or sacrosanct about "treating the relationship"; like most half-truths, the notion of "treating the relationship" is self-blinding. Focusing on the relationship per se does not implicitly reflect an understanding of systems theory. One can focus on the couple from a rational, linear cognitive-behavioral perspective (e.g., Masters and Johnson)[10] as well as a psychoanalytic one (e.g., Kaplan). The major question in treating the relationship is: How sophisticated is one's understanding of the ways systems actually operate? The system is often best dealt with by the therapist making his/her alliance with the individuals as separate entities, as a systemic intervention. Focusing on the relationship *doesn't* dictate making the primary alliance the one between the therapist and "the marriage." Cross-modality interventions are possible: (a) focusing on an individual to unbalance a relationship, (b) focusing on the relationship to unbalance an individual, and (c) making an alliance with both spouses to unbalance the *marriage and both* individuals.

Sometimes one *can* "treat the couple" as a single entity, but this approach rarely produces the enhanced differentiation necessary for *intense* intimacy and eroticism. More often than not, prior attempts at fusion perpetuated (if not created) their presenting problems; a therapist's focus on "treating the relationship" only exacerbates the situation. Couples often require treatment *because* they try to "work on the relationship" or "make a commitment to the relationship."

"Treating the relationship" doesn't require losing sight of the individuals: It involves, in fact, *seeing the individuals in the system*. The solution often requires breaking "relationship problems" into component interlocking individual issues, and working with them isomorphically.

---

[10]The characterization of Masters and Johnson's approach as a cognitive-behavioral orientation is my own; many other clinicians have described their work similarly (e.g., LoPiccolo, 1978; Nichols, 1984; Witkin, 1980). Leiblum and Pervin (1980) point out that Masters and Johnson's publications stimulated great interest from self-described behaviorists. However, Masters and Johnson don't describe themselves as behaviorists; in fact, they don't categorize their approach at all. At one point, they described their approach as "atheoretical" because it did not fit within any approach they were familiar with. More recently, Heiman and Grafton-Becker suggested that Masters and Johnson's approach could *possibly* be conceptualized in a systemic framework; however, this is clearly a retrofitting of theoretical schemas:

> The heart of Masters and Johnson's approach, sensate focus with its gradual increase of sexual stimuli, can easily be conceptualized as a generic systems intervention; the sexual relationship is a patient overwhelmed with anxiety, and each member of the couple helps put "the patient" at increasing ease. However, Masters and Johnson never claimed to be systems theorists (or behaviorists, although their techniques, as we have mentioned, are often viewed as emerging from that school). Part of their program's effectiveness is that they devised a treatment that worked very well for most symptomatic, nonphysically based sexual problems. One could call it a "universal prescription" (cf. Selvini-Palazzoli & Viaro, 1988). (1989, p. 61)

Presenting suggested modifications to the *couple* seems obvious; even when successful, however, this strategy obviates the crucible of differentiation. When interventions are presented *individually*, the crucible is set: *Unilateral* (rather than conjoint) tasks embrace level-2 intimacy and enhance differentiation.

> A great deal has been learned about the concept of differentiation by observing the obstacles people encounter in trying to raise their basic level during the course of family psychotherapy. A person with the ability and motivation can, through a gradual process of learning that is converted into action, become more of a self in his family and other relationship systems. This process of change has been called "defining a self" because visible *action* is taken to which others *respond*. . . . When someone attempts to be more of a self in a relationship system, the absolutely predictable response from important others is, "You are wrong; change back; if you don't, these are the consequences!" In fact, if such responses do not occur, one's efforts to define more of a self are probably inconsequential. (Kerr & Bowen, 1988, p. 100)

Strategically, primary alliances with the spouses *as individuals* rather than as a couple are contrary to patients' anticipations of conjoint therapy. People thinking about divorce often seek an individual therapist, fearing a marital therapist will sell out his/her individual interests in favor of perpetuating the marriage. Likewise, people seek individual therapy or individual sessions in conjoint therapy to screen their thoughts in private before presenting themselves to the spouse. This involves more than simply wanting to clear one's thoughts or wanting more time for intensive self-focus; the goal is often to modulate what the spouse gets to see of them (i.e., the antithesis of intimacy).

Steve, for example, originally requested individual consultation for his problem of low sexual desire and intermittent erectile difficulty during coitus. Steve and Nancy had been married for almost 30 years, during which time they had had "wonderful" sex except for the last two years. Steve said Nancy was proficient in bed and a "really great" sex partner for him; by his report, their sex was very intimate with lots of inventiveness and creativity. Nancy had begun to complain about his "lack of communication," "lack of affection," and his lack of sexual desire; sexual frequency had dropped from three or four times per week to about once per month.

Steve thought that the problem was that his wife's body was aging and he didn't find her physically attractive anymore. However, he could never tell her this, he was quick to add. Steve felt that his wife was "highly sensitive" and needed constant affection and reassurance; he was sure she would be very hurt to know his feelings towards her.

When Steve reported not really enjoying sex for the last two years, I asked him what he thought about during it. Steve said he thought about "satisfying" Nancy. On closer inspection, this meant he wanted to make her reach orgasm and get it over with. Steve found his mind wandering during sex, sometimes thinking that he just wanted to "shut her up" for the next several weeks. After listening to his description of Nancy being "highly sensitive," I suggested that this was his way of saying that he found her to be highly emotionally reactive, dependent, insecure, and demanding. Steve had two reactions: (a) it was true, and (b) this was an awful thing to say and feel, *about someone else* — acting as if feeling this was tantamount to doing something to Nancy, and implicitly suggesting that she *should* take his feelings as a reflection on herself.

I asked Steve if he thought Nancy knew about his thoughts and feelings during sex; he looked perplexed. He had never considered this before, and wasn't sure. I suggested that the implications were interesting either way; Steve asked me to explain.

I pointed out that if his wife didn't know his feelings during sex, then his prior report that they had intimate sex for many years was not very credible. If they were truly intimate all these years, then wouldn't his wife be aware of his mental state during sex? Wouldn't she be aware that she was no longer in emotional contact with him? More accurately, Steve's report raised the question of what he regarded as intimate sex, and what in fact was happening in the sex they did have.

What if, on the other hand, his wife *was* aware of his mental attitude towards her and, in the face of that knowledge, was demanding more of the same? That raised the possibility that perhaps his wife was not as interested in *intimacy* with him as he thought; she might *want* to be serviced by him as long as he kept his feelings to himself and proved to be a proficient technical partner.

Steve was uncomfortable with both sets of implications. Having walked in thinking that his situation was both clear and unsolvable, suddenly Steve was in the crucible.

Steve returned to the next session, stating that the intervening week had been an emotional roller coaster. He had been withdrawn and contemplative after the session; his wife immediately sensed this and pursued him for an explanation. Steve avoided disclosing his consultation with me; she persisted, complaining they never talked anymore. He still resisted; Nancy would not let it go. Eventually, they had a "knock-down drag-out fight." Steve chose this moment to tell her that he did not find her sexually attractive anymore.

Hurt and "wounded," Nancy said that she knew she was not as attractive as she used to be. At first Steve disagreed and tried to reassure her. She became inconsolable, and increasingly labile. Steve said he felt angry and caught in a no-win situation, "having finally told her what I was thinking." Nancy threatened to leave and packed her bags. At that point Steve thought he had nothing to lose: He told her his whole theory about not find her aging body attractive, giving a full account of his thoughts. The ensuing fight raged for hours into the night.

Steve never clearly defined himself with Nancy until he thought she was on her way out the door. Whenever he thought the marriage might survive, he lied *in the name of protecting his wife and the marriage.*

Not surprisingly, the evening concluded with Steve and Nancy having very intense sex, which was repeated the following morning. Nancy was still distraught the next day, until she called a friend for a referral for a therapist for herself. Suddenly she was calm and reintegrated rapidly.

When asked why they had "great sex" after the fight, Steve suggested it had been so long since their last sexual encounter. This "horniness" theory might explain the first night, I suggested, but not the subsequent morning. Moreover, unless her body changed significantly while they were fighting, he experienced desire and "great sex" both times with the same body that had (to Steve's way of thinking) previously precluded it. Steve's phenomenological experience did not jibe with his theories about his lack of sexual interest.

This discrepancy contained a clue about a possible solution, as well as a hint about why it hadn't occurred yet. The difference, I suggested, might have been his *telling her* about his "sagging flesh" theory, even though the theory itself did not seem to be true (i.e., level-2 intimacy). Steve presented himself as he saw himself, defining himself in front of his wife. Said differently, when *he* was intimate with *her*, Steve felt sexual desire and intensity. On the other hand, Steve only did that when he thought the relationship was over; when he thought it might continue, he dodged.

Conjoint treatment offered numerous opportunities for isomorphic intervention. Individual therapy played into Steve's tendency to modulate his self-presentation according to Nancy's anticipated reaction and Nancy's tendency to take Steve's behavior as a reflection upon herself. Steve initially assumed that conjoint treatment was an implicit commitment to continue the marriage; this was exactly the type of contract that would cause Steve to *not* be intimate or have desire for sex. Steve saw his lack of sexual desire as his "excuse" to leave: A return of sexual desire required greater self-disclosure and maintaining himself. If Steve was going out to a world full of women, on the other hand, he might want to learn to stand on his own two feet with one before he went.

Steve was in the crucible: survival of the marriage and successful divorce hinged on the very same acts. Holding onto himself (rather than his wife) gave him the best strategic positioning, whether he remained in the marriage or left. Making the alliance with *both* spouses as separate people didn't permit Steve to avoid making a clear presentation of self; the same alliance increased Nancy's ability to differentiate herself from her husband. Engaged in this manner, one partner's development drove the other's forward to greater capacity for intimacy and eroticism. Conjoint treatment embodied the intimacy both said they wanted (but were insufficiently differentiated to tolerate).

David Kantor's (1980) four-level developmental framework provides a convenient means by which to understand Steve and Nancy's situation from a multisystemic perspective.

> Level 1. *Meaning structures*: The personal meanings individuals bring to and acquire in the system: their histories, myths and lores, icons or symbols, the things they notice and talk about.
> Level 2. *Action structures*: The behavioral repertoire.
> Level 3. *Strategic structures*: Characteristic interactional patterns and sequences reflecting hierarchical rules and alliances.
> Level 4. *Model structures*: Drawn from the elements of the prior three levels, model structures contain each spouse's ideals, goals, and relationship values, including the perceived core purpose of marriage.

Kantor's four levels organize the diverse topics that have been discussed thus far:

- *Meaning structures* = object relations issues, unresolved individual conflicts, level of differentiation, history of the dyad and families of origin.
- *Action structures* = sexual and nonsexual behavior repertoire.
- *Strategic structures* = interactional patterns, sexual initiation patterns, courtship rituals, incongruous power hierarchies, extended family structure.
- *Model structures* = beliefs and paradigms on a macro level: implicit marital contracts, level-1 or level-2 intimacy, the "meanings" of conflict or low sexual desire.

In Steve and Nancy's case, the sexual behavior pattern (action structures) yielded information contrary to the stated model structures. Confronting this led to shifts in interactional patterns (strategic structures), which opened the way to potential changes in object relations issues and level of differentiation (meaning structures).

In an elicitation approach to sexual-marital therapy, model structures and attributional meanings of behaviors are embedded in patients' sexual behavior. These competing meanings and models are missed when sex therapy focuses upon the couple's behavioral exchange only to discern techniques ineffective for arousal and orgasm.

When couples enter treatment, the breakdown of spouses' competing model structures are glaringly obvious in their repertoire and styles of interaction. Couples expect the therapist's focus to remain on this level of "action structures." The therapist's behavioral suggestions tend initially to confirm this presupposed focus on sexual technique. Thus, it is particularly striking to couples when the therapist utilizes their own (sexual) behavior to move to meaning, strategic, and model structures (levels 1, 3, and 4). Where the couple previously saw only ineffective physical contact, the therapist highlights (a) the embodiment of each partner's unresolved issues, (b) partners' interaction patterns, *and* (c) a vehicle for resolution.

Kantor (1980) offers an important hypothesis that *marital crises involve normal developmental tasks*. Ritual impasse represents " . . . a positive assertion and representation of identity, an opportunity for transformation, a scenario for family development . . . involving an assertion by the individuals that their inner meanings are not to be ignored and that they see themselves as transmitters of legitimate ideal values" (1980, p. 147).

Kantor hypothesizes:

> *A normal developmental crisis is an identity struggle taking place on all four system levels.* The more outward features of the crisis are: (1) a temporary collapse of the system's problem-solving capabilities, that is, a breakdown in its *steering mechanisms* (events occurring at the pattern level of organization); and (2) a constriction and rigidification of its behavior (at the action level of organization), that is, a gravitation into stuck *psychopolitics*. (p. 146, italics original)

Kantor suggests that identity crises can result in two developmental changes: (a) increased structural complexity and efficiency of the relationship, and (b) increased richness in the internal life of the individuals and their communicational complexity.

Differentiation, anxiety tolerance, and the capacity for intense intimacy and eroticism are forged within the sexual crucible *if the couple can hold on* through the ritual impasse. In the process, *intense* conflict is an anticipatable and necessary occurrence.

Utilizing Intense Conflict

The real elegance and power of the sexual crucible approach become evident with couples having extremely high or low relationship conflict. The latter will be considered in the subsequent chapter; highly conflicted couples, often

considered unamenable to sexual therapy (and an anathema to many therapists) will be addressed here.

Treating couples with extreme relationship discord embraces the very process of people holding onto themselves rather than their spouse; conjoint
treatment becomes the literal and figurative embodiment of differentiation and
intimacy. As people gain insight into themselves, the partner is sitting right
there, watching. There is no "delayed broadcast" of self that allows for editing;
people start living their intimacy "televised live and on the spot."

When one partner redefines his/her identity and position in the relationship, what often starts out as defiance of the partner becomes an act of self-
confrontation. Although there is less "thumbing of noses" at the partner, the
other spouse often continues to take it that way nonetheless; the second
spouse refuses to recognize any possible motivation of the first that is not self-
referential. The inability to "permit" the first spouse to have his/her own
personal crucible reflects the underlying emotional fusion.

This situation creates the opportunity to construct a second, interlocking
crucible for the second spouse. The purpose here is *not* to directly support the
first spouse in his/her fledgling attempts at differentiation; that would undermine his/her efforts. Moreover, it isn't necessary: what is upsetting the partner
is the first spouse's *success* in functioning more independently. The second
spouse's *insistence* on taking the other's behavior personally constitutes another
channel of "prime time intimacy" being broadcast live and in color in front of
the partner.

Focus of Interventions

From an ego psychology perspective, encouraging both partners to hold onto
themselves rather than negotiate away their fragile self-definition involves
"approaching from the side of the defense." Necessary ego-strengthening and
increasing differentiation occur by the therapist taking each partner's perceptions at face value, encouraging each to respond to his/her own reality, rather
than that of the partner.

When one perceives one's partner as an invader broaching the walls of one's
psychological integrity, it makes little difference whether the conflict involves
giving oneself up to a partner who actually needs to dominate and control or
giving oneself up to the embodiment of one's introject of a controlling,
dominating parent (they often coincide). The crucible is still the same: the
conflict of giving oneself up to one's fears (whether externally or internally
based) or holding onto oneself and going *through* one's fears. It makes little
sense at such times to suggest that patients are, for the most part, struggling

with projections of their own object relations issues (even when this is the case). To do so negates patients' reality in the interest of "helping" them, patronizingly encouraging them to distrust their own perceptions and rely on the therapist. Accepting help on these terms undercuts the very differentiation that is so badly needed.

Couples often have to reach a point of relationship destabilization in order to reintegrate at a higher level of differentiation and anxiety tolerance. The stabilization that subsequently occurs reflects more than just the partners' having "cooled off" or scared themselves and backed down. *In reaching the brink of terminating the relationship, partners recognize that it is their refusal to accept responsibility for their own lives that makes power struggles and withholding fights possible. "Power struggles" and control fights are issues only as long as the pair remains emotionally fused.* This sobering and differentiation-enhancing realization makes it easier for them to handle the prospect of separation, and easier to stay together in an unfused fashion.

Use of Touch

It is possible to use physical contact between spouses having varying degrees of conflict, including open hostility and *extreme* resentment. In the latter case, the use of touch is totally contrary to conventional wisdom, which is perhaps why it works so well; it is another example of isomorphic multisystemic interventions. The strategy involves redefining the scope, nature, and purpose of physical touch to increase differentiation and modify the strategic balance in the dyad; "unhooking" physical contact from its common meaning as an expression of caring, commitment, or desire to pleasure the partner. The stated purpose remains consistent with the notion of the elicitation window: for each person to use touch in the dyad as a way of understanding what he/ she has contributed to the current difficulties (particularly nonsexual ones) so that he or she can avoid creating similar problems for himself/herself in this or any other relationship. There is no commitment to either the partner or the marriage; the commitment is to *self*.

Detaching touch from "desire to please the partner" is a particularly interesting point. Many couples are so thoroughly fused and rancorous that they willingly forego their own pleasure in order to deprive the partner. Unhooking touch from desire to please the partner creates a sudden transformation in the power hierarchies between the spouses. Whereas physical contact in the midst of strife is often seen as a selling out of self, the paradigm shift permits it to be used as an ultimate demonstration of relationship with self.

In accepting the use of touch in the relationship for *personal development*, the identified patient unilaterally changes the basic nature of the sexual relationship and the overall relationship dynamics. One spouse's sexual interest or behavior can no longer be used as a reflection upon the other. The impact that this has on the relationship, and on the two individuals, is profound.

Couples expend time and energy constructing the ritual impasse; it contains encoded information on the four levels Kantor (1980) conceptualizes. Spouses can use the current context to work on themselves, and then move on or stay together in more productive ways. Given the choice between this and taking the additional time to construct their issues with new partners, most couples take the current opportunity. When one spouse uses the current relationship, including the current hostility, as a way to learn to maintain him/herself and take care of "individual" difficulties, the implicit capacity for a more self-contained and self-respecting exit from the relationship suddenly cools both spouses' threats to leave. The power of the elicitation window emerges as the asymptomatic partner's dependency for validation and security becomes manifest.

Increased destabilization and rigid psychopolitical positions create a crucible of *internal* conflict. The difference between statements designed to torment the partner (or gain strategic position) and those that lead to differentiation and intimacy is in the therapist's use of the crucible. Ultimatums issued to one's partner always contain an often overlooked self-addressed ultimatum as well; threats diminish when the therapist changes their vector by encouraging partners to maintain their integrity by carrying through on self-declarative statements. Realization of the inability to trust *oneself* (rather than one's partner) changes the locus of conflict. When the individual is torn between holding onto him/herself and holding onto the relationship at any cost (i.e., giving up his/her self-definition and integrity), the crucible of differentiation emerges. *Differentiation breaks the sexual "choke hold" of incongruous power hierarchies and sexual withholding in marriage.*

"Normal" Sadism – Tearing Someone's Heart Out

Intense conflict is one of the darker sides of marriage; sadism is one of the darker sides of eroticism. The lousy blowjob and the "wham bam" may be born in ignorance, but marriage is where both are perfected. Marriage is where one learns to "screw" one's spouse two ways at once—withholding the erotic gratification the partner craves *while* having sex. "The Japanese have a word for it," said J. P. McEvoy, "It's judo—the art of conquering by yielding. The Western equivalent of judo is, 'Yes, dear'" (in Peter, 1980, p. 324).

Jokes about the masochism of marriage are commonplace; *sadism* directed towards one's spouse, however, is rarely acknowledged.[11] Recognizing sadism is one's partner (or oneself) when the relationship is rancorous is difficult enough to tolerate; seeing it surface without apparent provocation when one's spouse appears generous, considerate, and loving is something else again. It creates the crucible of whole-object attachment: accepting sadism as a part of *everyone*.[12] This painful awareness is best used to (a) increase one's own ability to self-soothe, (b) increase one's acceptance of existential separateness, (c) increase one's respect for *friendship* in marriage.

The dynamics of "normal" marital sadism are intuitive, paralleling every child's dependency on his/her mother's body for physical and emotional gratification. Even women who take pleasure in giving life and nourishment sometimes experience the impulse to deprive the child of the *pleasure* of the breast (i.e., providing physical "nourishment" while withholding the *giving* of it). Mothers sometimes feel frustrated and angry about the infant's desire for her body, feeling that joint-ownership has suddenly occurred or that she no longer belongs to herself. The resulting resentment surfaces in being deliberately slow to respond, and shoving her breast in the child's mouth with the angry (withholding) thought, "Here, take it, God damn you."[13]

In daily life, folks deliberately/unconsciously frustrate the salient underlying needs of loved ones while (eventually) responding to the manifest request. One husband, for example, emotionally tortured his family (including the family dog) by making them whine and complain about his "procrastination," which *he* then complained about and used to rationalize further non-performance.

Sadism is the undisclosed interpersonal component of "procrastination." It

---

[11]*Sadism* is defined in the American Psychiatric Association glossary (1975) as "Pleasure derived from inflicting physical or psychological pain or abuse on others. The sexual significance of sadistic wishes or behavior may be *conscious* or *unconscious*. When necessary for sexual gratification, [it is] classifiable as a sexual deviation (p. 136)." *Sadistic personality disorder* appeared in the DSM-III-R as a proposed diagnostic category needing further study. The criteria included (a) humiliating and demeaning others, (b) lying to inflict pain, (c) restricting the autonomy of people in close relationships, and (d) manipulating others in order to establish compliance and dominance. *This diagnosis is not applicable if sadistic behavior is only directed towards the spouse.*

[12]The reader may recall the importance given to Fairbairn's (1954) concept of the "bad" libidinal object of childhood (i.e., the parent who tantalizes the child into painful hope and longing), and "the vampire model of sex" (Chapter Seven). *Not wanting to want* as attempted self-protection from the pain of desire was also discussed in Chapter Nine.

[13]This is the "bad breast" that Melanie Klein (1935, 1946) talks of; Klein also discusses "vampire" introjects and oral sadism.

also surfaces in the *partial* withholding of gifts that never seem to be quite right or are given or received with little thought. *Mercy fucking* withholds the *sweetness* of sex, tearing out the heart of a monogamous spouse by withholding the final piece of *giving* while leaving no easy recourse. Sadism permeates the self-presentation, "You don't appreciate that I am doing as much as fast as I possibly can to improve our sex," *when this is not the case.* In *The Age of Reason*, Tom Paine (1794) wrote, "Infidelity does not consist in believing, or in disbelieving, it consists in professing to believe what one does not believe."

There is a sadist inside each of us; marriage shoves one's nose into it if one has the integrity to look. The following is a case example of how these issues commonly play out in marriage; what is unusual about this couple is their ability to respond to the ensuing marital crisis. The dynamics described are not gender specific; the spouses' respective roles are often reversed. The narrative is framed using the concept of the crucible as a naturally occurring process, although this notion was unknown to couple. The vignette illustrates how moderately differentiated couples are sometimes able to resolve their difficulties without the assistance of a therapist (and raise their level of differentiation in the process).

Max and Renee's relationship wasn't very different from many others. Renee was rarely orgasmic with a partner when they started dating, and then only with great difficulty. Anxious and physically ill-at-ease, her style of sexual initiation was to signal Max in a childish, non-erotic way and then wait to be the object of his sexual aggressiveness. Although she displayed little initiative to improve their style of sex, she became regularly orgasmic through Max's patience and considerateness. Max thought that time and effort would eventually lead Renee to be more sexually aggressive in a more mature adult fashion. In the subsequent eight years of stalwart encouragement, this was not to be.

Over years of prodding, the "good sex" got better but the "bad sex" didn't; bad sex occurred about as frequently as the good. Sex was satisfying for Max when Renee put out the effort—but Renee was usually lazy in bed. Only once or twice in all those years was she willing to hump until she came; she wasn't willing to work up a sweat.

In particular, Renee expected Max to bring her to orgasm through cunnilingus (her favorite sexual style). She rarely initiated fellatio, however, and gave up receiving oral sex when Max insisted he would only do it when he received in kind. Renee relied on a vibrator in combination with rear-entry coitus to satisfy her.

Renee eventually allowed herself to "fuck"[14] Max in female superior coitus; after

---

[14]See Chapter Fourteen for a discussion of the non-pejorative aspects of *fucking*.

some years, she was willing to "do" Max when she performed fellatio. More generally, she closed her eyes, tuned Max out, and expected him to "do" her.

Max wanted Renee to "wake up" and be with him during sex; Renee told Max she didn't know what he meant and put the responsibility on him to make her understand.

Over the years, the explanations for Renee's passivity changed but never disappeared. If Max wasn't stroking and reinforcing her, this became the ostensible "reason" why Renee wasn't more passionate; she complained that he only touched her when he wanted sex. Max tried touching more often outside the bedroom; Renee felt like he was "always pressuring her" for sex.

If Max didn't initiate, sex rarely occurred. If Max waited to see what subsequently happened, nothing did (or was short-lived). When he brought this up again, Renee accused him of partial culpability for not having brought up the topic in the interim.

Max tried touching her more often, but insuring that it didn't lead to sex. That actually worked sometimes, except that when Renee *did* decide she wanted sex, she expected Max to get things started (or at the very least, to "share equal responsibility").

When they were in bed and Max didn't "get things started," Renee's notion of sexual aggressiveness was to announce her availability by pulling one of his arms toward her. This wasn't done in the style of a "roll in the hay" or "wrestling"; there was nothing seductive or flirtatious about it. It was more like "OK, now do something, turn me on." Max longed to feel *her* eroticism, to be the object of *her* sexual aggression.

On some of the rare occasions Renee did initiate, her lack of emotional involvement and physical inactivity became so pronounced that Max gave up in frustration. When confronted, Renee "acknowledged" that she really didn't "feel like it" or had changed her mind. When Max exploded in anger and pain, Renee criticized him for losing his temper, particularly since she was "just answering his questions" and "he was the one who stopped the encounter."

Renee complained that Max was always correcting her, that his *real* purpose was to make her feel diminished. Max then took the tact of positive reinforcement: He commented on her slightest effort to improve their sex. But it didn't lead to continued improvement—Renee became complacent and lazy in subsequent encounters. When Max pointed this out, Renee encountered that Max was never satisfied, and that just the other day he had said how wonderful their sex was.

Renee met Max's attempts to modify their style *during* sex with the complaint, "Why can't we just do it; why are you assuming that I won't do it good?" When Max waited till they were done, Renee responded, "Why didn't you say something?" or "I feel like you are rating me, judging me."

Renee couched the problem as an autonomy and control issue (e.g., "Why do we have to do it *your* way?" "I just happen to like it differently than you do"). She sidestepped the self confrontation that (a) *she* controlled the style, content, and occurrence of sex, (b) Max was actually being deprived of *his* preferences, and (c) Renee's behavior was not simply a matter of "preference." The erotic aggression that Max wanted to experience from Renee surfaced the same way Renee's aggression surfaced in the remainder of her life: as *passive-aggression*.

Periodic fallouts over sex were culminated by Renee stating that she finally wanted to pursue better sex with Max; Renee then claimed it was Max who kept sex from progressing if he remained skeptical and guarded. Max pointed out that even when sex had gotten better after prior confrontations, it regressed after a week or so. Renee countered that his guardedness was a self-fulfilling prophesy. The burden fell upon Max to swallow his pride and anger to keep the future of the marriage alive.

Renee trapped Max every time she backed herself into a corner through her own avoidance. Max couldn't take the pressure off of her without giving up his own preferences. Max was even willing for Renee to make a clear statement that she honestly didn't want or care if sex improved; he would make his own choices based on that. But he was trapped between Renee's unwillingness to risk losing him by not keeping him *wanting*, and her unwillingness to confront her sexual inhibitions.[15]

Max knew full well what it was like to tear a woman's heart out—it had happened to many women who dated him over the years. He was mortified when several healthier girlfriends confronted him; after many years of therapy, he finally was able to make friends with women—to consider his impact on them. Renee was one of the women he subsequently befriended; now he was on the receiving end.

Never stopping to think that the issues at hand might involve matters of personal integrity, Renee was mortified to recognize that she had violated her own. The issue wasn't that her grudges against Max or her own fears weren't valid. It was that she withheld from him in the guise of "I am doing the best that I can, I am really trying." Renee's less-than-genuine self-confrontation masked the attitude, "I will get around to it when I feel like it, until then you can wait; *you* be uncomfortable rather than me."

Folks often overlook their sadism because they are looking for the feeling "I deliberately want to hurt you"; they overlook, "If you really love me, you will be patient (forever)." The obvious self-interest and "selfishness" mask the component of "It's OK with me if the person I love hurts because I don't want to deal with myself." The attitude involves (a) denial of the spouse as a separate individual, (b) acceptance that he/she will hurt by one's (in)activity, (c) acceptance of one's misrepresentations, and (d) just a touch of enjoyment that the spouse is unhappy—sometimes more than just a touch.

The part that really upsets folks is the aspect of *intent*. People use the inevitable and predictable impact of personal problems as a way of depriving or punishing others. It isn't that this point is too sophisticated for the average

---

[15]See Chapter Twelve for discussion of the two-choice dilemma.

person to understand; folks' ability to work the sexual system is intuitive, as is their understanding of the impact on the partner. Suggesting that awareness of this process is repressed doesn't mean that it is totally repressed; on the other hand, people who can't tolerate recognizing the slightest hateful and sadistic impulse in themselves (i.e., total repression) tend to be extremely pernicious to others. Recognizing sadism in oneself or one's partner requires recognizing that one can (and often does) love and hate the same person at the same time (Chapter Seven).

This line of examination doesn't mean that personal problems are necessarily created to deprive one's spouse. One might suggest Renee's difficulties with intimacy and eroticism were caused by (a) fears of personal rejection, (b) fears of losing a cherished loved one (Renee still lingered over the death of a parent), (c) low anxiety tolerance, (d) fears of success, (e) interpersonal insecurity, (f) etc.

The issue of sadism concerns that iota of choice people usually have, which (if nothing else) surfaces in *motivation* to change. Whether or not the backlash of the personal problems is *inflicted* is usually evident in the effort put forth to change. Renee knowingly let Max languish, ignored the double-binds she put him in, disregarded his anguish, rejected his efforts to help, and even attacked him verbally during sex. This is what normal marital sadism looks like.

Max and Renee entered an intensely painful period after one relatively pleasant sex experience in which he tried to engage her verbally; Renee responded saying, "I'm not a dog you can make jump through your hoops." Several days later their young son commented for the first time on the tension and strained interaction between Max and Renee, showing some signs of strain himself—the situation had hit critical mass.

Each partner entered a separate but interlocking crisis; resolution involved the destabilization which Renee both feared and constructed. Max, for his part, had to extricate himself from being victimized by his own monogamous commitment; his crucible involved several pieces:

- Controlling himself rather than trying to control Renee. This involved soothing himself over Renee's ability to force him to choose among giving up the sex he wanted, giving up monogamy, or giving up the marriage.
- Recognizing that Renee would *always* be able to withhold a part of herself, and moreover, she could refuse to share particular sexual experiences he craved.

- Soothing the anger/shock that his "gut sense" was right about Renee; he had preferred to believe her, rather than himself.
- He had to reject all "mercy fucks." Although Max wanted to rationalize that these were better than nothing until better sex came along, he knew that (a) "better" never would happen if he did, and (b) the "bad" sex they had was worse than none at all.

For Renee, a different crucible was no less gut-wrenching:

- Confronting her impulse to withhold from Max and hurt him, while being fully cognizant that she loved him at the same time. Did she have the integrity to confront a part of herself that she found repugnant?

The self-confrontation involved seeing how she instilled in Max the ever-present hope/hunger that better sex might yet happen. It was right under her nose—the flip-side of her desire that he not lose faith or patience with her. This actually involved choosing between her fears of losing Max and her feelings about how she treated him: Renee didn't think Max would love her if he saw the part of her she refused to see in herself.

- The time had passed for "admitting" that she sometimes deliberately withheld from Max or deprived him as a by-product of her attempts to protect herself. The critical task was not insight, but rather, *doing something*.

"Doing something" involved temporarily relinquishing her self-protection and her counter-claims of frustration and disappointment. It involved not asking for "support," "understanding," "more time," or "commitment" from Max, nor letting her anxiety intolerance control her any longer. It involved growing sexually the way everyone does: *by doing it*.

Once finally in crisis, Renee rose to the occasion. She took responsibility for herself as an end in itself, and was able to find new alternatives: Renee recognized that mastering her fears and increasing her ability to self-soothe offered her the sense of security she always sought; she finally found the only balm there is for truly loving at a profound level.

Moreover, she found this didn't involve acquiescing to Max or abandoning her self-interests; it actually offered a better way to *pursue* them. Confronting herself and taking care of this matter actually kept the crucible going farther than Max might have ever thought. When she subsequently confronted him about her own dissatisfactions in the marriage, he had less room to maneuver and faced a much tougher partner. He couldn't use her own non-performance as a way of justifying or explaining his own; maintaining his own integrity, moreover, required engaging in the same type of self-confrontation he had seen Renee accomplish, and for which he begrudgingly respected her.

In the sexual crucible, partners drive each other's development forward on many levels by the process of *self*-confrontation.

> There is something about being known by another person for a very long time that is hard to convey to people who are about to split up. They don't understand the gift they give themselves by refusing to lose faith in another human being. (Prather & Prather, 1990, Introduction)

> Your partner can offer you but one thing, the opportunity to make peace. (Prather & Prather, 1990)

We began this chapter by discussing the role of anxiety and anxiety tolerance in personal (and especially, sexual) development. Working with extremely conflicted couples can be a thoroughly gut-wrenching experience for a therapist. One of the "payoffs" is the opportunity to work with such couples as they approach the crucible of an *extremely pleasurable* relationship; the payoff for the therapist is ironic, in that this too is often fairly anxiety-provoking. In the next chapter, we shift our focus to the upper end of the continuum of sexual pleasure. Later on (Chapter Sixteen), we will address the role of the therapist's ability to modulate the affective wallop of participating in the sexual crucible at either extreme.

CHAPTER FOURTEEN

In Pursuit of Sexual Potential

The pursuit of sexual potential is an "adults only" activity by virtue of the personal maturation and tolerances required. These requirements include (a) being seen and known at profound levels (e.g., eye contact and "I" contact during sex), (b) focusing on eroticism and transmission of "vibes," (c) tolerating wall socket sex, and (d) self-soothing the pain of intense eroticism and intimacy.

The struggles and triumphs of this process are illustrated through a lengthy case example of a couple in their sixties.

It has been proposed in previous chapters that most people never reach their sexual potential, and those who do are often in the fifth and sixth decade of life. To many clinicians, this is the antithesis of the expected; "older" people are often thought to be more difficult to work with than those who grew up in the 1960s and 1970s. It is often overlooked that older adults, having witnessed transient friends and fads, are often better able to differentiate themselves from ill-fitting social values and adopt their own sexual behavior as a praxis for living.

It has also been proposed that the sexual crucible is a powerful vehicle for exploring the limits of one's sexual potential. A case example of two mature people exploring the limits of their sexual potential in the sexual crucible is a way of bringing both points into focus.

CASE EXAMPLE: MR. AND MRS. KENNEDY[1]

Mr. Kennedy and Mrs. Kennedy, both in their early sixties, originally consulted me for a problem of intermittent erectile dysfunction that had existed throughout their three-year marriage. Both had been widowed in their fifties;

---

[1]Publishing this case example has reqired mastering my *own* discomfort; I am still slightly uncomfortable. *Unabashed eroticism is almost entirely nonexistent in the professional sexual literature.* Sexuality textbooks are *devoid* of eroticism. This material is offered here in the same spirit with which my patients pursue their sexual potential: as an act of integrity.

Mr. and Mrs. Kennedy married after a year of courtship. This was the second marriage for him and the third for her. Mrs. Kennedy was a trim and attractive woman with both class and spunk. She acknowledged her previously satisfying sexual encounters with her two husbands as openly as she admitted they were not otherwise particularly "nice men": Her first marriage ended in divorce around her husband's philandering, and the second was acrimonious until that husband died. Mr. Kennedy, on the other hand, was a gentleman as far as she was concerned; she just wished he could loosen up a little in bed and get over his erectile difficulty.

Mr. Kennedy *did* epitomize the positive aspects of a *gentle*man; he was generous and considerate but not without backbone. He had been married only once to his childhood sweetheart; they had been virgins when they met, and he remained monogamous all his life. His first wife died after a long lingering illness; Mr. Kennedy loved her dearly. After an appropriate time of mourning and loneliness, and with some misgivings about disloyalty, Mr. Kennedy met his current wife who lit up his life. Mr. Kennedy proclaimed himself an "old school" man with traditional values, and in some ways this was true. By Mr. Kennedy's standards, sex with his first wife was "terrific"; his idealization of her made it difficult for him to see that it had been, in fact, quite conventional, if not restricted. On the other hand, Mr. Kennedy was a fairly realistic and adaptive man in many ways, and willing to learn from his own experience. He was a bit intimidated by Mrs. Kennedy's prior sex life, but at least on an intellectual level he accepted that this occurred before she even knew he existed. He had the wisdom not to ask for details, and Mrs. Kennedy didn't offer any.

Mr. Kennedy labored under the feeling of being responsible for "running the show, sexually." He felt diminished and threatened when his wife made suggestions; Mrs. Kennedy restricted herself accordingly. Mr. Kennedy had intermittent loss of erection during intercourse from the outset of the relationship; as time progressed, it happened more frequently and earlier in their encounters. The thought that "old age" might prevent him from satisfying his new bride only complicated things. A trip to his urologist failed to reveal a source for his difficulty; papaverine self-injection had been suggested but Mr. Kennedy rejected the option. Mrs. Kennedy didn't know what to do with her sexual frustration or anger. She just wanted to keep from doing anything that might make her husband's wounded pride worse. Mrs. Kennedy felt unsure of her appropriate role in this situation; she rejected the Phyllis Schlafly approach to womanhood as "unbelievable" and saw "bra burners" as too militant. She complained that there were no good role models for a woman her age.

In contrast, Mr. Kennedy was fairly sure of his: The man's role was to be captain of the ship. Unfortunately, he was doing a lousy job of steering the sexual relationship, and his rudder wasn't functioning too well either. Mr. Kennedy was only experienced with coitus in missionary position and his erectile difficulty precluded even that. When he lost his erection, Mr. Kennedy assumed the event was over. Mrs. Kennedy learned to keep herself indifferent and unaroused as self-protection from frustration. She was quite open to other forms of sexual interaction, but Mr. Kennedy never initiated anything else; he felt doing other behaviors only highlighted the inadequacy of his penis, and Mrs. Kennedy didn't think that was the best time to introduce innovation, which might make him more awkward.

Over the course of time, Mrs. Kennedy's lack of sexual interest became increasingly obvious, which bothered Mr. Kennedy even more. Both had the sensation of "drifting apart," at the same time that their caring and enmeshment kept them from saying and doing new things to help themselves. Eventually, Mr. Kennedy agreed to Mrs. Kennedy's tentative, periodic suggestions that they seek treatment.

From the outset, Mr. and Mrs. Kennedy were treated in a highly formal manner; the aura of professional "distance" eased Mr. Kennedy's damaged self-esteem as well as their concern about impropriety. Mr. Kennedy had serious misgivings about sexual-marital therapy, seeing it as "airing dirty laundry" and violating the sanctity of the marital bedroom. Mr. Kennedy entered treatment requesting directions from the therapist the way one might talk to an automobile mechanic; unfortunately, giving him what he wanted would have further undermined his tacit role-definition and sense of competency.

To further complicate matters, Mr. Kennedy was approaching retirement age as a senior manager in a medium-sized firm where he had worked for many years. He had always been a "team player," although the business owner rarely compensated him for his loyalty and hard work. The owner often said that the management team was like a family and could not favor one "son" disproportionately. Mr. Kennedy said that he worked hard as a matter of personal pride; however, he was angry about being exploited and fearful of being pushed aside.

Mr. Kennedy was used to giving instruction, not taking it. The therapist approached Mr. Kennedy by pointing this out and suggesting the role of "consultant" for himself, which Mr. Kennedy accepted. Rather than establishing a formal ban on intercourse or giving direct suggestions, the therapist offered that Mr. Kennedy merely stop doing whatever had been ineffective up to now; together they could figure out what to do next. Mr. Kennedy left the session complaining that he felt like a "damn fool paying another damn fool," but did he it; in the third week of treatment he had repeated erections for sustained periods on three successive nights. Mrs. Kennedy even joked that he was "poking" her back as they lay in bed. On the fourth night, he initiated intercourse and remained erect until both he and Mrs. Kennedy reached orgasm. Fortunately, Mrs. Kennedy required only a few minutes of penetration; she was multiply orgasmic. However, a subsequent evening ended in secondary erectile dysfunction; Mr. Kennedy lost his erection during thrusting.

Mr. Kennedy returned to his next session in a much happier frame of mind. He apologized for calling the therapist a fool; he said *he* was still a fool, but a happy one. Mr. Kennedy sat smiling with his arm around his wife's shoulder during the session; for her part, Mrs. Kennedy glowed slightly. Mr. Kennedy reported that their problem was fixed; they had intercourse spontaneously with no problem. Both were obviously pleased, but there was an air of tension between them. Neither was too secure in their "cure," and there was an unspoken anxiety that it would return. Moreover, Mrs. Kennedy wasn't as eager to leave treatment; she was hoping to improve more that just her husband's erections.

Therapist: You don't have to worry about having the problem again. (pause)

Mr. Kennedy (somewhat hesitantly): What do you mean?

Therapist: You will have it again. I might be wrong, but I think you can count on it. So instead of being nervous that it *might* happen, you can rest assured that it will.

Mr. Kennedy: That is no comfort.

Therapist: Would you prefer false reassurance, sir? I am happy for you on your progress. At least you know that the problem is not written in stone and that you can get somewhere with it. But you both seem acutely aware that it is not well cemented in yet. I think that is good judgment on your part. Unless you want to leave your sex up to fate, or refrain from intercourse three weeks before you want it, you might want to learn more about your sexuality. To some degree, your penis is still running your sexuality.

Mrs. Kennedy: How long will this take?

Therapist: It's up to you. Actually, we could terminate now. You have literally gotten exactly what you said you wanted. You wanted "to be able to do it like you use to, like everyone else"; well, actually you have now done both. You have done it, and with lots of anxiety and insecurity. Your bodies have done what you think they are supposed to and we have fulfilled our original contract. I know that you are afraid I am interested in buying a Mercedes, so we can stop here if you like.

Mr. and Mrs. Kennedy looked at each other and decided not to stop "quite yet."

The Beginning of Intense Sex

Mr. and Mrs. Kennedy returned to report a marked improvement in the quality of their interaction. Although they never labeled it as such, it was the start of their experimentation with *wall-socket* sex.

Mr. Kennedy: I was out of town for most of the week, so we only got together for sex once.

Mrs. Kennedy (smiling): Complaining?

Mr. Kennedy: No. I guess I'm still concerned that Doctor Schnarch will think we aren't doing it often enough; besides, we're paying for this so we might as well get our money's worth. But I don't think that the sex, the one time we had it, could get any better.

Therapist: I doubt that, regardless of whatever happened.

Mrs. Kennedy: Well, we certainly are going to have to get more exercise if we are going to do it.

Therapist: How *did* you do it?

Mrs. Kennedy: Well, when Tom walked into the bedroom, he knew that something was up. I was wearing a nightgown that I really think is sort of spicy, but I haven't worn it since our honeymoon.

Mr. Kennedy: Yeah, I remembered it; I liked it.

Mrs. Kennedy: Then we did a lot of kissing. I had some thoughts after our last session, and this time I decided that I was not going to just be kissing him while I was a little disappointed that he is not doing it the way that I really like . . . (looks at Mr. Kennedy to see his response). Well, are we going to be really honest here?

Mr. Kennedy: Helen, just say want you want to say.

Mrs. Kennedy (To therapist): This may sound immodest, but *I* think *I'm* a good kisser . . . (smiles). Well, I do. Anyway, I had shown Tom how I like to kiss, and I could tell that he always was trying too hard. He'd move his tongue in my mouth mechanically; technically he'd do exactly what I asked but his tongue was too rigid, too harsh. You know, your mouth should be soft, like butter . . . (looks over at Mr. Kennedy who is chuckling). Oh, you! (Mrs. Kennedy makes a mock "swat" of her hand at her husband.)

Mr. Kennedy (laughing): I didn't say anything!

Mrs. Kennedy (to therapist): Normally one of us would get frustrated, so it was simpler to let him kiss me any way he wanted to, or not do it at all. He has never been much of a kisser. I mean, I could kiss all night! This time I thought, I had the sense that he was really wanting to do it. So I just calmed myself down. I think he sensed it, because after about five minutes of kissing, which we never do, his tongue got soft and we started playing with them.

Mr. Kennedy: I never understood what it was Helen wanted. I would move my tongue like she asked, but she always got frustrated with me, which really got my goat. Now I understand what she really wanted. I *felt* her tongue. I just thought I was suppose to stick my tongue in her mouth and move it around.

Therapist: Sounds not too different from what you folks have described actually goes on during intercourse.

Mr. Kennedy: Well . . . I never thought of it that way, but maybe it is. I know this, it was like we were "doing it" with our mouths. I never realized her mouth could feel that good to me. I mean, it was soft and warm. We played back and forth, trading the lead about whose tongue was doing who. It was like playing mind games with our mouth. I mean, I *thought* we were doing that (voice trailing, suggesting a need for Mrs. Kennedy to respond).

Therapist: Are you saying that as a self-declarative statement or as a question needing confirmation from your wife?

Mr. Kennedy: What do you mean?

Therapist: Are you certain that this is what *you* were doing?

Mr. Kennedy: Yes.

Therapist: Are you certain that this is what you and your wife were doing?

Mr. Kennedy: Yes.

Therapist: What if your wife says that she didn't have the same experience? Will you throw away your own experience and tell yourself that it didn't happen?

Mr. Kennedy: Is this another example of me trusting my own experience? If I don't do that, then I really am a fool. I don't really get this, though; how could it be real if she didn't feel it too? (pause) I guess if she didn't feel that we were playing that tongue game, she missed a hell of a good time.

Mrs. Kennedy: I didn't miss it. I know that you could feel me, 'cause I felt you; it was like we were in synch. It made me very happy.

Mr. Kennedy: Well, it certainly made you aroused, too!

Mrs. Kennedy: (nervous laughter) Stop that, you are making it sound too sexy.

Mr. Kennedy: Well, if you are going to talk like that, so am I. Besides, we aren't saying anything he hasn't heard before, and isn't that the whole point of what we are sticking around for? I mean, I may be showing my stupidity, but I never connected with anyone like we did when we kissed the other night. If you knew we were missing that, no wonder you have been angry at me. That was fantastic. I could do that for an hour.

Therapist: Well, maybe you will.

Mr. Kennedy: You mean, if I'm smart I will.

Therapist: You sound plenty smart. (to wife) It sounds like you both had a good experience at home, which has further utility here in my office. You are obviously a woman who knows about eroticism and likes sex, and you are old enough not to have to play adolescent games about it. I say that as a compliment. What is your hesitancy to have that competency, and your eroticism, surface in your discussions with me?

Mrs. Kennedy: I don't know.

Therapist: Well, what are you focusing on when you say it sounds too sexy?
(long silence)

Mrs. Kennedy: I know that you are a professional and all that, and I know that this is going to sound stupid . . .

Therapist: You haven't done anything stupid so far . . .

Mrs. Kennedy: I know that you spend all day talking to people about sex . . . but I get real uncomfortable with you *seeing* me sexually.
(pause)

Therapist: I am not disagreeing with you when I ask: in what way?
(long pause)

Mrs. Kennedy: Do you ever fantasize about your patients?

Therapist: I know that now *I* am the one who sounds stupid, but let me ask: what difference would it make to you if I did or I didn't?

Mrs. Kennedy: I am uncomfortable with the idea of you thinking of me in bed.

Therapist: Mrs. Kennedy, I have the deepest respect for your ability to be direct about this; it reflects considerable maturity and strength that will help you later on. I am also going to take your question very seriously, because it is absolutely appropriate. Have you sensed any inappropriate sexual interest or arousal from me towards you?

Mrs. Kennedy: No, I know that you are too professional for that; I know this sounds stupid.

Therapist: It doesn't sound stupid at all; quite the contrary, I am impressed with what you are bringing up here. I said that I had faith that if you were willing to go about your business and learn from your interaction with Mr. Kennedy, what was important would surface; perhaps it is right now. There are many therapists who have not mastered their own sexuality, who "poach" on patients in subtle, if not blatant, ways. You are quite right to be concerned about this. If I am a good sex therapist and I am acting appropriately, you don't need to trust me; and if I am acting inappropriately, you have no business trusting me. So don't "trust" me and don't take anything for granted; watch me very closely. See if I have an inappropriate sexual interest in you.

Mrs. Kennedy: I don't really think that you are like that.

Therapist: Mrs. Kennedy, the issue, if I understand it, is not whether I am "like that," but rather, if *you* are like that. The issue is not whether you can "trust me," but rather whether you can trust *you* if you sense in me what you now fear. What I mean is, can you can handle yourself *if* I am like that.

Mrs. Kennedy: How do you mean?

Therapist: Well, in the event that you sensed that I had some inappropriate sexual interest or thoughts about you, two choices come to mind. One is, do you have the strength and willingness to terminate treatment with me, even if it seems that treatment in some ways is going quite well? My guess is that if I had those sorts of feelings, you would sense them. Most women are quite sensitive to those sorts of "vibes" from men.

Mrs. Kennedy: Actually, I used to feel those sorts of things around my father. He was an alcoholic, and when I was in high school, I couldn't stand to be alone with him or have him touch me. Nothing overt ever happened, of course, but I could feel it. I learned to play down my attractiveness all the time I lived at home; even after I got married to my first husband, I didn't like to be alone with my father. I am still always cautious when I meet a man that I not look him in the eye or be too attractive or flirtatious or do anything that might make him think that I find him attractive.

Therapist: Why not?

Mrs. Kennedy: If he thought that I found him attractive, then he might expect me to have sex with him.

Therapist: What difference does it make what *he* expects?

Mrs. Kennedy: I just always have . . . I think many women do.

Therapist: I am sure they do; however, the question is, do you want to spend the rest of your life restricting your eroticism like many women do, taking responsibility for making sure that your husband gets an erection and that other men don't?

Mrs. Kennedy: I don't want to be considered a "cock tease." That is what we use to call it.

Therapist: Are you planning to put the make on men walking down the street?

Mrs. Kennedy: (laughing) I hadn't given it much thought, to be quite honest.

Therapist: At the moment, we seem to be talking about just three men: your husband, your father, and your therapist. Displaying your eroticism with your husband is a challenge that I think you both are increasingly up to handling. As for your father, did you ever tell anyone what you felt?

Mrs. Kennedy: No, there was nothing to tell. Nothing really happened that I could point to, and my mother never would have believed me. We weren't as open about this sort of thing as society is today; now you read about this sort of thing every time you pick up the paper.

Therapist: So, how many years have you been hiding your sexuality?

Mrs. Kennedy: Since I went through puberty, almost 50 years. I mean, I didn't hide it with my former husbands, but as for other men, yes I have.

Therapist: Well, you are 63 years old; perhaps you would like to get to the point in your lifetime when you modulate the display of your eroticism based on what *you* think, rather than on what someone else, including me, thinks of you.

Mrs. Kennedy: How do I do that?

Therapist: That is the second option I alluded to before. Do you have the strength to utilize me and my expertise to your own advantage, or are you going to modulate what we talk about, and how we talk about it, because you are going to take responsibility for keeping me "in line"? In other words, are you going to let *my* sexual impulses control *your* treatment, or are you going to scare the hell out of yourself and master yourself and your eroticism right in front of me?

Mrs. Kennedy: I feel sort of guilty even making an issue of it, like suggesting that you would even waste your time thinking about me, us. I know that therapists are suppose to keep a professional distance from your patients.

Therapist: I encourage you to see it your own way, because that is the way that you'll see yourself. *I* take what you are doing as a point of courage and mutual respect. What you are describing with your father is sort of like psychological sexual abuse. I think you are taking treatment quite seriously. You have managed to develop a way to have this emerge that may permit you to work out this issue with your father. At this point, getting into "did it really happen" would be a digression. You told me that this was your reality; the question is, can you validate your own reality and operate out of it? That is why I did not answer your question about my thinking about you in sexually inappropriate ways. If you sense the same for me and you *don't* terminate, you really *do* need a therapist.

Mrs. Kennedy: Well, I don't want you to get the notion that I am prissy or a prude. I don't respect that in women.

Therapist: Mrs. Kennedy, you have shown yourself to be a very gutsy woman.

Mr. Kennedy: Do you want to hear the rest?

Therapist: The rest of what?

Mr. Kennedy: What we did.

Therapist: There's more?

Mrs. Kennedy: I've been monopolizing the conversation. Tom, you tell him.

Mr. Kennedy: We did some new things we never did before. Helen lit some candles and we lay in bed. It was beautiful; a lot prettier than light from the TV or from the adjoining bathroom. All these years and I had never done that. I had this blue steel hard-on and didn't want to waste it. But we were kissing and everything was really different; I thought it was my duty to mount Helen, but she told me to lie alongside her and stroke her, and this time I listened.

Therapist: What was it like?

Mr. Kennedy: (wry laughter) Different!

Therapist (smiling): So I gather; different in what way?

Mrs. Kennedy: Tom was touching my breasts and thighs, and my vagina, and between my vagina and my bottom. (embarrassed smile) It felt good to be touched real lightly and I asked him to go back and do some more. We have never done anything like that before.

Therapist: (to husband) What was it like for you?

Mr. Kennedy: It was incredible! I felt so free and relaxed. I knew that Helen really wanted me and I liked that she asked; I didn't have the feeling that she was ordering me around or correcting me like before. She had an orgasm while I was touching her with my hands; we eventually had intercourse for me. I lost part of my erection, but I still continued until I came; it really didn't bother me like it use to. I want her to teach me what she wants; I can be a real quick study (seductive glance toward his wife).

Therapist: My compliments, sir. You sound like you have reached a point in your life where you don't have to have all the answers and can tolerate having an equal as a sexual partner. That is quite an achievement for any man. I may be wrong, but would you have been capable of not having all the sexual answers when you were 20?

Mr. Kennedy: No, I guess not.

Therapist: You are a living demonstration of why people rarely reach their sexual potential until the latter years of life.

(brief pause; Mr. and Mrs. Kennedy look at each other, smiling and joining hands)

Therapist: (to wife) Did you anticipate that you would come in and tell me all the details of this, even while it was going on?

Mrs. Kennedy: (smiling) Well, doctor, it wasn't like I was thinking of you at all at the time; but, yes, I knew it would make me nervous to tell you, but I would do it.

Therapist: Why?

Mrs. Kennedy: (glancing at her husband) Because I am committed to this lug. He is the kindest man I have ever met. I am not opposed to a good screw for its own sake, but I want to have it with *him*.

Therapist: Well, then, there is another interesting aspect to the issue of your being afraid to display your eroticism with me.

Mrs. Kennedy: What is that?

Therapist: Even knowing that you were going to tell me about it, it didn't stop you. You were still able to maintain your eroticism, and push it further than you were totally comfortable with, both at home and here with me.

Mrs. Kennedy: I never thought of it that way.

Mr. Kennedy: I'm impressed. Hell, I was impressed the other night.

Therapist: I'm impressed now. I am sure curious where you are both headed.

Mr. Kennedy: What should we do from here?

Therapist: Since you are enjoying touching each other, some variants of what you have developed on your own might be useful. (A brief discussion of positional variations of genital and nongenital touching ensues.)

Mr. Kennedy: Can you be more specific about which of these we should do?

Mrs. Kennedy: I know, "Do whatever we like, and learn from it."

Therapist: It sure doesn't seem to be hurting you any.

In the next session, the Kennedys reported further gains.

Mrs. Kennedy: I know that this is going to sound strange to you, but it doesn't to me.

Therapist: I am learning that whenever either one of you tell me something is going to sound strange or stupid, it is going to be important.

Mrs. Kennedy: I realized that my vagina belongs to me.

Therapist: That's remarkable.

Mrs. Kennedy: No, I'm serious.

Therapist: Why won't you let me be serious too?

Mrs. Kennedy: I guess I just find it hard to believe that a woman my age is just finding out that her genitals belongs to her. I mean, isn't possession suppose to be nine-tenths of the law?

Therapist: That's not hard to believe at all; lots of women die, never having gotten that clear in their heads. How'd you get this clear to *you*?

Mrs. Kennedy: Tom was touching my vagina this week, and I did it different from the inside of *me*.

Therapist: How do you mean?

Mrs. Kennedy: I guess I figured out that either I concentrate on the sensations in my vagina when my partner is touching me, and tune him out so I can have my orgasm, or I let him do what he wants to my crotch and tune myself out and go elsewhere mentally. Either way, I never have control of me with a man really being there.

Therapist: You're doing it again.

Mrs. Kennedy: Doing what?

Therapist: Working on two levels. What you are telling me reflects some resolution of the issue you mentioned last session about how sexuality was handled in the house with your father; this involves possession of your own sexuality. It also sounds like you are recognizing that you are never really intimate with your husband when he is touching your vagina.

Mrs. Kennedy: How do you mean?

Therapist: You don't tend to maintain a clear presentation of yourself in close proximity to your partner. In this case, you are describing openly retaining control of your own vagina when your partner is touching you or is in you. In the mental style of intercourse you are describing, either you leave or you have him leave, so to speak.

Mrs. Kennedy: You're right! I never thought of it in that way.

Therapist: Well, in spite of not thinking about it, you seem to be quite capable of doing it. If I got it straight, you are doing it right this moment: giving a clear presentation of yourself in front of your partner. Maybe this is what intimacy is all about.

Mrs. Kennedy: Well, it feels good, but not entirely.

Therapist: For sure; that is what it's like.

Mrs. Kennedy: Well, this time I *did* stay in control of myself; in control of my vagina to use your terms. I told him to slow down; I didn't just let him do whatever he wanted and I didn't block him out.

Mr. Kennedy: I could feel the difference. Her instructions never made sense to me because I was trying to *think* my way through them. This time I could *sense* her and what she wanted; her talking to me in that low breathy voice also helped (laughter).

Mrs. Kennedy: It was strange, I felt so open to him, but I didn't feel vulnerable.

Therapist: How did you do it?

Mrs. Kennedy: I . . . I mean I'm a little ashamed to say this . . . I used to do this ridiculous "scoot" backwards towards the headboard, moving my bottom away from him. Tom would put his finger in me before I was ready, and I'd be dry and it would hurt; at the very least it didn't feel good. I felt like I couldn't say anything to him; it would hurt his feelings. I didn't want to do anything to make the problem with erections get worse.

Mr. Kennedy: I always *knew* I was doing something wrong.

Mrs. Kennedy: Well, this time he was getting a little too eager to do it. I asked him just to play with the outside of me, my vagina. Just the lips. I think we had a good time. He kept looking in my face to see my reaction, and I didn't tune him out. I looked back. In fact, one time he did it so good touching me lightly, that it tickled. I "scooted backwards" but I was laughing; Tom had this worried look on his face at first, but then he laughed too. I had to tell him to firm it up a little. It was fabulous.

Therapist: What was it like for you, sir?

Mr. Kennedy: I got quite an education. Helen took me at my word. Helen directed my fingers till we found her "G" spot; I never heard of such a thing. Then we found some other spots she liked; they didn't have any alphabet to go with them though. (laughter) She felt very soft and smooth; I can't believe the difference in textures inside her. Whenever I used to touch her, I would just ram my finger in and out thinking it was like my penis. This time I did it like we learned to move our tongues, soft and feeling her. I rubbed her inside by the mouth of her vagina instead of thinking I had to get it all the way in back because my penis is supposed to be long.

Mrs. Kennedy: It's long enough, believe me.

Mr. Kennedy: I also did some oral sex on Helen. She asked me; she was real nice about it, not pushy or anything.

Therapist: What was that like for you?

Mr. Kennedy: It will take some getting used to, but it's not as bad as I thought. I had even suggested that once or twice with my first wife, but she wouldn't hear of it. Maybe she was more squeamish than I thought; but we were self-taught and we didn't know any better. I am starting to recognized what we missed. But at least I am glad that I have a chance to share this with Helen.

Therapist: (to husband) I am glad to see that you are not taking Mrs. Kennedy's retrospective report of tuning you out personally or feeling rejected now.

Mr. Kennedy: Well, I still get twinges, but I'm getting there; it's getting easier. It's sort of weird; she wants me more now, and although it means a lot to me, it doesn't mean the same thing to me that it used to. It's not life or death when we are in bed. Our sexual interactions make me feel good, and I feel good about Helen and me, but it is not like I need it as much.

Therapist: This is quite a compliment to you both: a woman who challenges herself to get control of herself, and moreover, to do so openly in front of her husband; and a man who does not feel controlled by his wife when she controls herself. Remarkable.

Mr. Kennedy: Don't many couples do this?

Therapist: Take a look around you and decide for yourself, sir.

"He Won't Lie Back and Receive"

Therapist: What's been happening since I saw you last?

Mr. Kennedy: Well, we have had a week of mixed successes.

Therapist: Mixed in what way?

Mr. Kennedy: I'll let Helen tell you about the good part, and then we can deal with the bad.

Therapist: I have this feeling that the bad is good, but let's go on and take a look.

Mrs. Kennedy: I kept watching the style, like we talked about; you were right, there were all sorts of messages in it.

Therapist: What did you see?

Mrs. Kennedy: I guess I never invited him in me, maybe because I never felt that my vagina belonged to me. I did something that "shocked" us both. We lit some candles so we could see, I brushed back my pubic hair, opened my labia, and let him look *inside* me. But it wasn't like being on a gynecologist's table; that's what it always seemed like when I read it in some woman's magazine. I was suppose to "show him" and look with a hand mirror, myself. I mean, I had done that myself. This was more like *us* doing it than following instructions; we thought about the options we discussed, and then did what *we* wanted to do. When I opened my lips, it wasn't like I was showing him a lab specimen. I opened me up slowly, I wanted to arouse him by watching me. I could tell he sort of liked looking. It made me really aroused for him. I felt really brazen; I liked it.

Therapist: How were you and your husband positioned?

Mrs. Kennedy: I lay on my back, face up, and Tom sat upright between my legs looking right into my vagina. I had one leg draped over each of his, with my legs bent and spread wide. We had kissed for a long time, and he didn't need to even touch me to get me wet.

Mr. Kennedy: It was the first time I have ever seen, *really* seen her vagina. I brushed my fingertips all around her pubic hair and the inside of her thighs. Then when she said she wanted to feel me touch her vagina, I gently touched the outside of the outer lips. They were red! I never saw that before.

Mrs. Kennedy: They were not! (embarrassed)

Mr. Kennedy: Yes they were; it was very special. I really didn't know what to think when Helen opened herself up. I could tell *she* was enjoying it. I wet my fingers in my mouth, and ran my fingertip up and down the length of her labia. It was great. When she spread them back I looked inside: I never saw *anything* like that. I always lay next to her, so even if I got a finger in, I could never look. There was one point, though, when I could tell that she expected me to shove a finger inside her and she wasn't ready; she started to move her knees together, just slightly. This time, though, I didn't get upset like I was doing something wrong; I would feel the feeling inside me, but I didn't give into it. I told her that I wasn't going to touch inside her until she was ready; it made me feel good to see her relax her legs apart. You could tell that the muscles in her thighs were soft and her skin relaxed.

Mrs. Kennedy: I never thought you wanted to look before.

Mr. Kennedy: I told you I can be a quick study on some topics. We did some other stuff, too. (to his wife) Should I tell him what you told me?

Mrs. Kennedy: (laughing) Hell, I can't believe what we have told him already. Go ahead and tell him anything you want.

Mr. Kennedy: She gave me a suggestion about oral sex. She suggested I put my tongue on her clitoris, with my finger inside her, and try to rub my nose. It was . . . well, it was interesting. Making love with my wife is like being with a young wildcat.

Therapist: Sound more like making love with a mature wildcat; the young ones are afraid to demonstrate that they know more about their vaginas than their husbands do.

(silent smiles; Mr. Kennedy and Mrs. Kennedy looking at each other and at me)

Mrs. Kennedy: Now, do you want to hear the bad part?

Therapist: Why is it bad?

Mrs. Kennedy: Because I was disappointed with Tom.

Therapist: Why is that bad?

Mrs. Kennedy: Well, maybe not *that* bad. Here we are doing all this great stuff, things are going better than they ever have; suddenly, it gets clear that Tom won't really receive from me. You were wrong: He *is* afraid of an equal.

Mr. Kennedy: It isn't that I don't want an equal, I just love turning you on and touching you. I really don't even care if we have intercourse anymore. (pause) Maybe it's that I don't feel comfortable not being the giver, I don't know why.

Therapist: Maybe there is an issue about equality here, but perhaps not quite what it seems at first glance. (to Mrs. Kennedy) I am not necessarily disagreeing with your interpretation; you may be right. I am curious why are you assuming that, if there is an issue about your husband not being able to tolerate equality, that it automatically refers to *you*.

Mrs. Kennedy: What else could it be?

Therapist: (looking at Mr. Kennedy while talking to Mrs. Kennedy) Maybe the person whom he refuses to accept as an equal is *himself*.

(long silence)

Therapist: (slowly, to Mrs. Kennedy) Your husband has made progress not taking your response or lack of it as a reflection on himself, when he is giving or wants to give to you. That is one thing; it is quite another for Mr. Kennedy to challenge his self-worth by not "producing" at all and placing himself in the role of the receiver. (to Mr. Kennedy) Correct me if I'm wrong, sir, but you feel the need to justify your very existence by being productive. It is when you *stop* producing that you really go into spasm. I appreciate that it is difficult to stop giving and take a turn receiving, particularly if you haven't paid your dues by doing your wife first. (voice soft) After all, who the hell do you think you are anyway, an *equal?* Where do you get off thinking that you are as good as anybody else? Let's face it, when you give, you ante up enough to be tolerated, right? When you stop putting out and take an equal turn, you are really tempting the gods, aren't you?

Mr. Kennedy: How'd you know?

Therapist: It's in the sexual style.

Mr. Kennedy: I guess I do feel that. I'm not comfortable if I'm not "paying the check" when I'm with friends. I never realized that I do that with Helen.

Mrs. Kennedy: Don't you think I want a turn "cranking your cord" too? Why should you get all the fun of seeing me turn colors?

Mr. Kennedy: I never thought about it that way. You make it sound like I am both selfish and unwilling to receive at the same time.

Mrs. Kennedy: Well, darling, I don't want to hurt your feelings, but you are, just a little.

Mr. Kennedy: (to therapist) What can I do about it?

Therapist: (softly) You can continue doing just what you are doing; I am sure that everyone else, except for perhaps your wife, will "love" you for it. Besides, if you stop, the gravy train is over for those who like the benefit of your insecurity, and they may not be laudatory of the change. On the other hand, if you have the guts, you can lie back and let your wife *really* take care of you, physically. What you need to deal with will be right there. You will feel either wonderful or very insecure; you can have a good time or fight with yourself. Neither is likely to kill you. (tone lightening) In fact, if this is going to have some benefit beyond just touch, you will probably have to feel good enough to feel really guilty or insecure. Let me help you have a really rotten time, it's my specialty: let her give to you before you do her. If you have the courage, maybe you can go home and feel good enough to feel bad. If not, maybe you can just feel bad about not feeling good. There is no point about feeling bad about feeling bad, and it takes too much integrity to feel good about feeling good.

Mr. Kennedy: That sounds good to me.

Therapist: That's too bad.

Mrs. Kennedy: Not to me, I'm getting better at being bad. (seductive smile)

Therapist: So why is this part, about Mr. Kennedy not being willing to receive, "so bad"?

Mrs. Kennedy: Well, I guess it's not perfect.

Therapist: As long as you want perfection, you can count on a lot of things feeling bad.

Mrs. Kennedy: I'll settle for having it real good.

Therapist: Apparently not yet you won't; maybe you are on the way. Actually, as long as you demand that things be perfect, you won't have to deal with things being too good at all. Maybe you will make it, though. (pause) Actually I fail to see the bad part in the "bad part." What has been lying dormant is finally starting to surface through your sexuality. (To Mrs. Kennedy) Until you reached the point that you really wanted to pleasure your husband, and the sex got good enough to trigger his feelings of unworthiness, you could bypass this. I guess when sex was lousy and periodic, Mr. Kennedy was getting what he thought he deserved. (pause, tone lowering again) If you want to be really helpful to him, don't help him. Your husband is a very proud man, and he is going to have to handle himself on his own. The best you can do is stay out of his way. You, on the other hand, may need to accept that you cannot make him see his own self-worth; the very attempt is an inherent contradiction. If you really have faith in him, leave him alone. If you are not willing to let him fail and take the loss that it will represent to you, then you can get "helpful" and screw it up.

Mrs. Kennedy: No . . . I will leave him alone on this.

Therapist: Besides, it occurs to me that there is an additional advantage to *you.*

Mrs. Kennedy: What's that?

Therapist: It will help you deal with not having it perfect.

Mrs. Kennedy: How so?

Therapist: (gently) What will happen to you if Mr. Kennedy makes it? (pause) He is already an unusual man, and you clearly love him. If he masters himself in a way that few men do . . . what will you do when he dies? You both have already lost a spouse, so it's hard to play adolescent games like "it won't happen" or "we will go together." Whatever you may do, this time you love with your eyes open. You gave up two men whom you didn't think that much of; will it be "good enough" to give up a great man?

(long silence; Mr. Kennedy reaches out for his wife's hand as her eyes fill with tears)

Mrs. Kennedy: Let's go find out.

"It's a Stinkin' Job But Somebody Has to Do It"

Mr. and Mrs. Kennedy returned to the subsequent session in obviously high spirits. Their eyes were bright and sparkling. I found myself instantly happy for them as I met them in the waiting room. They were bubbling over with good news; on the way into my office, Mrs. Kennedy related that her husband's employer had called at home at a time that they had set aside for themselves. Mr. Kennedy did something "out of character": He told his boss he would call him back at a later time and got off the phone. Mr. Kennedy chuckled with pride at his wife's remark.

Mrs. Kennedy: (seating herself next to her husband in the office) That's not all he did!

Therapist: What else did he do?

Mrs. Kennedy: He really got into receiving from me . . . up to a point.

Therapist: (to Mr. Kennedy) You did "not doing"?

Mr. Kennedy: (quietly, with proud smile) Yeah, it was a stinkin' job but somebody had to do it.

Therapist: How'd you "not do"?

Mr. Kennedy: I "didn't do" twice. The first time I just touched Helen, and then she did me. The second time, I went first.

Therapist: Did you touch your wife while she was touching you?

Mr. Kennedy: No, but I had to struggle with myself; I won.

Therapist: Did you find your mind wandering?

Mr. Kennedy: Yes. I kept thinking that I was suppose to do her, even though I knew that she was getting pleasure out of doing me.

Therapist: What do you make of it?

Mr. Kennedy: I don't know . . . I get nervous. Besides, I had enough, and I wanted to please her.

Therapist: You had enough what?

Mr. Kennedy: I don't know, enough pleasure? I had the impulse to start touching her, but I didn't.

Therapist: It's hard just to receive, isn't it?

Mr. Kennedy: Yeah, harder than I thought.

Mrs. Kennedy: (smiling) He did real good, though. And I made it hard for him, too. I really got into giving to him. He finally let me bring him to orgasm with my hand. I used some of the options we talked about last session. He was a little awkward about some of it, but he hung in there.

Mr. Kennedy: (smiling) And *you* were totally comfortable with the whole thing?

Mrs. Kennedy: No, but I'm enjoying learning.

Mr. and Mrs. Kennedy had experimented with different positions of her stimulating him manually; they found that having Mr. Kennedy standing or kneeling on the bed worked better than lying on his back. Mrs. Kennedy pulled downward slightly as she stroked his penis in this position; it allowed Mr. Kennedy to feel his own erection better and he felt less helpless when receiving. Mrs. Kennedy liked it because it had a different ambiance from lying in each other's arms. She developed the pattern of lightly oiling her hand and her husband's penis, giving it long, slow strokes. She stopped at the top of the stroke with the head of his penis in her hand, and finished by bumping the heel of her hand gently but firmly into his pubic bone. Working in conjunction, they found that Mrs. Kennedy was pretty good at doing this from the outset; she got even better when she added a more pronounced upward pull. Mrs. Kennedy enjoyed the feeling of her own sexual prowess, and the "power" of having her husband "by the dick" and feeling him shudder under her administrations.

Mrs. Kennedy: I joked with Tom that I wasn't just going to "jerk him off"; I did say that I might "push and pull him off" though. I could tell when he was about to orgasm; he started holding back. He couldn't just let himself come right away. I told him it was OK, but he wouldn't listen to me.

Mr. Kennedy: I wanted to make it last; it felt so good. Besides, I always do that; I do it for her.

Therapist: How do you try to make it last?

Mr. Kennedy: I think about something else.

Therapist: That's a very common approach: "I feel so good, I think I'll tune out my wife and make it better." Why do you do it?

Mr. Kennedy: I don't know; I always thought I did it to make intercourse last longer so Helen could orgasm. In this case, since we weren't going to have intercourse, it doesn't make sense.

Mrs. Kennedy: Well, don't do it on my account; I want to see you really lose control of yourself for once.

Therapist: (to Mrs. Kennedy) You want your husband to have enough control of himself to stop monitoring and give himself up to the moment? (smiling) Boy, you sure are hard on a fella! It's hard to tolerate that intense intimacy, him letting you see him like that.

Mrs. Kennedy: (smiling) That's what I want.

Mr. Kennedy: (smiling, tongue in cheek) I think I'm up to it.

Therapist: Well, let's see what happens.

As the couple left the session, Mr. Kennedy walked closer than usual as he took my extended hand to our customary handshake. He held my hand and looked at me, eye to eye, several seconds longer than would be appropriate in a social setting. His eyes and his mouth smiled; he nodded as he said, "Thank you for all that you have been doing with us."

The subsequent several sessions were remarkable in the deepening of intensity in eroticism and intimacy, as well as the ego-strengthening that occurred. Mrs. Kennedy almost crackled with electric energy; she was becoming "feisty in her old age," as she put it. She respectfully challenged her husband in discussions about world politics and in the bedroom. The increasing begrudging respect between them was obvious and fruitful; when they had sex, there was increasing room for a facilitative level of aggression. Both Mr. and Mrs. Kennedy reported more profound orgasms than they had ever experienced. Mr. Kennedy increasingly permitting himself to receive, and Mrs. Kennedy was enjoying being able to "crank his cord"; both experienced enhanced self-esteem and sexual prowess.

Mrs. Kennedy really liked to make Mr. Kennedy groan, which he did with some reluctance. It was only after some intensely pleasurable sessions in which his wife moaned and laughed with obvious delight that Mr. Kennedy became acutely aware of his own inhibition about making noise: His orgasms were always silent. He felt somewhat inadequate compared to Mrs. Kennedy's lack of inhibition; a healthy sense of competition was surfacing. For her part, Mrs. Kennedy felt deprived; she still felt him holding back and wanted him utterly abandoned and "out to lunch."

On one occasion in particular, Mrs. Kennedy "did" Mr. Kennedy. He had been particularly generous with her, and she decided to "return the compliment." She started doing him manually in the manner they had developed. Whenever Mr. Kennedy closed his eyes, she talked to him seductively and got him to look at her. She did things to entertain him visually, like looking in his eyes, talking about the heat in her loins, how good his penis looked to her, or moving her body suggestively. She held his penis firmly like she knew he liked; Mr. Kennedy later said she had a "greedy" look in her eye. When she could feel his penis throb on the march to orgasm, she backed off just a notch and kept him on the edge. When Mr. Kennedy sensed what was happening, he laughed weakly; his own pleasure was the object of the joke. Rather than holding back, she could feel him offering himself up to the moment. She could tell that this was a watershed experience for him. Next time, they experimented with oral sex.

Mrs. Kennedy: (smiling) I used some of the techniques we talked about, and improvised from there.

Mr. Kennedy: (laughing) It was mind blowing!

Therapist: (smiling) Interesting pun; was it *that* good?

Mrs. Kennedy: You bet. First I just licked him all over; I caught him right after he showered, and he tasted fresh and clean and just a little salty.

Mr. Kennedy: She said I was better than Godiva chocolate; she *loves* Godiva chocolate!

Mrs. Kennedy: I even licked his balls. I could tell he wasn't expecting that; even though he didn't seem to like it as much as when I sucked his penis, I think Tom is game for just about anything at this point.

Mr. Kennedy: (tongue in cheek, quietly) Try me.

Mrs. Kennedy: Then I started in with my hand on his penis, just like he likes. I took him in my mouth, but not enough to gag me. Oral sex on a man is the one thing that I had never really gotten totally comfortable with. I kept the entire length of his penis wet with saliva from my mouth, like we talked about. I always had a problem thinking I had to swallow my own saliva, which was hard with his penis in my mouth; I was afraid I would bite him (laughs). This time I let the saliva flow out my lips, and used my hand to work it down his shaft. I didn't feel obligated to just do him with my mouth, and I didn't feel the pressure to keep doing it till he came; I got to have fun working him over. What part of him that wasn't in my mouth, I stroked with my hand. I would stop sucking him from time to time, and do him with just my hand and look at him or kiss him. I could tell that he was loving it.

(Mrs. Kennedy looks over at her husband, who is beaming, and continues) When I wanted him to come, I started to move my mouth and hand in unison, like a big vacuum. The feeling of my own sexual power was exceptional! When he got close to coming, things got really interesting. I wasn't just doing him to make him come; I was taking my time so my mouth didn't get tired and I wasn't rushing him. I wasn't ready to try swallowing his cum yet but I wanted to let him shoot in my mouth; I knew Tom wasn't totally comfortable with this either, but I wanted him to experience it. I put my tongue in the back of my mouth so when he came it wouldn't shoot down my throat. I think seeing him ejaculate so many times recently, and us daring ourselves to taste it when it was on my hand really helped. Anyway, I let him come in my mouth; I let it just flow down his penis with the rest of my saliva. It wasn't bad at all. Also, this time I didn't stop when he came, and he didn't either; he just kept coming and coming. I just eased up a little but didn't stop altogether. I didn't know a man could orgasm like that; they seem to just have these little ones. This was an *ORGASM!* (Mr. Kennedy actually blushes at this point.)

Mr. Kennedy: (laughing) My body was a wreck afterwards, I had muscle spasms in my legs, and I could hardly walk.

Mrs. Kennedy: Good for you, you deserved it.

Therapist: Well, I have some notion of what the answer will be, but let me ask directly; (to Mr. Kennedy) what was it like from your side of your penis?

Mr. Kennedy: Exactly like she described it; except, I really remember "the quiet." Aside from seeing this great lascivious side of her, I remember "the quiet."

Therapist: What "quiet"?

Mr. Kennedy: I remember having this acute awareness of my body arched backwards as I knelt on the bed, seeing my wife's body in the candle-light. I could feel every muscle in my body pulled tight like I was a drum. She was beautiful; she was pumping this energy into me right through my penis. You may think this is funny, but I kept thinking that this was some kind of pagan ritual, like a high priestess sent to me by the gods. We had candles lit and the room was beautiful.

Therapist: (softly) It sounds lovely.

Mr. Kennedy: I remember the quiet in the room. Sometimes I thought I heard a remote sound come from somewhere, but it was like in another world. It was as if time had stopped, you know; like we were in an isolation chamber, like a cave. Sometimes I heard her emitting this low throaty moan as she did me, like she was chanting, like a Buddhist monk. My penis was the sacrament. It was so deafeningly quiet, I almost found it unnerving. Just me, Helen, and the bed existed; the world stopped at the boundary of our bedroom. I never heard such quiet be-fore. I could even hear her hand sliding on my penis, and the sound of her sucking me. I even remember the slurping sound and the popping sound of her mouth coming off the end of my penis. The moment was just profound. I didn't try to come, and I didn't try not to come. It was like she was going to take it right out of me; she wanted my cum. We were like two separate people and a unit at the same time. We were communicating, connected through my penis.

(brief pause, Mr. Kennedy's eyes fill and his wife reaches out to take his hand. He continues) And when I came . . . I am embarrassed to say this . . . I had tears in my eyes. I heard before of women crying when they came, but I always thought it was because they were thinking of something sad in their past. I never heard of a man crying when he came. I mean, I thought . . . "this is what it's like when God touches you, and Helen is my blessing." All this is going on in my head while I'm coming; I felt profoundly separate from Helen and yet I was acutely aware of her and *with* her. I was part of everything and everyone, and yet absolutely on my own. The quiet was deafening. (slowly glancing over to Mrs. Kennedy) Why are you laughing at me? (starting to laugh with her)

Mrs. Kennedy: (tears running down her cheeks, smiling) I am not laughing at you, honey. I am really moved by what you just said. What you are saying about "the quiet" being deafening is beautiful; I experienced it myself. It was really special to me. And I am really happy that you know about "the quiet"; I never called it that, but it is a good way of putting it. (starting to laugh) But I'm laughing because "the quiet" wasn't the only thing that was deafening. When you came you were bellowing, "Oh my God," and really *grunting*, and not just once, my dear. I never heard you do anything like that before; honey, it was *great*. I mean, *I* actually got self-conscious for a moment; I thought someone might hear us, and then I thought "go ahead, let them." I finally got to see you be unselfconscious in bed, and it was as good as I imagined, maybe better. You are a real *animal*.

Mr. Kennedy: (astonished laughter) I have absolutely *no* memory of doing that.

Mrs. Kennedy: (laughing, looking in his eyes) *I* will never forget it.

Therapist: (to Mrs. Kennedy) You're doing it again.

Mrs. Kennedy: (laughing) What am I doing this time?

Therapist: The issue of being afraid of sexual vibes from your father. Do you want me to hear your "Let them hear me, I don't care" remark only on one level?

Mrs. Kennedy: Funny that you should bring that up. I was thinking about him last week, not just about being disappointed that I didn't get the father I wanted. I thought about whether he and my mother ever experienced the pleasure that Tom and I are. I thought of him being frustrated all the time, and maybe not knowing what he was after or how to get it. I guess my mother was more controlling than I realized; I stopped seeing her so much as the victim. I could think of my dad seeing me as sexual, and not be frightened by it; I was just sad.

An Invitation to "Regression"

Therapist: How are things going?

Mr. Kennedy: You won't believe how much is going on.

Therapist: Try me.

Mr. Kennedy: Well, a lot is happening with my job. It is finally clear to me that there is no clear hierarchy in the upper management of the business. The owner is afraid to stand on his own two feet, everyone "yeses" him, and he plays the role of the arbitrator. Everyone wants me to take responsibility for making sure we make a profit. I work my ass off and do more than anyone else; my associates, who basically do nothing, want to make sure no one gets more of a bonus than they do. My boss says that he would have trouble with the other managers if he gave me more. So, I told him that he could give the other managers just as much responsibility and overtime work, too. I finally said I wanted to be compensated proportionately for my efforts and responsibilities. He told me that I was being disloyal and selfish; he really pulled out all the stops to get me to buckle under. I told him this was *business*. He was shocked and pissed off at first. He told me that I was making problems between him and the other managers. I finally told him he could choose which manager he wanted to have problems with, but that I had a family and my own self-respect to take care of.

Therapist: Well . . . ?

(Mr. Kennedy smiles.)

Mrs. Kennedy: He got the bonus he wanted!

Therapist: My deepest respect and congratulations.

Mrs. Kennedy: We also ran into a problem with the sex; it didn't cave us in like it would have in the past, but we wanted to talk it over with you.

Therapist: Like what?

Mr. Kennedy: We had intercourse; we tried rear entry for a change, but it wasn't very good. I lost my erection and it wasn't arousing. It was sure a disappointment after our last sexual experience.

Therapist: Were you expecting it to be like last time?

(Mr. Kennedy and Mrs. Kennedy look at each other, and then nod.)

Mrs. Kennedy: Yup, I guess we were, sort of; I never realized it at the time, though.

Therapist: Then I guess this is another good "bad" experience.

Mr. Kennedy: (laughing) OK, I know that I should be dying of gratitude that I had a lousy experience, but would you please explain this one to me.

Therapist: Well, you are welcome to see it anyway you like, but it occurs to me that sex is finally good enough to push you to the limits of your own tolerance. Last week the issue was could you tolerate having it, and this week the issue is can you tolerate not having it. You have made a lot of progress freeing yourself from what you thought were other people's performance expectations; have you now established last week's tran-scendent sexual experience as the new performance standard for your-selves?

Mr. Kennedy: I never thought of it that way; I guess *I* did, at least. (to wife) How about you?

Mrs. Kennedy: I guess I did too; I was expecting it to be the same.

Therapist: Well, if you are going to be able to have it that good, you are going to have to be able to tolerate *not* having it that good. You have to be willing to enjoy it while you have it, and be able to soothe yourself when you don't.

Mrs. Kennedy: I thought a lot about our discussion about one of us dying; it really hit home. We aren't kids anymore. I'd be lying if I said I was comfortable with this idea, but I'm working on it. I plan to love him while I got him. But I never saw that it also came up *this* way, tolerating the loss of really good sex.

Therapist: It's the same thing.

(long silence; Mr. and Mrs. Kennedy look at each other and hold hands)

Mr. Kennedy: I think I had a different problem; maybe it's the same thing and I just didn't recognize it.

Therapist: What happened?

Mr. Kennedy: My problem was that I couldn't feel her when I was inside her.

Mrs. Kennedy: Maybe I am too slack after all these years. I told him maybe he needs a young filly.

Therapist: I think the woman he wants is you. We have no reason to assume that Mr. Kennedy's lack of feeling has anything to do with your vagina; I'm not ruling it out, we just have no reason to jump to that conclusion.

For one thing, it is not a position that your husband is used to. (to Mr. Kennedy) How did you do it when you couldn't feel her?

Mr. Kennedy reported some degree of physical awkwardness and emotional anxiety in his initial exposure to rear entry vaginal coitus. They had difficulty attaining the same degree of emotional connectedness they had come to anticipate with other techniques they had mastered. All told, Mr. Kennedy experienced a significant diminishment in the total stimulus level he derived from this encounter. He reported a common pattern in which he began thrusting fast and deep to stimulate himself inside Mrs. Kennedy's vagina. Very soon, Mr. Kennedy's thrusting had a paradoxical result: he was thrusting so fast that he had little sensation and little friction. Originally educated in the "more is better" school of sexual technique, Mr. Kennedy never thought to calm down and do it *slow*. This, together with the performance expectation developed from their prior encounter, created a significant reduction in awareness of penile sensations. This same pattern of rapid thrusting leads to retarded ejaculation in some men; Mr. Kennedy just lost his erection as his fatigue and anxiety mounted.

Therapist: Well, at least you can see how you *used* to approach intercourse. Why not move your penis in her like you have learned to move your tongue?

Mr. Kennedy: (grins) Well, that approach seems to have worked so far.

Therapist: It's your penis and it's up to you how you move it, but you might try moving slower and shorter strokes.

Mr. Kennedy: Like how?

Therapist: Maybe you can see how *little* you can move your penis and still feel it. If you want friction, stop hammering away and see if you can move your penis to the point that you can just barely begin to feel your wife's vagina sliding on you. You could move back and forth just enough to feel her tugging on you, as you change direction in and out. You can do this with your penis deep inside, or you can do this with only the head in the opening of Mrs. Kennedy's vagina.

Mrs. Kennedy: Sounds good to me.

Mr. Kennedy: You mean you don't need me deep inside you.

Mrs. Kennedy: (making an obvious pun) Read my lips.

Mr. Kennedy: Oh, you are so *bad*! (laughing) I never expected old age to be like this.

Mrs. Kennedy: You can be old by yourself, you old fart! I'm still young. Those young bucks better watch out. (Mrs. Kennedy slaps his leg, laughing.)

Mr. and Mrs. Kennedy's presentation could easily have been taken as a regression, if accepted in line with their initial presentation and their fears. In actuality, it was more like a crisis of faith, a question of ego-strength. Rather than regression, however, the event became a springboard for progress. The ensuing weeks brought other increments in intensity that further challenged the limits of their development.

Discussion during therapy sessions returned to the topic of "doing" and "getting done." Initially, Mr. Kennedy assumed this referred to "giver" and "receiver" roles. However, with some intrepidation on everyone's part, we embarked on an exploration of "fucking." Drawing upon their experience with manual and oral sex, Mr. and Mrs. Kennedy distinguished the subjective experience of "fucking" from the restricted context of intercourse, and the phenomenological roles of "fuck*ee*" and "fuck*er*" from "making love." That led to discussion of "humping," "grinding," and other aspects of sexual aggressiveness. All the while, the underlying issues of Mr. Kennedy's anxieties about "receiving" were increasingly resolved at deeper levels.

Mrs. Kennedy started doing "Kegel" exercises to increase vaginal muscle tone and bladder control; she did them every time she stopped for a red traffic light. One day she came home highly aroused with the delightful report that she was fantasizing about Mr. Kennedy while she was doing it and started to lubricate in the car. That evening they had sex instead of dinner. Mr. Kennedy climbed into bed first to await his wife, lying face down, relaxing. To his surprise, Mrs. Kennedy climbed on top of rather than next to him. She reached up, held his wrists in place, put her hips against his buttocks, and *ground* him. Almost reflexively, Mr. Kennedy stiffened; his issues about masculinity and relinquishing control were pushed to the limit. Mrs. Kennedy was about to give up, thinking she had gone too far. At just that point, however, Mr. Kennedy began to relax and enjoy it. It took 24 hours for Mr. Kennedy to talk with his wife about his experience; he wasn't entirely comfortable with this new behavior, but he was game for another try.

The spillover from this event surfaced in Mr. and Mrs. Kennedy's subsequent experimentation with rear entry coitus. On their next encounter, Mr. Kennedy was in less hurry to penetrate. He simply ground her buttocks with his pelvis for a while without attempting intromission; they just moved in rhythm, with no break in contact of their hips. Both Mr. and Mrs. Kennedy reported increased relaxation in this activity. Mr. Kennedy reported learning to insert his penis all the way and then move it just enough to feel the tug of his wife's vagina on him without sliding. He had no difficulty "feeling" her vagina from thereafter.

Although not inherent in rear entry coitus, it was in this position that Mr. and Mrs. Kennedy really began to explore the psychological dimensions of their eroticism. They began to experiment with different mind sets and styles in the same anatomical position. Sometimes, Mrs. Kennedy would "take charge"; Mr. Kennedy would remain quiet and receptive after penetrating his wife and she would slowly move her hips and "do" him. She would also reach down and gently cup his scrotum or rub her nails on it while he was inside her. She surprised both of them with her comfort in touching her own clitoris while in this position. It was on just such an occasion that Mr. Kennedy had another "quiet" experience:

Mr. Kennedy: I was surprised to have that feeling again, while inside her like that. It was timeless; just me inside her with my penis, rocking with her. Not humping against her or even grinding, just rocking in motion together. She was gently rubbing the hair on my scrotum, and whispering, "Baby, baby." I couldn't see her eyes, but I could smell her and I sensed her with me. I closed my eyes, and I saw her smiling at me; I thought I was in heaven. I had this fantasy that she was the embodiment of womanhood, sent to make peace with me. It was so peaceful.

On other occasions, things got more rambunctious, and Mr. Kennedy was the "doer." Mrs. Kennedy lowered her shoulders and chest to the mattress, turned her head to the side, and emitted a low guttural, "OK, now *do* me, baby, do me *good*." One particular time, Mr. Kennedy started out with slow shallow penetration and "innovated" circular thrusting, brushing his public hair against her buttocks as he moved his pelvis side to side as well as in and out. He concluded with deep thrusting and hard pounding, but he didn't stop when he orgasmed. He enjoying the feeling of "grinding" her, even after he had ejaculated and lost his erection. Later, as they lay in each other's arms, they joked about the noises made by the air he had pumped into Mrs. Kennedy's vagina.

Mr. Kennedy: My orgasm was a complete surprise to me. Normally, I can feel it happening before it starts. This time I had no idea I was about to come. I was totally caught up in the experience, and it sort of "snuck up" on me.

Mrs. Kennedy: (smiling) He was in rare form again.

Mr. Kennedy: I heard myself making noises; I was vaguely aware of it but I didn't bother to control it. It was like the noises were coming out of my guts rather than my throat.

Mrs. Kennedy: Are you going to tell him the other part?

Mr. Kennedy: (slowly) Well, the other part had me sort of shook for a while. I didn't tell Helen for several days, because I didn't know what to make of it, myself. I had this visual experience. There was a brief period where my eyes were so tightly clenched that I suddenly realized I could see *through* them. First I thought I was hallucinating. Then I realized it was really happening; I could see Helen and the room.

Mrs. Kennedy: (laughing) Now look at what we've done. He is turning into a sex machine. *I've* never had a visual experience like that. I told him I'm going to climb on top of him and give myself an hallucination, too.

It was not as though rear entry coitus was the path to salvation; it was simply a position that Mr. and Mrs. Kennedy enjoyed. It was also a *useful* position; they became adept at using it to push their own development forward. However, it was not the only position that they did this with: Mr. and Mrs. Kennedy became increasingly adept in pushing each position to its potential.

In one occasion of oral sex, for example, Mrs. Kennedy opened the encounter by putting her index finger in her vagina and running it under Mr. Kennedy's nose and upper lip. He was stunned, and pleased by her brazenness; she gave him a smile that heralded the encounter to come. Mrs. Kennedy put her hands under her buttocks, raising her hips to offer herself to his caress; she rolled her pelvis and thrust against his tongue. Mr. Kennedy decided this was also the time to add oral stimulation to his wife's perineum; he had easy access in this position. Mrs. Kennedy started talking while he did her. Up to now "talk" consisted of "I love you," "that's good," groans, and aspects of technique. This time, however, she started "doing" him "aurally" while he did her "orally." It was like a feedback loop: from her mouth, to his brain, out his mouth to her vagina, and then back out her mouth. It was a startling increment in intimacy. Afterward they kissed deeply; deep "french" kissing, not the perfunctory kiss that makes one partner feel dirty for having the other's genital juices on his/her mouth. Mrs. Kennedy described it as the kiss that pushed her to embrace her own body as clean and acceptable, once and for all. Eventually, Mr. and Mrs. Kennedy went through "guilt" for not having intercourse more often and preferring oral sex:

Mr. Kennedy: We realized we were feeling this "guilt" and tried to figure it out. I think we felt were *supposed* to have intercourse. It is weird, like the sex police were going to come in our bedroom and say, "Stop having oral sex with your wife, you have a duty to have intercourse," like someone is keeping track.

Therapist: Sounds like you are well on your way to getting over keeping track.

Mrs. Kennedy: Well, it has taken us a while, but we are finally getting it through our heads that our bodies and our lives belong to us. Well, really, each to ourselves.

Mr. Kennedy: We also considered if our focus on rear entry and oral sex was an avoidance of face-to-face intercourse.

Mrs. Kennedy: I didn't think this was true because we now look *inside* each other when we have sex orally, manually, or in rear entry; I guess I just know what I like! (laughs) But, it was a pleasure to go along and let him check it out. So we did it face to face, but it was nothing like the old "missionary" way. I was on my back with my heels in the air; Tom picked my legs up over his shoulders, and put a pillow under the small of my back. We joked that if our bodies got stuck in this position, it would give the ambulance attendants a shock.

Mr. Kennedy: I made sure that we both looked at each other, all the way through. I had an orgasm and never looked away. It wasn't just looking *at* each other, it was looking *inside* her. I saw her face get this questioning look at one point, and I just opened myself up and let her look at the love I have for her; she started smiling and then I got really happy and I came.

The Approach of Termination

Mr. Kennedy: I really didn't understand when we first came in here what you meant when you talked about me being tense during sex. I kept looking for something like anxiety attacks or fear of failure. Now I have a profound sense of relaxation when we are together, in and out of bed, that I never knew existed. It is what I imagine babies feel, only better. (Mr. Kennedy reaches out to Mrs. Kennedy and strokes her hand.) We can do it in a few seconds now. It almost makes me want to tense up sometimes when I relax that much. I have to soothe myself down; I have to tell myself that I can put my armor on quickly when I need to.

Mrs. Kennedy: When I really let myself reflect on what has happened to us in such a relatively short period of time, and how we might have missed out on this, it makes *me* tense. (talking about Mr. Kennedy) Now I realize how lucky I am to have him in my life.

Therapist: I hope you enjoy him during the time that he is on this earth, and are willing to let him go when it's time.

Mrs. Kennedy: I believed that foolishness about people "being made in heaven for each other" when I met my first husband. Then I had the feeling we were the marriage made in hell. I don't think my relationship with Tom was made in heaven, although I think we will end up there, together. If we are soulmates, we earned it ourselves. I want to see him be happy; the part about giving him up when he dies, I'm still working on that part.

Mr. Kennedy: I don't want to lose Helen either; I am just thankful for the time we have had, and will have, together. I never thought my life would turn out like this. No one will ever believe us about this experience; we can't even tell our friends. Maybe I know one man who might, and I'm not too sure even he would understand.

Mrs. Kennedy: Besides, we can see many of our friends have their own problems now, even the ones we used to admire and think were perfect. I have a friend who thinks she is really sexually daring; she once masturbated with vegetables. I know she feels very superior to me, and I think she would be floored if she really knew me now.

Therapist: What about taking people on the level they can handle?

Mr. Kennedy: When you realize how few people are really capable of being a friend, it makes you stop and cherish your partner more deeply. And, we do cherish the few friends we really have. I keep thinking this is *hubris*, but it feels more like reality to me; it frightens me to see what I now see, and it frightens me to think that I never used to see it.

Mrs. Kennedy: We wanted to ask you, what do we tell our kids about this? I want my grown kids to know what we have learned, particularly my daughter. She is married with kids of her own. I know that she and her husband have problems from time to time. I mean, I'm not going to talk to them about our sex life like we talk with you, but I want them to have the benefit of what we didn't even knew existed.

Therapist: What makes you think they haven't already started to get that? They are watching you and getting an education about what the potential of the later years of life are about.

Mrs. Kennedy: Yes, you're right. But, I would like to be able to sit down and tell them something.

Therapist: Well, you folks are clearly moving towards termination. I will be happy to discuss talking with your kids. It is a good sign; you don't sound defensive about being in treatment.

Mr. Kennedy: No, we started out that way, but now we're proud.

Therapist: I am very glad that you chose to do it with me. On the other hand, you are offering me the opportunity to act like the great sex kahuna one more time. Part of terminating involves being willing to trust yourselves and live with the last bit of uncertainty. It means giving up cross-checking your perceptions with me.

Mrs. Kennedy: It will be hard to stop seeing you.

Therapist: It will be for me also.

Mrs. Kennedy: I'm sure there is more we could learn.

Therapist: I'm sure there is; that is why there is one thing in particular that will be the last thing we share. You will have to learn to give me up voluntarily, to leave here even though you enjoy it and there are some things left undone. The last things you learn, you will learn without me. The last thing you learn with me will be saying goodbye to something you still value. You can always come back, but you can't leave with that anticipation. Our goodbye is a preparation for the final goodbye between the two of you.

OVERVIEW AND INTEGRATION

Range of sexual experience and depth of involvement are only two parameters of sexual potential. Mosher's (1980) model of three dimensions of sexual experience (Chapter Three) is an attempt at a topology for an incredibly broad typography; the content and context of sexual experience are as varied as human emotion.

One might think of sexual experience as a *language of expression*: some people are mute, some are sexually aphasic or dyslexic, many have a small utilitarian vocabulary, and a few are wordsmiths who use their broad vocabularies articulately.

Mosher pointed out that depth of involvement in sex can vary from superficial to profound; people differ in their enjoyment and engrossment in sexual linguistics. Some are only interested in sexual activity as pragmatic conversation, others enjoy "talking" just to be sociable, and some become enthralled by a particular sexual topic, style, or partner. A smaller group appreciate eloquent sex as an art form. Such people may not be fond of "idle chatter." They can become profoundly engrossed with someone who has a mastery of the language of sex and the imagination and creativity to use it; they are simply intrigued by the process of exchanging meanings with a fundamentally separate person.

The problem of sexual "languaging" is literal as well as metaphorical. Discussing intense eroticism and intimacy (and why people avoid both) is troublesome, in part because appropriate conceptual guideposts and professional lexicons are almost nonexistent.

> Although this subject [person] was compelled to use the conventional term "orgasm" to describe her experience, this was only because our language is deficient in terminology to describe adequately the full range of bodily erotic experiences, especially mystical and celibate beatitudes, ecstasies, and pleasures. But one thing is certain. The familiar truths about sex and conventional routes of sexual expression begin to appear as one largely overworked possibility among many. The erotic sense of one's own body, one's attractiveness to others, and the meaning of gender, orgasm, and psychosexual development can no longer be explained with prevailing concepts and theories. (Sovatsky, 1989, p. 163)

Clinical conceptualization and evaluation often reduce sexual languaging ability to vocabulary. The range of sexual behaviors in which one engages is not as important as the range of emotion and meanings that can be contained and conveyed in such behaviors. For example, the fact that partners engage in cunnilingus, fellatio, or "missionary" coitus actually offers relatively little information; the *style* of these behaviors, however, is far more revealing. One can see from the preceding case description that questions like "Do Mr. and Mrs. Kennedy do a particular behavior?" or "Do they like it?" are so inarticulate that they block the pursuit of sexual potential and utilization of sexuality as an elicitation window.

More sophisticated and discerning ways of looking at sexual style exist outside contemporary practice. The Kama Sutra,[2] for example, discerns 64 coital positions and examines subtle nuances of *biting* and *scratching* (Douglas & Slinger, 1979).[3] *Noises* made during sex, volitional and nonvolitional, are

---

[2]The Kama Sutra is the earliest surviving Hindu love manual, written around the second century A.D. by Vatsyayana, and translated in 1883 by Sir Richard Burton.

[3]Douglas and Slinger quote from the Kama Sutra: "When a man bites a woman, she should do the same with double force. Thus, a *Point* should be returned with a *Rosary of Points*, and a *Rosary of Points* with a *Broken Cloud*, and if she feels chaffed, she should immediately begin a love quarrel with him. At such times she should take hold of her lover by the hair, bend his head down, kiss his lower lip, and then, in the intoxication of her love, she should shut her eyes, and bite him in various places" (p. 246).

discussed as ways of releasing emotional "blockages" and categorized in great detail. Citing a discussion in Taoist texts of nine different ways a man can move his penis, Douglas and Slinger offer yet another meaning to the sexual crucible: *Nine styles of moving the Jade Stalk while inside the Female Crucible* (p. 264).

Facial expressions during sex were studied as part of Eastern sexual doctrine to gain understanding of the sentiments associated with eroticism. A seventeenth-century painting of a Taoist couple having sex, for example, depicts the woman looking into a mirror to examine her facial expressions (Douglas & Slinger, 1979, p. 236). Many of the Tantric sexual positions utilized to gain spiritual transcendence involve prolonged eye-contact.

BEING SEEN AND KNOWN AT PROFOUND LEVELS
Eye Contact

Monkeys, apes, and humans engage in complex visual communication by way of more highly developed facial musculature and expression than found in other vertebrates. Eye contact in sexual initiation, a common aspect of primates, is often overlooked in studies of hormones and sexual behavior (Dixon, 1990).

This form of sexual communication *during sex* is often overlooked in humans as well. Eye contact *during* sex is rarely addressed in the clinical literature. This is noteworthy since (a) eye-contact ("flirting") appears to be a sexually arousing "phylogenetically ancient" trait occurring in a wide range of cultures (Dixon, 1990),[4] and (b) the physiological capability for sustained eye contact during face to face intercourse facilitates the uniquely human capacity for intimacy during sex.

At first glance, it seems surprising that this capacity is not exploited by contemporary treatment approaches; upon reflection, it is not. In its focus on sexual (dys)function, sex therapy has emphasized the use of touch, but not the use of *feeling*. Our initial discussion of sexual potential (Chapter Three) mentioned that modern sex therapy encourages eye closure, "tuning out" the partner, and focusing on the tactile sensations in one's body. In that discussion, "a therapy that encourages people to tune in" the partner was conceptualized. That kind of treatment might not be desirable to everyone; some people don't want to *feel* while "copping a feel." Even working with those who *do*, it's hard

---

[4]This is the third aspect of eroticism encountered thus far that highlights the role of sociobiology in human evolution; the evolution of noncyclical sexual interest and pairbonding (see Helen Fisher (1982) in Chapter Twelve), and the emergence of the neocortex and the capacity for intimacy (Chapter Four) are the other two.

to help them have sex that feels personal—hard for married couples to *know* each other in the sense that the Bible takes for granted.

One way to accomplish this is through eye contact during sex (i.e., literally "seeing eye to eye"), although folks are often reticent to play with this aspect of eroticism. A series of vignettes have already illustrated this point: (a) the 1991 AASECT presentation where not one therapist in the audience regularly considered whether patients could have eyes-open orgasms (Chapter Three), and (b) the cases of Paul and Sarah (Chapter Eleven), and Mr. and Mrs. Kennedy, who learned to do exactly that.

As indicated above, our real focus is *style of behavior* rather than sexual behavior per se. Although eye contact during sex is itself a major sticking point for many couples, it actually comes in many *styles*. These styles change as couples progress through three stages (for those who persevere): (a) eye contact, (b) *prolonged* eye contact, and finally, (c) *letting your partner see you.*

Couples who develop the ability to have eye contact still have a way to go to establish "I" contact! Seeing I to I—two people letting themselves see and be seen behind the eyeballs (i.e., looking inside *each other)—is something else again.*

George Leonard (1989) describes the experience of allowing himself to be *seen* during sex.

> For me, the erotic encounter is ecstatic in the dictionary sense of the word. It takes me out of my set position, my stasis. It permits me the unique freedom of stripping away every mask, every facade that I usually present to the world, and of existing for a while in that state of pure being where there is no expectation and no judgment. The act of love, at best, is an unveiling. Layer after layer of custom and appearance are stripped away. First goes clothing, then every other marker of status and position: job, title, honors, monetary worth. Propriety must also go, and with it pride. My freedom lies precisely in surrender, in my willingness to relinquish even my hard-won personality (*persona*, Greek for "mask"), my image of who I am in the world and what I should be—my ego. If I am willing to travel this far and expect nothing, then nothing can go wrong. There are no "sexual problems," no "sexual solutions." There is no technique. I am as a god; whatever happens happens.
>
> And it is in this state of surrender, of not-trying, that my full erotic potential is realized. For I am now willing to lose everything and find nothing. All that has maintained me in the ordinary world is of no use here—grammar, syntax, sensory acuity. Even differences of gender fade away in the climatic rhythm of our joining. I am not male, my love is not female. We are one, one entity. Through the tumult of love, we have arrived at a radiant stillness, the center of the dance.

At this point, there is a choice that lies beyond conscious choice; predisposed by trust, commitment and passion: to travel even beyond space and time and enter a sublime darkness. Seeing nothing, hearing nothing, I am totally connected with my love and, through her, to all of existence. What was veiled is unveiled, what was hidden is revealed; beneath all appearance, beyond all customary distinctions, there is a deeper self that wears no mask. In the darkness, there is an illumination. I love, I have found nothing and all things. (Leonard, 1989, p. 79)

If it is this wonderful, why don't people want to be seen during sex? If the problem was merely body image, it would be easier to resolve. The problem is *the reluctance to be seen on the inside and felt*. It is in this sense that sex therapy has emphasized physical contact and avoided *feeling*. In the present discussion, *feeling* takes on new meanings, as in feeling *"vibes"* and touching each other emotionally. *When touching and feeling reach this depth of profoundness, many people bail out.* Although it will not be mentioned repeatedly in this discussion, we are essentially talking about differentiation and the capacity for self-validated (level-2) intimacy.

"I" Contact

Couples can look each other in the eye but still not let each other *look* inside. People have an innate ability to avoid "I" contact during sex. Eventually, they can learn to look *into* each other during sex, and tell when their partner (eyes opened or closed) is *not available*. Anyone can, although not doing so avoids many upsetting implications—the training starts early in childhood (Chapters Seven and Eleven).

This same phenomenon occurs between therapists and patients all the time. You look people in the eye, their eyelids are up, but their emotional "shades" are down; you can't see past their retinas. *You (and they) can tell when you are really seeing inside them, and they* know *when they are letting themselves be seen.*[5]

---

[5]This material is applicable to more superficial (yet still meaningful) levels of object-relations and existential issues than I am discussing. Unless I am mistaken, readers may confuse the two without realizing that I am referring to a more profound level of "being seen" than many people experience. This deeper level of experience is, in itself, curative and healing; in therapy, it becomes the portal to teaching self-soothing (discussed in Chapter Seven, and detailed in *The Intimacy Paradigm*). "I" contact during eye contact was illustrated in the vignettes of Mr. and Mrs. Kennedy, and Paul and Sarah (in Chapter Eleven).

The therapy I conduct reached new depths when I began discussing *intangibles* with patients who had been with me for a while. The approach requires assuming they can tell the difference when they are really letting someone *see* them. This line of discussion opens the door to inquiring about this level of contact in their marriage, why they never say anything about what they know in this regard, and why and how they do or don't pursue it.

Surprisingly, many people are reluctant to acknowledge they can tell when they allow themselves to *see* and *be seen*.[6] When patients try to reference this experience by reflecting back on sexual encounters, they often have difficulty; many have never experienced it in that context. More often, however, the problem is that *people lie about being able to feel each other: They lie that they do when they don't, and they lie that they don't when they do. Seeing and being seen often become a crucible of integrity*.

Establishing that patients know about *seeing* and *being seen* from personal experience is a strategic intervention: It removes room to maneuver and avoid the issue, like acting as if they don't know what I am talking about or asking me to "explain." Verbal explanations fall short and discussions about "object relations" have little utility: (a) They lead to conceptualizations and cognitions that fail to capture the right tone, and (b) it insures that the topic of conversation won't occur. Patients encourage intellectual or philosophical discussions to avoid the experience itself.

I can't *prove* patients know what I am talking about—I can't even prove that the phenomenon exists. I can only demonstrate its existence by referencing their personal experience. Besides, the important internal referent is *experiential*: The best referent is one *I* know they have experienced—times it has occurred in treatment with *me*.[7] Patients ultimately acknowledge this awareness; in so doing, they reconstruct the same level of interaction in the session. This experience seems to make people heal and grow.[8] It is, however, exceedingly hard to tolerate.

Ask folks why they look away or break off contact when it is feeling good:

---

[6]Leonardo Da Vinci said there are three classes of people: *those who see, those who see when they are shown, and those who do not see* (quoted by Madariaga, *Saturday Review*, April 22, 1967).

[7]Separate and apart from its utility in this regard, there is something wrong (from my perspective) if this highly intimate experience never occurs with a patient. It is diagnostic as well: I find no point in broaching the topics discussed here with such people until it does.

[8]This involves a mutual shift to a metalevel, discussed in Chapter Four regarding Chelune, Robison, and Kommor's (1984) notion of intimacy as intentional metacommunication.

They know exactly what you are talking about, but exceedingly few can tell you *why* they do it. The most common answer is something like:

> I know this doesn't make any sense. This feels real good and I know you're not going to hurt me. I just get nervous, "twichy-like," like it feels too good or something. I don't know, it makes me feel weird to be talking about it. I've never acknowledged this with anyone in my life.

Letting someone look inside you is an ultimate demonstration of integrity. Acknowledging this "I" to "I" while it is happening often provokes chortles and guffaws of laughter—and bittersweet chest pains, too. Patients get embarrassed about *being seen* being seen. When couples (at low levels of differentiation) attempt this after bitter long-term conflict, they often become highly emotionally reactive and reflexively defensive (see Chapters Seven and Eight).

"Focusing," "Vibes," and "Contagion"

"Seeing behind the eyeballs" is merely *one* aspect of sexual potential. Other related *intangibles* involve the focusing of eroticism and the transmission of "sexual vibes" (emotional contagion). Douglas and Slinger (1979) write that the erotic power of the mind was well known in the Orient:

> A couple should be aware of their movements during love-making and should try to manifest them as artistically as possible. This helps to focus the minds and emotions of the partners, enabling the channeling of energy and the transformation of ecstasy into the visions of unity. When lovers hold in mind and enact the multifarious sexual roles, they can build up to orgasm consciously. This is one of the secrets and goals of Tantric love-making. (p. 218)

Consider how women who can orgasm solely through fantasy *focus* their eroticism. They use mental imagery, subtle isometric self-stimulation, intense sensate focus, and most of all, they channel their own erotic energy into an intense, laser-like focus. In coupled sex, a partner on the other side of that kind of focused eroticism is in for a *jolt*. It can be intimidating to be paired with a person who can do it to that degree—there are not many people around who can. Partners of people with lesser but still significant ability to access their eroticism are often intimidated as well.

This scenario is not very different from men's reaction to women who can have multiple orgasms. The issue isn't just a feeling of "not being able to keep up"; it is a little awesome to be with someone who is multiply orgasmic, given that many people (a) can't delay their orgasm and do so only once, (b) can't make themselves come even once, or (c) require great effort. There is considerable variety of ability to access/focus one's eroticism.[9]

The notion of focused eroticism is not particularly esoteric. People encounter it *every day* while walking down the street, making eye contact with someone they find attractive: Eyes meet, and they realize they are really *looking* at (and *seeing*) each other—both liking what they see. They can *feel* each other. Sometimes it happens when two strangers stand several feet apart in an elevator, neither looking at the other, both watching the floor numbers light up.

Clinicians and the general public take this for granted in daily life. Social psychology can document that it happens and predict the social behavior surrounding its occurrence; we can't, however, explain *how* it happens psychophysiologically. Kerr and Bowen's (1988) concept of *a general emotional system*, however, offers a basis for tentative clinical formulation: *This is nothing more than the erotic form of emotional contagion* (Chapter Seven).

Contagion is the interpersonal broadcasting of emotion found in many species, which includes (a) the ability to send and receive information on a kinesthetic level, (b) with or without concomitant cognitive awareness or understanding. Wilson (1985) and Kerr and Bowen (1988) hypothesize that humans share an interpersonal "emotional" network as do ants, bees, dolphins, and whales, which have sophisticated communication systems (e.g., for locating food or danger and mobilizing others); bees do it so well, it contributes to a gender transformation in a male when the queen dies.

The notion of emotional contagion of eroticism is no different from Kerr and Bowen's (1988) conceptualization: *Feeling* another person's eroticism isn't any different than being "infected" with their anxiety (or pain, love, or anger). The conception of eroticism as contagious permeates common parlance (e.g., lascivious, licentious, dissolute) and obscenity law's view of eroticism as *dangerous* (see Table 11.1 and footnote #7, Chapter Eleven).

The counterpart to sending erotic "vibes" is the ability to receive/read them from others. People know the feeling of being "undressed" or violated by the way someone else *looks* at them; they know when to avert their gaze from someone approaching on the street—they can *feel* it. This is not just a question

---

[9]The fact that women still *fake* orgasms, and men worry about being "faked out," is testimony to the fact that many people coexist at the other end of the continuum of emotional contact. There is *no* possibility of faking being *seen*—one can feel the emotion "shades" are still down. Orgasm-faking reflects how little "*I*" contact couples commonly have when they copulate.

of physical proximity or dominance displays. Common social behavior revolves around this ability.

Until fairly recently, men have been socialized to be the "senders" of this erotic energy, and women the "receivers." Men learn that part of their gender role involves doing this with women who are total strangers; women learn that acknowledging this transmission is tantamount to accepting a proposal for sex. Reciprocal "vibes" make folks feel like they are "doing it" (which is exactly the point we are building to). In more recent times, women feel greater license to "send" sexual vibes—and men have experienced varying degrees of relief, flattery, and intimidation. *But exceedingly few people focus their eroticism and broadcast it through eye and body contact during sex*. Married couples often crave doing in the bedroom what they did before marriage walking down the street with just a look.

Why is it that people don't want to be *seen* or *felt?* It is because eroticism is like a thumbprint, as personal and unique as the shape of one's genitals. "*I*" contact about eroticism is an extremely powerful form of level-2 intimacy. Part of it involves simply acknowledging that one really *has* eroticism; the other part involves what one's erotic map looks like.

Robert Bly (1990) offers another link between the disclosure of eroticism and the impact of the family, previously discussed in Chapter Eleven. He addresses the aspect of men's masculinity often referred to as *phallicness*. Paraphrasing his message for applicability to both genders, Bly suggests that men and women are afraid of the power of their *male* and *female essence*.[10] This essence constitutes a significant part of eroticism. He describes many people's personal experience: Encountering one's eroticism is a scary, risky proposition, requiring the courage to accept the "*nourishing* dark side of oneself."

Bly's thesis explains the reluctance for "*I*" contact during sex. Accessing one's sexual energy is not compatible with certain contemporary notions of "niceness" and tameness. People lock up the "wild, hairy" side of themselves and turn control of it over to their parents—both generations are ambivalent about eroticism. People explore their eroticism secretively and furtively, hiding it once again and acting like it never happened; they do it with their parents, and they do it with their spouses (particularly after an intense intimate-erotic experience). "We've all replaced the key [to our eroticism] many times and lied about [having taken] it (Bly, 1990, p. 13)."

When one partner accesses and focuses his/her eroticism (all other stimula-

---

[10]Bly refers to this aspect of masculinity as the *deep male* or the *Hairy Man*.

tion remaining constant), the well-attuned partner experiences a corresponding shift in sensation/arousal. Both can *feel* the difference. This is the backbone
of Tantric and Taoist Yoga, and the Kama Sutra; it fits within the dimension of
psychological processes which contributes to *total stimulus level* in the quantum model (Chapter Two).

It is hard to get Westerners to even discuss the existence of this energy,
much less to get two partners to practice focusing this energy/consciousness
simultaneously (and deal with all the stages of development necessary to get to
this point). This energy, which fuels the profoundness of sexual experiences, is
conveyed through the "*I*" *contact* of *having one's eroticism felt and seen*; a particular genre of this will be mentioned momentarily.

WALL SOCKET SEX

Prior chapters proposed that couples' sexual styles are determined by the
unresolved issues they are trying to avoid; selection has relatively little to do
with the physical efficacy of particular sexual techniques. As the foregoing
case example illustrates, efficacy has more to do with the ability to maintain
oneself as the intensity and salience of eroticism and intimacy hit new heights.
Venturing outside the *range* and *depth* of one's preferred sexual style pushes the
envelope of one's personal development; herein lies the use of the elicitation
window and the sexual crucible.

Level of differentiation becomes an increasingly crucial factor in this process. As the case of Mr. and Mrs. Kennedy demonstrates, people carry a level
of anxiety that they often don't know about; this anxiety is *below* the baseline
levels by which they judge themselves subjectively anxious. Getting people to
calm down enough so that they cease to have sexual dysfunctions or anxiety
attacks is one thing—it is quite another to get them to *really* relax.

Profound relaxation and involvement in an alternative sexual reality require
terminating what Harry Stack Sullivan (1953) referred to as "security operations": subtle but constant monitoring of the world for potential signs of
threat. Low-level tension is worn like emotional body armor (Adler, 1951), a
state of alertness offering the fantasy of self-protection from sudden threats
and disappointments. People find it difficult to let go of this low-level anxiety
and become *quiet*—this is what Mr. Kennedy "heard" when he finally *relaxed*.[11]

---

[11]A complete treatment approach for reaching this level of *quiet* is presented in *The Intimacy Paradigm*; if it can help people reach this level (and produce *wall socket sex*), you can imagine its utility in
reducing anxiety in the treatment of overt sexual dysfunctions. It is probably not too early, however,

Sexual repertoires, however, are specifically designed to circumvent this occurrence. *When patients report being "relaxed," they are referring to the absence of massive anxiety, and the intactness of security-operation-maintaining low-level anxiety.* When sex becomes profoundly intimate and erotic, individuals experience the curious phenomenon of *not wanting* to relax any further, and encounter additional anxiety if they do.

Pushing the reluctance to relax offers further opportunity to enhance differentiation, resolve object relations issues, and increase the ability to self-soothe. The resulting tranquility sets the stage for experiences of eroticism and intimacy that challenge the essence of one's self-worth. Nonvolitional and nonselfconscious "sexual abandon" occurs in the context of *a tranquil but firm grip on oneself.* Whereas couples may have previously complained of sex being "rushed," *both* partners often experience a disquietingly but pleasurable level of intensity when the pace is slowed sufficiently.

Progress in the sexual crucible is generally indicated by the emergence of *wall-socket sex*, a term originally suggested by a couple in the course of treatment.[12] The couple compared the unanticipated "energy" of their erotic connection to one of sticking a finger in an electrical outlet. *Much to their surprise, it didn't involve sticking anything into any body orifice; it occurred in the context of nongenital touch.*

Defenses against intensely erotic and intimate connection are inherent in the way couples approach "massage" and traditional sex therapy prescriptions for "non-genital touch"; *this* is the stage of physical exchange at which couples are often best able to recognize and struggle with defenses against erotic "I" contact. The roles of "giver" and "receiver" in "non-demand, non-genital touch" don't necessarily require one to address the more intangible but salient dynamics of "doing" and "being done." One can "be the giver" without necessarily "doing the receiver." The sensations of "fucking" and "being fucked," in their most positive and loving connotations, are neither the same as coitus nor inherent in it.

It is exceedingly difficult for most people to really fuck *their spouse (in the most wholesome erotic sense of the word). If one is able to fuck (and many are not), it is usually done with someone else's wife or husband. The fallacy of the "whore-madon-*

---

to emphasize a point made repeatedly in that volume: The information in *The Intimacy Paradigm* has limited utility without a thorough understanding of the conceptual background of *The Sexual Crucible*. Techniques without a conceptual background make a clinician just a *technician*. Healers understand that healing is a *process*, not a technique. A collection of techniques is not a process; it often impedes the process of healing and growing.

[12]The occurrence of wall socket sex *below* the orgasmic threshold was depicted in Figure 9.4 of Chapter Nine.

na split" isn't that women can't turn their eroticism on and off between the bedroom and living room; the real problem is that people, male or female, can't crank loose their eroticism with the person they marry, period![13] Said differently, the problem isn't that folks put their spouse on a pedestal; it is that they put him/her on only *one* (where the spouse has to stand with his/her knees together)—if they put him/her on *two* pedestals, fucking would be a lot easier.

It is quite possible for couples to create the sensation of "doing" or "fucking" without any genital contact; it isn't that hard to do and doesn't take years of practice. It is a case, instead, of being able to *tolerate* it. Many married people have great reservations about *"fucking"* their spouse in any way (except perhaps euphemistically); at best, they permit themselves to fuck during the socially prescribed ritualized act of intercourse. *Fucking outside the context of intercourse* is often an extreme escalation in eroticism and intimacy which exceeds people's ability to self-validate in the context of their spouses; it is the embodiment of "eyeball-to-eyeball" "I" contact during sex.

Wall-socket sex offers multiple "shocks" that drive couples forward in a differentiation based, sexual-potential-focused, asset model of sexual-marital therapy:

- The shock of an *intense* erotic and intimate personal experience that seemly arises out of "nowhere."
- The shock that this occurs in behaviors other than intercourse and independent of orgasm.
- The shock of observing one's own intolerance and spontaneous withdrawal from such experiences.

---

[13]For men, this is the issue of "phallicness" to which Bly (1990) refers. A suitable corresponding concept for women has failed to emerge from the inherent masculinization of popular psychology and Western religion: *penis envy* or *phallic woman* is phallocentric, *femininity* is often mistaken for fragility, and *facho* is as misguided as *macho*. At best, women's sexual power is acknowledged as a *seductress* in reference to men; *butch* or *dyke* demonstrate the negative way autonomous potency in women is received.

In Eastern religions, the desired conceptualization is readily available. *Lingam* is the spirit of phallicness; *Yoni* captures the similar creative power of women. In fact, a Hindu myth exists that the gods *Shiva* (male) and *Parvati* (female) competed to see who could create a better race of people without the participation of the other. The *Lingajas* turned out to be stupid, feeble, misshapen creatures, whereas the *Yonijas* were a well-shaped, well-mannered, attractive race that beat the *Lingajas* in battle (Walker, 1983).

The sexual crucible is where men *and* women finally come to terms with the incredible power of female and male eroticism. Integrating unpretentious (*naked*) eroticism within a loving union is a potent grindstone. Accessing the *phallic* and *yonic* aspects of eroticism is the functional equivalent of resolving what psychoanalytic-oriented therapists refer to as the Oedipal/Electra complex.

- The shock of one's personal experience contradicting one's sexual belief system and prevailing societal wisdom.
- The cognitive dissonance of wanting-to-want intense sex but not pursuing it.

Wall-socket sex is a powerful means of exploring one's phenomenological reality. Sovatsky (1989) describes the common feeling of being a stranger in a strange land:

> It becomes very clear how sexual energy is both a basis for pleasurable sensation and a maturational force. In fact, one has the sense that the body is undergoing another kind of puberty, resulting in a transformation on a par with adolescence in terms of gender identity, bodily capacities, and sexual understanding. In other words, a whole new erotic universe emerges. (p. 163)

Wall socket sex is a distinctly adults-only event; it is not something teenagers and the immature really get to explore. Wall socket sex challenges one's sense of "entitlement," creating a need for increased self-validation while also producing the crucible that can create it. Wall socket sex is, in itself, a demonstration of increased ability to tap one's sexual potential. It negates a prevailing social reality and validates a more personal one: *Most sex is relatively mediocre sex, and common sexual boredom and minimal sexual desire often reflect good judgment.*[14]

*Wall socket sex presents the crucible of sorting out three challenges of self: (a) losing oneself, (b) the fear of self-*centeredness, *and (c) the capacity for self-*centeredness.

Many people avoid developing a *self* in the mistaken fear of becoming *selfish* (i.e., *self-*centered); in the context of wall socket sex this surfaces as fears of *hedonism*. Increased ability to center oneself (i.e., self-*centeredness*) is so antithetical to common experience that it triggers fears of becoming *self-*centered (i.e., totally self-preoccupied and indifferent to the partner's preferences). According to conventional wisdom, the degree of caring for someone is proportional to the ease with which one loses one's equilibrium with that individual (e.g., "head over heels over someone"; "s/he knocks me off my feet"); maintaining one's equilibrium is interpreted as *indifference*. Conventional wisdom tends to

---

[14]The observation that sex often improves on vacations stems from more than reduced interruptions and pressures. Sex often improves when one is removed from the things that define one's persona; the sense of being unknown in one's environment has a significant disinhibiting effect on displays of eroticism. The inability to do this "at home" reflects a need for greater differentiation rather than a change of scenery.

ignore reality: When people lose their equilibrium, they become completely *self*-centered until they regain it.

Self-Soothing and the Death of Narcissism

Increased ability to maintain oneself in close emotional proximity to the partner (i.e., level-2 intimacy), however, does *not* lead to invariant self-interest at the *expense* of the partner. One aspect of high-level differentiation is the ability to tolerate the tension inherent in recognizing the partner as a separate individual with competing preferences and agendas. Although well-differentiated partners *often* defer to the other's wishes, there is no loss of self associated with it.

Troubled couples aren't so lucky—partners often feel they have compromised themselves away, and (hopefully) will do so no longer. As individuals emerge from head-butting differentiation-enhancing highly conflictual periods they sometimes think, "I am going to be who I really am, and my spouse can take a hike if s/he doesn't like it."[15] However, this is *not* the attitude of someone who is self-*centered*; it *is* of someone who is *self*-centered or easily loses himself/herself. *When one is willing and able to hold onto oneself, there is no need to adopt this as a constant mind set.* The point is not to thumb one's nose at one's partner; rather, it is this: If one has to choose between holding onto one's partner and holding onto oneself, the choice is always the latter; letting go of oneself often guarantees the loss of *both*.

It isn't as simple as folks just wanting to interpret a spouse's *self*-sacrifice as a sign of "love" (e.g., "marriage takes sacrifice"). *People hate giving up the idea of eventually turning themselves over to someone else.* Intense relationship *discord* is a crucible in which spouses learn not to sell themselves out to a "*bad*" relationship. The fantasy remains, however, that one can, should, and will be able to turn over responsibility for self-maintenance in a "*good*" one.

Patients pursue therapy with the fantasy, "We are *two* because we don't get along; but we will become *one* when we resolve our differences." Learning that one must maintain oneself in a *good relationship* often comes as a utter shock and complete disappointment; this reality is avoided as long as the relationship remains combative. The desire to fuse and relinquish personal responsibility dies a slow and painful death.

---

[15]This often doesn't occur until the marriage looks to be over; ironically, this is often when it has a chance to survive (Chapter Thirteen).

A disquieting internal conflict mounts as long-sought improvements do not occur in anticipated ways. Spouses feel more intensely intimate *and* more separate, rather than isolated or "drifting apart." Fights about personal validity, the nature of reality, and pressure to compromise evaporate in increased *tolerance* for existential separateness. Individual and conjoint satisfactions emerge out of tolerance for being *two together* rather than a fused oneness. Each partner faces a choice: relinquish either the growing benefits of increased differentiation or the fantasies of fusion.

As the marital bed becomes the crucible of enhanced sexual development, it also becomes clear that it will never be a bed of roses. Given our biological heritage, impulses for sex with multiple partners will no doubt remain encoded in the cellular depths of the brain (Chapter Twelve). Monogamy may or may not reflect a higher state of development, but differentiation makes tolerating the tension inherent in honoring that commitment possible. Differentiation is what keeps this to a minor frustration instead of an internal war that can preoccupy the very center of one's existence (as it did in the theology of Sts. Jerome, Augustine, and Aquinas; see Chapter Seventeen).

The Pain of Intense Eroticism and Intimacy

Perhaps the most important reason why people avoid intensely pleasurable sex is also the least mentioned: *it hurts*. One of the more significant aspects of this pain was mentioned in Chapter Seven (page 192). At that time, we discussed the pain *"of what didn't happen"* and the working through of losses with parents and other emotionally significant figures.

This pain is tangible in sessions with patients exploring wall socket sex, and it is subject to the same emotional contagion as contagion of eroticism (discussed above). Induction of pain in the other spouse (and the therapist) occurs: When one spouse experiences this profound pain, it triggers similar feelings in the other. The result is reflexive (reactive) attempts by the other spouse to stop his/her own pain by pulling the first spouse out of his/her unfolding experience. Fights and other distractions (e.g., getting "helpful") are created to withdraw from profoundly intense sex and intimacy. This functions much like Melzack and Wall's (1965) pain-gate theory of pain control: creation of one pain to block awareness of another.

Intensely pleasurable marital sex triggers other painful unresolved issues. One involves relinquishing childhood fantasies of the prince or princess who will complete us (and whom, in turn, we will complete). Narcissism dies a lingering death, but it is its own punishment while it reigns. Highly conflictual relationships reinforce, and are reinforced by, infantile fantasies: Spouses continue to assume they picked the pauper instead of the prince. Highly pleasurable intimate marriages crucify the fantasy of the prince (and princess) and resurrect the partner, a dear uncommon commoner, who is "the chosen one" but still not the "one and only" of infancy.

> It was not until we started accepting each other as if we had been picked to be together by all the angels in heaven that we began to experience an arranged marriage. (Prather & Prather, 1990)

Greed (i.e., the *pseudo*-quest for perfection) comes in many forms; wall socket sex is where avarice is resolved. Alfred Adler (1951/1983) discussed negative reactions to attainment of cherished goals. Watzlawick (1989) recently suggested that nothing is more promising than an unfulfilled hope. Oscar Wilde noted life's two tragedies: not to get our heart's desire, and the other, to get it; Wilde thought the latter was worse. This is why: An intensely satisfying relationship carries the awareness of "not getting it all." Sebastian Moore (1989) (see Chapter Seventeen) discusses how the refusal to tolerate *loss* interferes with the attainment of intense desire:

> [We need to learn] the difference between liberation *from* desire (the latter equated with the insatiable self-promoting ego) and liberation *of* desire from the chains of my customary way of being myself. Two contrary views of asceticism present themselves here. The conventional view is that it means denying ourselves things we want. A more discerning and disconcerting view is that it means dropping things we no longer want, admitting to ourselves we no longer want them, and thus giving our journey, our story, a chance to move on. . . . (p. 91)

Intensely satisfying marriages trigger fears of engulfment, rejection, deprivation, and being controlled through one's own desire. Fears of pride, hubris, and the "evil eye" surface in many forms, including the fear of losing the good sex that one has achieved. Openly enjoying and acknowledging one's pleasure often feels like tempting fate (and one's partner) to withhold. Displaying one's eroticism can feel like playing with fire, particularly to those who modulate its expression in accordance with their partners' insecurities.

An increasingly satisfying relationship requires corresponding increments in the ability to self-soothe (Chapter Seven). Self-soothing is the balm that assuages "not having it all"; it also comforts the fears of losing what one has achieved. Intense desire and satisfaction are not safe until one can self-soothe one's own heartache, disappointment, and fears.

Contrary to rational logic, intense desire and *wanting* often become increasingly anxiety-provoking as the level of marital satisfaction increases. This phenomenon was previously discussed as libidinal "bad object" conflicts (Chapters Seven and Ten). Attempts to modulate these anxieties surface in the details of physical exchanges: Does the individual have the strength and integrity not to shy away from self-perceived pleasurable opportunities? The notion that "intense sexuality and intimacy are hard to tolerate" takes on a new level of significance.

Wall socket sex elicits residual fears of exceeding or usurping parents. Psychoanalytically oriented therapists will see oedipal issues; family therapists will see systemic homeostasis. Both vantage points are applicable to varying degrees at different times with different people. Profound sexual experiences trigger defenses in a way that pedestrian sex does not. Fears of evoking competition, jealousy, or painful self-reflection in parents, siblings, and friends emerge. Sons and daughters who longed for the opportunity to respect their mother or father become increasingly conflicted as their own development progresses; this conflict stems not just from the fear of "exceeding" one's parents, but also the reluctance to relinquish a fused attachment in lieu of *seeing* parents as separate adults like him/herself. The case of Sarah and Paul, the man who had slept in his parents' bedroom until age 13 (Chapter Eleven), offers just such an example.

A few months prior to the time of termination, Paul was seen individually at his own request. He wanted to discuss "oral sex," and Sarah did not want to be present for the discussion. The problem was that he could not really relax and enjoy receiving oral sex; he knew she did not want him to ejaculate in her mouth. The current discussion seemed more to do with sexual dynamics than sexual technique, since Sarah had been quite open to discussing oral sex per se in prior sessions.

As we talked, it became increasingly apparent that this was an issue about Paul's own sexual aggressiveness and "phallicness." By not participating in the session, Sarah had removed the possibility of my interfering by serving as intermediary. Paul would have to be assertive and maintain himself independently if he was to get what he wanted. Paul and I talked at some length about issues of "one-penis" and "two-penis" family systems and how the former raised conflicts in fathers and sons about adolescent prowess and aggressiveness. We considered this in relationship to his own childhood and his father's alcoholism and failure to thrive. We also discussed the significance of his own sons' increasing challenges to his authority.

We briefly discussed technique issues: differences between ejaculating in her mouth, her swallowing his ejaculate, and being able to stop worrying about her and focus on his own penis during fellatio. I made no attempt to encourage negotiation with his wife; Paul was on his own. Differentiation, phallicness, and running his own penis in discussing fellatio with Sarah all became one.

Paul and Sarah returned for their next session happy and smiling. As he entered my office, Paul said, "I have something I think you'll appreciate. It goes like this: You don't think your way to a new way of living; you live your way to a new way of thinking!" I was quite stunned with the elegance and appropriateness of his observation. But the best was yet to come.

Sarah seated herself saying, "I don't know what you both talked about, but I sure liked it. I never felt such an incredible jolt from Paul as when we made love after his last session. I couldn't take my eyes off him, it was so intense. I was just riveted in the experience with him. The sexual energy pouring out of him was exceptional." Paul remarked that he had not planned or done anything special, yet he knew that he had functioned in a qualitatively different way. He had thought a great deal about the session, and then "accessed something inside me and put it into what I did. It was not the technique, it was what I put of me into the technique. I don't know how to describe it, but I know that I can do it again."

It turned out, however, that Paul's difficulty was *not* resolved in this single "breakthrough." Sarah became comfortable and adept at oral sex; she *wanted* him to come in her mouth, hungering to "take him in" this way. Paul found himself "holding back" from the intensity of fellatio with his wife; he continued to have intermittent difficulty ejaculating.

Even after ejaculation was no longer an issue, *fucking* during fellatio took some additional development. Paul was a bit unnerved by Sarah's acceptance of his body and the power of her eroticism: She wanted to have fellatio in ways that made it clear to Paul that she was *doing* him. Doing *her* during fellatio brought up Paul's realistic concerns of gagging Sarah, and more fears about the destructiveness of his own sexual aggression. This remained an issue until the closing days of treatment. Part of Paul's retrieving the "key" to his eroticism (Bly, 1990) involved *fucking* during oral sex and announcing it in session. This report was part of our final meeting (described in Chapter Eleven).

SEXUAL TRANSCENDENCE

Where does the pursuit of sexual potential ultimately lead? If thousands of years of Eastern culture are any indication, it leads to transcendence of self and spirituality.

Sokol (1989) has written personal accounts of her own and other's transcendent sexual experiences. She notes her reluctance to publicly acknowledge what she found to be possible:

I was determined to investigate the experience and bring it fully into consciousness. At the same time, I was aware of my reluctance to confess the full ramification, because of the implicit demand to live a life that was based on that realization, and because of the possibility of disbelief and even ridicule from anyone I might have shared this with, except my husband. The ultimate taboo is not sexual freedom or death. The ultimate taboo is ecstatic self-transcendence. (p. 117)

Perhaps this hesitancy stems from the same source as does Sovatsky's (1989) observation that traditional sex therapy only makes a cursory approach to sexual potential.

Scientific theory allows little room for mystery, however, and so conventional psychology has explained the mystery away: Erotic feelings are merely the urge for genital orgasm, with little or no concern for the cycles of fertility or even balanced frequency. Psychology has limited eros to a certain set of behaviors, feelings, and images; in other words, it has turned eros into sex, and has taken upon itself the task of freeing us to have as much sex as we could ever want.

When eros is understood as mystery, however, traditional spiritual teachings about sex can be understood as an attempt to protect mystery from mundane explanations and profanations, rather than as a parental prohibition against certain activities. . . .

In short, a new history of modern sexuality has emerged that shows the limitations of the first wave of the sexual liberation movement. *The next wave, which promises a further integration of spirituality and passion,* has much to learn from yogic theories. (Sovatsky, 1989, pp. 160–161, italics added)

Douglas and Slinger, who know these Tantric theories, state:

Liberation, especially sexual liberation, must be oriented in a positive spiritual direction. If not, when the novelty of new sexual experiences has worn off, emptiness and meaninglessness inevitably result. (Douglas & Slinger, 1979, p. 11)

We conclude this chapter at the threshold of spirituality and sexuality. It may seem strange to make the leap from oral sex to sexual transcendence, but that is exactly what couples like Mr. and Mrs. Kennedy and Paul and Sarah experience in the exploration of sexual potential. We will return to this point in our final chapter. Before then, however, we will shift to gather in two major themes touched on throughout this book: the use of inherent paradox, and the role of the therapist in the sexual crucible.

CHAPTER FIFTEEN

Uses of Inherent Paradox in Sexual-Marital Therapy[1]

Although using paradox to treat sexual difficulties is not new, development of this modality has been restricted by the "rational" cognitive-behavioral approaches evolving from Masters and Johnson's legacy. Unwittingly, modern sex therapy creates its own inherent paradoxes which undermine treatment flow and successful outcome. A paradigm shift from "sex is a natural function" is proposed: Intimate sex is a developed ability and an acquired taste. Use of spontaneously occurring inherent paradox differs from "constructed paradox" (i.e., therapeutic double-bind) in numerous ways (e.g., no "bind" is constructed by the therapist; paradox is approached as a fact of life rather than as "pathology"). Inherent paradox is readily integrated into sexual-marital therapy and offers multiple advantages; foremost among these is enhancement of differentiation.

The use of paradox in the treatment of sexual-marital difficulties is not new. Victor Frankl (1967) was one of the earliest proponents of paradoxical psychotherapy. Weeks and L'Abate (1982) cite Frankl as using paradoxical intervention to reduce anticipatory anxiety as early as 1939. In 1946, Frankl reported the treatment of erectile difficulty by prohibition of intercourse (cited by Weeks, 1986). In this proscription, the patient was instructed to avoid the sexual behavior he was seeking help in mastering.

In his review of the literature, Stanton (1981) found that paradoxical intervention had been successfully used in the treatment of premature ejaculation and other sexual problems. Stampfl and Levis (1967) used implosion techniques, flooding individuals with sexual performance anxieties and fears of rejection to produce extinction of anxiety and avoidance behaviors. Milton Erickson used relabeling in a case of erectile dysfunction. He relabeled wed-

---

[1]An earlier version of this chapter originally appeared in L. Michael Ascher (Ed.). (1989). *Therapeutic paradox*. New York: Guilford Publications, and is used with the permission of the publisher.

ding night impotency as a "compliment," suggesting that the groom was so overwhelmed by the bride's beauty that he felt "incompetent" (Haley, 1973).

Like Frankl, Masters and Johnson used the ban on intercourse as a performance-anxiety-reduction technique. Others have noted that the ban on intercourse sometimes functions as a defiance-based injunction for individuals who have been resistant to having sex with their partner. However, deliberate use of the ban primarily as a defiance-based intervention was inconsistent with Masters and Johnson's orientation; the meta-communication of their approach is that the ban on intercourse is suggested to facilitate anxiety reduction, and compliance with therapist authority is crucial.

"Restriction of progress" (*defiance-based paradox*) approaches to sexual problems are more common to marital therapists who address the sexual difficulty as a symptom of the system. This approach anticipates that spontaneous symptom resolution will occur without using modern sensate focus activities when the system is reorganized; alternatively, this approach shifts to a more rational, logical approach once resistances have subsided. Defiance-based paradoxical approaches to modern sex therapy lack continuity in strategy because of the inevitable shift to nonparadoxical compliance-based prescriptions in the middle phase of treatment.

THE "MODERN" VIEW OF SEX AS A NATURAL FUNCTION

The exploration of paradox within sexual therapy has been restricted, in part, by the legacy of the rational, cognitive-behavioral approach from the seminal work of Masters and Johnson. Masters and Johnson advanced the viewpoint that patients should relax and let their bodies function as they are designed to do, proposing that *sex is a natural function*.

There is no doubt that this naturalized view of sexuality has an intuitive appeal to humanistic values. It certainly represents a vast improvement over the view of sexuality as sinful or dirty that characterized the rise of Christianity in Western civilization (Lawrence, 1989). However, the erroneous assumptions and attributions about the nature of human sexuality inherent in this relatively new view of sexual congress are only starting to surface in the minds of sexual health professionals (Simon, 1989).

Although there has been considerable societal benefit in the "naturalization" of sexuality, the notion that "sex is a naturally occurring, healthy function" is a strategically unreasoned position for sexual-marital therapy and the treatment of sexual problems. The naturalized view is basically a unidimensional intervention, aimed primarily at the reduction of performance anxiety and fear of failure; it assumes that people function primarily on a rational, conscious level. The naturalized paradigm of sex therapy ignores the wealth of experience from the fields of individual (psychodynamic/analytic) and marriage and family therapy, suggesting that unconscious and systemic issues are major determinants of individual behavior and the meaning attributed to that behavior.

The modern "naturalized" framework of sexuality creates an unfortunate paradigm, in which it is perfectly logical for the patient to ask, "If sex is a natural function, why should I have to do these strange behaviors you are suggesting for me? Other people don't need to do them to function normally." From this vantage point, seemingly logical anxiety-reducing activities can, paradoxically, have an anxiety-increasing impact on both the individual and the dyad. What at first glance would appear to reduce patients' performance anxiety and encourage them to "relax and let go" actually confirms their growing feeling of being "different" and inadequate compared to other people. Moreover, the naturalized view of sexual functioning reinforces patients' common belief that they should not be having their difficulty to begin with.

Behavioral suggestions of modern sex therapy lend themselves to being rejected on a purely cognitive, rational basis. Is it really logical that a woman who is unable to have orgasms during intercourse should avoid having intercourse as a way of eventually reaching that goal? Is it really considerate for a man, failing in his attempts to maintain his erection during intercourse, to stop trying to please his wife in this manner when both partners regard it as the only "normal" way? In so doing, won't he feel *more* insecure, more inadequate, and more selfish than he already does? From the patient's perspective, the most basic interventions of modern sex therapy appear to be inherently paradoxical.

By its very structure, modern sex therapy seems to stimulate resistance to itself; by its very content, it seems to be inherently paradoxical. These problems develop out of an inherently logical premise, creating a demand for patients to do something illogical. The attempt to present typical sex therapy interventions as logical and rational only compounds the conundrum.

What would an alternative paradigm look like? A nonrational paradoxical style of sex therapy will be presented in this chapter. This paradigm shift is based on a premise that even the most ardent proponents of "sex comes natural" usually will accept: *Although reproductive sex is a natural function, intimate sex is not. Intimacy during sexuality is an acquired skill and a developed taste.*

This seemingly innocuous (and rational) statement opens the door to a paradigm shift in both focus and dynamics in the treatment process. The full implications and application of this shift are outlined in *The Intimacy Paradigm* but several points will be made here briefly. First, it becomes immediately clear that the "sex is a natural function" credo is not fundamentally oriented towards intimacy (and may be antithetical to it); the alternative proposed above is consistent with the tenor and focus on intimacy presented throughout this book. Second, redefining the goal of sexuality as *intimacy* (a learned ability), rather than *"pleasure"* (a "natural" function), inherently reduces performance anxiety and fears of failure; the expectation of immediate success is diminished. Third, this framework provides an explanation for the couple's lack of success in the bedroom, reducing inadequacy feelings regarding prior spontaneous efforts. Fourth, and finally, this paradigm shift offers the clinician increased freedom in making a wide range of nonrational suggestions and interventions—generally revolving around spontaneously occurring paradox in the couple's sexual and nonsexual relationship.

INHERENT VS. CONSTRUCTED PARADOXICAL INTERVENTIONS IN SEX THERAPY

Watzlawick, Beavin, and Jackson (1967) distinguish three type of paradox:

> *Antimony*: paradoxical statements that are logical contradictions, mainly of interest to logicians, mathematicians and theoreticians.
>
> *Semantic antimony or paradoxical definition*: stemming from hidden inconsistencies in language structure, such as Epimenides' famous "All Cretans are liars" paradox.
>
> *Pragmatic paradox*: Often known as "double-bind" (Bateson, Jackson, Haley, & Weakland, 1956), and therapeutic double-bind (Watzlawick et al., 1967), this form of paradox comprises the foundation of most "paradoxical" psychotherapies. In this chapter, pragmatic paradox will be referred to as *constructed paradox*, reflecting the therapist's process of constructing therapeutic paradoxical binds that patients are induced to enter.

Watzlawick et al.'s category of "semantic antimony" (which they dismissed from serious consideration) is the focus of this chapter. This category will be referred to as *inherent paradox*, reflecting the therapist's process of focusing attention on preexisting paradoxes transparently embedded in the couple's reality. This is the same "inherent paradox" mentioned repeatedly throughout this book.

The concept of inherent paradox is expanded here beyond the limited scope of linguistic anomalies in "paradoxical definition" to include hidden inconsistencies in cultural sexual beliefs, practices, and values. Inherent paradox also arises from spouses' unresolved interlocking individual conflicts and the dynamics of relatedness between fundamentally separate beings (e.g., incongruous power hierarchies). Such conflicts and inconsistencies are often expressed in the simultaneous parallel meanings encoded in the couple's vocabulary of verbal and physical exchanges.

Constructed Paradox

In order to clarify the nature of inherent paradox, it is useful to examine constructed paradox, which is more familiar to many therapists. Paradoxical double-binds and constructed therapeutic counter-paradoxes are more than simple contradictory injunctions that leave the recipient no choice but to defy or comply with one admonition or the other. One requirement for constructed paradox to be effective is that the recipient must not be able to communicate with others about the paradoxical injunction itself. This is usually the rule in relationships in which pathogenic double-binds arise, and it is paralleled in the use of constructed paradox in treatment. Therapists generally refuse to discuss the "contradictory" or illogical nature of paradoxical suggestions and injunctions given to patients.

Another requirement of constructed paradox is that the recipient not be allowed to move to a higher level of abstraction or functioning in order to avoid the bind. That is, the therapist refuses to discuss the meta-communication within the paradoxical injunction or to discuss the injunctions as belonging to a therapeutic style known as paradox.

Constructed paradoxical interventions are often used as a way of dealing with patient resistance. In fact, one common guideline in the application of constructed paradox is that "straightforward" rational approaches are preferred as long as the patient or the relationship system is operating in a logical, rational manner. When the patient or the system appears to function in an irrational manner, the therapist shifts to constructed paradoxical interventions.

Constructed paradox has immediate appeal and face validity to therapists whose therapeutic approach generally involves construction of activities for patients to fulfill. Moreover, the proclivity of many therapists to see sex therapy as a behavior modification approach involving prescribed activities makes the use of constructed paradox a particularly attractive form of intervention. When therapists view patient noncompliance with prescribed activities as resistance to treatment and defiance of the therapist, utilization of other constructed prescriptions is quite inviting. The classification of constructed paradoxical interventions as compliant or defiant with the therapist's prescription (Rohrbaugh et al., 1981; Tennen et al., 1981) is fundamentally self-referential and subtly encourages an adversarial stance. Constructed paradoxical prescriptions often take on the quality of "blockbuster" interventions, delivered with great ceremony to the patient at the conclusion of a session. Emphasis is placed on the therapist's skill in delivering the constructed paradox, with a premium being placed on showmanship and benevolent cunning.

Inherent Paradox

Although Weeks and L'Abate (1982) dismissed the category corresponding to inherent paradox from serious clinical consideration, they did point out that the solution to inherent paradox is to promote a quantum leap in the complexity of the solution. Basically, this involves a paradigm shift in the process of going to a higher level of functioning. They offered as an example Bertrand Russell's theory of logical types, in which to establish the concept of a *class* of objects one must move to a level of abstraction higher than a collection of the objects that comprise the class. One can note a multitude of different types of chairs, but the leap to the concept of *furniture* is a shift in complexity of abstraction.

Resolution of problems in marital and sexual functioning stemming from inherent paradox requires shifting to a higher level of functioning. When the paradox results from embedded cultural values and beliefs, it is necessary to establish a viewpoint outside the culture from which the implicit cultural information can be viewed and examined. When inherent paradox results from interlocking unresolved individual dynamics, the solution requires more than an increment in emotional development for one or both individuals. It requires a paradigm shift in the way that existing information and perceptions are understood. From this vantage point, the individual can recognize that the current impasse reflects his or her own expectations and projections, rather than the simple validity of his/her perception of the partner.

Examining this from an alternative perspective, the requisite shift is in the level of differentiation. Without this increment in differentiation, the individual is trapped by a culture, a language, and typical personality development that are inextricably intertwined, reciprocally validating, and mutually perpetuating of inherent paradox. This perspective holds significant implications for therapists as well. Therapists whose professional identity is thoroughly enmeshed in the perpetuation of contemporary approaches to sex therapy are unlikely to recognize and appreciate the inherent paradoxes embedded in current practice. For example, attempts to treat inhibited sexual desire with the same sensate focus activities used for treating sexual dysfunctions is antithetical to the fact that it was the *failure* of such techniques that gave rise to the identification of lack of desire as a clinical problem.

It sometimes becomes apparent that the opposite of a shallow truth is generally false, but the opposite of a deep truth is generally true as well. Encouraging patients to be "selfish" in bed as a way of legitimizing pleasure and reducing performance anxiety often overlooks the fact that the partners have actually been demonstrating extreme selfishness for some time. Similarly, encouragement of childlike playfulness in bed overlooks the immaturity and lack of differentiation that often characterize adult relationships. Suggestions that becoming more *adult* rather than more infantile is the route to more intense sexual experience are quite paradoxical to contemporary viewpoints of sexuality. The idealization of childhood abdication of responsibility and avoidance of anxiety paradoxically reinforces preexisting problems and legitimizes patients' avoidance of the very activities that therapists suggest.

Inherent paradoxes that derive from contemporary language usage are relatively invisible until they are pointed out, at which point they become glaringly obvious. Consider a lovely statement like, "Wittgenstein has said that what can be shown cannot be said" (in Levenson, 1972, p. 167). Common phrasing, such as *getting*, *maintaining*, and *losing* an erection, *achieving* an orgasm, *giving* someone an orgasm, and *making* someone come, all perpetuate a performance ethic that is hard to disregard. Apfelbaum (1983) noted that many colloquialisms are half-truths that mask a corresponding contradictory half-truth:

> We are opposed to the use of slogans in therapy. They are unanswerable (at least by the client) and just pull for compliance. They also invariably are half-truths that make it harder for people to see the other side of an issue. Like the slogan that "you always do what you want." It is equally true that "you never do what you want." Or, take: "No one can give you an orgasm." That really sounds true. So does: "You can't turn yourself on." Or, take: "No one can tell you what *you* are feeling." It is equally true that; "Everybody knows what you are feeling better than you do." Or: "No one can make you do something you really don't want to do." It is also true that: "It is easy for someone to make you do what you really don't want to do." (p. 96)

Sometimes inherent paradoxes result from interlocking contradictions in male and female gender-role expectations. For example, a man is encouraged to define himself as sexually adequate by pleasing his partner. On the other hand, a woman is often sexually disinterested when she feels that her partner is more interested in fulfilling his role and demonstrating his prowess than in her own personal pleasure. A man who sets out to establish his competency and desirability by fulfilling his gender role is often at a loss to explain his wife's sexual disinterest—that is, until he thinks that it's his *wife's* gender-role training that is in the way! The fact that it is half-true only leads him farther off course from seeing himself.

Spontaneous paradox often results from splitting, isolation, and other intrapsychic defenses against the resolution of internal conflict. In their discussion of "symbolic interactions," Verhulst and Heiman (1988) describe inherent paradox resulting from interlocking unresolved individual issues:

> More recently, Elkaim (1986) has described how a double bind can develop between a couple's symbolic structures. He uses the term "official program" to describe the explicit request of each member of the couple for a change in the behavior of the other. In addition, he refers to the basic blueprint of how the world works, which each partner has drawn up in the course of his or her past, as that partner's "map of the world." For example, the double bind underlying a complaint of low sexual desire in a particular couple might be analyzed as follows: The wife's official program states, "I want my husband to have more sex with me." Yet her map of the world may be in contradiction with the official program, because of a deep-seated belief that sex is dangerous. Thus, messages from her "map of the world" state, "Do not have sex with me." A double bind develops if the husband has a complementary cognitive structure. His official program may read, "I want you to be less demanding in matters of sex"; this may be contradicted by his map of the world, which states, "I need to be pushed and encouraged because I am incapable of joyful sex." The reciprocal double bind in which both partners are locked is based upon a paradoxical interactional fit. If the husband initiates sex, and thus tunes in to his spouse's official program, he threatens her map of the world and "causes" her to push him away with excessive demands and criticism. If, on the other hand, the wife accepts her husband's behavior without making demands, she in turn threatens his map of the world. (p. 247)

Kerr and Bowen (1988) provide several examples of inherent paradox. One arises as a function of language, in which one partner asks the other, "Why do you do what you do?" Implicit in this simple interrogatory is the suggestion that the cause of the behavior is within the individual and independent of the asker's behavior. Another example derives from the characteristic interaction of poorly differentiated partners:

Both husband and wife are caught up in his or her own view of the situation. While both believe that for the marriage to improve it is the *other* that needs to change, in reality each contributes to the problem equally. The wife reacts when she feels unloved, ignored, and taken for granted; the husband reacts when he feels unloved, pressured to changed, and unappreciated. Each spouse is highly allergic to particular comments and actions by the other spouse; paradoxically, however, each spouse says and does things that invite the very comments and actions from the other spouse to which he or she is most allergic. A spouse who wants to be told he is "loved" reduces his chances of hearing it when he acts sullen if he does not hear it. People get "turned off" by one another's neediness. A spouse who does not want to be "dictated to" increases his changes of being dictated to by overreacting and rebelling against the perceived "domination" of the other. Rebellion invites efforts to control and efforts to control invite rebellion. The conflictual stalemate is created by these automatic emotional reactions and by the difficulty people have getting outside their own viewpoint sufficiently to allow them to think about the nature of the problem differently. (1988, p. 189)

While inherent paradox is not limited to the dynamics of sexuality and relationships, some of the most cogent examples are to be found there. Inherent paradox often surfaces at the interface between the drive for change and growth, and the drive for stability and homeostasis. For one example, chronically "helping" one's partner tends to cripple the one who is helped, and elevates the functional level of pseudo-self of the helper. For another, the tendency of undifferentiated partners who feel too "unloved" to elicit nurturance from each other further stimulates their fears of abandonment and reduces the sustainable level of intimacy.

Similarly, insecure individuals who perceive their partner as untrustworthy often attempt to have the partner prove that the perception is untrue. An increase in "trust" of the partner occurs at the expense of increased personal feelings of insecurity and self-doubt regarding one's perceptions. When it comes to fights about validation and dependency needs, most people willingly "put their finger in the pencil sharpener" one more time, when they are "hurt" that the partner doesn't get their point.

Contrasting Approaches to Paradox

Constructed and inherent paradoxes are contrasted in Table 15.1. Constructed paradox is sometimes used to push for omission or commission of particular

Table 15.1
Comparison of Constructed and Inherent Paradox

CONSTRUCTED PARADOX	INHERENT PARADOX
Patient cannot communicate regarding paradoxical injunction or meta-message	Therapist encourages discussion of paradox
Used when patient demonstrates resistance to change	Utilized throughout course of treatment
Paradox stems from single source or agent (e.g., a parent or both parents acting as contradictory locus of control)	Paradox stems from multiple sources (e.g., gender roles, sex myths, incongruous power hierarchies, interlocking unresolved personal issues)
Paradox is constructed by therapist	Therapist constructs or prescribes nothing
Patient is induced into the bind	Paradox is anchored in preexisting problems; no issue of "fit of intervention"; does not require strong alliance or rapport
Patient not allowed to shift to higher level of abstraction	Patient encouraged to make leap in complexity of solution and abstraction
Consistent with "no-growth" models	Consistent with developmental approaches
Emphasis on therapist's showmanship and "benevolent cunning"	Less adversarial or manipulative; more collaborative alliance; "observing ego"
Fuels "compliance" expectations and behavioral views of sex therapy prescriptions	No pressure for patient compliance
Conclusion: final "bind" left in place by therapist	Conclusion: freedom from binds of normality; acceptance of life as inherently paradoxical
Appeals to authoritarian therapists	Patient is encouraged to take charge; reinforces boundaries and autonomy
Oriented towards patient "resistance" and irrationality	Paradox as "normal" fundamental characteristic of complex systems
Links symptoms to others; puts partner "in charge" of symptoms	Strengthens differentiation and detriangulation
Paradox as pathogen; counter-paradox as counter-pathogen	Pathogen is intolerance for paradox and uncertainty; paradox is a fact of life rather than a "technique"
Therapist challenges the patient's system	Therapist must challenge his or her own development

sexual activities. In common usage, it is utilized by many therapists as a generalized systemic intervention, in the hope that the need to address stylistic details of bedroom behavior may be obviated. Whereas constructed paradox is generally employed only *after* the patient has demonstrated resistance to change, inherent paradox is utilized throughout the course of sexual-marital therapy; it provides a consistent treatment framework. This prepares individuals for the reality that marriage, intimacy—and sexuality for that matter—embody paradoxical elements at the most profound levels. Inherent paradox is quite consistent with an elicitation approach to sexual behavior, in which both the behavior and the inherent paradox contribute to the examination of individual and dyadic problems.

Exploration of inherent paradox keeps the focus on the problems that originally brought the couple into treatment, rather than on a "manufactured" problem of the therapist's design. Since the paradox is preexisting and "anchored" within the realities of the relationship, use of inherent paradox neither requires nor encourages greater "trust" or dependence on the therapist. It is instructive to watch couples attempt to subtly shift the therapist's position to one consistent with constructed paradox, because it is an easier position in which to deal with the therapist. "We didn't do what you told us to do" suggests that the conflict is between the therapist and the patients. The use of inherent paradox implicitly presents the therapist to the couple in a highly differentiated stance. The use of constructed paradox, in contrast, is a undifferentiated stance; in encouraging patients to either comply or defy, the therapist is telling them to *do something*.

In using inherent paradox in sexual-marital therapy, the goal is not merely the resolution of sexual dysfunctions but also the facilitation of complex functioning within the relationship. Rather than accepting paradox as pathology, sexual-marital therapy utilizes inherent paradox to develop tolerance and appreciation for complex functioning and the additional paradoxes that inevitably emerge in life. In the sexual crucible, the therapist encourages patients to discuss inherent paradoxes in their situation, violating one of the main rules of constructed paradox. Where inherent paradox results from underlying interlocking unresolved individual issues, it provides a vehicle for examination and resolution of developmental tasks.

For example, consider a man who believes his wife to be "sexually unresponsive"; in an effort to increase frequency of sexual contact, he initiated sex "all the time." Using constructed paradox, the therapist might prescribe that the husband initiate sex daily, "to insure getting the sex he needed" and "help his wife get over her 'inhibitions.'" When the man eventually feels coerced and rebels against the schedule of initiation, his frequency of initiation will probably diminish. Moreover, his resentment of "feeling pressured to have sex daily" will present the opportunity to experience what his wife has been feeling recently. (A potential pitfall might be that the intervention alienates the wife by making it appear that the therapist has ignored her feelings and validated the legitimacy of the husband's demands.)

In utilizing inherent paradox, the therapist might simply point out to the husband that the partner with the lowest sexual desire always controls the frequency of sex; the more he pressures his wife to have sex, the more he is dependent on her and the more control she has over him. Ultimately, the more he demands sex the less he is wanted, although he may eventually pressure his wife into having it. Moreover, the husband's frequent invitations allow his wife to remain passive, having sex when she wants it without ever initiating or having to *work* at it like he feels he has to. At the same time, the therapist can point out to the wife that there is no reason for her to have sex when she doesn't want it. On the other hand, she is participating in the construction of something else that she does not want: She is conditioning her husband to initiate sex far more frequently than he actually wants it, because he knows that she will respond when her guilt gets high enough.

The couple is caught in the grips of two simultaneous interlocking crucibles: When either partner escalates his or her entrenched position, it only further exacerbates the individual and mutual dilemmas. There is little need for the therapist to construct any additional paradox; all that is needed is an *illogical* solution for the inherent paradox that derives from seeming logical, reasonable positions.

Gordon (1988) has noted examples of inherent paradoxes in contemporary relationships:

> If you comfort (give to) me, you are more powerful than I am.
> I will not accept your comfort.
> If I comfort you, you are comforted.
> I resent you for being comfortable when I never can be. (p. 26)

> If you don't love me, stay with me, I will die.
> Therefore, I must cling to you no matter what the price.
> The more I cling, the more you feel smothered and distance.
> The more you distance, the more I cling. (p. 27)

An Extensive Case Example: Dr. and Mrs. Jones

Dr. and Mrs. Jones, both age 49, requested treatment for their sexual and marital difficulty. They had been married for 25 years and had two sons, ages 18 and 20. At the outset of the initial interview, the couple related that Dr. Jones was threatening divorce because of his wife's lack of interest in sex. After mentioning that her husband blamed all of their marital problems on her "frigidity," Mrs. Jones defensively reported that she was not "frigid"; she had been orgasmic until their marital conflicts became increasingly severe in the last 18 months. She also reported that her husband had difficulty with rapid ejaculation, which he refused to discuss with her and blamed on their infrequent sexual contact.

At a momentary pause in the middle of their initial interview, the couple had the following interchange:

Mrs. Jones: He really didn't want to come today. He feels like coming to treatment is admitting that there is something wrong with him. He could only come here by insisting that he is perfect and that the problem is me.

(Dr. Jones looked defensive about his defensiveness, confirming the accuracy of his wife's statement. Unfortunately, Mrs. Jones' statement made him less amenable to treatment.)

Dr. Jones: Well, I think that *we* should be able to take care of this. But I have also studied psychiatry during my medical school training, and I am enlightened enough to know that sometimes you have to go to a doctor to get something fixed even if it is an emotional problem. After all, that is my business too.

Therapist: I have seen a lot of couples, and it is fairly common for people to feel like coming to see a therapist, particularly about sexual and marital problems, is a de facto declaration of sexual incompetency and inadequacy. The funny thing about it is—I have never seen a truly inadequate man or woman in all the years I have been in practice. The truly inadequate ones don't come in here. To come to see me, people have to have some basic faith in themselves, faith that they can do better. The really inadequate people just hide in shame; just showing up here often makes people feel better after they get over the initial anxiety.

During the session, Dr. Jones claimed that he didn't care what anybody thought of him; he would say and do whatever he wanted. His statements seemed to be a declaration of counter-dependency, delivered as autonomy and independence. His style demonstrated his dependency on his wife; in the session, he could not complete one sentence if his wife gave any nonverbal indication of disagreement. He immediately turned to her to demand that she verbalize her disagreement, and then he argued with her. He could not even continue to look at the therapist to whom he was talking and continue with "his side" of recent events at home.

At one point, the therapist volunteered his surprise that Dr. Jones did not simply take the opportunity to continue telling his side of the story without stopping, an opportunity he would seemingly desire and demand. While then doing so, Dr. Jones repeatedly looked at his wife after every statement. The wife recommenced to make her typical minor signs of disagreement, which continued to infuriate him. As he talked, Dr. Jones' head swiveled rapidly with each statement, from the therapist to his wife, and then back again.

After several minutes, the therapist interrupted the husband, complaining that he (the therapist) was becoming "increasingly confused." In response to the doctor's question about the nature of the therapist's confusion, the therapist stated that he wanted the doctor to instruct him as to which of two messages the therapist was to listen to. On the one hand, the therapist pointed out, the doctor's verbal behavior suggested that he was very independent, if not indifferent, to his wife's opinions; Dr. Jones repeatedly demeaned his wife's ability to think clearly. On the other hand, the doctor's nonverbal behavior suggested that he was extremely attentive to her and accorded her opinions the greatest respect: his anger and head-swiveling actually reflected his valuing (but not tolerating) her opinions and his need for her agreement.

In pointing this pattern out to the husband, the therapist offered a tentative interpretation; perhaps the spouses were having difficulty resolving their difficulties because they didn't appreciate the whimsical, paradoxical nature of their relationship. The therapist suggested that, although it might appear that Dr. Jones was indifferent, he was highly emotionally dependent on his wife. Mrs. Jones merely smiled knowingly to herself, while her husband nervously and angrily turned to her and said, "You don't believe that, do you?" The therapist suggested that the doctor had actually just confirmed the interpretation with which he was disagreeing.

Note that the therapist never actually offered a defiance-based paradoxical suggestion for the husband to ignore his wife while talking with and looking at the therapist. Had this been done, it might have threatened the therapist's alliance with Mrs. Jones and removed the opportunity to interpret the husband's spontaneous behavior pattern. Instead, the therapist had only to utilize what was already occurring, without taking a personal position in the dynamic; the therapist could function as an uncommitted participant-observer with an alliance with both individuals.

Dr. Jones to therapist: I am not sure that I totally agree with you.
Therapist: I couldn't agree with you more, and everything you just said is absolutely true.
Dr. Jones: What is that?
Therapist: You are *not sure yet*. I encourage you not to agree with me. It is probably totally true that it is not *totally* true. It is a half-truth, like so many things in life and in your relationship. If you maintain your own good judgment, you will end up making up your own mind about the merit and meaning of this observation. Besides, if you are dependent on what your wife thinks of you, we won't get anywhere if I encourage you to become dependent on what I think also.

But, it *is* interesting that somehow you manage to make a statement that something might not be totally true, and make it sound like it is totally false. If I didn't listen very carefully, I might think that you were disagreeing with what I said, which you never literally did. Perhaps there might be *something* of value in the idea that you give your wife's opinions credit and that her opinion of you is crucially important to you.

At this point, Dr. Jones voiced a seemingly simple statement that reflected multiple levels of meaning: (a) an illustration of his view of autonomy as indifference and masculine impregnability; (b) his defiant attempt to hoist the therapist on his own petard; and (c) a common confusion of dependency with closeness and communication.

Dr. Jones: Well, if I was not emotionally dependent on her, then what would I do, never listen to her opinions? This is what she is already complaining about, and you seem to be telling me that I should be more like that.
Therapist: That is an interesting view of the potential negative effects that greater autonomy might create in your relationship. You seem to think that the sign of an emotionally independent man would be that he would be more indifferent and insensitive to his wife's opinions about him and listen to her even less.

On the contrary, a man who is really independent would be able to truly listen to his wife's opinions even more. And not because he believed they lacked any merit at all, or for the purpose of listening for their flaws and inaccuracies. Rather, he would listen to them to glean what partial truths she might have to offer him. He would be able to tolerate listening to opinions and facts that expressed alternative viewpoints and half-truths about reality, without hearing them as contradictions to his own.

(Therapist's pitch and volume dropping) He would be able to recognize that he and his wife exist in separate realities, not because they can't communicate or aren't compatible, but rather that they are inextricably separate people. He would be able to be closer and more intimate with his wife, not less, because he was willing and able to maintain himself as a separate person. Not in defiance of his wife, but because his feelings of self-worth and identity were not at issue. The inevitable surfacing of alternative viewpoints would highlight that he and his wife were two separate people and would never become one.

As the therapist's tone dropped, he emphasized the issues of aloneness and feelings of deprivation and emptiness the man was obviously feeling. In the last few minutes, Dr. Jones was noticeably overcome with feelings of sadness. The therapist offered him the following observation:

Therapist: I have another half-truth to offer. Sometimes couples fight because it is both their way of being as close as they can tolerate and a way of not being closer, although it looks like they are fighting *because* they are not closer.

Dr. Jones: I can't stand the fighting. When I come home, I want harmony. I grew up with constant fighting in my home, and with my aunts and uncles. I can't stand the constant need to be on guard. I didn't have any warmth or closeness when I was growing up, and I swore that my own family would not be that way.

Therapist: It is hard to have really intense intimacy and sex, because it requires two very separate people who can stand on their own two feet and tolerate the aloneness of being separate. The intense sex provides an intense awareness of closeness, but the closeness is highlighted by the awareness that the two people are actually separate and not fused. Only when both people accept that they will never know each other "totally" can they appreciate the full extent to which two people can become intimate and knowledgeable about what is going on inside their partner.

Dr. Jones (with humor in his voice): You mean we have to get more separate so that we can be closer?

Therapist: I couldn't agree with you more.

Dr. Jones: I am not saying that I agree with that.

Therapist: I agree with that too. By the way, any notion why the lack of certainty about something seems to mean to you that it is certain it can't be counted on?

Dr. Jones: Uhh, you mean like in my family, you could never count on anything if it didn't already happen? Something like that?

Therapist: Yeah, something like that. And you are uncertain whether or not you and Mrs. Jones will be able to resolve the sexual and marital difficulties between you and have better sex than you have ever had?

Dr. Jones: Correct. If I were certain that things couldn't get any better, then I wouldn't be here.

Therapist: Well, then look at the bright side. In the past, uncertainty meant that you were probably not going to get what you want. Now, uncertainty holds the possibility that you will. You just have to be able to tolerate the ambiguity while you both are creating new possibilities. If you need certainty at this point, the only way you can get it is by insisting on failure. If you want an opportunity at the best sex and relationship you have ever had, you better wish for ambiguity. Ironic, isn't it, you grow up not liking uncertainty, and now you have to hope for it. At least it tells you that maybe your marriage doesn't have to be like the home you grew up in.

At this point, several changes had occurred in the session:

- The alliance with Dr. Jones was much stronger and more collaborative, and he was less defiant. This was accomplished, in part, by reframing strength as flexibility.
- Mrs. Jones had observed the therapist deal with her husband in a way no one ever had. She also observed her husband to be more sensitive and needy, and less defiant and overpowering. Mrs. Jones intuitively knew this side of her husband, although when her behavior reflected this awareness it produced explosions in the relationship. Although never directly interpreted, the husband's reaction formation to insecurity, hunger for affiliation, and childhood deprivation surfaced in his pressure on her to perform sexually and avoid confrontations.
- There was greater congruence between the superficial content of the session and the underlying dynamics of the relationship. The power hierarchy had been rebalanced, without requiring the wife to be the identified patient.

- There was now greater tolerance for ambiguity, less need for immediate results, and reduced performance pressure on the wife to gratify her husband's insecurity by "functioning adequately."

There was also a reduction in the husband's potential defiance of any suggestion by the therapist to change their style of lovemaking; at the outset of the session, Dr. Jones would have taken any suggestion as an implicit indictment of his prior competency as a partner. At this point, however, the therapist laid the groundwork for future discussion of modifications in sexual technique to be couched as "the creation of ambiguity and the opportunity for new gratifications."

After several sessions devoted to "the problem of the day," Dr. and Mrs. Jones reported that their relationship was becoming increasingly stable and less volatile. Mrs. Jones suggested that perhaps the improvement was due to the therapist, which Dr. Jones took issue with. The therapist agreed with Dr. Jones, suggesting that any change that occurred was probably the result of something that the couple had done. Since it was not evident to them what had changed, the therapist made several observations:

- First, the therapist was happy that they were more comfortable with each other.
- Second, change did not apparently have to be as painful, difficult, or deliberate as they may have anticipated.
- Third, although they might not understand yet what had spoiled their relationship, and moreover, what it took to improve it, they could now use the ebb and flow in the relationship as a way of learning about it.

Dr. Jones began to complain that, "All this is well and good, but I don't see how it is helping us with our sex problem, which is what we came here for." The therapist suggested that Dr. Jones's comment was timely, because the couple seemed to be approaching the point that exchanging physical gratification might be congruent with the more positive emotional connection between them.

The therapist invited Dr. and Mrs. Jones to describe the manner in which they "made love," to which the couple responded with some discomfort and nervous laughter; they looked at each other and each invited the other to talk. Eventually Mrs. Jones described that it was invariably done late at night, in the dark. Her statement suggested that the lack of light was her husband's preference, and his discomfort appeared to corroborate this.

Further exploration revealed a typical pattern for couples with difficulty with ejaculatory control: "foreplay" consisted entirely of Dr. Jones' briefly kissing and fondling his wife, rapidly shifting to touching her genitals enough to permit hurried vaginal penetration. He refused to allow his wife to touch his penis, for fear of ejaculating prior to penetration. After approximately 10 seconds of penetration, he would ejaculate. Thereupon, Dr. Jones usually became upset and angry with himself and his wife; he alternately apologized to her and blamed her, implying that this would not happen if they tried more frequently. He would then withdraw into sullen silence. Mrs. Jones often made some attempt to console him, but lately she just withdrew to the bathroom to wash up. The couple seemed somewhat embarrassed about having revealed the "secret" details of their sexual encounters.

Therapist: What you are describing is a very typical problem. You are also describing a very common sexual style that both creates this type of problem and also results from it. Although you might think what I am about to say is odd—you have thought similarly about many of the things I have said so far. You might want to feel relieved that you have arrived at a common problem in the common way. If you are willing to change the way you use physical contact between you, at least for a brief period of time, you can probably turn this around.

Mrs. Jones: He won't make any changes, I have made several suggestions and he insists on doing it his own way.

Dr. Jones: Why should I have to change?

Therapist: I can't think of a reason why you *have* to change. It's your penis, and it's your relationship. You are not a man who will tolerate anyone telling him what to do, and that is as it should be. At least this way, you know that, success or failure, the responsibility is your own.

Dr. Jones: Why should I change? I am doing things the way that things are supposed to be done. The problem is her.

Therapist: I am surprised that you would really want to believe that. You seem to be a man who is used to being in control. When you suggest that your wife is the total problem, she also has total control of the solution. If this has been your attitude, no wonder you have been feeling frustrated and helpless to make changes.

Dr. Jones: What? What can we do?

Therapist: I can think of two possible approaches. One is to continue to believe that no change should be made in the way that the two of you have sex, and moreover, that the main problem is low frequency.

When you see it that way, it makes sense to try to solve the situation by pressuring your wife to have sex more frequently. And if that is what you really believe, then you also have the notion that no progress has been made because you have not pushed her hard enough. In that case, I have no choice but to encourage you to push her harder and to become more demanding of more frequent sex.

Dr. Jones: You want me to be more demanding?

Therapist: I don't want you to do anything. I am simply trying to help you follow your own good judgment. If I am not going to be duplicitous, and mean what I say when I encourage you to trust yourself rather than trusting me, I will *have* to offer to help you figure out more ways to pressure her and push her. On the other hand, since I have also encouraged your wife to trust herself as well, and she does not believe that simply increasing the frequency of sexual contact is the solution, I will also have to teach her how to maintain herself in the face of your pressure, so that we can have two strong, independent people. And as I hear myself say this, it doesn't sound like such a bad idea in any event. I have no difficulty supporting either of you in your own view of your difficulty.

Dr. Jones: Well, what if we were willing to change our sex?

Therapist: Well, there may be a therapeutic benefit in not changing, at least for right now.

Dr. Jones: And what is that?

Therapist: Well, if you change too quickly, you will not be able to find out what has been causing many of your difficulties. If you continue to do things exactly as you have done them, at least for a while, you will be able to get some insight into some personal difficulties that are transparent at the moment.

Mrs. Jones (picking at her husband): He won't even agree to turning the lights on.

Therapist: Well, that makes perfect sense to me. I can't think of why either one of you would want to put the lights on, although it really might help. If you put the lights on, your partner might see you!

Mrs. Jones: What is wrong with that?

Therapist: Nothing is wrong with it. It just sounds like more intimacy than either of you can tolerate.

Dr. Jones: It's more romantic in the dark.

Therapist: I am not disagreeing that you feel that way about it. In fact, it's useful to note that it seems that way to you. Because it allows us to begin to use your sexual behavior in a new way: to learn about the two of you in ways that are not available in your words.

In the dark, you can't really see who your partner is. You both want to feel that your partner is interested specifically in you, and not just in having sex with anyone. And yet you won't let her see who it is she is having sex with. You may believe that love is blind, but you are also insisting that it be that way. If it is more romantic that way for you, and I am not suggesting that it is not, then I wonder if what you are indirectly showing us is that you don't think your wife would really love you if she could really see you and know you, physically and emotionally. And I wonder if you are also suggesting that it is easier for you to expose the more romantic and tender side of you when you are somewhat hidden and so is her response to you.

Dr. Jones: I never thought about it in quite that way. I always hear about everyone else wanting to do it in the dark, too. (To wife) Well, are *you* so comfortable with the idea of the lights on?

Mrs. Jones: I always thought you wanted the lights off because you didn't like my body. I am not as young as I used to be.

Therapist: No one is as young as they used to be, but that is not the real issue. The more relevant question is whether or not you are more lovable and sexual than you used to be. Whether or not your husband has some discomfort with your body, it sounds like you *both* are somewhat ill at ease with being intimate during sex.

(Long silence, followed by Dr. and Mrs. Jones nervously laughing with each other)

Therapist: Well, maybe you two aren't the only ones with fears of really being loved and loving, and maybe you aren't the only ones with this type of sexual difficulty. On the other hand, I can't imagine that you go through other aspects of your life priding yourself on being just like everyone else, questing for being "average."

Mrs. Jones: Are you suggesting that we stop and turn the lights on? Donald will never go for that. He keeps insisting that we have to be more "spontaneous" when we have sex.

Therapist: That's interesting. Another way you folks are perfectly "normal." Lots of people keep stressing spontaneity because they are looking to feel something special and don't know what it really is. There is nothing special about spontaneous sex; it isn't as good as most people anticipate. Let me ask: What would you both prefer—having intercourse on the ride down from my office on the 5th floor of this building until you reached the guard downstairs, or taking a suite at the Regency, chilling a bottle of champagne, finding your partner in silk lounging clothes, and spending the whole morning with delicious fantasies of what comes next?

Dr. Jones: I'd settle for the ride down the elevator; the Regency never happens.

Therapist: As long as you are willing to settle for a ride down the elevator, why should it? If you are willing to settle for spontaneous sex, why should you get anything else?

Dr. Jones: Now it sounds like spontaneous sex is not the best sex.

Therapist: I think I best let you judge from your own experience, if you are willing to do some experimenting with both. But if you think sex should be a spontaneous event, perhaps you would oblige us with an erection now?

(Mutual laughter)

Therapist (changing the subject): What is your theory about why you are ejaculating so rapidly?

Dr. Jones: I get so sexually aroused, I can't hold back.

Therapist: You mean her vagina is so stimulating you can't tolerate it?

Dr. Jones: Yeah. And also the feeling of being close with her.

Therapist: Now I am confused. (long pause)

Mrs. Jones: What are you confused about?

Therapist: Well, I hear what your husband is saying, and perhaps now that I am confused, I understand why you both can't figure out what the sexual difficulty has been.

Dr. Jones: What do you mean?

Therapist: How long would you say goes by between the time you insert your penis in your wife's vagina and the time you ejaculate?

Dr. Jones: About 10 seconds.

Therapist: And how long could you last if your wife just stroked your penis with her hand, without attempting penetration?

Dr. Jones: We never do that, I want to come inside her.

Therapist: Well, if you did, what would you estimate?

Dr. Jones: Maybe a minute.

Therapist: A minute? Can your wife stimulate your penis with her hand real good?

Mrs. Jones: He used to complain that it felt too good, and he made me stop.

Dr. Jones: I didn't want to ejaculate before I was inside her.

Therapist: And how long does it take you to bring yourself to orgasm when you are by yourself?

Dr. Jones: I don't masturbate; I haven't done that since I got married.

Therapist: Well, take an estimate; would you bring yourself to orgasm in 10 seconds?

Dr. Jones: No, it was more like three or four minutes, but that was a long time ago.

Therapist: I understand. But what I am confused about is the pattern of what you are telling me. How do you make sense of the fact that you can last three to four minutes when you are stimulating yourself, one minute when your wife stimulates you manually, and 10 seconds of intercourse with almost no prior stimulation to your penis?

Dr. Jones: I can't take too much of the good stuff. Her vagina feels the best.

Therapist: Well, I have to accept what you are saying as your subjective experience of it, but it is getting more and more interesting. What if I told you that on a pure physiological level, masturbatory orgasms are more intense than coital orgasm, in part because you can pump in exactly the stimulation you like. Moreover, your wife can probably move her hand better than she can move her vagina.

Dr. Jones: I am not sure.

Therapist: Well, if I put a hundred dollar bill on the table here and told her she could have it if she could pick it up, which part of her anatomy would you tell her to use? (Lots of laughter) What is curious is that you have better ejaculatory control to the forms of stimulation that might actually provide greater intensity of tactile stimulation and less control in the one situation that offers the least. This is exactly the opposite of your theory that you ejaculate quickly during intercourse because it is "the good stuff."

Dr. Jones: I guess I don't know why.

Therapist: Well, maybe it is some other "stuff" that is making you ejaculate quickly?

Dr. Jones: Well, maybe it's best because I feel the closest to her when we have intercourse.

Therapist: How do you mean?

Dr. Jones: I start thinking about making love with her, and making her feel good; we get close, and I get so excited and aroused that I just come.

Therapist: My past experience with couples who have difficulties like yours is that they arrive at the same theory as you have, but actually are doing the exact opposite. Very quickly they stop thinking about making love and become preoccupied with the anticipation of *not* being able to make love. Rather than thinking about making your wife feel good, men in your situation usually start thinking about *not* being able to please their partners. As the time approaches for penetration, both partners begin to worry in silence.

Dr. Jones: Yes, I guess I do that. I never looked at it that way. (smiling)

Therapist: It's not a normal way to look at it. It's exactly backwards from the way that couples try to make themselves see what is happening. I see you have some appreciation of the paradox in all this. So . . . it doesn't sound like what is making you come more quickly during intercourse is the intimacy of the moment. Let me ask you another question. How do you try to delay your ejaculation during intercourse?

Dr. Jones: (embarrassed) I try to think about something else. . . . I know that I am suppose to be thinking about her, but if I do, I come.

Therapist: I am impressed at your ability to see that you are caught on the horns of a dilemma. On the other hand, you have hit upon the most common technique men use to delay their ejaculation: stimulus reduction. It doesn't work effectively in the long run and can eventually cause difficulty with erection, so I don't recommend that you continue it. But let me just point out that it cannot be that you are ejaculating more quickly during intercourse than during manual stimulation because it is more intimate, because you are actually trying to tune your partner out during intercourse. You are actually not very intimate when you are focused on failure, either. So if you are ejaculating quickly during intercourse, it isn't out of sheer amount of sexual stimulation, and it isn't because it is the most intimate form of sexual expression.

Mrs. Jones: Then what is it?

Therapist: I am not sure yet, but if you are willing to continue using your sexual behavior in the way that we have just used it, I am pretty sure that you will be able to figure out what the reason is and take care of it in the process.

At this point, the couple requested suggestions about how to go about this "new approach." Dr. Jones was more amenable to making some changes for a variety of reasons that were embedded in the interchanges of the session:

- The therapist engaged the partners in a mutual exploration of their sexual behaviors and perceptions in a problem-solving manner, piquing their curiosity and exploring the paradoxes of their sexual experiences as "normal" pitfalls.

- In addressing the paradoxes of their report, the therapist demonstrated humor and acceptance, and reorganized their experiences in new ways that permitted them to use their own thinking and resources. The therapist did not focus on technique as an end in itself, but instead used it to highlight aspects that may not have been apparent to the couple, offering meaning where there had not been even an inkling of a need for attention.

- The therapist demonstrated how the details of their sexual encounters could be used in nonblaming helpful ways, before any change in behavior was required. In so doing, the therapist demonstrated the utility in looking at the couple's spontaneous behavior, rather than focusing on getting the couple to do prescribed behaviors.

During this session there was a subtle paradigm shift, which allowed the couple to permit a tentative modification of sexual interaction without triggering the personal issues about adequacy and blame that previously precluded spontaneous change. At this point the therapist was able to recommend that the couple temporarily dispense with intercourse because it was "not useful," and take up more effective forms of stimulation. However, it is still required that the therapist avoid engaging Dr. Jones in a familiar power struggle.

Dr. Jones: Are you telling us to give up on intercourse altogether?

Therapist: I am not suggesting that you give up anything in any way, nor am I telling you to do it. I am merely remembering that you have been willing to throw away more intense forms of stimulation in lieu of less dense, less intimate, and briefer forms like intercourse. I am suggesting that you might want to do some things that will take care of some immediate problems. You both seem to be suffering from feeling emotional withdrawal from each other, including during sex.

I suggest that you do something that may allow you to be more intimate during lovemaking, and in fact, allow the two of you to put some lovemaking in the lovemaking. (To Dr. Jones) I also suggest that there is no real gift in your being willing to diminish the intensity of your experience in an effort to please your wife. It only seems to accomplish the opposite. I suggest that if you are willing to provide more intense pleasurable stimulation for each other, you may enjoy it more as well as enjoy it longer. That is your pattern, isn't it? You do last longer to more intense forms of stimulation?

Dr. Jones: I want to be able to do it like a man is supposed to do it.

Therapist: Well, then you have already succeeded. If you are willing to kill yourself, or at least your sexual pleasure, trying to measure up to your expectation of what a real man is, and you are still feeling inadequate, then I guess you have already made it to being a "real man." On the other hand, you are telling me that you like to feel that you are your *own* man. In that case, you need to do in your own bedroom what you think you ought to be doing, and not what you think someone else wants you to do, including what you think I want you to do. If you think it is in your best interest to have intercourse, I encourage you to do so. I am sure that you are a reasonable man, and you will do what you think is in your own best interest.

Dr. Jones: How will not having intercourse ever help me to have intercourse? (smiling)

Therapist: Dr. Jones, it looks like you are appreciating the paradox of living and loving. Look at the bright side: Having intercourse *hasn't* helped you to have intercourse. If it doesn't make sense, maybe there is new opportunity. Doing what makes sense hasn't gotten you anywhere. Besides, the more we talk in ways that don't make sense, the more it seems to make sense to you. That makes sense, right?

Dr. Jones (laughing): I don't know why I am laughing, I could never repeat what you just said, but I understood it and it makes sense.

Mrs. Jones (also laughing): Are you suggesting that we simply don't have intercourse?

Therapist: No, I am suggesting that if you really love each other, and you want to use your touch to express it, that you go home and do exactly that.

Dr. Jones: Like how?

Therapist: Well, if you want to feel that the sex is personal, why not do it in a personal way: Use some three-inch thick candles to light the bedroom, so you can see your partner seeing you.

Dr. Jones: Why three-inch thick candles?

Therapist: Because if you use narrow dinner taper candles, you have to think about the wax melting on the nightstand. It is a distraction from focusing on what is going on between the two of you, and there is already enough of that going on when either of you is thinking about failing. On the other hand, real intimacy is hard to tolerate, so if you need to worry about failing for a while, please feel free to do so.

Dr. Jones: I know I will still worry about coming too quick.

Therapist: That will be fine. If you are not going to be having intercourse, there is less external reason for you to do so. However, if you continue to be worried about failing, that is just fine. If it continues, it will be more of a clear reflection of things going on inside you, and we can use it very productively to find out what has always killed sex and intimacy for you. So actually, you can't lose either way. Either you will be able to focus more on the interaction between you, or you will find out what has always been in the way. Feel free to worry about ejaculating too quickly if that is what you seem to want to do, only this time also pay close attention to your thoughts and feelings at that moment, so we can use them.

Dr. Jones: Is this going to make her want to have sex more often with me?

Therapist: I can't guarantee anything. If *you* haven't been successful in making your wife have sex, and you are actually at home with her, then I know that *I* never will be able to *make* her have sex. On the other hand, I doubt that anyone *has* to make her have it. It sounds like your wife's lack of desire for the sex that the two of you have been having is a testimony to her good judgment. Sex has not been focused on pleasure, but rather, on avoiding failure. It sounds like the sex has been rather dismal for you both. *You* have been willing to settle for rather dull sex, as long as you get it frequently. If you think your wife has any good judgment, perhaps you can trust that when the sex gets worth wanting, she will want it. On the other hand, your struggles with yourself to get comfortable focusing on pleasure and tolerating the increased closeness will also be very helpful for your wife.

Dr. Jones: In what way?

Therapist: Well, I gather that she is not used to the idea that anyone would really want to be with her, just for her.

Mrs. Jones (suddenly in tears): I never think anyone could love me just for me, even my children. My parents were only interested in my not embarrassing them and doing good in school. They only paid attention when I was not measuring up to their standards. (Husband is suddenly very attentive and uncomfortable, recognizing the similarity of his own behavior with the report of her parents.)

Therapist: Well, then, if your husband could make some headway with giving up focusing on whether his penis shot off, and could look you in the eye while he touched you rather than preparing you to be penetrated, it might be very helpful in producing exactly the type of internal conflict you might need. As long as he continues to focus on ejaculation and intercourse, you might not like it, but it fits the style of interaction that makes sense to you. If he can light a candle, perhaps even get it himself, it will not make much sense to you in terms of "Why would anyone want to make me feel good for me?" But his progress would set the stage for your own. If you want to avoid the answer, keep the lights off and have intercourse.

The level of tension and defensiveness in the room was remarkably low. Dr. and Mrs. Jones sat quietly looking at each other, with neither feeling the urgency to speak.

Therapist: I guess this stuff works pretty good. You haven't even had to go home and do anything, and already you both are starting to use your sexuality in a new way, for both your development. Although you have different sexual symptoms, you have relatively similar issues underlying them. Both of you find it hard to accept that anyone could love you, want to please you or find you pleasing, if you are not trying to perform for them. (To Dr. Jones) I guess as long as you focus on whether or not you are going to fail, you don't have to deal with the nasty questions about whether the people you really love, love you if you stop performing and trying to measure up.

Dr. Jones: I guess my family wasn't much different. You could never satisfy my mother. And the only time the family talked, it was about a fight and someone being blamed. I never saw my parents exchange one shred of affection or a kind word. They just argued about whether my father made enough money and whether my mother spent too much.

Therapist: And what impact did that have on you?

Dr. Jones: I just tried to give her what she wanted and stay out of her way. But you could never succeed, because she always found something wrong.

Therapist: Well, since both of you have been really doing your part in this endeavor, I should also do mine. Now that I see where we are, I can suggest another modification that might not make sense to you. But it might make things more difficult for you because it will probably address these issues.

Mrs. Jones: Will it help us get over our problems?

Therapist: It will either help you get over them or make it clearer what they are about.

Mrs. Jones: What do you think will help?

Therapist: Do you normally touch each other at the same time?

Mrs. Jones: Unless he is just touching my vagina getting me ready for intercourse, yes we do. Why?

Therapist: Well, you might want to try taking turns touching each other, so that there is a clear giver and clear receiver at any given time. After one of you has a chance to receive, you could switch so that you each got some exposure in the opposite roles.

Mrs. Jones: Why would this help us?

Therapist: Well, it might help embody more clearly the very issues both of you seem to be struggling with: "Why would anybody really want me, to please me, just for me?" Simultaneous touch is just a convenient way to bypass this thorny question. It might also make it easier for each of you, as the receiver, to focus on the pleasurable sensations in your own body. Which will make you feel either much better or much more guilty and unworthy. And under the circumstances, I can't decide which would be better for both of you. I know it might not make sense, but I have this weird thought that having a good enough time so that you each felt unworthy might be a good thing for you.

Dr. Jones: It makes sense to me!

Therapist: I am sorry to hear that—maybe we are on the wrong track. (All three are laughing.)

Dr. Jones: I don't agree at all with what you just said.

Therapist: Once again, I agree with you completely. (Much laughter again)

Dr. and Mrs. Jones returned to report that they had set aside time to "touch" twice in the intervening week. They reported a marked reduction in estrangement and hostility between them both in and out of the bedroom. There was a notable softening in their eye contact during the session, and they had the look of a couple with a new, fragile sense of hope, which neither partner was eager to rupture.

They reported lighting candles for their physical contact, and Dr. Jones proudly reported that the encounter was actually more like "lovemaking" than when they had been having intercourse. He continued to have fears of ejaculating when receiving genital stimulation from his wife, but noticed a marked reduction in this regard. The wife was surprised and gratified by the encounter, complimenting her husband on his tenderness with her. To her surprise, she found it "nerve-wracking" to receive her husband's touch, although she seemed secure that he would not try to push her to have intercourse. The therapist congratulated Dr. and Mrs. Jones for making progress in reducing their fears of failure on the level of the immediate situation and on the longer-term issues.

The subsequent sessions consisted of increasing the amount of stimulation both partners could provide for each other and monitoring attempts on either one's part to avoid, reduce, or mitigate the resulting exchange of emotional and physical gratification. Such efforts were interpreted in a positive light of resolving the concerns about self-acceptance, bonding, and fears of loss in the context of the marital relationship and family-of-origin object relations issues. Within the subsequent three sessions (during which time they refrained from intercourse), they reported having their most prolonged erotic interactions ever, which further reduced the focus on intercourse. Dr. Jones became able to tolerate five minutes of intense manual and oral stimulation from his wife, and she, in turn, became increasingly responsive during the sessions as well as more aggressive in initiating.

The couple then asked when they should resume intercourse, clearly stating that both would follow the therapist's suggestion. The therapist pointed out that Dr. Jones was already able to tolerate far more intense stimulation during their current sexual activity than he had ever been exposed to during coitus. The therapist opined that Dr. Jones could probably last longer during intercourse than he had in the past, but questioned why they would want to return to a "less intense" form of stimulation.

The therapist suggested that if the spouses wanted to see how intercourse had destroyed their sexual relationship in the past, all they had to do was return to their prior style of focusing exclusively on it. On the other hand, if the couple wanted to use "simultaneous genital to genital" stimulation (involving vaginal containment of the penis), in addition to their currently successful activities, they could learn to master it as they had already mastered more difficult forms of stimulation. The couple was encouraged to make sure that, if they decided to add this form of stimulation, it was neither the first nor the last thing to occur.

The subsequent week Dr. and Mrs. Jones returned to report that they had decided to remain with their current activities and not add "the new activity." Thereafter, Dr. and Mrs. Jones returned to say that at the conclusion to a very pleasurable and intense session of noncoital lovemaking, they had "simultaneous genital to genital stimulation" for approximately four minutes.

Debriefing the Case Example

In this case, the therapist decided not to give detailed instructions about the nature of the touch in terms of style and location. The inherent questions of "massage" vs. more sensual caress, genital vs. nongenital touch, and the handling of orgasmic release were not discussed with the couple for several reasons:

- From an interpretive basis, the couple's own spontaneous construction and execution of the touching could be used more productively than behavioral activities directed toward rapid symptom relief. In the absence of detailed instructions, or in spite of them, the style in which spouses touch reflects their unstated and often unrecognized assumptions about themselves, their sexuality, and their relationship. In this manner, the therapist is able to use the prescription of touch both as a behavioral intervention and as a vehicle for eliciting unconscious aspects of both individuals.

- The constraints of available time and pacing precluded further discussion of technique. A productive, collaborative alliance had been established with the husband, allowing sufficient flexibility in his stance to modify his physical interaction with his wife. Further intervention might dilute the focus on alliance-building, or trigger his issues about autonomy, control, and status with the therapist. In subsequent sessions, when the therapist had demonstrated the process of debriefing and established a stronger alliance, greater clarity and refinement of bedroom suggestions could be established.

No major constructed paradoxical suggestions were delivered at end of the session to deal with "resistances." Instead, inherent paradox was used throughout the session, so that by the time behavioral suggestions were given, the push for homeostasis had already been reduced. The intent was to encourage activities that would address the sexual and marital issues undermining greater satisfaction. The therapist's focus on behavioral suggestions as a vehicle for resolution of family-of-origin issues, rather than merely as sexual technique, was paradoxical from the patients' perspective. There was a repeated shifting of frames of reference, from the individual to the interpersonal and back to the individual, reflecting the circularity of the processes involved.

The therapist's strategic stance, his affect during the banter, and the eventual alliance were also paradoxical from Dr. Jones' perspective. He was expecting that disagreement would lead to combat. Instead it led to further alliance, since the therapist did not become defensive, insecure, or invalidated by it. The therapist's stance was an embodiment of detriangulation. Dr. and Mrs. Jones were encouraged to be in control of themselves, reinforcing autonomy and boundaries; this is contrary to clinicians who use constructed paradox to link the symptoms of one individual to other people in the system (e.g., Palazzoli et al., 1978). The current approach demonstrated positive connotation by positive therapeutic *utilization*, rather than positive connotation through the attribution of benevolent intent. Therapeutic utilization of the interlocking unresolved issues of the partners *produces* the positive experience of the symptom, rather than encouraging naivete.

The sessions embodied Frankl's emphasis on the use of humor, allowing the patients to develop a more detached existential view of their problem and to shift from laughter to tears in very brief periods of time. The tone and style are somewhat similar to the unstructured hypnotic induction work of Milton Erickson (Erickson, Rossi, & Rossi, 1976). The reader may also recognize some similarity between the therapist's dialogue and the "confusion technique" made popular by Erickson. However, the purpose in the intervention described was not only to derail ("confuse") existing dysfunctional patterns, but also to encourage acceptance of uncertainty and paradox as a fact of stable relationships. Confusion became an opportunity for resolution rather than a source of anxiety.

A rereading of the dialogue will reveal that the therapist's statements were literally true and substantive, rather than merely being double-talk. Repeated statements that are paradoxical merely in the sense of being self-contradictory may diminish the alliance with patients. Patients sometimes respond to poorly implemented confusion techniques by deciding that it is the therapist who is confused. The exploration of inherent paradox avoids this pitfall through the presentation of statements which, although *seemingly* contradictory, absurd, or opposed to common sense, are compellingly true.

The use of inherent paradox is not without its limits. It is generally ineffective with very young children, mentally retarded individuals, and people who have sustained traumatic impairment of cognitive functioning. In the latter case, the problem is not one of perceptive ability; it is one of self-esteem and stigmatization. Recognition of inherent paradox tends to be confusing and disorienting; people with cognitive deficits attribute their confusion to impaired mental functioning, rather than natural reactions to insight. Inherent paradox is also not appropriate in crisis where suicide is an imminent possibility.

PARADOX IS NOT A "MAGIC" QUICK FIX

The need for certainty, lock-step reciprocity and intolerance of paradox obviates the possibility of spontaneous resolution of sexual and marital difficulties; it inhibits the emergence of complex systems. John von Neumann (1966) suggested that living organisms, organizations, and even machines have "complexity barriers." When systems of high complexity exceed the complexity barrier, new principles of organization and operation (meta-structure) emerge; this emergence allows development of ever increasingly complex adaptations. Below the complexity barrier, synthesis decays and simpler systems emerge (e.g., "stuck" families and couples). The mark of a complex relationship is the occurrence of inherent paradox.

In human relationships, the critical complexity barrier lies along the dimension of relationship differentiation. Above the critical complexity barrier lie true mutuality and tolerance for inherent paradox and chaos. Below the critical complexity barrier, low levels of differentiation require high levels of predictability in order to avoid generating anxiety; unfortunately, what becomes predictable is the *creation* of anxiety. As differentiation decreases, the probability that the relationship will generate anxiety progressivly increases; at the lower levels of differentiation, generation of chronic high levels of anxiety becomes predictable (Kerr & Bowen, 1988).

Campbell (1982) pointed out that systems shift from *predictability* to *probability* as they increase in complexity and sophistication. The ability of an individual and a relationship to function based on the *probability* of the partner's behavior, rather than on strictly enforced contingencies, is often crucial to enhancing intimacy, sexuality, and flexibility of the relationship. In his review of new studies of chaos, Gleick (1987) suggested that *flexibility and robustness* are critical aspects of all self-modulating systems. Flexibility concerns how well a system functions over a range of frequencies. Robustness refers to the ability of the system to withstand small jolts. All organisms, be they individuals, marriages, or families must respond to unpredictable and rapidly varying circumstances without becoming locked into a single mode of response.

True mutuality, based on differentiation, permits flexible adaptation to the ever shifting situations confronting a relationship; it requires flexible role definition of the partners and shifts to probabilistic functioning. Jeremy Campbell (1982) noted:

> . . . to understand complex systems, such as a large computer or a living organism, we cannot use ordinary formal logic, which deals with events that definitely will happen or definitely will not happen. A probabilistic logic is needed, one that makes statements about how likely or unlikely it is that various events will happen. The reason for this is that computers and living organisms must function reliably as a whole, even though their component parts cannot be expected to perform perfectly all the time. The parts function correctly only with a certain probability, and this probability must be built into the logic of the

system. The aim is to insure that even if single parts are very likely to malfunction, the chance of the entire system breaking down is reasonably small. (p. 105)

In considering the role of chaos in health, Gleick noted that "normal" processes we take for granted are often counter-intuitive (inherently paradoxical). He noted that a slight nudge to a linear system tends to keep that system off-track. However, a nonlinear system returns to the same starting point when given the same nudge. Moreover, a small change in one parameter of the system could push an otherwise healthy system across a bifurcation point into a qualitatively new behavior.

Resolution of inherent paradox involves a shift and escalation to a higher order of perspective (meta-perspective). It requires corresponding development of an *observing ego*, a tolerance for *ambivalence* and the simultaneous acceptance of *multiple realities*. Only by assuming a meta level can the individual tolerate ambivalence without conflict. On an intrapsychic level, this corresponds to the resolution of splitting, projection, and denial.

The requisite meta-level is not just the ability to observe one's own processes simultaneously with the reality of the partner. It is also the ability to accept that one's own immediate reality and responses are determined in some measure by one's own unresolved issues and unconscious processes, as well as by the position one occupies in the system. It is in the intolerance for inherent paradox, in terms of both content and degree, that each of us can see the side of ourselves that we refuse to see. It is for this reason that the use of paradox can be so valuable.

It may seem contradictory, if not paradoxical, that this chapter would discuss *truth* while also discussing relativity of perception. Simultaneous appreciation of constructivism, cybernetic epistemology (Keeney, 1983), and notions of a concrete external reality embodies the clinician's paradox. Eliminating this tension by restricting oneself to a single vantage point is as deadly to the development of a clinician as it is to the development of a relationship. Tolerating this tension spawns more elegant ways of understanding existence, as demonstrated in the work of Maturana and Varela (1987) and Jeremy Campbell:

> Above a certain level of complexity, there are intrinsic limits to a logical system, if that system is consistent. There will always be true statements which can neither be shown to be true nor proved to be false within the confines of the system, using the axioms and rules of the system. Moving outside the original system, enlarging it by adding new axioms or rules, might make the statement

provable, but within this wider metasystem, there would be other statements that could not be proved without further expansions, and so on without end. Perfect completeness is never reached. (Campbell, 1982, p. 109)

Referring to the work of Ilya Prigogine (1977 Nobel Prize winner in chemistry), Campbell notes:

The tendency to move forward toward a highly organized state, rather than backward toward a simpler state, is a property of open systems, those that exchange matter and energy with their surroundings. Open systems do not behave in the same way as closed systems, which for a long time were the chief objects of study in physical chemistry. Under certain circumstances, open systems reach a steady state in which they are far from equilibrium, or maximum entropy, and they maintain that state. They are highly "improbable," highly complex. What is more, such a steady state can be reached from different starting points, and in spite of disruptions along the way. (1982, p. 101)

If the couple has accepted the idea that sexuality, loving, relationships, and life itself is paradoxical in nature, there is increasingly little that the couple approaches as "contrary" to expectations. The couple develops a tolerance for ambiguity and an anticipation of uncertainty. What would previously be perceived as paradoxical, is now regarded as the "joke of life." The couple identifies such events as "what I used to think as paradoxical," in an ego-syntonic rather than ego-alien manner.

The therapist who loves the paradoxes of life can join with the couple in the final stages of treatment as simply another adult sharing an appreciation of the wonderful contradictions in the reality of our expectations and our childhood images. As the sense of "knowing wonderment" grows, the partners become their own sexual-marital therapists, increasingly able to modulate their sexual and other intimate behavior to cope with the ever shifting circumstances and day-to-day fluctuations that characterize the mutuality of a healthy relationship.

CHAPTER SIXTEEN

The Therapist's Involvement in Treatment

Being a therapist involves more than just techniques. The "person" of the therapist determines the most fundamental aspects of clinical practice: (a) patients' "characteristics," (b) "easiness" of treatment, and (c) existence of new "syndromes." The therapist's level of differentiation is a critical variable in ability to (a) detriangulate, (b) maintain clinical neutrality, and (c) tolerate the intimacy of treatment.

Given that therapists don't necessarily know any more about intimacy or have better sex or marriages than the general public, working in the sexual crucible is personally demanding. A therapist can't bring patients to higher levels of differentiation than he/she has reached. Moreover, long before ethics violations occur, violations of clinical integrity mark the point at which the therapist becomes the crack in the crucible.

Who defines the problem when a couple comes for treatment? Obviously patients do by deciding (a) they have a problem, (b) what that problem is, and (c) who has it (i.e., the identified patient). Obviously, the broader family system does, too, by defining (a) what is considered a problem, (b) molding family members' psychological functioning (i.e., introjects, ego structure, personal traits, etc.), and (c) differentially stressing particular individuals by virtue of their position in the system and increasing/decreasing the likelihood they will become symptomatic.

"Honoring the system" and believing that "the patient (or system) defines the problem" offers some therapists a satisfying egalitarian and "nonjudgmental" stance. But how do patients know that a psychotherapist is the right person to consult? Obviously, the problem was previously defined within the province of what therapists do. Who did that? Not a patient; it was a *therapist*.

As a subsystem of society, therapists define mental health "problems"; they do that at the time that they decide they can "treat" something. In announcing the availability of relief, therapists define the existence of disturbance; in announcing the potential for growth, therapists indict restricted development. Whoever decided that having patients "define the problem" was a good idea? A therapist. Who decided that who defines the problem could be a pitfall in treatment? Not a patient.

Therapists who "see" that a child brought for treatment is "really" the symptom-bearer of unaddressed marital problems violate the "patients define the problem" myth. The entire literature on psychotherapy, even systemic family therapy, demonstrates that therapists indeed define problems differently than do patients. Nor could it be otherwise: If the therapist's paradigm is identical to the patient's, nothing new can be offered in "joining the system." Long before the initial interview, the therapist and his/her colleagues participate in defining the problem.

So why do therapists like to believe that "patients define the problem"? No doubt it stems, in part, from attempts to avoid imposing biases on patients, and awareness of the enormity of therapists' responsibilities. Even if it were possible, however, it probably isn't good for patients alone to define the problem in treatment; it places responsibility on those with the least training to accurately diagnose the nature and extent of their difficulties. Not that therapists are omniscient, or that patients benefit from being relegated to a diagnostic classification or reduced to a disease; it's just that one can go too far in the other direction as well. Reliance on patients' self-definition of problems deifies social norms and discounts any value to modern science or the dialectic process between patients and therapist.

Patients *want* therapists' assistance in defining their problems. Aside from attempts to transfer personal responsibility onto the therapist, people legitimately seek consultation and evaluation. The quest to be "normal" in one's sex life and marriage is a more overriding concern than in most other areas of people's lives. Sometimes spouses can't agree about their sexual relationship, or they labor with a personal concern; others just want to know if marriages are typically as bad as theirs is. In these and many other cases, patients turn to health-care professionals to render an opinion about what is "normal."

In matters of law (and insurance reimbursement) the therapist defines the problem. Courts hold that patients are entitled to assume that a therapist's "expert" ability to diagnose and treat "disorders" will be utilized in the execution of his/her functions. Child-abuse reporting requirements are predicated on the assumption that patients cannot be relied upon to define the problem. Few therapists offer "patients define the problem" defenses in malpractice suits!

Should clinicians *not* tell men that deliberate mental distraction to delay ejaculation can lead to erectile dysfunction in later life? What about educating sexually inactive older couples that masturbation can reduce chronic prostatitis in men or that insertion of some penile shaped object can maintain vaginal elasticity in menopausal women? Some sexual symptoms are early indicators of underlying physiological difficulties; loss of erection, for example, may indicate incipient diabetes or a pituitary tumor. Working solely within self-defined problems incurs significant medical risks for patients and liability for the therapist.

The fact that patients define the initial point of engagement in treatment has nothing to do with a "value-free" stance on the therapist's part. While the thought that a therapist might "lay his/her values" on patients outrages some colleagues, others suggest that it can't be any other way.

Baker (1987) noted that conventional wisdom encourages clinicians to avoid values in the sexual arena and stick to "facts" and statistics. However, he suggested that such a posture ignores the "normative saturation" of clinical practice: Therapists and scientists cannot function without embracing norms which are themselves culturally bound. For example, therapists who see themselves as more "enlightened" than a couple arguing over whether to have a clitoridectomy[1] performed on their daughter don't recognize that (a) therapists' reactions are as culturally-determined as are patients', and that (b) "enlightened" clinicians of previous generations have, in good faith, prescribed surgery, acid burns, and thermoelectrocautery as "treatment" for masturbation. Suggesting that modern sexual and marital therapy has finally arrived at *real* enlightenment ignores our point of departure in Chapter One.

Baker counsels that clinicians can't avoid values because a truly scientific clinician could not be helpful; who should be treated and when to give information are not scientific questions, answerable solely with "facts." "Clinical judgment" (predicated on "prevailing scientific knowledge") is inherently value-laden, requiring constant scrutiny of the most cherished clinical truths and of the therapist himself/herself. State-of-the-art knowledge also reflects state-of-the-art ignorance.

Therapists' involvement in defining the problem goes beyond clinical judgment and personal biases. Treatment setting, institutional policies, supervisors, and financial pressures define which individuals have what "problems." High

---

[1]Genital mutilation (particularly of women) remains a not-uncommon practice in many parts of the world; it is often sought by well-meaning parents who want the best for their children, and performed by physicians who want the same for their patients. In many cases, it is done to presumably *enhance* future marital satisfaction.

patient volume, lack of privacy, and a "treat 'em and street 'em" atmosphere pervading some clinical settings determine whether or not a sexual or marital problem "exists" at all.

A patient complaining of erectile dysfunction and his wife were initially seen by a urology resident. The wife accompanied her husband to the doctor's office out of concern and desire to improve the situation. The resident interviewed the couple, ascertained no organic causes for the dysfunction, and left the room to report to his mentor. The supervising physician then saw the couple without the resident. The supervisor asked the wife to step outside while he talked to the husband alone. During this process, the supervisor learned that the man had no erectile difficulty in a secret affair, which provided very satisfying sex. The supervisor left the room, greeting the resident with an air of superiority. The supervisor announced, "He has no problem, there is nothing wrong there; he just doesn't like making love with his wife!"

While the urologist's statement was apparently true with regard to the absence of organic etiology, the question of whether or not there was a "problem" was clearly a matter of perspective. Although the urologist's biases are obvious in retrospect (one wonders what sex with his own wife was like), many mental health professionals fail to recognize similar problems in their own clinical practices.

Therapists participate in (a) defining the problem, (b) identifying the patient, and (c) delineating the patient's "characteristics." A recent live demonstration by a senior clinician drove this awareness home. The presenting problems were marital conflict over disparate sexual desire, the wife's inhibited sexual desire, and her pain during intercourse. Immediately prior to the interview, the therapist was told that the wife had been sexually abused repeatedly by her father during childhood; subsequently, the entire session was devoted to exploration of the details of these events. The therapist never elicited or examined the dynamic interaction between the spouses at home or within the session.

The therapist appeared fearful of confronting the rather ominous demeanor of the husband and of cracking their problem-maintaining veneer. In spite of the wife's reported dyspareunia and absence of vaginal lubrication during 70% of coital couplings, the therapist never questioned how the husband could not know that his wife was having pain during intercourse or why he continued if he did. The husband's emotional primitiveness and lack of empathy or emotional contact with his wife during sex were never addressed. The husband's statement that he "just liked sex" was never met with the question that it begged for: "What is it that you like about sex with your wife?"

The therapist neither challenged the husband's denial of masturbation nor questioned how he handled his own sexual urges, since his wife often refused sex. Given the wife's presenting complaints, this was not insignificant information. The therapist never addressed how the husband pressured the wife for sex or how his refusal to masturbate contributed to this. (A member of the audience later went so far as to suggest that the husband's reported lack of masturbation might reflect his own childhood sexual abuse!) The implications of the husband's recent pursuance of divorce proceedings were similarly lost in the exploration of the wife's prior sexual abuse by her father.

During the subsequent debriefing with the audience, the therapist commented offhandedly that he "might want to know a little more" about why the husband did not intervene when his brother repeatedly fondled the wife. Similarly, it was noted as "a little odd" that the couple's children knew all about the wife's sexual inhibition and teased her about depriving the husband. The possibility that this reflected the absence of appropriate emotional or sexual boundaries was not explored.

In commenting that the "warmth and caring" between the couple during the interview were palpable, the therapist was more accurate then he realized: The caring attitudes were a function of *the interview* situation and style, but not reflective of the problematic dynamics between the spouses. The interview as conducted permitted the husband to "support" his wife while she talked about her childhood abuse, which actually reinforced the husband's claim that her sexual disinterest was a function of prior abuse rather than something involving him. The interview allowed the wife to continue the facade that she would like to have sex with her husband if only she could and that she really felt badly about depriving him.

The complexities of clinical observation and intervention have been addressed by many authors. Harry Stack Sullivan's (1953) concept of the participant-observer underscores that the clinician determines, as well as observes, patients' "characteristics." Constructivism[2] doesn't mean "one can never know anything about patients"; it means instead that the clinician participates in bringing reality into view by his or her experience of it. Reality doesn't exist until one thinks it, recognizes it or, in the language of Maturana, "brings it forward." It *is* possible to say that another clinician missed some aspect of the

---

[2]Constructivism, a topic long debated within marriage and family therapy, involves the notion that there is "no direct correspondence between an event occurring "outside" of us and our inner experience of it. . . . the world as each one of us knows it is entirely constructed by ourselves (Keeney, 1983, p. 3)." Keeney (1983) proposes the same outlook as advanced above: "I hold that this position of "naive solipsism" is as limited as the view that there is a real world out there which our senses internally model. A more encompassing view is to see each perspective—naive solipsism and naive realism—as only partial glimpses of the whole picture (p. 3)." The fact that constructivism is rarely discussed in the sex therapy literature highlights its behavioral background and demonstrates the isolation of the sexual and marital therapy disciplines.

couple being interviewed. The first clinician elicits one view of a couple: how they act under the circumstances of his or her interventions. A second clinician brings forth additional aspects of the case. The mistake of constructivism occurs when one believes that any particular view is the *only* view, denying the simultaneous existence of multiple realities.

Probably every therapist has experienced a sense of personal threat from a patient at one time or another, or had some foreboding about confronting a crucial but anxiety-laden topic. Sometimes the therapist's lack of differentiation determines the course of inquiry; "clinical observation" becomes a convenient post-hoc rationalization for the therapist's decisions. Such a recognition requires constant scrutiny of one's personal and professional limitations.

We now shift attention to ways in which therapists participate in defining (a) an "easy" case, and (b) the "nature" of a clinical problem. Subsequently we will consider other aspects of the therapist's persona that affect treatment: (a) level of differentiation, (b) capacity for intimacy, and (c) clinical and personal integrity.

WHAT IS AN "EASY CASE"?

The foregoing vignettes illustrate that the degree of difficulty in treating a particular couple is not simply a function of the relationship's complexity or homeostatic resilience. "Easy cases" are also a function of the therapist, the therapist's approach, and the "state of the art." *"Easiness" refers to the absence of the therapist feeling threatened or stymied by patients' presentation (as evoked through interaction with the therapist).*

"Easiness" is subjectively defined relative to the breadth and depth of patients' and therapists' treatment goals, and what therapists expect will occur in the process of achieving them. When treatment focuses just on improving genital function, a case may look relatively "simple" because the scope of inquiry is sufficiently narrow (and termination occurs quick enough) to avoid opening up unresolved underlying issues.

Sexual desire and intimacy difficulties are often more complex than genital dysfunctions; as pointed out in Chapter Ten, however, this doesn't necessarily make them difficult to treat. Varying reports of difficulty reflect differences in therapists' approaches and skills, as well as the differences between various problems that superficially appear the same. A broad understanding of psychopathology and normal human development is *highly desirable* among clinicians who treat sexual dysfunctions symptomatically; it is *essential* for a clinician addressing the myriad problems that present as "intimacy difficulties." For example, encouraging the partner to be "closer" to a borderline patient raging at the spouse's emotional distance is generally a recipe for disaster. The borderline patient's rage expresses both sides of an ambivalent split-object attachment with the partner, demanding closeness in a manner that decreases the likelihood that it will occur. Effective sexual-marital treatment requires a skilled diagnostician who can recognize this and adjust the nature and pacing of interventions accordingly.

The therapist's involvement in treatment becomes obvious as soon as one questions the assumption that a case that "moves forward" rapidly is necessarily an easy case. Therapists who "educate" a great deal early in treatment find that superficially compliant patients look "easy" at the outset; overt conflict or patients' challenges to professional competency give such therapists more difficulty than scheduling problems or passive-aggressive styles. On the other hand, some therapists handle overt challenges at the outset of treatment better than those that manifest over time as diffuse excuses and disclaimers. Therapists who see the outset of treatment as a negotiation for expected patterns of participation experience initial struggles with silent or "anxious" patients as a *necessary* process that makes the later stages of treatment easier.

Ease of treatment involves congruence between the individuals, the systemic characteristics of the marriage and the extended family system, and the characteristics of the therapist. Beyond the obvious implications of "transference and/or countertransference" issues, congruence also involves the therapist's clinical paradigm. All else being equal, couples with complex interlocking issues will appear "easy" if the content of individual and dyadic issues and the dynamics of their subsystems lie parallel to the structure and style of the therapy. If the homeostatic patterns run counter to the style of treatment, then "resistance" becomes manifest and the therapist's valuation of the degree of difficulty increases.

Lastly, the therapist participates in the construction of "easy" or "difficult" cases through his/her conceptual and clinical sophistication. Sexual and marital problems can be readily conceptualized as a multiplicity of unidimensional levels (Figure 16.1). Some therapists recognize more sophisticated dynamic patterns within the couple and the treatment situation; they conceptualize on multiple, overlapping dimensions (Figure 16.2). Others develop even more sophisticated dynamic models, tracking particular issues *across* dimensions (Figure 16.3); finally, others understand and anticipate the simultaneous multidimensional impact of clinical interventions (Figure 16.4).

As the therapist's conceptualization of treatment becomes increasingly complex, and interventions and paradigms are developed to address that com-

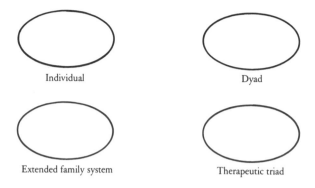

Figure 16.1 Multiple unidimensional model

plexity, the couple is *less likely* to be experienced as "difficult" to treat. This was the point of previous emphasis on isomorphic, synergistic, multidimensional, cross-modality intervention. Such interventions require a therapist who is able to function within a variety of conceptual approaches and clinical modalities, without becoming a believer in the inherent superiority of any particular one—that is to say, a therapist who can stand independent of the tools of his or her craft. Such a therapist can maintain a discerning observing ego with regard to patients, the clinical approach, and his or her own participation. The degree to which this is accomplished as a practical matter is a function of the therapist's level of differentiation.

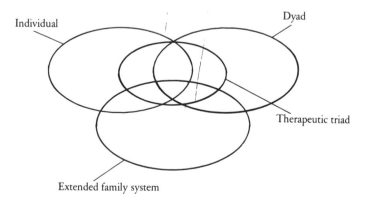

Figure 16.2 Multiple overlapping model

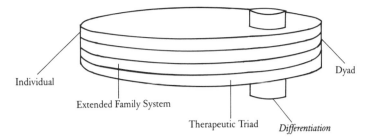

Figure 16.3 Three dimensional model

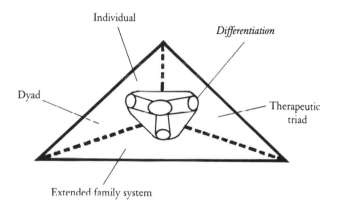

Figure 16.4 Systemic model

WHAT IS THE "NATURE" OF A CLINICAL PROBLEM?

Therapists' participation in treatment surfaces in even less obvious ways: the creation/"discovery" of new clinical phenomena. Something doesn't exist as something to treat until a therapist decides it is a syndrome in its own right and amenable to clinical intervention. For one convenient example, notice how the "nature" of low sexual desire has changed in the last 12 years (Chapter Nine); for another, consider the progression of modern "intimacy disorders":

> In the 1970s, a woman's problem was her "fear of success." No, said Colette Dowling[3] in 1981, women have a "Cinderella Complex"—a hidden fear of

---

[3]Dowling, C. (1981).

independence. No, said Robin Norwood[4] in 1985, women's problem is that they "love too much." Not really, said Melody Beattie[5] in 1987; women love too much because they are "codependent"—"addicted" to addicts and bad relationships. (Tavris, 1989, p. 220)

Knowledge of the "nature and course" of various sexual and marital difficulties is inherently tied to the methodologies through which they are viewed (e.g., process research, outcome studies); it makes no difference whether one considers the evolution of treatment for syphilis, chronic masturbation, or AIDS. When we "create" new diagnostic entities, prevailing treatments and their efficacy become critical determinants of what we "know" to be the syndrome's "course and progression." That is, of course, until another treatment comes along to which the syndrome responds quicker/better and looks different in the process. Until then, we don't know if treatment is as effective as possible, or perhaps interferes with some aspect of resolution; this process is called progress.

The emergence of "codependency" and "love/sex addiction" offers a particularly cogent example of the ways in which therapists define problems: The result has been the addition of an entire section in commercial bookstores in the last five years. Therapists and writers have literally created a socio-psycho-economic phenomenon through the publication of "popular" books and reciprocal endorsements, reinforced by auspicious contemporary forces affecting the mental health field in particular and society in general. The movement's emphasis on group approaches and "self-help" reduces per-unit costs, dovetailing with current pressures from insurance companies, HMOs, and other third-party payers. At the same time, it fuels an industry of clinicians by the collective financial lucrativeness such treatment offers.

Once a new treatment is popularized and enters the public's perception of contemporary psychotherapy, systemic impacts from the economic and social sectors drive it forward, adding the appearance of "proof" of broader professional acceptance than is the case. The fact that addictionology/codependency gained rapid acceptance is no assurance of accuracy or effectiveness.

The fact that an opinion has been widely held is no evidence that it is not utterly absurd; indeed in view of the silliness of the majority of mankind, a widespread belief is more often likely to be foolish than sensible. (Bertrand Russell, 1872–1970, in Seldes, 1985)

---

[4]Norwood, R. (1985).
[5]Beattie, M. (1987, 1989).

The Addiction Model's Flaws Make it Popular

Addictionology isn't a treatment for lack of differentiation; it is the embodiment of it. Fusion and borrowed functioning permeate the conceptual model (e.g., *victimization*) and infuse the clinical approach. Consumers are encouraged to err on the side of deciding that they *are* "addicts," at which time all behaviors become suspect signs of love/sex addiction until proven otherwise.[6] Carnes (1983) offers an example of diagnosis *based on the spouse's reaction*, exploiting the characteristics of poorly differentiated couples: A warning sign of sexual addiction, he cautions, "is when a spouse or significant other starts to feel victimized by the other's sexuality (p. 29)." The dangers of this approach were illustrated in the case example in Chapter Six.

Although addictionology speaks to people's experience, it does so in ways that interfere with amelioration. Katz and Liu (1991) point out in *The Codependency Conspiracy*, "When you're lost and don't know where to turn, the loudest, most compassionate voice you hear is probably the one you'll follow. . . . Unfortunately, the most alluring voice is not always the most helpful . . . (p. xii)."

Michael J. Bader's (1988) article, Looking for Addictions in All the Wrong Places, offers an insightful analysis, from which this section draws heavily; he writes:

> In truth, the addiction model, when applied to psychological and interpersonal problems and traits, contains unexamined assumptions and meanings that block attempts to understand these problems from both social and psychological perspectives. At the same time that the model strikes a chord in people, it renders attempts at deeper self-knowledge or critical analysis impossible. (p. 13)

Being self-destructively attached to an unsatisfying partner is apparently a common problem in our culture. "Rather than engaging in further analysis," Bader writes, "the reader has a kind of 'aha!' experience that involves locating himself or herself within this formal addiction framework (p. 14)." In identifying with the descriptions and analogies, however, people unwittingly buy the whole treatment philosophy and underlying *disease* model assumptions with-

---

[6]Patrick Carnes writes:

Level One behaviors [masturbation, discrepant desire in heterosexual relationships, centerfolds, pornography, and strip shows, prostitution, homosexuality] have in common general cultural acceptance. . . . Even the healthiest forms of human sexual behavior can turn into self-defeating behaviors—or worse—the victimization of others. (Carnes, 1983, p. 28)

out understanding or even recognizing them. Within the codependence/addictionology paradigm, for example, all addictions are assumed progressive and irreversible unless treated according to their prescribed methods. Ricketson (1989) spells out the message that frightens people into treatment and keeps them there: "Untreated codependency invariably leads to stress-related complications, physical illness, depression and death (p. 13)." In spite of Carnes' (1983) warnings of incipient pedophilia, voyeurism, and rape, the bread and butter of sexual addiction treatment remain people who have multiple sexual contacts with consenting adults.

To really see therapists' impact in defining problems and their treatment, one must recognize that what accounts in large part for addictionology's acceptance is its weaknesses rather than its strengths. Bader details a significant flaw *that accounts for the model's popularity*, its treatment approach, and the "nature" of the "disease": Addictionology is literally a half truth—telling the side of the story that people want hear, leaving part untold. The fact that some people experience some relief doesn't "prove" its conceptual accuracy or treatment efficacy. Kerr and Bowen (1988) repeatedly make the point that families and groups at the lowest levels of differentiation are able to relieve anxiety; it occurs, however, at the expense of individual functioning and development.

The addictionology/codependency/"adult child" literature flattens out childhood experience, blocking a clear view of one's parent as someone who had at least *some* volition intact. *The failure to exercise that iota of choice or willpower contains the awareness that at some level parents' behavior was deliberate and intentional.* Being told that parents were helpless makes the "wounded child" feel better, *but it is a lie.* Blaming a "disease" can be as pathological as falsely blaming oneself for what is really a medical illness.

Bader offers an alternative explanation to addictionology, pointing out the reason for the latter's phenomenal popularity: Some people feel responsible for disabled parents and repeat this pattern as adults *not* because of learned behavior or attempts to re-work past experience, but *because* of attempts to bypass traumatic truths about parents and oneself (including the realization that parents might have hated you regardless of their "addiction").

Appearances to the contrary, addictionology circumvents confronting oneself and one's parent. The "face to face" pseudo-confrontation that *does* occur is particularly insidious because it masks the absence of the real thing: confronting the parent one *knows* internally. Addictionology talks about intimacy, but doesn't encourage *looking* inside one's parent or oneself (Chapter Fourteen).

The "addict" avoids him/herself by not examining the dynamics underlying "loving too much" since the "disease" requires no further explanation. Over-compensatory solicitousness or self-abnegation is not examined for what it often is: denial of hatred for parents (and others), a desire to turn the tables on parents, revenge for feeling helpless, and denial of the wish to be free of them, profound disappointment and contempt for their weaknesses, devaluing them so as not to be further disappointed, the wish that they would die, and discomfort with adult eroticism.

Implications for Therapy

Patients unconsciously *know* what they feel, suggests Bader, even though they don't always know why they feel it. Sex/love "addictions" can't be corrected simply by cognitive rehearsal, injunctions to take care of oneself, or group permission and encouragement to be autonomous. The need for perpetual treatment results because "addicts" unconsciously *know* that childhood injuries and deprivations were often intended by parents who *really* used or abused them, however much they might deny it. This intuitive understanding makes "addicts" secretly resist the same theory they consciously embrace because it renders parents and self completely innocent. Addictionology plays the "addict's" game: proselytizing the dangers of "being in denial" while it is, itself, "in denial."

Addictionology emphasizes "addict's" self-flagellation, not recognizing that the real issue is *masochism*. Masochism has a strong relational component that revolves around attachment and defends against abandonment and existential loneliness. Self-defeating behaviors are resilient because they represent, in part, a defense against truly *seeing* the parent.

> The fact that relationship "addicts" feel that they are in the grips of a compulsion is often taken at face value by the addiction theorists and not recognized as disguised desire and attachment. (Bader, 1988, p. 97)

Collusion in the Treatment Alliance

Calling oneself an "addict" offers an identity to people with little solid-self; the label also offers instant acceptance, group membership, and a "hold-harmless" clause built into the program. Adoption of the "new speak" of addiction offers other "gains":

> As this new language of addictions becomes part of our daily discourse, including the discourse of psychotherapy, labels and catch phrases substitute for real understanding and analysis. A patient may say, "That's my ACA stuff," and invite the therapist to collude under the reassuring pretense that this phrase

explains something important, when in actuality it reflects the patient's desire *not* to analyze what s/he is really feeling. Once again, short-term relief is purchased at the cost of long-term cure and insight. (Bader, 1988, p. 98)

Sexual addiction theory and treatment involve a breach of integrity,[7] splitting off parts of the self and inviting "addicts" to have magical expectations of therapy. The result creates collusion between patients and therapists to avoid honest self-confrontation, a particularly troubling development in an approach prescribing itself for people whose commonality is a lack of personal integrity. Sex addiction/codependency treatments avoid a basic sense of *integrity* (i.e., solid-self, the basic ingredient in level-2 self-validated intimacy).

"Adult Children"

"Healing the wounded child" enshrines childhood narcissism, vulnerability, and dependency as the paradigm of intimacy and eroticism (i.e., level-1 intimacy); the codependence movement reduces grown men and women to "adult children." Although the term "adult child" originally meant "we are children emotionally," it now means being the child of a critical parent. Unfortunately, the original meaning is more applicable and important.

The codependency movement's answer to the emotional immaturity of adult children is to encourage more child-ness: Patients are told (a) to put their own well-being, desires, and needs first in relationships, (b) recognize their intrinsic worth, (c) learn to have fun, and (d) get in touch with the child within (Katz & Liu, 1991). Does the instant popularity of such programs reflect indulgence of the regressive yearnings of patients and therapists alike?

> Embracing, loving, nurturing, talking to, even taking the Inner Child for walks and car rides is a key component of the recovery program recommended by codependence leaders such as Bradshaw and Robert Subby, who encourages his fellow adult children to "sit yourself down somewhere in front of a mirror and imagine that the reflection you see is your own inner child. Look straight into his or her eyes and say: 'Thank you for not giving up.'" (Katz & Liu, 1991, p. 22)

---

[7]This statement does not reflect a moral judgment about compulsive sexual behavior; the SLAA (1986) handbook talks about sex and love addicts having violated, most of all, their own self-respect (p. vii). The topic of integrity of the therapist and the therapeutic process is discussed later in this chapter. A more complete discussion of addictionology theory and treatment is presented in *Addiction to Addictions* (Schnarch, 1991), a monograph available from the author. 101 W. Robert E. Lee Blvd., Suite 209, New Orleans, LA 70124.

A number of my patients have previously had long-term treatment for multiple "addictions" (e.g., sexual, drug, alcohol, codependence, gambling, smoking); the numbers are growing. First, one patient comes in and makes *dramatic* progress; then his/her "sponsor" comes in for a look. Gradually the word goes out through the incestuous addictionology network: You can only go so far in the addiction/codependency paradigm—then you "get stuck" or relapse.

We talk about integrity from time to time, but it isn't like being in church; it is more like a gut-check before parachuting from an airplane. Integrity means almost nothing to children (although getting caught does). We talk about taking care of Big Carl/Carla instead of Little Carl/Carla—taking care of infantile needs and tasks can get one only so far.

Two things commonly occur in treating self-defined "addicts": (a) They scare themselves with their progress, and (b) they scare themselves with the growing intensity of their sex and intimacy. Patients say that navigating the sexual crucible is often the toughest thing they have ever done in their lives; *no one* in the room believes in them when they start, and only one person believes that it can be done (i.e., the therapist). Watching such people become a Mr. and Mrs. Kennedy (Chapter Fourteen) is one of the greatest joys of this work.

Toxic Parent Theory

The reason for the sexual crucible's impact is reflected in how the topic of "toxic parents" is approached. The premise that adults are the way they are because of parental toxicity (pathology) ignores the many children of highly "toxic" parents who function quite well; the problem cannot simply be toxicity. "Toxic" parents tend to be extremely narcissistic people who inflict themselves upon children in ways that stunt the child's growth; they raise narcissistic undifferentiated children who are often toxic themselves, acting out their narcissism by blaming their toxicity on their parents and perpetuating it in yet another generation.[8]

The real problem, however, is not toxicity but rather the absence of a relevant emotional antibody (i.e., differentiation). The quest for a toxin-free emotional environment overlooks the lesson of the "boy in the bubble": Those who lack effective autoimmune systems must exist within a very limited and highly regulated artificial environment. It is no coincidence that people who

---

[8]This extreme narcissism has two components: (a) the "common" narcissism of childhood which the "adult child" never learned to modulate, and (b) the defensive over-compensatory self-indulgence the child takes on to compensate for an inept parent.

complain about emotional toxicity also complain about feeling controlled and restricted.

Is there any good derived from addictionology/codependence/wounded child/toxic parent approaches? One could argue that many people have become aware of self-destructive relationships and personal suffering; some feel understood and helped by such approaches. This point has some merit as long as one steers clear of an "opiate for the masses" argument; these approaches *stop* people from recognizing that the approach itself is self-limiting in the most subtle and pernicious ways. This is not, moreover, a cost-free treatment; the considerable amounts of money it consumes fuels the professional community's interest.

Other hidden costs are profound, even if not instantly obvious. Poorly differentiated therapists are swept up in the social movement, convinced that these difficulties require a "specialist"; patients are steered to "adult child" and "addiction" "experts," and therapists seek "specialty training." This is doubly unfortunate, because it gives the appearance of widespread clinical endorsement of this approach. Not succumbing to professional pressures and anxieties of the latest "pop" therapy is a demonstration of solid self—which brings us to the next step in examining the role of the clinician in sexual-marital therapy: *the therapist's level of differentiation.*

THE THERAPIST'S LEVEL OF DIFFERENTIATION

It is often assumed that therapists' "strategies" and behaviors are determined by higher cognitive processes and modulated emotions. As noted above, however, therapists (like patients) respond reflexively when anxiety and conformity pressure is high enough—an event more common in treatment than is often recognized.

Consideration of the therapist's personal development as a fundamental determinant of an effective working alliance, and as a primary treatment resource, lies outside the perspective of the professional sex therapy literature. Many of the concepts that underlie the original rationale for co-therapists in sex therapy (*e.g., patient advocacy, modeling, support, identification*) encouraged fusion and borrowed functioning rather than differentiation between patients and therapists (and between co-therapists); many co-therapy teams spent more time working on *their* relationship than on the patients'. A highly differentiated therapist, in contrast, is a fundamental requirement of the sexual crucible approach; modeling or identification is a secondary effect rather than a primary intervention. The major impact of the therapist's degree of differentiation occurs through anxiety modulation and redirection from the treatment relationship back into the dyad, and moreover, in the shift from interpersonal turmoil to inner conflict and resolution.

Case Example: The Role of Therapist Differentiation in Constructing the Sexual Crucible

The following example illustrates how the therapist's level of differentiation plays a role in the course of treatment; it illustrates, moreover, how a high level of differentiation is a basic requisite in the sexual crucible approach. The situation involves a consultation requested by a colleague for a difficult case involving a poorly differentiated middle-aged couple with a long history of marital discord.

Sharon constantly berated her husband's competency as a husband, lover, and father; Harry responded by passive-aggressively withholding from Sharon, to the detriment of his performance on the job and at home. In the course of treatment, the oscillations of accusations and counter-charges amplified to the point at which Sharon demanded that Harry leave the house. Eventually, Harry acceded to Sharon's demands, moving to an apartment in an apparent admission of inadequacy and personal failure.

Initially Sharon felt triumphant while Harry appeared vanquished, inadequate, and depressed. Treatment shifted from conjoint meetings to individual sessions with Harry, temporarily validating Sharon's claim that their marital difficulty stemmed from his deficiencies. After some very anxious weeks, Harry actually began to function better; he decorated his apartment, and became less depressed and less dependent on his wife. He began to feel better about himself and started thinking about relationships with other women, including sexual affairs.

At this point Sharon began to call the therapist, demanding that Harry's sessions focus on his "inability to make a commitment." As Harry's functioning improved, Sharon's security and "autonomy" deteriorated. Sharon reported finding the "insecurity and indecision" intolerable and precipitously began to demand "a commitment to the relationship" and agreement on monogamy.

Paradoxically, this increased Harry's desire for an affair. Sharon unwittingly stroked his ego with her own insecurity; moreover, Harry enjoyed the sweet revenge of his wife's anxiety about his possible liaisons. Although Sharon wasn't entirely sure she wanted him to return home, she was frustrated that some other woman might enjoy him. Now that he had lost 20 pounds, Harry felt stronger and more attractive. He was tantalized by the possible opportunity for the sexual experimentation which his marriage had "deprived" him. Furthermore, Sharon's push for commitment refueled Harry's longstanding fears of being entrapped and controlled.

Sharon's demands and threats escalated, including evening phone calls to pressure the therapist to induce Harry to "commit to the relationship." She reported anxiety attacks, sleep disturbances, and other somatic symptoms. Sharon threatened to terminate treatment and file for legal separation if she did not obtain a commitment to monogamy.

The therapist was faced with a choice in treatment paradigm and strategy. The therapist could do the "logical" thing and focus the couple on "negotiating" a "treatment contract" involving a "temporary no-affairs clause" and a commitment to "work on the relationship to help them resolve their differences." While this would reinforce the enmeshment that underlay the couple's difficulty, it would also temporarily reduce the therapist's anxiety. The therapist was tempted to rationalize this approach in the name of "stabilizing the situation" and because of fears that Sharon "could not handle the stress." However, the therapist had absolutely no worry of Sharon committing suicide or needing to be hospitalized. The therapist was feeling tremendously pressured and inadequate in the face of Sharon's demands and symptomatology; in effect, the therapist was being triangulated into the same position that Harry had occupied in the system.

On the other hand, use of the sexual crucible paradigm (which would focus on differentiation in the marital dyad) would require a highly differentiated therapist. The treatment format would be conjoint sessions. The interventions would involve making two simultaneous balanced alliances, one with each individual, rather than one with "the couple." The first would be with Sharon, in Harry's presence.

Attempting to negotiate a "no-affairs" agreement would have implicitly validated both spouses' belief that such an agreement was in Sharon's best interest; the therapist, instead, could take the position that a "no-affairs" contract perpetuated the same personal vulnerabilities that had brought Sharon to this point. Her longstanding insecurity about physical and emotional attractiveness had led her to take Harry's lack of sexual desire as a negative reflection on herself; now she was about to do the same thing with his possible desire for someone else.

A "no-affairs" agreement to soothe her immediate insecurities would deprive her of an opportunity to get control of her feelings of inadequacy once and for all. In the event of reconciliation, this would (a) leave her dependent on Harry for sexual validation, (b) make it safe for Harry to withhold the sex she demanded, and (c) perpetuate her attacks on Harry's sexual adequacy when he didn't make sexual overtures, further diminishing the likelihood of the marriage surviving. In the event of divorce, dependence on her dates for feeling desirable and adequate would be a bruising experience; either way, a no-affairs contract wasn't in her best interest.

Did Sharon believe that there wouldn't be other attractive women around or that Harry wouldn't be attracted to them if they had a "good relationship"? A no-affairs "agreement" would (a) make her *more* insecure and suspicious about Harry's behavior, (b) allow him to control her into controlling him, (c) keep her the scapegoat to Harry's displaced ambivalence about sexual experimentation, and (d) trigger Harry's fears of engulfment, leading him to act in ways that would make her even more insecure. Sharon herself complained that Harry was preoccupied with fears of being controlled.

The therapist could offer to help Sharon learn to calm her insecurities about desirability, femininity, and abandonment, and detach her self-worth from Harry's sexual behavior. The therapist might joke that Sharon should decide whether she wanted assistance in extracting a "commitment" from Harry or in becoming determined to "run like hell" if he offered one! This latter comment might add a much needed shift in tone to the therapy, introducing a note of levity and perspective on the "high drama" unfolding in the therapist's office.

Doing this in a conjoint session would probably have multilevel synergistic impact. It could reestablish a solid and invested relationship between the therapist and Sharon, offering her a course of action that addressed longstanding personal problems (sweetened by impulses of anger and defiance of Harry). Harry's motivation to have an affair would be minimized because of (a) less fear of Sharon controlling him, (b) less opportunity to hurt Sharon through his sexual interests or disinterest, and (c) the sudden shift in the power balance of the marriage.

This singular intervention involved a detriangulation that would markedly reduce the fusion in the dyad and settle both partners by redirecting their anxiety into two potentially productive internal conflicts. Utilizing the existing inherent paradoxes would probably "confuse" and disorient the spouses, further driving them inward and reducing the fusion between them.

The task of setting up the crucible for Harry would have started through the intervention with Sharon; putting the lid on would actually be quite simple. Harry expected the therapist to encourage delaying or foregoing his sexual experimentation. The therapist, instead, could talk openly with Harry (in Sharon's presence) about his possible interest in having an affair, freely acknowledging his sexuality, attractiveness, autonomy, and Sharon's inability to stop him from having sex with other women if he wished. *The key would be for the therapist to suggest that all Harry needed to do was openly declare this decision to his wife.*

In this actual case, the therapist seeking consultation felt that Harry was likely to become extremely anxious about openly acknowledging his sexual interests in front of Sharon or declaring his intentions. Harry was more experienced with defiance than autonomy; he was more prepared to fight about not being controlled than to decide how he wanted to run his penis (and the rest of his life). The therapist figured that Harry would challenge why he should let his wife know if he was having sex with someone else while they were separated. If he was really being separate and autonomous, Harry might suggest, why did he need to "report to her." Besides, the therapist anticipated, Harry felt no obligation to be "fair" with Sharon after years of abuse verbal.

The therapist's understanding of the concept of "fair" was as fused and undifferentiated as the couple's. The issue for Harry was not one of being "fair" to Sharon, but rather one of being "fair to himself." How could telling his wife that he was about to have an affair involve "being fair to himself," when she might decide to file for divorce? A highly differentiated therapist might suggest two possible ways.

First, Harry contemplated having an affair to find out what it might be like to be single and have relationships with other women. Harry acknowledged that this was intended as a testing ground to see if he might actually want a divorce. The therapist could suggest that Harry might not want to base such an important decision on a distorted picture of what it might be like to be single. Having a clandestine affair while holding onto Sharon and hedging his bets would give a distorted picture of "being single." Letting his wife know of his intent was being "fair to himself," in that going through the anticipation that she would leave him would give him a close approximation of having a relationship as a single man with another woman. Besides, if that was going to be part of the price of getting what he wanted, he might want to include this in his decision.

Secondly, Harry was starting to see himself as attractive and respectable because of how he maintained himself after moving out, doing things he was afraid to do or thought he couldn't do. In mastering his own anxiety, he had raised his own level of integration and self-respect. In fact, it was this new-found and hard-earned sense of integrity (i.e., solid self) that made him attractive to Sharon and made her nervous about losing him. Harry was faced with an inherent paradox: If he threw away his integrity and deliberately misrepresented himself in the process of exploring his own sexuality, he destroyed the very thing that made him sexually desirable to himself and his wife. Informing Sharon of his intent was being "fair to himself" in terms of not diminishing his integrity in the face of his fears of her anger or of being alone. This was the crucial difference between "reporting to his wife" and giving a clearly defined, highly differentiated, presentation of himself. If Harry wanted "intimacy" (i.e., level-2, self-validated intimacy), here was the opportunity.

The therapist might point out that Harry's fledgling sense of integrity and autonomy had involved a shift, from focusing on defying what Sharon thought of him to building a relationship with himself in which what he thought of himself was paramount. If Harry was indeed willing to throw away his integrity in order to rebel against Sharon, then he would merely replicate the same pattern that he had engaged in all the years of their marriage. If Harry needed to see this process once again, the therapist wouldn't stop him; in fact, the therapist would help Harry watch himself in the process.

Harry, much like his wife, wanted *two* simultaneous choices. He wanted to exercise his own gratification *and* control Sharon's options and behavior in order to keep himself emotionally stabilized. Harry was free to make any choice for himself, but he was only likely to get one choice at a time. That choice might even be to give up his own options and try to negotiate for Sharon to give up the same—but his choice would be a unilateral decision, with few, if any, enforceable contingencies.

As a whole, these interventions comprise a sexual crucible designed to increase each spouse's level of differentiation; Harry and Sharon might reestablish a relationship based on strength and differentiation rather than weakness and fusion. Alternatively, they could go their separate ways without years of legal battles recapitulating their emotional enmeshment. In watching the other confront him- or herself and *not* sell out to personal anxiety, each will have fought and bested the dirtiest fighter of all: himself or herself. No one would have to teach them to "fight fair." The best assurance of a fair fight is two individuals who can stand on their own two feet with their partner, steadfastly refusing to sell out their integrity.

The Crucible of Therapist Differentiation

What confronts any therapist using this approach is the requisite willingness to undergo a similar personal crucible. In this particular case, the therapist seeking consultation recognized that his personal vulnerabilities (e.g., differentiation and integrity issues in his own marriage, discomfort with anger) were affecting his handling of the case. The therapist's conflict about these personal issues was testimony to his own therapeutic integrity and commitment to help the couple. He understood, moreover, that helping the couple was not just a function of new insight or technique; it also involved his reaching a higher personal level of differentiation.

The construction of a sexual crucible generates considerable anxiety in the couple, and in the treatment alliance. This requires a therapist who can maintain him- or herself in the face of invitations to "focus on the relationship," teach "negotiation" and "communication," and foster "commitment to the relationship" as a dodge for patients' difficulties in establishing a relationship-with-self.

Focusing on the spouses as individuals rather than as parts of a marriage stimulates the lurking dread that the couple will separate or divorce. Many therapists don't *really* believe they haven't failed when a couple separates; it is often perceived as a failure of the marriage, the therapy, and the therapist.

Paradoxically, therapists' anxiety about couples' separating increases the likelihood that it will happen. Subtle and not-so-subtle encouragement to keep the relationship together "at all costs" systemically amplifies anxiety within the marital dyad. In highly fused couples, a "decision" to separate is *often* a ritual act through which spouses begin to differentiate; even a brief separation isn't an unequivocal step towards divorce. Such couples frequently reconcile (and do quite well in treatment)—*if* the therapist doesn't lose his/her nerve.

Couples frequently have difficulty moving on with their lives because they are unable to develop the "critical mass" or "critical pressure" necessary to accomplish the next developmental step or life decision. Some player in the system vents the pressure that causes both growth and discomfort. When therapy fails to assist couples, it is often because the particular therapeutic triad is similarly unable to generate and maintain an effective level of pressure.

The crucible of sexual-marital therapy can be thought of as a pressure cooker. It allows people to work at an intensity that would otherwise be above the couple's "boiling point." The sexual crucible pressure pot seals in the personal and interpersonal nutrients often lost to emotional simmering, stewing and deep-frying. This process requires a well differentiated therapist who can function like the modulating cap on a pressure cooker, gently rocking back and forth, keeping the pressure in, while keeping it from exploding. When the therapist's anxiety tolerance is exceeded, the crucible vents its energy without being able to build and maintain the critical pressure that drives personal development forward.

A therapist must be able to intervene in *two* directions with regard to anxiety: keeping the cauldron boiling while keeping it below explosive mass. Therapists face an inherent double-bind: patients complain that sex, their marriage, and therapy itself are boring or "going nowhere"; they similarly complain of too much anxiety when they venture into the unknown of "going somewhere new." Actually, these are two sides of the same coin, and the therapist who recognizes this sees these complaints as opportunities for invention rather than resistance. Particular suggestions are created for general systemic impact, for modification of destructive or ineffective interactions, for evocation of unresolved individual issues, and for illumination of the immediate pattern of behavior and expectancies surrounding the sexual encounter.

In doing this, therapists sometimes fear that the sexual crucible approach will "precipitate a psychosis" by "not respecting patient's defenses." Sometimes, however, respect for patients' defenses surfaces best in recognition of simple applied physics. The fear of precipitating psychosis is often based on a view of patients as empty and vacuous; the application of pressure and heat would seemingly crack them like an eggshell. There are some marginal individuals like this who generally exist on the fringes of society, modulating their equilibrium by controlling physical proximity to others.

Far more commonly, however, folks are not empty; rather, they are *full* of anxiety, anger, narcissism and discontent. Such people don't explode under pressure; they explode in attempts to *remove* the pressure. Said differently, it is the *lack* of pressure that precipitates the explosion. People who are continually erupting emotionally do so because they are habitually not under *enough* pressure; they are intolerant of the pressure of daily life and attempt to keep it that way.

Time and again patients who formerly presented themselves as crippled human beings emerge from the sexual crucible demonstrating dramatic improvements in ego functioning, resilience to stress, and reorganized family dynamics across three generations. Some of them have prior histories of extensive hospitalization, having established self-images and identities in their families as fragile "mental patients" requiring "careful" handling lest they "fall apart."

Therapists who prefer to focus on "pathology" will certainly find it in patients (and in themselves). While there is nothing empowering about ignoring the limits of patients' adaptive abilities, a therapist's fears often set the stage for the disintegration of patients' struggles for differentiation, in what looks like fragmentation of the patient's ego.

A therapist recently offered to "help" me recognize the "dangers" of the crucible approach. Even in her own practice as a traditionally trained psychiatrist, she had recently found it necessary to hospitalize the "fragile" wife of a couple she was seeing. She related the case of Keith and Lana, two people she described as relatively "weak" and highly fused. Lana wanted more "intimacy" and "closeness"; Keith was an abrasive, arrogant, cruel, and insecure man who belittled and dominated her. On a recent occasion, Lana "gave it her all"; although quite anxious, Lana made herself "vulnerable" by disclosing "a lot." Keith used the content of the disclosure to berate and humiliate her, to "shut her down." Lana then "decompensated," requiring institutionalization in a private psychiatric facility.

I pointed out that it was highly unlikely that Lana had disclosed "a lot"; people at low levels of differentiation do not tolerate the attendant anxiety. Generally, if at all, they disclose only a little and immediately see what response it elicits from the partner.

What seemed far more likely was that Lana reverted to fighting back from the underdog position she knew so well. Frustrated that she wasn't immediately reinforced for her "attempt" (a expectation encouraged by prevailing reciprocity-based notions of intimacy and from empathy and anxiety-reduction models of treatment), she had a temper tantrum that was elevated to the status of psychiatric high drama. The strategic advantage Lana gained by entering the hospital was not to be underestimated: draining Keith's financial resources and insurance benefits, leaving him with the household responsibilities, "tattling" on him to hospital staff and fellow inpatients, and forcing him to spend time attending "family sessions" at which she safely raged at him and sniped at his sense of adequacy and superiority. Moreover, Lana demanded nurturance from the therapist while raging at her as well. Even people who are "crazy" aren't totally crazy.

On the other hand, if Lana was truly interested in developing herself so that she could eventually stand on her own two feet with *anyone*, she could not have picked a better partner. If she kept challenging herself in the context of her husband, she would eventually learn to handle herself with him. She had already learned to do it from a position of "weakness" and she could learn to do it from a position of "strength." Yes, it would be hard, but so is life; if she wasn't ready to handle herself with him when things got hard, then she probably wasn't ready to live without him either.

Excluding chronic schizophrenic patients who think they are Jesus Christ or Mary Magdalene and those with organic psychoses, the *vast* majority of patients who are hospitalized in private facilities are never blatantly psychotic. Every patient's (and therapist's) reality-testing gets strained at times; "thought disorders" are a matter of degree and duration. The question is: when is hospitalization a necessity, when is it designed to give the patient a "rejuvenating vacation from stress," and when is the patient hospitalized to reduce the anxiety of some other member (including the therapist) when the system approaches critical mass?

Perhaps it is the case that some therapists *shouldn't* challenge such patients to grow. When the therapist's nonreactivity and anxiety tolerance are exceeded, the anxiety of the process vents through him or her and increases the likelihood that the patient will either be medicated or hospitalized. While it may seem negligent to characterize a potential psychotic break as a "temper tantrum," it is also self-serving for the therapist to suggest that he or she "can see the difference." When the therapist's level of differentiation is exceeded, the automatic reflexive responses that occur may *look* like higher cortical processes, but in reality they are window dressing for more primitive emotional responses that predominate at such times (Chapter Seven).

Therapists who repeatedly worry about precipitating psychosis in patients tend to be individuals who themselves have not achieved a significant level of differentiation; they are particularly reactive to patient anxiety. Such therapists underestimate patients' capacities to master the growth-producing challenges that the therapists themselves avoid. In the above example, the therapist actually encouraged Lana to "fold" by "cringing" in-session during Keith's attempts to undermine Lana's adequacy. Similarly, the therapist's attempt to "shield" and "support" Lana by intervening in the sometimes bruising exchanges gave a subtle message of disbelief in Lana's ability to increase her level of differentiation and learn to soothe herself. The therapist's fear for Lana's fragility interfered with the necessary exposure for growth. Moreover, Lana's pattern of controlling her marriage through displays of "fragility" was perpetuated in similar fashion in treatment.

Although certain therapeutic orientations are not pathognomonic in themselves, therapists at lower levels of differentiation gravitate towards clinical approaches which accommodate their personal needs:

- They ascribe, explicitly or implicitly, to models of *resistance* that are inherently self-referential (i.e., the therapist is the voice of "health" with whom the patient is not complying);
- they expect, implicitly or explicitly, to empathize or "love" patients to a higher level of functioning; and
- they ascribe to a model of therapy in which all power and responsibility emanate from the therapist, while simultaneously being unable to modulate the anxiety of professional practice in an increasingly litigious society.

The inherent paradox is that when patients hold onto such therapists for support and validation, they figuratively (and sometimes literally) embrace a major source of anxiety that exacerbates their own, and debilitates the efforts at self-modulation.

Triangulation and Therapist Neutrality:
Maintaining the Sexual Crucible

Effective treatment requires a tolerance for multidetermined sexual and marital difficulties. Partners tend to use half-truths as competitive mutually negating views of a singular reality, rather than as complementary simultaneous realities.

Therapists confronted with highly polarized couples locked in pitched battle often seek a "neutral" position by not "taking sides," as if "neutrality" were an end in itself. The fear (and actuality) of being pushed to "take sides" has immobilized many a therapist.

There is nothing wrong with "taking sides" as long as it is done strategically, rather than "adjudicatorily." Listening to both has little to do with spouses' perceptions of political neutrality: Both patients' views contain important information about the problem or, at the very least, about the problem-maintaining solutions they have tried.

Quite often the therapist has to take *no one's* side, but this too has little to do with neutrality. Simply rearranging the same limited pieces of data the patients have been shuffling is a sure route to treatment failure. The clinician must take a position that differs from that of *both* patients. Empathy, communication, and negotiation between their half-truths doesn't work because an effective solution lies *outside* the boundaries defined by their alternative positions.

The therapist's level of differentiation determines his/her capacity to unilaterally validate alternative realities that lie outside what either partner has heretofore been willing to consider, particularly when the therapist disagrees with both spouses on a point they happen to agree upon. Emergency room personnel *half*-jokingly say, "During a CODE, the first person's pulse to check is your own."

In this respect, the therapist's position in the sexual crucible is similar to that in strategic/structural therapy: Neutrality involves taking multiple positions, none fixed and each determined by what is necessary to drive the treatment forward at any given point. The therapist cannot be neutral in the sense of being uninvolved; therapeutic neutrality is the ability to remain both *deeply* engaged and yet emotionally untangled with the couple.

The notion that therapeutic neutrality is more determined by the therapist's personal level of differentiation than by any theoretical or technical sophistication is a sobering realization that stretches the fabric of therapists' self-acceptance and self-soothing. Kerr and Bowen note:

The ability to be in contact with a problem but not part of it relates to emotional neutrality and detachment. Neutrality does not mean a fence-straddling or a wishy-washy posture toward life problems. People are often so intense about "taking sides" on issues that an ability to see *both* sides is viewed as an unwillingness to take a stand. . . . Neutrality is reflected in an ability to be calm about what goes on between others, to be aware of all the emotionally determined sides of an issues, and to be aware of the influence of subjectivity on one's notions about what "should" be. Neutrality becomes differentiation when it is operationalized through one's actions in a relationship system. (Kerr & Bowen, 1988, p. 111, italics added)

Like any third party, and perhaps more so, therapists are subject to the couple's attempts to reduce anxiety through triangulation (Chapter Eleven). This view of therapist-patient interaction is sometimes mistaken as a "defensive" stance on the therapist's part to keep from being "taken in" by patient's "manipulations." A therapeutic stance in which the therapist "defends" against patients "defeating" him/her (or "the treatment") is an undifferentiated, over-personalized, and egocentric view that places the therapist outside the system and unaligned with patients. Triangulation is merely the playing out of natural ("normal") mechanisms of anxiety modulation in systems; it is no more adversarial than other systemic process.

The well-differentiated therapist, in contrast, *welcomes* attempts at triangulation as part of the elicitation process, and as opportunities to utilize his/her own differentiation in the form of *detriangulation*.

A basic tenet of systems therapy is that the tension in a two-person relationship will resolve *automatically* when contained within a three-person system, one of whom is emotionally detached. In other words, despite togetherness urges to the contrary, a problem between two people can be resolved without the "well intentioned" efforts of a third person to "fix" it. It only requires that the third person be in adequate emotional contact with the other two and be able to remain emotionally separate from them. The process of being in contact and emotionally separate is referred to as "detriangling." If the twosome does not triangle in a fourth person who is not detached, instead continuing to relate primarily to the third person who is, the twosome will bring their relationship back into equilibrium. (Kerr & Bowen, 1988, p. 146)

If a person can achieve more neutrality or detachment while in contact with the triangles that he is most connected to emotionally and then act on the basis of that neutrality, the tensions between the other two members in each triangle will be reduced. Emotional neutrality is reflected in a number of ways, two of which are especially relevant to triangles: first, the ability to see both sides of a relationship process between two others, and second, the ability not to have one's thinking about that process clouded with notions of what "should" be. (p. 150)

Kerr and Bowen state that detriangling is the most important "technique" in family systems therapy; it is ineffective, however, when it is attempted as a technique. *Detriangulation is more properly thought of as a spontaneous expression of the therapist's level of differentiation, from whence it derives efficacy.* The therapist's level of differentiation becomes a systemic intervention when he/she can be available, directive, and active, while remaining detriangulated.

Therapists must buffer patients' frequent attempts at triangulation to reduce the anxiety which is sometimes deliberately precipitated by the therapist. By way of example, consider three common occurrences which raise anxiety:

- Introducing a treatment paradigm that contradicts the half-truths both partners have maintained (e.g., pointing out inherent paradoxes).
- Rebalancing power hierarchies by confronting the spouse who presents him/herself as "pro-therapy" or who infantilizes the partner by being "helpful."
- Confronting the facade of a "good" relationship, prior "good" sex, and underlying hostility.

The therapist cannot assist patients to reach a higher level of differentiation than he or she has achieved. The therapist's anxiety tolerance and resilience to emotional contagion determine the point at which patients' pressures are vented through triangulation in the therapeutic relationship. The therapist's level of differentiation determines the degree of resiliency (nonreactivity) of the sexual crucible; the essence of any crucible is that its reactivity is lower than the raw materials contained for processing.

Mental health and other helping professionals pride themselves on the capacity to be both empathic and objective. This is not too difficult when the problems of the families being treated are under reasonable control. In more chaotic situations, however, the differentiation of the professionals is often lost and anxiety spreads like a forest fire through the interlocking triangles that surround the problem family. When this happens, *anxiety* of the therapist and staff has more influence on treatment decisions than do well-thought-out therapeutic principles. (Kerr & Bowen, 1988, p. 141)

An effective therapist modulates the display of *caring* as a therapeutic tool rather than indulging in a self-gratifying gush which reinforces patients' beliefs that their problems stem from lack of caring.

The therapist's empathy and caring cause him or her to *not* violate patients' autonomy or opportunities for growth. Effective caring involves self-discipline, rather than lack of boundaries; one's caring does not entitle one to trespass. The realization that the therapist won't drag patients forward (or shy away from anxiety) is productively anxiety-provoking at the same time that it is calming. The experience is the inherent paradox of detriangulation, the hall-mark caring-but-separate stance of differentiation.

THE THERAPIST'S ABILITY TO BE INTIMATE

If workshops and conferences in the health-care disciplines are any indication, marital and sexual therapists have increasingly become professional *theorists* and *technicians*, rather than *therapists*. There are those who focus on increasingly complex ways of "understanding" problems, openly acknowledging that they have no new solutions. On the other hand, there are those who promote specific techniques as if these were curative independent of the therapist utilizing them. What is often lost is a focus on the *person* of the patient in contact with the *person* of the therapist.[9]

Given that intimacy is the meta-dimension in which therapy occurs, the capacity for intimacy is one of the most relevant aspects of personal development for a therapist. Sexual-marital therapy is conducted in either a level-1 or level-2 paradigm of intimacy. The transitioning from a level-1 treatment paradigm to level-2 can be quite difficult.[10] Establishing a level-2 framework at the outset, on the other hand, creates a paradigm shift that ripples throughout treatment and grabs patients' attention. Therapists whose own views of intimacy involve reciprocity become hopelessly ensnared in patients' attempts to "find out more about the therapist because the therapist is finding out about them." Such clinicians often lose their personal solidity and stable therapeutic

---

[9]Brad Keeney (1983) offers the balanced perspective in which the above point is made:

> I prefer to view [an aesthetic understanding of change] as a contextual frame for practical action. A singular emphasis on pragmatics potentially leads to an ecological decontextualization of therapy where one's bag of tricks, cures, and problem-solving procedures is too easily disconnected from the more encompassing aesthetic patterns of ecology. Similarly, an esthetics of therapy without appropriate regard for pragmatic technique may lead to free-associative nonsense. (pp. 8–9)

[10]See the conclusion of Chapter Four regarding the transition from level-1 to level-2.

footing in coping with common challenges to their ability to remain differentiated.

Although patients often have intense unilateral intimate experiences, psychotherapy *can* be an extremely intimate experience for the therapist as well; treatment is often at its zenith when patient and therapist experience this simultaneously. Empathic involvement with a patient often creates a correspondingly intense self-awareness for the therapist. Like in intense sexual experiences, time stops and the alternate reality of the therapeutic hour becomes encompassing. All present have a profound sense of the others in the context of acute self-awareness. Participatory processes of patients and therapist are complementary and synchronous, but not identical (just like birthing a baby).

Intense therapeutic engagement cannot be forced through therapist self-disclosure, and moreover, "modeling" self-disclosure for patients rarely involves intimacy on the part of the therapist. What is generally disclosed by the therapist at such times has been previously well digested and involves little self-confrontation or acute self-awareness. Self-indulgent and self-aggrandizing therapist self-disclosure is neither intimate nor good modeling. Few therapists risk the self-disclosure of information that involves acute risk-taking or vulnerability (nor should it necessarily be any other way).

Beyond such misplaced efforts, modern psychotherapy discourages therapist-patient emotional intimacy in unforeseen ways. *It is rarely recognized that the concept of countertransference is antithetical to notions of intimacy in therapy.* The basic notion behind transference and countertransference concerns an inappropriate attribution, the content or degree of which is determined more by one's feelings for some other significant person than for the current individual. Although usually invoked in discussions of "negative" feelings towards the patient, the notion of countertransference implicitly regards "positive" feelings as unwarranted and primarily stemming from something other than the interaction between the patient and therapist. Transference and countertransference suggest, at best, a ceremonial display of self to the other, who never *really* sees or is seen.

A psychoanalyst circumvents face-to-face interaction because it limits engagement on the level thought to be most crucial to the therapeutic process: unconscious communication of projections from the patient. The "blank screen" clinical approach deliberately seeks to minimize conversational and social conventions that distract awareness from the psychoanalyst's associations, intuitions and feelings. In one respect, the process of the well-trained and highly differentiated psychoanalyst is intimate: the acute experience of self in the presence of the "other" (although these feelings are not disclosed as personal statements of self-definition).

However, the "blank screen" approach is occasionally utilized in face-to-face therapy as an adaptation to some therapists' lack of differentiation (although not conceptualized as such). Such therapists attempt to keep from being *seen* by patients; ironically, when done for this reason, it doesn't work.

At the other extreme from "blank screen" clinical approaches are the ones blissfully indifferent to the notion of transference and countertransference: *all* emotional exchanges are encouraged in misguided notions of honesty, intimacy, and "real emotional contact." Many approaches which recognize the *possibility* of true intimacy between therapist and patient also err in pursuing it as an end in itself, and as a necessary and sufficient vehicle of change. Such therapies often sit on the border of inappropriate patient-therapist contact and sexual exploitation. Both the "blank screen" and the "acting-out" clinical paradigms differ markedly from the Bowenian stance of *detriangulation*, which *requires* (a) a high degree of interaction *and* (b) the ability to modulate one's emotional reactivity.

Reflecting upon the foregoing discussion, one can legitimately ask: *What is the source and substance of health-care professionals' expertise in the area of intimacy?* Aside from reading clinical literature of generally dubious utility, what aspect of professional preparation supports therapists' implicit claims of special knowledge about intimacy? What facet of training increases a therapist's personal capacity for intimacy at work or at home?

Sexual and marital therapists don't necessarily know any more about intimacy or have better sex or marriages than the general public. At best, one might expect among therapists the same distribution of capacity for intimacy, problematic relationships, sexual dysfunctions, and psychopathology that one might observe in the general population. In fact, given the tendency for individuals to self-select careers in marital and sexual therapy in order to resolve their own personal problems, one could argue that the distribution might be significantly skewed towards the lower extremes.

It was previously mentioned that sensate focus exercises are not inherently erotic (Chapter Thirteen). Yet, the anticipation by many therapists that these activities are intrinsically pleasurable and arousing is testimony that these clinicians have never gone through the procedures they prescribe for others. One clinician with several years' experience allowed that she had "imagined" doing them; she recognized that she would have interpreted this same report as "resistance" if her patients responded similarly.

Folks don't recognize that therapists are simply "civilians" when they leave their offices; they are no more eager or able to go through the sexual crucible in their own relationships than are their patients. The *thought* of suggesting a voluntary ban on intercourse with one's partner, getting compliance, and concentrating on sensate focus activities makes many clinician anxious; actually *doing* it, all the more so. Sensate focus activities are no panacea, but many clinicians could benefit from the attendant differentiation that comes from driving their own relationships forward into greater intimacy and eroticism.

Conducting sexual-marital therapy pushes the clinician up against the limits of his or her personal development and unresolved issues. When that moment of self-recognition occurs in session, the therapist has his or her own personal intimate experiences; patients often become aware of this to varying degrees. If the therapist lacks the ego strength to tolerate this level of intimacy, treatment generally suffers. The notion that a therapist must be highly differentiated and capable of intimacy seems self-evident; embracing this in everyday practice is quite something else.

A bright young therapist consulted me about how I handled the issue of affairs. In the process, Conrad disclosed that he had several undisclosed affairs in the early years of his marriage. He had been monogamous for the subsequent 10 years and intended to remain so. Conrad described a satisfying relationship with his wife, which included both spouses having nonphysical friendships with members of the opposite sex.

The problem was that Conrad wanted to remain friends with Laurie, one of his prior lovers. Laurie was quite open about wanting to resume sexual contact; she "settled," however, for periodic nonsexual meetings in which she made seductive advances that Conrad ruefully declined. Conrad didn't want to reveal the prior affair nor give up contact with Laurie, and yet *he* felt that his prior and continuing behavior created a barrier to intimacy with his wife; moreover, his wife was already insecure and jealous about his current (nonsexual) female friendships. Conrad didn't feel totally clean and anxiety-free telling his wife that Laurie was "just an old friend"; it perpetuated the prior deception, particularly since Laurie wanted to continue the sexual relationship. Conrad had consulted many popular self-help books on "to tell or not to tell" but did not find the answer he sought.

The clinical point of Conrad's dilemma was that he became distracted and lost his resilience when patients presented issues involving affairs. It wasn't that he had anxiety attacks; he just began thinking about his own situation and failed to pursue avenues that might lead to a confrontation between the spouses. Even when Conrad saw such an opening, he lacked the personal belief that such crises could be successfully handled. Moreover, Conrad found it too self-disclosing (i.e., since the topic at hand was affairs) to disqualify himself from such cases on personal grounds.

To his credit, Conrad recognized that he had become the crack in his patients' crucible. Moreover, Conrad recognized that some of the pleasant memories of the affair contained elements of his eroticism that he still wasn't sufficiently differentiated to present and maintain with his wife.

It is only when the real-life implications of the therapist's level of differentiation are recognized that we as therapists begin to "squeak" uncomfortably in the heat of the sexual crucible.

Professional sex education occurs in informal interactions at conferences, meetings, and college seminars. Despite theories expounded in classrooms and colloquia, experienced professionals teach neophytes about human sexuality and intimacy in hotel rooms and bars, the same way that parents teach children through daily interaction in the home. If sexual or marital therapists have any greater capacity for intimacy and eroticism than the average individual in society, then one might expect that the leadership of these fields would embrace the highest personal achievement in this regard.

Unfortunately, one's dearest colleagues, well-respected leaders in the professional community as well as rank-and-file clinicians, often lead chaotic private lives. Their marriages are often barren, lacking the differentiation to drive the level of intimacy and eroticism forward through barriers of anxiety. One would think they "deserve better" and know how to get it; if warm personal regard and well-wishing from colleagues were sufficient, no doubt they would have it. The point here is not to disparage therapists for their shortcomings, but rather to underscore that clinicians are no different from their patients in the disinclination to undergo the crucible of differentiation. More respect must be accorded to the men and women who do so.

There is little in professional training that prepares psychotherapists to balance the demands of career and family; nothing obviates the use of professional obligations to avoid intimacy in personal relationships. Financial concerns, competition for patients, and time demands of adequate patient care are daily realities, but they don't preclude clinical practice from becoming the triangulated "other person" in a therapist's marriage.

Many reasons make it difficult for some therapists to reject patients' demands for late evening or weekend appointments. Once these demands are accommodated, however, these same patients often question the therapist's own intimacy needs and tolerance: "Why is he/she here with us instead of being at home?" There is a progressive paradoxical negation of sexual and marital therapy conducted after normal business hours.

Patients see the self of the therapist even in the structure of the clinician's practice. The therapist's willingness to be *seen* and to accept this as inevitable is a function of the therapist's capacity for intimacy. There is no safe haven for the therapist who hides from being known—that is, without diminishing the efficacy of the sexual crucible. The guideline for the therapist seeking to hone his/her craft is the same as that for the aspiring seeker of intimacy: *Live life so you have nothing to fear about what people know and see in you*.

BEYOND ETHICS: INTEGRITY

Ethics in sexual and marital therapy are often addressed because of the magnitude of damage created by ethical breaches. AASECT, AAMFT, and all mental health disciplines have established codes of ethics that prohibit overt sexual contact with patients. While this is applauded, our focus lies elsewhere: Is it possible to shift from the negative to the positive in discussing ethics, just as we have shifted our discussion from sexual dysfunction to sexual potential?

Charles Levy offers a realistic view of ethics codes:

> Codes of ethics are at once the highest and lowest standards of practice expected of the practitioner, the awesome statement of rigid requirement, and the promotional materials issued primarily for public relations purposes. They embody the gradually evolved essence of moral expectations, as well as the arbitrarily prepared shortcut to professional prestige and status. At the same time, they are handy guides to the legal enforcement of ethical conduct and to punishment for unethical conduct. They are also the unrealistic, unimpressive, and widely unknown or ignored guides to wishful thinking. The motivation to create a code of ethics may be a zeal for respectability. However, occupational groups are most often moved by a genuine need for guides to action in situations of agonizing conflict and by sincere aspirations to deal justly with clients, colleagues, and society. (Levy, 1974, p. 207)

In practice, professional ethics refers to questionable violations of minimal contractual obligations undertaken by the therapist in offering treatment to patients (e.g., Keith-Spiegel & Koocher, 1985). As such, ethical issues lie at the lower end of the continuum of therapist functioning. No matter how thoroughly defined, clarification of ethical violations doesn't orient the therapist toward helping people explore the limits of their sexual potential. At the opposite end of the continuum of unethical behavior, beyond the middle ground of ethical behavior, lies the arena of therapist *integrity*. Issues of therapist integrity (like patient integrity) have *everything* to do with sexual potential.

Integrity is one facet of an individual's relationship-with-self, a recursive aspect of differentiation. Integrity (rather than narcissism) is the fundamental basis by which one can accept his or her desirability and allow oneself to lie back, receive, and *relax* during sex. When narcissism is the primary foundation of self-perceived desirability, it renders the individual vulnerable, insecure, and unable to relax while being nurtured. When integrity is at the core of self-perceived desirability in contrast, the individual can unilaterally self-disclose, self-support, and maintain a sense of internal security that allows being nurtured and cared for.

Of all the ways in which people attempt to enhance sexual intensity, intimacy, and sexual desire, the one topic rarely discussed is the one for which there is no quick technique. It is also the one most expensive to develop. In matters of integrity there is no one else to fight with, no one else who can let you off the hook. Integrity is the manifestation of differentiation in which it becomes clear that autonomy is not simply defiance of others or "not taking any crap from anyone." Integrity involves not taking crap from oneself.

Integrity in therapy is similar to what Carlos Castaneda (1968) extrapolated from Don Juan's lessons about "the man of knowledge" and "the impeccable warrior." First, there was the need to know fear and not turn away from it:

Another necessity . . . was the need to experience and carefully to evaluate the sensation of fear. The idea was that, in spite of fear, one had to proceed with the course of one's acts. Fear was supposed to be conquered and there was an alleged time in the life of a man of knowledge when it was vanquished, but first one had to be conscious of being afraid and duly to evaluate that sensation. Don Juan asserted that one was capable of conquering fear only by facing it. (p. 198)

Then there was the need for self-mastery:

The constant renewal of the quest of becoming a man of knowledge was expressed in the theme of the four symbolic enemies encountered on the path of learning: fear, clarity, power, and old age. Renewing the quest implied the gaining and maintaining of control over oneself. (p. 199)

Personal integrity stemming from self-mastery has everything to do with one's feelings of sexual desire and wholeness, of feeling inherently desirable, and of feeling clean about being desirous. *In a sense, integrity is the sense of being desirable to oneself;* it is what permits an individual to desire intensely without fear of losing oneself in a relationship with another.

Money, power, and sex are the big three to which people sell out their integrity. Many people teach themselves that the price of sex *is* selling one's integrity, because that is what they insist on paying. It is revealing when an individual's most intense sexual experience *does* involve a loss of integrity.

Patients often think sex therapists look the other way about selling out a little integrity for good sex. In fact, many patients are *stunned* by the suggestion that integrity is more precious than sex, and paradoxically, integrity is the route to more intense sex. Integrity is directly correlated with sexual potential and the capacity for non-bypass styles of eroticism and intimacy. Integrity—and not just body posture and motion—is a central aspect of sexual *style*.

Issues of Sexual Attraction

The process of helping patients explore the limits of their sexual potential is mirrored in the therapist's quest for impeccability; that impeccability is quickly tested around issues of sexual attraction for patients. Long before the therapist's impulses are so out of control as to endanger his/her license, there is the loss of clinical integrity. A sexual or marital therapist is often assumed to be the ultimate partner; if the therapist is "grandstanding" or sexually interested in a patient (and then defensive when confronted or challenged), patients will *know*. Therapists who lie to cover themselves "mind fuck" patients, violating the integrity and intimacy of treatment. Although they may not be able to articulate this, patients generally sense it and the treatment alliance is fractured.

The issue is not the presence of the therapist's sexual impulses per se. One might argue that the therapist who is *unable* to tolerate such impulses curtails the use of an important dimension of meta-communication. Nor is the issue the strength of the impulses, or whether or not the therapist can control his or her behavior. The therapist who engages in exploitive sexual contact is clearly at the *bottom* of the spectrum under consideration. It is the more common and poorly defined *middle* of the spectrum that is of concern. That is to say, *violations of clinical integrity occur when the therapist becomes preoccupied with his or her own impulses, losing his or her solidity and ability to detriangulate.*

Therapists' integrity, like the word itself, stems from integration; that integration is a function of level of differentiation. *It is the therapist's integration, including his or her integrity, that helps patients differentiate and integrate themselves.* When the therapist has the sense of his/her own sexual impulses becoming embarrassing or self-diminishing and doesn't seek professional consultation or personal treatment, the crucible is ruptured.

Over the years, a variety of professional colleagues have sought my consultation about ethics violations involving sexual contact with patients. In almost every case, the therapist reported an awareness of unusually intense personal sexual interest in the patient, but disclaimed, "I could control it" or "I thought nothing would happen." In issues of integrity, the question of behavioral control is actually beside the point. The therapist knew that he or she had an impulse control problem that compromised his or her ability to maintain an impeccable position. While these therapists *might* have had sufficient clinical effectiveness to offer *some* modicum of benefit prior to the behavioral violation, they knew they were preoccupied with their own internal processes and operating in a diminished capacity. There was a secondary meaning to the therapists' assessment that "nothing was going to happen," regarding the efficacy of treatment.

When the therapist's *self-awareness* of an electric, erotic impulse causes him or her to lose a differentiated emotional stance, there is a violation of clinical integrity. At that point, the therapist is no longer able to use his or her intuition and feelings as a trustworthy tuning fork in empathic vibration with the patient. The therapist loses the ability to look beyond patients' eroticism to see their pain, and forgoes the use of patients' sexuality as a window of elicitation; the therapist becomes a voyeur who sees only his or her own reflection in that window. The point at which this happens is determined by the individual characteristics of the therapist rather than by some external measure of propriety. The therapist who has low intimacy tolerance shrinks from this self-evaluation, violating his or her clinical integrity and abandoning the patient in the process.

Do patients simply purchase the therapist's time, intellect, memory, and empathy? Or do patients pay for clinical skill? Clinical skill involves the use of the therapist's emotions both as a diagnostic tool and as the ability to "connect" emotionally while maintaining appropriate boundaries. Do patients purchase the right to expect that the therapist will monitor his or her level of functioning and seek appropriate recourse when impaired? Do patients purchase the right to expect that the therapist will go beyond monitoring minimal levels of functioning and seek his/her highest levels of personal development?

Given the absence of data suggesting that sexual and marital therapists achieve greater levels of differentiation than the general public, patients don't automatically get a therapist who can help them explore much of their sexual potential. Given the existing problems facing licensing boards and professional organizations certifying minimal competency of sexual and marital therapists, the notion of credentialing therapists as "sexual-potential-certified" makes the mind boggle. Each therapist remains his or her own regulatory agency on issues of clinical integrity.

Common Issues of Integrity

Integrity issues often arise in the same *dimensions* as ethical issues, although the *standards* are more stringent; violations of integrity occur at much higher levels of functioning than violations of ethics. What are often "grey" areas for ethical decisions are clear violations of integrity:

- Hurrying highly ambivalent patients into treatment where a laissez-faire attitude is more likely to allow patients to *complete* treatment.

One common example is the new patient who calls demanding an immediate appointment; the therapist senses that the immediacy is one aspect of the patient's problem rather than a reflection of an actual emergency. The therapist's prior experience in similar circumstances leads him/her to think that the patient is less likely to keep an appointment given for the next day than one set for a week later. However, the therapist has time available for tomorrow *and* next week, and he/she is hungry for billable hours. Does the therapist comply with the patient's stated demand (and the therapist's personal agenda) or respond from his or her own clinical judgment? Another example arises in inpatient programs for sexual perpetrators seeking to fill bed space; calls are received from potential patients across the country hurriedly seeking admission in order to *avoid* the local impact of their behavior and position themselves favorably in subsequent sentencing.

- Overstating one's competencies by innuendo or omission.

For example, does the therapist deliberately clarify the difference between a therapist who "does" sex or marital therapy vs. an AASECT certified sex therapist or an AAMFT clinical member? While the therapist may feel that such credentials offer no particular clinical advantage, depriving the patient of the opportunity to make an informed decision leaves the therapist vulnerable to subsequent challenges of motivation and integrity if and when his/her competency is questioned. A similar example involves misrepresenting practical experience as the equivalent of formal training in a particular sub-specialty.

- Holding onto patients for one's emotional or financial edification, when the patients' interests would be better served by another therapist or termination.

While one might rationalize that such cases are not ethical violations because patients derive *some* benefit from treatment, it becomes a violation of integrity when treatment fails to address the *core* aspects of patients' concerns. What of cases in which the patient reports benefit from treatment (and pays his/her bill), but the therapist's professional judgment suggests otherwise? Or consider a case in which the therapist continues with a couple who is significantly behind in payment without prior arrangement, because the therapist is afraid to confront the issue for fear that the couple will terminate and not pay off the account balance.

- Failure to confront patients' reluctance to confront the therapist about legitimate and appropriate grievances.

From time to time, every therapist becomes drowsy, bored, distracted, or inattentive during a session; his or her thoughts may turn to the prior patient or errands to run. Such events are potentially useful to treatment *if* the therapist is willing and able to use this recursively as an internal cue to some aspect of the therapist-patient interaction. However, in many cases the therapist literally "steals" time from the patient by substantively pursuing the tangential thoughts, fracturing the crucible by feigning interest and attentiveness.

Even this can be used productively by the therapist who discusses the way in which patients handle their awareness of the therapist's lack of attentiveness. Whether or not the patient reports such an awareness, the response will be relevant to some aspect of the patient's issues about intimacy and attachments. This type of intervention is an example of intimacy in therapy which intensifies the crucible. It requires a high level of therapist integrity and differentiation to make this type of self-declarative intervention; it must be done in a manner that does not blame the patient for the therapist's inattentiveness. Such an intervention encourages patients to trust their own internal cues but requires a therapist with a high tolerance for intimacy.

- Marketing statements and "hucksterism" in an atmosphere of increasingly competitive advertisements.

Can someone really learn how to be more intimate in an "intimacy workshop"? Does an "intimacy workshop" perpetuate the notion that intimacy is easy to achieve by doing particular behaviors? Does the advertising imply the opportunity for *significant* improvement, while any gains are likely to be modest at best? Do minor improvements in technique outweigh disadvantages of reinforcing level-1 paradigms that actually *limit* intimacy? Advertisements generally imply the opportunity to achieve the highest goals and ideals of relationships, rather than "minor improvements that will become roadblocks in the long run." Is the actual experience more geared toward helping participants recognize their *limitations* in being intimate, as an entrée into the therapist's ongoing practice?

THE FUTURE OF PROFESSIONAL TRAINING

Of all the myriad issues involved in the training and development of clinicians, the role of personal development is both the most critical and the thorniest. Far more trainees can be taught the theories and techniques of sexual-marital therapy than can be helped to become *therapists*. The notion that good therapy is an *art* that cannot be taught is a half-truth. Certainly, there are skills and techniques to be mastered; but, all things considered, level of differentiation is the single most important aspect distinguishing a therapist from a technician.

While differentiation cannot be taught, it *can* be systematically fostered and assessed through the content and style of professional training programs *if educators are willing to undertake the enormity of the project*. Such an undertaking would probably require changes in structure, content, duration, admission and graduation criteria, and faculty composition. It would raise numerous thorny issues along the way, but not any more than those raised when clinical supervisors and faculty currently permit a student to graduate despite grave doubts about his or her ability to function as a therapist.

It is not totally farfetched that patients might legitimately ask about the therapist's personal life in much the same way that they ask about other professional credentials. The foregoing discussion suggests that the therapist's level of personal development (i.e., level of differentiation and capacity for intimacy) is a crucial factor in what the therapist has to offer in treatment. Unfortunately, contemporary paradigms of psychotherapy have not come to grips with this dilemma. It is common practice to consider such questions from patients inappropriate and counterproductive to the treatment alliance. However, herein lies an inherent paradox. On the one hand, the patient always has the right to ask about the therapist's private life; on the other, the therapist can always refuse to provide such details. Yet patients will always be able to read the cues regarding the therapist's integrity. In this respect, the therapist's sexual behavior and emotional relationships are *never* private from the treatment process.

The point is not simply that the therapist will be revealed one way or another; rather, therapists who lack high levels of personal and professional integrity lose their resilience and their effectiveness. When the therapist reflects, "If people really knew me, they would think I am a sham," there is a disengagement from the patient. Poorly differentiated therapists sometimes create iatrogenic power conflicts by responding to patients' requests for personal information with defensive statements, such as, "We are here to discuss your issues, not mine." Therapist disclosure or "confession" often has a similar negative impact. The sexual crucible is ruptured while the therapist scrambles to cope with his or her sense of vulnerability in that intimate moment.

Clinicians sometimes ask how one shifts from using constructed paradox to inherent paradox and from standard sex therapy to the sexual crucible approach. Two "simple" suggestions come to mind. The first involves talking less and listening more closely to patients; the inherent paradoxes are embedded in patients' presenting situations and concerns. The second involves *entering* the same crucible of differentiation attempted with patients. This is not a form of professional training that many clinicians crave, but it is a necessary one. Therapeutic impact is not something one does for an hour, but rather something that stems from how one *lives* in relationship to family, friends, colleagues, supervisees . . . and patients.

Clinical integrity, like all forms of integrity, is an expensive commodity. It requires an inquiring mind that explores possibilities and implications, regardless of the internal conflict it generates in the therapist. Perhaps this is why it is so rare. One who aspires to help others explore the limits of intimacy and eroticism is obliged to enter the same crucible that he or she offers to others. It is a lot to ask of someone who simply wants to be a therapist. But can we ask any less?

CHAPTER SEVENTEEN

Sexuality and Spirituality

Spirituality is a relevant (and unavoidable) topic in working with couples' sexual-marital difficulties. It is also an important dimension in helping people reach their sexual potential. The sex-affirming Hebraic roots of Western civilization have been masked by Augustine's legacy of eroticism-hating sexual dualism, perpetuated by authoritarian-oriented Christian dogma, which negated the basic worthiness of human beings. The evolution of Western culture is a history of theologically based sexual oppression.

There are versions of Christian theology that affirm sex and the goodness of men and women; they provide a ready path for integrating sexuality and spirituality. One such path is outlined in this chapter. Spirituality, like intimacy, is a developmental task: One can appproach either from a stance of self-negation or self-affirmation. Desire is not a sin. Sin is the refusal to desire growth or exercise one's capacity for it; sin is the refusal to believe in oneself. Sexuality is the crucible of faith in which each of us struggles with the vision of our basic nature; it is where we see most clearly the face of the divinity we truly believe in.

Several years ago I had the good fortune to visit the "erotic" temples of Kajuraho in northern India. These ancient temples date back to the eleventh century, constructed about the time that the Roman Catholic church was building monasteries in Europe to solidify its program of clerical celibacy. These temples rise some hundred feet in the air, completely covered with exquisitely detailed figures providing an almost unimaginable education into the anatomical possibilities of human coupling and an appreciation of the beauty of the human body. One coupling depicted a man and woman engaging in rear-entry coitus; the man's index finger touched the sacral section of his partner's spinal column. This coupling actually displayed a highly evolved form of "sensate focus": channeling "psychic" energy to stimulate physical energy in the woman's *chakra* (center of energy located in the spinal synapses)! Clearly, this society had evolved its own notion of a sexual quantum model, well integrated with their prevailing understanding of human physical functioning.

Hindu Tantric Yoga stresses a view of physiology and spirituality in which one attempts to arouse the kundalini (sexual energy) located at the base of the spine and unite it with the lotus (highest and most powerful psychic power) located in the brain; the purpose is to gain spiritual energy and salvation. Ritual intercourse, preceded by careful preparation, prayers, and meditation, is seen as a cosmic experience. The fullness of human consciousness is thought to occur in the profoundly absorbing experience of an aroused kundalini, developed through the activation of sexual energies. Merging of sexual energies with another individual is considered as the most intense awakenings of consciousness. This is quite a contrast from a Western dogma that states that full human consciousness is achieved by suppression of these same energies.

However, the full impact of the temples lay both within their walls and in the bustling village surrounding them. While the exterior of the walls depicted every conceivable manifestation of erotic behavior, the interior chamber was unadorned. At the center of this circular chamber, some 15 feet in diameter, was a simple ceremonial bed platform, around which one could barely walk without brushing the plain stone walls. Inside the chamber, there was nothing to suggest it represented the culmination of a society that had developed sexuality as its religious core and as a means of spiritual worship and transcendence.

And yet, the *aroma* of the eight or ten sexually aroused visitors within the temple was striking. It was as if there were a sexual radiance, such as people experience during embarrassing adolescent arousal, coming from each of us; each of us vibrated in harmony with a sexual energy that seemed to come out of nowhere and everywhere. There were simple, knowing, friendly smiles between the men and women tourists who resonated with the moment; we probably would not have truly looked at each other if we had passed in a hotel lobby earlier that day. It was a very unusual experience, being highly aroused *for nothing or anyone in particular*. There was no impulse to start an orgy or even to pair up. There was this peculiar sense of eroticism and sexual desire emanating from each of us, in the context of an intense spirituality. It was not that any of us became more attractive at that moment; we simply became *desirous without an apparent object of that desire*.

To this Westerner's eyes, the cultural contrast of sexual values was stunning. Here was a religion that fully demonstrated acceptance of sexuality as part of men and women's spiritual life; it brought *eroticism* right into the tabernacle. How very different from the more austere and chaste presence in the altars of our churches and temples. Indian Hindu temples have a stone effigy of a penis (*lingam*) and a vagina (*yoni*) prominently displayed on the floor. In contrast, it was with great trepidation that I even *mentioned* the formal names for male and female genitalia when I was given the honor of presenting a sermon at a Unitarian Church recently.

ARE SPIRITUALITY AND MORALITY RELEVANT TO SEXUALITY AND SEXUAL-MARITAL THERAPY?

The relationship between sexuality and spirituality in Western religious cultures has received increasing interest in recent years (Curran, 1988; Genovesi, 1987; Guptka, 1987; Heyward, 1989; Holland, 1981; McMahon & Campbell, 1989; Metzger, 1989; Schulz & Raphael, 1989). It is no coincidence, however, that spirituality has been culturally and dogmatically defined as the province of clergy preoccupied with heavenly salvation rather than earthly delight; there is substance to the stereotype. As we shall see, the division of sexuality and spirituality in Western civilization has it roots in the rise of Christianity. However, the historical rending of sexuality from spirituality has placed the health-care professions in the same position as the laity: looking for legitimacy in the integration of the two in a professional (and personal) identity.

Helminiak (1989) suggests that the role of sexuality in one's spiritual development becomes obvious when spirituality is conceptualized as the integration of all aspects of the person and the actualization of one's fullest potential. Arguing that spirituality itself is a legitimate topic of professional concern, he writes that spiritual development is nothing other than human development viewed from a particular perspective in which it becomes the ongoing integration that results from openness to an intrinsic principle of authentic self-transcendence.

While Helminiak argues for the *legitimacy* of considering spirituality within modern sexual science, other authors approach the same integration as a *necessity*. Robert Baker (1987), for instance, suggests that the role of the clinician inevitably involves sexual philosophy:

> . . . [Consider] the values and theories that clinicians draw on when they advise their patients about sexual matters. For—in the clinical practice of medicine- the voices of contemporary clinicians preach what French philosopher—historian Michel Foucault refers to as the "great sexual sermon"—chastising the old order, denouncing hypocrisy, and praising the rights of the immediate and the real. Some protest that when competent clinicians discuss sexual matters with their

patients, they do so from a medical, therapeutic, or scientific perspective – they do not discuss these issues philosophically. Such a response reflects a common misperception of the nature of philosophical theory. No one wishes to challenge the proposition that, for the most part, when clinicians discuss sexual matters with their patients, they attempt to do so in a manner that draws appropriately on their scientific knowledge and therapeutic training. The point to be taken is that when sexual events conspire to force patients to engage their clinicians in discussions of sexual matters, the discussion necessarily evokes philosophies of sex, *not* because clinicians act in an unscientific or non-therapeutic manner, but rather because both science and therapy presuppose normative and philosophical commitments. Admittedly, these discussions may appear to be philosophically neutral to the participants, but that, as I shall show, is precisely the reason that these discussions become morally problematic. (p. 88)

Science and research are invariably influenced by values and philosophy, even with regard to what research is funded, what "knowledge" is pursued, how data are interpreted, and where (and if) research results are published. Perhaps most importantly, such values become so acculturated that they become transparent through universality; the problem is that values become noticeable only when consensus breaks down.

Baker refers to the modern clinician as "the true vicar of the values of twentieth-century society" (p. 93). He argues that patients would be better served by a clinician who took this inevitable role seriously than by a naive clinician who preached a valuational sermon by argument, authority, suggestion, and innuendo in the guise of scientific discourse.

Existential issues concerning the meaning of life and "the good life" invariably arise in the exploration of sexual potential, touching on spiritual matters. Many people who have "dropped out" of organized religion are shocked to find that exploration of sexuality often leads one to the core of spirituality. When one considers the alacrity with which childhood religious upbringing is hypothesized to cause sexual problems, it is hard to understand how a clinician could consider the topic outside the boundaries of professional purview.

Sexual health-care professionals occupy a unique position in the integration of sexuality and spirituality. Those not wishing to deal with this subject (if one ignores Baker's arguments of this impossibility) must remain aware of the absence of such integration within Christian-dominated Western society. McCartney (1987), for instance, has focused on the need for a new integration of sexuality and spirituality:

In a book written several years ago, Eugene Kennedy points out that compassionate religious leaders could do more to integrate human sexuality in people's lives than an army of sexual scientists, but that they have to give up their instincts to control men and women in order to achieve this. I agree with this insight and believe that the most positive contribution that Catholic moral theology will make to human sexuality is not in a discussion of the controversies . . . but with a new development now taking place, which looks not so much at sexual actions to determine their rightness or wrongness, but looks at human sexuality in the context of intimacy, spirituality, and interpersonal growth. (pp. 223–224)

What are the issues and difficulties involved in integrating sexuality and spirituality? McCartney suggests that the relevant issues are the relation of love and physical embodiment and the meaning of friendship and commitment, rather than focusing on whether premarital sex, homosexuality, and masturbation are always and everywhere wrong. H. Tristram Engelhardt (1987) proposes that sexual philosophy and morality can be conceptualized within two tiers, each one leading to its own conclusion. The first tier involves general *secular* concerns regarding autonomy, beneficence, and the keeping of promises; the second, *spiritual*, tier concerns which promises should be made.

Engelhardt suggests that spiritual morality involves issues that may be unique to sexuality, including one's understanding the "purpose" of sex and one's view of the good life. In contrast to attempts of Greco-Roman religions to promote "rationality" as the focus of sexual morality, sexual morality is not reducible to or defensible in terms of general rational considerations.

They depend on particular visions of the goods of sexuality, of the ways in which the unique urges and sensations of sexuality are to be orchestrated, experienced, appreciated, and realized against the backdrop of the reproductive, recreational, and social goals of sexuality. (p. 62)

DIVERSITY OF SEXUAL VALUES
WITHIN RELIGIOUS TRADITIONS

Many clinicians have little exposure to cultures that address sexuality in ways far different from organized Western religions and have little motivation to recognize the drastic transformations religious sexual values have undergone from early biblical times. Looking through the lens of prevailing Western Greco-Roman religions, through which a Westerner is unaware he/she peers, a clinician is likely to conclude that the core of religiosity is founded in asceticism. However, as we shall see, this conclusion is not warranted by the facts; what the casual conclusion reflects is the effect of the lens itself.

Francoeur (1991) has developed a convenient model for illustrating the wide diversity within even similar theological orientations with regard to sexuality. Within this framework, type "A" theologies are those that approach sexuality as dangerous, requiring the assistance of religion for *control*; in contrast, type "B" doctrines consider sexuality basically positive, and religion assists in bringing forth its fullest expression (Table17.1).

In order to understand the way in which scholars, laity, and even clergy could develop the notion of religion being inherently antisexual, we will

Table 17.1
Type "A" and "B" Sects Across Diverse Religions

RELIGION	TYPE A SECT	TYPE B SECT
Roman Catholic	Act-oriented natural law/divine order ethics expressed in formal Vatican pronouncements	A person-oriented, evolving ethic expressed by many contemporary theologians and the 1977 Catholic Theological Society of America study of human sexuality
Protestant Nominalism	Fundamentalism based on a literal interpretation of the Bible, as endorsed by the Moral Majority and the religious New Right; Seventh Day Adventists, Jehovah's Witnesses, Church of Latter Day Saints	An ethic based on the covenant announced between Jesus and humankind; examples in the 1970 United Presbyterian work-study document on Sexuality and the Human Community; Unitarian/Universalists, The Society of Friends
Humanism	Stoicism and epicurean asceticism	Situational ethics, e.g., the 1976 American Humanist Association's "A New Bill of Sexual Rights and Responsibilities"
Judaism	Orthodox and Hassidic concern for strict observation of the Torah and Talmudic prescriptions	Liberal and reformed reading of the Torah and Talmud
Hinduism	Ascetic tradition of monks with world-denying sexual abstinence; Yoga	Sacramental view of sex with worship of male lingam and female yoni; the Kama Sutra
Buddhism	Ascetic tradition of monks with sexual abstinence	Tantric traditions in which sexual relations are a path to divine union

From Francoeur (1991).

briefly track the evolution of sexual dogma in Western culture. At various points in this chapter, we will refer to notion of type "A" and "B" religious sects. Much of this discussion will concern Christianity, and perhaps type "A" and "B" sects may readily come to mind. However, Judaism, Islam, and even Eastern religions have sects demonstrating both the type "A" and "B" orientations to sexuality:

> While Hindu asceticism is practiced for life by a minority, most Hindus view sex, like material gain, as something to be enjoyed in moderation, without repression or over-indulgence. Sacred writings, devotional poetry, and annual festivals celebrate married love, the fidelity of women, and the religious power of sexual union. Typical of the natural approach Hinduism takes to sexuality is the report of Abbe Dubois (Rev. 53, 92) after he encountered a wedding procession whose highlight was a beautifully ornamented mechanized statute of a nude god having intercourse with a goddess. (Francoeur, 1991, p. 16)

Buddhism, Confucianism, and Taoism also display type "A" and "B" approaches.

> Following the Taoist principles outlined in the seventh century A.D. Art of Love, the goal of life is to cultivate sexual energy and unite Yin and Yang in every aspect of daily life. In sexual play these powers are aroused and in orgasm they are released from the body, passing into the partner of the other sex. The mutual exchange of Yin and Yang essences is believed to produce perfect harmony, increase vigor, and bring long life. (Francoeur, 1991, p. 19)

To put the subsequent discussion of Western religions in context, we should remember that Eastern and Western theological traditions differ greatly in the way that sex and transcendence are integrated. Even type "A" Eastern philosophies talk about natural disharmonies and tensions rather than original sin; in type "B" sects physical sensual pleasure (*bhoga*) is one of several paths to liberation and the union of the individual with the universal, and sexual relations are considered a path to integration and expanded cosmic awareness. Francoeur (1990) notes that Eastern views commonly celebrate sexual pleasure as a value in its own right, to be enjoyed for what it brings the participants; Kama, "the pursuit of love of pleasure, both sensual and aesthetic," is one of the four goals of life in the Hindu tradition.

In marked contrast to this is the notion of original sin in Western Christendom; Francoeur (1990) refers to this as the *monster in the groin* view of sexuality.

In the East, transcendence of human limitations and mortality is achieved by integration and increased awareness of the totality of . . . sexual and mental experiences. In Western Christian mythology, sex is a barrier to be overcome. In Christianity, humans are urged to transcend their mortality and achieve salvation by redemption and ascetic denial of the senses, especially the sexual impulses. (1990, p. 7)

Francoeur (1987a, 1991) has applied the "A" and "B" topology to wide variations of values, sexual and otherwise, within Christian doctrine (Table 17.2). A similar table of diversity could be constructed for Judaic and Islamic religious traditions.

Type "A" doctrines emphasize autocratic external (male) authority and a *sense of self-worth that is internalized from others*; creation has stopped, according to this view, and the Bible is best understood through traditional and fundamentalist interpretations. Type "B" theologies, in contrast, emphasize internal control and an autonomous sense of self developed through self-examination; God's plan is an ongoing evolution, requiring reinterpretation of the Bible in light of new understandings.

The emphasis on *becoming* and *emerging*, rather than *obeying*, is characteristic of *"process theology,"* a type "B" form of Christianity particularly compatible with the models of intimacy and sexuality developed in previous chapters of this book. Simmons (1987) characterizes the main points of process theology, as advanced by Alfred North Whitehead, as follows:

- God is the Creator whose very being is revealed through evolution and who, in turn, is affected by the processes of history and nature. God is both Being and becoming, since men and women effect and participate in God's future.
- God is love and His love is revealed in scientific perspectives of natural processes. Biology, psychology, anthropology, and phenomenological experience provide understanding of Scriptural insights regarding the power and the possibilities of love and sexuality. For example, spirituality, differentiation, object relations, and systemic processes are all subsystems of the grand system of human existence, and are manifestations of consciousness that Edelman (1989) demonstrated were rooted in evolutionary biological processes.
- Reality is in-process. Subjective consciousness and objective reality are integral rather than disparate. Consciousness, at least at extremely elementary levels, is present in all living things with each being affecting and being affected by the other. Psychosomatic wholeness (in

Table 17.2
Comparison of Sexual Values Derived From Two Distinct World Views Within the Christian Tradition

DIMENSION	TYPE "A" THEOLOGIES	TYPE "B" THEOLOGIES
Basic Vision	COSMOS – A finished universe.	COSMOGENESIS – An evolving universe.
Topology	Like the universe, humankind is created perfect and complete in the beginning. Theological understanding of humans emphasizes Adam.	Like the universe, humankind is incomplete and not yet fully formed. Theological emphasis has shifted to The Adam, Christ, at the end of time.
Origin of Evil	Evil results from primeval "fall" of a perfect couple who introduce moral and physical evil into a paradisiacal world.	Evil is a natural part of a finite creation, growth, and the birth pains involved in our groping as imperfect humans struggling for the fullness of creation.
Solution to the Problem of Evil	Redemption by identification with the crucified Savior. Asceticism, mortification.	Identification with The Adam, the resurrected but still fully human transfigured Christ. Re-creation, growth.
Authority System	Patriarchal and sexist. Male dominated and ruled. Autocratic hierarchy controls power and all decisions; clergy vs. laity.	Egalitarian – "In his kingdom there is neither male nor female, freeman or slave, Jew or Roman."
Concept of Truth	Emphasis on one true Church as sole possessor of all truth.	Recognition that other churches and religions possess different perspectives of truth, with some elements of revelation clearer in them than in the one true Church.
Biblical Orientation	Fundamentalist, evangelical, word-for-word, black-and-white clarity. Revelation has ended.	Emphasizes ongoing revelation and reincarnation of perennial truths and values as humans participate in the creation process.
Liturgical Focus	Redemption and Good Friday, Purgatory, Supernatural.	Easter and the creation, challenge of incarnation. Epiphany of numinous cosmos.
Social Structure	Gender roles clearly assigned with high definition of proper roles for men and women.	There being neither male nor female in Christ, gender roles are flexible, including women priests and ministers.

(continued)

Table 17.2
Continued

DIMENSION	TYPE "A" THEOLOGIES	TYPE "B" THEOLOGIES
Ecological Morality	Humans are stewards of the earth, given dominion by God over all creation.	Emphasis on personal responsibility in an ongoing creation/incarnation.
Self-Image	Carefully limited; isolationist, exclusive, Isaiah's "remnant." Sects.	Inclusive, ecumenical, catalytic leader among equals.
Goal	Supernatural transcendence of nature.	Unveiling. Revelation of divine in all.
Human Morality	Emphasis on laws and conformity of actions to these laws.	Emphasis on persons and their interrelationships. We create the human of the future and the future of humanity.
Sexual Morality	The "monster in the groins that must be restrained."	A positive, natural, creative energy in our being as sexual (embodied) persons. "Knowing," Communion.
	Justified in marriage for procreation.	An essential element in our personality, in all relationships.
	Genital reductionism.	Diffused, degenitalized sensual embodiment.
	Heterosexual/monogamous.	"Polymorphic perversity."
	Noncoital sex is unnatural, disordered.	Noncoital sex can express the incarnation of Christian love.
	Contraceptive love is unnatural and disordered.	Contraception can be just as creative and life-serving as reproductive love.
	Monolithic-celibate or reproductive-marital sexuality.	Pluralistic-sexual persons must learn to incarnate agape in all their relationships, primary and secondary, genital and nongenital, intimate and passing.

From Francoeur (1990).

which reason, emotion, and judgment are grounded in, and conditioned by, physiological processes) is the working model of being human. Body-soul dualism is rejected.

- Sexuality is integral to biological, psychological, and spiritual wholeness. Personal identity and the ego itself are distinctively sexual. Sex is neither disparaged nor glorified, but cherished and experienced in distinctively human dimensions. Asceticism is inconsistent with the needs of human nature, and celibacy is a lifestyle in which one fruitful and natural kind of experience is renounced for the sake of service to God and neighbor.

According to the *monarchical principle* of process theology, God is love and people's inherent capacity for love, developed through evolution, organizes human existence. Love is seen as the highest response of which any creature is capable, the highest moral achievement which makes community possible. Love is the moral norm by which sexual acts are measured, characterized by several features: (a) investment in the partner as an individual rather than solely as a means of sexual gratification; (b) fidelity to promises and agreements; (c) mutual interest in types of sexual play; (d) noninjury to the partner; and (e) responsibility for one's actions and for the well-being of the partner.

Process theology sexual ethics don't lapse into "anything goes" morality: Self-control and freedom are equally valued. Love requires constraint in sexual attitudes and actions if sex is to serve the purposes of love and not be a destructive force in the person's life. Sexual decisions are important because they may enhance or thwart personal development; people can develop the capacity to love as intended or can become unloving and thus fall short of God's intention. Both type A and B doctrines maintain concern for the "significant other" (the partner, the family and society) with regard to sexual conduct; they represent diverse approaches to the way that concern is developed and maintained.

Type B theologies are more supportive of the crucial importance of differentiation in human sexual and nonsexual development. This is not to encourage clinicians to indoctrinate patients in type B theology. Instead, this discussion should clarify the relative ease or discomfort particular patients may have in integrating the notion of the use of sexuality as a vehicle for human development.

Over the centuries, rigid authoritarian type A Christianity has become more like itself, giving rise to social problems (both historical and current) and alienating churchgoers to the extent that its own validity and relevance has been severely questioned. In the process, it has provided an ironic and striking demonstration of the importance of the type B emphasis on *becoming*.

As mentioned previously, inherent paradox sometimes becomes evident by simply collapsing time perspectives; this is the perspective that type A Scholasticism[1] lacked. Scholasticism produced unnoticed problems for itself which surfaced in three areas: (a) the nature of *grace*, (b) the relationship between God and the mortal world (i.e., nature), and (c) the relationship between God and the individual.[2]

Over the centuries, type A theologians emphasized *created* grace (i.e., justifying one's otherwise worthless existence through good acts as specified by the authority of the autocratic Chruch). Created grace was an entity in itself, through which people entered into a new relationship with God; this is commonly known as "letting God into one's life" which involves an entitative or ontological change in the human person (Haight, 1979). Theological problems eventually arose from ignoring the concept of an indwelling God as the ultimate root of man's value and validity.

> In so doing [Scholasticism] seemed to subordinate God's presence to existence; his indwelling, to this created change in a person's being. The problem, however, is that Scripture (especially Paul and John) seems to contradict this. There grace appears as first and foremost a communication of the personal Spirit of God who thus becomes present to human being[s] personally. The created effect within a person is precisely an effect or consequence of this indwelling and not the other way around. (Haight, 1979, p. 122)

While these differences may seem pedantic at first glance, they have vital importance for people seeking to integrate sexuality and spirituality. Momentarily we will examine the way in which this failed to happen in the evolution of Western culture and religion. It warrants outlining these issues (and how a twentieth-century type B theologian resolved them) to facilitate understanding the multisystemic impact of type A theologies for the last nineteen centuries.

The flaws in type A theologies surface around the *boundary* or interface between daily life (i.e., *nature*) and the spiritual plane (i.e., *supra-nature*[3]). In stressing the clear distinction between the natural and supernatural orders, Scholasticism viewed these two orders as separate and self-enclosed spheres of reality. Divine providence was viewed as *extrinsic* to daily life and nature.

---

[1]*Scholasticism* refers to the system of theology and philosphy of medieval university scholars from the tenth to the fifteen centuries, based upon Aristotelian logic and writings of the early Christian fathers; it is characterized by insistence upon traditional doctrines and methods.

[2]Haight (1979) gives an articulate explanation of the issues involved; much of this immediate discussion follows her analysis.

[3]Rahner's term was *supernatural*, although he did not use it in the sense of occult or magic.

In this view the supernatural order of revelation and grace is conceived of as being imposed on the human existence by an external decree of God, completely from outside nature, outside history, outside human experience. The connection of this religious sphere to a person's life is essentially one of authority and obedience. The apologetic and religious consequences of this view are most significant. If the human person is completely at home in the self-enclosed natural world, there is no reason or need why one should look for or be interested in a revelation. And should such a religious revelation be accepted, it will appear as a disturbance of our natural life and external force binding our freedom. Such a supernatural revelation will be completely unintelligible, but blindly obeyed, because it will respond to no need or desire grounded in natural experience and life in this world. (Haight, 1979, p. 125)

In Scholastic type A theologies, nature and grace are separate. Grace and the spiritual realm do not enter into human psychological experience, and have no part in a person's everyday experience of concrete living. There is heaven and there is earth, but there is no heaven-on-earth. Nature and grace (i.e., the supernatural) are minimally interpenetrating layers of reality (Haight, 1979).

The problems created by Scholastic dogma were addressed and resolved within Christian theology by Karl Rahner (1939/1968, 1941/1969, 1961). Haight (1979) suggests that Rahner is probably *the* leading figure in theology of the thirties, forties, and fifties to whom the new freedom and renaissance of Catholic theology can be attributed. Rahner bridged the dualism of Scholasticism (type A) by replacing it with an ontological one (remarkably similar to that of Maturana and Varela (1987)).

To Rahner (1961), (a) nature and the supernatural are distinct, but inextricably intertwined and interpenetrating, (b) spirit and matter are inseparable, and (c) grace is an intrinsic (vs. Scholasticism's extrinsic) part of human reality, even while remaining radically distinct from it. In *Hearers of the Word*, Rahner (1941/1969) sees human existence as fundamentally oriented toward God, and that God *is known* by living life and understanding history. Rahner offers a type B resolution of the type A problem, dealing with both the boundary issues of grace and spiritual plane:

Rahner's view of the experience of grace is a corollary of the theory of the supernatural existential. In brief, he says, first, that grace is experienced, but not as grace; it is indistinguishable from the stirrings of the transcendence of the human spirit. And, second, a person's experience of the supernatural call and address of God is never a perception or grasp of an object; grace appears rather as an unthematic horizon of transcendence. (Haight, 1979, pp. 126–127)

Rahner (1961) suggested that the ability to receive grace is an active quest, rather than a passive recipientship; in so doing we encounter the first echoes of a relationship between desire and grace which we will encounter in depth later in this chapter. *This is a critical step in the integration of sexuality and spirituality, for, as we shall see, Christianity has systematically set out to destroy sexual desire.* Desire or need in daily life was seen by Rahner as a call to salavation; while not a "saving grace," it was still a supernatural grace:

> The brilliance of Rahner's construction here is that it allows one to overcome extrinsicism and to view concrete nature as having an inner desire and need for the supernatural. All he adds is that this inner exigency is itself a gift of grace. (Haight, 1979, pp. 125–126)

According to Rahner's type B viewpoint, the primary meaning of grace is God's presence dwelling within people, giving life an intrinsic rather than extrinsic value, in much the same way that Martin Luther argued for. God's relationship with people is far more individually directed because that is where God dwells, available to the awareness of any human.

Rahner (1961) also clarifies other type A vs. type B differences in relationship-with-God. In type A, contact is intermittent; in Rahner's view, it is constant. In type A, there is often the unavowed view that "grace would no longer be grace if it were too generously distributed by the love of God! (Haight, 1979, p. 129)." In type B, there is more than enough for everyone, available through the relationship-with-self.

The problems of type A theology that Rahner (1939/1968, 1961) addressed implicitly involved *boundary issues* (i.e., the interface between God and people). As we shall see later in this chapter, Rahner suggests that *boundary experiences* (e.g., between people, or between people and life) are the crucible of transcendence and personal development wherein people experience grace in the concrete situations of daily life. Certainly, he demonstrates that they were the crucible of development for type A theology, which has been slow to rise to the occasion. When we return to integrate sexuality and spirituality, we shall find that the boundary experiences we repeatedly encountered in marital life (within the sexual crucible) are exactly the same boundary experiences which provide the portal of spirituality. First, however, we will examine how these issues have played out through the evolution of western civilization, in the arena of theology and sexuality.

THE EVOLUTION OF SEXUAL PHILOSOPHY
IN WESTERN RELIGIONS

Awareness of the variability of sexual theology in Western culture from biblical to modern times is conspicuously absent from contemporary society. Raymond J. Lawrence, Jr. (1989) suggests that this omission and widespread conflicts about Western sexual values are no coincidence. He proposes that these developments arise from the dualistic foundation of a powerfully sex-affirming Hebraic biblical tradition fused with the deeply sex-suspicious Greco-Roman tradition that later achieved ascendancy in Christianity. Lawrence documents the substance of this position in *The Poisoning of Eros* (1989), from which I have drawn heavily in this section. He writes:

> Popular opinion holds that Christianity brought a new sex ethics of chastity to a debauched Greco-Roman world. Michel Foucault and others have already shown the error of that opinion. The conflict was not between the orgiastic classical pagan culture and the chaste church, but between a sex-affirming Hebraic and a sex-negating Greco-Roman culture. Furthermore, that conflict has been brought forward into the present through the strange marriage of Christendom's baptized platonist ideology and its venerated Hebrew scriptures. (p. 1)

Ranke-Heinemann's (1990) *Eunuchs for the Kingdom of Heaven* notes that sexual abstinence existed in pagan cultures based on *medical considerations*; she cites the writings of Pythagoras (sixth century B.C.) and Hippocrates (fourth century, B.C.) as examples. She suggests that what Christianity brought was a *hatred of pleasure*, having its roots in Greek Stoicism (300 B.C. to 250 A.D.).

Sexual passion was not a sin in the Old Testament. From the Song of Solomon (7:6–10) we hear:

> How fair, how pleasant you are!
>
> O Love, daughter of delights,
> Your stature resembles the palm,
> Your breasts the cluster.
>
> Me thinks I'll climb the palm,
> I'll grasp its branches.
>
> Let your breasts be like grape cluster,
> The scent of your vulva like apples,
> Your palate like the best wine
> Flowing (for my love) smoothly,
> Stirring sleepers' lips.

I belong to my beloved,
And for me is her desire.

Within Judaism, sexual asceticism was never seen as a religious value; Rabbi Abba Aricha (c. 175–247) is quoted in the Jewish Talmud as saying "Man will have to render an account to God for all the good things which his eyes beheld but which he refused to enjoy" (Jerusalem Talmud, Qiddushin 4:12). Sebastian Moore, whom we will encounter later in this chapter, writes:

> Rabbi Akiba, the remaker of Judaism after the trauma of its break with its Christian progeny, called the Song of Songs the holiest book of the Bible, "the holy of holies." And according to a story in the Talmud, he was the only rabbi to see God in this life and survive. Shorthand: the only teacher who saw God and survived got sex straight! (1989, p. 11)

Minimum frequency of intercourse a Jewish man was expected to provide his spouse (depending upon the degree of manual labor of his avocation) was prescribed by religious text. Soldiers who might be traveling far from home were given leaves of absence from their sexual responsibilities. Jews were encouraged to copulate on the Sabbath because it was favored by God. Sexual intercourse was seen as a religious duty and a blessing, valued for the joy and pleasure of it even when procreation was impossible.

For sake of contrast, consider that abstinence from intercourse was superior even when procreation in marriage was possible in later Christian sexual theology. Christian medieval moralists argued that the Lord absents himself during copulation, and for various reasons encouraged abstinence from Thursday through Monday (especially Sunday), all feast days, for a month preceding Easter, Pentecost, and Christmas, several days prior to receiving the Eucharist, and the entire course of pregnancy. Married Christians often took communion only at the time of feasts, since they had to abstain from sex anyway; periods of prescribed abstinence often added up to a *minimum* of five months, causing the faithful to complain there wasn't much opportunity left over. Intercourse was also banned during menstruation, pregnancy, and wet nursing, making opportunities even slimmer.

Jews and Christians could both look forward to sex in heaven. The Christian's sexual liaisons, however, were going to be totally devoid of sexual desire or passion; intercourse and orgasm had no place there. Angels multiply without marriage and sexual reproduction. There had been no male and female "animal nature" in Paradise, either. Adam and Eve never had intercourse before "The Fall," according to Gregory (first century A.D.). Sexuality was

God's afterthought when he realized Adam and Eve wouldn't pass the test. Men and women being created "in God's image," was interpreted to mean "human nature without sexual differences."

The Rise of Christianity

With the rise of Christendom, interpretation of the Old Testament was given a new twist when read through the lens of platonism. The result, Lawrence suggests, was a distortion of Hebraic sexual ethics and an institutionalization of a pathogenic dualism that has existed until the present time. This dualism was the result of superficial acceptance, if not exhortation, of human sexuality as a gift from God; in theory, sexuality was something wondrous and beautiful (under prescribed circumstances), a reflection of God's wisdom and perfection.

Early Christian writers struggled to reconcile exaltation of virginity, celibacy and perfect chastity with sanctification of marital sexuality and childbearing, in the context of functional deprecation of sexuality. The result was a religious inherent paradox that shaped the course of Western civilization. Tertullian (A.D. 160–230) attempted to bridge the conflict by suggesting that a woman was a temple built over a sewer. Origen (A.D. 185–254), the most notable church father before Augustine, solved the dilemma by castrating himself (Money, 1985).[4] Origen's hatred of sexual desire led him to argue that Lot's daughters (who had incest with their father in order to conceive) were not as sinful as wives who had intercourse with their husbands out of "lust" (Ranke-Heinemann, 1990).

Compartmentalized sexual dualism is also apparent in the ambiguous messages and personal images of Christianity's most central figures. No less a personage than Albert Schweitzer joined the attempts to understand Jesus-the-man (as distinct from Jesus-the-Savior) which began in the age of Enlightenment and have continued ever since. In his prodigious *The Quest for the Historical Jesus*, Schweitzer (1906/1968) summarizes the myriad attempts to piece together the details of Jesus' life. Such efforts stemmed from a struggle to escape the tyranny of dogma, he notes, rather than purely historical interest;

---

[4]"There are eunuchs born from their mother's womb, there are eunuchs made so by human agency and there are eunuchs who have made themselves so for the sake of the kingdom of Heaven (Matthew 19:12)."

dogma did away with any reason to study the life of Jesus, providing instead a supra-mundane Jesus.[5]

Lawrence cites the research of other biblical scholars, as well as his own extensive work, suggesting that neither Paul nor Jesus was celibate; Ranke-Heinemann (1990) also provides additional support. In addition to numerous biblical citations, the presumption of celibacy is contradicted by what he and other theologians regard as strong circumstantial evidence to the contrary: (a) Jesus was probably in his fifties and at least his late thirties when executed; (b) he was a Jew raised in a polygamous Hebraic culture which expected men to marry at 18 and socially criticized or penalized them if not married by age 20; and (c) religious leaders in Hebraic culture were expected to marry and remain sexually active (all rabbis except one were married). Schweitzer (1906/1968) notes that Jesus was conservative in most things, including retaining the ritual worship of the God of Israel as sacred; this included attending synagogue, the scene of his earliest preaching.

It is ironic that the power of Lawrence's observation of Christianity's dualistic anti-sexual view is brought home not by his biblical arguments of Jesus' sexual activity but rather by our difficulty in even tolerating the question. If one has difficulty tolerating the imagery of one's parents' engaging in loving and intensely erotic sexual union, the very notion of a sexually active Jesus creates cognitive dissonance of a significantly greater magnitude. One might think that the ability to accept the sexuality and eroticism of Jesus might be Christendom's important contribution towards fostering acceptance of healthy family sexuality; unfortunately, Christianity's historical sexual dualism has precluded such a move.

Even people who have not been raised in a Christian religious background may experience some discomfort entertaining the very notion of Jesus as a Jewish man with genitals. The moment that you feel the imagery or the very proposition discussed above is blasphemous, debasing, or belittling of Jesus, you have elicited the *emotional* reality of seeing sex as demeaning and chastity as somehow a "higher" spiritual plane. If you feel that Jesus was "too pure" to

---

[5]Many secular scholars who studied the life of Jesus suffered broken careers. " . . . resolved as they were to open the way even with the seeming blasphemy," wrote Schweitzer, it was worse for priests who attempted the same. "The others, those who tried to bring Jesus to life at the call of love, found it a cruel task to be honest. The critical study of the life of Jesus has been for theology a school of honesty. The world has never seen before, and will never see again, a struggle for truth so full of pain and renunciation as that of which the Lives of Jesus of the last hundred years contain the cryptic record (p. 5)."

engage in sex or that he would have been "less pure" if he did, you have elicited the emotional reality that sex is dirty.

The point is lost if we get stuck pondering the question of whether or not Jesus actually was sexually active. The reality of sexual dualism becomes apparent in even considering the issue of *impulse*. What if Jesus was "above" having sex; did he ever struggle with hot sweaty imagery of someone he found sexually attractive? Did he make a furtive attempt at relieving himself through masturbation, even though it was proscribed by Jewish tradition and his own tenets? If Jesus' genitals and his impulses diminish his greatness, then how is a mere mortal to come to grips with his or her own sexuality?

Many others have had difficulty reconciling these issues. Pope Siricius (fourth century A.D.) promoted the view of a joyless Jesus who took no pleasure in the redemption process, and who would have chosen another mother to be born to if Mary had taken pleasure in giving birth to him. Jovian was one of the first in the Church to openly question Mary's virginity: He agreed that Mary may have *conceived* Jesus as a virgin, but suggested that she was not a virgin at *delivery* because her hymen did not remain intact. Jovian's biologically reasonable position was outrageous to pious ears (then and now)—he was excommunicated in 391 (Ranke-Heinemann, 1990).

But the issue of Mary's virginity illustrates Schweitzer's observation of repression-by-dogma; it potentially obviates the point of this discussion. More importantly, did Mary have sex with Joseph *after* she gave birth? Did she moan? Was she multiply orgasmic? Demetria Martinez writes in the *National Catholic Reporter*: "How did Mary feel during her pregnancy? What does it mean that the mother of God menstruated? Did Jesus enjoy eating? Did he feel sexual desire? The degree to which we flinch at these questions is a measure of how great the gulf is between faith and flesh (Martinez, 1991, p. 25)."

At this point, many individuals are tempted to retreat into recitation of the dogma that Jesus, as the Son of God, (or Mary) was above such impulses. But in so doing, two things occur. First, there is the sense of one's liturgy being under attack; in point of fact, all that is being addressed is the inherent dualism of sex being beautiful but sexual eroticism being base. Second, one retreats to a position from which the dogma becomes self-validating, but humans with human sexuality become invalidated.

Schweitzer (1906/1968) documented the easy way out of this dilemma: accuse an author who raises such issues of attempting to tarnish Jesus' image. Another might be to suggest that such an author obviously does not accept Jesus as the Messiah. The point here is that no disrespect is intended, and that tarnish is in the eye and the unconscious dualism of the beholder. The issue is not whether Jesus was the Messiah, but rather whether he would be less a Messiah if he had sexual impulses or had acted on them. What actually comes into question is not the validity of Jesus or his teachings, but rather the validity of the de-eroticized sexual dualism perpetuated from Augustine's time.

Whether Jesus is understood through the view of the Vatican or of dissident theologians, *any conceivable viewpoint accords Jesus the status of being one of the greatest, if not the greatest, spiritual leader and visionaries of all time*. His life, recorded by both disciples and foes, represents one of the *superlative* acts of self-differentiation from his prevailing culture. Jesus' crucifixion, in fact, was the punishment for his differentiation. But the notion of Jesus as the greatest man of all time is not enough to shore up the underlying antisexual viewpoint of Greco-Roman Christianity; the very notion of Jesus as a *man* who might have tasted the wonders of sexuality even once is intolerable. It clashes head on with the compartmentalized Christmas-time "babe in the manger" view of Jesus, totally devoid of eroticism and sexuality. And it is in this clash, this crucible of Jesus' image, that the inherent paradox of Christianity's sexual dualism is experienced. While worship of the Blessed Virgin has great significance to many people, it simultaneously casts sexually active married women in a disparaging light.

Ranke-Heinemann noted the impact on men and women, stating, "Face to face with a Lord of a Church who no longer reveals God's nearness to men and women and his compassion for them, because he has been made into the listless and lust-hating Christ of the bedroom inspectors and conjugal police, a person can no longer recognize himself as someone whom God loves, but only as someone who is impure and worthy of damnation" (1990, pp. 6–7).

Is it any wonder that so many people have difficulty integrating their spirituality and sexuality, when the image of our spiritual icons being sexually engaged is blasphemous? Is it a sign of individual pathology, or rather the reflection of pathogenic sexual dualism, when during church services a parishioner becomes both horrified by and preoccupied with his/her sexual fantasies of the saints? In Hinduism, for example, genital representations are visually prominent within temples, and their bible is replete with tales of the gods' sexual exploits and adventures. Yet Hinduism does not advocate promiscuity or temple orgies; women traditionally veil their faces and modesty is valued. Such customs stem from the *acceptance* of an ever present human sexuality, rather than the compartmentalization and rejection of it as sinful.

Augustine

In the 400 years between Jesus and Augustine, the Hebraic sex-positive view of sex was gradually rejected in favor of the sex-negative Greek philosophies of stoicism and gnosticism, which renounced sexual passion and erotic pleasure. Except for procreation, sex was quickly made a sin; joy and pleasure in sex even within marriage were considered antithetical to God's will. Intercourse was to be done at night in conjunction with preparation for sleep rather than intermixed with other daily activities.

When the Roman emperor Constantine adopted Christianity, it abruptly shifted from counterculture to mainstream religious dogma and was integrated into the social hierarchy. By the fourth century, Ambrose, Jerome, and Augustine established the ideal of virginity and sexual purity as the highest of Christian virtues. Jerome wrote that all sex was impure; he accepted marital intercourse because it produced new virgins. "Though God can do all things," Jerome wrote, "He cannot raise a virgin after she has fallen (Epistles 22)."

> Holy virginity is a better thing than conjugal chastity. . . . A mother will hold a lesser place in the kingdom of heaven, because she has been married, than the daughter, seeing that she is a virgin. . . . But if thy mother has been humble and not proud, she will have some sort of place, but not thine. (Jerome, in Seldes, 1985, p. 210)

Augustine, however, was the central architect of the sexual credo most identified with Western Christendom. Baker (1987) wrote of Augustine:

> The puritanical elements in Christian thought, although firmly grounded in St. Paul's Epistles, might never have become so prominent had it not been for the work of the Bishop of Hippo, St. Augustine (A.D. 354–430). For Augustine, and indeed, for all philosophical puritans, puritanism has little to do with sexuality, per se; it really concerns the proper relationship between mind/soul and body. At the heart of the theory lies the perception that one's moral stature and value as a human being is a function of the mind's ability to control the body. (p. 95)

Augustine perceived humans, and human sexuality, to be base and primitive in nature; it was only the unique capacity of "will" that made men and women superior "unnatural" animals. Thus, to be fully human and spiritual was to be at war with oneself (one's sexual impulses). "Succumbing" to "lust" devalued the gift of rationality and reduced men and women to the moral stature of barnyard animals. Augustine decreed that a baby was guilty of original sin because of the depraved nature of intercourse and because entrance to the world occurs "between the feces and the urine."

Lawrence (1989) clarifies the often-cited notion that intercourse was acceptable for procreative purposes within the confines of marriage; more accurately, it was at best *tolerated* in that limited context. In no case was marital copulation to be accompanied by the chaos of sexual passion. Augustine suggested marriage was improved by the speed with which spouses mutually consented to refrain from intercourse; continence from coitus was altogether superior to procreation, and other sexual variants that did not lead to procreation were proscribed. He briefly considered whether a faithless but celibate person was superior to one who was devoutly religious and married.

Augustine also *encouraged* the development of low sexual desire: demanding marital sex out of lust was a venial sin, whereas responding to such demands by performing intercourse without desire or arousal was not.[6] In Augustine's view, intercourse *without pleasure* had occurred in Eden before "The Fall."[7] Devoting an entire chapter of *The City of God* to the argument that man could fully control his organs in Paradise, Augustine suggested that man could have intercourse without pleasure in the same way that some people can wiggle their ears independently and regurgitate at will (Ranke-Heinemann, 1990).

It one asks him/herself why someone would want to marry at all under these conditions, the inherent paradox of a religion that also promoted marriage as a sacrament surfaces. The price for Augustine's saving mankind from itself was a theology that deliberately attempted to *create inhibited sexual desire*. In many people's minds, the Augustinian sexual ethic represents the epitome of Christian views of sexuality. For just that reason, many people have turned away from Christianity as a resource for integrating spiritual development with sexual behavior.

It is interesting to note that while Jesus' triumph of differentiation led to the creation of Christianity, Augustine's legacy (often accorded the weight of scripture) actually involved differentiating himself from the existent church hierarchy. Likewise, his personal life is a clinical study of differentiation from

---

[6]Subsequently, theologians argued whether a man's sin was greater with a beautiful woman or with an ugly one. One twelfth-century scholar suggested that sex with a beautiful woman was the greater sin because it gave more delight — and more pleasure was a greater sin. Another argued the converse, blaming women as the temptress of men: A man more compelled by a woman's beauty was less responsible, and hence, sinned less (Ranke-Heinemann, 1990).

[7]Augustine's logic was basically misogynistic: He argued that intercourse must have occurred in Paradise because there had to be *something* that woman offered man. He was certain that it could not have been companionship or intellectual conversation (Ranke-Heinemann, 1990).

his own mother, a topic that has received considerable attention from religious scholars. Lawrence notes that Augustine was so enmeshed with his intrusive, ambitious mother that he had to lie to her in order to escape from North Africa to Italy; she followed him there two years later. Soon after she arrived, Augustine abandoned his mistress of 14 years by whom he had a son.[8] Augustine then acceded to pressure from his mother and the church hierarchy and became engaged to a young and socially prominent heiress his mother selected to improve his social standing. Shortly thereafter, his mother moved in and kept house for Augustine and his son; she died a few months later. In the subsequent two years, Augustine was in a crucible of his own, primed to enter both a privileged social class and a prideful, increasingly self-serving clerical hierarchy he abhorred.

Augustine took another mistress during this time. He became more engrossed in Neoplatonic philosophy's strong Gnostic rejection of physical pleasure, seeking to transcend earthly issues to a remote spiritual plane somewhere "above." He eventually broke off the engagement, leaving Italy to join a monastery in Palestine.

This final outcome may reflect Augustine's belated attempt to differentiate himself from both his mother and an elitist imperial religious social order. Augustine's ecclesiastical emphasis on celibacy and his identification of sex with sin reflected, according to Lawrence, not only a renunciation of personal genital gratification but also a renunciation of contemporary Roman Catholic society. Augustine was not unilaterally focused on obliteration of sensuality and sexual desire; he was driven by a vision of society in which men and women renounced their individual agendas and pleasures in lieu of creating a community of love that included the have-nots.[9] The full negative legacy of Augustine's reversal from the Hebraic traditions required another 600 years to blossom; fully 200 violent years would be devoted in the Middle Ages to enforcing chastity, clerical celibacy, and monasticism.

One impact of this legacy is evident in the Penitence lists developed for the Church of England (and elsewhere). In the list drawn up by Theodore (c. 700, who later became Archbishop of Canterbury), premeditated murder

---

[8]Augustine practiced (rhythm) contraception, his son supposedly being a miscalculation. He became a fanatic against contraception upon his conversion. Paradoxically, "test-tube babies" produced by artificial insemination are banned by the Vatican, while actually embodying Augustine's ideal of conception without physical pleasure (Ranke-Heinemann, 1990).

[9]Ranke-Heinemann (1990), in contrast, describes Augustine as the man who fused Christianity into a systematic unity based on a hatred of pleasure, creating a fifteen-hundred-year-long anxiety-provoking hostility towards sex.

required seven years penitence, abortion necessitated 120 days, and oral sex required seven years, 15 years, or a lifetime of penitence. In another of his works, anal intercourse received 15 years penitence. This balance of punishment was maintained in other penitential lists. The thirteenth-century *Codex Latinus Monacensis 22233* stated that a wife's agreement to deviate from missionary positon coitus was as serious a sin as murder. Rear entry intercourse was permitted for medical reasons (e.g., obesity), as long as it was done with "pain in the soul" (Ranke-Heinemann, 1990).

The Middle Ages and Thomas Aquinas

Andre Lorde (1987) writes that attempts to separate the spiritual and the erotic reduce spirituality to a world of flattened affect—a world of the ascetic who aspires to feel nothing. The ascetic position, she believes, represents the highest fear and gravest immobility. The severe abstinence of the ascetic which has dominated Western culture and theology is not about self-discipline, she suggests, but rather, self-abnegation. While she argues that these remain present-day issues, self-abnegation was certainly what the Middle Ages were all about.

The obsession with salvation through sexual purity progressed within the church from Augustine through the subsequent eleven hundred years until the reformation triggered by Martin Luther. Vincent of Beauvias' *Speculum Doctrinale*, a manual on moral doctrine, was indicative of the tenor of the times; in it he specified that "a man who loves his wife very much is an adulterer. . . . The upright man should love his wife with his judgment, not his affections" (Money, 1985).

Thomas Aquinas (1225–1274), a Dominican monk, succeeded Augustine as the central author of Catholic sexual doctrine; he generally followed Augustinian doctrine but offered a somewhat more positive view of intercourse within marriage. Baker (1987) writes that Aquinas rejected the puritanical vision of a Creator who would fashion mind and body as eternal adversaries and human nature as a battleground between will and body. Aquinas saw the person as consisting of parts, including mind and body, each of which had specific uses intended by God's plan as revealed in nature. Any use of a part contrary to its intended end was immoral, perverse, and unnatural.

Since the goal of the sexual act was procreation, in Aquinas' view, contraception or masturbation remained unacceptable. He advanced a position of "sexual relationalism" in which marital coitus could be sinless, since concupiscence was compensated for by the good of procreation. Aquinas attempted to affirm sexual pleasure in theory, but was unsuccessful in avoiding the trap of condemning passion and sexual desire as destructive animalistic qualities antithetical to modulation and reason.

The medieval period was one of increasing extremism; rifts developed between celibate and sexually active clergy, and between an entrenched ecclesiastic hierarchy and all who opposed clerical hegemony. Within a Catholic Church that was becoming increasingly powerful as a stabilizing force in the midst of tumultuous geopolitics, the growing monastic movement set the stage for the institutionalization of celibacy and prohibition of clerical marriage. Many clerics, their families, and the general laity did not conform without a bloodbath. The mandate for clerical celibacy was strongly contested enough to split the church, requiring severe repression: In some places, priests were imprisoned for two years, publicly flogged, and then the process repeated.

There is a certain irony that synods of the Inquisition burned countless men and women for supposedly making people impotent or sterile by witchcraft, thereby rendering the conjugal act impossible or reproductively unfruitful! Emerging over a century after the torture-extracted confessions and burnings began, the synods' manual *Hammer of Witches* (1487) closely examined why God had given the devil particular power to bewitch coitus; the answer involved the loathsomeness of intercourse and original sin. There was still, however, the problem of dealing with "magic-induced" erectile dysfunction. In 1207, Pope Innocent III granted marriage dissolution to Philip II Augustus of France for this reason.

The extremism of the sexual purity crusade gave birth to emergence of the Cathar movement (the name deriving from the same Greek word for "clean" from which "catharsis" stems). This movement coincided with the emergence of "romantic" love in the secular world; troubadours (wandering minstrels) introduced the "heartache" notion of romantic love as it is known today. What developed was an image of love so pure that it could be consummated only in death; that is what the Cathars got. While Catharism was a fundamentalist derivative of Augustinian theology, it represented a threat to papal power. The movement itself was crushed, supplanted ideologically in the early 12th century by the naming of marriage as a sacrament and the rise of the cult of the Virgin Mary.

Unfortunately, this did not modify the Church's basic misogynistic orientation, which Ranke-Heinemann (1990) thoroughly documents. Christianity maintained the taboos against sexual contact with women who were menstruating. Women were encouraged to forego Holy Communion during menstruation throughout the Middle Ages; this was also used to keep women from holding office in the Church. Sex during menstruation became a *venial* sin around 1600, retaining its aura of improperness and lack of self-control.

Blood from childbirth, however, was considered more harmful than menstrual blood; thirteenth-century synods held that women had to be "reconciled with the Church" after childbirth before being allowed to reenter. Women who died in childbirth before "reconciliation" were often denied funeral service within the Church and were not buried in consecrated ground.

Martin Luther and Emmanual Kant

In the centuries of the Middle Ages, various individuals emerged within and outside the established clergy who reaffirmed eroticism and the pleasures of sexuality. Generally, they were dealt with harshly. As time wore on, however, even bishops and cardinals kept mistresses and fathered children whom they acknowledged.

With the sixteenth century Reformation led by Martin Luther, there was a return to the Bible as the ultimate authority against the corrupt papal hierarchy; simultaneously and not coincidentally, the Hebraic acceptance of sexual pleasure that had been expurgated was reestablished. Lawrence (1989) describes the Reformation as a defeat for the view of "salvation through sublimation or suppression of the sensuous and the sexual, and a victory for the body and sex and for a religion that affirms both" (1989, p. 170).

In contrast to the view that life was justified only through extreme piety and asceticism, Luther viewed the validation of human existence to be inherent in life itself. He rejected the notion of clerical celibacy as a requirement or as a higher plane of religious life; chastity was a godless vow boasting a superordinate faith. Likewise, the notion that marriage was a sacrament was also rejected.

Luther provided a well documented picture of himself as an earthy, sexually active man, almost startling in his humanness. Lawrence cites Luther as saying, "Nature does not cease to do its work when there is voluntary chastity. . . . To put it bluntly, seed . . . if it does not flow into the flesh will flow into the nightshirt" (Lawrence, 1989, p. 176). This view is consistent with other reports of Luther jesting at clerics who castrated themselves as acts of piety. Luther's own writings have led theologians and psychotherapists (e.g., Erikson, 1958) to conclude that his spiritual turning point (the so-called "tower experience," *Turmerlebnis*) occurred on the Wittenberg monastery toilet.

Within Protestantism, which emerged from Luther's legacy, clergy married; unmarried clergy were viewed with suspicion. Roman Catholicism continued to promote virginity, sexual abstinence, and clerical celibacy. And yet, the religious artwork of the Roman Catholic Counter-Reformation was unabashedly sensual, in marked contrast to the more austere Protestant religious symbols. Protestantism underwent another revision during the Enlightenment, in the personage of Emmanuel Kant (1724–1804). Baker (1987) writes of Kant:

> One of Kant's ambitions was to create a morality, founded in reason, that was entirely independent of presumptions about the nature, or even the existence, of god. While such an ethic necessarily eschewed concepts of sin and redemption, it incorporated, in suitably altered form, many of the concepts of the Christian moral theologians, particularly those of Augustine. Thus, Kant's theory retained the Augustinian idea of the conflict between the mind and body, except that, for Kant, the conflict was played out in terms of the tension between our rational will and our bodily inclinations. This conflict sets one of the major problems that Kantian moral theory addresses: the problem of determining the conditions under which more human interactions are possible. . . .
> For Kant, the primary moral imperative is to treat persons not merely as objects, but as moral subjects, – i.e., as autonomous rational agents, with purposes and projects of their own, who, as moral subjects, deserve the same respect that we would have others accord to ourselves. (p. 99)

The latter part of Kant's philosophy may sound surprisingly like "the golden rule." Kant's primary moral imperative embodied the functioning of a well differentiated individual who can see the partner as more than an extension of his/her own gratification. The concept of differentiation is appropriate in other respects as well: Kant's view of Enlightenment rejected dependence on autocratic clerical authority for guidance in lieu of trusting one's own reason. The Bible was subject to scrutiny and constructive criticism. But tolerance for differentiation existed within strict limits. Masturbation was unacceptable to Kant, as it was to Augustine and Aquinas. Only other-directed sexuality was permitted, albeit for different philosophical reasons.

In 1962, Pope John XXIII's Vatican II Council and the resulting encyclical marked the first significant shift within Roman Catholicism, from the Aquinian ideal of impersonal sex (i.e., for reproduction) to a personal and intimate view of sex (i.e., for family and love). The negative characterization of sex per se was not significantly changed. Masturbation remained theologically unacceptable, once again the reason being that it was not other-oriented.

The *other-oriented* aspects of these sexual philosophies is underscored for several reasons. First, it represents a marked difference from the *self-oriented* views of sensate focus activities used in modern sex therapy. Second, and more importantly, it raises the question of what orientation most facilitates the goal of a differentiation-based *other-oriented* sexual morality – that is to say, a sexual value system that is considerate of the partner as a separate individual and takes into account how couples actually become intimate (Chapters Four and Five). Third, and finally, the *other orientation* is highlighted for the reader in anticipation of the subsequent discussion of Sebastian Moore's thesis that *other-oriented* sexual desire reflects restricted spiritual development.

Modern Times

People who feel conflicts between their sexuality and spirituality are merely reflecting their Western heritage of Hebraic/Hellenic sexual dualism, which has created " . . . an obsession expressed on the surface as a longing for innocence but characterized covertly by a pervasive prurience" (Lawrence, 1989, p. 275). This was exemplified, in Lawrence's view, by Pope Pius XII's clarification in the final year of the Nazi holocaust (1944) that love was inferior to reproduction as motivation for marital sex; a similarly definitive statement on the Nazi death camps or Jewish genocide was never forthcoming.[10]

Paul Tillich (1936) and Karl Barth (1960) are perhaps the two most influential theologians (along with Karl Rahner) to emerge in the 20th century. Tillich's (1957) concern for self-actualization led him to consider sexuality from a viewpoint quite consistent with the notion of differentiation. He suggested that all human development, like adolescence, involved the struggle between the urge to self-actualize and the urge to remain in dreaming innocence; anxiety results from a move in either direction. Tillich considered the "fall from innocence" an upward fall. Both Tillich and Barth challenged conventional views of marital monogamy in their professional and personal activities. Tillich tried to keep his multiple sexual liaisons out of the public eye until his wife published an account of their marriage in 1973. Barth was more open about his bigamy, living his last 40 years with two women with whom he was sexually involved.

---

[10]Ranke-Heinemann similarly comments:

> Such absurdities are the results of mistaken sexual morality that after almost two thousand years is still not ready to give up its usurped dominion over the bedrooms of married people. It is astonishing how abundantly down through history one generation has intellectually begotten another generation of incompetent self-styled experts, surrounded them with a divine halo, devoting substantial portions of their lives to utter nonsense. This pseudo theological waxworks would make us laugh out loud, if we didn't know that its owners and operators have a lot of marital tragedies to answer for. (1990, p. 177)

Lawrence (1989) proposed a nonmonogamous ethic of "carnal reciprocity," in which "sexual self-actualization is preferable to sexual innocence, abstinence, and self-denial" (p. 247). His efforts to avoid the problems of sexual dualism and establish that sex is inherently good in and of itself led him to an extreme: Lawrence suggests, "where there are no contraindications, it is better to do it than not to do it" (p. 248) and with as many people as often as possible. Monogamy, in his view, is a unnecessary restriction on one of the most important sacraments of human experience; "marriage is to the church as Tar Baby was to Br'er Rabbit" (Lawrence, 1989, p. 273).

Lawrence's approach is much like that of Paul Ricoeur, who said, "When two beings embrace they don't know what they are doing, they don't know what they want, the don't know what they are looking for, and they don't know what they are finding" (Ricoeur, 1964, p. 140).

DESIRE AND SPIRITUALITY

There are several ways to conceptualize a resolution to the schism between spirituality and intense sexuality. One is to graft sexuality onto spirituality, like a botanical scion onto preexisting stock. Actually, this was tried in reverse in the grafting of Christian asceticism onto Hebraic sexual values, with obvious lack of success. Another, as Lawrence suggests, is to scatter eroticism in newly plowed terrain, secure in the knowledge that, given enough sex and partners, something new is likely to grow.

A third alternative involves that application of science and statistics. In the *National Catholic Reporter*, Father Andrew Greeley disclosed the results of his study to see if and how 1,450 married Catholics maintained "falling in love": 30% of those who showered *and* prayed jointly (presumably at different times) responded affirmatively. Only 20% of those who either showered *or* prayed together were "in love"; only 9% of those who did neither felt similarly. (Greeley, 1991, p. 20).

A fourth alternative is to create a paradigm shift. Sebastian Moore, a Benedictine priest, has taken this last approach, creating an ethic in which desire is the basic feature of spirituality itself.

Given the widespread clinical interest in problems of sexual desire and the earnestness with which Christianity systematically attempted to *create* inhibited sexual desire, Moore's perspective on the basic spiritual nature of sexual desire is unique and refreshing. It is one that can be readily integrated with our prior discussion of the crucible and sexual potential. Moore's remarkable books, *Let This Mind Be In You: The Quest for Identity Through Oedipus to Christ*

(1985) and *Jesus: The Liberator of Desire* (1989), provides much of the impetus for the discussion that follows.

In contrast to type "A" theology's spiritual *desire* devoid of sensuality, Moore's view is unabashedly erotic. For him, sexual arousal is the prototype of the drive for spiritual development. Moore promotes the notion of desire as inherently good; *self*, and belief in oneself, are good as well. Transcendent spirituality and religious conviction stem from a well differentiated self rather than feelings of dependency and inadequacy. Moore's theology is consistent with the diverse literatures of Freudian theory (although he takes issue with Freud at times in his later book), object relations theory, and research on early infant development.

Level-1 Spirituality

Moore postulates that desire occurs at one of two different levels of personal and spiritual development. At the beginning of life (*level-1 spirituality*), desire is the basic process by which human beings develop. Desire causes the infant to become aware of things occurring in and around him/her. The infant's initial state of continuous self-awareness lacks focus; it is shaped by movement from feeling empty towards those things that bring fullness and the satisfaction of desire. Although Moore never mentions object relations theory per se, his conceptualization offers an unusual link between spiritual development and the object relations concepts of introjection as reflected-sense-of-self-from-another:

> Now if self-awareness precedes and undergirds all *thinking* about myself, if I *consciously am* before I am able to say that I am this or that, then also I *consciously want* before I am able to say that I want this or that. As all my thinking about myself and my life depends upon a prior presence of myself to myself, so all my desiring depends on a prior *affective* presence of myself to myself. (1985, p. 15)

A child's feeling of desirability, co-requisite for emotional and spiritual development, stems from a sense of self as desired and desirable internalized from parents and caretakers. The child's introjected sense of self as desired and desirable is partially dependent upon parents' comfort with the sexual and nonsexual nuances of "desiring" the child. Incest, sexual abuse, and other unresolved emotional and physical boundary violations within the family interfere with children's spiritual development (in addition to their many other negative impacts); such events often distort desire as *bad* and create an avoidance of desirability. Moore hypothesizes:

> The desire to be desired stems from the certainty of being desirable: for it is *wanting to experience my desirability in action.* . . . Once I allow doubt as to the *existence* of this propensity or potential, the desire I am speaking of evaporates. (1985, p. 8)

Indirect desirability, experienced by reflection within the process of desiring another person, is the basic characteristic of level-1 spiritual development. At level-1, the source of personal desire and desirability is attributed to the significant other. This is the "normal" experience of desire, the level of spiritual development at which most people remain. People at level-1 spirituality are relatively fused and undifferentiated, limiting the range of self that can be displayed and the depth of intimacy achieved.

Unfortunately, a reflected sense of desirability, together with dependence upon being desired by another person, gives rise to the control struggles of childhood and later adult relationships. Level-1 desire reflects an undifferentiated attachment that is rife with potential for fights over autonomy and power; it is antithetical to individuation and emerges in patterns popularly referred to as "codependency." The common level-1 solutions are not "wanting to want" and/or attempting to become even more attractive to the other in order to bring him/her under one's own influence.

Moore doesn't focus on the systemic seeds of power struggles, control fights, or separation-individuation conflicts common to level-1 spirituality. However, he alludes to problems in what he calls the "magnet model" of desire:

> Now at the first, dependency stage, desire is much easier to talk about. The as yet unobtrusive presence of my own sense of being good leaves the other's charm the only force in the field. And so the simple magnet-model for desire easily inserts itself.
>
> This, I suggest, is how the simple magnet-model comes to impose itself, unnoticed, on philosophy. The philosopher's image of desire is "someone being drawn to someone or something by the latter's allure." Entirely in the shade is "someone being drawn to someone or something out of his/her own sense of being good." (1985, pp. 27–28)

At level-1 spiritual development, relationships are akin to those observed among young adolescents:

If you desire me, then I desire you because you desire me, since I don't desire myself. If I believe you instead of myself, perhaps I will come to accept myself. Paradoxically, this requires invalidating my own perceptions in the hope that I can develop a reflected positive sense of myself.

This is the level of spiritual development (and desire) at which many people remain: seeking God (and people) out of a sense of deprivation, unworthiness, and hunger. That it happens to be consistent with type "A" authoritarian theologies (and some contemporary psychological theories) is not difficult to understand. In *Solitude*, Anthony Storr (1988) points out that the period from birth to sexual maturity constitutes nearly a quarter of the total lifespan, longer than that of any other mammal. He notes that this extended childhood dependence on reflected desirability (while providing the opportunity to learn from one's elders) limits how far one can develop spiritually and emotionally; the power of solitude (i.e., a non-reflected sense of self) is often overlooked. Suggesting that man was not born just to obtain love from others, Storr writes:

> . . . attachment theory, in my view, does less than justice to the importance of work, to the emotional significance of what goes on in the mind of the individual when he is alone, and, more especially, to the central place occupied by the imagination in those who are capable of creative achievement. (p. 15)

Ascendance to Level-2 Spirituality

Reaching the transition point from level-1 to level-2 spirituality is in itself a developmental task. It involves the construction of the crucible of level-2 self-validated intimacy in which one confronts his or her rejection of self as unlovable and undesirable:

> This new moment, of self-acceptance in a love relationship, is the crucial moment. It is the watershed of all human relations. It is what most of us most of the time stop short of. For this is the vital point at which our belief in our goodness is not strong enough to carry us forward. It is always some, often subtle, self-rejection that hinders us from believing in another's finding us attractive and from seeing that the other does so when this happens. . . . And thus our weak sense of our goodness holds us short of interdependent relationships, and keeps us in dependent relationships. We are willing slaves to beauty rather than sharers in beauty. (Moore, 1985, p. 27)

This is the moment of intense intimacy in which a clear presentation of self is made, inviting the partner's open reaction. When the coreness of self being displayed and the salience of the relationship are sufficient, there is a test of *faith*: the faith in oneself as desirable, in and of oneself. At that moment of faith, there is a paradoxical sense of separateness coupled with an acute sense of oneself, in the context of an awareness of interdependence and participation with this other person. This is the epitome of the intimate experience described in Chapters Four and Five. Many such "moments of faith" are required in the transition from level-1 to level-2 spirituality for the construction of a solid self and an internalized sense of desirability. Such moments are seldom forgotten, however; they are the substance of knowing smiles as one celebrates one's life in the replaying of past memories.

Helminiak has written similarly of self-transcendence as a potential realized through constant self-questioning, evaluating, refining, and self-reforming. Responding to this challenge with growth requires the courage to explore, to risk, to change oneself, and to alter one's life. Helminiak underscored the inherent role of self-esteem in spiritual development, noting the enterprise to be risky and the experience of absolute freedom to be both frightening and paralyzing. Although he did not conceptualize this as differentiation, the commonality is unmistakable:

> The point is that spiritual development is an adult phenomenon . . . where adulthood is defined not by chronological age but by developmental achievement. In their stage theories of human development, Kohlberg (1969), Loevinger (1977) and Fowler (1981) all include a stage, first possible in young adulthood, that is characterized in some way or other as postconventional. It is to this postconventionality that the "self-critical" and "self-responsible" character of spiritual development points. A person at this stage of development is no longer wholly bound by the meanings and values that structure his or her social world. Rather one is capable of taking a critical stance toward one's social world and toward oneself, and on the basis of such criticism one structures one's life as he or she knows to be best. On the basis of one's own self, one chooses and makes oneself to be what one will be. One becomes one's own authority. (Helminiak, 1989, pp. 202–203)

The achievement of *level-2* spiritual development reflects a spiritual awakening involving a qualitative shift in the perceived *source* of desire. At level-2, there is a shift from a reflected other-oriented sense of desire to a *direct, self-oriented experience of desire*; personal desirability is experienced *internally*, stemming from one's core selfhood. Moreover, at this second level of desire, there is a shift in *object*; desirability and desire have no immediately apparent target. It is characterized by desire *for nothing in particular*, stemming from a sense of one's *own* desirability rather than a desire for a particular individual. This experience is the transcendence of the reciprocity model of intimacy (Chapters Four and Five).

> [Level-2 is] an experience in which arousal is *not* by desiring another person but *from within myself*. But this self-awakening, although it is not *caused* by desire, is certainly not *without* desire. On the contrary, those who break this new level of awareness speak of a great "longing" that comes with it. So what we have here is the reverse of the normal order in which desire for another awakes me to myself. Here the awakening to my self causes desire, a desire for I know not what, which we call longing. . . . This is the most revealing experience that we have: a sense that I am *in myself* and not relatively to other people and to my culture and race, carrying with it a longing for I know not what. It is a sense of luminous identity generating desire. (Moore, 1985, pp. 37–8)

For someone raised in Western religious cultures, initial experiences at the threshold of level-2 spirituality are paradoxical. There is a general anticipation that a heightened sense of spirituality brings with it *transcendence of desire*; type-A (level-1) theology suggests a model that heaven is the place where no one goes wanting. However, as one makes the transition to level-2, there is actually an experience of *increased* desire; it is a curious desire because it occurs in the context of fullness and richness.

> . . . the statement that vital [level-2] desire grows with its fulfillment does not adequately distinguish it from a phenomenon with which we are only too familiar: the more I get, of money, power, consuming, the more I want. The differentiating thing about personal desire is that it *desires* its own increase, as does the desire to know—I don't merely find myself wanting still more *once I've got what I wanted*. The lustful and the power-hungry do not *want* to want more. (Moore, 1989, p. 12, italics original)

Moore's distinction between (a) the desire-as-hunger model (i.e., desires cease once satisfied, such as the desire to be warmed and fed), and (b) a spiritual desire that grows through satiation, is familiar by now; Moore's non-deprivation model of level-2 spiritual desire is identical to the differentiation-based model of *passion* and *wanting* proposed in Chapter Nine. Said different-ly, level-2 spirituality transcends the prevailing "hunger" model of desire in modern sex therapy. Even more importantly for integrating sexuality and spirituality, Moore adopts the Rahnerian viewpoint of level-2 spiritual desire as embodied and invested in *daily* reality (including sexual desire); he avoids the leap of Gnostic-based Christian dualism to a separate/"higher" spiritual plane. Moore discusses this as the acceptance of oneself as inherently desirable and the embodiment of God-within: "We desire not because we are empty but because we are full" (1985, p. 15). One desires more deeply as a passion for life, rather than the yearning characterized by other-oriented, deprivation-based desire of level-1.

Transcendence to level-2 spiritual desire permits true *interdependence* between well-differentiated adults, in contrast to the dependency that characterizes level-1. As individuals and relationships shift from dependence to interdependence, dynamics become increasingly complex and interactions become less predictable. Moore writes:

> In place of the predictable (or at least treated as predictable) object, my desire now embraces the object in a wider context of a shared unpredictable interaction.
>
> What this means is that my desire has now become an investment of myself in a developing shared life, a commitment of myself to the unpredictable in hope. In fact my desire has developed into hope. The goodness that I sense as mine is now being invested in an ongoing, risk-laden, unpredictable, enormously promising interplay of *two* goodnesses.
>
> Now, whether I recognize this clearly or not, this new, deeper and more exacting direction of my desire is bringing me into a *new* dependence: a dependence on the total mystery that constitutes me, this unique good person, and supports my investment of my goodness in the risk-laden adventure of intimacy. The anchor of my new hope is goodness itself. This bears out a principle that I have come to see as bedrock to our whole quest for God: namely that we look to God, in hope, to the extent that we are investing ourselves in life's value and beauty, and not out of a *poor* sense of ourselves or a disappointed sense of life. . . . (1985, pp. 28–29)

The attainment of level-2 spirituality is the counterpart to von Neumann's (1966) notion of the *critical complexity barrier*, previously encountered in the discussion of inherent paradox (Chapter Fifteen). In the dual exploration of spirituality and sexual intimacy, an inherent paradox repeatedly emerges: the acute experience of self as god-within (the self as the center of the phenomenological universe) and the self as finite, inextricably separate, and peripheral but integral to a much larger overwhelming whole.

At this level, moreover, the paradox of ontological constructivism is resolved (Chapter Sixteen). "Consciousness at level-2 does not know the distinction between world-order and mind-order," writes Moore. "At that level, I am bathed in the original mystery of order coming out of chaos. My mind, as I try to work out the world order, is part of the very process of world order, *is* the world order as mind (1985, p. 51)."

It should be obvious that many of the processes that characterize level-1 spiritual development have similar but subtly different counterpart processes at level-2. For instance, there is a transformation of the magnet model in which desire and interpersonal attraction shift "from the simple pull of the beautiful other, through the phases and hazards of a relationship, to the pull of the mystery itself, the subtle 'come on' of a power utterly beyond our mind's grasp but able to communicate with us through love" (Moore, 1985, p. 29).

Although derived from a spiritual vantage point, Moore's view of intimacy as a fundamental human potential is remarkably consistent with the models of level-2 self-validated intimacy developed in Chapters Four and Five.

Intimacy, at least as it exists at level 2, becomes clearly distinguished from incorporation of the partner; desire and differentiation become synergistic. Moore says it best when he states:

> . . . Desire reveals its true nature when it comes into the moment of decision, either for the new initiate of self-exposure that makes possible interdependence, or for the cowardice that overshadows our society. Love is desire decided for. . . . Desire is most nearly itself when, asserting my own goodness which is its source, I pass from dependence to interdependence whose soul is hope. Then is desire most itself, so then am I most drawn—no longer by the obvious charm of another, but by the mystery that brings us together enlarging desire into hope. (1985, p. 30)

Ascendance to level-2 spirituality is marked by the experience of personal mysticism, a fitting framework for exploration of the mysticism of sexuality that affirms sexual pleasure and affirms the self. This is characterized by a sense of joining the human community, of being part of the intergenerational flow of life, and an abrupt cessation of the sense of isolation; it is the transcendence of existential separateness (Chapters Four and Five). This is accompanied by a profound sense of significance to one's life; such an individual often generates wonderful accomplishments, but the process and impact are quite different from those surrounding the achievements of an individual at level 1, who produces in the hope of becoming significant. Moore suggests "this luminous sense of myself is a sense of myself as somehow chosen, of my personhood as a destiny. This sense of being chosen by some mystery altogether beyond the mind's reach is the breakthrough experience out of which the whole of the Jewish scripture grows" (1985, pp. 37–38).

People at level-1 development are often not even aware of the existence of a second level of experience and functioning. Basically, the difference between level 1 and level 2 is a paradigm shift in spirituality, desire, and the perceived means to the "good life" that Engelhardt mentioned at the outset of the chapter. Some people may deny the plausibility of level-2 development and/or the crucial *qualitative shift* in desire and desirability that must occur. Moore writes, "Thus dependent on the other for my sense of self, I hardly suspect that there is a joy in being wholly myself, that there is a love for others in being wholly myself, of which the normal borrowed selfhood can give me no idea" (1985, p. 75). Once again, the spiritual path of desire and spirituality leads one back to our previous discussion of differentiation and intimacy.

The transition to level 2 doesn't occur by becoming engorged with a reflected sense of self-worth. Changing one's spirituality, one's relationship to God, is like changing one's sexuality in relationship to a partner: it starts with the individual drawing upon his or her belief in him- or herself. One can have faith out of acceptance and gratitude for one's current life and happiness or one can "bargain" one's faith in an attempt to "get gratified" without appreciating what one already is (or has). So, too, is it with sex.

True faith is not the balm of the weak, but rather the embodiment of one's strength and willingness to invest in the possibilities of life detected through one's experience. Similarly, one's sexuality can be rooted in weakness or strength. While both may involve copulatory behavior, the resulting experiences are often quite different when done from different levels of spirituality and desire. Conventional approaches to sexual therapy produce conventional levels of eroticism and desire; one might quite readily say that the orientation described in this book is an *abnormal approach designed to produce abnormal results*. The sexual crucible of sexual-marital therapy offers a vehicle for "post-conventional" sexual development and its integration with spirituality.

Self-awareness, Sin, and Resistance to Growth

Many people are reluctant, if not fearful, to enter such a pursuit; those who start the process inevitably back away in some fashion. As discussed in Chapter Fourteen, people are often reluctant to pursue the limits of their own sexual potential. Moore discusses this same phenomenon from the spiritual dimension; he considered *sin* to be the deep-seated refusal to grow. What Moore does is nothing less than finally confront the concept of human "animalistic" desire. There is a tendency to see the topic negatively when approached from a theological perspective. Pushing the issue, however, brings into view the disparaging Augustinian spiritual and sexual dualism regarding human "animal" nature that pervades Western culture. Desire is *clean* rather than base if one recognizes that people's "animal nature" is holy (in the way that grace permeates nature). Moore "stands Freud on his head," suggesting that while all desires are not "basic hungers," basic hungers are consistent with spirituality.

There may be something to the fact that those who study myths find there to be three universal themes: the meal as communion with the divinity, sexual union as similar communion, and one's life as a journey. "In other words," Moore writes, "food, sex, and death, the three points where our life is consciously animal, are sublated in the universal consciousness of humankind, into consciousness as dialogue with ultimate mystery. So to understand our basic hungers in terms of our eternal hunger is to go with the flow of all our psychic energy (1989, p. 12)."

Confronting the nature of sin and "animal desire" encourages people (a) to stop apologizing spiritually for their desire, (b) to recognize that men and women need not feel at war with their "animal nature," and most importantly (c) to recognize that sexuality *is a pathway* to spirituality. This understanding has been a fundamental aspect of type "B" Eastern religions for centuries. In contrast to type "A" Western theologies, which associate sin with excessive desire and covetousness, Moore offers us a paradigm shift: *Sin stems from a lack of desire for pleasure.*

> The sense of desirability, that directed me happily through life in infancy, now no longer works for me, for I am no longer just "this body." So my sense of being desirable ceases to be trustworthy as a guiding principle. I don't feel good with any conviction, and therefore I don't *do* what is good. . . . But how easy it is to *blame* the sense of being good and desirable that seems to have let us down. So we get the opposite version of what original sin is: original sin is the feeling of being good, it is "pride," it is "hedonism" . . .
>
> Because this mistake is so easily made, it has pervaded the Christian moral tradition, which has come to place original sin in feeling good instead of in feeling bad, which is where it should be placed, and the Christian moral tradition has laid itself open to those critics who accuse it of propagating the very disease it claims to be curing.
>
> Thus, we get the bad situation that while the best psychologists and counselors are coming to understand the root of our evil as a bad self-image, Christians tend to say to them, "You are leaving out original sin"—not realizing that these psychologists are, precisely, *pointing* to original sin. (1985, p. 83)

Original Sin

Moore suggests that massive evidence for the theory of evolution has made the old explanation of original sin nearly impossible to maintain, because it is difficult to think of the human race starting in a state of perfection in a universe where nothing else does. He proposes a *new* explanation in which original sin is the universal, culturally propagated and reinforced, human response to the trauma of coming out of animality into self-awareness, into "the knowledge of good and evil." This, he suggests, is the real meaning of the story of the Garden of Eden.

Original sin is a spiritual "not wanting to want": the lack of desire for growth. Sin is the belief that human nature cannot be changed and the *willingness* to live below one's potential at level-1 spiritual development. The origin of "sin" is one's reflected sense of self, and the resultant refusal to believe in oneself and strive for the realization of human potential (characteristics of level 1). A reflected sense of self is a result of human "historic generic genetic reality" (Moore, 1985, p. 69) as an animal species that evolved the capacity for consciousness which emerges rapidly during early infancy: the earliest awareness of self comes from assessing oneself by reactions from significant others.[11]

Moore's reinterpretation of original sin and the story of Genesis, and the integration of psychology and biology are quite consistent with many mainstream organized religions; the fact that it seems unthinkable (if not downright blasphemous) to modify basic biblical interpretations highlights once again the manner in which type "A" Roman Catholicism has permeated Western society. The full implications of Moore's breathtaking formulation of original sin are diverse and profound, taking off in two separate but related directions: (a) the impact of self-awareness, and (b) the role of faith. Each of these topics will be considered in turn.

Self-Awareness, Desire, and Intimacy[12]

Moore postulates that the two great childhood developmental crises (Margaret Mahler's separation-individuation process and Freud's oedipal stage) are "a shattering experience" (1985, p. 78) of self-awareness. The crisis of separation-individuation involves the initial realization of a separate, individual existence. The subsequent oedipal struggle, according to Moore, further reinforces

---

[11]Moore's concept of original sin as the result of bio-social evolution comes from a perspective quite familiar from our discussion of the capacity for intimacy (Chapter Four, e.g, Maturana & Varela, 1987) and pair bonding (Chapter Twelve, e.g., Fisher, 1982).

[12]Readers who follow the subsequent discussion from the simultaneous (isomorphic) "level-2" perspectives of spirituality and intimacy will find that both "fit."

the realization of separateness and the pain of desire, labeling hedonism as bad and carrying a threat of further feelings of abandonment. This frustrating send-off on life's journey creates a core dread of separateness implicit in all subsequent states of self-awareness. This primordial dread starts the habit of looking to others for reassurance (level-1 other-orientation). Paradoxically, looking to others for reassurance only stimulates the insecurity that an other-oriented sense of self-esteem brings.

This is the same pandemic "normal neurosis" discussed in delineating the difference between level-1 and level-2 intimacy. In fact, it should be clear that the two level model of intimacy proposed throughout this book and Moore's two-level model of spirituality and desire have more than a structural similarity. Both stipulate the fundamental importance of self-awareness in the phenomena each addresses. Both require/reflect/produce high levels of differentiation. Once recognized, the link between Bowenian theory and spiritual desire surfaces: Moore's suggestion that self-awareness is self-affirming, self-believing, and self-loving is grounded in what Kerr and Bowen (1988) referred to as solid-self *and* what Rahner (1941/1969, 1961) considered the indwelling grace of God.

Faith

Moore's point is the substance of level-2 self-validated intimacy: the strength to support oneself in moving forward, holding onto only oneself and life. "To not trust life," says Moore, "is to sink into a pathology (1989, p. 10)." It is what Bertrand Russell (in Seldes, 1985) referred to when he said that to fear love is to fear life, and those who fear life are already three parts dead. He addresses the same issues that Kierkegaard (1946) personified in his Knight of Infinite Faith, and which Stratton (1991) linked to the biblical story of Abraham and Isaac (Chapter Three): *When your life beckons to you like a lover, do you reach out with faith and desire or with suspicion and defensiveness?*

Faith is the application of differentiation in the everyday world. Basically, Moore offers a developmental model of faith that is analogous to Kerr and Bowen's scale of differentiation; faith, like differentiation, is a developmental process. Faith at level 2 involves holding onto oneself and not giving into fear when things do not seem to be going to one's liking; holding onto oneself for security involves coping with disappointments without losing one's sense of direction in life. Faith becomes a belief in oneself as a manifestation of the goodness of God, not an appeal as an insignificant creature to a greater power.

At level 1, there is a more primitive undifferentiated operationalization of faith. Faith is merely the anticipation that things and people will act consistent with the picture that we have of them in our head and their traditional role in a system. When people act "out of character," there is the sense of "losing faith" in them; the question then becomes whether one sees them as "unfaithful" (a level-1 response) or uses this difference to drive differentiation forward to achieve a "faith in oneself" (level 2).

And of what use is this faith? For facing the future, in the way that Friedman (1990) has Cassandra talk about anxiety intolerance and the need for certainty (Chapter Thirteen). Rahner looks towards the future in terms of transcendence-producing growth crisis and boundary experience:

> In seems to me that both Western and Marxist pathetic ideas of the future are always tempted to confuse this tomorrow, evolutionarily or, technically conceived, or both, that is already today, with the true future. To give the name "future" to plans plus the mere vacant passage of time dislodges the true relationship of man with the real future. I have nothing against planning, nothing against the pathetic idea that at least we are no longer simply manipulated but manipulating, that we now exist practically and not just theoretically, that we possess a futurology, know what we want, how we want our tomorrow to be, that we are no longer taken by surprise, make careful provision for ourselves, force upon the morrow the will of today. It is wonderful that we have all this, now that cunning human beings and human beings tortured by blind chance have discovered how to ensnare the future as their prey in the net of their own will, knowing how to build the streets on which their children travel.
>
> What is the future then? Just the secret opposite of what we are accustomed to call future, but which we denature to a piece of the present by our foreseeing and capable anticipation. The future is not where we are going but it is what comes to us of its own accord, if it so desires, and which we, strangely enough, have to contend. The future is non-evolutionary, unplanned, non-compliant in its incomprehensibility and infinity. The future is the silent lurker, who, if it jumps out on us, tears the nets of our plans which make our own planned and foreseen "future" into present. The real future is non-compliant, ruling us now and always. It is deliberate and silent, incalculable and yet patient, allowing us time because it has no need of it for itself since it never comes too late. (Rahner, 1969, p.64)

At level 1, faith is based on wishing that things will be the way that we want them to be, like a "wish list." Level-2 faith is the resolve to cope with and enjoy what the future holds. It involves relinquishing the narcissistic (level-1) hope/demand that the world will revolve around us and accepting/enjoying that we are a significant participant in a much larger process. At level 2, faith is the sense that the world is full of wonderment, but not necessarily one's lollypop; as the Rolling Stones said: "You can't always get what you want, but if you try sometimes, you just might find, you get what you need!"

CONCLUSION

Sexuality is plastic enough to permit wide interpretations of its nature and purpose. One has only to reflect on the transient history of sexual "facts" to recognize that sexuality is often the ultimate mirror in which we see only our view of ourselves. How quickly we have gone from "knowing" that a woman could not orgasm to "knowing" that she *must* have several.

Sex is plastic enough to permit wide interpretations of the nature of God as revealed in sexuality. There is a vast difference between the public construct of the God one acknowledges (if indeed, one acknowledges the existence of any), and one's private god-construct. Likewise, there is often a vast difference between one's conscious private god-construct and the one(s) that resides in the unconscious. Most people do not believe what they believe they believe.

The face of the private god we truly worship is latent in the style and content of our sexual behavior. It is evident in the politics of giving and receiving pleasure. Through sex, some of us worship in the dark, close-but-remote from the ones we love, praying to a God who ferrets out our deepest embarrassments and shortcomings. Some of us worship in the light, sharing and showing our faith in ourselves, praying to a God who smiles upon sex and who loves men and women for their strength. And the nature of our private deity may be most evident in the type of people we meet during solitary masturbation.

It is convenient to construct a distorted view of prior generations having been more pious from genuflecting to hell-fire and damnation, now that no one is alive to contradict it. Many have perished in crusades, Inquisitions and witch hunts in the name of salvation. Those who suggest that a return to yesterday will cure the ills of today that surface in the sexual realm ignore history: In the Middles Ages, when the church controlled every aspect of daily life, sexuality was certainly no better (and probably no less frequent) than today. If belief in a vengeful God is a deterrent to illicit sexual behavior, then how do we explain the escapades of Reverends Jim Bakker, Jimmy Swaggart, Martin Goreman, and priests who molest children?

What kind of God would make masturbatory orgasms physiologically more intense than coital orgasms, and then proscribe them?

This is not to argue that masturbation is good, acceptable, or even permissible. Rather, it is to suggest that those who regard masturbation as morally or spiritually wrong should reflect on the visage of God embodied in their sexual theology. Is masturbation the beneficence of a passive-aggressive God or do sexual values embrace a blasphemous visage of God?

Sexual potential is part of the goodness that dwells within people. The basic sense of goodness is one's relationship-with-self; the power that drives self-validating spirituality, desire, and intimacy stems in large measure from the goodness of sexuality. Sexuality is a quintessential boundary experience in which spiritual transcendence and grace await. If one believes that God created men and women and said "It is *good*," then how could one think God was overlooking their sexuality when saying it? When He said this, He was looking squarely *into* their sexuality.

If people's view of God is, indeed, a reflection of their sexuality, then perhaps it explains why some think God is dead. If people had more faith in themselves and in their spirituality, it might change the face of sexuality as we currently know it. Spirituality can be a powerful driving force in the exploration of sexual potential. And conversely, the exploration of sexual potential often awakens one's spirituality. Audre Lorde (1987) says that once we experience the fullness and power of our eroticism, we are propelled "in honor and self-respect" to aspire to our full potential:

> This is one reason why the erotic is so feared, and so often relegated to the bedroom alone, when it is recognized at all. For once we begin to feel deeply all the aspects of our lives, we begin to demand from ourselves and from our lives' pursuits that they feel in accordance with that joy which we know ourselves to be capable of. Our erotic knowledge empowers us, becomes a lens though which we scrutinize those aspects honestly in terms of their relative meaning within our lives. And this is a grave responsibility, projected from within each of us, not to settle for the convenient, the shoddy, the conventionally expected, nor the merely safe. (Lorde, 1987, p. 5)

Whether couples (or the therapist) profess a belief in spirituality, atheism, or agnosticism, the treatment paradigm of sexual-marital therapy will inherently contain some notion of the nature of sexuality, intimacy, and the purpose of life. I do not propose that a therapist advocate a belief in a spiritual God. That is a personal decision.

The position advanced here is that the sexual-marital therapist must be articulate and skillful in this area for two basic reasons. One is that many patients wish to integrate their sexuality and spirituality. The second is that most therapists do embrace, consciously or not, some notion of human development and see psychotherapy as facilitating that development. The practice of sexual-marital therapy provides an opportunity and a vehicle for profound personal growth, part of which is spiritual growth. A therapist would be negligent if he or she did not bring this opportunity to the awareness of his or her patients.

Love and Death

There is a simple elegance to the complexity of life, one that is oftentimes hard to bear. Life is difficult, but sweet. It takes strength and courage to reach one's sexual potential: the strength to believe in oneself, and the courage to use one's eroticism as a crucible for emotional and spiritual development.

We fear transcending ourselves. One of my patients, whom I greatly admire, currently sits at the boundary of transcending her long-term defense against life to a sex-positive self-affirming stance. She has already turned the corner on a history of sexual and emotional abuse, showing herself that she is worth saving and capable of it, too. In her deepest despair, she'd write me gut-wrenching letters about her past. Although she hasn't written for some time, she just wrote me this one:

> I feel as though I am in mourning. Perhaps I'm grieving over future losses that I may not have the strength to survive. These future losses include the loss of a therapist who is a "significant other" to me, and a loss of identity — if I see myself as sick and I give that up then is there any vision left of me? Death appeals to me because I perceive it as peaceful.
>
> My life has been filled with want. Unfulfilled desire is the form that want has taken most often. I chose not to long for that which is unattainable. It seems as though I am at a turning point and must decide if I'm willing to hope for a brighter future, and trust my capabilities to experience the future in a healthier way.
>
> I'm afraid of failing. I'm afraid of *rejection*. I'm afraid of not being good enough. I'm afraid that I may want too much — what is unrealistic to want?

Like her, we all face the crisis of faith in which we expose ourselves to life through self-willing spiritual desire. This is what "desire based on fullness" looks like in its fledging state. Faith is what drives us to face the fear of successful self-evolution, brought about by our own desire. We fear the unknown, we fear becoming someone we don't yet know, and yet, this is exactly why people enter therapy: to escape the problem-maintaining solutions that are known, and to become someone other than who we know ourselves to be.

We often don't understand our own reluctance to transcend ourselves in the very ways we wish we could grow. It is our original sin, our refusal to believe in ourselves. This refusal to accept our own grace is so profound, we don't recognize it: We attempt to protect ourselves from loss *now*, not realizing that our entire future is based on the hope that we will be someone new *who may not want the very things we now desperately attempt to keep*. We refuse to accept the possibility of self-transcendence, dreading instead not needing the things we now think we can't live without (even more than our dread of not having them). We look like the would-be travelers encountered in the Sufi tale at the outset of this book, stifled by our cabbage-baggage.

This fear of self-transcendence is actually the fear of *loving*, of being free *to want* and *to love*. Sebastian Moore asks, "Who *really* wants to feel like Jesus?" *Who really wants intense eroticism and intimacy? Who really wants to love?*

Readers may have noted that word *love* rarely appears throughout this book, and *lovemaking* is never used as a euphemism for sexual behavior. This does not reflect a belief that love and sex should be separate, nor that love is a topic unfit for discussion within the art and science of sexual-marital therapy. Rather, it reflects the difficulty of discussing this topic in a meaningful way and the distaste I hold for the casual, euphemistic, and bastardized use of the term. It also reflects my clinical impression and belief that all too few people reach that peak of human development in which both eroticism and the capacity to love are well developed and merged. Loving at the level that creates self-transcendence is, understandably, a rare occurrence.

This fear of self-transcendence which surfaces as fears of loving has several faces: love of self, love of another, and love of life itself. Loving oneself is not a simple challenge: Love of self brings with it a fear of death. The death of things no longer fitting, and the death of self which those things fit. Self-transcendence involves the death of the "old me" and the birth of the "new unfamiliar me." Loving is a self-mutating boundary experience triggered by one's own desire. Death goes beyond the death of self that comes with metamorphosis, the death my patient stares at. It goes beyond the troubadours' romantic view of love as "the little death." Love signals our eventual final death.

> It is quite erroneous to think that we do not experience death until we die. If we have lived at all, we already know it well. And our *memory* of having come into fuller life through it should affect the way we think about our certain final death. And if a person's growth is a progressive liberation of desire, and if the person's life moves inexorably toward death, then it would seem natural to regard death as the climax of this process. For something in us sees in death a cessation of our confinement to the space-time continuum, so we could put together this idea of deconfinement and the idea of a climax of liberation, a climatic growth crisis. The liberation of desire would then be the *meaning* of the ending of our space-time confinement. (Moore, 1989, p. 22)

Loving life itself carries with it the eventuality of physical death. Our fear once again demonstrates disbelief in our capacity for self-transcendence. It is as if we *really* can't conceive of life being just one more thing that we may not need after we go through the barrier experience. It is heartful to see how intricately living life (and death) as both *end* and *passage* involves transcending the refusal to want and developing desire based on fullness; it shows the craftsmanship of a godlike wisdom. Like love, life itself is something we won't let go of, but which we refuse to accept anyway.

Being unloved is a terrible thing . . .

We tend to ask, "Why me?"

The only thing worse is the terror of understanding and accepting the answer to
   the question we ask, when we sense that we *are* loved . . .

"Why me?"

The love of self and life, and the fear of one's own death, are often thought of as the ultimate self-transcendence. But it is rivaled by truly loving one's spouse; *this* is the ultimate grindstone upon which our ability to love and be loved is honed. The personal metamorphosis created by the death of a well-loved wife or husband is one we are often least prepared for, the one we sometimes think we can't transcend.

The strategy of pursuing a partner to protect oneself from heartache (or to soothe preexisting heartache) guarantees disappointment. When heartache is willingly accepted as part of loving a *good* partner in a *good* relationship, only then is it safe to love profoundly.

Loving is not for the weak. In the process of loving someone, particularly in a long-term relationship, something wondrous and awful happens. The partner becomes unique. When the partner dies, one might go on to bond with another. This other might also be a gratifying relationship. But when one loses a partner of some 30 years, the partner is irreplaceable: the events and developmental tasks of those years will not be repeated. The bonding that comes from standing in the presence of the partner while these steps are taken is not duplicated.

Losing a long-term loved one from a good relationship is irreparable. There is a hole in the fabric of one's life that is not filled by another. There is a cache of memories of good times shared and there is a great deal of *pain*. But these two heaps of pain and pleasure neither counterbalance nor neutralize each other's impact. One is left with both the pleasure and pain of having lost a valued partner. Desiring out of fullness makes this bearable, undertaken unwillingly and knowingly.

If the relationship has been a particularly rewarding and fruitful one, there may be a *great* deal of pleasurable memories—the joy of having bumped into this cherished person during his or her turn to walk the face of the earth. And just that much more pain as well. For such an experience reveals that there are often precious few people who can form that depth of bond. And so . . . one is left with a bounty of good memories and a wealth of pain. And the most terrible part of all, that few people anticipate, is that the loved one is not there to comfort you through their own death. This each of us must do, alone.

Another of the wondrous and terrible facets of love is that loving increases the capacity of the lover to love, making the loved one all the more dear and irreplaceable. And that makes the inevitable loss of the partner all the greater. If one has the courage, one reinvests this increased capacity to love, fully cognizant of the eventualities.

If one lacks the strength or the willingness to comfort and support oneself through the loss of this cherished loved one, there is an alternative escape route that many people take: to not love the partner too much. Many opt to lose a partner whom they do not cherish dearly, rather than lose a vitally loved one. The method of this "self-protection" is simple: Don't love the partner *too* well. In this way, the partner is lost just a little each day, rather than greatly all at once.

So one is well advised: Loving is not for the weak. One must be strong enough to love unilaterally. This is the final requisite for reaching one's sexual potential.

May we all develop the strength to love well.

References

Abse, D. W., Nash, M. E., & Louden, L. M. R. (1974). *Marital and sexual counseling in medical practice*. New York: Harper & Row.

Adler, A. (1951/1983). *The practice and theory of individual psychology*. Totowa, NJ: Rowman & Allenheld

Altman, I. (1973). Reciprocity of interpersonal exchange. *Journal of the Theory of Social Behavior, 3*, 249–261.

Altman, I., & Taylor, D. A. (1973). *Social penetration: The development of interpersonal relationships*. New York: Holt, Rinehart & Winston.

American Psychiatric Association. (1975). *A psychiatric glossary*. Washington, DC: Author.

American Psychiatric Association. (1980). *Diagnostic and statistical manual of mental disorders* (3rd ed.). Washington, DC: Author.

American Psychiatric Association. (1987). *Diagnostic and statistical manual of mental disorders* (3rd ed. rev.). Washington, DC: Author.

Andolfi, M. (1980). Prescribing the family's own dysfunctional rules as a therapeutic strategy. *Journal of Marital & Family Therapy, 6*, 29–36.

Apfelbaum, B. (1977a). A contribution to the development of the behavioral-analytic sex therapy model. *Journal of Sex & Marital Therapy, 3*(2), 128–138.

Apfelbaum, B. (1977b). On the etiology of sexual dysfunction. *Journal of Sex & Marital Therapy, 3*(1), 50–62.

Apfelbaum, B. (1977c). Sexual functioning reconsidered. In R. Gemme & C. C. Wheeler (Eds.), *Progress in sexology*. New York: Plenum Press.

Apfelbaum, B. (1983). *Expanding the boundaries of sex therapy: The ego-analytic model* (2nd ed.). Berkeley, CA: Berkeley Sex Therapy Group.

Apfelbaum, B. (1984). Professional sex films versus sexual reality. In R. Segraves & E. J. Haeberle (Eds.), *Emerging dimensions of sexology*. New York: Praeger.

Apfelbaum, B. (1985). Masters and Johnson's contribution: A response to Harold Lief and Arnold Lazarus. *Journal of Sex Education & Therapy, 11*(2), 5–11.

Apfelbaum, B. (1988). An ego-analytic perspective on desire disorders. In S. R. Leiblum & R. C. Rosen (Eds.), *Sexual desire disorders* (pp. 75–106). New York: Guilford.

Apfelbaum, B. (1990, February). Live clinical demonstration (pre-conference institute). AASECT annual meeting, Washington, DC.

Archer, R. L., & Earle, W. B. (1983). The interpersonal orientation of disclosure. In P. B. Paulus (Ed.), *Basic groups processes*. New York: Springer-Verlag.

Ascher, L. M. (Ed.). (1989). *Therapeutic paradox*. New York: Guilford.

Athanasiou, R., et al. (1970). Sex. *Psychology Today, 4*(2), 39–52.

Atwater, L. (1982). *The extramarital connection: Sex intimacy, and identity*. New York: Irvington.

Augarde, T. (Ed.). (1991). *The Oxford dictionary of modern quotes*. New York: Oxford University Press.

Avalon, A. (1974). *The serpent power: The secrets of tantric and shaktic yoga*. New York: Dover.

Bader, M. J. (1988). Looking for addictions in all the wrong places. *Tikkun*, (3)6, 13–16, 96–98.

Baker, R. (1987). The clinician as sexual philosopher. In E. E. Shelp (Ed.), *Sexuality and medicine: Ethical viewpoints in transition* (Vol. 2). Boston: D. Reidel Publishing Co.

Balint, M. (1952). *Primary love and psycho-analytic techinque*. London: Tavistock.

Bancroft, J. (1987). *Man and his penis: A relationship under threat*. Plenary presentation at annual meeting of the Society for the Scientific Study of Sex, Atlanta, GA.

Bancroft, J., & Wu, F. C. W. (1983). Changes in erectile responsiveness during androgen replacement therapy. *Archives of Sexual Behavior, 12*, 59–66.

Barbach, L. (1980). Group treatment of anorgasmic women. In S. R. Leiblum & L. A. Pervin (Eds.), *Principles and practices of sex therapy*. New York: Guilford.

Barbach, L. (1982). *For each other: Sharing sexual intimacy*. New York: Anchor Press/Doubleday.

Barlow, D. H. (1986). Causes of sexual dysfunction: The role of anxiety and cognitive interference. *Journal of Consulting & Clinical Psychology, 54*, 140–157.

Barth, J. (1960). *Church dogmatics III/4*. Edinburgh, Scotland: T & T Clark.

Bass, E., & Davis, L. (1988). *The courage to heal: A guide for women survivors of child sexual abuse*. New York: Harper & Row.

Bateson, G. (1951). Information and codification: A philosophical approach. In J. Ruesch & G. Bateson (Eds.), *Communication: The social matrix of psychiatry*. New York: Norton.

Bateson, G., Jackson, D., Haley, J., & Weakland, J. (1956). Toward a theory of schizophrenia. *Behavioral Science, 1*, 251–264.

Beattie, M. (1987). *Codependent no more*. New York: Harper & Row.

Beattie, M. (1989). *Beyond codependency*. New York: Harper & Row.

Beavers, W. R. (1977). *Psychotherapy and growth: A family systems perspective*. New York: Brunner/Mazel.

Beavers, W. R. (1985). *Successful marriage*. New York: Norton.

Beavers, W. R., & Hampson, R. (1990). *Successful families: Assessment and intervention*. New York: Norton.

Beres, D. (1956). Ego deviation and the concept of schizophrenia. *The Psychoanalytic Study of the Child, 11*, 164–235.

Berman E. M., & Hof, L. (1987). The sexual genogram—Assessing family-of-origin factors in the treatment of sexual dysfunction. In G. R. Weeks & L. Hof (Eds.), *Integrating sex and marital therapy: A clinical guide*. New York: Brunner/Mazel.

Bernard, J. (1977). Infidelity: Some moral and social issues. In R. W. Libby & R. N. Whitehurst (Eds.), *Marriage and alternatives: Exploring intimate relationships*. Glenview, IL: Scott Foresman.

Berscheid, E., & Walster, E. H. (1978). *Interpersonal attraction* (2nd ed.). Reading, MA: Addison-Wesley.

Bertalanffy, L. von. (1968). *General system theory: Foundations, development, applications*. New York: George Braziller.

Biddle, B. J. (1976). *Role theory: Expectations, identities and behaviors*. Chicago: Dryden Press.

Blau, P. M. (1964). *Exchange and power in social life*. New York: John Wiley.

Block, J. (1987). *The other man, the other woman*. New York: Grosset & Dunlap.

Bly, R. (1990). *Iron John: A book about men*. Reading, MA: Addison-Wesley.

Bowen, M. (1975). Family therapy after twenty years. In S. Arieti (Ed.), *American Handbook of Psychiatry: Volume 5. Treatment* (pp. 367–392). New York: Basic Books.

Bowen, M. (1978). *Family therapy in clinical practice.* New York: Jason Aronson.

Bowen, M., Dysinger, R. H., Brady, W. M., & Basmania, B. (1978). Treatment of family groups with a schizophrenic member. In M. Bowen (Ed.), *Family therapy in clinical practice* (pp. 3–15). New York: Jason Aronson.

Bowlby, J. (1960). Grief and mourning in infancy and early childhood. *The Psychoanalytic Study of the Child, 15,* 9–52.

Bowlby, J. (1969). *Attachment and loss: Vol. 1. Attachment.* New York: Basic Books.

Bowlby, J. (1973). *Attachment and loss: Vol. 2. Separation, anxiety and anger.* New York: Basic Books.

Bradshaw, J. (1988). *Bradshaw on: The family.* Deerfield Beach, FL: Health Communications.

Brazelton, T. B. (1978). The remarkable talents of the newborn. *Birth & Family Journal, 5,* 4–10.

Bullough, V. L. (1976). *Sexual variance in society and history.* New York: John Wiley.

Burgner, M., & Edgcumbe, R. (1972). Some problems in the conceptualization of early object relationships. Part II: The concept of object constancy. *Psychoanalytic Study of the Child, 27,* 315–333.

Burr, W. R. (1970). Satisfaction with various aspects of marriage over the life cycle: A random middle class sample. *Journal of Marriage & the Family, 32,* 29–37.

Byrne, D. (1977). Social psychology and the study of sexual behavior. *Personality & Social Psychology Bulletin, 1,* 3–30.

Byrne, D. (1983). The antecedents, correlates, and consequence of erotophobia-erotophilia. In C. Davis (Ed.), *Challenges in sexual science.* Philadelphia: Society for the Scientific Study of Sex.

Byrne, D. (1986). The study of sexual behavior as a multidisciplinary venture. In D. Byrne & K. Kelly (Eds.), *Alternative approaches to the study of sexual behavior.* Hillsdale, NJ: Erlbaum.

Byrne, D., & Schulte, L. (1990). Personal dispositions as mediators of sexual responses. In J. Bancroft, C. M. Davis, & D. Weinstein (Eds.), *Annual review of sex research: An integrative and interdisciplinary review (Vol. I).* Mount Vernon, IA: Society for the Scientific Study of Sex.

Calderone, M. S., & Johnson, E. W. (1981). *The family book about sexuality.* New York: Harper & Row.

Calhoun, J. B. (1956). A comparitive study of the social behavior of two inbred strains of house mice. *Ecological Monographs, 26,* 81–103.

Calhoun, J. B. (1963). *The ecology and sociology of the Norway rat.* (DHHS Publication No. 1008). Washington, DC: U.S. Government Printing Office.

Calhoun, J. B. (1971). Space and the strategy of life. In A. H. Esser (Ed.), *Behavior and environment: International symposium on the use of space by animals and men.* New York: Plenum.

Campbell, D. (1975). On the conflicts between biological and social evolution and between psychology and moral tradition. *American Psychologist, 30,* 1103–1126.

Campbell, Jeremy (1982). *Grammatical man.* New York: Simon & Schuster.

Campbell, Joseph (1949). *The hero with a thousand faces.* Princton, NJ: Princeton University Press.

Campbell, Joseph (1988). *The power of myth.* New York: Doubleday.

Canter, N. F. (1963). *Medieval history: The life and death of a civilization.* New York: Macmillan.

Carnes, P. (1983). *Out of the shadows: Understanding sexual addiction.* Minneapolis, MN: CompCare Publishers.

Castaneda, C. (1968). *The teachings of Don Juan: A Yaqui way of knowledge.* New York: Washington Square Press.

Chaikin, A. L., & Derlega, V. J. (1974). Liking for the norm-breaker in self-disclosure. *Journal of Personality, 42*, 117–129.

Chambliss, W. J. (1965). The selection of friends. *Social Forces, 43*, 370–380.

Chapman, R. (1982). Criteria for diagnosing when to do sex therapy in the primary relationship. *Psychotherapy: Theory, Research & Practice, 19*(3), 359–367.

Chelune, G. J. (1979). Measuring openness in interpersonal communication. In G. J. Chelune (Ed.), *Self-disclosure: Origins, patterns, and implications of openness in interpersonal relationships.* San Francisco: Jossey-Bass.

Chelune, G. J., Robison, J. T., & Kommor, M. J. (1984). Cognitive interaction and intimacy. In V. J. Derlega (Ed.), *Communication, intimacy and close relationships.* New York: Academic Press.

Clinebell, H. J., & Clinebell, C. H. (1970). *The intimate marriage.* New York: Harper & Row.

Colley, C. H. (1909). *Social organizations: A study of the larger mind.* New York: Charles Scribner's Sons.

Comfort, A. (1972). *The joy of sex, a gourmet guide to lovemaking.* New York: Crown.

Concise Oxford dictionary of quotations. (1981). New York: Oxford University Press.

Courtois, C. A. (1988). *Healing the incest wound: Adult survivors in therapy.* New York: Norton.

Csikszentmihalyi, M. (1990). *Flow: the psychology of optimal experience.* New York: Harper & Row.

Cuber, J. F., & Harroff, P. B. (1965). *The significant Americans: A study of sexual behavior among the affluent.* New York: Appleton-Century.

Curran, C. E. (1988). *Tensions in moral theology.* Notre Dame, IN: University of Notre Dame Press.

Dahms, A. (1972). *Emotional intimacy: Overlooked requirement for survival.* Boulder, CO: Pruett.

Dahms, A. (1976). Intimacy hierarchy. In E. A. Powers & M. W. Lee (Eds.), *Process in relationship* (2nd ed.). New York: West Publishing.

Davis, M. S. (1973). *Intimate relations.* New York: Free Press.

DeAmicis, L. A., Goldberg, D. C., LoPiccolo, J., Friedman, J., & Davies, L. (1985). Clinical followup of couples treated for sexual dysfunction. *Archives of Sexual Behavior, 14*, 467–489.

DeLora, J. R., & DeLora, J. S. (Eds.). (1975). *Intimate life styles: Marriage and its alternatives* (2nd ed.). Pacific Palisades, CA: Goodyear Publishing Company.

D'Emilio, J., & Freedman, E. B. (1988). *Intimate matters: A history of sexuality in America.* New York: Harper & Row.

Derlega, V. J. (1984). Self-disclosure and intimate relationships. In V. J. Derlega (Ed.), *Communication, intimacy and close relationships.* New York: Academic Press.

Derlega, V. J., & Chaikin, A. L. (1975). *Sharing intimacy: What we reveal to others and why.* Englewood Cliffs, NJ: Prentice-Hall.

Derlega, V. J., & Grzelak, J. (1979). Appropriateness of self-disclosure. In G. J. Chelune (Ed.), *Self-disclosure: Origins, patterns, and implications of openness in interpersonal relationships.* San Francisco: Jossey-Bass.

Derlega, V. J., & Margulis, S. T. (1982). Why loneliness occurs: The interrelationship of social psychological and privacy concepts. In L. A. Peplau & D. Perlman (Eds.), *Loneliness: A sourcebook of current theory, research and therapy.* New York: John Wiley.

Derlega, V. J., Harris M. S., & Chaikin, A. L. (1973). Self-disclosure and reciprocity, liking and the deviant. *Journal of Experimental Social Psychology, 9*, 227–284.

Diamond, M., & Karlen, A. (1980). *Sexual decisions.* Boston: Little, Brown & Co.

Dicks, H. V. (1963). Object relations theory and marital studies. *British Journal of Medical Psychology, 36*, 125–129.

Dicks, H. V. (1967). *Marital tensions: Clinical studies towards a psychoanalytic theory of interaction.* New York: Basic Books.

Dixon, A. F. (1990). Neuroendocrine regulation in primates. In J. Bancroft, C. M. Davis, & D. Weinstein (Eds.), *Annual review of sex research: An integrative and interdisciplinary review (Vol. I)*.

Donnerstein, E. (1980). Aggressive-erotica and violence against women. *Journal of Personality & Social Psychology, 39*, 269–277.

Douglas, N., & Slinger, P. (1979). *Sexual secrets: The alchemy of ecstasy*. Rochester, VT: Destiny Books.

Douvan, E. (1977). Interpersonal relationships: Some questions and observations. In G. Levinger & H. L. Rausch (Eds.), *Close relationships: Perspective on the meaning of intimacy*. Amherst: University of Massachusetts Press.

Dowling, C. (1981). *The Cinderella complex*. New York: Simon & Schuster.

Duffy, J. (1987). Sex, society, medicine: An historical comment. In E. E. Shelp (Ed.), *Sexuality and medicine: Ethical viewpoints in transition* (Vol. 2). Boston: D. Reidel Publishing Co.

Edelman, G. (1989). *The remembered present: A biological theory of consciousness*. New York: Basic Books.

Elkaim, M. (1986). A systemic approach to couple therapy. *Family Process, 25*(1), 35–42.

Ellis, A. (1960). *The art and science of love*. New York: Bantam Books.

Ellis, A., & Harper, R. (1977). *New guide to rational living*. Los Angeles: Wilshire Books.

Ellis, H. (1906). *Studies in the psychology of sex*. New York: Random House.

Ellis, R. (1980). The corona frenulum trigger. *Journal of Sex & Disability, 3*(1), 50–56.

Engelhardt, H. T. (1987). Having sex and making love: The search for morality in eros. In E. E. Shelp (Ed.), *Sexuality and medicine: Ethical viewpoints in transition* (Vol. 2). Boston: D. Reidel Publishing Co.

Erickson, G. D., & Hogan, T. P. (1981). *Family therapy: An introduction to theory and technique* (2nd ed.). Monterey, CA: Brooks/Cole.

Erickson, M. H., Rossi, E. L., & Rossi, S. I. (1976). *Hypnotic realities*. New York: Irvington.

Erikson, E. H. (1958). *Young man Luther: A study of psychoanalysis and history*. New York: Norton.

Erikson, E. H. (1959). *Identity and the life cycle: Selected papers*. (Psychological Issues, Monograph #1). New York: International University Press.

Fairbairn, W. R. D. (1954). *An object-relations theory of the personality*. New York: Basic Books.

Fairbairn, W. R. D. (1963). Synopsis of an object-relations theory of the personality. *International Journal of Psycho-Analysis, 44*, 224–225.

Feldman, L. B. (1982). Dysfunctional marital conflict: An integrative interpersonal-intrapsychic model. *Journal of Marital & Family Therapy, 8*, 417–428.

Feuerstein, G. (Ed.). (1989). *Enlightened sexuality*. Freedom, CA: The Crossing Press.

Fierman, L. B. (Ed.). (1965). *Effective psychotherapy: The contribution of Helmuth Kaiser*. New York: Free Press.

Fish, L. S., Fish, R. C., & Sprenkle, D. H. (1984). Treating inhibited sexual desire: A marital therapy approach. *American Journal of Family Therapy, 12*(3), 3–12.

Fisher, C. (1990). *Postcards from the edge*. New York: Pocket Books.

Fisher, H. E. (1982). *The sex contract: The evolution of human behavior*. New York: Quill.

Fisher, W. A. (1986). A psychological approach to human sexuality: The sexual behavior sequence. In D. Byrne & K. Kelly (Eds.), *Approaches to human sexuality*. Hillsdale, NJ: Erlbaum.

Fisher W. A., & Byrne, D. (1978a). Individual differences in affective, evaluative, and behavioral responses to an erotic film. *Journal of Applied Social Psychology, 8*, 355–365.

Fisher, W. A., Byrne, D., & White, L. A. (1983). Emotional barriers to contraception. In D. Byrne & W. A. Fisher (Eds.), *Adolescents, sex and contraception* (pp. 207–239). Hillsdale, NJ: Erlbaum.

Fisher, W. A., White, L. A., Byrne, D., & Kelly, K. (1988). Erotophobia-erotophilia as a dimension of personality. *Journal of Sex Research, 25*, 123–151.

Fogarty, T. F. (1979). The distancer and the pursuer. *The Family, 7*, 11–16.

Forrest, J. D., & Singh, S. (1990). Sexual and reproductive behavior of American women, 1982–1988. *Family Planning Perspectives, 22:5*, 209.

Forward, S. (1989). *Toxic parents*. New York: Bantam Books.

Fowler, J. W. (1981). *Stages of faith: The psychology of human development and the quest for meaning*. San Francisco: Harper & Row.

Framo, J. L. (1980). Foreword. In J. K. Pearce & J. L. Friedman (Eds.), *Family therapy: Combining psychodynamic and family systems approaches*. New York: Grune & Stratton.

Francoeur, R. T. (1987a). Sexual attitudes in historical and religious perspective. In R. T. Francoeur (Ed.), *Taking sides: Clashing views on controversial issues in human sexuality*. Guilford, CT: Dushkin Publishing Group.

Francoeur, R. T. (1987b). Postscript. In R. T. Fracoeur (Ed.), *Taking sides: Clashing views on controversial issues in human sexuality*. Guilford, CT: Dushkin Publishing Group.

Francoeur, R. T. (1990, February). The impact of religious beliefs on sexual behavior: A comparative view. Paper presented at the annual meeting of the American Association for the Advancement of Science, New Orleans, LA.

Francoeur, R. T. (1991). Current religious doctrines of sexual and erotic development in childhood. In M. Perry (Ed.), *Handbook of sexology* (Vol. 7). Childhood and adolescent sexology. Amsterdam: Elsevier Science Publishing Co.

Frankl, V. E. (1967). *Psychotherapy and existentialism: Selected papers on logotherapy*. New York: Washington Square Press.

Freeman, W. J. (1991). The physiology of perception. *Scientific American, 264*(2), 78–85.

Freud, S. (1905/1986). Three essays on the theory of sexuality. In A. Freud & J. Strachey (Eds.), *The essentials of psycho-analysis*. London: Hogarth Press & The Institute of Psycho-Analysis.

Freud, S. (1911/1986). Psycho-analytic notes on an autobiographical account of a case of paranoia (*dementia paranoides*). In A. Freud & J. Strachey (Eds.), *The essentials of psycho-analysis*. London: Hogarth Press & The Institute of Psycho-Analysis.

Freud, S. (1914/1949). On narcissism: An introduction. In E. Jones & J. Riviere (Eds.), *Collected papers IV*. London: Hogarth Press & The Institute of Psycho-Analysis.

Freud, S. (1915/1949). Instincts and their vicissitudes. In E. Jones & J. Riviere (Eds.), *Collected papers IV*. London: Hogarth Press & The Institute of Psycho-Analysis.

Freud, S. (1933/1966). Introductory lectures on psychoanalysis. In J. Strachey (Ed. and Trans.), *The standard edition of the complete psychological works of Sigmund Freud* (Vols. 15 & 16). New York: Norton.

Friedman, E. H. (1984). *Anxiety and the spirit of adventure*. Paper presented at the Networker Family Therapy Symposium, Washington, DC.

Friedman, E. H. (1985). *Generation to generation: Family process in church and synagogue*. New York: Guilford.

Friedman, E. H. (1990). *Friedman's fables*. New York: Guilford.

Fromm, E. (1941). *Escape from freedom*. New York: Holt, Rinehart & Winston.

Fromm, E. (1956). *Art of loving*. New York: Perennial Library (Harper & Row).

Gadlin, H. (1977). Private lives and public order: A critical view of the history of intimate relationships in the United States. In G. Levinger & H. L. Rausch (Eds.), *Close relationships: Perspective on the meaning of intimacy*. Amherst, MA: University of Massachusetts Press.

Gagnon, J. H. (1977). *Human sexualities*. Glenview, IL: Scott, Foresman.

Gallup, G. (1979). Self-awareness in primates. *American Scientist, 67*:417.

Garde, I., & Lunde, I. (1980). Female sexual behavior: A study in a random sample of 40-year-old women. *Maturitas, 2,* 240–255.

Genovesi, V. J. (1987). *In pursuit of love: Catholic morality and human sexuality.* Wilmington, DE: M. Glazier.

Gibran, K. (1923/1982). *The prophet.* New York: Alfred A. Knopf.

Glass, S. P., & Wright, T. L. (1977). The relationship of exramarital sex, length of marriage and sex differences on marital satisfaction and romanticism: Athanasiou's data re-analyzed. *Journal of Marriage &the Family, 39,* 691–703.

Gleick, J. (1987). *Chaos: Making a new science.* New York: Penguin.

Glenn, N. D., & Weaver, C. N. (1979). Attitudes toward premarital, extramarital, and homosexual relations in the U. S. in the 1970s. *Journal of Sex Research, 15*(2), 108–118.

Gordon, L. H. (1988). *A laundry list of marital mishaps, marital knots and double binds.* Falls Church, VA: PAIRS Foundation.

Gotwald, W. H., & Golden, G. H. (1981). *Sexuality: The human experience.* New York: Macmillan.

Greeley, A. M. (1991, Jan. 25). Healthy marriages are romantic ones, requiring mix of religion and sex. *National Catholic Reporter,* pp. 19–20.

Guerin, P. J., & Pendagast, E. G. (1976). Evaluation of family systems and genogram. In P. J. Guerin (Ed.), *Family therapy: Theory and practice.* New York: Gardner Press.

Guntrip, H. (1969). *Schizoid phenomena, object relations and the self.* New York: International Universities Press.

Gupta, B. (Ed.). (1987). *Sexual archetypes, East and West.* New York: Paragon House.

Haight, S. J. R. (1979). *The experience and language of grace.* New York: Paulist Press.

Haley, J. (1973). *Uncommon therapy: The psychiatric techniques of Milton H. Erickson.* New York: Norton.

Haley, J. (1976). *Problem solving therapy: New strategies for effective family therapy.* San Francisco: Jossey-Bass.

Harlow, H. (1976). *From learning to love: The collected papers of H. F. Harlow.* New York: Praeger.

Hatfield, E. (1982). Passionate love, compassionate love, and intimacy. In M. Fisher & G. Stricker (Eds.), *Intimacy.* New York: Plenum.

Hatfield, E. (1984). The dangers of intimacy. In V. J. Derlega (Ed.), *Communication, intimacy and close relationships.* New York: Academic Press.

Hatfield, E., & Walster, G. W. (1981). *A new look at love.* Reading, MA: Addison-Wesley.

Hatfield, E., Utne, M. K., & Traupmann, J. (1979). Equity theory and intimate relationships. In R. L. Burgess & T. L. Huston (Eds.), *Social exchange in developing relationships.* New York: Academic Press.

Hawton, K., Catalan, J., Martin, P., & Fagg, J. (1986). Prognostic factors in sex therapy. *Behavior Research & Therapy, 24,* 377–385.

Heiman, J., & Grafton-Becker, V. (1989). Orgasmic disorders in women. In S. R. Leiblum & R. C. Rosen (Eds.), *Principles and practice of sex therapy* (2nd ed.). New York: Guilford.

Heiman, J., & LoPiccolo, J. (1983). Clinical outcome of sex therapy: Effects of daily versus weekly treatment. *Archives of General Psychiatry, 40,* 443–449.

Helminiak, D. A. (1989). Self-esteem, sexual self-acceptance, and spirituality. *Journal of Sex Education & Therapy, 15*(3), 200–210.

Heyward, C. (1989). *Touching our strength: The erotic as power and the love of God.* San Francisco: Harper & Row.

Hinman, A. (1974). Marital problems in pediatric practice. In D. W. Abse, E. M. Nash, & L. M. Louden (Eds.), *Marital and sexual counseling in medical practice.* New York: Harper & Row.

Hite, S. (1976). *The Hite report*. New York: Macmillan.

Hof, L. (1987). Evaluating the marital relationship of clients with sexual complaints. In G. R. Weeks & L. Hof (Eds.), *Integrating sex and marital therapy: A clinical guide*. New York: Brunner/Mazel.

Holland, J. M. (Ed.). (1981). *Religion and sexuality: Judaic-Christian viewpoints in the USA*. San Francisco: The Association of Sexologists.

Homans, G. C. (1961). *Social behavior: Its elementary forms*. New York: Harcourt, Brace, & World.

Horner, A. J. (1979). *Object relations and the developing ego in therapy*. New York: Jason Aronson.

Humphrey, F. G. (1987). Treating extramarital sexual relationships in sex and couples therapy. In G. R. Weeks & L. Hof (Eds.), *Integrating sex and marital therapy: A clinical guide*. New York: Brunner/Mazel.

Hunt, M. (1969). *The affair*. New York: World.

Hunt, M. (1974). *Sexual behavior in the 1970s*. Chicago, IL: Playboy Press.

James, W. (1910/1983). *Psychology: The briefer course*. New York: Henry Holt.

Jerulsaem Talmud, Qiddushin 4:12, Robert Gordis, trans., cited in R. Lawrence (1989), *The poisoning of Eros*. New York: Augustine Moore Press.

Johnson, S. (1987). Personal communication cited in M. Scarf, *Intimate partners*. New York: Random House.

Jourard, S. M. (1968). *Disclosing man to himself*. New York: Van Nostrand Reinhold.

Jourard, S. M. (1971). *The transparent self*. New York: Van Nostrand Reinhold.

Kantor, D. (1980). Critical identity image: A concept linking individual, couple, and family development. In J. K. Pearce & J. L. Friedman (Eds.), *Family therapy: Combining psychodynamic and family systems approaches*. New York: Grune & Stratton.

Kantor, D., & Okun, B. F. (Eds.). (1989). *Intimate environments: Sex, intimacy, and gender in families*. New York: Guilford.

Kaplan, H. S. (1974). *The new sex therapy*. New York: Brunner/Mazel.

Kaplan, H. S. (1977). Hypoactive sexual desire. *Journal of Sex & Marital Therapy, 3*, 3–9.

Kaplan, H. S. (1979). *Disorders of sexual desire and other new concepts and techniques in sex therapy*. New York: Brunner/Mazel.

Kaplan, H. S. (1987). *Sexual aversion, sexual phobias and panic disorder*. New York: Brunner/Mazel.

Kasl, C. D. (1989). *Women, sex and addiction*. New York: Harper & Row.

Katchadourian, H. A., & Lunde, D. T. (1972). *Fundamentals of human sexuality*. New York: Holt, Rinehart & Winston.

Katz, S. J., & Liu, A. E. (1991). *The codependency conspiracy: How to break the recovery habit and take charge of your life*. New York: Warner Books.

Keeney, B. P. (1983). *Aesthetics of change*. New York: Guilford.

Keifer, C. (1977). New depths in intimacy. In R. W. Libby & R. N. Whitehurst (Eds.), *Marriage and alternatives: Exploring intimate relationships*. Glenview, IL: Scott, Foresman.

Keith-Spiegel, P., & Koocher, G. P. (1985). *Ethics in psychology: Professional standards and cases*. New York: Random House.

Kelly, K. (1979). Socialization factors in contraceptive attitudes: Roles of affective responses, parental attitudes, and sexual experience. *Journal of Sex Research, 15*, 6–20.

Kelly, K. (1983). Adolescent sexuality: The first lessons. In D. Byrne & W. A. Fisher (Eds.), *Adolescents, sex and contraception* (pp. 125–142). Hillsdale, NJ: Erlbaum.

Kelly, H. H., & Thibaut, J. W. (1978). *Interpersonal relations: A theory of interdependence*. New York: John Wiley.

Kelvin, P. (1977). Predictability, power and vulnerability in interpersonal attraction. In S. Duck (Ed.), *Theory and practice in interpersonal attraction*. New York: Academic Press.

Kerr, M. E., & Bowen, M. (1988). *Family evaluation*. New York: Norton.

Kierkegaard, S. (1946). Fear and trembling. In R. Brettall (Ed.), *A Kierkegaard anthology*. Princeton, NJ: Princeton University Press.

Kilmann, P. R., Boland, J. P., Norton, S. P., Davidson, E., & Caid, C. (1986). Perspectives of sex therapy outcome: A survey of AASECT providers. *Journal of Sex & Marital Therapy, 12*, 116–138.

Kinsey, A. C., Pomeroy, W. B., & Martin, C. E. (1948). *Sexual behavior in the human male*. Philadephia: W. B. Saunders.

Kinsey, C., Pomeroy, W. B, Martin, C. E., & Gebhard, P. H. (1953). *Sexual behavior in the human female*. Philadephia: W. B. Saunders.

Kirkendall, L. A. (1987). The sexual revolution is just beginning. In R. T. Francoeur (Ed.), *Taking sides: Clashing views on controversial issues in human sexuality*. Guilford, CT: Dushkin Publishing Group.

Klein, M. (1932). *The psychoanalysis of children*. London: Hogarth Press.

Klein, M. (1935). A contribution to the psychogenesis of manic-depressive states. *International Journal of Psycho-Analysis, 16*, 145–174.

Klein, M. (1946). Notes on some schizoid mechanisms. *International Journal of Psycho-Analysis, 27*, 99–110.

Kohlberg, L. (1969). Stages and sequence: The cognitive-developmental approach to socialization. In D. A. Goslin (Ed.), *Handbook of socialization theory and research*. Chicago: Rand McNally.

Kolodny, R., Masters, W. H., & Johnson, V. E. (1982). *Human sexuality*. Boston: Little, Brown.

L'Abate, L. (1977). Intimacy is sharing hurt feelings: A reply to David Mace. *Journal of Marriage & Family Counseling, 3*, 13–16.

L'Abate, L. (1986). *Systematic family therapy*. New York: Brunner/Mazel.

L'Abate, L., & Talmadge, W. C. (1987). Love, intimacy, and sex. In G. R. Weeks & L. Hof (Eds.), *Integrating sex and marital therapy: A clinical guide*. New York: Brunner/Mazel.

Laing, R. D. (1967). *The politics of experience*. New York: Pantheon.

Laing, R. D. (1970). *Knots*. New York: Vintage.

Lampe, P. E. (Ed.). (1987). *Adultery in the United States: Close encounters of the sixth (or seventh) kind*. Buffalo, NY: Prometheus Books.

Lawrence, R. J. (1989). *The poisoning of eros: Sexual values in conflict*. New York: Augustine Moore Press.

Lazarus, A. A. (1988). A multimodal perspective on problems of sexual desire. In S. R. Leiblum & R. C. Rosen (Eds.), *Sexual desire disorders*. New York: Guilford.

Lederer, W. J., & Jackson, D. D. (1968). *The mirages of marriage*. New York: Norton.

Leiblum, S. R., & Pervin, L. A. (1980). Introduction: The development of sex therapy from a sociocultural perspective. In S. R. Leiblum & L. A. Pervin (Eds.), *Principles and practice of sex therapy*. New York: Guilford.

Leiblum, S. R., & Rosen, R. C. (1988). Introduction: Changing persectives on sexual desire. In S. R. Leiblum & R. C. Rosen (Eds.), *Sexual desire disorders*. New York: Guilford.

Leiblum, S. R., & Rosen, R. C. (1989). Assessment and treatment of desire disorders. In S. R. Leiblum & R. C. Rosen (Eds.), *Principles and practice of sex therapy* (2nd ed.). New York: Guilford.

Leigh, W. (1985). *The infidelity report: An investigation of extramarital affairs*. New York: William Morrow.

Leo, J. (1987). The sexual revolution is over. In R. T. Francoeur (Ed.), *Taking sides: Clashing views on controversial issues in human sexuality*. Guilford, CT: Dushkin Publishing Group.

Leonard, D. (1991, March). Close encounters. *Child Magazine*, p. 58. (Letters to the Editor in June/July 1991 issue).

Leonard, G. (1989). Erotic love as surrender. In G. Feuerstein (Ed.), *Enlightened sexuality*. Freedom, CA: Crossing Press.

Lester, B. M., Hoffman, J., & Brazelton, T. B. (1985). The rhythmic structure of mother-infant interaction in term and preterm infants. *Child Development, 56*, 15–27.

Levay, A. N., & Kagle, A. (1977). Ego deficiencies in the areas of pleasure, intimacy and cooperation: guidelines in the diagnosis and treatment of sexual dysfunctions. *Journal of Sex & Marital Therapy, 3*, 1 (Spring), 10–18.

Levenson, E. A. (1972). *The fallacy of understanding: An inquiry into the changing structure of psychoanalysis*. New York: Basic Books.

Levine, S. B. (1988a). Intrapsychic and individual aspects of sexual desire. In S. R. Leiblum & R. C. Rosen (Eds.), *Sexual desire disorders*. New York: Guilford.

Levine, S. B. (1988b). *Sex is not simple*. Columbus: Ohio Psychology Pub. Co.

Levine, S. B., & Agle, D. (1978). The effectiveness of sex therapy for chronic secondary psychological impotence. *Journal of Sex & Marital Therapy, 4*, 235–258.

Levinger, G., & Snoek, J. D. (1972). *Attraction in relationship: A new look at interpersonal attraction*. Morristown, NJ: General Learning Press.

Levy, C. (1974). On the development of a code of ethics. *Social Work, 19*, 207–216.

Lewin, K. (1936). *Principles of topological psychology*. New York: McGraw-Hill.

Lewis, J. M., Beavers, W., Gossett, J., & Phillips, V. (1976). *No single thread: Psychological health in family systems*. New York: Brunner/Mazel.

Libby, R. W. (1977). Extramarital and comarital sex: A critique of the literature. In R. W. Libby & R. N. Whitehurst (Eds.), *Marriage and alternatives: Exploring intimate relationships*. Glenview, IL: Scott, Foresman.

Libby, R. W., & Whitehurst, R. N. (Eds.). (1977). *Marriage and alternatives: Exploring intimate relationships*. Glenview, IL: Scott, Foresman.

Lief, H. I. (1977). What's new in sex research? Inhibited sexual desire. *Medical Aspects of Human Sexuality, 11*(7), 94–95.

Lief, H. I. (1985). Evaluation of inhibited sexual desire: Relationship aspects. In H. S. Kaplan (Ed.), *Comprehensive evaluation of disorders of sexual desire*. Washington, DC: American Psychiatric Press.

Lief, H. I. (1988). Foreward. In S. R. Leiblum & R. C. Rosen (Eds.), *Sexual desire disorders*. New York: Guilford.

Lobitz, W. C., & LoPiccolo, J. (1972). The role of masturbation in the treatment of orgasmic dysfunction. *Archives of Sexual Behavior, 2*, 163–171.

Loevinger, J. (1977). *Ego development: Conceptions and theories*. San Francisco: Jossey-Bass.

Loomer, B. M. (1976). Two kinds of power. *Criterion, Winter*, 12–29.

LoPiccolo, J. (1978). Direct treatment of sexual dysfunction. In J. LoPiccolo & L. LoPiccolo (Eds.), *Handbook of sex therapy*. New York: Plenum Press.

LoPiccolo, L. (1980). Low sexual desire. In S. R. Leiblum & L. A. Pervin (Eds.), *Principles and practice of sex therapy*. New York: Guilford.

LoPiccolo, J. (1991, April). Post-modern approaches to the treatment of erectile dysfunction. Paper presented at the annual meeting of the Society for Sex Therapy and Research, Santa Monica, CA.

LoPiccolo, J., & Friedman, J. (1988). Broad-spectrum treatment of low sexual desire: Integration of cognitive, behavioral, and systemic therapy. In S. R. Leiblum & R. C. Rosen (Eds.), *Sexual desire disorders*. New York: Guilford.

LoPiccolo, J., & Stock, W. (1986). Treatment of sexual dysfunction. *Journal of Consulting and Clinical Psychology, 54*, 158–167.

LoPiccolo, J., Heiman, J., Hogan, D., & Roberts, C. (1985). Effectiveness of single therapists versus co-therapy teams in sex therapy. *Journal of Consulting and Clinical Psychology, 53*(3), 287–294.

Lorde, A. (1987). *Use of the erotic: The erotic as power.* Freedom, CA: Crossing Press.

Lowen, A. (1965). *Love and orgasm.* New York: Macmillan.

Lowenthal, M., & Haven, C. (1968). Interaction and adaptation: Intimacy as a critical variable. *American Sociological Review, 33,* 20–30.

Lowry, T. S., & Lowry, T. P. (1975). Ethical considerations in sex therapy. *Journal of Marital & Family Counseling, 1,* 229–236.

Lusterman, D. D. (1989). Crisis of infidelity: Marriage at the turning point. *Family Therapy Networker,* May–June, pp. 44–51.

Lusterman, D. D. (1990, May). *Treating the crisis of marital infidelity.* Pre-conference institute presented at the annual meeting of the American Association of Sex Educators, Counselors, and Therapists, Washington, DC.

MacLean, P. D. (1958). The limbic system with respect to self-preservation and the preservation of the species. *The Journal of Nervous Mental Disease, 127,* 1–11.

MacLean, P. D. (1972). Cerebral evolution and emotional processes: New findings of the striatal complex. *Annals of the New York Academy of Sciences, 193,* 137–149.

MacLean, P. D. (1982). On the origin and progressive evolution of the triune brain. In E. Armstrong & D. Falk (Eds.), *Primate brain evolution: Methods and concepts* (pp. 291–316). New York: Plenum.

Madanes, C. (1981). *Strategic family therapy.* New York: Jossey-Bass.

Maddock, J. (1991, May 4). Healthy family sexuality. Paper presented at the Annual Meeting of the American Association of Sex Educators, Counselors, and Therapists, St. Louis, MO.

Mahler, M. S. (1952). On child psychosis and schizophrenia. *Psychoanalytic Study of the Child, 7,* 286–305.

Mahler, M. S. (1968). *On human symbiosis and the vicissitudes of individuation.* New York: International Universities Press.

Mahler, M. S. (1980). Rapprochement subphase of the separation-individuation process. In R. F. Lax, S. Bach, & J. A. Burland (Eds.), *Rapprochement: The critical subphase of separation-individuation.* New York: Jason Aronson.

Mahler, M. S., Pine, F., & Bergman, A. (1975). *The psychological birth of the human infant.* New York: Basic Books.

Malone, T. P., & Malone, P. T. (1987). *The art of intimacy.* New York: Prentice-Hall.

Maltz, W., & Holman, B. (1987). *Incest and sexuality: A guide to understanding and healing.* Lexington, MA: Lexington Books.

Marcuse, H. (1955). *Eros and civilization.* Boston: Beacon Press.

Margulis, S. T., Derlega, V. J., & Winstead, B. A. (1984). Social psychological concepts of loneliness. In V. J. Derlega (Ed.), *Communication, intimacy and close relationships.* New York: Academic Press.

Martinez, D. (1991, Mar. 22). Eroticism: Reconnecting faith and flesh for God's sake and ours also. *National Catholic Reporter,* p. 25.

Maslow, A. H. (1968). *Toward a psychology of being* (2nd ed.). Princeton, NJ: D. Van Nostrand Company.

Maslow, A. H. (1971). *The farther reaches of human nature.* New York: Viking Press.

Masters, W. H., & Johnson, V. E. (1966). *Human sexual response.* Boston: Little, Brown.

Masters, W. H., & Johnson, V. E. (1970). *Human sexual inadequacy.* New York: Little, Brown.

Masters, W. H., & Johnson, V. E. (1976). *The pleasure bond: A new look at sexuality and commitment.* New York: Bantam Books.

Masters, W. H., & Johnson, V. E. (1985, June). Sex therapy on its 25th anniversary: Why it survives. Address to the annual meeting of the Society for Sex Therapy and Research, Minneapolis, MN.

Masters, W. H., Johnson, V. E., & Kolodny, R. (1982). *Human sexuality.* Boston: Little, Brown.

Masters, W. H., Johnson, V. E., & Kolodny, R. (1986). *Masters and Johnson on sex and human loving*. Boston: Little, Brown & Co.

Masters, W. H., & Sarrel, P. M. (1986). Sexual dysfunction as an aftermath of sexual assault of men by women. *Journal of Sex & Marital Therapy, 12*(1), 35–45.

Maturana, H. R., & Varela, F. J. (1987). *The tree of knowledge*. Boston: New Science Library.

Maykovich, M. K. (1976). Attitudes versus behavior in extramarital sexual relations. *Journal of Marriage & the Family, 38*, 693–699.

McAdams, D. P. (1984). Motives and relationships. In V. J. Derlega (Ed.), *Communication, intimacy and close relationships*. New York: Academic Press.

McCartney, J. J. (1987). Contemporary controversies in sexual ethics: A case study in post-Vatican II moral theology. In E. E. Shelp (Ed.), *Sexuality and medicine: Ethical viewpoints in transition* (Vol. 2). Boston: D. Reidel Publishing.

McMahon, E. M., & Campbell, P. A. (1989). A bio-spiritual approach to sexuality: The Christian search for a unification process within the human organism. In G. Feuerstein (Ed.), *Enlightened sexuality: Essays on body-positive spirituality*. Freedom, CA: Crossing Press.

McWilliams, P. (1971). *Come love with me and be my life*. Allen Park, MI: Versemonger Press.

Mead, G. H. (1934). *Mind, self, and society: From the standpoint of a social behaviorist*. Chicago: The University Press.

Melzack, R., & Wall, P. D. (1965). Pain mechanisms: A new theory. *Science, 150*, 971–979.

Metzger, D. (1989). Re-vamping the world: On the return of the holy prostitute. In G. Feuerstein (Ed.), *Enlightened sexuality: Essays on body-positive spirituality*. Freedom, CA: Crossing Press.

Miles, J. E. (1980). Motivation in conjoint therapy. *Journal of Sex & Marital Therapy, 6*(3), 205–214.

Miller, L. C., & Berg, J. H. (1984). Selectivity and urgency in interpersonal exchange. In V. J. Derlega (Ed.), *Communication, intimacy and close relationships*. New York: Academic Press.

Minuchin, C., & Fishman, H. C. (1981). *Family therapy techniques*. Cambridge, MA: Harvard Press.

Mischel, W. (1973). Toward a cognitive social learning reconceptualization of personality. *Psychological Review, 80*, 252–283.

Mischel, W. (1977). On the future of personality measurement. *American Psychologist, 32*, 246–254.

Mondadori, A. (1978). *Eros in antquity*. New York: Erotic Art Book Society.

Money, J. (1980). *Love and lovesickness: Science of sex, gender difference and pair bonding*. Baltimore: Johns Hopkins University Press.

Money, J. (1985). *The destroying angel*. New York: Prometheus Books.

Money, J. (1986). *Lovemaps: Clinical concepts of sexual/erotic health and pathology*. New York: Prometheus Books.

Moore, S. (1985). *Let this mind be in you: The quest for identity through Oedipus to Christ*. New York: Harper & Row.

Moore, S. (1989). *Jesus: The liberator of desire*. New York: Crossroads Publishing.

Mosher, D. L. (1980). Three psychological dimensions of depth of involvement in human sexual response. *Journal of Sex Research, 16*(1), 1–42.

Mould, D. E. (1980). Neuromuscular aspects of women's orgasms. *Journal of Sex Research, 16*, 193–201.

Moultrup, D. J. (1990). *Husbands, wives and lovers: The emotional system of the extramarital affair*. New York: Guilford.

Moustakas, C. (1961). *Loneliness*. New York: Prentice-Hall.

Moustakas, C. (1972). *Loneliness and love*. Englewood Cliffs, NJ: Prentice-Hall.

Murstein, B. I. (1974). *Love, sex, and marriage through the ages*. New York: Springer.

Myers, L., & Leggitt, H. (1975). *Adultery and other private matters: Your right to personal freedom in marriage.* Chicago, Nelson-Hall.

Neubeck, G. (Ed.). (1969). *Extramarital relations.* Englewood Cliffs, NJ: Prentice-Hall.

Newman, H. (1981). Communication within ongoing relationships: An attributional perspective. *Personality & Social Psychology Bulletin, 7,* 59–70.

A Newsweek poll: Mixed feelings about pornography (national survey conducted by the Gallup Organization). (1985, March 18). *Newsweek,* p. 60.

Nichols, M. (1984). *Family therapy concepts and methods.* New York: Gardner Press.

Nordine, K. (1987, September 22, 4:50 pm). Commentary. *All Things Considered.* National Public Radio.

Norwood, R. (1985). *Women who love too much.* New York: Pocket Books.

Palazzoli, M. S., Boscolo, L., Cecchin, G., & Prata, G. (1978). *Paradox and counterparadox: A new model in the therapy of the family in schizophrenic transaction.* New York: Jason Aronson.

Palazzoli, M. S., Cirillo, S., Selvini, M., & Sorrentino, A. (1989). *Family games.* New York: Norton.

Papero, D. V. (1990). *Bowen family systems theory.* Boston: Allyn & Bacon.

Patterson, M. L. (1984). Intimacy, social control, and nonverbal involvement: A functional approach. In V. J. Derlega (Ed.), *Communication, intimacy and close relationships.* New York: Academic Press.

Patton, D., & Waring, E. M. (1984). The quality and quantity of marital intimacy in the marriages of psychiatric patients. *Journal of Sex & Marital Therapy, 10,* 201–206.

Pearce, J. K., & Friedman, J. L. (Eds.). (1980). *Family therapy: Combining psychodynamic and family systems approaches.* New York: Grune & Stratton.

Perez, J. F. (1979). *Family counseling: Theory and practice.* New York: D. Van Nostrand Company.

Perlmutter, M. S., & Hatfield, E. (1980). Intimacy, intent, metacommunication and second-order change. *American Journal of Family Therapy, 8,* 17–23.

Peter, L. J. (1980). *Peter's quotations.* New York: Bantam Books.

Pfeiffer, E., & Davis, G. C. (1972). Determinants of sexual behavior in middle and old age. *Journal of the American Geriatrics Society, 20,* 151–158.

Pfeiffer, E., Vorwoerdth, A., & Davis, G. C. (1972). Sexual behavior in middle life. *American Journal of Psychiatry, 128,* 1262–1267.

Phillipson, H. (1955). *The object relations technique.* London: Tavistock Press.

Pineo, P. C. (1961). Disenchantment in the later years of marriage. *Marriage & Family Living, 23,* 3–11.

Pittman, F. S. (1987). *Turning points: Treating families in transition and crisis.* New York: Norton.

Pittman, F. S. (1989). *Private lies: Infidelity and the betrayal of intimacy.* New York: Norton.

Pittman, F. S. (1990). The secret passions of men. *Journal of Marital & Family Therapy, 17*(1), 17–23.

Pomeroy, W. B, Flax, C. C., & Wheeler, C. C. (1982). *Taking a sexual history.* New York: Free Press.

Prather, H. (1970). *Notes to myself.* Moab, UT: Real People Press.

Prather, H., & Prather, G. (1990). *Notes to each other.* New York: Bantam Books.

Putney, S., & Putney, G. J. (1964). *The adjusted American: Normal neuroses in the individual and society.* New York: Perennial Library (Harper & Row).

Rahner, K. (1939/1968). *Spirit in the world.* New York: Herder & Herder.

Rahner, K. (1941/1969). *Hearers of the word.* New York: Herder & Herder.

Rahner, K. (1961). *Theological investigations.* Baltimore, MD: Helicon Press.

Rahner, K. (1969). Christianity and the future. In *The future of man in Christianity*. Chicago, IL: Argus Communications.

Ranke-Heinemann, U. (1990). *Eunuchs for the kingdom of heaven: Women, sexuality and the Catholic Church*. New York: Doubleday.

Richardson, L. (1985). *The new other woman: Contemporary single women in affairs with married men*. New York: Free Press.

Ricketson, S. C. (1989). *Dilemma of love: Healing codependent relationships at different stages of life*. Deerfield Beach, FL: Health Communications.

Ricoeur, P. (1964). Wonder, eroticism and enigma. *Cross Currents*, Spring, 1964, 133–166.

Rimmer, R. H. (1977). Being in bed naked with you is the most important thing in my life. In R. W. Libby & R. N. Whitehurst (Eds.), *Marriage and alternatives: Exploring intimate relationships*. Glenview, IL: Scott, Foresman.

Robertson, Linda (1991, July). Personal communication.

Rohrbaugh, M., Tennen, H., Press, S., & White, L. (1981). Compliance, defiance, and therapeutic paradox. *American Journal of Orthopsychiatry, 51*, 454–467.

Rosen, R. C., & Beck, J. G. (1988). *Patterns of sexual arousal*. New York: Guilford.

Rosen, R. C., & Leiblum, S. R. (1987). Current approaches to the evaluation of sexual desire disorders. *Journal of Sex Research, 23*, 141–162.

Rosen, R. C., & Leiblum, S. R. (1988). Sexual scripting approach to problems of desire. In S. R. Leiblum & R. C. Rosen (Eds.), *Sexual desire disorders*. New York: Guilford.

Rosen, R. C., & Rosen, L. R. (1981). *Human sexuality*. New York: Alfred Knopf.

Rubin, Z. (1973). *Liking and loving: An invitation to social psychology*. New York: Holt, Rinehart & Winston.

Sager, C. J. (1976). *Marriage contracts and couple therapy*. New York: Brunner/Mazel.

Sandler, J., Myerson, M., & Kinder, B. N. (1980). *Human sexuality: Current perspectives*. Tampa, FL: Mariner Publishing Co.

Sarrel, P. M., & Masters, W. H. (1982). Sexual molestation of men by women. *Archives of Sexual Behavior, 11*(2), 117–131.

Satir, V. (1967). *Conjoint family therapy*. Palo Alto, CA: Science & Behavior Books.

Schacter, S., & Singer, J. (1962). Cognitive, social and physiological determinants of emotional state. *Psychological Review, 69*, 379–399.

Schaef, A. W. (1989). *Escape from intimacy*. New York: Harper & Row.

Schaefer, M. T., & Olsen, D. H. (1981). Assessing intimacy: The PAIR inventory. *Journal of Marital & Family Therapy, 7*(1), 47–60.

Scharff, D. E. (1982). *The sexual relationship: An object relations view of sex and the family*. Boston: Routledge & Kegan Paul.

Scharff, D. E. (1988). An object relations approach to inhibited sexual desire. In S. R. Leiblum & R. C. Rosen (Eds.), *Sexual desire disorders*. New York: Guilford.

Scharff, D. E., & Scharff, J. S. (1987). *Object relations family therapy*. Northvale, NJ: Jason Aronson.

Schlenker, B. R. (1984). Identities, identifications, and relationships. In V. J. Derlega (Ed.), *Communication, intimacy and close relationships*. New York: Academic Press.

Schover, L. R, Friedman, J. M., Weiler, S. J., Heiman, J. R., & LoPiccolo, J. (1982). Multiaxial problem-oriented system for sexual dysfunctions: An alternative to DSM-III. *Archives of General Psychiatry, 39*, 614–619.

Schover, L., & LoPiccolo, J. (1982). Effectiveness of treatment for dysfunctions of sex desire. *Journal of Sex & Marital Therapy, 8*(3), 179–197.

Schulz, D. A., & Raphael, D. S. (1989). Christ and Tiresias: A wider focus on masturbation. In G. Feuerstein (Ed.), *Enlightened Sexuality: Essays on body-positive spirituality*. Freedom, CA: Crossing Press.

Schutz, W. C. (1966). *FIRO (The interpersonal underworld)*. Palo Alto, CA: Science & Behavior.

Schwartz, M. F., & Masters, W. H. (1988). Inhibited sexual desire: The Masters and Johnson Institute treatment model. In S. R. Leiblum & R. C. Rosen (Eds.), *Sexual desire disorders*. New York: Guilford.

Schweitzer, A. (1906/1968). *The quest for the historical Jesus: A critical study of its progress from Reimarus to Wrede*. (J. M. Robinson, Trans.). New York: Macmillan.

Segraves, R. T. (1988). Drugs and desire. In S. R. Leiblum & R. C. Rosen (Eds.), *Sexual desire disorders*. New York: Guilford.

Seldes, G. (1985). *The great thoughts*. New York: Ballantine Books.

Selvini-Palazzoli, M., & Viaro, M. (1988). The anorectic process in the family: A six-stage model as a guide for individual therapy. *Family Process, 27*, 129–148.

Selye, H. (1956). *The stress of life*. New York: McGraw-Hill.

Sherfey, M. J. (1966). *The nature and evolution of female sexuality*. New York: Random House.

Sherfey, M. J. (1974). Some biology of sexuality. *Journal of Sex & Marital Therapy, 1*, 97–109.

Sherwin, B. B., Gelfand, M. M., & Brender, W. (1985). Androgen enchanges sexual motivation in females: A prospective, crossover study of sex steroid administration in the surgical menopause. *Psychosomatic Medicine, 47*, 339–351.

Simmel, G. (1908/1950). *The sociology of Georg Simmel* (K. Wolff, Trans.). Glencoe, IL: The Free Press.

Simmons, P. D. (1987). Theological approaches to sexuality: An overview. In E. E. Shelp (Ed.), *Sexuality and medicine: Ethical viewpoints in transition* (Vol. 2). Boston: D. Reidel Publishing Co.

Simon, W. (1989). Post-modernization of sex. *Journal of Psychology & Human Sexuality, 2*(1), 9–37.

Sloan, S. Z., & L'Abate, L. (1985). Intimacy. In L. L'Abate (Ed.), *Handbook of family psychology and therapy*. Homewood, IL: Dorsey Press.

Sokol, D. (1989). Spiritual breakthough in sex. In G. Feuerstein (Ed.), *Enlightened sexuality: Essays on body-positive spirituality*. Freedom, CA: Crossing Press.

Sovatsky, S. C. (1989). Tantric celibacy and erotic mystery. In G. Feuerstein (Ed.), *Enlightened sexuality*. Freedom, CA: Crossing Press.

Spanier, G. B., & Margolis, R. L. (1983). Marital seperation and extramarital sexual behavior. *Journal of Sex Research, 19*(1), 23–48.

Sprenkle, D. H., & Weiss, D. L. (1978). Extramarital sexuality: Implications for marital therapists. *Journal of Sex & Marital Therapy, 4*(4), 279–291.

Spring, I., & Manning, H. (1988). *Fifty hikes in Mount Rainier National Park* (3rd ed.). Seattle, WA: The Mountaineers.

Stampfl, T., & Levis, D. (1967). Essentials of implosive therapy: A learning theory-based psychodynamic behavior therapy. *Journal of Abnormal Psychology, 72*, 496–503.

Stanton, M. (1981). Strategic approaches to family therapy. In A. G. Gurman & D. P. Kniskern (Eds.), *Handbook of family therapy*. New York: Brunner/Mazel.

Steinberg, D. (1988). *Erotic by nature*. San Juan, CA: Shakti Press/Red Adler Books.

Stock, W. (1985). The influence of gender on power dynamics in relationships. In D. C. Goldberg (Ed.), *Contemporary marriage: Special issues in couples therapy*. Homewood, IL: Dorsey Press.

Storr, A. (1988). *Solitude*. New York: Ballantine Books.

Stratton, R. (1991). The knight of infinite resignation and the knight of faith in "Fear and trembling" by Soren Kierkegaard. *Delta Epsilon Sigma Journal, 36*, 30–33. (Barry College, Miami, FL)

Strauss, D., & Dickes, R. (1980). Adverse reaction of the apparently healthy partner in response to improvement in the overtly dysfunctional spouse. *Journal of Sex & Marital Therapy, 6*(2), 109–115.

Strean, H. (1980). *The extramarital affair.* New York: The Free Press.

Sullivan, H. S. (1953). *Interpersonal theory of psychiatry.* New York: Norton.

Sutherland, J. D. (1963). Object-relations theory and the conceptual model of psychoanalysis. *British Journal of Medical Psychology, 36*, 109–124.

Szasz, T. S. (1980). *Sex by prescription.* Garden City, NY: Anchor Press.

Tavris, C. (1989, Dec.). Do codependency theories explain women's unhappiness – or exploit their insecurities? *Vogue*, pp. 220–226.

Tavris, C., & Sadd, S. (1977). *The Redbook report on female sexuality.* New York: Dell.

Tennen, H., Rohrbaugh, M., Press, S., & White, L. (1981). Reactance theory and therapeutic paradox: A compliance-defiance model. *Psychotherapy, 18*, 14–22.

Thibaut, J. W., & Kelly, H. H. (1959). *The social psychology of groups.* New York: John Wiley.

Thompson, A. P. (1983). Extramarital sex: A review of the research literature. *Journal of Sex Research, 19*(1), 1–22.

Thompson, A. P. (1984a). Extramarital sexual crisis: Common themes and therapy implications. *Journal of Sex & Marital Therapy, 10*, 239–254.

Thompson, A. P. (1984b). Emotional and sexual components of extramarital relations. *Journal of Marriage & the Family, 46*, 35–42.

Tillich, P. (1936). *The interpretation of history.* New York: Charles Scribner & Sons.

Tillich, P. (1957). *Systematic theology* (Vol. 2). Chicago: University of Chicago Press.

Tolor, A., & DiGrazia, P. V. (1976). Sexual attitudes and behavior patterns during and following pregnancy. *Archives of Sexual Behavior, 5*(6), 539–551.

Tripp, R. T. (Ed.). (1970). *The international thesaurus of quotations.* New York: Harper & Row.

Tronick, E. Z. (1989). Emotions and emotional communication. *The American Psychologist, 44*(2), 1111–1125.

Van de Velde, T. (1930). *Ideal marriage: Its physiology and technique.* New York: Random House.

Verhulst, J., & Heiman, J. R. (1988). A systems perspective on sexual desire. In S. R. Leiblum & R. C. Rosen (Eds.), *Sexual desire disorders.* New York: Guilford.

von Neumann, J. (1966). *Theory of self-reproducing automata.* Arthur W. Burks (Ed.). Urbana: University of Illinois Press.

Wachtel, E. F. (1982). The family psyche over three generations: The genogram revisited. *Journal of Marital & Family Therapy, 8*, 335–343.

Walker, B. G. (1983). *The woman's encyclopedia of myths and secrets.* San Francisco: Harper & Row.

Walster, E. (1971). Passionate love. In B. I. Murstein (Ed.), *Theories of attraction and love.* New York: Springer.

Walster, E., Berscheid, E., & Walster, G. W. (1973). New directions in equity research. *Journal of Personality & Social Psychology, 25*, 151–176.

Walster, E., Traupmann, J., & Walster, G. W. (1978). Equity and extramarital sexuality. *Archives of Sexual Behavior, 7*(2), 127–141.

Walster, E., Walster, G. W., & Berscheid, E. (1978). *Equity: Theory and research.* Boston: Allyn & Bacon.

Waring, E. M., & Reddon, J. R. (1983). The measurement of intimacy in marriage: The Waring intimacy questionnaire. *Journal of Clinical Psychology, 39*(1), 53–57.

Washburn, D. A., Hopkins, W. D., & Rumbaugh, D. (in press). Perceived control in rhesus monkeys (*Nacaca Mulatta*): Enhanced video-task performance. *Journal of Experimental Psychology Animal Behavior Processes.*

Watzlawick, P. (1989, October). Addiction to ideas. Paper presented at the awards luncheon of the annual meeting of the American Association for Marriage and Family Therapy, San Francisco, CA.

Watzlawick, P., Beavin, J. H., & Jackson, D. D. (1967). *Pragmatics of human communication: A study of interaction patterns, pathologies and paradoxes.* New York: Norton.

Webster's New Universal Unabridged Dictionary. (1983). New York: Dorset & Baber.

Weeks, G. R. (1986). *Paradoxical intervention.* Paper presented at AAMFT Annual Conference. (Audiotape #505, Highland Indiana: Creative Audio Co. 1986)

Weeks, G. R., & L'Abate, L. (1982). *Paradoxical psychotherapy: Theory and practice with individuals, couples and families.* New York: Brunner/Mazel.

Weil, M. W. (1975). Extramarital relationships: A reappraisal. *Journal of Clinical Psychology, 31*(4), 723–725.

Weinberg, K. (1976). *Incest behavior.* New York: Citadel.

Weiner-Davis, M. (1990). Divorce busters. Paper presented at the annual meeting of the American Association for Marriage and Family Therapy, Washington, DC.

Weiss, H. D. (1972). The physiology of human erection. *Annals of Internal Medicine, 76,* 793–799.

Whipple, B., Ogden, G., & Komisaruk, B. R. (in press). Physiological correlates of imagery induced orgasm in women. *Archives of Sexual Behavior.*

Whitehurst, R. N. (1971). Violence potential in extramarital sexual responses. *Journal of Marriage & the Family, 33,* 683–391.

Wile, D. B. (1988). *After the honeymoon: How conflict can improve your relationship.* New York: John Wiley.

Willi, J. (1982). *Couples in collusion.* New York: Jason Aronson.

Williams, M. H. (1983). An unnoted inconsistency in Masters and Johnson's use of non-demand techniques: Retarded ejaculation. In B. Apfelbaum (Ed.), *Expanding the boundaries of sex therapy: The ego-analytic model* (2nd ed.). Berkeley, CA: Berkeley Sex Therapy Group.

Wilson, E. O. (1975). *Sociobiology: The new synthesis.* Cambridge, MA: The Belknap Press/Harvard University Press.

Winnicott, D. W. (1953). Transitional objects and transitional phenomena: A study of the first not-me possession. *The International Journal of Psycho-Analysis, 34,* 89–97.

Winnicott, D. W. (1960). The theory of the parent-infant relationship. *The International Journal of Psycho-Analysis, 41,* 585–595.

Winnicott, D. W. (1965). *The maturational processes and the facilitating environment: Studies in the theory of emotional development.* New York: International Universities Press.

Witkin, M. H. (1980). Sex therapy: A holistic approach. In B. B. Wolman & J. Money (Eds.), *Handbook of human sexuality.* Englewood Cliffs, NJ: Prentice-Hall.

Wolman, B. B., & Money, J. (1980). *Handbook of human sexuality.* Englewood Cliffs, NJ: Prentice-Hall.

Wynne, L. C., & Wynne, A. R. (1986). The quest for intimacy. *Journal of Marital & Family Therapy, 12*(4), 383–394.

Wynne, L. C., Ryckoff, I., Day, D., & Hirsch, S. (1958). Pseudo-mutuality in the family relations of schizophrenia. *Psychiatry, 21,* 205–220.

Yalom I. (1980). *Existential psychotherapy.* New York: Basic Books.

Zilbergeld, B. (1978). *Male sexuality.* New York: Little, Brown.

Zilbergeld, B. (1991, May 8). "Keeping Love Alive," Dotty Nathan Memorial Lecture of the Jewish Endowment Foundation. New Orleans, LA.

Zilbergeld, B., & Ellison, C. (1980). Desire discrepancies and arousal problems in sex therapy. In S. Leiblum & L. Pervin (Eds.), *Principles and practice of sex therapy.* New York: Guilford.

Zussman, Shirley (1985). Personal communication.

Subject Index

adaptive behaviors, situations beyond the range of, 220–23
addiction model, 517–19
  flaws in, 517–19
  paradoxical dealing with denial by, 519
  of philandering, 364
  social addiction to addiction, 66
Addiction to Addictions (Schnarch), 520
adult children, 341–43, 520–21
adultery, 351, 352
affairs, 206, 245, 282
  anxiety as a positive component of, 38
  caused by marriage, 352–53
  conducted by both partners, 378–79
  and differentiation, 370–72
  dynamics in, 378–80
  as elicitation window, 369
  and intimacy, 370–72
  incongruous power hierarchies in, 367–70
  motivations of "other person," 372–73
  myths about, 363–65
  sanctions against, 349–50
  sequential, 214
  and "sexual addiction," 353
  and stake in marriage, 373
  threatened by treatment progress, 245
  treatment approach, 367–372
  see also extramarital sex
Age of Reason, The (Paine), 415
aging:
  changes in, 53
  of a family system, 340–43

and intimacy needs, 6–7
and response thresholds, 26
services developed for the elderly, 86–87
and sexual potential, 431
AIDS, 86
ambiguity, tolerance for, 488–89
ambivalence, 238–42
  tolerance for, 222, 505
American Association of Sex Educators, Counselors, and Therapists (AASECT), 84, 146
American Psychiatric Association, 414n
androgen augmentation, 260
anorexia, 385
  and anxiety about individuation, 336–37
antimony, logical paradox, 475
anxiety, 37–41, 131, 169, 195n
  and anorexia, 336–37
  contagion of, 387n
  and family communication, 332
  "good enough" level of, 399
  in a "good relationship," 241–42
  in interconnected relationships, 321
  intolerance for, 385–91
  loneliness and, 107–9
  modulation by the therapist, 395–401
  pleasure, 387–91
  in premature ejaculation, 39–40
  raising in therapy, 534
  reducing by hospitalization, 530
  relief from, at low levels of differentiation, 518

613

inherent paradox (*continued*)
  secondary to strict religious upbringing,
    326
  treatment of, 292–304
  see also sexual desire, problems of
Integrating Sexual and Marital Therapy
    (Weeks and Hof), 180
integration, 222
  of behaviorism with psychoanalysis, 264
  of cognitive–affective states with physiologi-
    cal processes, 15
  of mind and body, 48–56
  of sex and marital therapy, 178–82, 394–
    95
  of sexuality and spirituality, 561
  the therapist's, 542
  whole object attachment and existential
    loneliness, 193
integrity, 521, 526–27
  beyond ethics, 540–45
  clinical, 543
  common issues of, 543–45
  crucible of, 458
  relationship to confusion, 404
  and sexual addiction theory, 520
  in therapy, 160, 540–42, 543–45, 547
  wall–socket eroticism stemming from,
    361
intercourse:
  prescribed by religious text, 563
  tolerance for, in Augustinian Christianity,
    569
interdependence versus dependency, 582
intergenerational triangulation, 204, 320–
    38
  and affairs, 372–73
  see also family of origin, triangulation
intimacy, 89–144, 173
  and acceptance, 102
  as an acquired skill, 173, 174
  and affairs, 370–72
  and approval, 103
  and the bypass approach, 135, 153
  and casual sex, 120
  versus closeness, 109–12
  and constructivism, 112
  defined, 109, 121–23
  definitional approach to, 90–92
  descriptive models, 92–95
  development of, in relationships, 125

dimensions of, 90–91
during sex, 455–62
dynamics at different levels of differentiation, 124, 129
and ego–structure, 194–95
and eroticism, 313
existential model of, 109–19
and existential separateness, 106–109, 116
expectations of, 125, 136–40
and expectations of trust and empathy, 103,
  131–32
and evolution, 2–3, 137–39
eye contact during sex, 455–59
as a fundamental human potential, 136,
  583
and gender–role behaviors, 68
as idiosyncratic experience, 133
and interpersonal systems, 110
intolerance of, xvii, 134–35, 153
intrapersonal and interpersonal systemic
  processes in, 121–22
and love, 100
level 1, 115, 117–18, 123, 157–58, 371
level 2, 116–19, 123, 371
  transition to, 117–19, 157–58
metacommunication of, 97–98, 123
as a meta–dimension of therapy, 535
model of, 19–20, 92, 115, 120–44
need for, 126–27, 126n
  defined, 183
normal neurosis and, 587
other–validated, 101–2, 106, 122, 123–
  25, 126, 130, 185
pain of, 467–69
quest for, 89–119
  by helping professionals, 9–11
reciprocity model of, 94–95, 102, 103,
  128
salience of, 91, 125
and self–awareness, 110, 586–87
self–disclosure in, 93–94, 97–98, 130
self–validated, xv, 102, 106, 122, 123–
  35, 126, 128–31, 184, 199, 371,
  579–80
sexual crucible model for, 173–75
and sexual expression, 176
therapist's ability for, 535–40
as threat, 143
tolerance, 124n, 125, 134–35, 174, 206
  defined, 183

Name Index